$3\frac{oo}{5}$

$\not{b}$

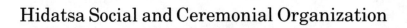

Hidatsa Social and Ceremonial Organization

Bears Arm, 1933.

HIDATSA SOCIAL AND CEREMONIAL ORGANIZATION

By Alfred W. Bowers

Introduction by Douglas R. Parks

University of Nebraska Press
Lincoln and London

Introduction to the Bison Book Edition copyright © 1992 by the University of
Nebraska Press
Manufactured in the United States of America

First Bison Book printing: 1992
Most recent printing indicated by the last digit below:
10   9   8   7   6   5   4   3   2   1

Library of Congress Cataloging-in-Publication Data
Bowers, Alfred W.
Hidatsa Social and ceremonial organization / by Alfred W. Bowers: introduc-
tion by Douglas R. Parks.
p.   cm.
Originally published: Washington, D.C.: U.S. G.P.O. 1963. (Bulletin /
Smithsonian Institution; no. 194)
Includes bibliographical references.
ISBN 0-8032-6098-9
1. Hidatsa Indians—Social life and customs. 2. Hidatsa Indians—Rites and
ceremonies. I. Title. II. Series: Bulletin (Smithsonian Institution. Bureau of
American Ethnology); 194.
E99.H6B67   1992
973'.04975—dc20   92-15146
CIP

Originally published by the U.S. Government Printing Office, Washington,
D.C., in 1963 as Bulletin 194 of the Smithsonian Institution, Bureau of American Ethnology.

CONTENTS

ILLUSTRATIONS

PLATES

(All plates follow p. 494)

TEXT FIGURES

MAPS

CHARTS

INTRODUCTION

By Douglas R. Parks

For most Plains Indian peoples their traditional religion, although alive through most of the nineteenth century, was generally no more than a memory during the early decades of the twentieth century. For many tribes—notably the Sioux, Pawnees, and Osages—Christian missionaries had begun proselytizing as early as the 1830s and by the end of the century had established congregations in the Indian communities; for the Sioux they had, moreover, effectively established literacy in the native language as well as a vast church network over numerous reservations. For other tribes like the Mandans, Arikaras, and Hidatsas, less populous and more remote from major paths of transcontinental travel and early Euro-American settlement, the full impact of missionization was not felt until much later in the nineteenth century; but even among these tribes native religious practices, at least in overt form, had given way by the close of the century to vigorous government and denominational efforts to suppress traditional beliefs and replace them with Christianity.

At the same time that missionary efforts were focused on the eradication of old beliefs and practices, traditional religious leaders of the nineteenth century frequently died unexpectedly from one of the many diseases, often of epidemic proportions, that recurrently afflicted Plains Indians throughout this period of drastic cultural upheaval. Although the deaths were not so detrimental to the religious life of the nomadic tribes, whose holy men typically dreamed their rituals and ritual paraphernalia anew with each generation, for the conservative semisedentary tribes, whose priests and bundle keepers guarded both legendary ritual shrines and accompanying secret knowledge that were generally imparted only late in life to novitiates, the early deaths were devastating for traditional religion. Through an unceasing process of attrition the knowledge and rituals of priests were removed from tribal life. Moreover, when tribal religious leaders and their rituals were clearly unable to control events and fend off adversity in a dramatically changing world, younger men, faced with unrelenting acculturative pressures to take on a new lifestyle, were no longer motivated to apprentice to elder tribal priests and bundle keepers in order to sustain a religion that had lost meaning and efficacy.

This late-nineteenth- and early-twentieth-century period, when not only religion but most of the overt symbols of traditional Plains Indian life were replaced by the accoutrements of contemporary rural American society, inspired a number of individuals—Indian and white—to preserve records of former lifeways while some people who knew the old traditions or remembered fragments of them were still living. Although these cultural recorders were sometimes enlightened army officers like Washington Matthews or the physician James R. Walker, they were generally anthropologists who visited a reservation for varying periods of time—sometimes a few days, often weeks or months, and only rarely for a year or more—to compile records that were as lengthy and informed as a combination of time, native cooperation, and other circumstances allowed. Only a few tribes, however, were distinguished by richly detailed, culturally insightful descriptions compiled from knowledgable participants in nineteenth-century ritual life. Among the rare studies that stand out from this period were those of the Cheyennes by George A. Dorsey, James Mooney, and George Bird Grinnell.[1] Several other tribes accorded exceptional attention at the turn of the century were ones for whom the record was compiled through the collaborative efforts of an anthropologist and an educated tribal member. Prominent among these were the Omaha and Osage studies of Alice C. Fletcher and Francis La Flesche, the latter a member of the Omaha tribe; and the Pawnee studies of James R. Murie, a mixed-blood Skiri who worked with several anthropologists, including Fletcher, George A. Dorsey, and Clark Wissler.[2]

Later, during the early decades of the twentieth century, the description of nineteenth-century Plains Indian life became more often the task of anthropologists alone, who worked with the few elderly people still possessing sufficient knowledge to reconstruct a meaningful portrayal of the tribal past. Among the tribes who benefited from protracted study and meticulous descriptions during this later period were the Pawnees (Alexander Lesser and Gene Weltfish), Crows (Robert Lowie), and Teton Sioux (Frances Densmore and Ella Deloria).[3] Of all tribes from this and the earlier period, however, few were accorded the lavish attention given the Hidatsas, whose nineteenth-century culture is one of the most richly documented in the Plains region—indeed, in all of North America. And representative of the finest material on this tribe is Alfred Bowers' *Hidatsa Social and Ceremonial Organization,* an ethnographic compendium that is now a classic in American anthropology.

THE HIDATSAS AND THEIR HISTORY

The first Europeans to encounter the semisedentary riverine tribes living in what came to be called the Upper Missouri region in the Dakotas were in the party of Pierre Gaultier de Varennes de La Vérendrye, a French trader from Montreal who set out in 1738 to seek a route to the Pacific Ocean and who in 1741 was followed by another expedition led by La Vérendrye's sons. Their contacts on these expeditions were only with the Mandans and Arikaras, however, and apparently not with the Hidatsas, whom they never mentioned by name. Sustained contact with the tribes of the region did not begin until the 1780s, shortly after the devastating smallpox epidemics of 1780 and perhaps earlier that swept across the plains and decimated many tribes, particularly the semisedentary ones living in compact villages. Tribes like the Arikaras and Mandans—and undoubtedly the Hidatsas as well—lost more than half their populations, and the survivors of each of these peoples, previously living in numerous villages distributed along the Missouri River, were forced to consolidate into two or three villages. Some six to nine Mandan villages clustered in the Heart River region prior to the epidemics were reduced to two, while at least ten, and perhaps as many as forty, Arikara villages along the Missouri south of the Cheyenne River were reduced to three.[4]

It is not clear precisely how devastating these early epidemics were on the people now known as the Hidatsas since contemporary historical accounts provide few clues beyond the indication that they, too, suffered the loss of entire villages. However, when Canadian traders from the north and St. Louis traders from the south visited them at the close of the eighteenth century, the Gros Ventres, as they were then known, were reported to have a population of two thousand living in three villages located near the mouth of the Knife River in present North Dakota; and living near them in two villages were the Mandans, who had fled north from the Heart River area to be close to the Hidatsas so that the remanant groups could provide each other mutual protection from the raids of such enemies as the Assiniboines, Crees, and Sioux.

These early traders, moreover, found the Hidatsas to be a diverse group of formerly—and still—autonomous villages that had converged on the Missouri at separate times, some relatively recently. The three village groups, each speaking its own dialect, were closely related to the nomadic Crows, who also comprised two or more divisions, each with its own dialect. The largest of the Hidatsa social divisions, and apparently the last to settle along the Missouri, were the

Hidatsa proper *(hiraáca),* whose own name for themselves was popularly thought to be related to the word *wirahǻci* or 'willows', giving rise in the nineteenth century to the occasional designation Willow Indians, Osier tribe, or People of the Willows. To the French and English traders, however, the Hidatsas were most commonly known as the Gros Ventres or Big Bellies, a name that in its French form is still used colloquially in the twentieth century on the Fort Berthold Reservation. Throughout the nineteenth century another common designation was Minitari, the Mandan name for them that is, interestingly, a borrowing into Mandan of the Hidatsa word *mirítaari* ('crosses the water'). Still another early designation for the Hidatsas was Fall Indians. Both it and the name Gros Ventre were also used to denote the Atsinas, an unrelated Algonquian-speaking tribe living in north-central Montana with whom the Hidatsas have frequently been confused. Because the two tribes were called by the same names, they were often erroneously thought to be related and were sometimes differentiated by specifying the Hidatsas as Gros Ventres of the Missouri and the Atsinas as Gros Ventres of the Prairie. Similarly, when referred to as Fall Indians, the Hidatsas were occasionally differentiated by a qualifier like the Missouri Fall Indians.

Living nearest to the village of the Hidatsa proper, and more closely associated with them in the early nineteenth century, was a smaller group, the Awatixa *(awatixaá),** whose closer relationship is depicted in the French reference to their village as the "Petit Village" and in Lewis and Clark's reference to it as the "Little Menetarre village," in contrast to the "Grand Village of the Minetarrees," which designated the Hidatsa proper. Nevertheless, according to native tradition, the Awatixa were the first group to reach the Missouri River from the east, settle there, and take up horticulture. The larger Hidatsa division arrived later and was, in contrast, the last of the three groups to give up a nomadic subsistence pattern for a semisedentary one.

Culturally and dialectally most divergent from the others was the Awaxawi *(awaxá'wi),* a third division formerly living farther south of the Knife River area and one that had associated most closely with the Mandans when the latter were still farther south near the Heart River. In the early nineteenth century the Awaxawi were often portrayed as a separate tribe, their more distant relationship to the other groups in part reflected in separate names used by early traders and travelers to designate them. Although also known by their own name for themselves, the French traders preferred to call them Gens des

---

*This name is sometimes anglicized in the twentieth century as Amatiha.

Soulier, Soulier Noir, or simply Soulier, rendered into English variously as "Shoe Nation," "Moccasin," and "Shoes Men." Another frequent designation that traders and travelers used exclusively for the Awaxawi was Wattasoon, their rendering of the Arikara term *wiitatshaánu'*, which is that tribe's name for all the Hidatsa groups, not solely the Awaxawi, and which translates both as 'well dressed men' and 'people of the water.'

From the close of the eighteenth century until 1837 these three groups continued to live in separate villages, but increasing intermarriage among them broke down the old custom of village endogamy and went hand-in-hand with a rapid process of cultural leveling of differences among the villages. In 1837 they and the other horticultural tribes of the Upper Missouri were devastated once again by a smallpox epidemic in which the Hidatsas lost some two-thirds of their population, the Mandans even more. In 1845 most of the survivors of the two peoples, whose histories had now become intertwined, moved north to establish Like-a-Fishhook, a combined village in which the Hidatsas and Mandans maintained separate sections. Later, the few Hidatsas and Mandans who had remained downriver came north to move into the new village with the others, and in 1862 the Arikaras, too, forsook their village at Fort Clark to consolidate with the other two tribes and form a third section in Like-a-Fishhook Village. There, within the fortified walls of a single, large village that afforded them protection against the constant raids of the vastly more numerous Sioux, each tribe attempted to recreate and continue the life it had known downriver.

Despite the separate sections in Like-a-Fishhook Village that enabled them to preserve their separate social and ceremonial organizations, for Hidatsas and Mandans the intermarriage and cultural exchange that had begun at the end of the eighteenth century continued unabated and, in fact, proceeded at an even accelerated pace since the surviving populations had become so small. For the Hidatsas, certainly, the three divisions were no longer able to sustain their past separate social and ceremonial organizations but were forced to forge a single, albeit heterogeneous, community.

Simultaneous with the progressive leveling of cultural and linguistic diversity from within, Hidatsa society was being transformed more radically from without by a combination of acculturative forces—U.S. Army troops stationed at posts near the Fort Berthold Reservation after 1864, Indian agency personnel resident on the reservation after 1868, day schools opening there as early as 1870, and missionary activity commencing in earnest on the reservation in 1876. Symbolically the old culture collapsed with the convergence of three fateful events: the last performance in 1879 of the Naxpike, the primary religious ritual of the Hidatsas; the subsequent disappearance of the buffalo in the early 1880s; and, perhaps even more fundamentally, the dissolution in the late 1880s of the old village lifestyle, when Hidatsa, as well as Mandan and Arikara, families were moved onto individual allotments. The latter change in particular forced these peoples to replace the overt manifestations of their cultures with at least the rudiments of those characterizing Anglo-American society.

THE STUDY OF THE HIDATSAS

When Alfred Bowers (1901–1990) came to the Fort Berthold Reservation in 1932 to begin a study of Hidatsa social and ceremonial organization, the Hidatsas had been living on family allotments or in small communities for over four decades. During that time they had experienced constant government efforts to transform them into self-sufficient small farmers or stock growers. Christian missionaries, particularly Congregational and Roman Catholic, had established churches in most communities on the reservation and for a period had operated boarding schools; the Congregationals had even ordained native lay readers and ministers among all three tribes. Day schools, which had been operating in most of the reservation communities since the late nineteenth century, as well as off-reservation boarding schools, which had taken Indian children to Hampton Institute in Virginia and Carlisle Indian School in Pennsylvania beginning in the early 1880s and later to other schools in the Dakotas, had produced several generations of educated tribal members. Nevertheless, the elder Hidatsas whom Bowers would interview had been born within the first decade after the abandonment of the Knife River villages and their parents had lived in those villages as adults, before the construction of Like-a-Fishhook Village. These elderly people living in 1932 represented the last generation who had experienced the former Hidatsa lifeway during its final decades in the mid-nineteenth century and thus provided one of the last opportunities to document that culture firsthand.

There were, however, many other writers who had preceded Bowers and had already created a rich documentary record. Among them were James Mackay and David Thompson, who were among the earliest fur traders to visit the Hidatsa villages at the end of the eighteenth century. Their descriptions, brief though important, were followed by those of a succession of travelers on the Missouri, beginning first with Lewis and Clark in 1804 and 1806. The most extensive and accurate portrayal of Hidatsa life from the early nineteenth century, however, is that of Maximilian, Prince of Wied-Neuwied, who wintered in the Knife River area in 1833–34 and made a careful, scientific record of the culture he witnessed that was well illustrated by Karl Bodmer, the artist who accompanied him. Subsequent nineteenth-century descriptions include the account of the fur trader Henry Boller, who from 1858 to 1861 lived in the trading post near Like-a-Fishhook Village and later published an entertaining and informative book recounting his experiences there; and the ethnographic and linguistic descriptions of the Hidatsas by the U.S. Army surgeon Washington Matthews, who from 1865 to 1872 was stationed at Fort Stevenson, the military post near Like-a-Fishhook. Although Matthews' ethnographic account in his single publication is short—the bulk is a grammatical sketch and dictionary of the Hidatsa language—it is nevertheless crucial for its late-nineteenth-century perspective.[5]

In the early-twentieth century several writers compiled records of nineteenth-century Hidatsa life. The first contributor was Edward Curtis, who under the auspices of financier J. Pierpont Morgan compiled a sumptuous, multivolume reference work entitled *The North American Indian* in one volume, which contains a long chapter depicting Hidatsa culture and mythology as well as an appendix providing a cultural summary, a sampling of songs and vocabulary, and five brief biographies of prominent tribal members. This ethnographic account was compiled from interviews with older Hidatsas during a visit to the Fort Berthold Reservation sometime shortly before 1907.[6]

Curtis' interviews at Fort Berthold were followed by studies there of three anthropologists—Gilbert L. Wilson, Robert H. Lowie, and Frances Densmore—who made more substantial contributions to the ethnographic record. The most extensive are those of Wilson, a Presbyterian minister whose avocation of collecting local Indian artifacts ultimately led him into a career as a professional anthropologist. In 1906, while making sketches at Fort Berthold to illustrate a children's book of Indian stories that he was preparing for publication, Gilbert and his brother, Frederick, met the Goodbirds, a Hidatsa family living there, and began to record ethnographic information from them. The following year George G. Heye, the New York collector who founded the Museum of the American Indian in New York City, sent the brothers back to Fort Berthold to purchase material culture specimens for him; and in 1908 Clark Wissler, the noted Plains ethnologist at the American Museum of Natural History, arranged support for the Wilson brothers to undertake a long-term study of Hidatsa culture under museum auspices. Gilbert committed himself to the plan and over the ensuing eleven years, from 1908 to 1918, he spent every summer but one on the reservation recording information on all aspects of Hidatsa life, and particularly material culture, his primary interest.

During twelve summers of field work Wilson amassed a prodigious amount of information, most of it in the form of long narratives taken down verbatim in English or English translation from his three primary sources, Edward Goodbird, his mother Buffalo Bird Woman, and her brother Wolf Chief. The material from each season was regularly sent to the American Museum in the form of notes that constituted field reports. Some of it was incorporated in *Agriculture of the Hidatsa Indians: An Indian Interpretation*, his 1916 doctoral dissertation in anthropology at the University of Minnesota. Other data were organized into monographs on the horse and dog and eagle trapping in Hidatsa culture; and still other narratives were published as the autobiographies of two of his adopted Hidatsa relatives, Buffalo Bird Woman and her son Edward Goodbird. (An autobiography of Wolf Chief was begun but never completed.)

When Gilbert Wilson died in 1930, a large portion of his ethnographic material remained unpublished, since he had preferred the role of collector to that of editor. So that at least some of this manuscript material might see print, Bella Weitzner, an associate of Wissler at the American Museum, took up the editorial task of arranging parts of it into one monograph on the earth lodge and compiling a summary of the remaining notes—a miscellaneous collection of data on subsistence, material culture, and the life cycle—into another monograph published much later. These publications, however, do not exhaust Wilson's total contribution to the record of nineteenth-century Hidatsa culture, since much of it still remains unpublished in his archived notebooks.[7]

The Hidatsa studies of Robert Lowie, who is most noted for his lifelong work with the Crows in Montana, were part of larger comparative investigations of Plains Indian ethnology undertaken while he was curator of ethnology at the American Museum of Natural History and were ones he himself undoubtedly pursued because of the close historical relationship between the Crows and the Hidatsas and Mandans. His Hidatsa field work at Fort Berthold, which overlapped with Wilson's and brought the two men into association, comprised no more than four months distributed over three summers in 1910, 1911, and 1913. During those periods Lowie interviewed at least five of the most knowledgeable elderly Hidatsas—Poor Wolf, Hairy Coat, Wolf Chief, Butterfly, and Buffalo Bird Woman—and employed Joe Packineau and Edward Goodbird as interpreters. As a result, Lowie published monographs on age societies and the sun dance *(naxpike)*, which were contributions to collections of descriptive and compara-

tive studies of these institutions among Plains tribes that were ultimately intended to elucidate their historical development and diffusion throughout the region. In addition, an article on kinship and a
third monograph focusing on the social organization of the Mandans,
Hidatsas, and Crows, both descriptive and historical, sought to document those cultural features that were shared by the latter two
tribes. Finally, during his 1911 visit to Fort Berthold, Lowie, recorded
four folklore texts, which were later edited and prepared for publication by Zellig Harris and Carl Voegelin.[8]

During the summers of 1912, 1915, and 1918, Frances Densmore,
the indefatigable ethnomusicologist who documented the music of
many American Indian tribes throughout her career, visited Fort
Berthold to record Mandan and Hidatsa songs. Her work there culminated in a collection exceeding one hundred recordings made on wax
cylinders and a descriptive monograph based on these recordings
that presents transcriptions of the songs, their lyrics, and associated
cultural information derived from interviews with the singers. For
the Hidatsas the latter included Butterfly, Good Bear, Holding Eagle,
Pan, and Old Dog, as well as James Driver, who represented a younger generation of singers. Although the book focuses on music, a considerable amount of ethnographic material, including myths, is
woven into the presentation.[9]

The folklorist Martha Warren Beckwith was the last student to
visit Fort Berthold during this early-twentieth-century period. She
came to record Mandan and Hidatsa oral traditions, fortuitously at
the same time Bowers was engaged in his own field work there and
was recording many of the same stories she sought. Working independently of him during three visits between 1929 and 1932, she collected over fifty narratives, all taken down in English translation,
that illustrate most of the genres of the two tribal storytelling traditions. For the Hidatsas her primary source was Bear's Arm, a respected elderly man with whom Bowers also worked; and his repertoire was expanded by several stories recorded from Mrs. White Duck
and Ben Benson, the latter a Mandan who knew both tribes' traditions. The collection, published shortly thereafter, is a valuable reference work notable for its copious cross-references to cognate stories,
themes, and motifs in the oral traditions of other Plains and Eastern
Woodlands tribes.[10]

Bowers' Mandan Studies

Alfred Bowers was not a stranger to Fort Berthold and the Hidatsa
community when he went there in 1932. Although born in Stanford,
Nova Scotia, on June 1, 1901, he came to the United States in 1907
when his parents homesteaded near Killdeer, North Dakota. Their

farm, located in Dunn County, was immediately south of the Fort Berthold Reservation, where contact with people from the reservation was inevitable. Bowers remembered vividly his first encounter when he was a boy. One day as he was playing outside, a group of Mandan and Hidatsa men came riding up on horseback to the house. They frightened him and he ran inside, Bowers reminisced, but when he came back outside with his mother to see what they wanted, the men apologized and indicated they were hungry. His mother fed them and they rode off. Years later, when Bowers began his work among the Mandans, Crows Heart remembered him and the incident, and that memory established a basis for their future relationship.[11]

After completing high school, young Bowers taught in rural schools in North Dakota while he pursued a normal school education, and in 1921, after qualifying to teach in a city school, he moved to Mandan, where he taught for several years. He then moved to Dunn Center, not far from his parents' homestead, where he served as head of the school system for four years. In 1927 he left North Dakota to attend Beloit College and after his second year there received a Bachelor of Arts degree in geology. As an undergraduate he took classes in anthropology taught by George L. Collie, who headed Beloit's Logan Museum and who persuaded Bowers to pursue a career in anthropology.

For the next three years, from 1929 through 1931, while he was a graduate student at the University of Chicago, Bowers undertook summer field research along the Missouri River in the Dakotas under the auspices of Collie and the Logan Museum. For Bowers it was a crucial period, when three men shaped his work and ultimately his career: Collie, who thought Bowers should confine his efforts in the Missouri Valley to the archaeology of documented Mandan sites; Faye-Cooper Cole, his advisor at Chicago, who wanted him to provide a cultural dimension to his studies by collecting ethnographic material from living members of the tribes whose prehistory he was investigating in order to reconstruct their nineteenth-century culture; and Frank G. Logan, founder of the Logan Museum, who urged him to record the life story of an elderly Indian in order to preserve a native perspective on the way of life Bowers would reconstruct. In the end Bowers and his three mentors agreed that he would accomplish all these complementary goals. And so for three summers, with funding from the Logan Museum, Bowers took students from Beloit to North and South Dakota, where they surveyed and collected materials from Mandan and Arikara sites. But more importantly, after carrying out a preliminary study on the Fort Berthold Reservation in 1929 to determine the feasibility of reconstructing aboriginal Mandan culture, Bowers returned there for a six-month period in 1930 and 1931, again with funding from the Logan Museum, to undertake a more thorough study of the tribe's social and ceremonial life in the nineteenth century.

During the initial visit in 1929, Bowers established the basis for his later Mandan work as well as his future study of the Hidatsas. With the aid of elderly members of both tribes, he began by making a census of the lodge groups in the Mandan and Hidatsa sections of Like-a-Fishhook Village and documenting the occupants of each lodge. Simultaneously he recorded data on individuals who owned sacred bundles and filled ceremonial offices, and then later prepared genealogies that in part allowed him to trace the inheritance of bundles and other ceremonial rights.

With this outline of Mandan social and religious organization in hand, Bowers returned in 1930 to record religious rites and the myths underpinning them. This endeavor was more delicate, since even though the older people had shown no hesitancy to discuss the possession or inheritance of bundles and ritual offices, they were reluctant, at least initially, to divulge sacred knowledge. Nevertheless, with the aid of his interpreter, Tom Smith, Bowers was able to plan his study and eventually overcome resistance to his recording nearly all rites. At the same time, he was able to record additional information on Mandan households not obtained in 1929, and by utilizing the genealogies based on household groups, he was able to determine the identity and household composition of the former Mandan villages at Fort Clark and the ones preceding them near the Heart River—an achievement essential to ascertaining the cultural differences that formerly had obtained between the villages and that were still preserved in the memories of the older Mandans he interviewed.

The Mandan study that emanated from this work is a combination of two sets of interdependent data. The first part is a description of social organization—of households, clans and moieties, and villages— the kinship system and its terminology, and the life cycle. Following this background, which explains how an understanding of social relationships is crucial for comprehending religious organization and ritual transmission, are accounts of all the ceremonies Bowers was able to record. Those accounts, which comprise both myths and reminiscences, are presented in transcribed narrative form, sometimes condensed but generally given verbatim as they were recorded in the English translation the interpreter had provided as the elders recounted the narratives in their native Mandan. Preceding each narrative or set of narratives, which actually forms the descriptive core of the ceremony, is an introductory section in which Bowers backgrounds the account. The presentation, then, is one in which the anthropologist privileges through texts—the origin myths that explain the ritual symbols and acts as well as segments of personal histories—the native conception of what constitutes the important features and significance of the ceremony. The anthropological narrative, in contrast, provides the backdrop and thread that ties the whole together.

After completing the study, Bowers deposited the manuscript and field notes on which it was based in the Logan Museum, which had funded his field work. Later, in 1932 and 1933 while he was studying the Hidatsas, he expanded his earlier report with additional information on Mandan social and ceremonial life, particularly eagle trapping. Again in summer 1947, while recording the autobiography of Crows Heart, then ninety-two years old and the lone survivor of his original group of Mandan informants, Bowers verified his earlier data on social organization. In 1950 a revised manuscript, incorporating his original report, the additional data, and summaries of two other papers—one on Upper Missouri archaeology and the other on Mandan and Hidatsa history—was finally published as *Mandan Social and Ceremonial Organization.*

BOWERS' HIDATSA STUDIES

In spring 1932, at the urging of Faye-Cooper Cole, who continued as his faculty advisor at the University of Chicago, Bowers submitted a proposal to undertake an analogous study of Hidatsa social and ceremonial organization, since this tribe, too, offered a rare opportunity for such an investigation—and one that would complement the Mandan. Although during the nineteenth century Hidatsas were culturally similar to Mandans—a similarity resulting from a century and a half of close relations and progressive intermarriage—they nevertheless differed in fundamental ways. Both peoples were semisedentary horticulturists who shared many overt lifeways, but the Hidatsas were actually latecomers to the Missouri River area, and for them horticulture and the earth lodge domicile were late acquisitions derived from the Mandans, who had practiced corn cultivation and lived in earth lodges for many centuries. As Bowers notes, in the seventeenth and eighteenth centuries the peoples now known as the Hidatsas and Crows were an aggregate of related but dialectally and culturally diverse bands and villages that were moving across the northern plains, by tradition out of eastern North Dakota, where some thought they originated in the area of Devils Lake. Their history during this period, and even into historic times, was a fluid one in which some groups settled along the Missouri River and others proceeded farther west, while still others moved back and forth between the two; but ultimately, because of historical vicissitudes, the groups coalesced into the two tribal entities known historically as the Hidatsas and Crows.

Despite their similarities, numerous fundamental features distinguish Hidatsa culture from that of the Mandans as well as the Arikaras, who were also horticulturists along the Missouri River. Among the most salient are the lack of village or band sacred bundles, which characterize not only the Mandans but even more fundamentally the Arikaras farther downriver, and the lack of a separate ceremonial lodge or area in the middle of the village, again an integral feature of Mandan and Arikara ceremonial life. There was no consensus among Hidatsas on their origins as there was among the Arikaras and even the Mandans; and, in contrast to the traditions of the other two tribes, Hidatsa origin myths are common Plains myths integrated into a larger interrelated history. The Hidatsas, in short, illustrate a people who share the fundamental cultural features of nomadic Plains societies but who relatively recently took up the lifestyle of the semisedentary riverine tribes represented by the Mandans, and more remotely the Arikaras, who in turn had influenced the Mandans.

Bowers' proposal for the Hidatsa investigation was in many ways a replication of his Mandan study. It began with the same methodological approach: to make a census of the 1870 population, securing name, age, sex, and clan of each individual; to map the lodges in Like-a-Fishhook Village and record their occupants; to map the cornfields and correlate their ownership and inheritance with the ownership and inheritance of earth lodges; and to record genealogies based on the census that would take families back to their former villages. Based on his earlier work, he listed twenty-five ceremonies known to exist among the Hidatsas and proposed to document them as well as any additional ones he should discover. Again, as in the Mandan study, he emphasized the importance of recording the myths that explained the basis for a rite: "From my experience with the Mandans, I feel that too little emphasis has been given heretofore to the sacred mythology of the American Indians. These groups think of the Mythological Period as but a few centuries ago and it is in these myths that we find the native's explanation for the origin of the natural and the social order."

After explaining the difficulties of obtaining ritual knowledge among the Hidatsas—difficulties he felt certain he could overcome by patience and familiarity—he explained the need for such a study. Very little about their ceremonial life had been recorded because of the difficulty in securing information. Lowie had had no success, and Wilson had been able to document only two ceremonies. Noting that such a study was still feasible because most of the rituals had been performed within the last forty years and their associated bundles were still preserved and treated ritually, he argued that it would allow anthropologists to compare Hidatsa with Crow religious life and thereby provide an important historical perspective on two closely related Plains peoples. He contended, moreover, that no study of Hidatsa social organization would be complete without a thorough knowledge of their ceremonial organization and that a complete account of their rituals would illustrate how one people had conceptually united the natural and social orders.

To accomplish the Hidatsa project Bowers proposed taking it beyond his Mandan study in several methodologically significant ways. Most important was his stated intention to learn the Hidatsa language and record narratives in it rather than solely in English translation as he had done previously. Recognizing the importance of the linguistic dimension to such a study, he also recommended that application should be made to the Committee on Research in Native American Languages for funding to enable him to record Mandan texts as well, an urgent need since the language was dying out and it was a task he could accomplish in the course of the Hidatsa project. Furthermore, now that suitable recording instruments were available, he requested that one be purchased so that he could document the songs that were integral to all ceremonies. Finally, he suggested that since no archaeological investigations of Hidatsa sites had ever been made, he would map all known village sites and secure cross-sections of the refuse piles there, and further proposed that he devote a portion of his time to archaeological study to broaden scholarly knowledge of the prehistory of the horticultural Missouri River tribes.

The proposal was funded by the Rockefeller Foundation, and on August 8, 1932, Bowers described his situation in a letter to Cole:

> I am settled conveniently here at Elbowoods in the government hotel in the agency village right in the midst of the Hidatsa camps. The hotel has four rooms and there are two roomers at present. We get meals at 20 cents and room for $10. a month which was cheaper than I could feed myself. I need to take my lunch out when working which is extra. So far I have been able to get an informant who is on friendly terms with the man running the electric light plant so he lives right here on the job all the time. I may have to spend part of my time away up in the hard-boiled section where the die-hards live but at present I am able to get what I want from informants living within 25 miles of the agency.
>
> . . . I have been working on the Thunderbird bundle since last week, during spare moments, taking down the myth in the native Hidatsa language. Writing phonetically is a slow, tedious task. I

have a new interpreter since my man of former seasons [Tom Smith] is seriously ill of heart trouble caused, as the old men say[,] for violating some of the native customs while working with me. One old man asked me if I was feeling well, but having been tipped off ahead of time, I told him I was in the best of health.

I am finding work for several years and doubt very much if I shall ever be able to finish by next June or July as I had hoped on the funds available. I could do much more work were I to dispense with the native texts but I feel that I am learning the language as I go and hope to do my work without an interpreter later on.

By the end of the month Bowers reported to Cole that for the past two weeks he had been working on the *naxpike,* or sun dance, taking down its myths in Hidatsa but expressing concern that, even though he had become skilled in writing Hidatsa, transcribing texts in the language was a slow, tedious task. So slow, in fact, that

I fear that I shall be obliged to give it up. Every day brings light on new bundle rites so that there may be at least 50 of them, each separate with its own mythological setting and duties in the general tribal religious scheme. This work is immensely interesting but extremely difficult, in spite of my familiarity with every old man of the tribe.

In the same letter he told how he had had a Mandan name bestowed on him the previous evening:

The Indian Fair ended last night. I was called out in the center yesterday and presented with the name Four Bears by the old Mandan at whose home I camped the two seasons when working with the Mandans. The naming was strictly according to tribal custom, full consideration being given to clan etc. By virtue of the intimate friendship with Crows Heart, they considered me of the Chicken clan and looked for the name of the most distinguished Chicken clansman. The old men were nearly all night selecting a name and running down the question of its eligibility, etc. Mandan Four Bears was the last regular chief of the Mandans; he died of smallpox in 1837, but 25 years later an Hidatsa took the name from the Mandans. The giving of a name, even, is a complex rite, and involves the whole question of kinship relations, with reciprocal obligations. In view of the fact that the giving of the name was wholly of their own free will, and since I was the only white to get one according to their statement at the time of conferance, I felt it was a tactful act to accept gracefully and thus widen the feeling of goodwill between myself and the two tribes for it would react favorably to me in my work with them.

In a letter to Frank Logan and his wife, Bowers described the name bestowal ceremony in greater detail, providing an instructive ethnographic account in its own right:

I want to tell you about the ceremony held at the dances last night at which over a thousand Mandans, Hidatsas, Crows, Arikarees, Santee Sioux, Tetons, Pawnees of Oklahoma, Otos of Nebraska, Cheyennes, Arapahoes, Yanktons, and other tribes were represented and at which I was invited to come forward and take and perpetuate the name, Four Bears, in honor of the Mandans' greatest leader, who died in 1837. It was rumored several days before the tribes met that the Mandans, for the first time since the smallpox scourge of 1837, were to take into the tribe as a leader one who was working with them to record their history. The old men met on the evening of the 25th of August and spent all night checking up their memories concerning the history of the war record of the Mandan Four Bears and determining if the name was eligible and if the family descended from him would part with the name. They agreed and the old men made presents to the family for the name. I had brought 24 red pipes from Pipestone, Minnesota, to give to the old men which I stepped forward and presented to them as their names were called.

After the presentation of each pipe the old women dressed in beautiful elk-tooth decorated dresses and fine feather headdresses danced around us, singing the victory songs which they always did when a man returned successfully from a war expedition. This they did after each pipe was given. After I was through, Crows Heart, the man with whom I lived when working for the Logan Museum stepped forward and speaking in the Indian language which was interpreted in several languages said in about such words as these:

"One hundred years ago we were a numerous and happy people, with no fear of our enemies. Our people were brave and proud of their great leaders. Foremost of our leaders, and the bravest and wisest of all of them was Four Bears. He fasted in the Okipa for four days and he fasted nine days on a hill without food or water to get a God who would bring him success in war and make him a great leader among his people. Once he captured a herd of horses from the enemy and brought [it] to our village alone. He revenged the murder of his brother by walking 250 miles to the Arikara camps where he entered their camp by night and killed singlehanded in bed the man who murdered his brother. He was braver than the Cheyenne and once challenged their chief to a dual singlehanded. All these things he did to raise his name before the people and to spread the word to the enemy that the Mandans were the bravest people on the earth. Twenty five years later, a young war-leader of the Hidatsa was given the name Four Bears. He, too, distinguished himself as a great man. He ruled his people wisely and all looked to him for advice. He marched with a few men thru enemy territory to Fort Laramie, Wyoming to make the treaty with the whites which last year paid each of us $1400 and today we are rich and own fine homes and many cattle. Three years ago a young man came to my house and lived with me while I related the glories of our history. Sioux, Arapaho, Crows, all of you, listen to my words. Ours has been a noble history and we are proud of it. This young man became my closest friend and I have looked to him as a 'younger brother, my clan brother' and we have exchanged many presents. All the tribe is his friend and all say he is a good man and working for our good. Last night at a general council we looked about for the name that would be most honorable to give him and the tribe has agreed that only the name of their greatest chief would be suitable. We are aware that to give this name is to lose it from our tribe forever [and] were we not proud of him and certain that he will always consider himself one of us [we would not do so].

"My tribesmen, are there any who object to naming him Four Bears? Did I not as a small boy fast on the hills until the Gods sent me a vision that I would be successful in war and leader of my people? Do you remember that I suffered in the Okipa ceremony, that I hanged from a cliff all night with thongs thru the flesh of my chest, that I dragged buffalo skulls by thongs thru my back, and that I led a thirsty stallion with thongs thru my legs and that each time the gods sent me a vision that I would be successful in war? Do you forget the time I killed two Chippewas singlehanded when none other was so brave as to venture in the deep grass where they hid? Do you remember when I avenged the death of a clan brother by the hands of the Sioux? All these things I did for the good of my people and the clan. Today I stand before you and say that we have another leader who is the friend of all of us. Whenever he meets us he is our friend. His name from now on is Four Bears. If there are those who object, speak. Fellow Mandans, speak the name of our new son or brother according to your clan."

Then we walked around the inside of the circle and the Mandans called Mato Topa (Bear Four), the Hidatsa, Daxpits Dopash, and each of the other tribes the words in their language. When we were through passing through the lines, Crows Heart explained that from now on I should be so called and that all the tribes should extend me the courtesy given other Mandans. That Mandans should ask my advice and I theirs. Already an old woman with stomach trouble has called on me to advise her if she should go to the hospital.

I am interested to know if there will be any additional medicine bundle rites brought to earth as the result of this newly added prestige. I am sure that all this will lighten the job of investigating the Hidatsa religion study I am making. I enjoy this work and, of course, feel quite honored to have been shown this honor in view of the fact that the Mandans have not given a white a name like this since before the smallpox when Joseph Kipp was so named. There is a prejudice against it for fear that one will not come back and thus the name will be taken away from the tribe, especially the important names for all would agree that to sell a name or give a name not owned would bring no end of bad luck to the tribe.

On September 26, Bowers again wrote the Logans, telling them that he was planning to go on a Mandan eagle-trapping expedition. He had hoped, he said, to go with a Hidatsa group, but since he was not sufficiently acquainted with the men in their parties, he fell back on the company of his more intimate Mandan acquaintances. Afterwards, on November 11, when he wrote Cole's secretary about fiscal matters, Bowers mentioned the trip and told her that just after the party's earth lodge and eagle-trapping pits been prepared for use at the trapping site, a heavy snow fell and forced them to give up the expedition, but fortunately not before he was able to get a full acount of the rituals that opened the eagle-trapping season.

Over the ensuing months Bowers' letters to Cole describe a winter busy not only with field work but also personal matters. The young anthropologist temporarily lost his family farm in Dunn County to the tax collector and during the spring struggled to regain it by trapping beavers to sell for their pelts, while at the same time he became embroiled in state political maneuverings to replace the director of the North Dakota State Historical Society, a position that Bowers himself sought unsuccessfully. At the same time, however, he recorded a seemingly endless amount of data, working at times in his hotel room and at other times in the homes of his informants, wherever possible using his typewriter to record narratives dictated in English. Illustrative of his experiences is a description in a letter to Cole written on January 12, 1933:

> I have been working on the stories of the Gods and Holy People of the tribe, thinking no ceremony would have any meaning until I was familiar with these stories. The way it looks now it will take me a year to record all of them. It is an immense job for there is often hesitation in telling them. One man told me he knew 100 sepa-

rate stories of First Creator, Coyote, and I think there will be that many, alright. One cannot understand their beliefs of the origin of the universe, its people, and its ceremonies unless he knows them. I did not want to go into them but I found that I had to for First Creator is the Servant for all ceremonies, which is pretty good evidence of the great antiquity of the Coyote Trickster in their traditions, I believe, tho Dr. Radcliffe-Brown might not agree with us. I have given up all hope of finishing all the work I wanted to by June for each day brings out new leads that I wish to follow. Too, I am not wise enough to separate the religious life from the social life, or even the techniques. It is all woven to-gether and one helps to explain the other. In a story today, I found that the Buffaloes got into much trouble because too few bulls monopolized the cows and it led to trouble of all sorts until First Creator killed the tyrants off. Then he said, "That is bad for man or animals; men can have one, two, or three wives, but men who take more leave some without wives and in time there is trouble. From now on, men should not marry too many women at one time." My informant said, "You see, First Creator used the case of the buffalo to illustrate how we could get along best to-gether."

Throughout the spring Bowers' success in recording material continued unabated, once again expressed in a letter to Cole on May 9 that also provides a humorous allusion to one of many nagging problems:

My work is getting to the place now where it requires most careful planning to avoid repetition and provide for the filling of obvious gaps. If the religious characters would remain a speckled eagle or coyote instead of changing so much, it would simplify the work considerably. It is too bad that the Indians when evolving their system of gods did not call in an Anthropologist, or at least an efficiency expert.

In June, when Bowers was planning a six-week tour of the reservation to obtain residual information on minor ceremonies, Edward Kennard, a Columbia University graduate student working under Franz Boas, arrived at Elbowoods to begin a study of the Mandan language. Since Kennard had no camping equipment—a necessity for working with reservation people not living near Elbowoods—Bowers invited him to accompany him and share expenses. Kennard accepted the offer, and his presence, it seems, stimulated Bowers to propose to Cole that in August, when his current grant would expire, he should undertake a linguistic study of Hidatsa parallel to Kennard's with Mandan, a proposal that also revealed the extent to which Bowers' work with the language had progressed:

I began to take religious rites in text and spent over a month at it. Finding the work too slow, I felt that I would never get thru in a year, in view of the evident wealth of religious lore. During the past year, hearing the language spoken daily I have come to understand much of the structure and have mastered the sounds. With this Mr. Kennard working on the Mandans, we could travel together and compare notes frequently, thus being of considerable mutual aid. It will take him six weeks to get to the place in Mandan that I now hold with the Hidatsa and by the time I finish my ethnological work, I could pick up the other for the balance of the season. I realize that my linguistic training has not been as thorough as in other fields but he has found my phonetic chart of the Mandans essentially the same as he secured and the rules of vowel changes with accent that I first noted as well. I think it would be a fine chance to get in some work on the Hidatsa since there is so much work being done on the Siouan languages.

Although this proposal, unfortunately, never materialized, Bowers persevered with learning Hidatsa and in late June wrote Cole that he had worked part of the preceding week without an interpreter and even took his notes in the language, commenting that the only disadvantage to such a procedure was that he could not use his typewriter but must handwrite notes.

Bowers' work, which continued through the summer, included several weeks of camping in the remotest part of the reservation, where he attempted to record ceremonial information from the "die-hards," members of the dissident Crow Flies High band that had left the reservation in 1870 and lived near Fort Buford at the mouth of the Yellowstone River until they were forcibly returned to Fort Berthold in 1894. His efforts, however, were less than successful; in fact, he wrote:

I never found such hard sledding in all my work here as I have had with this Crow Flying High Band and when I say tough, I mean tough enough. They still go out on the hills crying all night, never venture into a Christian Church, and carry an inherent dislike for all whites. If I had time, I know that I could get next to them but even with the best of secrets, others do know something of it so I have much second hand information on most of the things they own.

On August 1, when his funding was exhausted, Bowers completed work at Elbowoods and, with no prospects of employment or additional support, moved back to his farm, where he fixed up a granary in which to live, since the renter's family occupied the house. In a letter to Cole on June 8, he summarized his endeavor over the preceding year:

With the difficulties one encounters yet in any study of the religious societies of the Plains, I feel well satisfied with the results I have secured. I do not mean that I have done everything . . . but I do feel that I have sampled every medicine ceremony and can give a very concise account of them all. . . . when I come to write the material up, I will find obvious gaps which may or may not be filled at this late hour, but in certain respects my data is more complete than that of most workers in the Plains.

First I wish to review again my method of procedure. When beginning work, I saw that to get a desirable picture of the religious life of a tribe not numbering more than 500 since the smallpox epidemic of 1837–38, I could control my data by taking a census of 60 years ago from the older people. . . . With that as a beginning, I traced back each line as far as informants could remember. In a few cases as leading religious leaders, these blended into the mythological period and went back to "the beginning of the world," which was to be expected. Then I had a desirable informant tell me the religious rites each person owned and in that way I found a relative who had inherited these rights to the ceremony and asked them for their information. In a few cases I could not find descendants and was obliged to rely on others who could give more or less complete accounts.

I took as my first job knowing the owners of the rites 60 years ago, that of getting the traditional origin of the rite and found that in the natives' minds the "story" of how the ceremony came to the tribe more important and more secret than an actual account of how the ceremony was performed. Before attempting a formal description of the various ceremonies, I undertook the writing of endless numbers of these origin stories which brought [out] the interrelation of certain ceremonies and which defined the rules of the rites.

I do not know what your personal opinion is of the great emphasis I placed on these origin rites but to me they were the most essential part of the religious beliefs and I do not believe that anyone is in a position to analyze the religious life of the tribe I worked [on] or any other tribe until he knows these accounts well. Getting these stories was the most difficult part of my work and a piece of work that many are apt to neglect because of the reluctance of the Hidatsa to relate them.

Personally, I set out to show how the religious structure was set up and stayed after these until I had all of the important origin stories recorded.

In the past, as you know, Kroeber, Spier, Wissler, and some of the minor anthropologists have used certain traits as, for example, dancing around the central pole, sexual freedom, etc., as found in certain ceremonies of different tribes to illustrate diffusion. For the Historical School, the traditions I have recorded will be just as usable. In fact, Boas has used mythology of the Plains tho never carrying it as far as we could to-day with the added information at hand. . . .

Gaining familiarity with the traditional origin of many ceremonies, the formalized rites, then takes on new meaning. Songs mean little to the study except that where the words mean the same in two tribes. . . .

My last step was to trace down the inheritance of rites and establish the rules. This I did with great care and detail and feel that I made a definite and accurate account of that aspect of the investigation.

We know from historic data that there was a progressive reduction in the number of villages of the Hidatsa and Mandan and that in former times these villages were often widely scattered so that when a certain ceremony was to be held, it was not possible to bring owners of certain ceremonies over great distances to perform their respective parts. I was interested in learning what would happen in the case of a division of the tribe or village and found that in 1870 the Hidatsa divided because of a quarrel and lived 200 miles apart until brought together by the government by force. I took a careful census of that section of the tribe, traced out what ceremonies remained with each section and how they adjusted themselves to the separation, keeping up the religious life. To my knowledge, this has never been done heretofore. My results were surprisingly fruitful and threw much light onto the dynamics of the religious life.

Like so many anthropologists of his generation, Bowers was not able to write his study of Hidatsa social and ceremonial organization once he had completed his field work; nor was he able to get additional funding in the 1930s to continue and expand his research while the opportunity still existed. With no income that would allow him to return to Chicago to continue his studies, he went back to his farm and then accepted a position as county extension agent for the Department of Agriculture in Mountrail County, a demanding job that nevertheless allowed him occasional evenings to work with his data and weekends to drive to the reservation for an afternoon of work with his Hidatsa friends. For several years he sought employment with the Indian Service, thinking that his anthropological training would appeal to the Collier administration, and hoped to be assigned to the Fort Berthold Reservation, where he could continue his studies; but the efforts were fruitless.

During the ensuing years he continued to work at first sporadically, and beginning in 1936 more steadily, with his Mandan and Hidatsa materials. Although in less frequent letters to Cole he mentions filing and cross-filing the data, the concern he expresses most often is the form in which they should be presented, since both Cole and Paul H. Nesbitt, Collie's successor as director of the Logan Museum, were urging him to prepare the materials for publication. By now he had several sets of data—Mandan and Arikara archaeological notes from his early work for the Logan Museum; Mandan notes on material culture; and Mandan and Hidatsa ethnographic notes embracing religious life, social organization, and mythology—and he was uncertain how most effectively to arrange them, although his inclination was to compile four monographs: one on Mandan archaeology, one on traditions and mythology, one on religious and social organization, and finally one on Mandan material culture.

In 1940 and 1941, apparently with financial support from the Logan Museum and the assistance of his wife, Gladys Monson Bowers, whom he married in 1939, Bowers completed one manuscript on Mandan archaeology and two others on Mandan and Hidatsa ceremonialism. Finally, in January 1947 he was able to return to the University of Chicago to continue study and work with his materials under the supervision of Cole and a young social anthropologist recently added to the department, Fred Eggan, who had formerly been a classmate of Bowers. The two-year period there, which included a short field trip back to Fort Berthold in summer 1947 to record Crows Heart's autobiography, culminated in a dissertation entitled "A History of the Mandan and Hidatsa," for which he was awarded his doctorate in anthropology in 1948. The following year Bowers accepted a teaching appointment at the University of Idaho, where he founded the department of anthropology and remained until retirement. It was there that he completed *Hidatsa Social and Ceremonial Organization* in 1962, nearly three decades after his field work.

THIS BOOK AND BOWERS' WORK

Bowers' monograph on the Hidatsas is a composite of materials written at different times that reflects a combination of academic influences, some obvious and others only inferential. Certainly his teachers at Beloit College and the University of Chicago—Collie, Nesbitt, Cole, and Radcliffe-Brown—who represented a variety of perspectives, are clearly manifested throughout the book, but in Bowers' eclecticism are also found traces of earlier anthropological hallmarks exemplified by Alice C. Fletcher's study of the Pawnee Hako and Alfred L. Kroeber's mapping of Zuñi households.[12]

Foremost, however, the book is a description of Hidatsa social organization and ceremonial life that parallels his earlier Mandan book and is, accordingly, divided into two parts. The first one, in which Radcliffe-Brown's influence is most clearly discerned, is a portrayal of social organization that comprises detailed descriptions of Hidatsa village and tribal organization, the clan and moiety system, the kinship system, the life cycle, the age grade societies, and warfare. The second part, the description of ceremonial organization, discusses supernatural power and the relationship of individuals to it, the mythical period in Hidatsa history, and each of the ceremonies known to the Hidatsas.

Although Bowers supplements his description of Hidatsa social and ceremonial life with material from the historical and ethnographic literature—from the rich accounts of Thompson, Maximilian, Curtis, Lowie, and Wilson—it is essentially a presentation of the data he himself recorded, presented verbatim in narrative form, although frequently condensed when the narratives were too long to be quoted in full. In the introduction, after noting that most anthropologists are silent about their field methods and analytic techniques, Bowers provides an explicit account of his own methodology that was unusual for its time. Characterizing his approach as the "creatively historical method"—one that combines Boasian historicism and its concern for ethnographic detail with British structural-functionalism and its concern for understanding social structure and kinship—Bowers endeavored to reconstruct Hidatsa culture as it existed in 1836, just before the last major smallpox epidemic, by interviewing elder Hidatsas who had experienced the former lifeways during their youth, and by working back in time by means of genealogies, inheritance patterns, reminiscences, and oral traditions. And, following Boas, he felt compelled to record his interviews as texts in the native language, a method he utilized during his initial work but abandoned after the sheer bulk of data he attempted to record precluded it.

Preceding these two main parts of the book is an historical overview, apparently written in the 1940s, that summarizes references to the Hidatsas appearing in eighteenth- and nineteenth-century sources and that in turn briefly relates these historical accounts both to Hidatsa traditions of their own origins and to the archaeological record. At the end of the book, in an essay written sometime after 1956, Bowers concludes his presentation with an interpretive chapter situating Hidatsa prehistory and post-contact history within the context of northern Plains culture history at large. It synthesizes an array of interdisciplinary data—archaeological, historical, and cultural—portraying the early-eighteenth-century cultural landscape in the Dakotas as one of small, culturally and linguistically related groups, usually individual villages, that were shifting locations and functioning independently of one another rather than in concert as tribal entities. Only after the late-eighteenth-century smallpox epidemics, when the native populations were drastically reduced, did these groups consolidate into larger tribal groupings and develop complexly integrated social and ceremonial systems. For the Hidatsas in particular, Bowers contends, this was a period in which a diverse population underwent significant cultural enrichment under Mandan and Arikara influence. Though not a novel observation for the Upper Missouri peoples now known as the Hidatsas, Mandans, and Arikaras, Bowers' emphasis on independent small-group inter-action and movement, where alliances and antagonisms transcended cultural relationships, is important for modern students who all too often project the tribal entities of the historic period back into prehistoric times. At the same time this interpretative essay illustrates the interests of contemporary archaeologists—represented by his teachers Collie, Nesbitt, Cole—to link the historical cultures of living peoples with their prehistoric remains.

What especially distinguishes Bowers' work, in addition to its recognition of kinship as fundamental to an understanding of Hidatsa social and ceremonial organization, is its foregrounding of native Hidatsa conceptions of their social and ceremonial world and the recognition of individual variation and perception in shaping that world view—or, more appropriately, those world views, since the culture Bowers reconstructed was not static or homogeneous but rather diverse and changing. Thus the description of ritualism is arranged within a Hidatsa chronology, in which individual ceremonies are presented in the perceived order of their adoption into Hidatsa society in mythological times and are interrelated as Hidatsas understood them. Similarly, the ceremonial accounts themselves focus on the "stories" of each ritual—the sacred and secular traditions in which appear the origin accounts of the rituals and the instructions for the symbols and ritual acts comprising the ceremonies—as well as the reminiscences of individuals who had participated in or witnessed ceremonies performed in the nineteenth century. These myths, legends, and personal reminiscences, as Bowers so aptly notes, are after all the very sources of information to which any young Hidatsa man or woman must have had recourse when learning about the ceremonies. It is this Hidatsa perspective that he wished to convey.

Concomitant with his concern for presenting the material from a Hidatsa perspective, Bowers explicitly states that he attempted to minimize his own intrusion into the documentary process, assiduously avoiding the two criticisms Hidatsas most commonly voiced of academics who came to study them: that either the anthropologists tried to answer their own questions or that they cut off their informant's explanations with the statement that what was being said was not important. In contrast with the practice of other field workers of his time, Bowers allowed, and even encouraged, these native voices to speak freely, to tell without interruption the formal myths explaining aspects of their culture and, when describing social patterns, to digress when excursions into another area seemed to produce noteworthy cultural information.

The result of Bowers' methods is a unique book important not only for its incomparable richness of ethnographic description of a Plains Indian social and religious system but also for its enduring value as a cultural document that lets native Hidatsas—the people who lived and knew that nineteenth-century culture—describe it in their own words. This is a precious record, compiled just before the last individuals who knew that lifeway passed on, concluding a period in human history that will never again be witnessed. Because of Bowers' interest and perseverance in preserving a vital part of this history, as well as his perspicacity in documenting it as faithfully as he could, readers today and in the future—native Hidatsas no less than academics and the public at large—who wish to gain an understanding of a nineteenth-century Plains Indian society and its religion will forever have the opportunity to acquire an insightful portrayal in this description.

NOTES

1. Washington Matthews, *Ethnography and Philology of the Hidatsa Indians,* U.S. Geological and Geographical Survey, Miscellaneous Publications no. 7 (Washington, D.C., 1877).

James R. Walker's major publications are "The Sun Dance and Other Ceremonies of the Oglala Division of the Teton Dakota," American Museum of Natural History, *Anthropological Papers* 16, pt. 2 (New York, 1917); Walker, *Lakota Belief and Ritual,* ed. by Raymond J. DeMallie and Elaine A. Jahner (Lincoln: University of Nebraska Press, 1980); Walker, *Lakota Society,* ed. by Raymond J. DeMallie (Lincoln: University of Nebraska Press, 1982); Walker, *Lakota Myth,* ed. by Elaine A. Jahner (Lincoln: University of Nebraska Press, 1983).

George A. Dorsey's Cheyenne studies are published as *The Cheyenne: Ceremonial Organization,* Field Columbian Museum *Publication No. 99,* Anthropological Series 9, pt. 1 (Chicago, 1905), and *The Cheyenne: The Sun Dance,* Field Columbian Museum *Publication No. 103,* Anthropological Series 9, pt. 2 (Chicago, 1905). Mooney's work on the Cheyennes appears in *The Ghost-Dance Religion and the Sioux Outbreak of 1890,* Bureau of American Ethnology Annual Report 14, pt. 2 (Washington, D.C., 1896) (reprint, Lincoln: University of Nebraska Press, 1991), pp. 1023–38, and *The Cheyenne Indians,*

American Anthropological Association Memoirs 1 (Lancaster, Pa., 1905). Grinnell brought together his ethnographic material in *The Cheyenne Indians: Their History and Ways of Life,* 2 vols. (New Haven: Yale University Press, 1923; reprint, Lincoln: University of Nebraska Press, 1972); mythologic and other stories are collected in *By Cheyenne Campfires* (New Haven: Yale University Press, 1926; reprint, Lincoln: University of Nebraska Press, 1971).

2. Alice C. Fletcher, *The Hako: A Pawnee Ceremony,* Bureau of American Ethnology Annual Report 22, pt. 2 (Washington, D.C., 1904); Fletcher and Francis La Flesche, *The Omaha Tribe,* Bureau of American Ethnology Annual Report 27 (Washington, D.C., 1907).

Francis La Flesche's studies of Osage rituals are *The Osage Tribe: Rite of the Chiefs; Sayings of the Ancient Men,* Bureau of American Ethnology Annual Report 36 (Washington, D.C., 1921); *The Osage Tribe: The Rite of Vigil,* Bureau of American Ethnology Annual Report 39 (Washington, D.C., 1925); *The Osage Tribe: Two Versions of the Child-Naming Rite,* Bureau of American Ethnology Annual Report 43, pp. 23–164 (Washington, D.C., 1928); *The Osage Tribe: Rite of the Wa-xó-be,* Bureau of American Ethnology Annual Report 45, pp. 523–833 (Washington, D.C., 1930); *War and Peace Ceremony of the Osage Indians,* Bureau of American Ethnology Bulletin 101 (Washington, D.C., 1939).

James R. Murie's Pawnee work includes "Pawnee Indian Societies," American Museum of Natural History, *Anthropological Papers* 11, pt. 7 (New York, 1914); *Ceremonies of the Pawnee,* 2 vols., Smithsonian Contributions of Anthropology 27 (Washington, D.C., 1981; 1 vol. reprint, Lincoln: University of Nebraska Press, 1989); and a manuscript with George A. Dorsey, "The Pawnee: Society and Religion of the Skidi Pawnee," which is being edited for publication by Douglas R. Parks. Mythology recorded by Murie is published in George A. Dorsey, *Traditions of the Skidi Pawnee,* Memoirs of the American Folk-Lore Society, vol. 8 (New York: Houghton, Mifflin, 1904); and Dorsey, *The Pawnee: Mythology,* Carnegie Institution Publications, no. 59 (Washington, D.C., 1906).

3. Alexander Lesser, *The Pawnee Ghost Dance Hand Game: A Study of Cultural Change,* Columbia University Contributions to Anthropology 16 (New York: Columbia University Press, 1933); Gene Weltfish, *Caddoan Texts: Pawnee,* Publications of the American Ethnological Society 17 (New York: G. E. Stechert, 1937).

Robert H. Lowie's studies of the Crows include "Social Life of the Crow Indians," American Museum of American History, *Anthropological Papers,* 9, pt. 2 (New York, 1912); "The Sun Dance of the Crow Indians," American Museum of American History, *Anthropological Papers,* 16, pt. 1 (New York, 1915); and separate studies of religion, mythology, art, and material culture published as American Museum of American History, *Anthropological Papers,* 21, pts. 1–5 (New York, 1917–24) and 25, pts. 1–2 (New York, 1918–22). A summary of these detailed studies appears in *The Crow Indians* (New York: Farrar and Rinehart, 1935).

Frances Densmore, *Teton Sioux Music,* Bureau of American Ethnology Bulletin 61 (Washington, D.C., 1918; reprint, Lincoln: University of Nebraska Press, 1992); Ella Deloria, *Dakota Texts,* Publications of the American Ethnological Society 14 (New York: G. E. Stechert, 1932).

4. For the early history of the fur trade on the Missouri River, see Abraham Nasatir, *Before Lewis and Clark: Documents Illustrating the History of the Missouri 1785–1804,* 2 vols. (1952; reprint, Lincoln: University of Nebraska Press, 1990). Preston Holder, *The Hoe and the Horse on the Plains: A Study of Cultural Development among North American Indians* (Lincoln: University of Nebraska Press, 1970), provides an introduction to the early history of the horticultural tribes of the Middle Missouri and a contrastive study of their lifeways in relation to those of the nomadic tribes. Roy W. Meyer, *The Village Indians of the Upper Missouri: The Mandans, Hidatsas, and Arikaras* (Lincoln: University of Nebraska Press, 1977), presents a chronological history of the Mandans and Hidatsas and their relations with the United States.

5. Accounts of eighteenth and early nineteenth century visitors to the Hidatsas are brought together in W. Raymond Wood and Thomas D. Thiessen, eds., *Early Fur Trade on the Northern Plains: Canadian Traders among the Mandan and Hidatsa Indians, 1738–1818* (Norman: University of Oklahoma Press, 1985). For Lewis and Clark's observations of the Mandans and Hidatsas, see Gary E. Moulton, ed., *The Journals of the Lewis and Clark Expedition,* vols. 3 and 4 (Lincoln: University of Nebraska Press, 1987). The account of the Hidatsas and Mandans by Alexander Philip Maximilian, Prince of Wied-Neuwied, appears in his *Travels in the Interior of North America, 1832–1834* (1839–41; reprinted as vols. 22–24 in Reuben Gold Thwaites, ed., *Early Western Travels, 1748–1846,* 32 vols. (Cleveland: Arthur H. Clark, 1904–1907); Bodmer's illustrations are reproduced in *Karl Bodmer's America,* ed. by William H. Goetzmann et al. (Omaha and Lincoln: Joslyn Art Museum and University of Nebraska Press, 1984).

Henry A. Boller, *Among the Indians: Eight Years in the Far West, 1858–1866* (1868; Lakeside Classic reprint, ed. by Milo Milton Quaife, Chicago: R. R. Donnelley & Sons, 1959; abridged reprint, Lincoln: University of Nebraska Press, 1972). Matthews, *Ethnography and Philology of the Hidatsa Indians.*

6. Edward S. Curtis, *The North American Indian,* ed. by Frederick Webb Hodge, vol. 4, pp. 129–72, 180–211 (Cambridge, Mass.: University Press, 1907; reprint, New York: Johnson Reprint, 1970).

7. Gilbert L. Wilson's major publications are *Goodbird the Indian: His Story Told by Himself to Gilbert L. Wilson* (New York: Fleming H. Revell, 1914; reprint, St. Paul: Minnesota Historical Society Press, 1985); *Agriculture of the Hidatsa Indians: An Indian Interpretation,* University of Minnesota Studies in Social Science 9 (St. Paul, 1917; reprint entitled *Buffalo Bird Woman's Garden: Agriculture of the Hidatsa Indians,* St. Paul: Minnesota Historical Society Press, 1987); *Waheenee: An Indian Girl's Story Told by Herself to Gilbert L. Wilson* (St. Paul: Webb Publishing, 1921; reprint, Lincoln: University of Nebraska Press, 1981); "The Horse and Dog in Hidatsa Culture," American Museum of American History, *Anthropological Papers,* 15, pt. 11 (New York, 1924); "Hidatsa Eagle Trapping," American Museum of American History, *Anthropological Papers,* 30, pt. 4 (New York, 1928); "The Hidatsa Earthlodge," American Museum of American History, *Anthro-*

pological Papers, 33, pt. 5 (New York, 1934); Bella Weitzner, "Notes on the Hidatsa Indians Based on Data Recorded by the Late Gilbert L. Wilson," American Museum of American History, *Anthropological Papers,* 56, pt. 2 (New York, 1979). Carolyn Gilman, Mary Jane Schneider, et al., *The Way to Independence: Memories of a Hidatsa Indian Family, 1840–1920,* is an extensively illustrated exhibit catalog that includes cultural and historical sketches of the Hidatsas based on the Wilson materials. Wilson's manuscripts in the Minnesota Historical Society have been published in a microfilm edition.

8. Robert H. Lowie's publications on the Hidatsas include "Societies of the Hidatsa and Mandan Indians," American Museum of American History, *Anthropological Papers,* vol. 11, pt. 3 (New York, 1913); "The Kinship Systems of the Crow and Hidatsa," *Proceedings of the International Congress of Americanists* 19:340–43 (Washington, D.C., 1915); "Notes on the Social Organization and Customs of Mandan, Hidatsa, and Crow Indians," American Museum of American History, *Anthropological Papers,* vol. 21, pt. 1 (New York, 1917); "The Hidatsa Sun Dance," American Museum of American History, *Anthropological Papers,* vol. 16, pt. 5 (New York, 1919); Lowie, Zellig Harris, and C. F. Voegelin, *Hidatsa Texts,* Prehistory Research Series, 1(6) (Indianapolis: Indiana Historical Society, 1939).

9. Frances Densmore, *Mandan and Hidatsa Music,* Bureau of American Ethnology Bulletin 80 (Washington, D.C., 1923).

10. Martha Warren Beckwith, *Mandan-Hidatsa Myths and Ceremonies,* Memoirs of the American Folk-Lore Society, vol. 32 (New York: J. J. Augustin, 1938).

11. Material for reconstructing Alfred Bowers' work with the Mandans is taken largely from his correspondence with Faye-Cooper Cole in the papers of the Department of Anthropology, Special Collections, Regenstein Library, University of Chicago. Other details come from interviews with Bowers in Moscow, Idaho, July 12 and 13, 1985, and from an obituary in the *Lewiston Morning Tribune* (Lewiston, Idaho), August 8, 1990.

12. Fletcher, *The Hako: A Pawnee Ceremony*; Alfred L. Kroeber, "Zuñi Kin and Clan," American Museum of Natural History, *Anthropological Papers* 18, pt. 2 (New York, 1917).

PREFACE

During the spring of 1932, the late Dr. Fay-Cooper Cole invited me into his office at the University of Chicago to examine a project which the late Dr. George L. Collie, curator of the Logan Museum of Beloit College, had formulated to investigate the archeology of the historic Hidatsa sites near the Knife River in North Dakota; the investigation was planned to include interviews with the older Hidatsa men and women concerning an interpretation of their ancient way of life. When the depression deepened, the Logan Museum was unable to finance these researches. Since our preliminary investigations had indicated that there were only a few well-informed old Hidatsas living who were familiar with their aboriginal culture, Dr. Cole suggested that I work with them for at least 1 year and investigate every aspect of their former culture before they passed away. Hidatsa archeology could be done later. In the meantime, under the influence of Dr. A. R. Radcliffe-Brown and Dr. Robert Redfield, my own principal interests had shifted away from archeology.

Dr. Cole secured a grant from the Rockefeller Foundation for 1 year's investigation of Hidatsa culture. During the depression, expenses were less than we had calculated and after 9 months in the field I was able to handle the Hidatsa language without the services of an interpreter; therefore it was possible for me to remain at Fort Berthold Reservation for 15 months. It was our understanding that a request would be made for additional funds to report the findings, but since funds were not available in 1933 I obtained employment with the U.S. Department of Agriculture, where I worked for several years. However, as time passed, it became evident that I was losing my understanding of the Hidatsa language; in the period 1939–46 Dr. Cole sent me additional funds to engage interpreters to translate passages that were no longer intelligible to me and to recheck some of my field data.

From July 1932 to September 1933 I lived at Elbowoods, N. Dak., where Mr. and Mrs. Hal O. Simons, who were employees of the Government as Farm Agent and Postmistress respectively, provided me with living quarters. Off-reservation I made my home with Mr. and Mrs. George A. Boomer, of Oakdale, whom I had known for many years. I look back with warm memories to the time I spent in their homes.

However competent informants may be, it takes good interpreters to bring out the information one seeks. Tom Smith, my first and oldest interpreter, had worked with me in assembling the data I used for my Mandan study. He had attended school at Hampton, Va., as a young man, but had returned home to hunt buffaloes and participate in the ancient ways. He had done much of the preliminary work in acquainting the older Hidatsas with the nature of the study to be made and had assisted me in preparing a preliminary census of lodge groups as of 1870–72, even before the Hidatsa study was undertaken. Without his help I could not have secured the data I received from a few of the more conservative non-Christian Indians. When I came to Elbowoods in 1932 he had already written me that his health was not good. I found him too ill to work for me, but he did give me much assistance in selecting good informants and he talked to them of my work when he saw them. He died about 2 months after this study was begun. He had told me that Sam Newman would be an excellent interpreter if I could get along with him. Mr. Newman was without question the most competent interpreter I ever used. He had had extensive experience interpreting for various Government officials. Although he was with me most of the time for 9 months, I cannot say that I came to know him well. He never discussed his family or neighborhood matters with me. He always came on time, even though the winter of 1932–33 was a severe one, with deep snow. He would come to my informant's home, take off his heavy wraps, sit at his place at the table, and, without commenting on any of the events of the day, say, "Will you read me the last paragraph, please, so I can collect my wits?"

I used James Baker as interpreter during the late winter while I worked in the Independence district of the Fort Berthold Reservation and lived in his home. Jim, as he was known by everyone, made no claim of competence as an interpreter, his only experience being with White stockmen of the district who came to call on non-English-speaking Indians about ranching problems. He was warm and friendly, and we became close friends and kept track of each other as long as he lived. Whereas Sam Newman's facial expression never changed throughout the day and one would have never been able to anticipate humorous or serious matters coming up in translation, Jim was continually responding to the informant. One moment he would say to me on the side, "Get ready to shed tears" or "You are going to get a laugh out of this" or "Hold onto your hat." Sam Newman's precise manners and lack of response to emotional scenes was always bringing informants up short of tears. This was not so with either Tom Smith or James Baker. Informants freely expressed their emotions to them, laughing at the obviously humorous events of their lives and weeping on recalling the death of their loved ones in war or epidemics. These were my interpreters, all of whom have long since died.

My informants, too, have long since passed away, Crows Heart being the last to die, about 13 years ago. Joe Ward, the younger son of Hairy Coat (see pl. 2) who had come from Awatixa village on the Knife River, was the first to die. In fact, the data he supplied I recorded while making the Mandan study during odd periods when no Mandan informant was immediately available. He would have been an easier informant than his brother, Bird-Lying-Down, as he was an elder in one of the Christian churches at the time of his death. His death made my work much more difficult, for, even at that late time, some informants were reluctant to discuss the details of their various ceremonial bundles and lore.

Bears Arm (frontispiece) was a brilliant man with a tremendous memory for detail, but, more important to me, he had given much prior thought to the interrelationships of the various aspects of Hidatsa culture. His home was near the Elbowoods Agency, and people from the most distant ends of the Fort Berthold Reservation found a hearty invitation to come in and spend the night with him. Sometimes these old people would stay up all night telling of past events. He told me, when I first discussed with him the matter of serving as an informant, that he had long recognized how the younger people were losing interest in the old ways and that the old people visiting at his place were glad to find one who wanted to know everything about the Hidatsa ways and history. I was very fortunate to find a man of Bears Arm's understanding with whom to shape the design of this study. His father, Old-Woman-Crawling, was born at Awaxawi village and his mother, Many Growths, was from Awatixa village. I addressed Bears Arm as "father" and he addressed me as "son."

Wolf Chief was an old hand at dealing with anthropologists, for he had been an informant for Dr. Gilbert L. Wilson, Dr. Robert H. Lowie, and Edward S. Curtis. He lived at Independence and I had come to know him beforehand as he claimed me as a fellow clansman of the Prairie Chickens. Unlike Bears Arm, who was a man of great dignity, Wolf Chief was easygoing and inclined to laughter. He had a tremendous memory for details, but he was not the great synthesizer Bears Arm was. He died during the spring of 1933 while this field study was being made but after I had completed my work with him. Thinking he would not live much longer, he had asked me, if I were around when he died, to come to his funeral and shed a tear on his grave, which I did.

My experience with Four Dancers, of the Speckled Eagle clan, whom I addressed as "older brother," was somewhat different from my relationships with the others. He was the only male descendant of the Earthnaming bundle owners from whom I could secure data concerning the Earthnaming ceremony for Poor Wolf, having no sons, had not given his daughter, Mrs. White Duck, a coherent picture of this important ceremony. When I drove up to Four Dancers' home he was quite surprised when I addressed him in the Hidatsa language and told him why I was there. We talked a while and then he said, laughing, "You talk just like an Awaxawi." All my associations with him were without the aid of an interpreter. Even at this late date, after nearly a century of living together, the older people still had slight dialectic differences which they associated with the various original community groups. I took down everything he said in Hidatsa text and we got along very well together. He gave me much valuable data on the Earthnaming and related ceremonies that the other informants were unable to provide. I learned from him much about the internal stresses that so often got out of hand and led to the disruption of communities, such as had occurred when the Crow-Flies-High group, with Four Dancers' father as ceremonial leader, had moved out of Fishhook Village to Fort Buford when he was a small boy.

The weakness of this study is in part due to the few convenient and outstanding female informants near my headquarters. I relied entirely on Mrs. Good Bear—she addressed me as "grandfather"—for information on those ceremonies in which she had participated with her husband. Most of the information on the Sun Dance came from her. She also contributed much material on lodge groups with which she was familiar, both Mandan and Hidatsa. I relied on Mrs. White Duck—I called her "father's sister" and she called me "son"—for an understanding of the woman's role in Hidatsa community life. She told me very early in my study with her that she thought the woman's role in warfare was as important for the success of the expedition as those who were away to war, and that the success or failure of a war party depended as much on what women at home did while the warriors were out as on what their male relatives looking for their enemies did. I learned much from her, and what I have written of the woman's role is largely her contribution.

I did not use Crows Heart very much during the initial study except for those ceremonies that were clearly of Hidatsa origin, since he came from a mixed Mandan–Hidatsa household. However, during the summer of 1947 I spent several weeks with him recording his autobiography, and I did draw heavily from these notes for an interpretation of many aspects of Hidatsa culture. He was the first of my informants to apply their kinship terminology to me, calling me "younger brother."

Without the help of these older Hidatsa informants, this study could not have been made. All of them were born about 1850–60 and were adults at the time of the Custer massacre. They had been participants in their ancient ceremonies. They were the last survivors sufficiently informed to provide an accurate picture of their former culture. Other weaknesses in this study are due to my own shortcomings; I never observed the culture I was studying. When such a wealth of information is at hand, it is not always easy to extract the most pertinent patterns of a culture for analysis or to see life as the informants did without actually living it.

I have had much assistance from many people. I am deeply indebted to the late Dr. George L. Collie of the Logan Museum, Beloit College, for starting me off into the field of Plains researches. The late Dr. Fay-Cooper Cole followed my progress in the field and guided me skillfully toward the attainment of my objectives in the Hidatsa studies. Dr. A. R. Radcliffe-Brown guided me toward an understanding of the synchronic approach to the study of society as a system, which was essentially the image of the Hidatsa that Bears Arm was always describing for me. Dr. Radcliffe-Brown would have been greatly impressed with Bears Arm. Nor had I gone far in my field investigations before I discovered that theoretically, under the Hidatsa kinship system, an individual might stand in several different relationships to another. At first I was inclined to believe that there were errors in my recording or that informants were confused. I drew these matters to the attention of the late Dr. Robert Redfield. He called for examples and was able to demonstrate to me that, in fact, individuals could stand in a number of different relationships, each social situation determining the relationship that would prevail.

In January 1947, I went to Chicago to prepare manuscripts from my field notes on the social and ceremonial organization of the Mandan and Hidatsa and Great Plains archeology under the direction of Dr. Cole. When he retired from the faculty of the University of Chicago, the supervision of these researches went to Dr. Fred Eggan with whom I worked until July 1, 1949, when I joined the faculty of the University of Idaho. I am deeply grateful to Dr. Eggan for his assistance. During my first years on the University of Idaho faculty, it was difficult, because of my heavy teaching load and large classes, to devote much time to this report. Three years ago my teaching load was reduced by one-fourth so that I could devote time to the preparation of this report and other researches in the Plains which the University of Idaho had sponsored.

Dr. Robert L. Stephenson, chief of the Missouri Basin Project, River Basin Surveys, Smithsonian Institution, suggested the incorporation of various old maps of the Hidatsa sites near the Knife River that had been made by personnel of the North Dakota Historical Society many years ago, and Russell Reid, superintendent of the Society, furnished me with these maps. Dr. Stephenson provided a reconstruction of Rock Village of the Awatixa (pl. 1), made by Don Hartle for the River Basin Surveys. James Macduff, of the Geology Department, University of Idaho, processed the village maps of the Knife River sites for publication. All the other maps and drawings were prepared by Dale Ludick, of the Geography Department of the University of Idaho. Leo D. Harris made the photographic studies of Bears Arm (frontispiece) and of Drags Wolf and Foolish Bear (pl. 12). The turtle effigy (pl. 6) was photographed by Russell Reid for Logan Museum of Beloit College. All other original photographs were taken by the author. It is a privilege to express my thanks to all these people and many others who have helped me in one way or another in the preparation of this book.

Finally, I must express to my wife, Gladys Monson Bowers, my deep appreciation for her great help in typing rough and revised copies of my extensive field notes on Hidatsa mythology and traditions as well as the final manuscript. We have worked together as a team during the entire period this report was in preparation.

ALFRED W. BOWERS,
University of Idaho

February 1962

*   *   *   *   *   *   *

NOTE

The variation in the spelling of "AwaxEnawita" and "Itisuku" in the text and in the charts arises from dialectic or individual differences in pronunciation. The final vowel "u," "a," or even "E" comes out short and unaccented cn the ends of compound words and to the listener may sound like *u* as in "up," *a* as in "anon," or E as in "met."

HIDATSA SOCIAL AND CEREMONIAL
ORGANIZATION

By Alfred W. Bowers

INTRODUCTION

Anthropologists are usually silent with respect to their field methods and their manner of handling research data in the final preparation of reports. When the researcher lives with the people he is investigating and writes about a way of life that he is able to observe, one may presume that most of what he records is the result of personal observations supplemented by direct inquiry. When I studied the Hidatsa Indians in 1932 and 1933, and for short periods thereafter, little of their ancient way of life remained, and a description of what I saw then would have told me little of the ancient culture that I was endeavoring to reconstruct.

The Hidatsa of the Fort Berthold Reservation provided an excellent laboratory for the employment of the "creatively historical method" so commonly used by those of us who have directed researches in the Great Plains area. At the time I undertook this study, the older Hidatsa men and women had lived much as their grandparents had when the first fur traders and explorers visited them at their ancient villages downstream on both banks of the Knife River. This was the last chance anthropologists would ever have to get first-hand information from those who had lived by the ancient culture.

Much had already been written about the Hidatsa. Some of this information was very good; much of it omitted material we should have about these important agricultural communities. They had been variously known as Big Bellies, Gros Ventres, Ehart-sah, Minnetarees, Minnetarees of the Willows, Wandering Minnetarees, Minataries, Minitaries, Mahaha, Maxaxa, Awatixa, Amahami, Awaxawi, Ahnahaway, Gens-di-foulers, Mirokac (collectively with the River Crow), and by other names. This array of proper names for various segments of the total population told us little of their original community social organization. The first extensive study to employ the name "Hidatsa" as a tribal designation was written by Wash-

1

ington Matthews (1877), assistant surgeon of the United States Army, while stationed at Fort Stevenson near Fishhook Village. Since that time, all students of the culture have identified them as Hidatsa, and other proper names have tended to drop out of the literature except in Government reports.

All the informants for this study were born within 10 years after the abandonment of their old villages near the mouth of Knife River. Their parents all were adults before Fishhook Village was built in 1845, and they had referred to three contemporary settlements which they identified as Hidatsa, Awatixa, and Awaxawi, these three and no more. The three ancient villages were remembered by my informants, for it was the custom of many families to return to these sites and to point out to the younger people the depressions of lodges where certain relatives had lived, their graves, or earth rings on the prairies where various ceremonies such as the Naxpike or Wolf ceremonies were held. Wolf Chief, Crows Heart, and Bears Arm pointed out many of these features to me, identified even earlier sites in the Sanger vicinity, and explained many things that might have otherwise gone unrecognized.

As this study progressed, it was evident that some cultural differences existed between villages and that there should be some consistent way of identifying these former separate and independent communities. The tribal name "Hidatsa" was generally in use by this time, although it had been employed by the people themselves only to identify the inhabitants of the largest village community situated on the north bank of Knife River. I decided to continue the use of the term "Hidatsa" when speaking of the entire population or when referring to customs and practices that appeared to be common to all three communities. I have identified the people of the middle village as "Awatixa," the name by which they were designated by the others. The small group, somewhat more diverse in dialect and culture, I have designated as "Awaxawi." Unlike their near neighbors, the Mandan, they had no tribal name until given one by early traders. Since many situations arose during the preparation of this manuscript when it was necessary to distinguish the community group known as "Hidatsa" from the other communities, I have employed the term "Hidatsa-proper" when referring to them.

This study of the Hidatsa actually began several years prior to the field studies of 1932 and 1933 when, as a graduate student in anthropology at the University of Chicago and graduate assistant for the Logan Museum of Beloit College, I collected much archeological data from ancient earth-lodge sites along the Missouri. Although the ancient sites of the Hidatsa at, and downstream from, the mouth of the Knife River have never been extensively studied by archeologists, surface features of these sites are still clearly distinguishable, and river cutting frequently exposes large sections of some of these sites and their associated artifacts. Extensive digging by local artifact hunters at the old village of the Awatixa north of Stanton, N. Dak., has opened up deep cross sections of stratified refuse with the lower levels, producing many pottery types identical to those found at the oldest traditional sites of the Hidatsa in the Sanger area but not characteristic of the contemporaneous modern sites. Perhaps the strongest evidence in the archeology of the region indicative that the Hidatsa groups when first reaching the Missouri were culturally more unlike the Mandan than in later years, as mentioned in both Mandan and Hidatsa traditions, is the fact that the late prehistoric and historic archeological inventories of the two tribes are essentially identical. Researches in Hidatsa social organization and ceremonialism point to similar intertribal cultural borrowing even within the memory of informants or of their parents.

Rarely does the researcher in an Indian tribe have available so rich a source of archeological, historical, and anthropological information when undertaking a detailed analysis of a small segment of the total culture of a people as was the case with the Hidatsa. We can trace their group movements through the earliest historic accounts and the statements of qualified informants from data they secured from grandparents who saw the first White traders to reach their villages. We can compare their prehistoric culture, as revealed by their traditional village sites, with that of their immediate neighbors, the Mandan, and even with their more remote neighbors, the Arikara.

The literature on the Hidatsa is extensive, even though the early fur traders, explorers, and others tended to view them as the "poor relatives" of the Mandan, giving us rather extensive accounts of the life of the latter and sketchy accounts of the former. Among the first contributors to our knowledge of the Hidatsa were Boller, Kurz, Lewis and Clark, Charles Mackenzie, Maximilian, Palliser, Thompson, and others (see Bibliography). In the middle of the past century, studies by Hayden, Matthews, Morgan, and Schoolcraft appeared. During the first quarter of this century, various aspects of Hidatsa culture were studied by a generation of trained researchers, among whom were Beckwith, Curtis, Densmore, Hyde, Lowie, Pepper, Will, and Wilson. All of them contributed important information on some aspect of Hidatsa culture and provided background data for this study.

The primary purpose of the present study was to reconstruct the aboriginal culture of the Hidatsa as it would have been observed about 1836, prior to the last major smallpox epidemic. It would have employed the synchronic approach to the understanding of the

Hidatsa at a moment in time. However, as the study progressed and as I became aware that my informants all recognized marked changes in their way of life from that of their grandparents, I decided to deviate from that plan wherever there was pertinent and authentic knowledge of historic cultural changes. My employment of the diachronic approach was especially applicable to particular aspects of their culture such as the age-grade system. In other areas of their culture, such as their kinship system, there was little evidence of cultural change.

Extensive use has been made of the voluminous source material on the Hidatsa. I have tried to combine all that has been written about them with my personal observations of their ancient sites and culture and what information I was able to glean from native informants. My aim has been to produce a study of the personal and intimate relationships of individuals and organized groups living together within a complexly integrated social-ceremonial system that was undergoing significant cultural enrichment under the influence of their agricultural neighbors until terminated by the heavy losses suffered during the smallpox epidemic of 1837 and the destructive influences of subsequent White encroachments upon their community and ancient wildlife resources.

The Hidatsa were not a homogeneous people. The knowledge of one was not that of another, save as exists between individuals as to sex and age, so characteristic of very primitive hunters and gatherers. The Hidatsa had a firm economy based on hunting and primitive hoe gardening. There was much specialization; one could have learned this from the literature.

My first problem was to select informants who possessed special knowledge. I had become acquainted with most of them beforehand while making the Mandan study with the help of Tom Smith, who was in their age-group and knew each of them well. We had anticipated difficulty in getting informants to reveal certain religious lore, and it was necessary, in some instances, to assure the informant that what he told us would not be revealed in his lifetime so that we would not be interfering in the orderly transfer of this knowledge to Indian purchasers. This rule was never broken. When what we recorded of a religious nature was not repeated by us, or informants learned that we never talked about what they told us should be treated secretly, confidence between us grew. When resistance was met in securing sacred lore and the informant was otherwise well informed, we would work with him on routine social patterns and try again. Usually, after getting acquainted with each other, the informant would slowly edge into the sacred area of his experiences and submit to detailed inquiry. Eventually there was not an informant that

I could not have interviewed on any aspect of their culture; any gaps in our knowledge of Hidatsa social and ceremonial life are of my own oversight.

From my experiences with the Mandan, I decided to investigate household and kinship ties first and then relate sacred bundles and rites to households and lineages.   The Government census and tribal roles for 1870 and 1880 were obtained in advance, studied, and partially memorized.   Without revealing this fact to my informants, I then made up my own census as of about 1872, using Bears Arm, Mrs. White Duck, and Mrs. Good Bear as informants.   This was the only instance in which I used several informants simultaneously. This census by households was taken by securing, first of all, the names and relationships of the occupants of the three informants' own households and then moving to those households to which they had been related or where they visited most.   These three informants finally came to a number of households about which little was known, and information on them was secured from other informants. On the basis of the principal occupants of these household groups, extensive genealogies were then made extending family lines back to the three contemporary villages at the mouth of Knife River, Rock Village, and a fifth community area near Square Buttes of which my informants knew little.   Residence at Scattered Village (Awatixa) on the north bank of the Heart River at Mandan, N. Dak., was not borne out by these genealogies.   However, the data on household groupings is in essential agreement with the Government records when one takes into account the fact that the small log cabin was introduced at this time—what the Government counted as two or more households (lodges set side by side, perhaps joined by a hallway) my Indian informants counted as a single household.

The next step was to establish the clan membership of all individuals reported, the approximate age of each person, village of birth, and all known tribal and personal sacred bundles and rites in which the individual had held ownership and special roles.   Most of this was known in a general way, at least, through ritual observations or by word of mouth.   Nevertheless, inquiries with other informants brought out further information about certain lesser known bundles, especially those of a personal nature.

Understanding the social position of mixed families, where the husband and wife were of different tribes (primarily Crow, Mandan, Arikara, and Assiniboin) was more difficult.   In one instance, the husband would be a Mandan and in another, a Hidatsa, but no rule of residence seemed to apply.   It was finally established that mixed households should be classified as Hidatsa only in those instances in which they participated primarily in Hidatsa activities.   I had

had some misgivings as to whether it would be possible to relate lineages and household groups to the three former villages at Knife River, but I found that informants were more certain of the old village ties than of actual clan membership. I had to rely on moiety membership for some individuals whose precise clan membership was not known.

The genealogies were further extended as the study progressed and additional informants were used. Constant reference was made to them throughout the field study period. They provided me with precise information on the inheritance of sacred bundles, bundle complexes, and rights—often at variance with the ideal patterns— and indicated that certain ceremonies or age-grade societies were found only at certain villages. Differences in village clan systems were also determined by these genealogical records. They were especially valuable in ascertaining changing trends in intervillage marriage between clans while living in the old villages and intra-village marriages after the survivors united at Fishhook Village. It was further established that intervillage marriage and marriage with the Mandan or other tribes was virtually nonexistent prior to the building of Fishhook Village in 1845 and common with the Mandan, but rarely with the Arikara, after that date. With this information at hand it was possible to view in brief outline most of the important sacred bundle systems even before investigating the details of the associated rituals.

At the time this study was made, there were many more old Hidatsa men and women than were interviewed. Some, whose parents had not been important leaders and who were not from households owning important bundle rites, were not used in the investigation. Access-ability in the reservation was also an important factor. Where several shared unique information, I tended to go into great detail with one informant and merely recheck with another. Informants were both Christian and non-Christian, the latter tending to be more conservative in divulging sacred lore but equally cooperative in routine matters. Even the Christian Indians were not entirely unrestrained in divulging knowledge of their parents' sacred rites. They would speak freely of general matters concerning these bundles; but would sometimes wait for a while before relating the sacred myths and usually did not like to have pictures taken of the sacred bundles. There was a common reluctance to sing any of the sacred songs. Mrs. Good Bear, for instance, was a devout Roman Catholic who attended Mass regularly and who spoke freely with me concerning her deceased husband's and her role in the Naxpike (Sun Dance) ceremony. She knew all the songs used, but could not be prevailed upon to sing them or repeat the words of the songs. Wolf Chief, a Congregationalist, told how he had been in several close brushes with lightning after he allowed Gilbert L. Wilson to take the Water-buster (Thunder) clan bundle to New York City, and had been afraid of lightning ever since.

I discovered that all informants were unwilling to talk in the presence of visitors, regardless of the subjects being studied. In former times it was considered bad taste to enter uninvited when one was telling stories or giving certain information to another and the only trouble encountered was with young men not familiar with this custom.

The kinship charts were prepared primarily from the combined genealogical data of all my informants. At this time (1932) there were no important variations in the terminology and categories with the exception of those of the father's father's sister and daughter-in-law. Some claimed the former was a "grandmother" while others thought she would be a closer relative by some other extension of the kinship system. Daughter-in-law terminology also differed between villages. It was found that many factors of social partic-ipation affected the relationships between individuals and extended the system to include nonrelatives, age-grade associates, ceremonial participation, adoption of children and ceremonial adoptions by both men and women, and equation of Hidatsa with Mandan clans. All these produced systems of interaction between individuals in which two people often stood in several relationships to each other. This was not mentioned specifically by informants and came out in the study of various customs.

All of my informants had had previous experience with anthro-pologists and claimed that no two of us worked the same way. I heard several criticisms of us, chiefly that we either tried to answer our own questions or that informants were cut off by saying that what was being told was not important. I tried to avoid doing either, for I had a year to make this study and I was as interested in what my informants thought about their cultural values as in what they did. Each informant was encouraged to digress when one social pattern reminded him of something else, or when his excursions into another area seemed to produce noteworthy cultural data. Since the Hidatsa explain much in their culture by means of formal myths, they were encouraged to relate the myths as they had learned them. Lest continuity be broken, I usually avoided interrupting informants and held back my questions until a narrative had been completed.

I followed few fixed rules in getting at the data, and these were subject to change whenever the situation warranted. I frequently requestioned an informant months later on obscure points. The old people generally knew who would be the best informed in certain areas of their culture.   Wherever possible, I relied heavily on direct information from the informant's parents or a relative who had lived in the same household.   One who had bought ceremonial rights or had paid a person for specific information was considered to be a better informant than one who had not done these things.   Information from an individual who had served as understudy to a ceremonial leader in performing a ceremony was highly rated as was that from one who had been a ceremonial "father" when another was buying ceremonial rights and bundles.   I discovered that mere participation in a ceremony as a young man added little information that one could not have acquired as an eyewitness to the event.   At all times I have had before me notes on the source and the conditions under which the informants gained their information and have tried to weigh this in my analyses.

From the beginning of the field study, I recognized that the Hidatsa learned much by means of sacred and secular myths and that the symbols and ritual acts performed could best be understood in terms of the instructions in these myths.   So I always took them down in essentially the form in which they were related to me, making allowance for some alteration both in form and meaning inevitable in translations.   After I acquired some understanding of the Hidatsa language, they were recorded in native text without an interpreter and translated later.   These myths often revealed interrelationships, native attitudes, and values not otherwise apparent.

Their mythology and traditions as recorded provide an important body of original source material on Hidatsa literary style and form, but in too great detail to be used unedited in this study.   They appear in this report in summary form, expressing what I thought were the important points the speaker was trying to communicate.

The various sections dealing with Hidatsa ceremonial organization were arranged, in part, chronologically according to native traditions at the time of their adoption in mythological times.   This chronological order was broken, however, beginning with "The Thunder Ceremonies," in order to treat groups of related rites as complexes. Some of the rites of the complex—the Thunder ceremonies, the Wolf ceremonies, or the Buffalo Calling ceremonies—are believed to go back nearly to the beginning of time.   Other related rites were adopted from time to time thereafter.   Because the informed Hidatsa believed these rites were interrelated, I arranged them in this way.

Finally, I have tried to present a detailed account of the social and ceremonial life of the Hidatsa in the image they had of their way of life.   To do this, I have frequently resorted to the same sources of information a young Hidatsa man or woman would have—sacred and traditional myths—and have presented them herein as a summary of the myth.   In other sections of this study I have presented brief segments of personal histories, believing that a correct presentation of the social and ceremonial organization of these people should be meaningful to those who worked so long with me when it was being recorded.

HISTORICAL AND CULTURAL BACKGROUND

The first reference in the literature to the Hidatsa as an independent tribal group was made by Thompson (1916, pp. 209–242), who visited the villages of this tribe and of the Mandan in 1797. Prior to that time, owing to the similarities between the cultures, tribal differences apparently were not recognized by the early White traders; all these earth lodge village groups living upstream from the Heart River were known as Mandan, from the name given by the Assiniboin to the more numerous and sedentary tribe. The Mandan, prior to the 1782 smallpox epidemic, must have greatly outnumbered the population of the three Hidatsa villages. The latter, however, were not recognized as separate tribal and linguistic groups until White traders had come to live in the villages and had actually learned the native languages. When Thompson visited the five village groups of Hidatsas and Mandans, his information was obtained from traders who had married into the tribes and were living in the villages.

In 1738, La Vérendrye (1927, pp. 290–360) visited earth lodge village groups on the Missouri downstream from the traditional village sites of this tribe believed, on the basis of archeological findings, to have been occupied at this time. Although there is no reference in La Vérendrye's account to visiting groups other than the "Mantanees," he may have seen the Awaxawi group of Hidatsa who were then more closely associated with the upstream Mandan village groups.

Mackintosh, in 1773, reported that the Mandan were living on both banks of the Missouri with from 9 to 13 villages and many thousands of warriors (Schoolcraft, 1851, vol. 3, p. 253). However, no reference is made to other tribal earth lodge groups. His estimation of the Mandan population is obviously excessive and it is to be presumed, on the basis of traditional and archeological evidence, that some Hidatsa village groups, particularly the Awatixa and Awaxawi, were also included in these figures.

Although the M. Bellen map of 1755 was the first to show the location of the Mandan villages, indicating that the Mandan and Arikara were separated by a stretch of about 300 miles on the Missouri River, no reference is made to the Hidatsa in relation to these other earth-lodge groups (Winchell, 1911, p. 47). The Laurie and Whittle map (1782) enumerates and locates a number of tribes heretofore not reported (ibid., p. 56).   It resembles Bellen's map in that the Mantons River still was not recognized to be a section of the Missouri.   The Mandan lived along the Mantons River, which flowed to the southeast. Their nearest neighbors were the Nadouasis who had left the head-waters of the Mississippi, crossed the Red River, and were living below the Mandan villages.   Immediately to the west of the Mandan villages were the Snake Indians; the Assiniboin were to the north. The Arikara were to the southeast along the Missouri River, and the Tetons occupied the prairie region between Lake Traverse and the Missouri River.[1]

During the entire period of recorded history, beginning with Thompson in 1797 and continuing to 1845, the Hidatsa recognized three independent but closely related village groups whose relative size remained unchanged.   Of these groups, the Hidatsa were the most numerous and exceeded the other two in total numbers.   The Awatixa were intermediate in size, while the Awaxawi have never exceeded 20 earth lodge household groups in historic times.   Thompson (1916, pp. 235–236) visited these groups when they were in their winter villages and gave the following figures for households by village groups: (1) Awatixa, 31 earth lodges and 7 tipis; (2) Hidatsa, 82 earth lodges; (3) Awaxawi and Mandan, 52 earth lodges (15 Awaxawi and 37 Mandan); (4) Mandan, 40 earth lodges; and (5) Mandan, 113 earth lodges.   For 190 Mandan lodges he estimated the population to be 1,520 and for the Hidatsa (Fall Indians) 128 lodges and 7 tipis he gave a population of 1,330.[2]

Even as early as 1797 two contradictory accounts of the history of the Hidatsa were recognized by Thompson; that they were formerly agriculturalists living at the headwaters of the Red River, and that they were nomadic and came from the north to settle near the Mandan, where they adopted agriculture and fixed villages.   The same con-tradictions appear regularly in subsequent accounts, and similar information was given to me by Hidatsa informants when this study was made.

LeRaye, in 1802, identified two village groups of Hidatsa; the Hidatsa-proper occupying the large village (site 35) on the north bank of the Knife River and the Hidatsa group, better known by the natives as the Awatixa, immediately opposite on the south bank (site 33).   The Awaxawi, whom he called Gens-di-foulers, had an independent village (site 32) 3 miles below the Awatixa (LeRaye, 1908, p. 169).   He estimated the population of the two Hidatsa

---

[1] Bellen probably errs in placing the Arikara so far downstream.   There is much archeological evidence that several Arikara village groups were at this time upstream from Pierre, S. Dak., in a region not well known to explorers.

[2] Identification of these village groups was by my native informants.

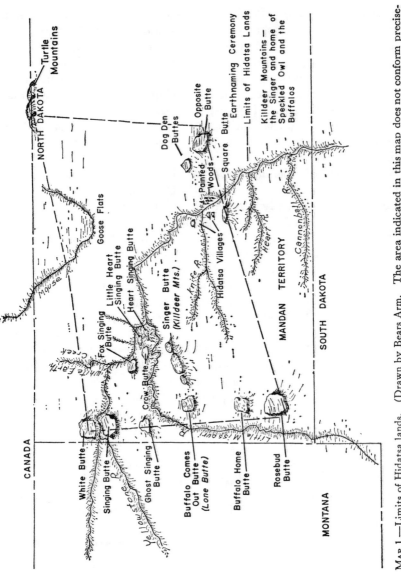

MAP 1.—Limits of Hidatsa lands. (Drawn by Bears Arm. The area indicated in this map does not conform precisely to that given in the narrative, because Bears Arm was an Awaxawi.)

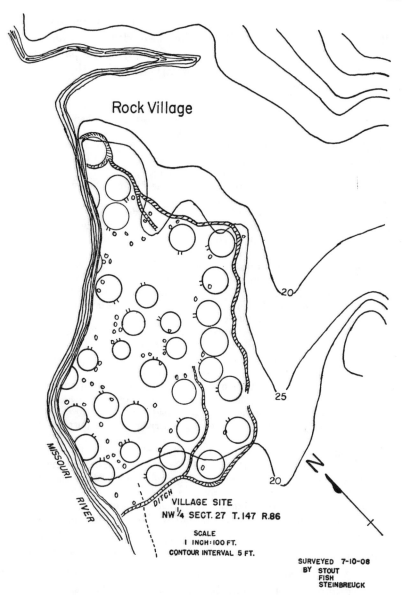

MAP 2.—Map of Rock Village.   (Courtesy North Dakota Historical Society.)

villages to be 600 warriors and 2,500 inhabitants.   It is of significance for a reconstruction of Crow–Hidatsa group relations to note that, on the basis of information obtained from the various Crow bands, the Ehart-sah (Hidatsa) were still considered to be a Crow band although the two other Hidatsa village groups, the Awatixa and Awaxawi, were not so considered.

Lewis and Clark (1804–05) wintered near the Mandan and Hidatsa villages. They also grouped together two Hidatsa village groups, the Hidatsa and the Awatixa (sites 35 and 33) as a separate tribe to distinguish them from the Awaxawi. Concerning the earth lodge villages at this point they wrote:

The villages near which we are established are five in number, and are the residence of three distinct nations: the Mandans, the Ahnahaways [Awaxawi],[3] and the Minnetarees [Hidatsa and Awatixa].

On the same side of the river, and at a distance of 4 miles from the lower Mandan village, is another called Mahaha [The Mandan name for the Awaxawi]. It is situated on a high plain at the mouth of Knife river, and is the residence of the Ahnahaways . . . [They] formerly resided on the Missouri, about 30 miles below where they now live. The Assiniboins and Sioux forced them to a spot 5 miles higher, where the greatest part of them were put to death, and the rest emigrated to their present situation, in order to obtain an asylum near the Minnetarees . . . their whole force is about 50 men.

On the south side of the same Knife river, half a mile above the Mahaha and in the same open plain with it, is a village of Minnetarees surnamed Metaharta[4] who are about 150 men in number. On the opposite side of Knife river, and one and a half miles above this village, is a second of Minnetarees, who may be considered as the proper Minnetaree nation [Hidatsa]. It is situated in a beautiful low plain, and contains 450 warriors.

. . . The Mandans say that this people came out of the water to the east and settled near them in their former establishment in nine villages; . . . The Minnetarees proper assert, on the contrary, that they grew where they now live . . . They also say that the . . . Minnetarees of the Willows,[5] whose language with very little variation is their own, came many years ago from the plains and settled near them. Perhaps the two traditions may be reconciled by the natural presumption that these Minnetarees [Hidatsa] were the tribes known to the Mandans below, and that they ascended the river for the purpose of rejoining the Minnetaree proper.

The inhabitants of these five villages, all of which are within the distance of 6 miles, live in harmony with one another. The Ahnahaways understand in part the language of the Minnetarees. The dialect of the Mandans differs widely from both; but their long residence together has insensibly blended their manners, and occasioned some approximation in language, particularly as to objects of daily occurrence and obvious to the senses. [Lewis, 1893, pp. 196–200.]

Although Lewis and Clark's analysis of the history of Hidatsa village groups is somewhat confusing, many of these conflicting traditions can be resolved by examining the Hidatsa not as a tribe but as independent village groups. Both the LeRaye and Lewis and Clark accounts agree in designating the Awaxawi, although dialectically related to the others, as somewhat removed culturally. Lewis and Clark further

---

[3] Village group names in brackets are my interpretations.
[4] The Mandan name for Awatixa meaning "Scattered Village." Another Mandan equivalent is "mitoxtᴇ" which is the name by which the Mandan also speak of the village on the present site of the city of Mandan, N. Dak.
[5] So far as we know this name was applied only to the Hidatsa, never to the Awatixa or Awaxawi. Note that the Awatixa at this time recognized dialectic differences with the Hidatsa and that the Mandan tradition of a Hidatsa migration to the Missouri as nonagriculturalists is denied by the Awatixa as applying to them.

indicate that the Hidatsa (Minnetarees of the Willows) and Awatixa (Minnetarees-proper of Metaharta) have had independent histories. The former, as a nomadic group, came recently to the Missouri from the northern plains to Heart River where they became known to the Mandan before taking up residence north of Knife River. The Awatixa claimed long residence on the Missouri as an agricultural group. This distinction between nomadic (Hidatsa) and sedentary (Awatixa) Hidatsa groups must have loomed prominently in their minds, for they distinguished these two groups when they wrote:

. . . As Captain Clark was about leaving the village, two of their chiefs returned from a mission to the Grosventres [Hidatsa] or wandering Minnetarees. These people were camped about ten miles above, and while there one of the Ahnahaways [Awaxawi] had stolen a Minnetaree girl. [Ibid., pp. 219–220.]

It appears that Lewis and Clark were aware of differences between the two principal Hidatsa village groups, the Hidatsa-proper and the Awatixa, since they refer to the group living on the north bank of the Missouri as the Minnetarees (Hidatsa), and those on the south bank (Awatixa) as the Minnetarees, surnamed Metaharta. Inasmuch as the names employed to designate these village groups are of Mandan origin, it would be well to examine Mandan interpretations of them. According to my Mandan informants, the word "Minnetaree" referred only to the nomadic ethnic group which arrived at the Mandan villages near Heart River from the northeast in late prehistoric times. Having tasted the Mandan corn, which they learned to cultivate during a short residence there, they were advised by the Mandan leaders in these words:

It would be better if you went upstream and built your own village, for our customs are somewhat different from yours. Not knowing each other's ways the young men might have differences and there would be wars. Do not go too far away for people who live far apart are like strangers and wars break out between them. Travel north only until you cannot see the smoke from our lodges and there build your village. Then we will be close enough to be friends and not far enough away to be enemies. [Crows Heart.]

Once this group became established on the Missouri near the mouth of Knife River, a separation occurred to produce the Hidatsa who adopted agriculture and built Hidatsa village 35 on the north bank of the Knife River. The remainder removed farther upstream and became the Kixa'ica' or 'Those Who Quarreled Over the Paunch,' the present Hidatsa name for the River Crow. According to Mandan interpretations, neither the Awatixa nor the Awaxawi was involved in this more recent migration, both being older agricultural groups on the Missouri. The Mandan relate the Awatixa to the western Crow from whom they are said to have separated by mutual consent while living on the Missouri between the mouths of the Knife and Heart Rivers. They viewed this early separation as a gradual one due to their long western migrations out onto the Plains. Eventually the western ones moved permanently into the upper Little Missouri River region to take up hunting. The smaller group remained on friendly terms with the Mandan living in the Painted Woods region intermediate to the Knife and Heart Rivers where they practiced agriculture. This seems to be a reasonable interpretation, for the Mandans who supplied much of the data recorded by Lewis and Clark in 1804 were aware of the different cultural histories of the three Hidatsa village groups and the Crow.

Concerning the Awaxawi, if we are to rely on traditions and interpretations of Mandan and Awaxawi informants, we must conclude that they represent an independent village group who arrived on the Missouri after the Awatixa and Mountain Crow and prior to the Hidatsa–River Crow; that they were agriculturalists prior to their arrival on the Missouri as indicated by the Thompson account; and that they were, owing to their small numbers, closely associated for defense with either the Mandan or the more sedentary Awatixa during the 18th and first half of the 19th centuries. The archeological record of their traditional villages on the Missouri River further strengthens native beliefs of the relative periods of the occupation along the Missouri by these three village groups and the Mandan.

In 1806, Alexander Henry recognized the Saultier (Awaxawi) to be an independent tribe, writing:

These people are an entirely different tribe from the Big Bellies and Mandanes;[6] their language resembles that of the latter more than that of the former, but is not the same.[7] Their long intercourse with those people has tended to this similarity of language, and from proximity they have acquired the manners and customs of the other nations, though they continue to live by themselves. They have the reputation of a brave and warlike people. They formerly sustained a three-years' war with the Big Bellies notwithstanding the latter were then ten times their number.[8] They held out with the greatest resolution and disdained to submit till the others, finding it impossible to reduce them, unless by extermination, proposed to make peace. Since then they have lived in amity. They are stationary, like their neighbors, the Mandanes, with whom they have always been at peace, and have acquired more of their customs and manners than those of the Big Bellies, who continue to view them with an envious eye. [Henry, 1897, pp. 343–344.]

Henry estimated the size of the villages to be: Awaxawi, 40 lodges; Awatixa, 60 lodges; Hidatsa, 130 lodges. These are unquestionably overestimations, since lodge outlines at these villages show Hidatsa site 35 to have 83 earth lodges, Awatixa site 33 to have 49 earth

---

[6] Hidatsa and Awatixa village groups at this time lived in the same two villages as reported by Lewis and Clark previously.

[7] Henry errs. It was a Hidatsa-Crow dialect.

[8] Traditionally this was with the Hidatsa, not the Awatixa, and was brought about by the unwillingness of the Hidatsa to permit settlement on the Missouri upstream from the mouth of the Knife River in traditional Hidatsa hunting territory.

lodges, and Awaxawi site 32 to have approximately 20 lodges. The exact number at the latter site is not definitely known, since the site has been partially destroyed.

Bradbury (1904, vol. 5, p. 162) also distinguished the Awaxawi as a separate tribe from the other two Hidatsa village groups of which he said "It is stated by Mr. Lewis that the two villages or bands can raise six hundred warriors but the number at this time is probably much less." It was at this time, according to traditions largely substantiated by recent tree ring studies, that one group under Strong Jaw moved out of the Hidatsa village to build on the Little Missouri near the mouth of Cherry Creek (Will, 1946). Concerning the Awaxawi, Bradbury (1904, p. 163) wrote that—

In our way to the Mandans we passed through the small village belonging to the Ahwahhaways, consisting of not more than eighteen or twenty lodges. This nation can scarcely muster fifty warriors, and yet they carry on an offensive war against the Snake and Flathead Indians.

Catlin in 1832 did not recognize the Awaxawi as a separate tribe, writing:

The Minitarees (people of the willows) are a small tribe of about 1,500 souls, residing in three villages of earth-covered lodges, on the banks of Knife river; a small stream, so called, meandering through a beautiful and extensive prairie, and uniting its water with the Missouri. [Catlin, 1841, vol. 1, p. 185.]

Catlin identified Awatixa village on the south bank as the principal village; it consisted of 40 to 50 earth-covered lodges (see map 5).

Maximilian (1906, pp. 230–231) in 1833 reported that the Hidatsa groups were in the same villages as when Charboneau came to the Missouri in 1797. These were sites 35, 33, and 32. However, 6 or 7 years prior to 1797 it would appear that the Awatixa and Awaxawi were not living at the mouth of Knife River, for Maximilian describes an attack by the Sioux on Hidatsa village (site 35). These two incidents provide a minimum date for the final union of the three Hidatsa village groups at the mouth of Knife River where they remained in close associations until 1837 when they scattered to escape a second smallpox epidemic. The Maximilian account would indicate that immediately after the smallpox epidemic of 1782, the Awatixa were in Rock Village (site 53) upstream from the mouth of Knife River, the Hidatsa were at the mouth of Knife River in village site 35, and the Awaxawi were downstream near the Mandan of the Hensler-Sanger region where ruins of their villages were described by Lewis and Clark in 1804. This date for the occupation of Rock Village would agree with Curtis' (1907 a, p. 131) account.

Bears Arm, one of the principal informants for this study, stated that his mother, Many Growths, was born at Awatixa site 33. Immediately after the smallpox epidemic of 1782, the Awatixa abandoned

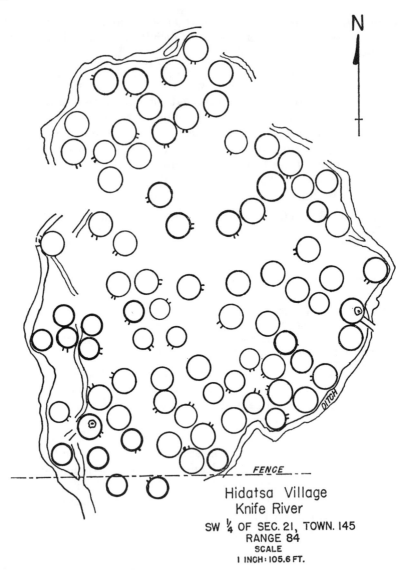

N

Hidatsa Village
Knife River
SW ¼ OF SEC. 21, TOWN. 145
RANGE 84
SCALE
I INCH : 105.6 FT.

MAP 3.—Hidatsa village site 35 on the north bank of the Knife River. (Courtesy North Dakota Historical Society.)

their old village 34 and removed to Rock Village, where Bears Arm's maternal grandmother was born.   According to Bears Arm, the village group which we know as Hidatsa comprised both an agricultural and nomadic population prior to 1782.   The ratio of nomads to agriculturalists varied from season to season.   Their principal headquarters was on the north bank of Knife River (site 35) from which they ranged upstream along the Missouri, the tributary regions to the west, and the Mouse River and Devils Lake regions to the northeast.

The Awatixa at this time, he stated, were agricultural and lived much like the Mandan who placed great emphasis on agriculture. They had lived at site 34 for a long time, at first with the Mandan and Awaxawi living downstream to the Heart River and beyond, the Crow to the west, and the other Hidatsa–River Crow group to the northeast and upstream as nomads.   The Awatixa were then the most

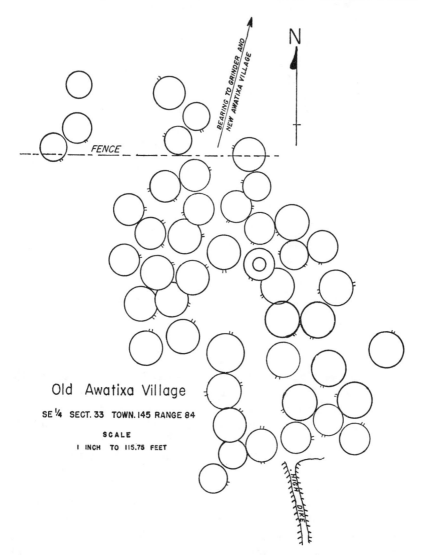

Map 4.—Old Awatixa village at the mouth of the Knife River.   (Courtesy North Dakota Historical Society.)

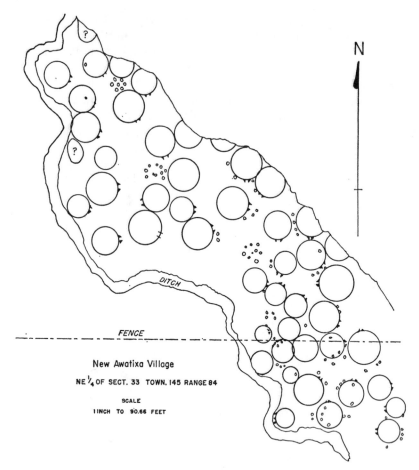

MAP 5.—New Awatixa village at the mouth of the Knife River.   (Courtesy North Dakota
Historical Society.)

northern agriculturalists along the Missouri River.   Concerning the
Awaxawi, where his father was born, Bears Arm stated that this group
was once more numerous and lived to the east as agriculturalists on
the streams of that region and later at Devils Lake.   There the
Hidatsa–River Crow (called *Miro'kac* prior to the separation) found
them and concluded that they were related since their languages were
mutually intelligible.   Reaching the Missouri, the Awaxawi lived in
the Painted Woods region around the Square Buttes where they
remained on friendly terms with the Mandan of that and the Heart
River region, and the Awatixa of site 34 on Knife River.   Prior to
the epidemic of 1782, the enemies of the earth-lodge groups, particularly the Sioux, were not numerous.   The Arikara were more numerous
and aggressive at that time and carried on constant warfare against

their upstream neighbors. There were fewer Assiniboin and they rarely wintered on the Missouri River upstream from the earth lodge villages at and below Knife River. The Hidatsa and River Crow hunted on that stretch of the Missouri between the Knife and Yellowstone Rivers and were numerous enough to withstand the Assiniboin.

It was during this time that the Awaxawi moved upstream and attempted to build a permanent village above Knife River only to be driven out by the Hidatsa. War broke out between them and was continued for 3 years during which time the Awaxawi moved downstream near Fort Yates and built a village near the friendlier Cheyenne. This conflict with the Hidatsa and temporary residence below the Mandan traditionally is prior to 1782, according to Bears Arm, as the Awaxawi were in the Painted Woods region during the first smallpox epidemic.

Awatixa traditions provide little information on their early history and migrations, for they claim to have always occupied positions on the Missouri, principally around and upstream from Painted Woods (Washburn, N. Dak.). They have no traditions of permanent residence elsewhere. It was in this area that they believe the clans and all of the rites relating to the Sacred Arrows originated. From all information provided by traveler accounts, Mandan informants, and Awatixa traditions, it appears that this group lived in that area for at least three centuries. They claimed to be the descendants of an original population which came down from the sky to Charred Body Creek situated a few miles below the present town of Washburn. Their traditional history is chiefly an account of the cultural development of tribal ceremonies pertaining to this village site, the sites of the Hensler-Sanger region, and site 34 at the mouth of the Knife River. References to legendary incidents occurring elsewhere are exceedingly rare. They speak of moving downstream to the north bank of the Heart River while still a part of the Crow (Mountain or Western Crow) where certain incidents occurred prior to the removal of the latter to the western Plains in company with a few Mandan families. They claim Rock Village above the Knife River was built after the epidemic of 1782 when the Hidatsa consisted of both nomadic and agricultural groups. They also mention in the Waterbuster bundle myth, a temporary village built farther upstream and below Shell Creek. This site is said to have been built prior to the arrival of the Hidatsa–Crow. Nor are the Awatixa unique in claiming exclusive cultural development in one area along the Missouri River, having first been created there by culture heroes who brought the original "parents" of the tribe down from the sky; some Mandans have a similar legend to account for the original creation of the earth and the human population of the region at the mouth of the Heart River.

According to both Awatixa and Mandan traditions, once the original populations were established, other related groups moved to the region and joined them. There is much archeological evidence in the earth lodge sites of the area to support the general outlines of tribal histories as given by native informants. Will (1946) has dated certain sites of the Heart River region as representing an early agricultural population at the Huff site. On the basis of changes of frequencies of pottery types, I have shown that a continuous cultural development occurred in that region even predating the Huff site (dated as 1485–1543) and continuing to the historic period (Bowers, MS.). Typological differences exist between these earlier traditional Mandan sites and those believed by both tribes to have been occupied by the various Hidatsa village groups. On the oldest identified horizons, the Mandan sites show many middle Mississippi cultural traits. The Hidatsa show stronger Woodland influences. Mandan pottery had a high frequency of plain or polished (body) wares while Hidatsa pottery had a high frequency of check-stamping and cord-roughening. These differences were less pronounced in the historical period sites. Mandan village sites show fixed lodge arrangements with an open circle or ceremonial area within the village, a specialized ceremonial lodge with structural features of the older rectangular lodges, and the common use of bastions. The Hidatsa never preserved a fixed ceremonial area within the village, nor is there reference to lodge orientation within the camp area. Even in historic times, the Hidatsa had no ceremonial or tribal lodge for their ceremonies. Nor do those Hidatsa sites known to have been occupied prior to the smallpox epidemic of 1782 show well-defined fortifications, although the Mandan were building strongly fortified villages before A.D. 1500.

Trade sherds appearing in Mandan sites after 1550 indicate that the first Hidatsa groups, probably the Awatixa and their closest Mountain Crow relatives, reached the Missouri about that time or a little later. Awatixa pottery and culture in general were influenced by the Mandan far more than were Mandan cultural traits influenced by the Awatixa, indicating that the first contacts were made by an Awatixa invading group fewer in number than the contemporary Mandan. That contacts were not entirely broken between the various Hidatsa–Crow groups is indicated by the close similarity in their languages. If we assume a distribution of Hidatsa–Crow groups in accord with their traditions (from the Red River and its western tributaries westward in the headwaters region of the Sheyenne and James Rivers, the Turtle Mountains, the southern loop of the Mouse River and onto the Missouri upstream from Washburn, N. Dak., thence westward onto the Little Missouri to its headwaters and the Yellowstone River to the Powder River), we have an area which reveals materials of unusual uniformity. Temporary campsites found along the rivers reveal pottery complexes characteristic of this older Hidatsa earth lodge culture on the Missouri. Temporary nonagricultural sites are found east and west of the Missouri; permanent sites are found on the lower section of the Sheyenne River where it empties into the Red River and again in the Devils Lake region where evidences of agriculture are indicated. It appears that only in the central portion along the Missouri, around Devils Lake, and in the lower Sheyenne River region, was agriculture regularly practiced by the Awatixa and Awaxawi. Evidences of occasional agriculture upstream from the mouth of the Knife River is indicated by numerous small storage pits, scapula hoes, and charred corncobs. The corncobs could have been brought in by trade, but it is unlikely that scapula hoes and storage pits would have been used unless some agriculture was practiced. The archeological evidence indicates that agriculture was not important upstream from the Knife River until historic times, but earlier attempts at farming are indicated by numerous temporary sites in that region.

The late prehistoric and protohistoric locations of the village groups comprising the Hidatsa tribe are pretty well defined by traders and native accounts which can be authenticated by archeological record. The Awaxawi were intermediate in position on the Missouri to the Mandan and Awatixa, living in the Painted Woods region as agriculturalists. The Awatixa, though formerly most intimately associated with the other agricultural groups, the Mandan and Awaxawi, rather than with the nomadic Hidatsa–Crow groups, were by this time in closer associations with the Hidatsa who occupied the north bank of the Knife River and the area upstream from that point. The final separation of the Hidatsa and the River Crow traditionally occurred during this period after a quarrel over the disposal of a buffalo's paunch. The archeological record upstream along the Missouri and Yellowstone Rivers, however, would indicate that this Hidatsa–Crow population was composed of numerous bands which gradually moved apart as some members took over agriculture while others remained on the Plains permanently as hunters.

It would appear that even the Hidatsa-proper did not make the decision to settle in earth lodge villages quickly but, rather, were indifferent to agriculture for quite a while. The smallpox epidemic of 1782 and the westward movement of the Assiniboin and Sioux changed the picture on the Missouri; it was the sedentary peoples who suffered most from smallpox. The more nomadic Hidatsa were compelled to make a decision between reuniting with the River Crow or moving in with their linguistically closer relatives living near the

Knife River. It was during this period, 1782–1800, and as a result of some serious losses at the hands of the Sioux, that the three Hidatsa and the nine or more Mandan village groups reorganized for mutual defense. In 1790 a large force of Sioux attacked the Hidatsa; because of the distance between the villages, the Awatixa at Rock Village and the Awaxawi, who had survived an attack on them and the Nuptadi Mandan, were unable to provide assistance. Nevertheless, by 1796 the Mandan groups had all moved out of the Heart River region and had consolidated their position in a limited area immediately below the Knife River Hidatsa villages.

Close intervillage and intertribal cooperation developed. One group of Arikara, who previously had had close ties with the Awigaxa Mandan near the Grand River, moved north at this time and settled nearby at the Greenshield site opposite Washburn. They did not get along well with the other Mandan and Hidatsa groups and were soon driven out. The Awaxawi had abandoned their village near Square Buttes after the epidemic of 1782 to live in one of the Mandan villages. However, once the earth lodge population was concentrated near the Knife River, they moved into a village of their own (site 32) situated between the Mandan and Hidatsa. There they continued to live as an independent village group until after the epidemic of 1837. They then abandoned their own village organization and united with the Awatixa.

The Hidatsa, Awatixa, and Awaxawi occupied the same village sites between 1795 and 1837 although the Hidatsa-proper had some difficulty in integrating their population. Quarrels occasionally broke out, one resulting in the building of Cherry Creek Village on the Little Missouri River. These close contacts, between slightly different cultural groups of Hidatsas and Mandans endeavoring to preserve their independent village systems, resulted in the breakdown of cultural differences through intergroup borrowing and intermarriage. Nevertheless, something of the cultural differences between these groups is still preserved in native interpretations and traditions. The assimilation process of the Hidatsa groups was rapid after 1782.

With the heavy losses suffered from smallpox in 1837, a second period of reorganization followed. Many living at Hidatsa village considered rejoining the River Crow. In fact, many did move there permanently. Other Hidatsas from this village moved upstream when the epidemic broke out and built an earth lodge village near the mouth of the upper Knife River which they occupied until 1845. The Awaxawi and Awatixa remained on the Knife near the Mandan until 1845, when, in company with the Nuitadi Mandan, they undertook the building of Fishhook Village where they were rejoined by many Hidatsa households. The problem of resolving several traditions was not an easy one. None of the groups composing the population of Fishhook was sufficiently numerous to survive in an independent village. Were it not for the pressures of nomadic enemies, the remnants of each village would have lived alone. Those Hidatsa who were unwilling to continue as agriculturalists at Fishhook moved west and united permanently with the River Crow.

In the chapters that follow, through field investigations and interviews with many Hidatsa informants, I have examined the cultures of the three original village groups, recorded cultural differences where it was possible to do so, indicated something of the cultural elements common to the three groups, and have traced out in some detail those cultural processes and native concepts of the history or "road" by which the Hidatsa groups achieved the cultural status they knew when Fishhook Village was abandoned for the move onto the reservation. The Hidatsa still (1932) think strongly in terms of these original village groups.

HIDATSA SOCIAL ORGANIZATION

The Hidatsa employed the term "chief" to designate anyone who, by virtue of his authority at any particular moment was recognized as leader of a group of people, whether a segment of the village group, a village group, or the entire population of the three villages and such other organized groups as might be residing with the Hidatsa at that particular time. Leadership was graded in much the same manner as was the male and female population comprising the age-grade system. The Hidatsa had, in 1932, a rather clear understanding of the character of the tribal leadership prior to the epidemic of 1837 when the population lived in three independent villages. According to my informants, these villages had had no tribal council until after the epidemic of the 1780's, as the villages were widely scattered along the Missouri and its tributaries and contacts were not numerous. At that time, the Awaxawi were below the Knife River near Square Buttes, and the Awatixa were in their old village on the south bank of the Knife River where they had lived for a very long time. The Hidatsa-proper comprised a loose association of closely related bands that ranged northward along the Missouri and Lower Yellowstone, the Little Missouri, Mouse River, Turtle Mountains, and even the Devils Lake region. Occasionally the wandering Hidatsa groups would all move back to the north bank of the Knife River to plant corn but, just as often, they remained on the prairies during the summer, hunting buffaloes. These northern Hidatsa bands collectively greatly exceeded the Awatixa and Awaxawi in numbers and consistently resisted their efforts to move above the Knife River. Each Hidatsa band was under the leadership of a strong chief who had considerable prestige with his group. The Awatixa, who had a traditional history of long residence in earth lodge villages on the Missouri, had a more complex village system of chieftainships based on hereditary bundles and offices, "ward" leadership to supplement and reinforce tribal chiefs, and clan inheritance of rights and privileges. The ceremonial aspects of their village life were organized around a

26

village or peace chief and the war activities around an outstanding war leader. The Awaxawi, although sedentary like the Awatixa, lacked clan inheritance rights and privileges. The ceremonial and peace functions at Awaxawi were vested in the Earthnaming bundle owner while the war activities were organized around the strongest war leader.

The smallpox epidemic of the 1780's greatly reduced the tribal population, and the subsequent westward movement of the Assiniboin caused the Hidatsa and Awatixa village groups to attempt a union. At this time the Awatixa built Rock Village upstream from the Knife River. The effort was unsuccessful because of conflicting bundle rights and the jealousy of the chiefs. After a few years, those who desired to remain agriculturalists returned to the Knife River. The Awaxawi left Painted Woods and built 2 miles below the mouth of Knife River, the Awatixa were situated on the south bank of the Knife, and those Hidatsa who chose to ally with the other two village groups settled on the north bank. A few Hidatsa families joined the Crow, and others followed them, a few families at a time, until after 1845. Except for the short residence at Rock Village, this was traditionally the first time that the Hidatsa village groups had lived within a few miles of one another. This was done to offer better opportunities for mutual defense and still retain the original village groups. The Hidatsa lived in about 130 lodge or household groups, the Awatixa in approximately 50 household groups, and the Awaxawi in about 20 household groups.

COUNCILS

For mutual defense against common enemies, around 1797 or 1798, the three villages established a tribal council composed of the most distinguished war leaders of each village. Council membership has been reported by my informants as totaling 10, with the head chiefs of Hidatsa and Awatixa as additional members, and as 12 in number by Curtis (1907 a, vol. 4, p. 182). Their duties were concerned only with general matters concerning warfare and the mutual assistance of the villages. They made peace with neighboring villages and discouraged efforts of the enemy to make alliances with one village to the exclusion of the others. This tribal council was first established before 1800 and continued until the three village groups united to build Fishhook Village in 1845.

When the smallpox epidemic broke out in 1837, the council was composed of the following men (according to Bears Arm who secured this information from his father, Old-Woman-Crawling, who came from Awaxawi):

Hidatsa Village	Clan membership
Wolf Chief	Three-clan moiety
Two Nights	Waterbuster
Gives-Away-his-Arrows	Prairie Chicken
Bloody	Awaxenawita
Runs	Waterbuster
Awatixa Village	
Blackens-his-Moccasins	Waterbuster
Young-White-Bear	Maxoxati
Stirrup	Knife
Two Tails	Maxoxati
Awaxawi Village	
Crow Bull	Awaxenawita
Roadmaker	Waterbuster

This tribal council was composed of persons whose names commonly appear in the journals of travelers and traders of that period. The village representatives of the tribal council were outstanding individuals, respected primarily for their good judgment and military accomplishments, who were members of their respective village councils from which they received their authority. When a member died or lost prestige, as in the instance of One-eyed Antelope who stole a woman and killed her husband when he returned from warfare to claim her, the position was not filled until the next year at the time of the summer buffalo hunt and the Naxpike ceremony. There were no regular meetings of the council. If one of the members had something to discuss with the others, he would have a feast prepared and the matter was discussed at that time. On other occasions, as when a pipe bearer arrived for the purpose of arranging a peace treaty or the peaceful admission of his band for trading, the council met to determine the attitude of the people. The council frequently would refuse to discuss matters with young men of an enemy tribe, knowing that such an arrangement did not carry the authority of the band leaders. It appears that the council also had an earlier understanding with the Mandan, for in his journals of 1806, Alexander Henry wrote of a party of Arikara that had arrived at the nearby Mandan villages to arrange a treaty:

About 30 Big Bellies soon arrived on horseback, at full speed; they brought an interpreter with them. This party consisted of some of the principal war chiefs, and other great men, who did not appear well pleased, but looked on the Pawnees with disdain. After some private consultation they desired the Pawnees to return immediately to their own villages and to inform their great war chief, Red Tail, that if he sincerely wished for peace he must come in person, and then they would settle matters, as they were determined to have nothing to do with a private party of young men. [Henry, 1897, p. 335.]

When it was not possible to arrive at a unanimous decision, the council would endeavor to influence the minority group or a decision was postponed for a later date. Because of the numerical superiority of the Hidatsa-proper the other two villages frequently gave in, particularly in matters concerned with the protection of the villages. This led early travelers to refer to the domination of the other two villages by the Hidatsa-proper. This was probably only partly true for either village group could have moved away and settled at any time provided they did not establish a permanent earth lodge village upstream from the Hidatsa-proper. In matters for the common good, the council was an effective organization. There was no tendency to include Mandan representatives in the council even though the two Mandan village groups lived only a few miles below the Awaxawi. Instead, the two tribes maintained independent councils which met jointly from time to time to discuss common problems. Each tribe defended the villages of the other tribe from attack and peace treaties were not entered into by one tribe unless the other was included. With one exception, that of the Nuptadi who did not go upstream when the other Mandan accompanied the Hidatsa groups in 1845 to build Fishhook, preferring an alliance with the nearby Arikara, this rule was followed until the people went onto the Fort Berthold Reservation.

This federation of Hidatsa villages served a useful function in breaking down the borders between village territorial grounds, thus eliminating one longstanding cause of intratribal friction. In 1750, the Awaxawi controlled the river region opposite the present town of Washburn and hunted on the flats and along the small streams in that region, the Awatixa controlled the Knife River valley westward toward the Killdeer Mountains, and the Hidatsa claimed the region along the Missouri upstream from the mouth of the Knife River. When the three village groups settled on the Knife, however, separate village hunting grounds were no longer recognized. Each group hunted on the others' territories or hunting parties were comprised of household groups from each of the villages. Nevertheless, the Hidatsa-proper felt a prior claim to the region upstream from the Knife and consistently refused to permit the Awatixa, the Awaxawi, or the Mandan to build earth lodge summer villages above them on the Missouri. In 1845, because the wood had been largely consumed at the Knife River, the Hidatsa-proper contemplated moving upstream to the Lower Yellowstone to join the River Crow. The Awatixa, under Four Bears and Missouri, preferred to move to Fishhook Bend and there build a permanent village. The former raised no objection to a village at that point since they contemplated moving still farther upstream. In the spring, however, when a trading post was established at that point, the Hidatsa-proper also decided to settle there. The upstream position in relation to the other groups of the Hidatsa was never relinquished. An attempt at this time to establish a separate Hidatsa-proper village near the present town of Sanish, N. Dak., failed due to the greater strength of the Assiniboin. For a number of years after the three Hidatsa village groups united at Fishhook, each former village group continued to occupy a separate winter village; in each instance we find the Hidatsa-proper occupying the upstream position. The Hidatsa-proper did not contribute to the organization of the original "building" ceremonies at the time Fishhook Village was built in 1845, these rites being largely performed by the leaders of Awatixa, Awaxawi, and the Nuitadi Mandan, but their strength was not great enough to survive alone as an independent village group. Cultural differences between villages caused endless friction; the Awatixa and Awaxawi were more conservative than the Hidatsa-proper in the preservation of longstanding organized rites, and the latter placed greater emphasis on individual vision experiences. When an opportunity arose to settle near a Government fort at Fort Buford shortly after 1870, many Hidatsa who had earlier failed in maintaining a summer village near Sanish, again moved upstream to live. It is this group that now occupies the upstream end of the Fort Berthold Reservation around Shell Creek.

The stability of the original three Hidatsa groups is indicated by the traditions and mythologies identified with these groups, the archeological evidence of long residence in recognized village sites, and the persistence of the original groups in maintaining and preserving their identity in the face of forced union for mutual defense against common enemies. One cannot say that they were primarily economic groups, for if that were so, after the epidemic of the 1780's the Awatixa and Awaxawi collectively were not as numerous as either village group had been before the epidemic. It appears to me from native accounts, that the reluctance to unite was due to different cultural histories, differences in ceremonial and social organization, a strong sense of village solidarity, and the unwillingness of recognized leaders to share their hard-earned positions with others of comparable status.

Some of the cultural differences can still be identified from an analysis of bundle rites and the traditional knowledge of the older Hidatsas. Since the Awatixa have contributed much to the ceremonial rites at the building of the last important village, the Fishhook Village, some of the basic cultural characteristics of that group will be indicated first. This Hidatsa group had traditions of long residence on the Missouri; in fact, this group claims to have settled the earth from a village in the sky which distinguishes them from the other two groups which claim a common kinship by virtue of a common origin from the underworld. In spite of their traditional origin from the sky, the oldest culture-bearing levels in the Awatixa sites show features which are characteristic of the other Hidatsa sites on the Missouri as well as to the east and southeast of the region. The Awatixa culturally occupied a position intermediate to the other two Hidatsa groups on one hand and the Mandan on the other. The basic Hidatsa–Awaxawi inheritance pattern of sacred rites and objects was from father to son; the Mandan practiced clan inheritance of bundles, particularly ancient tribal bundles. The Awatixa had a dual system; that is, most bundles were inherited through a "father-to-son" relationship but a number of other important bundles were owned by the clan and transmitted to another member when one holding the bundle died. The Waterbuster and Knife clan bundles were owned collectively by the clan members of Awatixa village. While living at the Knife River, and after the other two bands had built villages nearby, those of the same clan in the other villages at first claimed no rights in the clan bundles; it was not until the three Hidatsa groups united at Fishhook in 1845 that clan rights extended to the other groups. The Shell Robe belonging to the Prairie Chicken clan of Awatixa was actually kept by the Mandan during the last century. Nevertheless, rights in the bundle were claimed by all Mandans of the Prairie Chicken clan regardless of the village they lived in, and by the Awatixa. More recently, after uniting at the mouth of the Knife River, rights were extended to include persons of the Prairie Chicken clan at Awaxawi and Hidatsa. The Awatixa, according to traditions, brought the Sun Dance (Naxpike) down from the sky and taught the rites to the other Hidatsa groups. They shared with the Mandan the custom of arranging skull circles near the scaffolds for the dead as shrines to the Sun Doing bundles and transporting back to the villages skulls of those who had died or had been killed when away from home. This custom was not generally practiced by the other Hidatsa groups. They did not establish "mourners' camps" as did the Hidatsa and Awaxawi, rationalizing this practice by the other two groups on the basis of a quarrel—not a part of their cultural history—which occurred prior to the separation of the Hidatsa-proper and River Crow.

Awatixa village organization differed slightly from that of the other Hidatsa groups in the absence of an Earthnaming bundle with rites defining village hunting territory. It was claimed that the highest ranking leadership was vested in the holders of the Knife clan bundle (Three-clan moiety) and the Waterbuster clan bundle (Four-clan moiety): Stirrup and Blackens-his-Moccasins, respectively, just prior to 1837. The village had no open circle or lodge arrangement other than the close grouping of lodges according to nearness of kin.   The village was, however, divided into four "wards," each under the supernatural protection of a prominent man selected for his part in the ceremonies conducted for the gods of the direction which he represented.   These four men, known as "protectors of the people," were esteemed ceremonial leaders and occupied a status position equal with that of the two village chiefs and other select members of the village council distinguished either for their knowledge of sacred lore or for distinction in warfare.   Although the dual chieftainship of the Mandan and the other Hidatsa groups prevailed, the distinction between war and village chiefs was less evident due to the greater prestige of the Waterbuster and Knife clan bundles.   The entire population was organized by the age-grading of both men and women.   The Black Mouths served as police and enforced the regulations of the council composed of older men.

The Hidatsa-proper and Awaxawi village organizations differed from that of the Awatixa in many ways.   Both groups traditionally arrived rather recently on the Missouri.   Since that time the Awaxawi were in intimate and continuous contacts with the Mandan, particularly those at Painted Woods.   According to traditions, the Awaxawi came to the Missouri as a small agricultural group and settled in the Painted Woods region.   They represent the most diverse dialectic group and were believed by Lewis and Clark to be a distinct tribe (Lewis, 1893, p. 196).   During their short residence on the Missouri, they have been on friendly terms with the Mandan with whom they cooperated in the performance of tribal rites and, before reaching the Missouri, with village groups of agricultural Cheyennes near the headwaters of the Red River.   In spite of dialectic differences and their greater emphasis on agriculture, they more closely resemble the Hidatsa-proper culturally than either the Mandan or Awatixa.   Hidatsa and Awaxawi clans apparently did not own ceremonial bundles;[9] all inheritance was from "father" to "son."   Authority was vested in a council of head men who had attained eminence by the performance of rites or successes in warfare.   The top leadership of the council was represented by the owner of the Earthnaming bundle, who organized the rites relating to the various buffalo-calling ceremonies which defined village hunting territorial rights, and the principal war leader.   Thus the socioceremonial and the war-making activities of the village were symbolically separate as represented by two head men.   Traditionally, the top leaders of the ceremonial activities are said to have held precedence over the war leaders.   In recent years, due to the increased war activities of the tribe in its struggle for survival, the war leader

---

[9] One exception—the notched sticks for the Tying-the-Pots ceremony.

took precedence and the owner of the Earthnaming bundle was his representative in the village. As at Awatixa, special leaders were selected when the occasion arose: directing the summer hunt, managing the winter camp, or traveling beyond the summer village. Villages were divided into four "wards" with a bundle owner, whose gods were of the direction selected, serving as "protector of the people." The Black Mouths were subordinate to the council of older men and policed the village.

The village council was of indefinite size, since elevation to membership was based on personal achievements and public acclaim. Although it was composed chiefly of those who had passed the Black Mouths in age, it was essentially a group of mature men. Since the Black Mouths must be kept informed of council decisions, they usually met together whenever any matters of great importance were being discussed. It was the privilege of each person to speak, but one's prestige was based chiefly on age and accomplishments; those with mediocre records carried little influence. If a young man with a good record presumed to influence the older men, they would usually say to him:

You are young; you have a good record. Do not assume responsibilities of this kind too soon. If you seek to influence us, it may be that you are not ready. Then you might "kick the stone." There is plenty of time. When you are older and have demonstrated your ability in other things, the people will want you to be their leader. In the meanwhile, be kind to the old and the very young; be industrious and generous. Do not ask to be our leader. If you do all the things that a chief must do, the people will ask you to help when they think you are ready.

The high respect for age indicated by the attitude of individuals toward their older brothers and fathers, an organized age-group to the next higher one, and the buying of sacred bundles from older people, is expressed in the attitude of the people toward the council. Normally, one's position and prestige in the council was slowly attained. One who had distinguished himself in a chiefly way frequently did not attend meetings until he was called in to render an opinion or to assist in solving some difficult problem. Since to act as a group, all sub-groups and households should have a voice in decisions, important matters were frequently discussed for quite a time in order that all households might have an opportunity to express an opinion. In the organization of the council the "crier" or announcer held an honored role comparable to that of "First Creator" in the ceremonies. He announced meeting dates and the purpose of the meeting so that each household could be adequately informed of the matters for discussion.

It was the privilege of each household to send an older person to express opinions. In the event that a number of related households opposed the proposition, measures were taken to win their approval or the matter was dropped. We find, for example, instances of peace emissaries being received by the council but acceptance being delayed until those households which had recently lost members in warfare against the tribe had indicated their willingness to accept the peace offerings. The council could not accept the peace plans if a household refused to approve. Usually, families were given horses and other goods in considerable quantities as symbols of respect to the dead members of the households, at which time objections were withdrawn. Although on the surface these gifts may appear to outsiders as bribes, to these people the offering of gifts was a symbol of respect. If the returned leader of an unsuccessful war expedition did not fast long enough or inflict personal torture sufficient to console the families of those killed, the council frequently was thwarted in its efforts to win their approval of the matters under discussion. In the face of continued resistance by the households, the council was unable to function. Even as peace negotiations could not be completed except with the approval of the interested households, neither could the village function as a unit in other matters. Thus, at best, the council was only as strong as the bond which held households together. The council could not prevent households from withdrawing from the village whenever they wished to establish independent villages. Through the police, however, it could enforce rules of behavior as long as the household groups remained in the village.

The attitude of a dissatisfied group obviously took a different form when enemies pressed them from all sides. On the other hand, a group could lose prestige by making unreasonable demands. Informants will say that decisions were always unanimous and that decisions were not made until a solution was reached that was acceptable to all. Nevertheless, we have a number of council decisions which were not unanimous and can observe the reactions that followed. Since conditions of warfare were difficult during the winter due to deep snows and the ease of tracking the enemy, pressures of enemy groups were not as great. Under these conditions, the village group was frequently unable to agree on a common winter camping area and small segments of the population would break away against the better judgment of the older and more experienced leaders. The council could not exert physical force to drive them back into the group but they could throw the weight of tradition against them by publicly invoking the gods sending the winter buffalo to send them no buffaloes. Cherry Necklace was selected by a majority of the combined Hidatsa, Awatixa, and Awaxawi during the autumn of 1862 as "leader of the winter camp" but was opposed by some households because he had already served in that capacity a few years earlier during which time members of these households died. These deaths were blamed on their leader since he was held accountable for any deaths or accidents occurring during the winter. Cherry Necklace could have reinstated himself in their esteem by "sacrificing" for the dead, that is, making offerings of goods and fasting a short time away from the village, but he chose instead to disregard the matter. Now he was chosen again by the other households because there had actually been many buffaloes in the vicinity of his camp all winter but some families chose to oppose him on the grounds that he had brought them bad luck intentionally as proved by his disregard for their deceased relatives. Thus a stalemate developed and no compromise could be reached. They went into two winter camps: one under Cherry Necklace and the majority of the population together with the police organization, and the other a few miles nearer the summer village. Rumor reached the unorganized camp that their relatives were concerned for the safety of this small group and that Cherry Necklace had pointed his pipe to the north and invoked the gods of that direction to send the people back by sending the buffaloes only to his camp where the long established buffalo calling rites were being performed. Soon rumors also reached the little camp that Cherry Necklace had also pointed his pipe to the south and directed the Sioux to attack the undefended camp to bring them back. When the buffaloes came south to Cherry Necklace's camp but did not continue southward to the other camp and scouts discovered strange human tracks in the woods near the little camp, relatives went to the little camp and begged them to join them for mutual defense and offered them goods to show their respect, treating them as mourners.

From the foregoing accounts, we have seen that prior to 1837, each village group had its own council and police force and operated pretty much as an independent group with prescribed territory on the Missouri for permanent summer villages and separate hunting territory. The traditions indicate that the territory controlled was sharply reduced during the latter part of the 18th century due to epidemics and an intensification of warfare when neighboring groups received firearms and moved westward into territory formerly controlled by these and the Mandan village groups. With the reduction of controlled territory, and the resettlement of the three village groups near the mouth of Knife River, a tribal council was established for effective cooperation between village groups, its membership consisting of some 12 members of high status. This system was not of long existence, beginning shortly after the 1782 smallpox epidemic and ending with the union of the three village groups to build Fishhook Village in 1845.

Various writers have written of the first building of Fishhook Village but the particular rites employed on this occasion have significance only when analyzed in the light of the former village systems of the three Hidatsa and one Mandan group that comprised the original population at the time of its founding. Each of these village groups had suffered severe smallpox losses 8 years before and the intervening period was one of general disorganization. No doubt the original village groups would have remained independent and separate villages had the pressure of enemy groups slackened, for we have seen that although the Awaxawi numbered only 18 or 20 households prior to the epidemic, they had shown no inclination to assimilate with any of the other village groups. During this period of social disorganization, the Hidatsa and Mandan village groups accepted the Arikara [10] as equal partners because of common enemies, the Sioux. The three Hidatsa groups and the Nuitadi Mandan chose to move out of the Knife River region because wood was getting scarce. One Mandan village group, the Nuptadi, preferred to maintain an independent village near the Arikara rather than join with the Hidatsa. The Nuptadi Mandan group had many kinship bonds with the principal Yankton bands under Medicine Bear, a Sioux chief, whose mother was a Nuptadi Mandan taken prisoner when the Sioux sacked and burned the village near Painted Woods during the 1780's. She was a small girl at the time and was reared by the Sioux, later marrying a Sioux. Her son distinguished himself and became head chief of one large band of Yankton. It was said that he always had a compassion for the Nuptadi Mandan and liked to visit them because he had so many relatives in that village. Other Mandans taken prisoner at the same time and adopted by the Sioux likewise claimed kinship with this Mandan group which remained back at the Knife River when the Fishhook Village was built.

The smallpox epidemic of 1837 had cut deeply into the earth lodge population on the Upper Missouri; even a majority of the original tribal council died at that time. Of the three Hidatsa village groups, the Awaxawi and Awatixa suffered the heaviest losses; this was due to the nearness of their villages to the Mandan where the epidemic first broke out. At this time, the Hidatsa-proper were on one of their periodic upstream migrations and were dispersed into several bands. The period 1837–45 was one of indecision; the Awatixa and Awaxawi were so few in numbers that they were obliged to seek assistance of the Mandan and Arikara for protection from the Sioux. The Hidatsa-proper, in part, lived in a strongly-fortified village north of the present town of Sanish while others moved westward and joined with the River Crow from whom they had separated when they

---

[10] The Arikara were themselves the remnants of a large number of independent village groups.

adopted agriculture and settled at the Knife River. The Awatixa, with a long history of life in earth lodge villages, chose to remain agriculturalists as did the Awaxawi who were few in number and unable to maintain an independent village organization. The Nuitadi Mandan, finding conditions intolerable with the Arikara, who had moved in on them after the smallpox epidemic, indicated a preference for the Awatixa and Awaxawi near whom they had lived for a long time and with whom some households were related through marriage.

The Awatixa, Awaxawi, and Nuitadi Mandan then organized a council headed by Four Bears, son of Two Tails of the original council, who was at that time the most distinguished war leader. He was entrusted with the physical defense of the people, and Missouri was selected to organize the ceremonies of establishing the new village which was to be built upstream from the mouth of Knife River but below the Hidatsa-proper. Although the selection of the site is clothed in traditions, the Like-a-Fishhook Bend was an ideal site for defense. The role of the supernatural in determining where to build is indicated by the complete absence of references to the many advantages of the site for the summer village. It was on a low bend overlooking the Missouri with the river at the edge of the village, steep banks on three sides, an abundance of timber growing in the valley and reaching up to the edges of the village on two sides, suitable soil for gardens in the timber, and a broad, flat, grassed prairie with an unimpaired view which extended back from the unprotected side of the village where horses could be better protected while grazing.

During the period 1837 to 1845 the Hidatsa were unable to operate as a tribal unit. The more sedentary Awatixa and Awaxawi preferred to continue the old cultural pattern based on agriculture. The Hidatsa-proper, with a short traditional history of agriculture on the Missouri after separating from the River Crow with whom they had still maintained close contacts on the Missouri above Knife River, preferred to accept an invitation to rejoin the Crow. When the final decision was made and the site of the new village had been selected, the Hidatsa-proper were ready to move upstream in the spring and separate permanently from their more agricultural relatives. Some Awatixa and Awaxawi families, however, decided to abandon agriculture and move upstream, while several Hidatsa-proper families moved downstream to continue agriculture.

Boller (1868, p. 242) gives essentially the same account of the events leading up to the building of Fishhook Village. He wrote:

. . . At last they determined to seek the Crows and unite with them again. They deserted their village, abandoned their corn-fields, left the bones of those once loved and lost, and severing all old ties, crossed to the east shore of the Missouri, and started on their pilgrimage.

It was in the fall when they arrived at the site of the present village. The Four-Bears thought it would be a good place to winter in, ... When spring came, the Fur Company's steamboat arrived, and at the urgent solicitation of the Indians, a trader was left with a few goods.

The squaws cut and dragged timber for a fort; the Gros Ventres gave up their idea of rejoining the Crows, ...

Although the original Hidatsa village group broke up at this time they took little part in the village-building ceremonies. The top chieftainship was patterned after the former Awatixa village system in which the Waterbuster clan owner was village chief and Missouri was selected to manage the ceremonies of laying out the village and designating the ward leaders or "protectors of the people." The war chief was likewise selected from this village group, Four Bears being selected for that position.

The top leadership in 1845 when the village was built was as follows:

Head Chiefs.—Missouri River from Awatixa, village chief and keeper of the Waterbuster clan bundle; Four Bears from Awatixa, war chief and owner of rights in Daybreak and Sunset Wolf ceremonial bundles; and Big Hand from Awaxawi, First Creator impersonator and announcer for the chiefs.

Protectors of the People.—Big Cloud (Fat Fox) from Awaxawi, Thunder bundle and protector of the east direction; Bear-Looks-Out from Awaxawi, Old-Woman-Who-Never-Dies bundle and protector of the south direction; Bobtail Bull from Awatixa, Thunder bundle and protector of the west direction; Bad Horn from Hidatsa, Bear bundle and protector of the north direction; and Big Hand from Awaxawi, village announcer.

This group was entrusted with the supernatural protection of the village. Four Bears, the war chief, took no part in the ritual organization of the village other than outlining the limits of the area on which lodges were to be built. In deference to the wishes of the Mandan families, they laid out an open-circle area within the village near the riverbank on the southwest section of the village which was reserved for their ceremonies, sacred cedar, and ceremonial lodge. The Mandan were organized independently by the Okipa members under the direction of Big Turtle and Flying Eagle. The Mandan did not have enough households to complete the open circle and others also selected lodge sites there.

From the time of its first construction, the village life was a compromise of several village systems. A distinct ceremonial center with lodge orientation had never before been reserved in Hidatsa villages farther downstream, according to native traditions. This is borne out by archeological evidence in the three villages at the Knife, Fort Clark Station, Bagnall, Gaines, Mile Post 128, Upper Sanger, and other traditional sites, although the surface evidence at Upper Hidatsa site 35 suggests a small area not occupied by lodges. The still distinguishable large open circle described by Kurz (1937), Boller (1868), and Matthews (1877) at Fishhook Village, suggests the village arrangement of a dozen or more Mandan sites found between the mouth of the Knife and Cannonball Rivers, some of which were occupied as early as the 15th century. The open-circle area had never been considered a sacred phenomenon by the Hidatsa as it was by the Mandan; even today there is no religious taboo against describing it although the writer sometimes encountered this in his work with the Mandan. Nevertheless, it was a convenient place to assemble on social and ceremonial occasions. Although the Hidatsa never performed tribal rites at the sacred cedar, as did the Mandan on all ceremonial occasions, the Mandan ceremonial lodge situated adjacent to the open circle to the north and facing the sacred cedar became increasingly popular with the Hidatsa. Because of its great size, the performance of ritualistic feasts formerly held in any large earth lodge were often held in this lodge.

The council continued to be the principal policy-making body. Any chief could call a council meeting merely by preparing a feast for its members. The village was occupied only during the summer period while the gardens were being cared for; the population would leave in late fall for the eagle-trapping camps and winter villages when the danger of massed attacks against them lessened. At first the population tended to retain its identity according to the four original village groups from which it was derived. The council was selected from the population at large without regard to original village origin, the only qualifications being that one was in the age-group above that of Black Mouths and had distinguished himself in warfare or had participated in recognized ceremonial and social activities. Until the Nuptadi Mandan joined the earlier population at Fishhook, one large Black Mouth society functioned to preserve order until the population went into winter camps. The society then broke up into separate camp segments based on their original village ties.

Unless enemies were numerous, it was customary even as late as the 1860's for the Hidatsa to go into three separate winter camps and the Mandan into a fourth some distance away. In some instances the camps were many miles apart, at other times only a few hundred yards apart; nevertheless this breaking up into separate camps, however close they were, was a device for expressing each group's feeling of "separateness." There were intergroup gambling contests for adults and games of skill for the children, but in the summer village the population was intermixed so that an outsider would scarcely have been able to detect the existence of different social groupings.

Under the direction of the council, the village was fortified. A large bell was obtained and rung each day by a Black Mouth to announce that the gates were open for the horses to go to pasture. The bell was again rung in the evening to announce that the gates were soon to be closed and that the people should come in from their work. Once the gate was closed, all sections of the village were guarded to keep out intruders, and only those who could be identified were admitted. Unauthorized war parties were forbidden to go out and the rewards of their successful expeditions were depreciated.

LEADERS

War

It was in this atmosphere that Fishhook was first built and administered until the last Mandan village group and the Arikara settled at the village after 1860. Prior to that time, the people at Fishhook were largely at the mercy of the Assiniboin and Sioux whose war parties against the Arikara and Nuptadi Mandan living below the Knife were harbored and fed both going and coming and the group felt obliged to tolerate them—even though it was common for a young man to be sent out on the sly to warn the people downstream. During this time several large-scale attacks were made on the village, each of which was driven off under the skillful leadership of Four Bears who is today still considered one of their most distinguished war chiefs. The role of the village or religious leaders has been largely obscured by the numerous exploits and the bravery of this military leader. His prestige was so great that all respected him as the savior of the village. Before his death in 1861, he had convinced the Nuptadi Mandan and the Arikara that their position would be more secure if they came to Fishhook to make their permanent home away from the Yanktons who greatly outnumbered them and were determined to extend their range northward from the Heart River to include the large Painted Woods bottoms admirably suited for winter camps.

The role of the council has been largely obscured by the social stature of this Hidatsa leader, but numerous incidents reflect the influence of the bundle owners expressed in the objective acts of the war chief. At the time the Arikara were invited to move north and join the other earth lodge people at Fishhook, they chose to build instead on the opposite bank in two separate villages and with that end in view "planted" their medicines there. That is, they had covered certain tribal bundles, indicating that the villages should be erected at that spot. The Hidatsa-Mandan council sent word across with Four Bears that the Arikara should move across and build with the others but they told this delegation that they had put their medicines in the ground at that place and planned to build there. Then the bundle owners entrusted with the rites of the "protection of the people" selected Wooden Bowl to take the pipe to the Arikara and ask them to come but they still refused to accept the pipe. Standing before them, Wooden Bowl raised his pipe so all could see, saying, "My medicine is the bear who lives above. These people have refused to take the pipe so I ask you, my god, to send them across in four days."

Wooden Bowl returned and told the people how he had invoked his god, the bear, to compel the Arikara to comply with the orders sent across by Four Bears and his council. In a few days a large party of Sioux came and camped beside the Arikara. They got along very well for a few days and then a quarrel broke out between an Arikara and a Sioux in which both tribes became involved. The Mandan and Hidatsa crossed to the aid of the Arikara even though they had "called down the gods" on them with the result that the Sioux were driven off. Then the Arikara crossed and joined the Hidatsa and Mandan where they remained until the reservation was established.

On another occasion, the Hidatsa were informed in 1851 that they should send representatives to Fort Laramie for the purpose of entering into a treaty with the Government concerning tribal territory. Again we find the real authority asserting itself in the persons of those bundle owners possessing supernatural powers. Among these were the two Earthnaming bundle owners whose rites were concerned with certain hills and other landmarks believed to be the homes of various supernatural beings, foremost of which were those believed to be connected with the increase of the buffalo herds. When the delegation was selected with Four Bears as leader, Guts and Poor Wolf instructed him relative to tribal territorial claims based on the area traditionally associated with their bundle rites. It was on the basis of this information that the delegation entered into a treaty with the Government.

A chief was considered great if he could command the respect of the village for a long time. The principal war chief's position and reputation varied according to residence. He was essentially a summer chief and connected with the summer village life during which time warfare was actively conducted. Although he would still be an important person during the winter period, when warfare was usually discontinued, the winter chief or leader of the winter camp took precedence over all other males. Unlike the winter chief, who was appointed annually and rarely succeeded himself, the principal war chief continued as long as he retained the good will and respect of the entire community. When dissatisfaction developed, the tactful chief invited in those who expressed opposition to him in an effort to dissipate conflict, showed other evidences of generosity and good will, or suggested that others take over his work. He was still an important member of the council. In any event, when the principal war chief grew old he tactfully relinquished his position to a younger man who had passed Black Mouth age.

When Missouri River grew old and his Waterbuster clan or Skull bundle was relinquished to Small Ankles, the latter never attained the eminence of the former owner. The top ceremonial leadership reverted to the system formerly in practice at Hidatsa and Awaxawi where the principal role was delegated to the owner of the Earth-naming bundle. Since, with the union of the Hidatsa-proper and Awaxawi, two bundles were in existence, complications developed. Guts, who came from Hidatsa village, was a much older man than Poor Wolf, the bundle owner from Awaxawi, and should have held seniority, but he had the reputation of bringing bad luck to all war parties he accompanied. None would follow him as war leader and the warriors tried to keep him from accompanying them. In time, people thought that he had committed some errors when buying the bundle and his prestige was very low indeed, however hard he tried to win successes in warfare. Poor Wolf, the other bundle owner, although a younger man, had some military successes. He was always kind to the old and the poor, and had bought rights in this and several other bundles. He was active in many additional ceremonies and showed great interest in the people's welfare. He was selected as principal village chief after he had shown good judgment while serving as one of the leaders of the Black Mouth or police society. With the death of Four Bears and the selection of Crows Paunch as war chief, Poor Wolf became the village chief over the objections of the younger men still in the Black Mouth society. Guts then relinquished his rights in the Earthnaming bundle to his son, Bobtail Bull, of the younger set who had a good reputation in every way and none of the bad luck that had plagued his father. Bobtail Bull was very popular with his own age-grade group and was a recognized leader of the younger "set" as Poor Wolf was of the next older age-group. As holder of the Earthnaming bundle of the former Hidatsa village on the Knife, he was held in high respect by those formerly belonging to that village. By tribal custom when all other things were equal, precedence was given to age. Poor Wolf rightfully occupied a position superior to Bobtail Bull, who was some 10 years younger, but each had an Earthnaming bundle although from two different villages on the Knife River. This was a new situation, for in the old villages there was only one bundle to a village and it could not be subdivided.

Opposition to Poor Wolf and Crows Paunch came largely from the former Hidatsa village group with short traditional permanent villages, for this group was traditionally more like the Crow with fewer formal ceremonies. The Awatixa and Awaxawi had placed great emphasis on the formal ceremonies of long traditional existence as the basis for societal welfare and indicated that, with the exception of Bobtail Bull, the others had not made outstanding contributions to the ceremonial life of the village. The younger men replied that this was true but that they had done individual fasting and had more scalps, war honors, and stolen horses than those who were always hanging around the village begging goods of their relatives to pay for the ceremonies. It was in this atmosphere that the people lived during the latter part of the 1860's. Under other circumstances, one group would have broken away until the differences had been reconciled but this was impossible at the time because of the pressure from the Sioux.

During this time the conservative element centered its attack on Crow-Flies-High whose relations with Bobtail Bull were essentially that of a war chief to the village chief except that this relationship did not have universal approval. Crow-Flies-High's parents had died during the smallpox epidemic of 1837 and he was reared by women of his clan. His father was the owner of an Old-Woman-Who-Never-Dies bundle which was "put away" when he died. While fasting as a young man, Crow-Flies-High dreamed of the bundle which was interpreted as a supernatural instruction to perform the rites and take up his father's ceremonial rights with the tribe. Instead, he made up a personal bundle of those articles seen in his dream and otherwise disregarded tribal practices of "taking up the father's gods." Thus, the old "holy" men got neither a big feast nor fine goods and Crow-Flies-High received neither promises of success in warfare and everything that he undertook nor the promise that he would some day become a chief. Still, he was very successful whenever he went out to war whether under someone else or as his own leader. The older men said that his luck would surely give out, but it never did. Fearing that he would lead the young men to their deaths, the old men would advise the young warriors not to go out with Crow-Flies-High; but they would sneak out and return with war honors. All this was very disturbing, for Crow-Flies-High and his friend Bobtail Bull were both members and leaders of the Black Mouth society as well.

To reinforce their positions, Crows Paunch and Poor Wolf selected from the council four men older than themselves to serve as "protectors of the people" according to ancient custom, but many of the younger group ridiculed these four men, calling them, "protectors of our chiefs who are no good." About this time, the Government established Fort Buford near the mouth of the Yellowstone and younger men from the village served as scouts. Trouble broke out at the village when the Government rations were being distributed; some younger men accused Crows Paunch and Poor Wolf of showing favorites and retaining too large a share for their own families. Fights broke out, but Bobtail Bull quickly asserted himself as leader of the opposition and urged moderation. He promised that if his supporters would take no drastic steps or resort to fighting, he would serve as their peace chief, take them upstream, and ask the Government for permission to build a village near the fort. Since there were many buffaloes farther west and the young men could get positions as scouts, he felt that the people would be happier there. The next day his followers commenced packing and left the village shortly thereafter. Some Mandans discovered that they too had not been treated fairly by their chiefs in the distribution of goods and decided to go along also. At this time, the Mandan had two sets of head men: those representing the Nuitadi Mandan who came to Fishhook in 1845 when the village was first built, and those of the Nuptadi Mandan who arrived in the early 1860's. Flying Eagle, the chief of the Nuitadi Mandan, also decided to go upstream, for the people no longer recognized his authority and talked about him when he was not present, saying that he was selfish. A few Mandan families went with him.

The character of this conflict expresses numerous situations which would have taken a different form in former times. In the first place, it was wrong for younger men to question the authority of the older men, irrespective of their relative ceremonial and military achievements. This questioning of authority led to the fast breakdown of the age-grade structure. A drift away from the organized and formal public rites was indicated by the willingness of young men to go to war with one who had not obtained his full military authority in the customary way. Although the practice of seeking personal supernatural guidance was characteristic of the Crow and numerous other adjacent tribes, the Hidatsa had gone one step further and had made supernatural quests a prerequisite for entrance into the formal bundle rites having group recognition and participation. A final point was the length of the feud and the unwillingness of either group to take the customary steps to separation into a separate camp, either permanently or until the differences had been corrected, knowing that should the smaller group move away and suffer severely from enemy attacks, their leaders would lose face and those who followed them would be ridiculed by their relatives who had wisely taken no part in the separation.

In this instance, the separation "worked." The group had the protection of the U.S. Government. Buffaloes were numerous, so the people lived well. In fact, there was an upstream migration of individual families to join the group, which was an affront to the leadership at Fishhook. More than that, the four "protectors of the people" named did not prove to be wise selections; Sitting Elk murdered Edge-of-Rock in a drunken brawl. This disposed of two members of the group: Edge-of-Rock, who was dead, and Sitting Elk, who was banished and taken in by the U.S. Army stationed at Fort Stevenson. Of the other two members, Knife, the Long Arm impersonator of the Naxpike ceremony, moved to Fort Buford and joined the Bobtail Bull group; Cherries-in-Mouth had family troubles and with no wives to provide big feasts for his friends was no longer able to entertain and people no longer sought his advice.

This was the situation at the time that the Government was taking over the social and economic life of the Hidatsa. The two groups visited back and forth and assisted each other in the performance of ceremonies. There was no thought of intergroup warfare and neither group defended those who got into trouble at home. The relationship between villages was essentially the same as existed a century earlier while living in the three villages on the Knife River. There was a general drift away from the formal public ceremonies at Fort Buford while the other group continued about as before. In time, Crow-Flies-High as military leader assumed the principal role as had Four Bears a number of years earlier; Bobtail Bull, as village or peace chief was not so frequently mentioned. At the present time, the descendants of this group live largely in the Shell Creek section of the reservation and are spoken of as the Crow-Flies-High band. They still consider themselves to be a separate group which had its origin several centuries earlier when they separated from the River Crow to occupy the river section north of the mouth of the Knife River.

Summer Camp

The accounts given above have been devoted to the three original village groups, the Hidatsa, the Awatixa, and the Awaxawi. These were the summer village groups which were formerly further subdivided into winter groups until the pressure of enemies and reduced numbers caused further integration so that the summer and village populations were composed of the same households. The social, ceremonial, and economic life of the summer village was more complex than that of the winter camps, even in later years when the population of each summer village occupied the same winter camp. Summer was a period of intensive activity for the women and many of the older men in the gardens, planting and caring for the growing crops of corn, beans, squash, and sunflowers. There were corn scaffolds to build or repair, former seasons' crops to be restored, cache pits to be built, and many other duties relating to the production, curing, and storing of the crops. This was the period of small hunting expeditions into the adjacent areas and one large communal summer hunting expedition organized so as not to interfere with the caring for the gardens.

Summer was also the period of greatest war activity. When the last snows were thawing, the rivers were clear of ice, the horses had regained their strength, and the men talked of warfare; even those too old or too young to participate actively talked about it. Those intending to go out cried and fasted on the prairie, offered feasts to the older men for assurances of successes and advice, and looked to their riding equipment and ceremonial bundles as plans were formulated to leave the villages in search of their enemies. Simultaneously, enemy groups moved from their wintering grounds to the summer ranges while their young men made similar plans to raid the Hidatsa and other earth lodge villages. Although the Hidatsa emphasized warfare and encouraged the young men to carry on continuous warfare against their enemies, and all males hoped to show publicly symbols of their military accomplishments, it was necessary for the village at times to restrict military activities so that enough able-bodied men were always at hand to defend the aged, the women, and the children from attacks on the village. In these situations the role of the top leadership, the council, and the dual chiefs armed with the authority of public opinion, becomes evident; a war leader asked to remain in the village when many parties were out was acclaimed as highly as those who had returned with military honors. Since the protection of the village was primarily the duty of the Black Mouth society, the status of that group which effectively protected the village from attacks was greatly enhanced; its members automatically became members of the council when relinquishing their society to the preceding age-group. Not only must the village be defended from attack but the women must be protected while working in their gardens or getting wood. All these activities required close integration of the entire population.

This was the period of greatest ceremonial activities. All of the corn, snake, and rain rites were performed at that time; likewise the Naxpike (Sun Dance) and Wolf rites were held during the hottest part of the summer. The Hidatsa liked a well-performed ceremony but, by virtue of the inheritance pattern, there were frequently more ceremonies promised than it was possible to perform adequately. In these situations, the older men could postpone the performance of a particular rite until the succeeding year simply by informing the pledger that "since you have pledged the ceremony, it is the same as though you had gone through with it." The postponement had the sanction of the group and the authority of the council was never questioned. Informants say that to question the authority of the council would have brought bad luck which was just what the pledger was endeavoring to avoid by pledging the ceremony. Village estimations of young men's bravery and fortitude were made largely on the basis of observations of the older men at the important summer ceremonies. When the population occupied the three villages at the Knife River, there was a large measure of competition between youths of different villages to outdo each other in the endurance of pain and the old people would encourage this competition by telling their young men that they should be brave and not show any signs of fear in the presence of their people from the other villages or of enemy groups who might be present.

The summer camps were situated on grassed terraces above wooded bottoms and out of the reach of floods. The construction and maintenance of these villages was a greater task than was necessitated by the winter villages. The large summer earth lodges, large drying scaffolds, and the storage pits all demanded a great deal of labor. During later years there were fortifications to build and maintain. In time, fuel became a problem and it was necessary to rely more on driftwood or trees and branches cut from timber farther upstream and floated down to the villages. Nevertheless, the stability of, and the long residence in, these summer villages is indicated by native traditions substantiated by travelers' accounts, the depth of refuse accumulation, and the concentration of lodges on their village sites at the Knife River and downstream along the Missouri to the vicinity of Square Buttes.

INTERTRIBAL VISITS

Both intratribal and intertribal contacts were most numerous during the period of summer village occupation. Visits were both economic (alien groups came to trade for garden products) and social in character. At this time it was necessary to watch the hotheads to prevent quarrels, and to protect the village should trouble threaten. The Black Mouths met continuously during the visiting period, forbade young men to leave on war expeditions lest the village be left defenseless, and frequently recalled parties outside the village when word was received that an alien group was approaching. There were also continuous contacts with other Hidatsa village groups and the

Mandan. In later years such visits were deemed a necessity in the winter camps also, occasioned by the proximity of enemy winter camps attracted by nearby trading posts.

The Hidatsa visited alien groups a great deal, even those groups against whom they conducted intermittent warfare. There were numerous friendships between individual Hidatsas and members of alien bands who customarily came to the villages to trade for corn. In return, a prominent Hidatsa would pledge a return visit at some future date at a rendezvous out on the prairies. As far as I know, these small group visiting trips were only to those bands which came regularly to the villages to trade. A Hidatsa would select as a "son" a prominent member of the visiting band, usually the leader of the band, and announce that he would come to visit sometime during the summer. In the interim both "father" and "son" would prepare the goods and paraphernalia necessary for the adoption ceremonies. The father would first prepare, or have prepared by some member of the Adoption Pipe fraternity, the principal ceremonial object; a wooden pipestem decorated with redheaded woodpecker scalps, eagle feathers, and horsetail hair hanging as a scalp. He would also secure a good buffalo horse, complete sets of clothing for the son and family, and other fine presents such as robes, guns, and bows and arrows. In the accumulation of the necessary things, he received assistance from his own and related households, and from the members of his own clan and age-grade groups.

When the time came for the adoption rites to be given, frequently a large part of the village indicated a desire to go along for the purpose of trading corn for robes, horses, and other things. The father in the adoption rites became the leader of the party since it was his ceremony. If a large number of families were involved, including small children, and the trip would take them through enemy territory, the party was organized in essentially the same manner as the summer buffalo hunt. Since the party was burdened with sacks of corn and other garden products, they traveled slowly. The leader was responsible for the safety of his party and invariably employed those Black Mouths in the party to assist in the policing of the group. If the leader was especially popular and the group represented most of the village population, the Black Mouths accompanied them as the recognized police force while the defense of the village was left to those left behind and the men of an adjacent village.

One adopting a son of an alien group endeavored to make a good display of wealth, and his relatives would feel obliged to go along and assist him in his efforts lest the enemy groups think little of the Hidatsa. If a man had little following and the others thought that his trip was unwise, it was usually canceled on the advice of the older men and the rites were held when the alien group came to the village. Nevertheless, trips, sometimes involving a large percentage of the village population, went far out onto the prairies even as far as the Black Hills and Powder River, traveling as an organized group and through territory occupied by unfriendly groups to reach the band where the adoption was to be made. To command the confidence of a large party, the leader must have distinguished himself on former occasions. To lead a party far from home on one of these combined adoption and trading expeditions added greatly to one's reputation. Frequently, the top leadership of the summer village and other adjacent Hidatsa or Mandan villages went along on these trips but their social position at the moment was inferior to the one who had organized the party and they were subject to the same rules as the others. The leader surrounded himself during the trip with the other distinguished men of the tribe; they met at his lodge to eat, smoke, and discuss the affairs of the day. In all matters of procedure, however, he was the final authority, for he was responsible for the safety of the most distinguished chiefs as well as the women and children.

Arriving at the enemy camp, he set up a separate camp in a circle, policed the camp lest the young men get into quarrels, and directed the negotiations with the alien group. The people looked to him for instructions through his announcer as on the summer hunt. Rigid discipline was necessary to avoid quarrels or, if quarrels broke out, immediate steps had to be taken to settle them before they got out of control. Although the rules of hospitality prescribed that one who had entered the camp or village and had been fed and sheltered was to be protected, young men sometimes did not observe these rules. For that reason, the police authority was important in keeping one's own group from committing an unfriendly act which would involve the safety of the entire party. One who had wide "relationships" with alien groups and could bring them to the villages to trade for corn enjoyed a high prestige. Leadership of trading parties provided one of the avenues by which Hidatsa chieftainship was developed.

Sometimes, however, smaller groups of related households traveled out from the villages for the purpose of visiting "friends" in neighboring tribes. Although small groups did not go far from the villages, care had to be taken against attack by an enemy war party. Instances of the attack and extinction of these small parties must have been rare indeed, for informants could recall few traditional examples. These small visiting groups were never as elaborately organized as the summer camp. The character of the organization was determined by the size of the party and the likelihood of being attacked. If the party was merely a group of individuals accepting invitations to come visiting, usually the most distinguished war leader was selected or the people accepted his leadership without the formality of a selection. More often, however, these visits were for a specific purpose; to invite the alien group to come to trade, to observe ceremonies, to partake in the winter hunts, or to instruct the Hidatsa in some ceremony or dance which appealed to them. Although the group lacked the formal organization and specialization of duties so characteristic of the summer camp, the essential features were there: a leader was appointed or one assumed that position by virtue of his personality and prior experiences; the older men were consulted when crises arose; and younger men served as scouts. The principal difference was the absence of an organized police group. Being better able to travel unobserved, the party avoided battle by seeking cover, and prohibiting noises and fires whenever, in the opinion of the leader and the older men, the situation warranted. One wonders why, in view of the teachings of the older men when the youth of the village were seeking supernatural guardians, these measures were taken. Evidently, the Hidatsa were practical about these religious matters.

Summer Hunt

One of the most important activities of the summer camp was the summer buffalo hunt which, invariably, affected the entire tribe. These hunts were not tribal activities in the manner of the Plains nomadic groups, who assembled as a unit during the summer for the large buffalo hunts and tribal Sun Dance activities, but rather a village activity in which all except the old participated. It was a recognized unit of the total social and economic activities of the village and seems to have been a custom of long standing. After the corn had reached knee-height, and the fixed summer rites such as the Naxpike and Wolf Ceremonies had been performed, there was a slack period of about a month before the time came to harvest the crops. The summer hunt was designed to come at this time. In former times, it was often customary to go out 100–200 miles from the village to cure meat and hides, leaving behind an older woman of each household, the small children, and enough older men to defend the village from burning. In later years, with reduced numbers and villages closely built for mutual defense, groups cooperated for the defense of the villages and older people. Either the older people would move to one village, or they would keep in close touch with each other, or one village would not go out until the others had returned.

The older men planned the summer hunt several months in advance from reports of war parties and others who had been out from the villages to learn the disposition of enemy camps as well as the location of the herds. From this information they determined the region where the hunt would be held. The principal problem was that of transporting the cured meat and hides.

The summer herds generally were largest to the southwest of Knife River between the Killdeer Mountains and the Black Hills, but the problem of transportation overland was greater than when the hunt was held upstream from the summer villages, for then the hides could be used for boats and the cured meat could be floated down to the villages. If the reports indicated an abundance of buffaloes adjacent to the Missouri or its larger tributaries, the Hidatsa preferred to go in that direction. However, the buffaloes usually—especially after a severe winter—left the river valleys, which had been stripped of all grass, to summer on the higher lands away from the principal streams.

Some time before the village group was to leave on the hunt, the council of older men selected a hunt leader. Although all men aspired to be selected as leader once, many never received that distinction chiefly because there were too many eligible for the honor. The selection was made on the basis of one's personal record; he should first of all be one who had been a successful "leader of the hunters" on a former summer hunt, have the buffalo represented in his sacred bundle, and have the confidence of the group. This leadership was an outlet for those who had not been previously afforded the distinction of serving as leader of the whole group. As a rule, former winter camp leaders were not selected or, if they were considered, they usually declined in favor of one who had not as yet been so recognized. The principal war leader was rarely selected and his role was a subordinate one during the period of the hunt.

The council considered different men until one could be selected with unanimous agreement of the group. Rarely did a minority group hold out, for it was believed that when the people quarreled over the selection of the leader, bad luck would surely follow. The fear of responsibility for prolonged debate was sufficient to quickly break down most opposition. As soon as the leader was selected, the council's announcer called the name of the leader and the time of departure. Although the council delegated authority to direct the group, the wise leader solicited the assistance of the council as representatives of the various households in order that he could keep in close contact with his group, learn their difficulties of travel, and know of their wishes. Once the leader was selected, and before the party left for the hunt, his lodge became headquarters for the council. The old men would drop in through the day to eat and discuss details of the contemplated hunt. Some would tell of a household with no horses or riding gear, of others whose men had all been killed in a recent battle, and of the little problems of preparation for the trip. A good leader was one who could organize the group to travel without laggards. So he would send word by his announcer to those with a surplus of horses to lend assistance here and there or a word of criticism to another household that was not providing adequately for some of its members. But many of these details were more tactfully handled by dropping a hint to the council member most closely related to the distressed household.

Since the gardens were so important to the Hidatsa, the summer hunt was not scheduled to leave until the corn was knee high. When the date for the hunt was announced, the women looked to their gardens, completing the hilling of the plants and pulling the last weeds; the men repaired their riding equipment and checked their weapons. But the sharp dichotomy of work was not as apparent as during normal times. Men did many duties otherwise reserved for the women. They would assist in the gardens, spread out the tipis for inspection and last-minute repairs, and attend to last-minute matters so that the household would be ready to move out of the village when the signal was given. Everyone worked hard to get ready, for the summer hunt was a happy event in Hidatsa life. It was an opportunity for the younger boys and girls to travel and see new things. Riding horseback together in groups, boys were often mounted three or four to a horse. They ran races, sang songs, and galloped back and forth from the front to the back of the line.

The older boys and young men would dress up and watch for opportunities to talk to their girls whose mothers were otherwise engaged in caring for the household's equipment. But this flirting was often a front to conceal their inner feelings about the torture ordeals that would be expected of them once the group was out in the buffalo country. Many had already pledged to draw buffalo heads or to be suspended from some cliff while on the summer hunt; others knew that their "older brothers" would bring up the matter once they had reached the hunting grounds.

The welfare of the whole group was the leader's responsibility, but the council was always invited to assist him. The leader's position was at the head of the line with his announcer who rode back and forth informing the people from time to time of matters affecting the whole group. The Black Mouths policed the party, driving stragglers back, assisting the laggards or those encountering difficulties of travel and looking after the general welfare of the group. The leader called upon men younger than the Black Mouths to serve as scouts, riding ahead and watching from the hills for evidences of enemies or of buffalo herds.   Each group of scouts under a leader selected by the summer hunt leader was assigned an area to cover; these groups were changed from time to time so that their horses were not tired excessively.   Often these scouts were 40 miles or more in advance of the main party.   As the group moved along, the leader designated the evening camping places for several days in advance.   These sites were selected because of water, fuel, and ease of defense; a level flat adjacent to a stream usually was selected because it provided protection from the creek bank on one side and water for themselves and their animals in case of attack.   Since they frequently went to the same general area to hunt each year, certain named camps were used.

The camp circle was always used.   The leader's household set up two tipis, one for the leader and his council and the other for his household, at the head of the line.   Those at the back end swung in a circle so that the household at the rear of the line placed its tipi to the left of the leader's council lodge.   The Black Mouths moved back and forth to see that the tipis were spaced properly to complete the circle and yet leave sufficient room to bring in the horses.   When the tipis were set up, rawhide ropes were strung between each tipi forming a corral into which the horses were driven for the night. While the tipis were being set up, the horses were freed of their burdens and taken to pasture by the younger men below the status of Black Mouths.   While some young men kept the horses together so they would not stray, others rode out to serve as scouts in guarding the group against surprise by enemy horse-raiding parties.   Before dark, the horses were brought into the enclosure and guarded during the night.   Special attention was given to the horse guard while the Black Mouths kept scouts out in all directions near the camp to forestall sudden attacks on the party.   Young men were permitted— in fact, they were encouraged—to go out to hunt small game such as antelope, deer, and elk or even to surround a small herd of buffaloes. Except for small quantities of dried corn and corn balls, no other food was taken on the summer hunt; the party relied on the game brought to camp each day by the scouts and small hunting parties sent out whenever animals were discovered at hand.   They moved along leisurely from one camping spot to the next, stopping to permit the women to dig wild turnips or to pick Juneberries and chokecherries whenever the quantity of these foods warranted the delay.

As the party approached the customary hunting grounds, they stopped from time to time to permit those having sacred bundle rites relating to certain buttes and sacred spots to make appropriate offerings for the replenishment of the herds or for a distinguished individual to pray at some traditional fasting spot where he had formerly received supernatural experiences. When the buffalo appeared in great numbers, the leader, with the advice of the council and the information supplied him by the scouts, selected the camping place where the hunt would be held. The camp was always placed near good water, either a large spring or a creek, and a supply of wood from which to construct the drying frames.

The final organization of the hunt was not completed until the camp had been set up. Then the leader of the summer hunt selected the "leader of the hunters" whose duty it was to organize the surround and direct the rites of taking the buffaloes. In the selection of this man, the camp leader always named a person of a younger age-grade group, one who had formerly shown skill in hunting buffaloes and had the right to pray to them. Generally, the one selected had just recently obtained or had made the pledge to obtain his sacred bundle. Thus he was given an opportunity to test the bundle's supernatural powers. Except for the camp leader, who always remained in camp, and those Black Mouths who were selected to protect the party, all other males were given definite assignments. The younger boys herded the horses while the old men assisted by hauling poles into camp and setting up the drying frames. Young men acted as scouts watching from the hills to prevent attack. All men not otherwise assigned were expected to assist in the surround.

The surround was a group activity and anyone hunting alone was severely punished by the Black Mouths. The "leader of the hunters" planned the attack and arranged the riders. Before the hunters made the attack, all dismounted and stood around their leader while he prayed to his bundle for good luck and to the buffaloes, who were given a small offering placed on a buffalo skull or a stick, asking them not to send him bad luck or to gore the hunters. In return for good luck, a feast was promised the buffaloes at a later date. Without the rites, it was believed that the buffaloes would break up into small groups and run out between the hunters. All manners of misfortunes are said to have befallen those who did not fast properly or who, in other ways, violated the rules relating to the buffalo rites. When the hunters had good luck and everything went well, the "leader of the hunters" was acclaimed as a future leader of the village. On other occasions, when their horses stepped into badger or gopher holes, or the buffaloes were difficult to handle, people talked of his bad luck and sought to explain it in terms of improper fasting or ritual performances. The leader would then ask to be relieved of his responsibility to his hunters, and would ask the camp leader to select another to complete the surround.

As soon as the surround was completed, word went back to the camp for the people to come out and help with the butchering. At first the women would come out to assist, but, in time, as the supply of meat reaching the camp grew, the women would stay in camp curing the meat and hides while men with packhorses would butcher and transport the meat and hides to camp. Meat and hides were taken to a number of convenient parts of the camp and piled in heaps. There was no particular attempt at supplying one's own household; coming in with meat, one would look across the camp circle and select a collecting point where the pile was low and there unload his meat. Old men and women alike assisted as their strength permitted, if doing no more than standing nearby to keep the dogs away. Old men who never assisted in getting wood or poles for the summer village would work enthusiastically hauling poles for additional drying frames. From time to time, if the meat was not taken from the piles for curing fast enough, the camp leader would go around the circle and urge the people to work faster. Until the meat was taken from the communal piles for curing on household scaffolds, it remained group property and could be taken by anyone able to cure it. Due to the division of male labor at this time, many households would have no hunters and butchers out, but in the manner of distribution of the meat and hides, all shared according to their ability to dry and store the meat. Nor was the capacity of the households to care for the meat and hides equal. Some households would have four or more middle-aged women of good health and wide experience in caring for meat, while others might have only one woman who was in ill health or was burdened with several small children. Under normal conditions, the women of a household would often fill all drying space quickly. While their meat dried, they would assist their less fortunate clanswomen or brothers' wives. The tribal rule that "the clan looks after its own" certainly applied to these situations. There was a great deal of mutual assistance between related households on these occasions.

Evenings were spent in dancing and feasting. For many young men, however, once the first large kill was made, it was a period of fasting for supernatural instructions. In these camps, self-torture took two forms: (1) dragging of buffalo heads through the camp by means of thongs in the skin and flesh; and (2) suspension from cliffs or trees. The Hidatsa, like the Mandan, thought of the various supernatural beings as having homes near the summer villages or in hills and other places on the prairies. Believing that it was easy to get supernatural guidance from the buffaloes, many sought visions during the summer hunt. Generally, a number of young men were fasting on hills or dragging skulls through the camp at the same time. These personal vision quests and brief stops for an individual to make a personal offering when passing a butte or other spot were the principal religious expressions while on these summer hunts. In no instances were any of the important village ceremonies performed.

By contrast with the nomadic tribes, this period was not one for reorganizing the tribal structure, selecting new chiefs, joining military societies, or any of the other group activities. For the Hidatsa, the summer hunt was primarily an economic activity. Even the leadership of the summer hunt was in hands other than either the summer village or winter camps. Its internal organization and economic aspects show close similarity to the nomadic groups in that the camp was organized around a recognized leader and a police authority and that the camp circle was employed. But the top leadership differed from that of the nomads. The leader was selected for a specific time, that is, from the time the group left the summer earth lodge village until it returned about a month later; the nomadic leadership was, except in a few cases, for no specific period. The summer war chief and village or peace chief seemingly had no greater authority than any other distinguished person and was restricted by the same rules as were other people. For the nomadic groups, there was a leisureliness that the Hidatsa could not enjoy since the hunt must be completed in time to harvest the crop.

As soon as the party returned to the village, the summer camp leader's duties terminated and the established village leaders took over. The summer buffalo hunt thus was one of the outlets for leadership to which all aspired as a mark of public esteem.

WINTER CAMP

After the return from the summer hunt, and the completion of the harvest, the group disbanded to form winter camps. These were in sharp contrast to the few but permanent summer villages to which they returned each spring. According to traditions, prior to the appearance of the strong Siouan bands and the Assiniboin, the summer villages were unfortified and the population was widely scattered over a broad site situated to exploit adjacent corn grounds. This is certainly true, for only in the ruins of the later sites do we find evidences of fortifications and ditches. In traditional sites such as Fort Clark Station and the settlements at Sanger, lodges were widely scattered over broad river terraces. The pressure of enemy groups also produced changes in the winter village structure. In contrast to the summer village sites, which are still easily identified by deep refuse and lodge pits, winter camp sites are exceedingly difficult to find even when taken to the actual locations by older informants who lived there. These were temporary sites located in the heavy timber for protection from the storms. The wood was used for lodges, fuel, and feed for the horses. The site was selected solely on the basis of the wood supply and observations that the buffalo sought shelter there during the colder months. The lodges were neither large nor carefully constructed, and the eagle-trapping lodge was of common use. In the fall, after the garden products had been stored away, the population of any of the summer villages would disperse into several groups to seek shelter on the Missouri or one of its tributaries. There, under the leadership of an eagle-trapping bundle owner, eagles and other large birds were caught until ice began to form along the edges of the streams. If the crops were poor, they usually remained in the eagle-trapping camp until spring, depending on the hunt, and returning in the spring by bullboat, floating down their lodge goods, dried meat, and hides. Not uncommonly, while the Crow were on the Little Missouri and Lower Yellowstone and before enemies became too numerous, these winter hunting parties would go overland to the Little Missouri nearly to its source to trap eagles and hunt until spring and return to the summer villages by water, using the larger hides for boat covers to float the party and the goods. There was a revival of this practice after the railroads went through and the Sioux were put on reservations, but the distances traveled were not as great as formerly.

The winter camp organization was much simpler than that of the summer village. The top leadership was vested in a "winter camp chief" selected by the council, and his authority was only for the period out of the summer village. According to tradition, the winter camp system was based on that of the eagle-trapping camps; one leader functioned with full authority and responsibility for the welfare of the group. His duties were to supervise and organize the camp for the duration of the winter until they returned in the spring. He selected the winter campsite with the advice of the council, determined the time for moving, and generally supervised the group very closely. He set the time for the winter ceremonies, regulated camp activities during sanctioned rites and fasting for the winter buffalo-calling ceremonies, and placed restrictions on family movements beyond the camp whenever the enemy was about or when the herds were observed to be moving toward the river bottoms. The winter camp leader was held responsible for any misfortunes that befell members of the party, even such trivial matters as accidental broken limbs. Once having suffered misfortune, a household preferred to avoid going out with the same leader unless he compensated the unfortunate ones with gifts of one sort or another. The same responsibility rested with one leading the winter camp in later years even when the total village population was in a single camp. Every ambitious male aspired to be winter chief at least once in his lifetime although men usually refused to serve more than twice. His authority and responsibility were great. He received credit for all enemies killed during the winter, but he was likewise held responsible for any killed by the enemy even though it was not customary for the winter camp chief to engage in active warfare except when the village was attacked.

About the year 1863, Cherries-in-Mouth was winter camp leader. He had fasted much and had been given credit, as war leader, for five Sioux killed a few years earlier in a winter battle at Saddle Buttes. During this battle Red Leaf had been shot through the lungs but had recovered. In 1863, however, Red Leaf overexerted himself while hunting, and the old wound opened causing him to bleed to death. This was considered equivalent to losing a man in warfare and the death went against Cherries-in-Mouth's record.

The winter camp leader was selected by the council on the basis of his military record, interest in public matters, participation in village and tribal rites, generosity and kindness to the old, good judgment, and personality. Ownership of winter buffalo-calling rites and good standing with the various households were of importance, for the leader must have the confidence of the people. He could direct the buffalo-calling rites personally, or he might cooperate with others having a good reputation in "bringing the buffaloes." Likewise, he must have the good will of the households or the population would be likely to break up into smaller camps. Since much good will was obtained by generosity, selfish persons or those with an unhappy home were disregarded. Humility when selected was a prime virtue as the leader was expected, by custom, to express his own incompetence without the assistance of his sacred bundles and the advice and assistance of the older men. The leader's lodge became a meeting place for the village dignitaries to eat and sleep while discussing matters for the good of the group. The leader selected his own announcer, a clansman, usually an older and distinguished individual who had acted as assistant in many ceremonies. There were few rules, but those that were made were enforced by the Black Mouths. It was customary for the summer village leaders to rest from their summer duties and to relinquish their responsibilities to the newly selected leaders.

Nowhere in the Hidatsa culture do we find clear-cut distinctions between military aspects and village or peace functions—war chiefs performed numerous rites and village chiefs often went on military expeditions—but winter camp leadership was more clearly indicated as an extension of the role of peace or village chief to the winter camp, for this was a period of little military activity.

The Hidatsa relied heavily on the winter buffalo migrations onto the river bottoms both for their primary source of food during the winter months, and for a surplus to carry them through the spring months when they were engaged in agricultural pursuits. Frequently the winter herds did not come onto the river bottoms, especially when the season was mild. Then the winter camp suffered. Whether the winter was mild or not, the rites to the winter herds began with the winter solstice and continued until either the herds appeared or the population divided into smaller hunting groups to seek other game such as deer and elk in the undisturbed wooded areas. They did not normally rely heavily on the garden products for winter subsistence. Some corn and other garden products were taken to the winter camp to vary the diet, and periodic trips were made to the summer village to open caches for additional garden products, but the Hidatsa endeavored to save their produce for use while at the summer village.

The winter leader never relied solely on the supernatural powers of his own sacred bundles. He would pray frequently to his gods to send good luck and the herds, but his principal duty was to organize and regulate the winter rites. Ambitious younger men who had recently received visions would go to the winter leader for interpretations of their dreams. A good leader was one who could stimulate interest in winter fasting, for it was to his credit to have many young men out in the forests or on the hills fasting during cold stormy weather when the "calling the buffaloes" rites were being celebrated. If the fasters succeeded in bringing the buffaloes, that is, if the buffalo herds began arriving while one was fasting or shortly thereafter, particularly if the herds appeared on the day indicated in the dream, fasters were praised by the people without in any way detracting from the reputation of the winter camp's leader. From native accounts recorded when making this study, we find numerous instances of young men first coming to the attention of the people as potential tribal leaders as a result of their successful fasts during the winter camp period.

Winter fasting followed two distinct patterns; fasting for personal vision instructions, and fasting for the specific purpose of bringing the winter herds. The former affected but few people, chiefly the household of the faster, and generally went unobserved by the population at large unless the personal torture was so severe that his clan relatives or age-grade society members were obliged to intervene. In the latter instances, the entire population was affected. It had the sanction of the winter camp leader and those working with him in the management of the camp, and restrictions of one sort or another were invariably imposed on the whole population while the fast was on.   Commonly, when one with recognized supernatural powers volunteered to fast at a distance from the camp, fires were extinguished, all loud noises were prohibited, and hunters were forbidden to leave camp.   The entire population fasted while men and women alike addressed prayers to their sacred objects.   When the sun set, the faster returned to the camp and the fires were rekindled.   Fasting continued daily for 4 days, after which, if no buffaloes appeared, the faster terminated his fast by either promising the herds in a stated time or offering some excuse for his failure.   The women's White-Buffalo-Cow society also fasted daily during the coldest days, with the camp organized in the manner described above.

The first approach of the winter herds toward the river bottoms was the signal for increased ritualistic action to "keep them coming." The camp was strictly policed to prevent premature hunting.   Wood cutting was prohibited, and fires were extinguished if they were up-wind of the approaching herds.   Scouts kept watch of the progress of the herds and reported regularly to the camp leader.   The individual households which had sacred bundles including buffalo skulls made offerings of food and calicoes to each bundle, while households having no such bundles made similar offerings to those of closely related households.   During the approach of the herds, the Black Mouths were on constant guard to see that no person hunted prematurely; there are traditions that on some occasions the police killed individuals disobeying their orders.   In the memory of the oldest Hidatsa, however, there were few intentional violations of the orders; hence the punishment was less severe.   In any event, the Black Mouths had the authority, fortified by public opinion, to take such measures as they deemed necessary to enforce the "no hunting" orders of the winter chief.   According to informants, the buffalo herds were easily startled when they first reached the wooded bottoms from the prairies—in fact, whenever a herd first moved to a new pasture—and it was necessary to leave them undisturbed for a few days to graze and get settled in their new environment, or they were likely to move on. During this time, Wolf Chief said that it was very hard indeed to restrain one's self, particularly when the children were crying from hunger and cold.   The people stayed within doors and could often see the buffaloes walking between the lodges or hooking at dogs that had not been securely tied.   When the time came to kill, even in later years, restrictions on the use of firearms were enforced.   These restrictions placed the young men unskilled with bows and arrows at a disadvantage.   After two or three large surrounds had been completed and enough meat had been secured for the winter needs (and the meat-curing capacity of the women had been reached), all restrictions were removed and those who desired additional meat went out in small parties and hunted whenever they wished. With the arrival of the winter herds, the ritualistic activities diminished. Those who had pledged summer ceremonies used the period for exceptional efforts to obtain large quantities of meat and robes. The pledgers hunted continuously and the women cured meat and tanned robes with the assistance of their female relatives. The people would say that the pledger's prayers for a good living for his people were being answered when, during his period of preparation, the winter herds were unusually large. "The gods he was buying had sent the buffaloes," they would say.

The winter camp leader's responsibilities ended with the return to the summer village. When enemies were far away, the families leisurely returned to the summer camp in small groups of related households, assisting each other with the loads and the care of the children. If, however, signs of enemy war parties had been reported or there were other reasons for believing that an attack might be made, the group moved as an organized party with the leader to the front and the Black Mouths in charge to see that none dropped out of line. Should a household encounter difficulty in traveling at the pace set by the leader or the loads fell from the horses, others gave immediate assistance so that all were adequately protected. Each individual killed or wounded represented a mark against the leader's record. Therefore, the good leader was careful to maintain discipline and to prohibit individual and disorganized breaking of camp unless danger of attack was very remote. He lacked authority to prevent segments of the group from leaving the main party, establishing temporary hunting camps out in the hills, and following the buffaloes moving out from the river valleys with the first general thaws. He was not, however, responsible for the safety of these small hunting parties once they had fallen out of line.

These spring hunting camps were not without leadership. The principal purpose of these side trips was to obtain an additional supply of fresh meat. The older men met and selected from their number one who had formerly enjoyed good luck while making the "surround" and who had bundle rights which included the sacred buffalo skull. The organization of the camp was essentially the same as for the larger summer buffalo hunt. These hunts were known as "in-between" hunts as they were conducted after the winter camp had broken up and before the summer village was reoccupied. Guards were placed around the camp but the Black Mouths no longer functioned as an organized group except when the entire winter encampment moved out onto the hills as a group. Instead, the leader selected various younger men who served without regard to age-grade affiliations. The old people today identify the thousands of boulder outlines on the prairies adjacent to the river valleys as former tipi outlines of these "in-between" camps occupied in the late winter and early spring as precautions against sudden flooding of the river bottoms. From all available evidence it appears that with the arrival of the Sioux and Assiniboin, the "in-between" hunting camps were less common and that when brief expeditions were made onto the adjacent prairies, greater emphasis was placed on organization for defense.

As the groups moved back into the summer village, the summer chieftains assumed command, and the winter camp leader became merely a distinguished member of the council of older men. If the population at large was well cared for, had no suffering or deaths, the winter camp leader was highly acclaimed. If there had been an unusually large number of buffaloes nearby, the people would say that not in years had there been so many buffaloes, and would recount the fine winter they spent. They would show their esteem after returning to the summer camp by preparing feasts from the garden products which had been sparingly used during the winter, and invite the winter camp leader and his family. Other households perhaps, were not so successful: one member of the household had died or had had an accident; their horses had been taken sick and died or had strayed away to be captured by raiding parties; their best buffalo horse may have broken a leg or been gored by a buffalo. All these and other misfortunes went against the winter leader's record. They would tell their friends of their misfortunes and criticize the leader behind his back even though he had been their best friend before going into the winter camp.

Custom provided numerous measures for restoring good will and the wise leader was certain to take quick action. If the discontent arose from the killing of a member of the household by a known enemy, the leader would often organize a retaliatory war party or designate one to go out and take the scalp of the particular enemy or one of his near relatives. This type of war honor, going out for a specific person, particularly if unaccompanied far from the village, was of the very highest. In recent years, the Hidatsa had a wide acquaintance with enemy groups and frequently the person killing a Hidatsa was known in the village. When the individual or war party returned successfully, the scalp was taken to a sister of the one mourned. She carried the scalp during the war dances and sang the praises of the one who had returned victorious. No longer did the household criticize their winter leader; in fact, they would be the first to nominate him as winter leader for the succeeding year.

Frequently, however, one did not take such positive action. Hearing that a war party was going out, the former winter leader might make offerings of gifts and recite a prayer for the success of the party. If the expedition was successful, out of gratitude to the former winter camp leader who had assisted them ritualistically, he received the scalp which was taken to the mourners, especially the sister or mother, and carried in the dances. Then the matter was forgotten. For minor misfortunes such as the natural death of a relative, feasts and presents were sufficient to establish a feeling of good will between them. Then the people would say, "Think nothing of it; one can't live forever." Wolf Chief tells of a little boy who told the winter chief that their winter chief was no good because his bow string kept breaking, and the winter chief had a new bow made with a stronger string; after that the boy had no trouble with his bow. When the parents heard of the incident they scolded the boy, for they considered it impudent for a child to speak of an elder in that manner.

SUMMARY

The Hidatsa used the term "chief" very broadly to designate anyone who was at the time in a position of leadership and authority. Every important situation required leadership. We have shown above that there was a feeling of clan leadership in matters concerning the clan; that each age-grade as an organized group had its complement of officers; and finally that responsible leaders were recognized in the general administration of the summer and winter villages. These by no means exhaust the list of organized groups recognized by these people. These units varied in size from the community to small economic groups, such as fish trapping, and from permanent groups to those of short and temporary existence.

The wide selection of leaders and the numerous opportunities to "lead" are consistent with their concepts of supernatural powers and the promises of the tribal ceremonial leaders when young men organized and planned their lives. On every important occasion, when a young man distinguished himself in warfare, personal torture, or ritualistic purchases, the leaders assured him that his ultimate goal should be that of "leader of the people."

Because "supernatural power was measurable," it increased by the performance of certain rites and other practices and, in like measure, was exhausted in combating the daily risks. As the individual assumed greater responsibilities within the group, these powers were exhausted at a greater rate. An individual, therefore, should not remain in authority too long and no man aspired to continuous leadership. In applying this concept to group leadership, we find constant changing of top leadership as the situations of life changed.

The opportunities to lead enumerated above indicate only a few group situations, but they represent the largest groups for which leadership was provided. In this category should be included the organization of the village for the purpose of corralling buffaloes near the village. Since this activity had important ceremonial aspects and was a part of a group of related rites, it is analyzed under "Hidatsa Ceremonial Organization" (pp. 282–476).

The Clan and Moiety System

The clan—a named matrilineal group—was an important feature of Hidatsa social, economic, and ceremonial life. At birth, the child became a member of his mother's clan or, if the mother was clanless because she had belonged to a different tribe, the child assumed the clan of the other children of the household. In spite of the traditional late arrival of the Hidatsa-proper and the Awaxawi on the Missouri River, the clan names as now employed are concerned with incidents or events occurring along the Missouri River and in no instance reflect incidents or events relating to their former residences to the east or northeast. The traditions and mythology indicate that two different clan systems were once in vogue: (1) the 13-clan system of the Awatixa; and (2) the 7-clan system of the Awaxawi and Hidatsa-proper.

ORIGINS

Reference to the Awatixa system of 13 clans is found in the myths of the Sacred Arrows which relate that when this group came down from above to inhabit the earth, their culture hero, Charred Body, selected 13 household groups to represent the 13 parts of the sacred arrow. Each household group established a matrilineal lineage; marriage within the household was prohibited. Since the population of this mythological village was small, people were able to remember their relatives. Because of the rich land Charred Body had found below at Painted Woods, with its extensive wooded bottoms for agriculture and the large herds of buffaloes on the adjacent prairies, the population increased rapidly and broke up into 13 small local groups of related kin. At that time the groups were exogamous and lived near each other for protection from certain local evil spirits who resented the occupation of the area by Charred Body's people.

During mythological times, these groups were named for incidents involving them. Of the 13 original groups, 8 received names which still designate existing clans. Of the other five lineages, nothing is remembered, and it is assumed by the Hidatsa that these groups died out or united with other named groups.

The Hidatsa-proper and the Awaxawi informants claim never to have had more than seven clans. Genealogies of the three Hidatsa groups indicate that the eighth clan, the Xura, was found only at Awatixa. They also claim short residence on the Missouri, coming to this river as large village groups without clans. It is to be presumed that they had matrilineal lineages, in view of the method whereby clans were introduced into the village population; when a clan name was adopted from some incident involving a group of males, the name was extended to include the mothers, sisters, and sisters' children. In this manner, according to mythology, every person in the tribe in time became a member of a named clan. This system of extending clan membership obviously is acceptable to the Hidatsa, for they show that whenever a considerable number of female prisoners were taken, in a few years all were incorporated into the clan system by the same methods as nonclan Hidatsa were integrated when the clan system was adopted.

Native concepts of clan origin are of two kinds: (1) the origin of the clan from a single female of a household group coming down from the sky with Charred Body; and (2) a local group accustomed to living together. We shall see that numerous bundles were inherited by clans of the former group but less characteristically by those of the latter.

The clan names with two exceptions are nontotemic and refer to incidents involving a few people. The *Maxoxati* clan receives its name from *maxoxi*, which refers to the dry dust that formed from the decaying of the earth lodge rafters and dropped down continuously, and *ati* meaning "lodge." The *Métsiroku* clan means literally "knife people" and refers to an instance of wife-purchase with a stone knife. The *Apukawiku* clan receives its name from *apuka* meaning cap or article of clothing worn above the eyes to shade them from the sun and *wiku* meaning "low." The clan name was derived from the supernatural experiences of Packs Antelope with the Thunderbirds and the Grandfather snake of the Missouri who killed by means of lightning which flashed from his eyes. When he returned from his exploits with the supernatural, he shaded his eyes to protect the people. The three clans listed above are grouped together and are known today as the Three-clan Moiety.

The Prairie Chicken clan was believed to have once been a separate village group. The name was derived from the fact that members of this group were noisy like the prairie chickens. In another myth, the Prairie Chicken clan began from the custom of a war party to camp at night in the bushes, the berries of which were eaten by the prairie chickens. The *Awaxɛnawita* clan derives its name from the childhood custom of building tiny villages with wet clay. Later the people saw hills upstream and nearly opposite the present city of Williston, N. Dak., that reminded them of the work of small children. The people camped there three times; hence the name *Awaxɛñawita* taken from *awaxɛ* meaning 'hill sliding down' and *nawi* meaning 'three.' The *Miripáti* clan derives its name from a quarrel that occurred in the village. The *Miripáti* separated and built near the village of the *Xura,* who, at that time, had a separate village. Water was brought from the river and stored in bladders for use in case of a prolonged attack. One man became angered because of the cowardice of his people and cut up the waterbag hanging in his lodge; after this the group was known as *Miripatihɛ* from *miri* meaning 'water' and *pati* meaning 'to break open.' The *Xura* clan, which in recent years has functioned as a named lineage in the Waterbuster or *Miripáti* clan, is believed to have been a separate village at one time. The name is derived from the noise of the cicada. The village, except for one woman and her baby daughter, disappeared mysteriously during the night. The survivors moved to the village of the Waterbusters of Awatixa and formed a friendship with that group.

The *Itisúku* clan received its name from the custom of being out to the front of the war party along the edges of the hills overlooking the Missouri. Once a group of young men called on Old-Woman-Who-Never-Dies at her lodge near the Red Buttes and she promised them success in warfare. When they returned to their homes, they called themselves *Itisúku.*

In addition to the eight clans listed above, there were a few members of the Speckled Eagle clan in the tribe. According to tradition, this clan was of Mandan origin although many members can no longer trace their lineages back to any particular Mandan village group. They lived principally at Awaxawi village. According to the Mandan, however, the Awaxawi Speckled Eagles were people who moved to Awaxawi at the time of the destruction of Nuptadi shortly after 1780. Like the Mandan Speckled Eagle clan, they have been assimilating with the Prairie Chicken clan in recent years and marriage with the Prairie Chicken clan is now generally disapproved.

CLAN MEMBERSHIP AND AFFILIATIONS

A census by informants of the Mandan and Hidatsa living at Fish-hook Village in 1872—subsequent to the removal of the Crow-Flies-High band—showed the following population by clans: [11]

Hidatsa clans:	In Hidatsa households	In Mandan households
Maxoxati	62	12
Knife (Mɛtsiroku)	35	17
Low cap (Apukawiku)	14	0
Prairie chicken	62	5
Awaxɛnawita	44	21
Waterbusters (Miripati)	62	12
Xura	1	10
Itisuku	16	4
Mandan clans:		
Waxikɛna	1	29
Tamisik	43	93
Prairie chicken	10	60
Speckled eagle	9	10
Other tribes:		
Arikara	3	29
Blackfoot	0	2
Crow	4	2

While the Mandan and Hidatsa seemed in general agreement as to whether a mixed household was Mandan or Hidatsa, no definite rule could be made. Although children generally claimed to belong to the mother's tribe, there were numerous exceptions to the rule as in the case of Bad Gun, one of the Mandan chiefs, whose mother was a Hidatsa and whose wife was also. Tribal affiliation seemed to be based even more on the individual's participation in social and ceremonial functions. In other similar situations a man and the household would have been classified by the informants as Hidatsa. The extent of Hidatsa-Mandan intermarriage prior to 1872 is indicated by the figures for households. These figures do not include one faction of the Hidatsa who moved away about this time and were accompanied by a few Mandans. We see that there were 296 Hidatsas living in recognized Hidatsa households while an additional 63 belonging to Mandan clans lived in the same households as did 3 Arikaras, and 4 Crows who were brought there by marriage. In addition, there were 81 persons belonging to Hidatsa clans who were living in recognized Mandan households housing 192 persons of Mandan clans. More than 80 percent of this intermixture of Mandans and Hidatsas occurred after 1850.

---

[11] These figures do not include those individuals of alien groups who have been adopted and assumed clan affiliation.

The Three-clan moiety was composed of the Maxoxati, Knife, and Low Cap clans. Although differing greatly in relative size, each was of equal status in the moiety. In recent years it has become common practice to identify oneself as "three clan," and in some instances the actual clan membership is not now known. The other moiety is spoken of as the "Four-clan moiety" although it actually comprises five clans, excluding the Speckled Eagle which is of Mandan origin. The clans of this moiety are grouped into phratries of linked clans. One phratry is composed of the Prairie Chicken-Awaxɛnawita clans. In mythological times, so the people say, the Prairie Chickens would kill and scalp people of the other clans. They lived in a separate village near Expansion and above the mouth of the Knife River. The people of the Awaxɛnawita clan went to the people of Prairie Chicken village and said, "It is not right for us to fight, for we speak the same language." Then the Prairie Chicken people "united" into a friendship band with the Awaxɛnawita people. When no other relationship was known, persons of the two clans treated each other as distant clansmen. Nevertheless, marriages between the two clans were common. The close ties of the Waterbuster, Xura, and Itisuku clans are indicated by the mythologies. When the Xura village group moved away and disappeared, one household joined the Waterbusters of Awatixa village and is now largely incorporated into that clan as a named lineage. The union of the Waterbusters into related clans is of long standing, according to the mythology, and stems from the belief that at one time a minor group of Waterbusters, who later were identified as Itisuku, went on the warpath together. The tables show that this phratry was largely exogomous. This is consistent with native beliefs that the Prairie Chicken and Awaxɛnawita intermarried more frequently than the Waterbuster-Itisuku.

Table 1 was prepared from genealogies of the Hidatsa and Mandan living at Fishhook Village in 1872 and was compiled from the information supplied me by about 15 informants. Table 1 enumerates marriages which were of some permanence and does not include brief elopements. These marriages were, in general, those that occurred between 1825 and 1885. Approximately 80 percent of the marriages occurred after 1855 while the Mandan and Hidatsa were living at Fishhook Village. Figures for the Mandan are included in the table to indicate the extent of intertribal marriage.

Table 1 shows that of 128 marriages within the Hidatsa tribe, 7 were within the clan. According to custom, it was considered improper for one to marry a person of the same clan, but the instances of marriage with one of the father's clan are equally rare. This is in sharp contrast with data from the Mandan genealogies which show a frequency of nearly 25 percent. Table 1 shows 59 marriages with

TABLE 1.—*Mandan and Hidatsa intermarriage by clans*

Clan	Hidatsa Three-clan moiety			Hidatsa Four-clan moiety					Mandan moiety I		Mandan moiety II	
	Maxoxati	MEtsiroku	Apukawiku	Prairie chicken	AwaxEnawita	Miripati	Xura	Itisuku	WaxikEna	Tamisik	Prairie chicken	Speckled eagle
Maxoxati	3	6	3	8	8	13	1	–	2	7	1	–
MEtsiroku		2	1	5	7	9	1	2	–	5	9	3
Apukawiku			–	1	–	–	–	2	–	1	–	–
Prairie chicken				–	16	16	3	5	1	2	3	2
AwaxEnawita					1	8	–	5	1	6	2	1
Miripati						1	–	1	–	4	1	3
Xura							–	–	–	–	–	1
Itisuku								–	–	1	–	3
WaxikEna									–	7	7	2
Tamisik										4	20	2
Prairiechicken											2	6
Speckled eagle												–

TABLE 2.—*Mandan and Hidatsa intermarriage by moieties*

Moieties	Hidatsa Three-clan	Hidatsa Four-clan	Mandan moiety I	Mandan moiety II
Hidatsa three-clan	15	57	15	13
Hidatsa four-clan	57	56	13	31
Mandan moiety I	15	13	11	31
Mandan moiety II	13	31	31	8

Mandans, or the equivalent of approximately 1 out of 3 marriages. During the same period, Mandans married with Hidatsas in the ratio of 59 to 50.

In theory, moieties were not exogamous. This is in sharp contrast with the Mandan who claim that prior to the smallpox epidemics, moieties were exogamous. Table 2 shows the same marriages when grouped according to moiety. It shows that of the 128 Hidatsa marriages, 57 were between opposite moieties while 70 were within the same moiety. Moiety exogamy was most generally observed by people of the Three-clan moiety with only 15 exceptions. The figures for the Mandan seem to verify native traditions of former moiety exogamy; 31 marriages were between opposite moieties while 19 were within the moiety. The figures indicate that in cases of intertribal marriages, even for the Mandan, there was no tendency to select mates of the opposite moiety.

At the present time the Mandan clans are equated with certain Hidatsa clans. The Mandan WaxikEna equals the Hidatsa Maxoxati; the Tamisik equals the Knife; the Mandan Prairie Chicken equals the Hidatsa Prairie Chicken; the Mandan Speckled Eagle equals the Hidatsa Speckled Eagle. As stated above, those of the Hidatsa Speckled Eagle clan claim to be descendants of Mandans who moved to Awaxawi village after the first smallpox epidemic. According to traditions, the equivalence of the Mandan Prairie Chicken clan was originally with the Prairie Chickens of Awatixa village, who owned a Sacred Robe bundle in common. It was customary for these people to meet whenever the ceremony was being performed. Inclusion of the Prairie Chicken members of Hidatsa and Awaxawi villages in these rites did not occur until after the three Hidatsa villages united for mutual defense after 1837, at which time all Prairie Chicken members, irrespective of village origin, met when the rites were being performed and were entitled to receive goods and honors. Marriage within the clan was then no longer considered proper. The equating of the other clans occurred within the memory of the older people living in 1932 when this study was made. When they were young, opinion was divided; some thought that it was proper for persons of the Knife clan to marry Mandans of the Tamisik, since the couple was of different tribes, but others disapproved. The same views prevailed for the WaxikEna and Maxoxati clans. By 1880, when such marriages occurred, disapproval was general.

Equating of clans was extended to include the moieties as well. Except for the Awatixa, who claim to have once had a 13-clan system which at this time seems forgotten, there was a marked difference in the number of Mandan and Hidatsa clans. The Hidatsa Three-clan moiety was equated with the Mandan WaxikEna-Tamisik moiety founded by Lone Man and comprised the survivors of the Six-clan moiety; the Hidatsa Four-clan moiety became equated with the Mandan Seven-clan moiety founded by Clay-on-Face of which only two clans, the Prairie Chicken and Speckled Eagle, survive.

The Hidatsa clan names have remained unchanged during the entire period of recorded history. This is in sharp contrast with the Crow among whom names were changing during the memory of old informants. With the exception of the Prairie Chicken and Xura clans, Hidatsa names were nontotemic and more closely resemble the Crow than the Mandan who had, in one moiety, Prairie Chicken, Speckled Eagle, Bear, Badger, Red-Hill-People (snake), Crow, and Bunch-of-Wood People. In spite of their traditional late separation from the Crow, none of the names of Crow clans show similarity to those of the Hidatsa nor do the Hidatsa have traditions of clan relationships to specific Crow clans. Those Hidatsa who have had intimate contacts with the Crow during the period of readjustment subsequent to the smallpox epidemic of 1837, when many Hidatsa lived temporarily with the Crow, are aware of the presence of clans among the Crow but in no instance do they equate the clans of the two tribes. Those Crow who settled with the Hidatsa soon affiliated with a Hidatsa clan group.   Such has also been the case with persons of other tribes settling at the villages.

The role of the Hidatsa clan, with a few exceptions, is essentially the same as that of the Mandan.   It is composed of a named group of relatives tracing their origin back to separate households of Charred Body's village and to names subsequently given to the group during their residence on the Missouri River.   The clan is an outstanding feature of Hidatsa social organization but it has its economic and ritualistic aspects as well.   It extended kinship relationships to the limit of the village and the tribe, not to discount a more recent extension by means of "clan equating" to include the Mandan as well. Based on a "sibling" relationship between clan members, one classified as "brothers" and "sisters" those of one's clan.   By the same principle, the persons of the father's clan were "fathers" or "father's sisters."   These were the most important kinship extensions, since they comprised an individual's important relatives.

CLAN DUTIES AND RESPONSIBILITIES

The clan was responsible for the care of its own members.   These obligations were expressed in many ways.   Old people and orphans were cared for and often taken into the households of clan members. When the wife died, the man generally left the household to live in one where the females were of his clan.   One would go preferably to the sister's or sister's daughter's household; otherwise he would take up residence with any member of his clan with whom he was well acquainted.   From the number of instances of change in residence of old men whose wives had died and the attitude of those providing care for them, I feel that they were welcomed through a sense of obligation.   These old men were respected and welcomed members of the household and played an important role in informing the younger people of tribal lore and traditions.   Since those attaining prominence in the tribe were required to display considerable knowledge of tribal traditions and mythology, particularly those defining proper conduct, these old men sold their stories and received goods, horses, and honors, in proportion to their knowledge in these matters.

It was the duty of the clan to assume responsibility for the care of orphans.   The Hidatsa interpret an orphan to be one whose father and his brothers, mother and her sisters, married sisters, and able-bodied maternal grandmothers were dead.   Then the clan took over and provided a home.   The number of such cases was quite large after 1800 owing to epidemics and enemy attacks on small hunting parties of both sexes.   It is interesting to observe that some of the most distinguished Hidatsa of the 19th century were left orphans in 1837 by the inroads of smallpox.   Occasionally a childless couple received permission of the clan to adopt one of a different clan. These children invariably joined the clan of the female caring for them.

The clan was responsible for the behavior of its members. It was the duty of older persons of the clan to instruct and supervise the children as they grew up. At first this responsibility was assumed by the "older brothers" of the household: one's own older brothers; the mother's brothers and the mother's sisters' older sons; the maternal grandmother's brothers; or any other males residing in the lodge and classified as "older brother." Also included were the females of the lineage residing in the same lodge. As a child grew up and moved more freely about the village, it was the right as well as the duty of an older person of the clan to step in and correct any child who violated village rules and customs, and to lend assistance on various occasions. Discipline usually took the form of a mild reminder of misdeeds. In more extreme offenses—hitting smaller children or girls, playing in lodges containing certain sacred bundles, destroying property, attempting rape, or stealing—any older clan member conveniently at hand could step in and inflict punishment by beating or ducking the offender in the river.

It was the duty of the clan not only to discipline its own members but also to protect them from the attacks of others. When a mature person violated tribal custom and caused people to talk of his misdeeds, the whole clan was shamed. People would say that the clan had been negligent in its duties or he would have behaved properly. Often some woman would neglect her gardens and steal from others' gardens. People in the village would talk of strange tracks seen in their gardens and of stalks from which corn had been stripped. Watching late at night, someone would see a woman or sometimes several women leave a certain lodge and go toward the gardens. Knowing that the women of that household had been neglecting their garden or had failed to plant a crop that year, the observer would conclude that these women were out stealing. A thief's clan would usually attempt to break up the stealing without the assistance of the injured parties, lest the Black Mouths be called upon to investigate the affair. Each sex tended to discipline clan members of its own sex. Women of the clan would lie in wait to catch her. Seizing her they would throw her down and beat her with sticks, straps, and even hoe handles until she confessed her errors and promised never to steal even so much as the smallest and most worthless thing again. If she fought back, the punishment was likely to be extremely severe. When she promised to forego stealing in the future, she was taken to the lodges of her clan members and given food, clothing, and sometimes even horses. Once the stealing was stopped, it was considered improper for people of other clans to discuss the matter lest the same misdeeds be committed by members of their own clan. Had the stealing continued, it would have been the right of others to demand payment of any member of the thief's clan. Probably more important for the peace of the village, this practice of punishing a clan member kept conflicts localized and confined within a segment of the total village group and limited the duties of the organized village police to matters involving the population at large.

One's clansmen played an important role in directing and supervising the fasting of its younger members. When a number of young clansmen had reached the age of 12 to 14, older people of the clan would say that it was now time for them to take fasting seriously. Several related households would discuss the matter and decide to send the boys to some secluded spot under the direction of an older clansman where they would be supervised and instructed in fasting. A fasting shelter would be erected where the director could eat and smoke and those who wished to could sleep. Each faster would select a spot on the side of a clay bank, beside a pile of rocks, or near a bush too small to offer shade or protection from the hot sun, where he would stand during the day and far into the night. He was taught how to cry to the gods for successful dreams; afterward he would be recommended for a chance to join some war leader to secure from the enemy that which the holy ones had promised him in the dream. During the time the boys fasted, the leader observed their behavior and watched to see that food or water was not being taken on the sly. Those who pursued extreme measures to induce good dreams were publicly praised in the village and were told that they would surely live good lives.

The clan further assisted its young men by encouraging fasting and participation in all ceremonies providing opportunities for public fasting. The most popular rites in this class were the NaxpikE (Sun Dance) and the Wolf ceremonies which emphasized warfare. The clan furnished goods and horses for a younger member to give during the ceremony to certain "fathers" and others in exchange for customary services relating to the acquisition of supernatural powers. When the young clansman endured unusual suffering during the ceremony, the clan would voice its approval and bring goods to the ceremony in such quantities as to embarrass the other clans whose members had endured less suffering or had shown fear during the torture feature.

The clan protected its members from outside attack, whether by a member of the village or by an outsider, and resented infringement by another in the disciplining of a member. Because of these important functions of the clan, the father's role as a disciplinary officer · exceedingly unimportant. Had the father scolded his son or hit he would have been severely criticized by both his son's and his own clan. When a clansman's wife was stolen, the whole clan felt injured and would assist the one whose wife had been stolen by demanding payment collectively from the aggressor's relatives and clans. Since some of the aggressor's relatives usually had advance information that an elopement was contemplated, it was customary for them to take goods and horses to the injured man even before he discovered his loss and had enlisted the assistance of his clan; otherwise they were permitted to kill the aggressor's horse and cut up his property.

The clan revenged the murder of a member by killing the offender and demanding goods of his clansmen as indemnity. There is no recorded instance of murder by one of a different clan in recent years so it was not possible to study a case history of manslaughter. When a person killed another of the same clan, restitution was between households. Since the clan as an organized group could not extract indemnity from itself, the matter was allowed to drop if the murderer escaped from the village. During the last century there have been at least three murders committed within the clan by males while intoxicated. In two cases the murderer was aided by his household in making his escape while his household and closer clan relatives made restitution to the dead man's household. The third case was committed during a drunken brawl after the Agency was established and was handled by the North Dakota courts. In former times, murder was of such great importance that the Black Mouths took charge immediately to see that matters did not get out of hand, otherwise a portion of the population was likely to break away and establish an independent village. In former times when the Hidatsa occupied three villages, since each village had essentially the same clan representation, murderers escaping from one village were not secure in another one because of the presence there of the murdered one's clansmen. Generally they would escape to the Crow but frequently the Mandan or Arikara would harbor them. At first those of Hidatsa village who had committed crimes against persons of the Prairie Chicken and Speckled Eagle clans were prohibited refuge with the Mandan, where these clans were also represented. Because of the numerous marriages between the Mandan and the Hidatsa villages of Awaxawi and Awatixa, it was never considered safe for men of these villages to seek refuge with the Mandan. After the Mandan moved north to the region of the Hidatsa villages near Knife River, refuge with the Mandan was less common due to the equating of the Mandan and Hidatsa clans and intermarriage between these village groups. One-eyed, a chief of the Hidatsa, is said to be the last from Hidatsa village to seek temporary refuge with the Mandan with whom he lived for a short time after killing a clansman whose wife he coveted.

Clan cooperation was expressed in many ways. In addition to assisting and caring for the old and the orphans, women who were ill and could not do their work were assisted in caring for their households and gardens. One might even be brought into the lodge of clanswomen and nursed back to health. Goods and horses were contributed when a clansman performed a ceremony. Men of the same clan gave up their wives for an unmarried clansman or one whose wife was in advanced pregnancy when a ceremony was being performed, in order to enhance the prestige of the clan. When a clansman was killed in warfare and his clan brothers did nothing about it, people of the other clans would accuse them of being cowards. The highest honor was shown one who had organized his fasting so as afterward to avenge the death of a clan brother. In every instance, the clansmen brought out goods and property for the victory dances when one of its number had returned successfully from war.

At death, both the person's own and the father's clan had important duties. Generally, the members of the father's clan who officiated were selected in advance, sometimes years beforehand. It was the duty of the clan to provide goods, horses, and food for the funeral rites as payment for the official mourners who comprised the adults of the father's clan. Not uncommonly one who was believed dying would call in the close relatives of the father's clan, either men or women, who would paint and dress the dying person even before death occurred. The clan members would begin bringing in the property and displaying it on lines within the lodge where those caring for the sick person and friends coming in for a last visit could observe them. It was believed that a lavish display of goods expressed the generosity and solidarity of the clan. The sick person was happy in the belief that in the spirit world he could boast of the goods that had been disposed of when he was sent away. The clan had no other role when death of a member occurred. Individuals of the father's clan were in charge of the last rites. A dying person called in those who were to be present to perform the funeral rites, otherwise the family would make the selection. They would say to the people selected, "We want you to bring the robe; your son (or daughter) is ill and about to leave you."

Those selected talked to the "son" or "daughter," telling him not to be afraid; that all people must die sometime; that they would see their people in the spirit village and to greet them. Some dying persons had many messages to carry to relatives in the spirit world. The Hidatsa preferred to be dressed and painted when death occurred, so, not uncommonly, a person would be painted and dressed several times before death occurred. Brave men wounded in battle, knowing they were dying, often asked to be painted so that they could dance before the people to show their bravery. The people of the father's clan would sing the victory songs and praise their "son" while his own clansmen wept at the thought of losing one of their members. In such circumstances the "blood father" occupied an intermediate situation. He would weep with his son's clansmen, cut his hair, and inflict physical pain on himself as did the females of the son's family and clan. The degree of self-torture was usually in direct proportion to the son's bravery and whether the father would be left sonless. A man grieved loudest and longest for an only son.

The final rites were held at the grave or scaffold where the body was taken by persons of the father's clan and either placed on a scaffold or interred, according to the wishes of the deceased or his nearest clansmen. Those officiating, people of the father's clan, and visitors, were given the goods collected by the clan for its deceased member. According to tradition, the Hidatsa more frequently buried their dead outside of the village than did the Awaxawi or Awatixa. In this respect, the latter groups more closely followed the later Mandan practice of placing the dead on scaffolds. The archeology of the three Knife River villages supports this native belief; individual burial pits and mounds are exceedingly numerous adjacent to Hidatsa village although exceedingly rare at the other villages.

The father's clan had other important duties in addition to officiating during the death and funeral of a son. They generally named their "sons" and "daughters" and frequently, in the case of children dying young, the same person giving the name was selected to "bring the robe" when the child died. Informal feasts were also given to the people of the father's clan from time to time. Everyone was expected to give feasts. Those who had a surplus of food and property were expected to share it from time to time with the elderly, but more particularly with the people of the father's clan. One looked to the people of the father's clan for formal instruction in fasting and rituals and paid for that service. With few exceptions, organized ceremonies likewise passed from one man to another standing in the relationship of "son." The father and the people of the father's clan were respected relatives; they took little part in the routine training of their "sons" and "daughters." In ritualistic training, however, they assumed a dominant role, for, at birth, a "son" or "daughter" received a name taken from these ritualistic possessions believed to afford supernatural protection. All through life the people of the father's clan offered prayers and sold sacred objects and rites to the "sons" and "daughters"; and in death they disposed of the body with appropriate rites to send the spirit away. On some occasions, special rites were performed years after the death of a "son" or "daughter" who had died away from the village, at the time when the skull was brought back and placed at a skull shrine.

The clan, particularly a large one, played an important role in uniting households and integrating the village population, and it brought together many households for common efforts. Thus we find that the amount of goods required for the purchase or performance of a ceremony was far in excess of one person's ability to acquire. Ceremonial demands, in general, were not difficult burdens for one belonging to a large clan since all people of the clan were obliged to assist to avoid censure from the other clans and to save face. Only in the case of small clans was the burden heavy; this may explain the tendency of the small clans, such as the Xura and Itisuku, to affiliate with larger ones. The obligations of the clan in elevating a person to chieftainship were so numerous that a small clan was at a distinct disadvantage.

Not only did the clan play an important role in the integration of household groups comprising the villages but it united households with those of other villages. The degree of cooperation between persons of the same clan but of different villages was largely a matter of distance. According to the opinion of informants, well supported by archeological evidence, the villages were quite widely separated when the population was large and their enemies were not so numerous. The villages were largely endogamous due to matrilocal residence which kept the women tied to the households of their mothers. Males were reluctant to move from their mothers' villages where they had all of their closest social and ceremonial ties. We can assume that, because of the similarity of clan names and groupings, the clan system as we know it today was established long before 1796 when the three village groups occupying sites within 3 or 4 miles of each other at the mouth of Knife River were visited by early travelers. In relations between villages, the clan was the principal integrating force. Visitors from adjacent villages were housed with clansmen and frequently assisted and participated in the ceremonial activities of fellow clansmen. Although there were minor dialectic and other cultural differences which distinguished villages, a common clan system played an important role in holding the tribal population together and avoiding intervillage warfare.

By 1825, and after a quarter of a century of intimate contacts with the Mandan, refuge there was no longer offered to those who had murdered a tribesman. This is undoubtedly due to the equating of Mandan and Hidatsa clans prior to that period. At this point it is interesting to note that even though the Crow-Flies-High band of Hidatsa separated from the Fishhook Village about 1872 under conditions approaching civil war and established a separate village of their own, those who got into trouble at either village were not accepted by the other because of the strength of the clan ties. Neither Big Wind, who committed manslaughter at Fort Buford, nor Sitting Elk, who committed the same offense at Fishhook and under similar circumstances—killing a clansman while intoxicated—dared flee to a Hidatsa village. Big Wind fled to the Crows and Sitting Elk fled to Fort Stevenson and asked protection of the U.S. Army. It is interesting to observe, and it is important for this study to note, that the custom of village groups to break up whenever irreconcilable internal conflicts arose did not weaken authority of the clan.

HIDATSA MOIETY CONCEPT

In contrast with the Mandan, the Hidatsa moiety concept was of less social and economic importance. In this respect the Hidatsa seem to have occupied a position intermediate between the Mandan, who had a highly developed moiety concept, and the Crow where the moiety was unknown. Nowhere in the Hidatsa ceremonialism does one find moiety seating of fasters or participants as practiced by the Mandan in their important summer Okipa ceremony. We find the Hidatsa fasters in their important summer Naxpike and the Sunset Wolf ceremonies sitting around the periphery of the sacred lodge without regard to moiety. Hidatsa fasters, when participating in the Okipa ceremony, would sit by moieties and, so far as possible, by equated clans. Although the Hidatsa relate the myth of the creation of the earth by two heroes working on different sides of the Missouri River, they obviously borrowed the myth from the Mandan in very recent times. Their ceremonies in no way celebrate the event nor are the culture heroes represented in the rites identified with clan or moiety as did the Mandan; nor does one find culture heroes responsible for the establishment and naming of moieties as with the Mandan. The concept of the moiety is highly developed and permeates the entire Mandan ceremonial structure and one would conclude from their traditions that the clans came later than the moiety. References to Hidatsa symbolic representation of the moiety is limited to the Eagle Trapping and related ceremonies which, in every respect, show greater similarities to the comparable Mandan rites than any other common ceremonies. In fact, the similarities in the rites and mythological interpretations were so great that in a former paper (Bowers, 1950, pp. 206–254) I treated this aspect of their cultures together, the differences between the two tribes being no greater than between different bundle lines of the same tribe. I interpret this similarity of Eagle Trapping rites, techniques, and beliefs as pointing to recent diffusion from the Mandan. This similarity seems also to substantiate Hidatsa traditions of an eastern origin from a wooded region not suited for eagle trapping by the techniques in vogue on the Plains. If we eliminate those moiety concepts associated with eagle trapping and related economic activities, little or nothing of the moiety concept remains. We find the Hidatsa dividing the buffaloes taken from corrals by moieties but the rituals of corralling buffaloes are associated with the eagle trapping bundles and, more particularly, the sacred snares of that bundle.

One finds reference to moiety division of eagle trapping sites with the Missouri River serving as the dividing line between moieties, but a survey of site locations recalled by the older people shows no such division (ibid., p. 213). I found that informants unacquainted with the eagle trapping rites had no knowledge of territorial moieties. Lowie (1917, p. 21) speaks of moiety eagle trapping grounds on which other trappers could not trespass. Case histories show that these are basically clan grounds—linked-clans and moiety ties applied only when no clansman used the site—at least so far as ownership and use were concerned in the 19th century. A new trapping site was the property of the man who erected the lodge and supervised the selection and excavation of the trapping pits. So long as he lived, the site was his own to use or to lend. When he died, the site became the preferential property of the clan and not of his son who inherited the bundle rites. Here we have two rules of inheritance in conflict with each other, namely, clan inheritance of trapping sites and father–son inheritance of bundles. The Mandan, with a highly developed system of clan inheritance of property and bundles, provided for simultaneous transfer of both the site and the sacred bundle to a younger clansman.

Lowie (ibid.) refers to moiety division in council and mentions the greater number of chiefs in the Four-clan moiety. Chieftainship seems to have been unaffected by moiety affiliation; instead, it was a mark of individual stature based on personal accomplishments. Moreover, there were more people in the Four-clan moiety, my count showing 237 individuals in the Four-clan moiety and 185 in the Three-clan moiety. In addition to sitting and debating issues by moiety in early treaty discussions and other business dealings with the U.S. Government, each moiety had a spokesman; one who was held in high regard by the tribe. In the division of Government allotments, goods were divided into two equal parts and the members of each moiety took from their pile. The same rules applied when dividing corralled game.

The moiety defined relationships when clan relationships did not apply. When parents were of different clans of the same moiety, one occasionally hears reference to honors shown the opposite moiety, honors usually limited to those of the father's clan. Case histories show a greater tendency of the Mandan, in the same situation, to offer presents to all clans except that of the mother. My case histories show that rarely did an Hidatsa ask one of the opposite moiety to cut the flesh and insert the thongs for fasting; this was the special duty of one's father's clansmen, irrespective of his moiety affiliation.

In the light of recent data obtained from the Mandan, I believe that the Hidatsa moiety concept developed recently from a clan system similar to that of the Crow after their settlement on the Missouri. It was not exogamous nor were there traditions of former marriage exogamy. The Mandan, on the other hand, had traditions of moiety exogamy and the table shown indicated even during the last century a greater tendency toward moiety exogamy than for the Hidatsa.

THE KINSHIP SYSTEM

Not only the daily social and economic life but much of Hidatsa ceremonial life as well was patterned by the kinship system. Kinship was based on socially recognized genealogical relationships which extended to the limits of the tribal group. For many individuals, the culture heroes were also included in the kinship structure. Alien populations likewise were included in the kinship groups in instances where

TABLE 3.—*Hidatsa kinship terms* [1]

Number [2]	Term [3]	Meaning	Symbol	Used by
1	*igá*	Mother	M	m.s., w.s.
2	*tatE*	Father	F	m.s., w.s.
3	*iuku*	Older brother	OB	m.s.
4	*isúku*	Younger brother	YB	m.s., w.s.
5	*itawíu*	Older sister	OSi	m.s.
6	*itakísu*	Younger sister	YSi	m.s.
7	*itáru*	Older brother	OB	w.s.
8	*irú*	Older sister	OSi	w.s.
9	*itáku*	Younger sister	YSi	w.s.
10	*ikú*	Grandmother	GM	m.s., w.s.
11	*arutága*	Grandfather	GF	m.s., w.s.
12	*irisú*	Son	S	m.s., w.s.
13	*iká*	Daughter	D	m.s., w.s.
14	*isáwi*	Father's sister	FS	m.s., w.s.
15	*itawapisá*	Grandchild	Gch	m.s., w.s.
16		Wife	W	
17		Husband	H	
18	*iráti*	Sister's husband; wife's brother.	SiH	m.s.
19	*itúgu*	Son's wife	DinLaw	m.s., w.s.
20	*itúti*	Daughter's husband	SinLaw	m.s., w.s.
21	*úuku*	Brother's wife	BW	m.s.
22	*itú*	Brother's wife; husband's sister.	BW=HSi	w.s.
23	*itutága*	Wife's mother	MinLaw	
24	*itaitága*	Wife's father	FinLaw	
25	*isikisú*	Husband's brother; sister's husband.	HB=SiH	w.s.
26	*irakúu*	Pal		m.s., w.s.

[1] *u* as *u* in *up; i* as *i* in *it; a* as *a* in *anon; E* as *e* in *met*.

[2] The numbers correspond to the various kinship charts.

[3] The symbols correspond to the various kinship charts.

contacts were numerous and continuous. The accompanying charts summarize the important features of the Hidatsa kinship system. Charts 1 and 2 illustrate by means of conventional diagrams the kinship terms used by a male ego and by a female ego.[12] The system can be conveniently described by an analysis of its terminological structure, the behavior of reciprocals, and the life cycle of the individual. For convenience in analysis, English terms will frequently be employed, but these terms should be understood in reference to native meanings which are determined by the applications and the social behavior involved.

The Hidatsa kinship system is of the "classificatory" type in that collateral and lineal relatives are classed together. The father's brothers are classed with the father, and the mother's sisters with the mother, while separate terms are employed for the mother's brother and the father's sister. Grandparents are distinguished according to sex, and grandparent terms are extended to their siblings of the same sex. The maternal grandmother's brother is an "older" or "younger brother" (*iuku* or *isúku*, m.s.); the maternal grandfather's sister is a "grandmother" except in those instances where the maternal grandfather and the father are of the same clan when she is classed as "father's sister"; the paternal grandmother's brother is a "father" and the paternal grandfather's sister is sometimes a "grandmother." In the parent's generation there is a separate term for the "father's sister," and her husband is classified as a "grandfather." There is no separate term for the "mother's brother." Instead, he is classified with ego's brothers, being either "older brother" or "younger brother" depending on whether he is older or younger than ego. The mother's brother's wife, woman speaking, is classified with her brother's wife and her husband's sister as "sister-in-law" (*itu'*). A man classifies the "mother's brother's wife" (*úuku*) with his brothers' wives and his wife's sisters.

In ego's generation, siblings are distinguished according to age and sex, while parallel cousins are treated as siblings. A female uses the term *itáru* and a male the term *iuku* for an older brother; both employ *isúku* to designate a younger brother. A female employs the term *irú* for an older sister and *itáku* for a younger sister; the children of sisters are designated as sons and daughters. A male designates "older sisters" as *itawíu* and "younger sisters" as *itakísu*, their female lineal descendants likewise being classified as "older sisters" and "younger sisters" depending on their age.

---

[12] The kinship system is still in operation (1933) among the older people so that it is possible to get a rather detailed account of the terminology and most of the social usages.

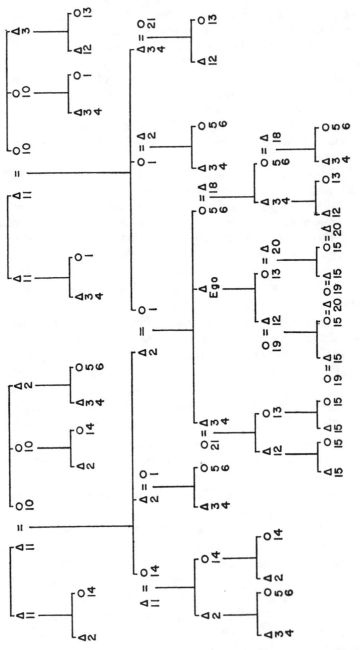

CHART 1.—Hidatsa kinship system; ego=male.

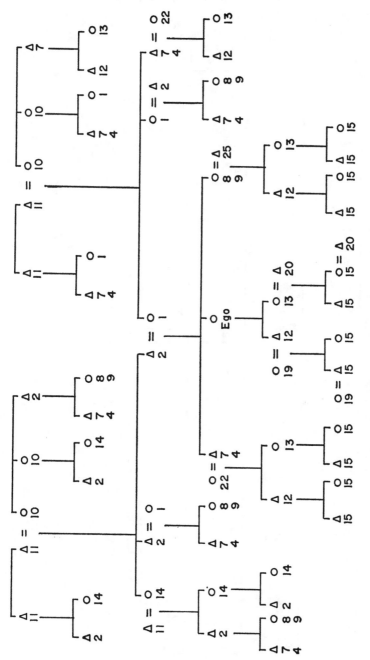

CHART 2.—Hidatsa kinship system; ego=female.

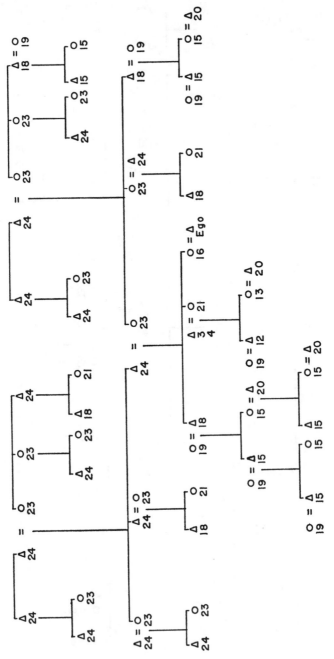

CHART 3.—Hidatsa affinal relatives ego=male.

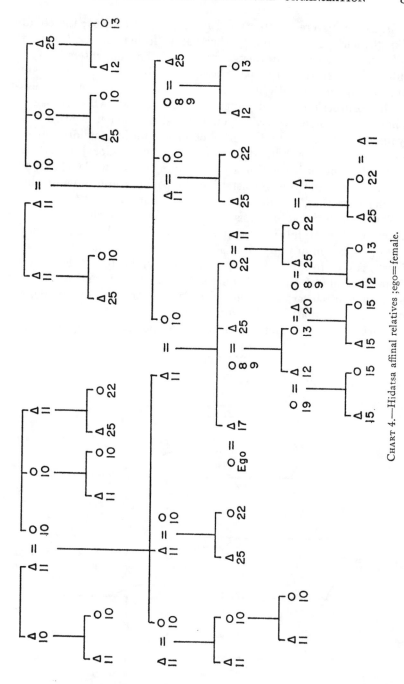

CHART 4.—Hidatsa affinal relatives; ego=female.

Cross-cousins are differentiated from parallel cousins; the children of a "father's sister" being "father" and "father's sister," while the children of "mother's brothers" are "sons" and "daughters." In the children's generation, a female classifies her brother's and her sister's sons and daughters with her own sons and daughters. A male classifies his brother's son and daughter with his own while the sister's children are "older sister," "younger sister," "older brother," and "younger brother." In the grandchild generation, children of sons and daughters are "grandchildren," sons of "older brother" and "younger brother" are "sons" and "daughters" while children of "older sister" and "younger sister," male speaking, are "older brother," "younger brother," "older sister," and "younger sister."

This conventional analysis does not throw much light on the nature of the Hidatsa kinship system. Obviously, the system is not organized on any principle of "generation" except for lineal relatives. A clue to the basis of organization is indicated in the grouping of descendants of the "father's sister" and "mother's brother," by individuals of either sex of the "sister's" descendants by a male, and by the rule of matrilineal descent.

Charts 5, 6, 7, 8, and 9 illustrate the Hidatsa kinship system by

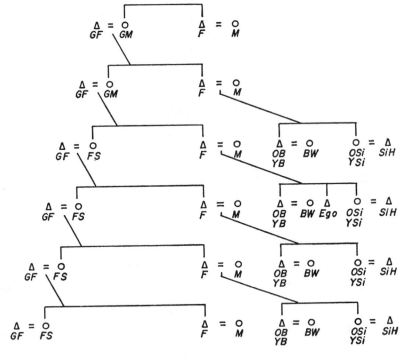

CHART 5.—Father's lineage; ego=male.

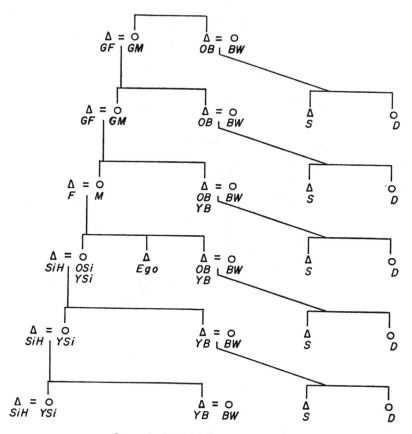

CHART 6.—Mother's lineage; ego=male.

means of lineage diagrams and indicate that the form of grouping is a "vertical" one based on matrilineal descent, rather than a "horizontal" one based on bilateral descent. In ego's father's lineage all the women are "grandmothers" or "father's sisters" and all the men are "fathers." All men marrying women of the father's lineage are "grandfathers" regardless of their age and all wives of "fathers" are "mothers"; sons of "fathers," regardless of their ages, are "older brother" and "younger brother" and their wives are "sisters-in-law" (*úuku*), male speaking; (*itú*), woman speaking. Daughters of all "fathers" are "older sister" and "younger sister" and their husbands are brothers-in-law (*iráti* for male ego and *isikisú* for woman speaking). For male ego, all females of the father's matrilineal lineage classified as *úuku* are potential wives in the event of the death of a "brother." For female ego, all males of the father's matrilineal lineage classified as *isikisú* are potential husbands in the event of the death of a "sister."

In ego's own lineage, the mother's matrilineal lineage, we find a

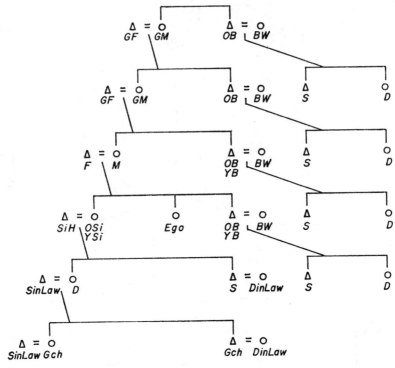

CHART 7.—Mother's lineage; ego=female.

greater differentiation of relatives. These are ego's closest relatives and, since descent is matrilineal, the position of a female ego is conceptually somewhat different from that of a male. The female relatives of a male ego are differentiated as "grandmother," "mother," "older sister," and "younger sister"; for a female ego the female relatives are "grandmother," "mother," "older sister," "younger sister," "daughter," and "grandchild." A man's male relatives of the lineage are "older brother" and "younger brother." A woman makes greater differentiation of male members of the mother's lineage; males of her own or preceding generations are differentiated on the basis of age as "older brother" or "younger brother"; those of the first descending generation are "sons"; those of the second and succeeding generations are "grandchildren." Husbands of females of the lineage are classified as "grandfather," "father," and "brother-in-law" by males of the lineage whereas females of the lineage classify males married to females of the lineage as "grandfather," "father," "brother-in-law," and "son-in-law." All females married to men of the lineage are classified as "sisters-in-law" (úuku) by males of the lineage. Women, on the other hand, distinguish two groups of

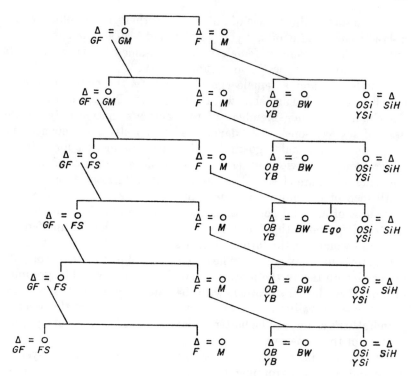

CHART 8.—Father's lineage; ego=female.

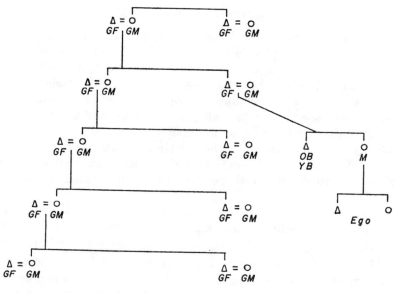

CHART 9.—Mother's father's lineage; ego=male or female.

"sisters-in-law": the spouse of an "older brother" is an "older female in-law"; the spouse of a "younger brother" is a "younger female in-law." The "younger female in-law" classification is extended to include spouses of "sons" and "grandchildren."

A male ego and a female ego also classify the children of male members of the lineage somewhat differently. A male ego classifies the children of male members of the mother's lineage only on the basis of sex as "sons" and "daughters" irrespective of their age and generation. A female ego makes the same distinction for children of her own and previous generations but children of males of succeeding generations are classified as "grandchildren" irrespective of sex.

All men of the mother's father's lineage are called "grandfather" regardless of age and generation, and all women of the same lineage are called "grandmother" or "father's sister" by both male and female. Men and women of the father's father's lineage are not usually recognized; instead, they are classified in relationship to other kin with closer kinship ties to the mother's matrilineal lineage. The grouping of the father's father's brothers with the paternal grandfather, whereas informants generally were uncertain of the classification of the paternal grandfather's sister, can be better explained by the practice of equating siblings of the same sex.

The lineage diagrams are the basis of the Hidatsa kinship system. They indicate the grouping of kin, determine the applications of kinship terms, and regulate the behavior and social relations of every Hidatsa within the village group.

KINSHIP EXTENSION

The extent to which the Hidatsa recognized kinship is important both from a comparative standpoint and also from that of social integration of the village group and the relations of the villages to each other and to neighboring alien social groups. The Hidatsa have numerous methods of extending the scope of the kinship system which result in the general belief that all people of the village and the neighboring Hidatsa villages were in some way related to each other. Actually, by the extension of the kinship categories to comprise the entire village and tribal group, an individual generally stood in two or more relationships to all persons not of the immediate related households.

In addition to the socially recognized genealogical relatives mentioned in the preceding charts, a person was believed to be a blood relative to everybody in his own clan even though this relationship could not actually be traced. A person was similarly related to all members of his "linked" clans and moiety. Since, with two exceptions, the same clans existed in the other Hidatsa villages and were equated with the Mandan clan system, further groups of relatives were established that cut across village, tribal, and linguistic lines. A person was related to everybody of the father's clan, "linked" clan, and moiety; this relationship also extended to the other Hidatsa villages and to the Mandan. There is no evidence of similar extensions to include the Crow clans. Kinship was additionally extended to include the mother's father's clan which was conceptually independent of the father's clan except in instances where the father and mother's father were of the same clan and lineage. Such instances were rare, the higher frequency of merging of the two lineages by the Mandan being due to the clan inheritance of tribal bundles associated with female inheritance of the lodge and matrilocal residence.

"Adoption" rites were of common occurrence. All men of distinction, and some women as well, adopted "sons" from clans and lineages not otherwise closely related, thereby establishing closer relationships with new sets of relatives. Moreover, "adoption" ceremonies with persons of different Hidatsa villages and of different tribes established kinship relations beyond the village unit to which the individual belonged. A "peace" chief was expected to perform many of these adoption ceremonies to cement the village with other nearby village and band units, thus encouraging intergroup visiting and trading.

The Hidatsa highly respected those of the village who had wide "relationships" with alien bands. As far as it is possible to determine, all council leaders had established, by means of the adoption ceremony, "father–son" or "friend–friend" relationships with a number of distinguished men of other tribes. Even the children established "friend–friend" relationships with individuals of the same age and sex by the formal exchange of clothing and presents. Although women occasionally adopted "sons" or "daughters," their relationships usually were based on "father–son" relationships existing between males of their households. Thus, if a woman's brother adopted a "son" she became his "father's sister"; if her husband did the adopting, she became "mother." Nevertheless, the culture provided many extentions of "kinship" reaching beyond the limits of the tribe and materially affecting intertribe activities and behavior.

From observed cases of cultural borrowing between tribes in historic times, we find that these intertribal kinship groups have been the principal avenue of cultural transmissions. Unfortunately, the number of observed cases is not sufficiently large to determine whether this was the sole avenue of cultural borrowing. About 1870, a band of Santee Sioux from Devils Lake introduced the Grass Dance to the Hidatsa who bought the right to perform the dance. According to the Hidatsa purchase pattern, if the sellers were treated as "fathers" then the sale was outright, as in the instance of the age-grade transfers. The Hidatsa therefore treated the Santee Sioux as "friends"; a relationship that existed between groups of individuals of the same age or that prevailed when one earth lodge group transmitted a society dance to another earth lodge group not having the society. The same year that the Grass Dance was bought by the Hidatsa and a few Mandans, visiting Crows watched them dance and invited them to visit the Crow for the purpose of selling the right to dance. Before selling to the Crow, officers of the Hidatsa Crazy Dog Society sold them the right to use certain emblems of that society for the dances—even before the dance rights were sold to the Crow the same year. When the visiting Crow invited the Hidatsa to return the visit and bring the Grass Dance to them, the matter of sale was discussed. The Hidatsa were unwilling to sell in the sense of relinquishing their rights, which would have happened had a "father-son" relationship been established. The Crows, therefore, agreed to a "friend-friend" relationship so that the Hidatsa could transmit the right and the information while still holding their own rights. Then each member of the society selected a friend to whom he supplied a duplicate set of the society equipment. Another instance of cultural borrowing between the Assiniboin and the Hidatsa is evidenced in the case of the Horse Ceremony. Before the rites were transmitted to individual Hidatsas, a "father-son" relationship had existed for some time; then on the initiative of the Assiniboin "father" the rights to doctor horses and to perform the ceremonies were sold. In the two instances of sale to Holding Eagle and to Big Black, the cultural borrowing (buying in this instance) was through the medium of an existing intertribal kinship relationship.

Marriage resulted in the acquisition of an additional set of relatives and altered the previously established classification of relatives. Marriage between persons of the same clan regardless of village residence and between close blood relatives was disapproved of. During the last century, the members of the Mandan Prairie Chicken clan have come to be viewed as "related" to the Hidatsa Prairie Chicken clan and marriage between Prairie Chicken members has been universally disapproved. Also in recent years, the Xura clan has been reduced to a lineage of the Waterbuster clan and marriages between the two are discouraged. It has not been considered proper for the Speckled Eagle clan to marry with the Prairie Chicken clan although a few have done so. Other than these restrictions, there were no clan limitations to marriage and there is no evidence that the moiety in any way regulated marriage. An additional set of relationships through marriage with persons of other tribes, particularly the

Crow, Sioux, Assiniboin, and Chippewa, commonly occurred. Visiting between related people of the Hidatsa villages and groups of relatives of other tribes was of common occurrence.

In the event of the separation of a couple with children and the subsequent remarriage of the wife, an additional set of relatives was acquired. The wife would no longer recognize her former husband's relatives based on marriage but would classify them according to the various categories employed previous to their marriage. The former husband would do likewise with the woman's relatives. The children would recognize the stepfather's relatives as though they were their own father's as long as the stepfather performed his social and economic duties as a father. Whether the biological father and his relatives were ever recognized would depend on the assistance that they gave in rearing the children and the attitude of the stepfather. Should the stepfather fail to perform his duties as a father, the children's affections were usually transferred to one of the mother's sisters' husbands. This was an important matter to a young person who must make a decision as to the "father" he would recognize when participating in the social and sacred rites of the community. Since the father, the stepfather, and the mother's sisters' husbands were frequently of different clans, the decision had an important bearing on the selection of ceremonies in which he would participate. Should a young man, however, distinguish himself in warfare we find, from a study of genealogies and case histories, that the father invariably began showing new interest in a neglected son.

Members of an age-grade society treated each other as related kin of sibling grouping although all of the clans of the village were generally represented in the membership. Members assisted each other in warfare, ceremonial functions, and on any other occasion when such group action would enhance the prestige of the society. Although age-grade purchase was a group action, instruction and preparation of the symbols of the society were individual in nature and involved intimate personal relations between the seller and one to four "sons" by the extension of the kinship system. Each organized men's society thought of the next higher society collectively as "fathers" and the next lower one as "sons." Women of an organized women's society likewise thought of each other as "female siblings." The clan principle was not closely followed by females, the sale being made to "daughters" who were daughters of female members of the clan or of the father's sister's clan. Either group, however, addressed a woman as "daughter" and the collective transfer was considered a "mother-to-daughter" transfer. The comrade or pal relationship (irakúu) that existed between individuals was extended to men's societies in their relationship to the women's societies. Each of the women's societies had a "pal" society which assisted during the performance of their organized social and ceremonial functions.

The Hidatsa treated the Whites married into the tribe as a single clan of male "brothers."

Ordinarily, adoption of a child took place when parents separated or the mother died. Usually the mother's relatives adopted and cared for the child. The first responsibility for the care of an orphan rested with the child's mother's sisters. If one of these was childless, she would invariably adopt the child and care for it; the husband's opinions were not solicited. If the child had no close "mother's sister" the responsibility rested with the father's sister; she commonly asked for the child even when there was a mother's sister to care for it, but to relinquish a child under those circumstances was considered improper and one so doing would be the subject of severe criticism by the other members of the child's clan.

In extreme crisis situations, such as the occasional destruction of a large part of the village population by warfare or epidemic in which a number of the households were broken up, extreme measures of reorganization were necessary. During the smallpox epidemic of 1837, when more than half of the Hidatsa died, children were cared for by their nearest kin—the first responsibility rested with the mother's own sisters and the maternal grandmothers; second were the father's brothers' wives or the father's sisters. Those having none of these relatives were cared for by women of the clan. A few instances were cited where orphans were adopted by women not of the above groups because of unusual circumstances such as being left childless with no child of the clan available for adoption. In cases such as the latter, the child so reared invariably disregarded his blood kin and clan and adopted the clan and kin of the person raising him. Should such a person endeavor to marry one of his own blood, however, he would be advised not to do so. Adoption of children of alien tribes, when the parents were unable to care for them or they had been abandoned by their parents while trading at the Hidatsa villages, was of common occurrence. The cases usually involved children whose father had been killed or died and whose mother was unable to travel with and care for a small child. These children when adopted frequently assumed the position of a child who had died, while the kinship bonds with the blood relatives were never broken. They could return to their own tribe when grown and nothing would have been done to prevent it. In fact, it was a common occurrence to return to visit the blood relatives, and no war party would have knowingly attacked a band from another tribe coming to the village to visit relatives.

Another group adopted into the villages was composed of prisoners, comprising women, small children, and even babies, when it was possible to bring them back safely without danger from counterattack. A woman sometimes would ask a brother leaving for war to bring her a child, to replace one that had recently died, instead of a horse. Women prisoners were taken as wives and their children captured with them lived in their mother's household. Motherless children were adopted and cared for by other households. If a girl was approaching marriageable age, she was usually taken into a household without formal adoption and assisted the women of the household until she could be married to some young man who would assist in the hunting. The most illustrious prisoner to become a member of the tribe was Bird Woman, the Shoshoni guide for Lewis and Clark in 1805–1806. By residence at Awatixa village, she became a member of the Itisuku clan.

Within the village, those men owning ceremonial rights that included a buffalo skull were collectively spoken of as "fathers." Women of comparable status were addressed as "father's sister." The kinship system also comprised the culture heroes and various sacred objects. Woman Above, Old-Woman-Who-Never-Dies, the field mice, the corn mill, and the Holy Women were referred to as "grandmother." Fire and Missouri River clan bundle deities were "grandfathers." Sun, Moon, Two Men, Buffalo Bull, and many others were "fathers." In every situation of a sacred character, there existed a kinship relationship between the sacred characters and objects on the one hand and the bundle owner and purchaser on the other.

The numerous methods of extending kinship within the village invariably brought about situations in which a Hidatsa had a choice of two or more relationship terms for the same person. A few case records will indicate the general underlying rules for determining kin not in the direct bloodline. Chart 10 illustrates several alternate relationships between Bears Arm and Walks. Bears Arm always called Woman-in-Water a "father" because Woman-in-Water and Old-Woman-Crawling were of the same clan and were presumed to be related through "clan sisters" further back, although they could not trace out actual blood sister relationships since Woman-in-Water's female lineage was of Awatixa village while Old-Woman-Crawling's mother's lineage was from Awaxawi village. Bears Arm explained that Medicine Robe was, by the extension of his mother's lineage to include those of her clan, actually an "older sister" since he and Medicine Robe were of the same clan and that would have made Woman-in-Water a "brother-in-law." Bears Arm placed greater emphasis on the "sibling" relationship existing between males, in this instance Woman-in-Water and Old-Woman-Crawling, than a similar

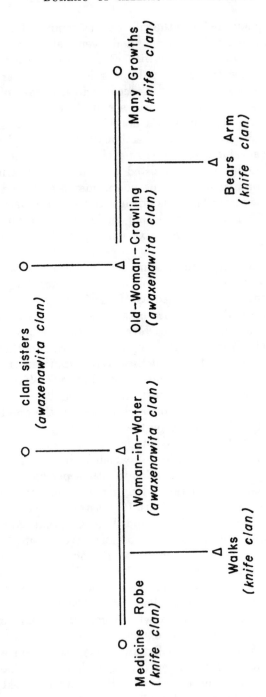

CHART 10.—Relationships between Bears Arm and Walks.

sibling relationship between Many Growth and Medicine Robe. He always addressed Woman-in-Water as "father" and Medicine Robe as "mother." Although by this reasoning, Walks should have been a "son," this would have been inconsistent with clan exogamy. He always called him "brother," claiming that common sex was again the important factor.

In the case of Yellow Coat (Chicken-Can't-Swim) of the Itisuku clan (see chart 11), Bears Arm called him "grandfather" by this reasoning: he first showed that nowhere in his known matrilineal or patrilineal lineages were there any lineal or collateral relatives married to persons of the Itisuku clan. Yellow Coat's wives, however, were of the Prairie Chicken clan as was also Bears Arm's maternal grandfather, so Bears Arm called each wife "grandmother" and Yellow Coat "grandfather." He could have addressed Yellow Coat as "father" since the Itisuku clan was of the Four-clan moiety to which Bears Arm's father belonged, but he considered the other relationship a closer one. He could also have called Yellow Coat "grandfather" through Breathing, Bears Arm's paternal grandfather who was also of the Prairie Chicken clan, but he considered Bear-Lying-Against-Tree, the maternal grandfather, a closer relative than Breathing. Bears Arm called Two Bulls a "grandfather" who, although a son to Good Squash, was also of the same clan as Bear-Lying-Against-Tree. He could also have called Two Bulls a "brother-in-law" since Bears Arm and Chippewa Woman were of equated Mandan and Hidatsa clans and would have so classified Two Bulls had there been no other relationship. He considered relationships with Mandan individuals on the basis of equated clans closer than moiety relationships within his own village and tribe.

Bears Arm (Knife clan) called Cherry Necklace (Maxoxati clan) a "brother" because both were of the Three-clan moiety, and the wives "sisters-in-law" because there were no persons of the Maxoxati clan in Bears Arm's lineages; neither were there persons of the wives' clan in his lineages. None of Bears Arm's relatives had ever adopted a "son" or "brother" in Cherry Necklace's lineages. The moiety was, in this instance, the last resort in establishing relationships.

The evidence indicates that the moiety or the "linked" clan served as the basis of extending kin only when lineages did not apply. The Three-clan moiety, consisting of the Maxoxati, Knife, and Low Hat clans, comprised one group of linked clans. The Four-clan moiety had two groupings or phratries: Phratry I comprised the Prairie Chicken, Speckled Eagle, and Awaxenawita clans; Phratry II comprised the Waterbuster, Xura, and Itisuku clans. Thus, a person would call females of the Prairie Chicken, Speckled Eagle, or Awaxenawita clans "father's sister" when the father belonged to

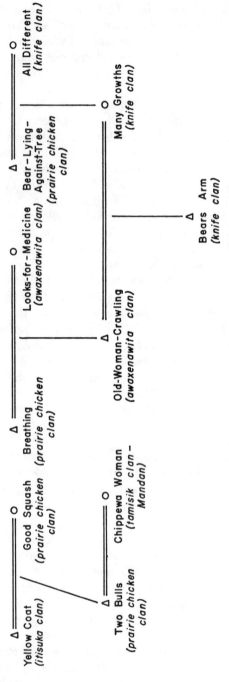

CHART 11.—Relationships between Bears Arm and Yellow Coat.

one of these clans. This was an important relationship for the Hidatsa because of the numerous situations when one was expected to offer presents to males and females of the father's clan.

This "father's sister"-"sister's son" relationship would, unless broken by closer ties established by marriage, extend to all of the father's sister's female descendants as well as to the female members of the father's clan. Chart 12 illustrates this point. Old-Woman-Crawling could call Bear Woman and Hunts Turnips "daughters-in-law," since they were his wife's mother's brother's wife and sister-in-law. The Hidatsa, however, preferred not to employ classifications based on affinal relationships when other relationships were applicable, due, I believe, to the instability of marriages. In this instance Old-Woman-Crawling never classified the two women as "daughters-in-law" but rather as "sisters" because they were of the same clan. Bears Arm called them "father's sisters" since they were of Old-Woman-Crawling's clan but they were Bears Arm's mother's mother's brother's wife and wife's sister. He called Bears Nose an "older brother" but called the women "father's sisters" instead of "sisters-in-law." Bears Arm, on the other hand, called Bear Woman and Hunts Turnips "father's sisters" even though Bear Woman was married to his mother's mother's brother. In his own age group was Medicine Woman, daughter of Bear Woman, who also might have been classified as a "father's sister." However, she was a "closer" relative to Bears Arm than her mother, Bear Woman, being the daughter of Bears Nose (Knife clan of Bears Arm) whereas Bear Woman was only his wife. From Bears Arm's point of view Medicine Woman was a blood relative while Bear Woman was not.

Lying Chicken stood in several relationships to Bears Arm. In the first place he was the husband of Hunts Turnips, whom Bears Arm called a "father's sister," and was therefore a "grandfather." Likewise he was a "brother," since Bears Nose was a "brother" to both: to Bears Arm by being his mother's mother's brother and to Lying Chicken since they had married sisters. Old-Woman-Crawling called Lying Chicken "brother" because they were of the Four-clan moiety. When Lying Chicken—who, by all standards of kinship extensions would have been classified as a very distant relative indeed—married, Old-Woman-Crawling adopted him as a "son" since Lying Chicken gave promise of becoming a distinguished warrior, and thus new and permanent relationships were established between two sets of relatives. Bears Arm continued to treat Medicine Woman as a "daughter"; Lying Chicken became Bears Arm's "brother," a relation that could not be broken during their entire lifetime except in the event of cowardly acts; Hunts Turnips and Bear Woman became Bears Arm's "sister-in-law."

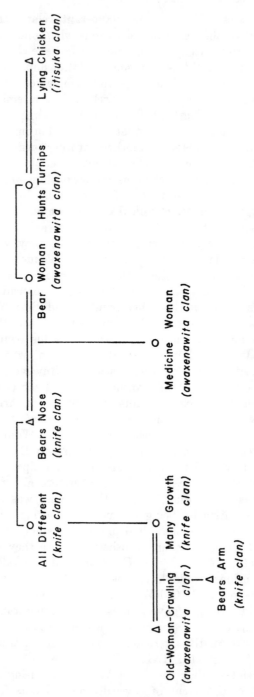

CHART 12.—Relationships between Old-Woman-Crawling and Bear Woman.

All other things being equal, relationships through persons of the same sex were closer than through opposite sexes. Frank Packineau, Low Hat clan, and his wife, Rattles Medicine of the Maxoxati clan, both belonged to the Three-clan moiety with Bears Arm who was of the Knife clan. Bears Arm would classify Packineau as an "older brother" and Rattles Medicine as an "older sister" prior to their marriage, but after they were married he could not do so since that would imply that Frank Packineau had married his sister. Bears Arm could continue to call Rattles Medicine a "sister" and then Frank Packineau would be a "brother-in-law" or he could call Frank Packineau a "brother" and Rattles Medicine would be a "sister-in-law." Bears Arm chose the second alternative because he considered relationships established between individuals of the same sex closer than with the opposite sex. Bears Arm's sister, Wolverine, employed the first alternative, calling Rattles Medicine a "sister" and Frank Packineau a "brother-in-law." Informants recognize that relationships based on moiety membership are remote and not ordinarily employed.

Formerly, the village residence was also a factor in determining relationships when no known lineal or clan affiliation existed. Persons of the same village were considered closer even when no actual relationships were known. Since Rattles Medicine and Bears Arm were of parents coming from Awaxawi village, whereas Frank Packineau was from Awatixa village, in former times Bears Arm would have considered Rattles Medicine a closer relative of the Three-clan than Frank Packineau and would have called her "sister" and Frank Packineau "brother-in-law." This distinction was rarely used after the remnants of the three Hidatsa village groups united following the epidemic of 1837.

Out of the numerous alternatives, the selection made by the individual determined his social position in relation to others. A woman of the Xura clan might call an individual of the Maxoxati clan a "son" whereas he would call her "father's sister" while her husband called the same individual a "brother-in-law" because the man of the Maxoxati clan had married a "sister." Lead Woman (see chart 13) called Old-White-Man a "son" as he was the son of a member of her clan. She also could have called him a "grandfather" since Old-White-Man was Lead Woman's husband's sister's husband, but the latter relationship would be based on marriages and could be dissolved at will whereas neither Lead Woman nor Old-White-Man could change their clan affiliations. Also, by maintaining a "father's sister" status to Old-White-Man she was eligible to receive presents during social and ceremonial occasions. Crows Heart could have called Old-White-Man a "grandson" but he never did, always calling

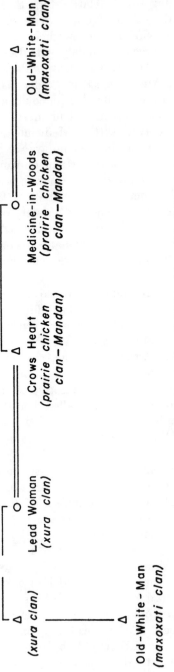

CHART 13.—Relationships between Old-White-Man and Lead Woman.

him "brother-in-law." In either instance Old-White-Man was an affinal relative. Crows Heart considered a relationship to Old-White-Man through a sister "closer" than one through a wife.

The above examples illustrate the methods of determining extended kin. The Hidatsa considered everyone of the tribe a relative and there is evidence that the extension of the kinship system, to include the Mandan through the equating of Mandan and Hidatsa clans, is of recent development. One's relationship by blood and lineage is the basis from which extended kin groupings are determined. There are so many factors involved in the classification beyond the blood relatives that no fixed rule can be made. The relationship is largely determined by social participation. Although the Hidatsa kinship system is not a "clan system" the importance of the clan, phratry, and moiety, in regard to kinship has been indicated by the foregoing discussion of the kinship extensions. Other extensions of the kinship system are brought about by ceremonial adoption and cooperation in the organized ceremonies and age-grade societies; these extensions go beyond the limits of the village and tribe. The general outline of social behavior prevailing between relatives was the basis for socially recognized relationships with groups of extended kin.

KINSHIP BEHAVIOR

Reciprocal obligations and duties between relatives were important elements in social integration. The basic relationships were those existing between members of the elementary family, the household, and the related households. Although the basic relationships are those which apply to parents and children, because of descent and residence factors, relationships of a more distant order play an important part among the Hidatsa. Within the elementary family there are nine possible combinations of relatives or reciprocals: mother–daughter; mother–son; father–son; father–daughter; husband–wife; older sister–younger sister; older brother–younger brother; older brother–younger sister; older sister–younger brother.

Within the parental household groups there are also these important reciprocal relations: mother's brother–sister's son and daughter; father's sister–brother's son and daughter; grandfather–grandchild; grandfather–daughter-in-law; grandmother–daughter-in-law; father-in-law–son-in-law; mother-in-law–son-in-law; brother-in-law–brother-in-law; sister-in-law–sister-in-law; brother-in-law–sister-in-law.

The general pattern of behavior prevailing between these pairs of relatives should throw much light on the native values ascribed to the terminology and indicate the relationship of the individual to the family, the household, and the other household groups comprising the village unit.

MOTHER–DAUGHTER

The relationship between a mother and her daughter was an exceedingly close and intimate one. It was based on kinship ties, lifelong residence together, common occupations, and common sex. The mother was the principal instructor in both economic and ritualistic matters. She taught her daughters to cook and care for the lodge, grind corn, tan and decorate hides, sew, butcher and cure meat, and to perform all of the special tasks. If, for instance, the mother was a potter and owned particular designs, the daughter was expected to buy the complete rights and continue the designs unique to that female lineage.

She instructed her daughters in the care of the gardens, the planting of the seeds, the pulling of weeds, the curing and storing of the garden products, and the performance of those rites celebrated while engaged in agricultural activities. She taught them good manners toward visitors and strangers and particularly toward prospective husbands. She selected her daughter's first "ceremonial" mother at the time of her daughter's first introduction into and participation in the age-grade societies. She also was the principal one to advise the daughter in premarital sex matters and, with the assistance of the other "mothers" and "older sisters," kept a watchful eye to see that these instructions were obeyed. The mother assumed an important role in the marriage of the daughter, for no well-trained daughter would want to marry a man disapproved of by her mother.

A woman's deepest affections were for her own daughter, but, in a household where there were many others standing in a mother–daughter relationship, diverse female work patterns developed. Thus, one or two "mothers" commonly worked together in the gardens while the others were in or about the lodge preparing the meals, tanning and working with hides, or performing the multiple tasks of the household. When there was urgent need of extra help in the gardens, one of the "mothers" would take all of the household "daughters" to the fields where they worked together. Here the daughters were watched to see that they performed their work.

A mother who had given her daughter good training preferred to have her live in the same lodge after marriage and to assist her as she grew old, hence the tribe was strongly matrilocal. The mother was always present when a child was born to her daughter; if the daughter was living in another lodge, she invariably returned to her mother's lodge to give birth to the child. The mother advised her daughter in the care of the child and would offer such assistance as she could without taking over its actual care. A mother might punish her child by denying her privileges or by scolding her, but physical punishment by whipping was almost entirely unknown. An older brother might shake her and ask her to come back to her senses but the usual procedure was to scold her or to offer positive rewards in return for good behavior.

Although residence was normally matrilocal, it was not customary for several sisters with different husbands to occupy the same lodge. The Hidatsa believed that it was hard for men married to sisters and living in the same lodge to get along together. If one husband was ambitious and a good hunter, he would be praised by the female owners of the lodge and only poor hunters or unlucky warriors with little pride would continue to live there. The first residence was invariably patrilocal whenever insufficient time had been allowed for the preparation of the son-in-law section of the lodge.

Informants all thought that a woman had more "mothers" through the father's clan than in the mother's clan. This is consistent with the extension of the "mother" relationship beyond the immediate households. In the mother's lineage and clan, only her household sisters and those females who were daughters of the maternal grandmother (rarely was the great-grandmother known) were classified as "mothers"; all other clanswomen were classified either as "older sister," "younger sister," "daughter," or "grandchild," depending upon their relative ages and other factors. Within the household there were frequently other "mothers" of different clans when the father had not married sisters. A female classified as "mothers" all spouses of men of the father's clan. Of this group of "mothers" close bonds of affection and respect were often shown due to the practice of looking to the members of the father's clan for instruction and assistance in ceremonial matters.

Since the wife contributed significantly in goods and services whenever a man performed a ceremony and shared in his purchases, her advice was widely sought by a "daughter" through her husband. In visiting other villages, one felt free to move in with a household whose female members were classified as "mother" by the extension of the kinship relationships when it was not convenient to stay with a "sister."

Mother–Son

The relationship of a mother to her son was almost as close as to her daughter since it was based on kinship ties. It was, however, different from the mother–daughter relationship due to sex dichotomy, division of labor, and matrilocal residence. A mother taught a son early in life to play boys' games, to dress like boys, to be brave, and at all times to avoid female avocations lest he be "blessed" by one of the female deities and become a berdache. Naming, games, and terms of address all emphasized a son's masculine character and discouraged him from participating in female activities. He was permitted to own property in his own right and to dispose of it; he was taught to use bows and arrows and to hunt small animals and birds; he was instructed in the importance of warfare, fasting, and hunting, and was discouraged from gardening and wood gathering.

The mother contributed much time to advising her son, as a child, a duty that was largely taken over by her brother as the son approached the age of puberty. She would advise a son in matters dealing with ceremonial participation, contribute goods for his use in the ceremonies, and direct his efforts in securing proper visions. The mother was his closest relative and the one who did most to organize her cooperating group to contribute material assistance consisting of goods, horses, and food for a son's age-grade and other purchases. Although a mother would have a direct interest in selecting a daughter-in-law who would make a good wife, she would not ordinarily say a great deal when she disapproved, leaving the matter to her brothers and older sons to decide. If they, too, objected to the marriage, there would be no goods put up, in which case the other family would generally withdraw the marriage offer.

A young man was expected to obey his mother. If she was growing feeble and had no daughters to help her in the lodge and her gardens she, in consultation with her brothers, frequently selected a young woman as wife for her unmarried son at home with the intention of bringing the daughter-in-law into the lodge to help her and to inherit the lodge and gardens when she herself was too old to manage the household. In such cases, she enlisted the assistance of the other females of the lodge and her brothers of other households to put up the necessary goods and horses to complete the marriage. This was a happy arrangement for a woman without female descendants. She could keep her son at home to hunt and provide for her household. Situations of this nature required respect and cooperation between the females, the mother on the one hand and the wife on the other.

A man was expected to look after his mother, irrespective of his residence, and to take an interest in her welfare. As a newly married man he was free to return to his mother's lodge at any time, and if he wished to give a feast for his friends or respective relatives, it was always given at the mother's lodge. She and her daughters were expected to meet him when returning from a successful war expedition and to sing his praises—or to torture themselves if he died or was killed. A man would return often to his mother's lodge for meals and, should he return to the village from hunting and find his wife out of the lodge, he would leave most of his meat with his wife's household and return to his mother's lodge to eat, for it was not considered proper to be in the lodge alone with only his parents-in-law.

His horses were grazed and cared for by the younger members of his mother's household and most of his personal property was kept there. Although he was expected to hunt for the wife's household when living with her people and to supply meat for her to take to her parents, a man's interest was at first primarily with his mother's group. The mother would be ashamed of a daughter-in-law who failed to keep her husband's clothing mended and his moccasins in good repair. If he needed a good horse and his wife's people had none, he could use freely those of his mother's household. The spoils of war went to his mother and her female relatives and they were expected to mourn longest if he lost his life.

FATHER–SON

The father's relationship to a son was quite different from that of the mother. In the first place, they were of different clans; but it was to the father and his clansmen, nevertheless, that the son looked for formal training in the ceremonies. The two parental groups comprising the father and his brothers, and their sisters and their children, on the one hand and the mother, her sisters, and brothers on the other, were sharply differentiated both as to lineages and functions. The father's obligations were both economic and ritualistic. He should provide for the family by hunting game and protecting them from their enemies. In the Hidatsa's mind, however, this was not an essential function, for households were known which had had no adult male for a decade or more and in which the members lived very well by exchanging garden produce for other necessities. A man's status in the wife's household rose as children came along. He was never present at the time of the birth of his child. Once it appeared that the infant was going to live (at the age of 10 days or so), however, he took the leading role in securing a name for it. He could give the child a name from his own ceremonial rites but ordinarily a man preferred to widen the field of supernatural forces working for the child's welfare by selecting another of the same clan to give the child a name suggested by the namer's ceremonial rites. Even at the age of 10 days a child's individuality was reconized. When approaching the person who was to supply the name, the father would say "My son who has just come to live with us asks you to give him a name and to receive these goods." The father's brother or sister supplying the name would pray to his or her sacred bundles to send the child good luck and the father would do likewise. Each time thereafter when the father offered the pipe and food to his sacred bundles, he would ask that they send his children good luck and keep them healthy. He would continue this practice until the son's security was assured by owning sacred bundles of his own.

It was considered improper for a man to urge a son to participate in sacred rites. This belief stemmed from traditional lore that an individual's role in the sacred rites would be revealed in due time by vision instructions. Hence the father taught by example rather than by direction. At all times the initiative came from the son or his son's older brothers. Although the Hidatsa made little distinction between the father and the father's brother and received instructions from both, it was from one's own father that ceremonial rites were normally obtained, although one was not denied rights to bundles owned by the father's brothers or even husbands of the mother's sisters when the proper vision instructions were received.

The cultural patterns provided many situations for the extension of this father–son relationship to more distant or attenuated "fathers." A man's closest ties were with his own father if his parents were not divorced. The father's brothers were next in importance. In the purchase of a ceremonial bundle a "ceremonial" father was selected to instruct the "son" and to prepare a new bundle. He was one of the father's clan but rarely of known blood relationship. This selection brought together distant "fathers" and their relatives, which thereafter increased cooperation between these two groups of relatives. Feasts were given by each group to the other and, in the performance of other rites at a later time, the "ceremonial" father's children, now standing in close sibling relationships, were expected to assist.

A "father" coming upon a "son" who had just killed an animal should be given the choicest parts and the hide without asking. It was expected that he would praise his "son" upon returning to the village, or condemn him if the gift was not a generous one. Since a man's status was raised through his relationships with "fathers," no person hoping to be shown honors and respect would deny a "father" meat even should it mean returning to the village empty-handed. Wishing to save an animal for one's family, it was a more common practice for a man killing an animal and knowing that "fathers" were hunting nearby, to move away from the kill and pretend that the animal had escaped until the meat could be brought to the village undetected.

It was a man's highest aim to have many "sons" and "daughters" both of his own and through extension of the kinship system; he was then assured of many presents and other honors during his lifetime. He received goods, horses, and the right of ceremonial intercourse with the "sons'" wives; in return he sold sacred rites, performed sacred rites, and taught tribal lore to his sons. If a son died, the father or his sister must, when asked, "bring the blanket" to wrap the body in, take it to the scaffold or grave, and send the spirit away.

A father, on request and for pay, instructed a son in the arts of warfare and horse stealing but avoided taking him on his own expeditions. He would supply objects from his own sacred bundles for the son to wear until he had sacred objects of his own and the son was expected to pay the father with horses taken. There was always an aloofness toward the father that never entirely disappeared. Although a young unmarried man would go out hunting alone with his father and would be taught many things, most that one learned of secular matters was taught by an older brother or one standing in that relationship. The Hidatsa have a saying that if a chief's son has many "older brothers" he will become a chief also, but if he has no "older brothers" his father will spoil him.

FATHER–DAUGHTER

A father's relationship with a daughter was even more distant than that with his son. It was expected that he would provide meat for the household but he had few other economic duties. He was not present at her birth, but he did provide a name for her or he selected another of his own clan to name her. He was usually consulted by his wife and her brothers when a husband was being selected. He might even give a horse to the other family if he thought much of his daughter. A man avoided being in the lodge alone with a daughter after she reached the approximate age of 10 years. Often through life he offered the pipe and food to his sacred bundles, asking for her continued success and good health. In later years she was expected to assist in the preparation of goods and food for her brothers' ceremonial purchases from the father. A daughter's attitude toward the father was largely determined by the compatability of the parents; if the parents had cooperated in the ceremonies and there was good will between them, the father was highly respected as the owner of important bundles. Although a daughter rarely inherited important bundle rites from the father, the culture provided some ceremonial rewards to the sisters assisting a young man in purchasing their father's ceremonial rites. Due to the division of labor between sexes, a daughter learned little from her father of the daily skills and practices. In the event that the mother died, unless a sister or other female replaced her through the operation of the sororate, the father usually returned to his sister's household to be with people of his own clan until he could remarry into another household.

HUSBAND–WIFE

The relation between a husband and wife varied widely with different couples and changed gradually from the time of marriage to old age. Probably the majority of couples got along very well, particularly when the young people made their own choice of mates and were assisted subsequently by their relatives in completing the marriage ceremonies. Residence was, in theory, matrilocal. A study of 39 lodge groups at Fishhook Village as of 1872 shows that 22 were matrilocal, 11 were patrilocal, and 6 were both patrilocal and matrilocal. A young married man was expected to live with his wife at her lodge and to hunt for her family except when: his mother had no grown daughters at home; he was an older man long married and needed a young wife to help his aging wives; or his wife had several brothers-in-law already living in her mother's lodge.

At first the bond between the husband and wife was weak and easily broken by the husband if they were living in the wife's lodge, and by the wife if she was living with her husband's people. This was probably due to jealousy since the husband would frequently continue to see girls he had "run around" with before marriage and husbands were suspicious of their wives and always checking up on them to see if they had dropped their former sweethearts. There was a saying that a young married couple would get along better when their children came. This was generally true.

There was a marked sex dichotomy in labor and in ownership of property. The woman cared for the garden, cured the meat, tanned hides and made the clothing, supervised building the lodge, and did all of the household work. The man hunted, cared for the horses, assisted in the heavier work of building and repairing the lodge, went on war expeditions for horses and scalps, and carried out most of the ritualistic activities.

Sexual relations were avoided during menstrual periods and there was segregation during that time. Although sexual relations were not taboo during pregnancy, it was customary for the parents-in-law to offer another daughter or one standing in that relationship as second wife when the first one was in advanced pregnancy, since intercourse was not considered wise after the fifth or sixth month. In a population with a ratio of nearly three females to each male, rarely was it impossible to supply a second wife. This was obviously an insurance against having the man running around with other women and possibly losing him as well.

In the wife's lodge a man could divorce his wife by simply picking up his things and walking out—or his wife might tell him to leave. When living with the husband's household, a man would generally hesitate to tell a wife to leave unless she was one he had married without the exchange of goods between families. Instead, he would probably go out visiting to another village and stay away until the news reached him that the wife had returned to her people. Adultery and mistreatment were the most common grounds for divorce. Usually the families would attempt to patch up differences between them. If a man had been unusually mean to his wife and she had run away or sent him away, he would usually, when desiring a reconciliation, send his sister to straighten matters out. In cases of separation the children customarily stayed with the mother.

The ties that held husband and wife together were, to begin with, affection or respect for their parents and, later, children and common interests in household and village activities, particularly those of a ritualistic nature. After a few years of married life when the husband and his wife or wives had adjusted their lives to each other and the children were coming along, marriages were quite stable; only during the first years of adjustment were divorces common. The extended household tended to maintain its structure in spite of numerous divorces and separations.

OLDER BROTHER–YOUNGER BROTHER

A very close bond of mutual assistance and affection prevailed between brothers of approximately the same age. This was based on common blood and residence. Age was an important factor in determining the relationship between brothers. Brothers would tease each other a great deal but quarreling was largely unknown due to the early training of the household in which harmony between persons of the same clan was emphasized. The closest bond was between "brothers" of the same household, and little distinction was made between one's own brothers and the sons of mother's sisters living in the same household. Of the other households having close "brothers," those in lodges occupied by the mother's sisters were considered closer brothers than children of the father's brothers; the former were not only "brothers" through blood sisters but were also of the same clan.

The universal rule that it was the duty of the clan to discipline its own members might well have been restated to say that it was the duty of the older male members to discipline and train the younger male members since much of the actual training of boys and young men was directed by their "older brothers." Age was an important factor in determining whether one gave or received advice. My informants frequently mentioned accepting advice and instructions from "older brothers" who, at most, were only a few months older. In one instance, Wolf Chief had told a male clansman that he would do as the other advised because he was the older and therefore would understand such things better—actually, the difference in age between them was at most not more than 3 months.

An older brother would advise his younger brother in competitive contests or in hunting small game and take an active interest in the things he was doing. If the older one had been away to war and had won honors, he would relate his experiences and encourage the younger man to follow his ways. If the difference in age was not great, they would play together, hunt together, chase girls together, and fast together in the same ceremonies or at the same places away from the village. They would assist each other in putting up goods to hear the sacred myths or ask the mother to help them with feasts to their "fathers" who were to pray for them to be successful in war expeditions.

Older brothers already established in the ceremonies would help the younger ones in their ambitions to secure a good wife, honors in war, and rights in ceremonies and age-grade societies. In fact, a younger brother not making suitable progress was severely criticized by older brothers. It was the most distinguished older brother's right to discipline those not showing special interest in warfare and ritualistic activities. An older brother rarely punished a younger one unless the other clan members of the household demanded it. Finding a group of boys abusing a girl, he would feel obliged to whip and cuff the young boys of his own clan and related households at once and see that the girl got back to her lodge without further trouble. Having once punished his own brothers, the girl's brothers could not punish them again. Learning of the attack, "older brothers" of the other boys involved in the attack would hasten to punish their relatives to avoid having their property cut up and their horses shot by the girl's relatives. Boys caught stealing were also punished by whipping or ducking in the river to avoid ridicule and retaliation. Older brothers, being around more with their younger ones, were expected to keep an eye on them to keep them out of trouble and to avoid situations requiring the intervention of the Black Mouth society.

Inquiry among the older Hidatsas revealed that only a few had ever been whipped or ducked by an older brother but all had been scolded at one time or another. Those who had been both ducked and scolded thought that the scolding was the more severe punishment, for invariably it was done in public or word of it got around. In any event, it was not held against an older brother afterwards since there were so many situations when he could and did offer assistance. They would assist each other in progressing through the age-grade societies and if their age differences were not very great they often bought societies simultaneously. They would have feasts prepared to show honor and respect to the same older people, fast together, dance together, and even hunt together alone when there were no reports of enemy activities about.

Unless there was a great difference in age, they would go on raiding parties together under the leadership of a war chief and assist each other in capturing horses. In situations of extreme danger, a brother's first duty was to protect the other one even when the odds were against him. Should one be killed by the enemy, his brothers were expected to avenge his death. One who succeeded in killing the particular enemy responsible for the death of a brother was highly respected and Hidatsa traditions are rich in accounts of brothers going out alone to waylay and kill the person responsible for a brother's death. Like the Mandan, there was a special design to be worn indicating that the wearer had gone out alone far from the village to kill and scalp one enemy.

It was a man's duty to see that his deceased brother's widow and children were cared for. He held first right to marry the widow and she ought not remarry with another until her husband's brothers had made their views known. A man felt strongly obliged to marry a widow who had mourned long for her dead husband. A single man would ask a brother for his wife to assist in certain ceremonies and one should not refuse his request. If one or more of a man's wives wished to go out with her male relatives and their wives to get meat, and the husband found it inconvenient to go along, he would frequently send a younger unmarried brother in his place to hunt for the women and even to assume his own rights and duties. Older men and women involved in this temporary husband–wife status explained that this was done to keep other men from running off with these unattended women. Under no circumstances was a brother permitted intimacy with a brother's wife without the other's permission. A man would tease his sister-in-law and tell her that she should go out with him on the prairie or go visiting the Crows, but she was expected to accept these overtures as a form of teasing and never take them seriously. If a woman made overtures to her husband's brother and he was "unable to resist," the woman and not the man was punished, for it was said that women should have greater controls of their sexual impulses than men. A brother was not expected to hold a grievance against another brother; in fact, when conflict situations arose, brothers invariably banded together. There are numerous references in the mythology to widespread chaos in the village stemming from quarrels between brothers.[13]

---

[13] See "The Legendary Period," pp. 297–308.

OLDER SISTER–YOUNGER SISTER

Except where there was a marked difference in age or ability, there was little difference in behavior between this set of relatives. Where there was a marked difference in age, the older sister acted more like a "mother" to the younger one. The bond between sisters was very strong, being based on close blood ties, residence, sex, occupation, and lifelong residence together. As children they played together around the lodge. Later they worked together in the gardens or about the lodge and cooperated in the same household activities. Quarrels between sisters were rare and of little consequence. Unless there was a marked difference in their ages, they were commonly married to the same man. There was a strict rule that the oldest sister should marry first and ultimately become the female head of the household. The younger sisters were expected to marry the same man as they, in turn, reached marriageable age. When differences in age were great, however, younger sisters frequently had a different husband and commonly moved to a different lodge unless the husbands were of great difference in age. The oldest sister or sisters married to one man normally inherited the lodge, garden plots and tools, and the household goods. There was little distinction in behavior between sisters of the same or of different mothers, provided they were reared together in the same household. With few exceptions, sisters reared their deceased sister's children. Since descent was matrilineal, children of sisters were adopted without changes in clan affiliation or kinship terminology.

When a husband maintained two households, the wives were often of different clans. Then the sister bond was not as close; in fact, there frequently was mild antagonism toward each other. The attitude of sisters of different households depended in large measure on the attitude of their mothers toward each other.

Sisters cooperated in preparing food and goods for ceremonies performed by their husbands and brothers, working together as a team. This relationship of two or more sisters working together and taking over the role held by the mothers formed the basis for the continuity of the Hidatsa household. Brothers were expected to marry and move away, but the sisters' obligation to the household was primarily that of preserving its continuity.

BROTHER–SISTER

A strong bond existed between a brother and his sister, based on common blood and residence combined with common economic and ceremonial interests. They played together until they were 6 or 7 years of age, after which they tended to avoid each other when other relatives were not present. Early in life, division in their play and work activities was emphasized by the parents lest a son take an undue interest in girls' toys and dress and become a berdache. Thus, a boy was treated like a boy and a girl like a girl so that a brother and sister quickly developed many different interests. Less concern was shown over a girl who played with bows and arrows than was shown over a boy who played with a ball or doll.

It was not considered proper for an adult male to carry on prolonged conversations alone with a sister, particularly if they were alone in the same lodge. A man would have a great deal in common with a younger brother or an older sister but very little with a younger sister. An older sister would tan hides and make clothing for a brother even when he lived in another household. It was expected that he would frequently return to eat with the sister's household. They aided each other in assembling goods whenever one of their relatives was giving a feast, and a brother often gave horses or other property for a sister at dances. Each would put up goods when the other married and do all that they could to bring honor to the sister's household. A sister would look to her brother for help against an abusive husband and one frequently hears an informant say even today, "She got pretty saucy with her husband for she had many brothers." However, brothers did not always defend a sister from her husband's wrath. If she was found meeting a lover in the cornfield or while out for wood, the brothers would do nothing when she was severely beaten. If the husband was a good provider for the household, the brothers would recognize this and endeavor to put her straight. (Although no one thought the less of a runaway woman who returned to her husband, everyone thought ill of a man who cried around because his wife had left him and who made overtures to get her to return.)

When there were several mothers in a lodge there were likely to be brothers and sisters of different ages. If the mothers had died or were feeble, the younger brothers and sisters were invariably cared for by older sisters living in the lodge with their husband. These older sisters cared for them as they did their own children and the children would come to respect their older brother-in-law and treat him as a "father." Although older brothers had an interest in the household, living in a different lodge after marriage their interests were divided. They would advise and discipline their younger brothers and sisters but the principal responsibility for their training rested with the older sisters. A married brother would bring meat to the family and see that they were provided with horses for his brother-in-law's use. In return he would get assistance from his sisters in his social advancement.

A sister would fast and pray for her brother's success when he was away on a war expedition and she should be the first to meet him outside of the village when he returned. Then he was expected to give her the horses he had taken. All his war activities were directed toward the enrichment of his mother's household and, in return, his sisters were expected to inflict the most severe personal self-torture and to mourn longest were he to be killed.

Mother's Brother–Sister's Son; Mother's Brother–Sister's Daughter

There is no distinction in the terminology for a mother's brother; he is an "older brother" or "younger brother" depending on their relative ages. The sister's children are "brother" and "sister," older or younger, depending on their relative ages. In the Hidatsa matrilineal system the mother's brother is a very important relative even when married and living in a different household. The most distinguished mother's brother was usually considered the head of the mother's household and the actual direction and supervision of the "younger brothers" was his responsibility. It was his chief duty to direct their interests so that they would bring honors to themselves and distinction to their household. He advised, punished, and praised them; he organized their fasting and games of skill and instructed them in tribal lore.

He would advise a "younger son" in marital matters and give material assistance if he approved of the match; rarely would a young man marry someone of whom his mother's brother disapproved. He would condemn a "sister's son" for being derelict in his ceremonial duties while offering assistance with goods and horses. Until a young man had made considerable advancement in the ceremonies he would not tease a "mother's brother," but should he have the good fortune to exceed his adviser in amassing war honors, he would invariably tease his "mother's brother" saying "I went in where the fighting was heaviest and see all the honors I have, but you must have been somewhere else for I see you do not have as many honors."

Unlike the Mandan, who transmitted most of their tribal bundles from mother's brother to sister's son or ones standing in that relationship (except those owned by the clan or reserved for women), sacred bundles passed from father to son. Therefore, the sister's son or daughter did not look to the mother's brother for ritual training.

The relations of a girl to her mother's brother were less restrained. He would give assistance at her wedding or settle domestic quarrels in the household, but the role he took depended on the assistance asked of him by his sister.

FATHER'S SISTER–BROTHER'S SON; FATHER'S SISTER–BROTHER'S DAUGHTER

The father's sister occupied a position similar to the father in the ceremonial life and distinguishable only by tribal limitations placed on the activities of females. It was her right and duty to be present when a brother's child was born and to receive presents for rituals performed at the time of its birth and naming. Most female babies were named by the father's sister or a woman standing in that relationship, the name being taken from ceremonies in which she held rights with her brother. She was paid by the child's clan relatives. The sum was large if a distant "father's sister" was giving the name but only a token payment was made if she was the child's father's own sister or the maternal grandfather's sister.

The father's sister was expected to pray often for her brothers' children so that they would be healthy and grow to maturity. In later years it was expected that they would honor her by giving her goods and horses during ceremonies and social events. Should her brothers' children be sickly, she was expected to come and assist them with the doctoring and "bring the blanket" if death occurred. Even though she might be younger than the deceased "brother's child," it was her duty to officiate at the funeral, when requested by the deceased's clan relatives, and to send the spirit to the "home of the dead."

Having assisted her brother each time he made ceremonial purchases, she was likewise considered to have supernatural power controls, and presents were due her each time honors were shown her brother. The father's sister played an important role in the transfer of the age-grade societies owned by women. She selected as a "daughter" first those who called her "father's sister" and instructed them in the ritual of the society being purchased.

The father's sister took no part in the marriage of her brother's children; neither was it her duty to give presents to the sister-in-law's household. Marriages were in no sense religious in nature.

GRANDMOTHER–GRANDCHILD; GRANDMOTHER–DAUGHTER-IN-LAW

In general, grandmothers treated their grandchildren kindly and looked after them much the same as the "mothers" of the lodge did. A child saw more of the maternal grandmothers since they usually lived together in the same household. These old women, too old for active work in the gardens or for heavy work around the lodge and village, usually cared for the grandchildren of the lodge. They would make toys, offer advice, relate myths and traditions, and teach skills they had themselves obtained. For this advice and instruction the children were advised to make payments to them even though they might be of little value.

A grandmother might sleep with her granddaughter and watch her to see that the boys did not molest her, going out with her after dark when the granddaughter had business away from the lodge. A grandmother was with her granddaughters more than with a grandson. A grandmother would tease her grandchildren about their associates and they would do likewise, but teasing was mild out of respect for her age.

A "grandmother" had a right to meat being brought back to the village and, learning that a hunting party was approaching the village, the old women of the village would walk out to the point where the hunters would pass and sit down to await the men with their loads. Each hunter was expected to give meat to those women whom he addressed as "grandmother" irrespective of the lodge in which she lived and she, in turn, should sing one of the songs of praise. Any young man wishing to become a village leader must be generous to the "grandmothers."

A grandmother might adopt a child whose mother and mother's sisters had died and care for it until it was old enough to marry. In return, the child was expected to care for the grandmother during the latter's old age.

The paternal grandmother was treated with respect due to her position as mother of the father from whom one received training in the ceremonies. She was not teased; in fact, she was feared and highly respected if her husband owned important ceremonial bundles. Since men were afraid to marry the widow of one who had important sacred bundles, even the grandchildren feared her and treated her with a certain reserve when she came to call. This difference seems to have been less apparent when she lived in her son's lodge. As children grew older the paternal grandmother played a greater role in the ritualistic training than did the maternal grandmother and, being of the father's clan, her knowledge of sacred matters was solicited and paid for on numerous formal occasions.

Other "grandmothers" were those women whom the husband called "mother," "father's sister," or "grandmother." They, in turn addressed the young man's wife as "daughter-in-law" to distinguish her as being not of their blood. If living in different lodges, the "grandmothers" always treated her with respect. The situation was somewhat altered with time when living together in the husband's household where none of her sisters-in-law lived. Although the wife preferred to live in her own household, frequently the husband had no sisters to care for his parents and payments were made to the daughter-in-law to come to the husband's lodge to live. This was a good arrangement for the husband's people, for, provided they chose a good daughter-in-law, they would have help around the lodge and in the gardens. When the daughter-in-law was treated well and got along with her husband's family, she gradually assumed the position of "one of the family" with the arrival of children. She inherited the lodge, gardens, and lodge property. After a number of years of harmonious residence together, the mother-in-law would say that her daughter-in-law was just like a daughter and would begin to call her "daughter" and the daughter-in-law would address the mother-in-law as "mother." This change in terminology was based on common residence, common interests in ceremonial bundles held by her husband, and lodge inheritance. There was not, however, a corresponding change in terminology for the husband's father, brother, or sister.

GRANDFATHER–GRANDCHILD; GRANDFATHER–DAUGHTER-IN-LAW

A child showed somewhat different attitudes and feelings toward the mother's father than toward the father's father due to the inheritance of sacred bundles and rights from the latter. Residence was also a factor. A child normally saw more of the mother's father, so it was this relative who contributed most to his early training in games and hunting. The grandfather would make toys for his grandsons and teach them games. As the children grew older he would show more attention to the grandsons, instructing them in the art of hunting and warfare although not actually participating in those activities himself. A grandfather might mildly tease his young grandchildren and they would reciprocate. With age, however, the children learned to respect and fear their grandfather (particularly if he was an important leader in the ceremonies) and the teasing lessened.

A grandfather might scold one who was lazy or disrespectful and might even hit one with his cane when they were residents of the same lodge. The mother's father, due to his position as the ranking male member of the lodge, was entitled to meat brought in by a grandson married into another household merely by walking up when the hunter was entering the village and saying, "We are hungry." Should a child lose both parents, the maternal grandparents might adopt the child, otherwise the child should be cared for by the paternal grandparents.

A woman classified as "grandfather" all those whom the husband called "father" or "grandfather." The men, on the other hand, distinguished her from their blood relatives by classifying her as a daughter-in-law. She was treated with respect, and teasing was improper. She was expected to respect them in return, feed and shelter them, and treat them at all times with kindness. The penalties for those who are unkind to the husband's father are well illustrated in numerous myths. Women who were kind to their husband's father were believed to have good luck all through life.

The grandparents' roles in the preservation of the tribal traditions and cultural heritage were important. It was considered proper to shift the physical responsibilities to persons of middle age, allowing older people more leisure time. Thus, while the father was engaged in warfare, hunting, or preparing for ceremonial feasts and rites, and the mother and her sisters were busy in their various economic, social, and ritualistic enterprises, the grandparents were free to teach. It was the pattern of the culture for the younger people to seek out the knowledge and skills possessed by the older people, particularly those of their own households. In return, the society offered many rewards to those possessing unique skills and knowledge. It seemed to this writer that Hidatsa interest in the history of their tribe and its institutions is not unique among the older people today.

Much of their culture was transmitted through purchase from those of the previous generations who had bought from their elders. Thus, arrows were made only by those with ceremonial rights in bundles carrying arrow-making songs; pottery was made by those with bundles associated with Old-Woman-Who-Never-Dies; basket-making was practiced by those with Holy Women rights; fish, eagle, and game traps were controlled by those with Black Bear rights; and bullboats and earth lodges went with River bundles. Since these skills were related to the principal bundles from which the original rights were given, there was an aura of sacredness about them. A person wishing to learn to chip flint and to make arrows could buy the rights and receive the instructions from those with the sacred bundle or he could buy the rights from one who had bought secondary rights from the bundle owner. In practice, it meant that a young man would go first to the people of his own household, generally a maternal grandfather, for instruction and training. The same rules would apply to a woman wishing to obtain the knowledge of pottery making. One did not have the right to make those things or perform those rites which were privately or group owned without first getting permission. Thus, much of the knowledge which one acquired during his or her lifetime, often at a high price, was shared with the younger generations, while the goods received in payment helped to sustain them in old age.

MOTHER-IN-LAW–SON-IN-LAW

A man classified as "mother-in-law" all those females that his wife and his own brothers' wives classed as "mother," "father's sister," and "grandmother." In theory, all of a woman's sons-in-law's extended "older brothers" and "younger brothers" were also "sons-in-law" but ordinarily these extended kin were not so recognized.   There was complete avoidance of recognized sons-in-law, but the limits to which the taboo extended were largely determined by the associations of extended "brothers."   The avoidance taboo would invariably extend to two households, the wife's mother's and the wife's father's sister's, but generally there were four or more lodges in which the son-in-law could not carry on a conversation with the older females.

When residence was matrilocal, a separate section on the left side of the lodge was prepared for the son-in-law and his wives; here he was expected to stay when the "mothers-in-law" were in the lodge. Should they meet in the entrance to the lodge or out in the village, they would turn their heads and appear not to recognize each other.   Unless the son-in-law's section was ready when the marriage was completed, the newly married couple would live with the husband's people until it was ready.   However, if the family was in urgent need of a hunter, quick work was made of finishing the repairs.   When residence was patrilocal, the taboo caused little inconvenience to the husband. He was free to move around his mother's lodge at will, help himself to the food at the fireplace if the women were away, clutter up the lodge with his riding equipment, and have friends in at any time.   In his wife's lodge he had none of these privileges.   Conversations were relayed through the wife as intermediary.

The son-in-law could break this taboo by taking a scalp in warfare and bringing it to any one of the numerous women classified as "mother-in-law."   One of the women then would carry the scalp during the victory dances and proclaim her new "son" so all could hear. Then all would know that he no longer avoided her.   He would address these "mothers-in-law" thereafter by the same terms as his wife did.   Scalps were never brought to the mothers-in-law unless one was living in their lodge.   To have done so while living with his own people would have been grounds for much teasing on the part of his joking relations.   They would say, "That foolish fellow must not trust his wife; perhaps he is getting his mother-in-law on his side."   Others would say, "Perhaps he is going to give up his wife and marry his mother-in-law."   In any event, the taboo was never broken down when the man was living with his own people.

The scalp was a mark of prestige; to give it to the wife's household instead of his own was to bring extreme honors to them.   They would dance and sing his praises.   Apparently the wife's family did not expect the first scalp.   When, however, he had taken scalps on several occasions without honoring the wife's people, his omission was viewed as an insult.   Their joking relations would say "We heard that your son-in-law won great honors the last time he was to war but I don't suppose you would know anything about that," or "We heard he meant to bring you a piece of it but a White man gave him a bottle of whisky for it.'' Repeated successes in warfare without recognizing the mother-in-law often led to divorce. Giving the mother-in-law a scalp was no guarantee that the marriage would be successful, but it did help in changing the status of the son-in-law in the wife's household. He could help himself to food when the women were out, bring in his friends, and do about as he would in his own household. Although his status was somewhat improved after children had come, there was still general avoidance unless the taboo was broken in the above manner.

Father-in-law–Son-in-law

Although the taboo was not as extreme in the case of father-in-law and son-in-law, it was not considered proper to sit around and visit. If they had business to transact, they discussed it and then separated. The same reserve prevailed through life and was not modified by long residence together or the presentation of scalps to the mothers-in-law. The avoidance was not as strict when the father-in-law and son-in-law were of the same clan, for there were many situations when cooperation outside of the household was necessary. Unlike the Mandan, there seems to have been no effort to get a son-in-law of the same clan.

Brother-in-law–Brother-in-law

This was a relationship based on marriage. One classified as brothers-in-law the husbands of "sisters" and the "brothers" of one's wives. In terminology and behavior no distinction was made between the two groups. There was mutual assistance between them. Brothers-in-law generally hunted together and if one was unmarried and living in the same lodge, they would pool their meat and bring it to the same household. The wife's brother would bring back horses from raids and give them to his sister for her husband's use to show respect for his sister's husband who was hunting to provide for the family. Assistance was interpreted in terms of the welfare of the sister's household since it was not considered proper to give a brother-in-law horses when residence was patrilocal.

There was usually a certain amount of rivalry between them in ceremonial matters. Although a woman would assist either a brother or a husband in obtaining sacred rites, a man would receive assistance from a brother and a sister but never directly from a sister's husband.

When the wife had small brothers whom she was caring for in the lodge, her husband frequently assumed the role of a "father," providing for the younger "brothers-in-law's" physical needs and instructing them in sacred matters. If a man was mean to his wife, beating her too severely or accusing her falsely, brothers-in-law were likely to interfere, especially if the man was not a good provider or was not the owner of important sacred bundles. The Hidatsa have a saying that "a woman won't take much abuse from her husband if she has many brothers." Other times one will hear them say, "She was saucy to her last husband too because she had many brothers and now she is a widow again." Nevertheless, a husband could make certain demands of his wife that even her brothers would not question. Should her husband whip her for failing to perform her duties, the brothers were unlikely to do anything about it.

Sister-in-Law–Sister-in-Law

In this class are the females the husband calls "sister" and the wives of those men she addresses as "older brother." It was customary to distinguish age by classifying the spouse of a younger "brother" as a daughter-in-law when the difference in their ages was 10 years or more. There was mutual assistance between sisters-in-law, irrespective of their residence. They normally were in different households but, in any instance, helped each other, working on robes, or curing meat while out with hunting parties. When a man prepared food and goods for a ceremony, his principal assistants were his wives and his sisters. They shared the confidence and respect of a common man. Returning from the hunt, each should be cared for; finding his wife out visiting, he would go to his sister's lodge to eat.

Brother-in-Law–Sister-in-Law

A woman classified as brother-in-law all males her husband classified as "older brother" and "younger brother," and the husbands of women she classified as "older sister" and "younger sister." By the extension of the kinship system, a female had many brothers-in-law and a male had many sisters-in-law. By the operation of the sororate and levirate, all of a woman's "brothers-in-law" were potential husbands, and all of a man's "sisters-in-law" were potential wives. Rarely, however, did a blood brother assume the duties of a deceased brother, chiefly because he was usually already married into a different household. If he was getting along well there he would be likely to invite trouble since jealousies would be sure to arise. A single man would often be teased by his joking relatives, but if he was attached to his brother's children more than to some young unmarried woman he would usually take his brother's widow in order to provide for the children. It was usually a more distant "brother," however, who married the widow. Instances of marriage to a deceased wife's younger sister were even more rare, chiefly because seldom were any available. If the family intended to have sisters marry the son-in-law, the marriages were already completed before the death of one of the sisters. It was common occurrence for two brothers actively engaged in warfare together to promise each other and their wives that, in the event one brother was killed, the other would marry the widow and care for her children. Then friction rarely developed between the two households.

A brother-in-law would tease his sister-in-law a great deal, often carrying the teasing to the point of vulgarity. He would accuse her of love affairs with decrepit old men or little boys and ask her when he could take her out. Often when the husband could not get away for a hunt planned by a few households he would send a brother in his place to look after his wife, hunting and butchering for her. Supplying a wife for a brother to use in a ceremony or age-grade purchase was a common occurrence. Cooperation between brothers-in-law and sisters-in-law in ceremonies was the usual practice since a man making these purchases would have the assistance of his wife and his brothers as well as his wife's sisters.

Friend–Friend

This was a relationship prevailing between two males or two females. The selection was made by the individuals themselves and was of an informal nature. They would play together. Men in later years hunted or went to war together. The only bond was a common liking for each other. A list of a dozen or more sets of friends showed that rarely were they of the same clan. Age and compatability seemed to be the basis for these associations. It was of common occurrence for two male friends to marry two girls who were friends or for a man to marry two girls who were close friends.

Joking Relative–Joking Relative

This is a relationship between related kin with a difference in the degree of teasing depending upon the relationships between the opposing parties. The term "joking relative" applied, in descending order of activity, to persons whose fathers were of the same clan; sisters-in-law and brothers-in-law; persons of the same clan; persons whose fathers were of the same moiety or "linked" clans; and grandparents with grandchildren.

It was the right of the "joking relative" to criticize an offender of tribal custom and standards, and one was obliged to accept it in good grace. Men would tease one who had less honor marks or had not stolen many horses. Even a member of the village council was not above criticism. Crows Heart had distinguished himself in warfare and for a number of years had the highest war record of the Mandan and Hidatsa. Still, his joking relatives would tease him, saying that he was once brave but now that there were no enemies around, he was even afraid of the snakes.   On one occasion he and a number of his Hidatsa inlaws were returning from visiting the Sioux on the Cannon-ball River.   They stopped in the shade along the river to eat and rest. While the men were sitting there he looked around and his joking relative asked him if he was afraid of snakes.   While they were dozing, a bullsnake crawled over his arm.   His joking relative saw the snake and waited for Crows Heart to jump away so that he could tease him but Crows Heart, pretending to be sleeping, waited until the snake had crawled half way through his hand and then threw it at his joking relative, striking him on the chest.   Not being prepared for this sudden turn in events, his joking relative jumped away.   Crows Heart then said, "Now I see that my joking relative is not very brave.   He went out to war all the time but he never won many honors.   When there were enemies to strike, he must have been somewhere sleeping."

The most severe criticism was leveled at one who had been cowardly. A joking relative was expected to save another in danger and failure to do so would have brought down upon the person such criticism that he would have been ashamed to appear in council or to offer advice on village matters.   If one was angry at a joking relative and was the possessor of greater war honors, he could say "That is how I strike my enemies" and administer a severe blow to the other who could not, on penalty of loss of face, strike back.   Often brothers returning from a successful war expedition with scalps would search out a joking relative who had not shown much interest in warfare or had not struck the enemy when out.   Seizing him, they would hold him and cut his hair off, telling him that it was a man who looked just like him that they had scalped.   Then it was the right of the victim to demand a good horse in return.

It was the duty of the joking relatives to criticize one who made unjust claims of bravery or industry and to set him aright.   As a rule, the severity of criticism and teasing was influenced by age.   Individuals with a great difference in age criticized and teased each other less severely even though they were children of men of the same clan, for one was supposed to show due respect for age.   The degree of teasing was also affected by residence.   Those living in the same lodge were supposed to live together harmoniously; therefore, the more distant "joking relatives" were the ones who were most active.

The importance of the joking relative cannot be overemphasized. No one, from the highest chief to the lowliest orphan, was exempt from these relatives.   If criticism and teasing were not taken in good grace, one was certain to lose prestige.   If one resorted to force, public opinion and, if necessary, the Black Mouths could interfere.   However, since the clan should discipline its own members, it seems that matters never got entirely out of hand.

LIFE CYCLE

Most social, economic, and ritualistic activities were more complex sets of relationships than was indicated above in the analysis of general attitudes and behavior patterns prevailing between pairs of relatives. Relatives had prescribed duties and obligations for every important occasion in the life of a Hidatsa. Some insight into their general attitudes and behavior patterns is indicated by tracing an individual from birth to death. Since no effort has heretofore been made to bring together the important events in the life cycle of this tribe, it is particularly appropriate that these specific aspects be examined in relation to the total cultural setting.

BIRTH AND NAMING

It is rather difficult to get adequate information on Hidatsa beliefs concerning conception and birth. On inquiry about the physical nature of conception, informants invariably mention "spirits" entering the mother's body, causing a baby to develop there. Although they frequently cite instances of virgins giving birth to babies who grew up to become culture heroes, they consider humorous any suggestion that unmarried girls of recent times gave birth to children without actual intercourse. On the other hand, they recognized that all married women did not have children.

The spirits destined eventually to become human beings, like those that will become animals and birds, were believed to inhabit certain hills in their traditional territory. Three of these hills are remembered: one is near the mouth of Knife River; a second is on the Heart River; the third is southwest of Dickinson, N. Dak., and east of the Little Missouri River. Each hill was believed to be an earth lodge in which the babies lived and were cared for by an old man. Women would put toys at the foot of these hills if they wanted children. It is of significance that in the memories of my informants, only the hill near the Little Missouri and farthest from their villages had been visited by childless women. Matthews (1877, p. 51) indicated that men were accustomed to fast at these hills when desiring a son. If this was true, the custom has fallen into disuse. According to native beliefs, children desiring to leave the hill and be born, must crawl across a ditch within this earth lodge on an ash pole. If they succeeded in reaching the opposite side without falling into the ditch, they would be born into the tribe soon afterward. One time when Cherries-in-Mouth, Cuts-his-Hair, Sitting Elk, Puts-His-Hair-Away, and Crows

Heart were out on the warpath under the leadership of Cherries-in-Mouth, Crows Heart wanted to go onto the Baby Hill near the Little Missouri to look around, but the leader said, "We came out to look for our enemies, not babies' tracks." Shortly afterward, however, the entire party went to Buffalo Home Butte nearby to see if the buffaloes had been coming out of the cave recently. They made offerings of eagle feathers to the buffalo spirits residing in the hill and asked the buffaloes to come out faster, for the number on the earth was not very great at that time.

It was believed that the tracks of the little babies and buffaloes could be seen under the rocks and in the caves of those hills where they were believed to reside. Some people would claim that they could remember things before they were born. Sitting Elk [14] of the Hidatsa and Standing Bear of the Mandan would claim that they could even remember each other when they lived in the Baby Hill. Standing Bear was in the lead and they came to the washout with a small pole as a bridge. Standing Bear crossed safely but Sitting Elk fell from the pole after he had reached the opposite side, so he was delayed. Standing Bear was born first. Although they were born of different mothers, Standing Bear would call Sitting Elk his "younger brother" for they had started out of the hill at approximately the same time. Standing Bear said when they grew up, "I crossed the bridge and went on but Sitting Elk nearly fell in. That is the sign that I am going to live to an old age but Sitting Elk will not grow old." Standing Bear and Sitting Elk called each other brother even though the former belonged to the Mandan Tamisik clan and the latter to the Hidatsa Waterbuster clan.

The concept of the origin of humans from spirit homes was extended to other animal life as well. There were numerous Buffalo Spirit homes where offerings were made for the propagation of the big mammals. [15]

From the ceremonial myths believed to be of Awatixa village origin, it appears that they, unlike the Hidatsa and Awaxawi, thought that they came from the sky in contrast to the other groups who tell of the first settlement of the earth from people coming from underground. Sometimes a person would say that he came from above when he was born and that, when he died, he would return to the land above. Then the people would say that he talked just like an Awatixa. Frequent reference is made in the sacred myths to former existence in the sky. A common theme of these myths is that one's former existence will be revealed by visions. The Hidatsa also believed that the spirit babies would play with sticks and were so rough that some

---

[14] He had a Naxpike bundle but was obliged to leave the village after he murdered Edge-of-Rock, a clansman.

[15] See Earthnaming Rites, pp. 433–436, for these spirit homes,

would be hit on the base of the spine producing a purple mark which was distinguishable for several months after birth.

If a pregnant woman ate the pancreas, or killed snakes or any animals, she would have a difficult delivery. She should not eat or look at a rabbit or the child would have a split lip. If she ate eggs, it was believed that the child would awaken early in the morning and keep the people awake. She should not quarrel and become angry or the child might come too soon and die. If she braided grass and made a ring of it, or picked up a ring of braided grass, the male child might be deformed. It was believed that working in the cornfield was good for a pregnant woman, for the baby would then be strong but not so large as to make delivery difficult. The older women would tell their daughters having their first babies that if they kept busy and did not think about it, the delivery was always easier.

Regardless of residence, it was customary for a woman to give birth to her first baby at her mother's lodge assisted by her female clanswomen. Various household rites were employed when delivery was difficult. If delivery was further delayed, her husband's sister and mother were expected to contribute assistance. If their measures failed, certain women having both sacred rites and practical knowledge relating to childbirth were called in and paid to assist the women. The otter was believed to possess the supernatural power to make delivery easier. Other doctors used black root, scrapings from the turtle, or pulverized rattlesnake rattles taken with water to induce delivery.

It was the maternal grandmother's responsibility to care for the child, and bury the placenta or wrap it and place it out of the reach of animals. The child was wrapped in soft tanned hide and placed in a cradle made of buffalo hide. The household group made the cradle, the men providing a young buffalo's hide which the women tanned prior to cutting and sewing the parts together.

The child was taken from the cradle twice a day to be washed and cleaned. The rites of naming the child were viewed as the formal way of introducing him to his father's relatives. Often a child was named by the maternal grandfather living in the lodge and only a nominal payment was made for the service. When the child was named by someone outside of the household—a "distant" father or father's sister—it was customary to procure a supply of fresh meat and garden products, take the child to the person giving the name, and pay him with the food. The richer families usually gave a horse also. The name given was taken from some incident or association with the name-giver's sacred bundle. The person giving the name would first pray to his or her medicine bundles. When a boy was to be named, one would ask his sacred things to give him good health so that when he grew up he would be helpful to his people and brave in battle. They would ask that he live a long useful life and be a leader among the people, kind to the old, and have much to show for his efforts. One would ask that a girl be industrious and good to her people so that she would sometime have a happy home with a good hunter and warrior as her husband.

Prior to receiving a name, children occupied a marginal position between the spirit world and the mother's household. Should they die unnamed, they were wrapped and placed without ceremony in a tree with other unnamed children. From there the spirit left the body and returned to the Baby Hill or other place from whence it had come, while the body was thought to be consumed by Sun and his sister, cannibals of the upper world. Only rarely did an individual "know" the hill or place to which a child returned; this information usually was revealed to the child years later during fasting.

Birth and naming made the child a member of the mother's household and clan while additional transitional rites between birth and the attainment of adulthood were the means of establishing new sets of relationships, some of which were with people outside of the village and tribe. The naming ceremony also introduced the child to the people of the father's clan. The child's position was then complete as far as the immediate parental clan groups were concerned. It was further believed that one's "real" person was not revealed until fasting had been undertaken seriously. Then one's spiritual father would come to him and enumerate the things the young man should undertake to help his people.

TRAINING AND CEREMONIAL PARTICIPATION

The early training of a Hidatsa child was largely entrusted to the mother, with assistance from the other females of the lodge. When the mother was ill or died during childbirth, it was not uncommon to give the child to another woman to care for and to adopt. At an early age, boys began to receive training different from that of girls. Boys were trained in games of hunting and warfare by the older men, especially the grandfathers, of the lodge, or by the younger men of the lodge who were classified as "older brothers." The father's role, particularly as far as it concerned his first son, was likely to be one of aloofness and distance if living in the wife's lodge. He was expected to hunt for the household and help protect the village from its enemies. Thus his attention was directed toward other matters. He was expected to show respect for his son by neither scolding nor punishing him. When a child was old enough to walk, he was usually in constant company with the other children of the lodge and their closest relatives of related households. An older brother would look after a younger one, seeing that he did not get hurt or stray away, pulling him back when approaching too close to the horses or when in danger of falling into an open cache pit. A younger sister would be given into the care of one of the older sisters of the lodge. Those a little older would teach the younger ones games which they had learned from those a little older than themselves. Thus the knowledge possessed by the older siblings was passed down to the younger ones. Most of a boy's economic training came from the maternal grandfather and the older brothers—less frequently a brother-in-law—while his ritualistic training was reserved for the father and the people of the father's clan. Except for ritualistic training, most of the cultural heritage was transmitted informally. A girl received most of her training from her mother and the older women of the lodge. Although her own mother was closest to her, as a rule, all lodge females would give advice and training directed toward her welfare and upbringing. The household was sharply divided as far as its child-training functions were concerned; one looked to the mother's lineage for economic and social training while the father's lineage assumed the responsibility for ritualistic training.

A boy was discouraged from playing with toys usually used by girls while, to a lesser degree, girls were not encouraged to play with boys' toys. "Spin the top" was the first game played by very small boys while the girls of the same age would play with marbles and beads. Usually the maternal grandfather would make the top and show the little boy how to spin it. The maternal grandmother or some other old woman of the lodge would supply the toys for the little girls and show them how to string the beads or roll the marbles.

Even though men had firearms, the boys had bows and arrows. It was said that a Hidatsa boy grew up with a bow and arrows. He was given a bow and blunt arrows as soon as he was able to use them. At first he would use them around the lodge, shooting into the coals or at targets made of grass set up against one of the lodge posts. Girls of the same age would have a ball to roll and kick. Gambling was common and encouraged by the adults. A boy would invite another of an adjoining earth lodge to come over and shoot at a target, usually a stuffed rabbit skin, and the one who hit it would take both arrows. The old men of the lodges would join in the contest, betting things for their lodge members, and pitting lodge against lodge. It would not be long until the young boys of the same age were shooting at moving objects with greatly improved bows and arrows. Wolf Chief said that he was not more than 6 years of age when he began testing his skill with other boys in the game of "tied up," one involving shooting arrows into a stuffed bird thrown into the air by some old man. Each contestant would usually have some old man and older brothers there advising him, showing him how to lead the moving object so as to hit it.   In none of my accounts was there reference to the father's participation in these games.

While boys of 6 or 7 years of age were gaining proficiency in the use of bows and arrows, the girls would play "kick ball" or learn to sew clothing for their dolls.   The women would encourage the little girls to care for their younger sisters and encourage the boys to pro- tect and look after their younger brothers.   Little boys just learning to use the bow and arrows would help the older ones to surround small patches of brush where rabbits were known to stay and to keep them from running out while they closed in on them.   Frequently 100 or more children, both boys and girls, would surround a patch of brush to enclose the rabbits.   Then the older boys would teach their younger brothers how to hit moving targets.   According to the reminiscences of numerous informants, this must have been common winter sport for Hidatsa children.   Each child was entitled to the animals he had killed, identification of his rabbits being made by special markings on the arrows.   Returning home with his rabbits, the parents would praise him and say that he would surely be a great hunter and warrior when he grew up.   Informants related that they went out to surround rabbits while still so young that it was necessary for their older brothers to carry them through the deeper snowdrifts. Some older person would act as "crier" for the boys and call through the village that the little boys should get their weapons and come out for the rabbit hunt.   Here we see, even in the childhood games of boys under 10 years of age, elements of the adult social pattern: the organized age-group with an announcer; the leader; the cooperating group; and the approval of society as a whole, expressed by praise for those who had demonstrated exceptional skill.

Concepts of reciprocal obligations were taught early in life.   A boy would get his bow and arrows from his maternal grandfather who, in turn, should be presented with some of the rabbits, gophers, or prairie chickens shot with them.   A girl would do favors for her "grandmothers" who had made toys for her or had taught her how to decorate things with beads and quills.   Informants spoke warmly of these relatives and the reciprocal relationships of their childhood.

The discipline of little boys and girls was a household responsibility and the duty of the older members of the clan.   In some situations they learned about the police.   When word was sent through the winter camp that everyone should be quiet, for the buffalo herds were approaching the river, freedom of movement about camp was often permitted by the Black Mouth police society provided there was no noise.   One informant said that when he was 6 years old he was sliding downhill with other boys and girls of his age when word went around that the buffaloes had appeared on the hills opposite and that everyone should be quiet. The children forgot about this order and began to shout. The police appeared carrying their clubs. Seeing them, the children ran for home for they had been told that the Black Mouths killed people who did not obey their orders and there was nothing the people could do about it.

There were always a number of old women in the village who encouraged boys to be active so that they would become good hunters and warriors when they grew up. In the fall, when the corn was in the milk, one of these old women would invite the boys and girls under 10 years of age to come to her garden where she had prepared roasted corn on the cob for them. The girls would stand around the fire where the corn was roasting while some old man would line up the boys for a footrace to be run to the fire. The girls would shout as when someone returned from the war with horses and scalps while the boy who ran fastest was praised and told that he would surely be the first of his group to strike the enemy. Boys were always running footraces in imitation of the young men preparing for war. Some of these courses were 5 and 6 miles in length. The older men would encourage them to race, and commonly bet on their relatives.

Girls' training was quite different from that of the boys. They cared for their younger brothers and sisters when the women were out of the lodge. As they grew older they were taught to cook, care for the lodge, make and repair clothing, and care for the gardens. Even the heavier work in the gardens was performed by the females of the lodge. Although old men too feeble to engage in hunting or warfare would frequently assist the women of the household in clearing brush, repairing fences, or even hoeing the garden if the work proved too much for the women, boys and young men were never permitted to assist. This prohibition was fortified by ritual beliefs that those young men who performed women's customary duties were more likely to dream of the Woman Above and become berdaches. This resulted in a distinct sex dichotomy of labor. The only common exceptions were butchering and retrieving wood from the river.

Children were taught, when 4 or 5 years old, to respect the sacred bundles hanging at the head of the lodge. They were told by their clansmen that these bundles were gods and that they should "cry to these bundles" whenever they thought of them to get good luck. All "older brothers" were not equally entitled to discipline a younger one. Special rights and obligations were held by those who had shown bravery in war. Age and experience were important, for a boy only 2 or 3 years older would teach the younger one all that he knew. An "older brother" who had been unusually brave in battle would make it a point to watch while going through the village for younger ones who were not doing right and scold them. Frequently he was an older brother by the extension of the kinship system to include males of the same clan. Finding the boys playing rough or teasing the girls, he would seize one of his own clan and duck him in the river or hit him with a strap saying, "This is the way I hit the enemy." They would say that boys who fought with the girls would not be brave in battle.

Older brothers, particularly the mother's brothers, were the ones to prepare the younger ones for their first fasting. The first fasting was customarily begun at the age of 7 or 8 years. It was customary for a boy of that age to accompany a brother a few years older to the ceremonial grounds and stay with him. Advice and direction was given by a brother who had fasted often. A boy 7 or 8 years old would be afraid to attend alone, but it was considered great sport to fast if accompanied by an older brother. Seeing that his son was making plans for his first fasting, the father would take some object from one of his sacred bundles and place it on a stick to be set up in front of his son at the ceremonial lodge. Relatives—father's and mother's—would praise him and call his name as he walked to the ceremonial grounds, saying that he would surely be a brave man when he grew up. The household would bring presents to the ceremonial grounds and give them to people of the boy's father's clan who, in turn, would pray for the success of the "son." Small boys were not expected to stay at the ceremonial grounds for the entire 4 days but they were expected to stay for a short time. Usually most of the small boys had left the ceremony by the end of the first day. On future occasions, they would stay for 2 or even 3 days. By the time a boy was 15 or 16 years of age, fasting was taken more seriously, for he was then reaching the age when he should be going out on his first war expedition. Fasting introduced a boy to a new set of relatives, particularly the "ceremonial" fathers; the prominent men of his father's clan.

When the boys reached the age of 11 or 12 years, they would run in gangs chasing the girls. The older brothers would criticize the younger ones for dressing up in their finest clothes and watching the girls all the time when they should be fasting or caring for the horses. At this age, boys often made a great deal of trouble around the village. Those who took little interest in training for warfare would dress in their best clothes and loaf around the village or at the trading posts watching for the girls. The girls were taught not to be intimate with these boys for they would be poor hunters and have no war records. Nevertheless, gangs of boys would watch for girls to catch them alone. It was considered great sport to catch a girl who was being watched especially closely by her female relatives. Girls would be scolded for carrying on an affair with the boys, while nothing was usually said to a boy unless he gave so much attention to the girls that he neglected other duties. Cases of rape were common. The offender might be severely whipped by the girl's brothers or the man's sisters might try to restore good relations by expressing regrets and giving her household a horse or other valuables. The young man would lose face as it was considered cowardly to force a woman into sexual relations against her will.

It was at this age, when the young boys were getting into mischief and just before they were old enough to go on war expeditions as camp tenders, that they joined the Stone Hammer society. At the age of 12 to 15, boys organized and bought the society from the older boys who were ready to buy the next higher one. As members of the Stone Hammer society they were expected to confine their mischief to those times when the society was meeting. They would announce their meetings in advance so that all would hear; then those who failed to protect their food were likely to lose much of it during the night. The society owned a stuffed mouse to which they prayed, asking it to help them find the best food. The leader would tie the mouse in his hair before going out on a raid for food. The members would grease their bodies to make seizure difficult, paint their bodies with the distinctive society markings, and tie up their hair in a knot. If a lodge door was securely barred, entrance was often made down the chain suspended from the smokehole or poles were removed from the side of the lodge. Old people would often place their meat between robes on the bed so that they would waken if someone attempted to move it. Frequently old men would stay up all night talking and smoking around the fire with the meat in a conspicuous place near them to encourage the boys to attempt to slip in quietly and remove it. This was considered good practice for stealing horses when older. Other households would set up various traps to warn them that prowlers were at hand. This was considered good training for entering a Sioux camp undetected when out raiding horses.

When one was caught stealing, his hands were tied in back of him and around one of the large lodge posts. His associates would return to the lodge where the society had its headquarters to report the misfortune. The society would collect goods and follow the leader to the lodge where its member was being held prisoner and form a circle around him crying. The old people would scold them severely for attempting to steal their best meat. Then the boys would offer some of their goods to free their member. A high price was always set, not expecting that it would be paid, but not infrequently the boys paid up without dickering. Old women would warn them that the next time they would keep them tied up longer and it would cost them more to get their member back. It was understood that if the boys failed once, they would continue until they succeeded. When they were successful in stealing from a lodge, the old woman of the household would prepare a feast for them. They would smoke the pipe she had filled and had ready for them; then they would enjoy the food, singing and dancing while they ate. After that it was considered improper to steal from that household. Wolf Chief said that during the time he was a member, he had been in many of the Arikara lodges and all of the Mandan and Hidatsa lodges looking for food. This training in entering a lodge undetected was considered good training for entering an enemy camp at night.

A boy was encouraged to fast during all ceremonies that included fasting rites. At the age of 15 or 16 he was constantly reminded to fast by his "older brothers" if he did not join in the ceremonies. He was scolded publicly; even his mother would cry because the family was poor and her son was not doing anything to help them. When there were a number of boys of approximately the same age in several related households, the bravest and most distinguished older brothers would frequently select a man classified as "father" who had led war parties to take the boys out from the village, there to supervise their fasting and suffering. He would see that they cried to the holy things and did not take food or water. He would suggest that the boys cut off a finger, cut flesh from their body, or be suspended from a tree or bank by means of thongs put through the skin to induce dreams from the spirits. Those who agreed were tortured by the man in the manner that they chose. He would promise the bravest ones that they could go out with the next war expedition.

Because of the numerous enemy tribes near at hand, it was necessary for the Hidatsa to herd their horses continuously during the daytime and bring them in at night. Except when snow was on the ground, scouts were kept out beyond the range of the grazing animals. A common arrangement was to place the horses in charge of the younger boys, while those who had been to war acted as scouts to signal in case an enemy war party was discovered. Frequently, several older boys would take out the horses and train the younger ones. Those showing sufficient skill in handling horses were invited to accompany war parties and assist in driving back the captured animals.

The most distinctive feature of Hidatsa child training was its uniformity. Irrespective of the unequal and changing status positions of the various households, each child had essentially the same opportunities. Some households would have no fathers to whom the boys could go for ritualistic training; nevertheless, they could attain eminence by following the instructions of the older persons of the household. One could acquire the sacred bundles and ceremonial rights owned by a deceased father provided he showed bravery in battle, was industrious, and married well. Nevertheless, a young man was greatly handicapped by having no father to whom he could go for early guidance in ritualistic matters. He was further handicapped belonging to a household without an adult hunter, for it never received the same share of hides and could not put up as much goods in the ceremonies. Likewise, having no mature male to assist in the ceremonies, the household did not receive many gifts during the ceremonies. Due to the heavy losses of males as war casualties, it was not uncommon for a household to be without a male provider for several years, during which time the children were growing up, for the Hidatsa population was composed primarily of women and children.

Although the products of the community summer hunts were equally available to all households, as were the animals taken in corrals during other seasons, they did not always resort to these methods of securing game. The people of the clan would provide their basic necessities and the women of the household would trade garden produce for meat and other things. A boy would frequently stay out of an age-grade society in which he should belong because he felt that his people could not spare the goods. At the same time, other boys would take the honored positions because their families were wealthy and showed good prospects of a continuous income from prominent positions held in the various tribal ceremonies. Death of a father was a serious blow to a young man's ceremonial ambitions—chiefly because one was expected to pay "ceremonial" fathers for their advice and, frequently, the household was poor.

The Hidatsa say that the best husbands often were those who had no fathers or became orphans too late to be adopted; they had to work hard to get ahead. The sons of eminent men were the ones to lead the war parties but the poor boys were often the ones to capture most of the horses. Difference in wealth was reflected in the course of a young man's interests. One who was poor and felt unable to accumulate the goods to buy the deceased father's rites, generally established personal bundles based on his visions preliminary to later tribal bundle purchases when he had prospered. The richer boy, while still a relatively young man, would perform the formal ceremonies and obtain the same rites as his father owned. A young man's interest, whether in warfare and hunting or in rituals, was usually evident before he had married. This was partially determined by his birth—into a household that either did or did not possess many rights in ceremonies. In either instance the course followed to attain eminence was difficult and exceedingly competitive.

A young man usually received his first serious training in the hardships of warfare and hunting at one of the formal ceremonies which included fasting and torturing as a part of the rituals. By participating with the household furnishing the goods and horses as gifts to the ceremonial fathers, one could enhance the status of the person putting on the ceremony. The demands were so great that only those who were married could initiate a ceremony. However, any young man (more particularly, those classified as "younger brothers") was obligated to put up goods and to fast whenever a ceremony involving fasting was being given. The distinguished war leaders would come to watch the young men and to observe their response to hunger and pain in order to get only the most promising ones for their war parties.

It was considered a great honor to be invited to go out with the higher-ranking war leaders. Parents discouraged their sons from accompanying those leaders with poor reputations. Boys who were alert, good runners, and ambitious were soon invited to go along with war parties to serve as camp tenders. They were expected to care for the fires, bring water, and do the cooking. If there were two or more boys along, the leader would observe their response when camp duties were assigned them. Should he need a green branch to hang sacred objects on and there were four boys in camp, at his request all four were expected to jump up and bring the branch even though one could do it. Boys knew that they were being watched and that those who were lazy would not be invited out again soon. Returning home, it was expected that the leader would praise publicly those who had shown interest and had obeyed his orders. As time passed it became more difficult for the lazy boys to join war parties under the more successful leaders.

Offensive warfare provided a young man with many opportunities to learn skills in locating horses and attacking or evading the enemy. There were also opportunities to observe and participate in rites not practiced in his own household. The ambitious leaders encouraged fasting by the camp tenders, offering as rewards the opportunity to serve as scouts on future expeditions. At this point in a young man's training, the father's experiences and training were solicited directly by a son. The father would outline in detail his experiences in fasting, the dreams he had received, the ceremonies he had performed, and his military achievements. He might even "give" his son those horses and scalps which the former had been promised in his dreams but which, for one reason or another, he had not yet possessed. When a young man had reached the point where he sought advice in ritualistic matters, the "older brothers" became an assisting group, supplying goods, horses, and other necessities as payments to the father or "ceremonial fathers." The Hidatsa believed a young man wishing to get ahead should have many fathers praying for him.

Thus, the father generally directed his son to other "fathers" and payments were made to them individually for their ritualistic instructions and prayers.

Even those eligible by the rules of inheritance to purchase the father's sacred tribal bundles, believed to go back nearly to the beginning of time, were not exempt from military duties. Every sacred bundle was in some way concerned with warfare even though its principal functions were to bring the buffaloes, catch eagles, insure good growing conditions for crops, or attain other social values. In the competition for high status, those who had performed many ceremonies and had publicly disposed of a great deal of wealth were not expected to have as many war records to show as those who had distinguished themselves largely in warfare.

A girl's position was much different from that of a boy. She usually remained a lifelong member of her mother's household, brought her husband there to live, and inherited the lodge and lodge property, including the gardens, when the older female members of the lineage died. Her training was in domestic tasks so that she could marry a good provider. Her affections and interests were with her brothers even after they had married and moved to another lodge. She would put up goods when a brother returned from a successful war expedition, fast for his success while he was away, and have first claim to the horses he had captured, even when he lived with his wife's household, provided she ran out to meet him. She fasted less than her brothers, never tortured herself while seeking a vision, and generally kept the first name given her for her entire lifetime. She was taught to avoid the village ceremonies during her menses lest she undo all the rites, and, if on eagle-trapping expeditions or small hunting parties, to report her condition so that appropriate sacred songs could be sung to send away bad luck. There were no organized puberty rites but many simple household rituals relating to agriculture which she was expected to observe. A girl was trained to become a good gardener and housekeeper, and a skillful tanner and decorator of hides. It was customary for the household to arrange her marriage soon after she had reached puberty.

MARRIAGE AND THE HOUSEHOLD

Marriage did not involve more than a few Hidatsa households at most and was never a public event. Frequently only the two households of the couple were involved. Courtship was usually carried on openly and people would see that the couple were showing affection for each other. When a girl was a good worker, and neither she nor the man had been married before, his older brothers and sisters would see the couple together a good deal in the village, perhaps noting that the girl had accepted his pemmican at a ceremony, that she was wearing his beads, or that when he was away from home herding the horses or hunting she would pass his mother's lodge several times a day. They would tell their younger brother that he should marry the girl. Frequently a young man would be reluctant to suggest marriage, fearing that her family would demand more horses than could be spared yet being reluctant to suggest that they elope for fear that her family would resent the suggestion and either keep a closer watch on her or marry her to someone else. When the brothers and sisters suggested the marriage, a young man was free to bring up the matter, knowing that his family would put up horses for him. My informants claimed that they never gave any thought to the matter of close relationship at first, for their older people were quick to disapprove of courtship with one of the same clan or of a too close blood relationship.

A young man preferred to marry without putting up horses. His joking relatives would be sure to tease him for buying a wife otherwise. However, few households permitted their daughters to marry for the first time unless the husband's people delivered the number of horses demanded of them. If the girl agreed she would say to him, "It is all right, but I will have to ask my mother first."

Even though the young man was acceptable, the first thing the mother would ask was, "How many horses did he promise us?" Rarely did a young man offer horses, preferring to get married without relinquishing them. To discourage undesirable marriages, the mothers would tell how hard they had worked to bring the girl up well while the young man ran away or never seemed to get any honors when at war; how he loafed while herding his brothers' horses and had not given them good care; how he never showed interest in hunting; how he slept late every day and never seemed to find anything to do. If the girl still expressed a desire to go through with the marriage and, if necessary, live with her husband's people, the older brothers were appealed to in an effort to prevent elopement. They would restate all of the young man's faults and if there was still danger of an elopement, the children of her father's clan (the "joking relatives") might participate. The girl could persist in the marriage and escape the household's criticism, for "a mother should love her daughter." There was no escape from the father's clansmen's children, however, for they were scattered throughout every Hidatsa village to which she might go. Nevertheless, once the marriage was completed, people preferred not to talk about it.

If the proposal was acceptable, the woman's household set the day for the marriage and the number of horses that would be expected.

The man would inform his household of the number of horses that the girl's family wanted and his mother's sisters and brothers would meet and decide which horses to give. The man's sister would take the horses to the other lodge beforehand and leave them. Meanwhile, food was being prepared for the wedding feast. When the horses arrived, the girl's mother would invite her male relatives and their families to come for the feast. The sister's older brothers and mother's brothers present at the feast were given the horses brought from the young man's household; they then gave an equal number of their own horses to the girl's mother who, on the day of the wedding feast, took them to her son-in-law's household, tied them up, and left.

The groom's relatives, the household and those whom he classified as "brothers" living in other lodges, came to the groom's lodge at the appointed time. The women from the other household, including the bride, came to the groom's lodge with all of the food needed for the feast and the horses given by the wife's household. The bride remained and all of her household left. A robe was placed on the floor for the marrying couple to sit on. At this point the groom was expected to appear bashful so that his brothers could tease him. The husband's relatives passed around food and then began presenting the bride with goods which were to go to her mother's household. At the same time the bride gave the horses to her husband's people. When the exchange of goods was completed, word was sent by the bride to the other household who sent female members over to take the things away. This completed the ceremony.

In this instance, the initiative being with the husband and his relatives, residence was patrilocal. Few families were willing to relinquish their females, however, and it was customary to prepare a separate section of the lodge for the son-in-law and his family, after which a horse and other property were taken to his household with a request that he bring his wife back to her own household. If the wife's sisters and their husband or husbands were already occupying the lodge with their wives' older relatives, it was not uncommon to permit a younger daughter to take up residence with the husband's people. An ambitious man generally did not like to live in a lodge with his wife's sisters and their husbands unless the two men belonged to the same clan.

Marriage was as frequently initiated by the woman's household. People who had raised their daughters well would look for an ambitious young man who was a good hunter and warrior, showed great interest in rituals, and was good-natured and kind, to become their daughter's husband. When a marriage was planned by the woman's household, the older women of the lodge would go to the females of the other lodge and get their approval even before the matter was discussed with the prospective husband. Once the proposition was agreed to by the females of the two households, the man's older brothers were instructed to go to him and break the news that his people wanted him to marry the girl. The older brothers were selected since one was expected to obey them and because they would be assisting in supplying the horses and goods for the wedding. When the initiative was with the girl's people, they would indicate the number of horses that they would put up. They selected the day for the wedding, took the horses and food to the husband's lodge and returned for the presents given by the husband's relatives. A few days after the ceremony, the wife's brothers took a horse, gun, or other things used by a man in hunting and invited him to move over to their mother's lodge.

Frequently a man was poor and had few relatives to assist him in completing the marriage ceremony, particularly when he belonged to a small clan. Several informants referred to the marriage of Two Shields whose close relatives had all died years before. He had lived from lodge to lodge while a young boy. When he was old enough to go out hunting, he would volunteer to go along at every opportunity. There was a household that had four daughters. They had been brought up well by their people and never ran around with the boys; instead, they had the reputation of being good workers and kind to the old people. Their parents talked of marrying two of them to Two Shields. Informants were not sure why Two Shields could not have the other two daughters as well but they thought that the household wanted at least two sons-in-law to help them. When the matter was discussed with Two Shields, it was agreed that he must not ask for the other sisters or have an affair with them.

Concerning this marriage Crows Heart said:

Two Shields was not good looking; sometimes he acted queer and did not seem too bright; he didn't take much interest in rituals and sometimes he did not even seem to respect those things; sometimes he would steal and once his clansmen beat him for taking things. But he was a good hunter and liked to go out hunting. It seemed that even though he was not too bright, he did understand the habits of the wild animals.

When the people heard that Tucks In wanted to marry his daughters to Two Shields they said, "We think you are foolish to give your daughters to that man," and Tucks In replied, "You people do not know it but I want to eat meat; that is why I want to give my daughters to that man. I know he does foolish things and does not care about the holy things but he is nevertheless a good hunter."

So Tucks In and his wife gave two of their best buffalo horses to Two Shields and he married the two girls and came to Tucks In's lodge to live. Since Two Shields was an orphan and had no regular lodge he did not put up anything. Tucks In had two sons and they would go out hunting and bring in all the meat that the household could use. The family treated him well for he was a great help in getting meat and they did not want to lose him. It was a good place to go visiting. There was always plenty of food, for Two Shields hunted and the women worked hard in the gardens.

People were soon saying that Tucks In was a great man for he was very generous; whenever one went to that lodge, he would find it full of their relatives. The women were busy all the time tanning robes to sell to the trader to get guns and ammunition for Two Shields and his two younger brothers-in-law. One time he found some stray horses and gave them to his father-in-law.

Two Shields was such a good provider that Short Bull offered him his daughter named Spotted Woman. Then Two Shields had two lodges to provide for and Tucks In's relatives didn't come so often. He would stay at one lodge for a short time and then he would move over to the other lodge. When hunting, he would take the meat to the lodge where he was living at that time and the women of that lodge would take part of it to the other family. But the lodge where he lived would get the greater share. If either family had objected to the arrangement, it would have got no meat.

He left Spotted Woman because her family was not satisfied with the arrangement. If the family had wanted him bad enough they could have given him another horse and asked him to come back but I guess they were glad to be rid of him for they had another man in mind.

Although Two Shields was a good hunter, he was not too smart. One time the Fort Buford band was up near Poplar hunting and the men found a gray mare that was so wild they could not catch her. Two Shields threatened to kill her but the older men who understood the holy things said, "You must not kill that horse; it may be that she comes out of the earth and goes back in again when she has enough to eat. That is why her mane and tail are so long. Horses are holy. If you kill her, she may bring you bad luck."

Two Shields did not believe that so he waited for her at a waterhole and killed her. The people said that he would surely have bad luck. More than twenty years later, after the people were put on the Reservation, Two Shields, while mowing hay, was cut on the foot and bled to death.

It was not uncommon for a family to attempt to marry their girls to men who were already married and had families. If the two households were related and the women were of the same clan, this prearranged plan was often very satisfactory, particularly when a shortage of eligible husbands existed. This arrangement was often made between related households so that each could have the services of a good provider. It was less likely to be more than a temporary arrangement when the second household was not on intimate terms with the other one. Then each household would try to outdo the other and in the end one would become tired of the arrangement.

Owing to the greater risks taken by males in warfare and hunting, adult females greatly outnumbered the males, often 2 to 1. Monogomy was rare. Divorce was common. When there were children, families were less likely to break up. While making this study, the Hidatsa said that Wolf Chief was one who had more than the usual number of wives. Wolf Chief enumerated his various marital ventures and seemed proud of many of his conquests. His only regret was that with so many wives, he was childless in his old age. The variety of ways in which he obtained a spouse and the complexity of his marital relations are given below in his own words:

When I was 18 years old and single I had a dream of four frames surrounding my father's sacred bundles, the outer one being old and broken down. I remembered my dream and told my father how I saw willows in a circle like the fishtrap and that there were four concentric circles with the outer one broken down. He said, "I often think of the way that you and your friends play here in front of these skulls [16] and now this dream has been given to you by these 'grandfathers.' It means that you will give the 'walking' ceremony four times and make your wives 'granddaughters' of the buffalo bulls.[17] It also means that you are going to live to be an old man for the last circle of sticks is old and broken down."

I thought that I would have my wife "walk" with the buffalo when I married and then I would surely have a long life. While the other young men of my age were out looking for the enemies, I used to dress up and go out through the village looking at the girls; but one day the enemy came to the village and I thought that this time I will surely have to fight. I went out and, being brave, I was to the front chasing the enemy when one man turned and shot my horse, killing it. When the fight was over all my "fathers," the men of the Waterbuster clan, were proud of me because I was so brave and sang the honor songs.

When I came back to our lodge, a girl stepped up in front of me and I asked what it meant. She asked where my bed was and I showed her. I felt bashful for I was only 18 at the time. Her name was Different Snake; she had been married and was separated from her husband. She said "You are not supposed to go out tonight."

Seeing us together at my bed, my mother came over and said, "Will you want any supper? It seems that I have a daughter-in-law." Different Snake said that we should go to bed so she took off my moccasins and leggings. When she came near me I was not bashful any longer and possessed her. In the morning my mother got up and prepared breakfast for us and we sat together on a robe she spread for us. When it was daylight I was bashful again and did not talk much with Different Snake.

I did not love her for she had come to me without being asked. I was fond of another girl who had not been married so I thought as I sat there eating my breakfast, "I will go out and stay away for a while; it will be better to separate from her."

I went out and did not go back for 4 nights when I heard that she had left. While I was out I met the girl I liked and she said that she had heard I was married. I told her I did not like Different Snake. She told me that I should go back as I was married but I told her that I would not. I kept seeing her and 3 nights later I got her to come with me to my mother's lodge. She was Brown Blossom, a Mandan. The families exchanged presents after she came to live with me.

Now that I was married, I thought that I should give the "walking" ceremony. I thought that Brown Blossom was quite young and might not obey me so I mentioned the matter to my father. My father said, "We will tell your mother about it and she will advise you. Since you have really promised, you should not back out. When your mother comes in we will have her explain it to your wife, also to your mother-in-law, and it may be that they can persuade your wife to help."

---

[16] The Waterbuster clan bundle. See pp. 467–473 for the rites.
[17] The Painted Red Stick rites. See pp. 451–463.

The women all agreed to it, thinking that it would make me a good husband; then my wife would be with me always and we would have a good living. My wife's brother said, "It is a great thing for it is hard to do. If he puts you in the ceremonies that way, it is like giving you to the gods. Then the gods will take good care of you. You must not be bashful or refuse the holy men for they are doing that for your welfare."

When everything was arranged between my wife's relatives, I talked to her about it, telling her how much I wanted to give the ceremony and have her "walk" with the gods and become a "granddaughter" to my fathers [18] but that I hated to ask her. She immediately replied "It is all right; my people have advised me to do this for you, for then you will stay with me. It will show that we love and respect each other and that you want to get along with me and not leave me."

My father said to me, "I think this is a good thing you are doing. I had your mother in the same ceremony and she was always the right kind of woman after that. Your wife is old enough to understand and this way you will have a good living and she will be faithful to you. If you give it four times as in your dreams you will be a great man and have good luck and a good home. You must go onto the lodge and announce the ceremony saying, 'I am promising to light the fire and give you the light. I promise to make feasts for my fathers all over the world. I want to see my people well fed with enough food for a good living.' "

Brown Blossom was in the ceremony 2 nights, going to the various holy men and saying, "I will take you out," but each would pray for her in the lodge instead of having intercourse with her. My father had told me not to think about it if I saw her going out, saying "If you think of your wife when someone takes her out, you will not be successful. When I was doing my part in the same ceremony, sometimes the men took my wife out and other times they gave her the red sticks to press to her chest. Then when we went to bed I could always tell the difference for it seemed that she smelled good and had new life."

I happened to look in the direction of the door and saw that Walking Chief of my father's clan, the Waterbusters, was taking her out. When they returned, I asked her to go to Poor Wolf, Waterbuster Clan, and he prayed for her. The next day she hid and was afraid to go through with the ceremony. I thought that I would not be able to finish the ceremonies; then I would surely have bad luck for not finishing what I had promised the gods. I went to a clan brother, Knife, who said, "My younger brother, you do not need to stop the ceremony. All the women married to men of the Prairie Chicken clan are eligible to go in with you and help you out. So you can use my wife for the next 2 nights."

I was angry at my wife for hiding. My people thought that some women were afraid of the ceremonies and that I should not beat her. I began seeing Iron Woman every day and 5 days after the ceremony was finished she told me that my wife was seeing Small Bull. He had gone along when the women were picking Juneberries and had picked for my wife. I was angry at my wife so I brought Iron Woman to my father's lodge without paying her, for she was looking for a man at that time. Then I had two wives. After 4 days with two wives, during which time I directed all of my attentions to Iron Woman, the other took her things and left. I was glad that Iron Woman was looking for a man and had told me about my wife's affair with Small Bull for, by getting her, my "joking relatives" no longer teased me about my wife who ran out on me at the ceremony. So I proved to them that I could get plenty of wives, even without paying horses for them.

---

[18] Heretofore she was a daughter-in-law to Wolf Chief's "fathers."

While I lived with Iron Woman, another young woman named Folds-her-Robe would watch for me and stop to talk. I liked to have her stop me that way for some of my "joking relatives" were sure to see us. This made Iron Woman angry, but she did the best she could to hold me. In a few months I brought Folds-her-Robe to my father's lodge but I did not have to put up any horses for her either. Then I had two wives who said mean things to each other all the time. I got tired of their constant quarreling and used to go out through the village looking for other young women. When I came back I would find that they had been fighting. I would talk to both of them and try to make peace between them for it had not been long since my other wife, Brown Blossom, had walked out and hidden during the ceremony.

My mother would keep saying to my wives, "After a while you women will have children and then you will get along better together."

Buffalo-with-Grey-Penis was going out hunting with his wife and wanted me to go along. I wanted to go for he was a good hunter and his wife was my "grandmother." They came to my mother's lodge and invited my two wives to go along for they knew that I would not trust them alone in the village. I got powder and bullets from the trader. I left Iron Woman with my parents for she did not care to go along. We set out afoot, just the four of us, and walked to the mouth of the Little Missouri where we camped. We hunted up the Little Missouri where we shot elk and cured the meat, drying it over a slow fire. In all we killed five elk and two deer. We made four bullboats of the four elk hides to float the meat and the four of us to Fishhook Village. Before we returned, the women divided the meat equally between them. When we reached the bank at the village my wife called her brother, Old Bear, and her sister, who was Buffalo-with-Grey-Penis's wife's sister, and the two came to the river bank. I thought that since the meat belonged to my wife, it was her right to dispose of it as she wished, so I took my gun and personal things and went to my mother's lodge.

My wife came in shortly afterward with a bundle of meat as large as she could carry on her back; what she could not carry she had given to her brother and sister. Bringing so much meat to our lodge made my mother very happy, for my wife did not have to do that since she had many relatives. My mother set to cooking some of the meat. Iron Woman was still in the lodge but she did not say much. She was as surprised as the rest of us that Folds-her-Robe had brought us so much meat. Folds-her-Robe was with me all the time and sat down with me when the food was ready but my other wife would not join us. My mother dished out her share and took it to her. When I looked at her from where I sat eating with Folds-her-Robe, she would put her head down and would not talk. Then she refused the food, picked up two dry robes she had been decorating, and went out. After she left, my mother told me that she had heard in the village that Iron Woman's people had told her to come back home for Wolf Chief had left one of his wives and would do it again for he was not good to his wives.

While I had Folds-her-Robe with me, I found another girl that I became fond of so one day I hid myself out in the woods so that I could talk to her. My wife must have suspected us for she came along and found us talking. When I went home she was angry. She turned her face from me that night; in the morning she would not eat so I went out for a while visiting my friends. When dinner was ready, she refused to eat and cried, saying to my mother, "I have been doing the best that I can for your son, going out after meat, and caring for his things. Now I do not think I can get along with him." Then she picked up her bedding and walked out.

When I got back my mother told me what had happened but I did not say anything for I knew another girl who had not been married. I liked this Bird Woman very much but it was awful hard to see her alone. Her mother watched her all the time and never let her go out alone. Her father never paid much attention to her for while he was caring for this family he was also running around with other women all the time. His wife did not worry for she was caring for, and was good to, her husband's mother who was old. They had lived together so long that she no longer paid attention to his love affairs and knew that he would always come back. It was a long time before I was able to get Bird Woman alone where I could talk to her, for William Bell was watching to catch her alone to talk to her, too, even though he was also watching for Looking-for-Sweetgrass. At last she learned that I was watching and following her and that I wanted to marry her. She made it as hard as possible for me to talk to her. One night I met her and asked her to marry me. She said, "You are married; you don't need me." When I told her that I had sent my wife out she said, "I am not a foolish girl; I won't marry you unless you give me a horse."

I gave her the horse which she took to her brothers who gave me a poorer one in return. Then she came to my parents' lodge to live. Bell married Looks-for-Sweetgrass. That summer we were out hunting along the Yellowstone for we heard that there were many buffaloes out there. Because my wife was young, I took my sister along to teach her how to cure meat and hides. I had a good running horse and killed several buffaloes so we had plenty of meat and hides. We were hunting about 10 miles from the Yellowstone and my father said that we should take care when skinning the buffaloes not to cut holes in the hides or they could not be used for bullboats. My father thought that we would need four bullboats for our meat so my wife and I went out to get the poles. While we were cutting the poles, scouts rode by and called that a small herd was nearby so I left my wife to finish trimming the poles while I went out for another hide for the boats.

When I came back with the hide, from a distance I saw two people talking together. I discovered that it was William Bell talking to my wife. Then I remembered that I used to meet his wife before he married her and could have taken her away from him instead of marrying Bird Woman so I did not worry. When I came back to camp my sister was worried because Bird Woman had not come back and thought that she might have drowned. She kept looking out and wondering about my wife's disappearance until I told her that my wife was out with William Bell.

My sister said, "She went out after some wood; it is too bad; I thought she would be different from the others."

I said to my sister, Brown Woman, "You can divide the meat and bullboats so that she has half. I know William Bell's wife for I have talked to her before. I do not think it will be very hard to get her to come over here with us."

I went to her lodge after dark and lay down close to it so that I could look in and see which side she was sleeping on. When it was quiet inside, I went up and lifted the cover, for their tent was a frame covered with robes. At first she was startled. I told her who I was and added, "Your husband is out in the brush with my wife." That made her very angry. I said, "I do not think your husband is coming back tonight so there is no reason to be afraid if I come in with you." So I pulled off my clothes and crawled under her blanket and told her to do the same. My brother-in-law, White-Finger-Nails, who was the brother of Bird Woman, was sleeping in the lodge so we made enough noise to make sure he knew what was going on. I thought this would shame him so my wife's brothers would scold Bird Woman.

During the night Bell came in and, seeing that we were together, he went out again. In the morning I took Looks-for-Sweetgrass back to my mother's camp. She brought her share of the dried meat with her. Some families were bringing down their meat with horses but ours was using bullboats. My new wife and I painted up and dressed in our best clothes so everyone could see how happy we were. Others were floating along, too, but we kept a little to the side of the others. I was singing the Fox Society songs as we floated along but at the same time I had my eyes on some other girls. This way I got separated from my family. Hearing a noise, I saw that my new wife and Bird Woman were fighting with bullboat paddles so we paddled off where Bird Woman could not hit her.

When we got back to the village, Looks-for-Sweetgrass gave all of her meat to her mothers, sisters, and brothers. Then she came to me at my mother's lodge. I liked her for she did such fine quill and bead work so I kept her for a year. During that time I again had the 4-day walking ceremony for the buffaloes. We went through it together and while she was taking the kettles back after the ceremony was completed, I stopped to smoke with some of my friends. I caught her standing with White Belly, one of my friends, holding hands. I said to them, "You two people stand there very pretty," but my feelings were badly hurt for he was a clansman. I went back home and closed up the door so there was no chance for her to get in. I knew he would take her out.

Now that I had gone through the ceremony with Looks-for-Sweetgrass, I was sure that I could get a good wife who had not been married. I found a girl named Otter who was the daughter of Red-Buffalo-Cow, the head chief of the Nuptadi Mandan. I tried hard to get her, for none of the young men could boast that they had possessed her. We could see that she warranted that good reputation; she worked hard and never seemed to want to get away from her mothers to talk to the men. It took me a long time to marry her for she wanted three horses while I tried to marry her without putting up horses. I tried to get her to love me; I tried to get her to go out with me alone on the prairies. She refused each time I asked her. I could see that her people were not worried for they had confidence that she was not going to elope. At last I had to give in and put up the horses. My brothers and sisters helped me and we had the feast at my mother's lodge. Immediately, her family paid me a horse to come to my wife's lodge to live.

Red-Buffalo-Cow was good to me. We were of the same clan and he treated me like a brother. He would say to me, "Sometime you must invite the old people to eat with you here and then you may become a chief, too." This was much different than in the Hidatsa lodges where the fathers-in-law were not as friendly. At that time I was strong enough to stand many hard hunting trips without eating during the day. I would go out hunting often and we surely had a good home. I had two mothers-in-law there. The Government issued out two guns to each tribe and my father-in-law got one with many shells. He said, "My son-in-law, here is a gun for you; now you can kill all the game you want."

He had other daughters; All-Comes-Out was about 2 years younger than Otter, and Antelope Woman was much younger. One day when Otter was several months pregnant, my father-in-law said to me "I am well satisfied with the way you treat us, bringing in meat from the hunt and bringing me the candy and goods from the trader. We do not think we can find a better husband for our daughters so you can have All-Comes-Out but not Antelope Woman, for it is up to her whom she marries since she has been married before." I took All-Comes-Out without putting up any horses and was with her all the time while Otter was pregnant. The baby was a boy; my father-in-law named him Standing Coyote from a dream in which he saw a coyote standing looking out over the land.

I slept with All-Comes-Out while Otter was nursing Standing Coyote. Antelope Woman's mother and sisters talked of giving me Antelope Woman, too, but I did not learn of that until later. One day I lay in bed with the rear curtain raised for it was hot in the earth lodge. I had just come from bathing in the river and was lying in bed naked. Antelope Woman came around to the back of the bed and said, "I will lie beside this man." I moved over and she crawled in with me. While I possessed her, my oldest wife lifted the curtain and told us it was wrong so Antelope Woman left. Then I went outside and stayed in the village until late that evening. Otter met me when I came in and said "Why don't you go to your new wife? I saw you in there. You have treated my younger sister like a dog. You can leave. We are not dogs."

I left because it was their lodge. I did not mind so much leaving my wives even though Otter had been in the walking ceremony twice with me for she was not a blood relative. It was hardest to leave my son. When the other women heard about it, there was trouble in the family, for Antelope Woman had been married before even though she was the youngest of the three sisters. The family did not object to my coming to see the boy, for it was not my fault, and then I stayed with All-Comes-Out again. Otter would quarrel with me even though I did not stay with her since she was nursing the baby. One day she said to me, "Why don't you go back to Antelope Woman and leave All-Comes-Out alone? Antelope Woman may have a disease and then you will pass it on to my sister, All-Comes-Out. We have had plenty of chances to marry. You are not the only eligible husband around here." That made me very angry so I left Red-Buffalo-Cow's lodge.

Two days later my mother said, "Your mother-in-law was here while you were out; she wants you to come back."

I replied, "I do not think I will go back; they made me angry telling me that I was not the only man and that the other girl might be diseased."

A few days afterward I had my eyes on another girl named Rubs Herself and I thought that I would like to marry her. I stood around near her lodge, trying to get a chance to talk to her. At the same time, White Belly was watching for her. Then I learned that she had married him. I had met her once alone and talked to her. I was hurt when I learned that another had got ahead of me. I still tried to talk to her but it was much harder now that she was married. One dark evening I saw her in front of her husband's lodge and seized her saying, "I have tried hard to see you."

She said, "You must not do that for I am married now and they might hear you." Her husband did hear us and came running out so I ran off before he could see who was with her.

It was customary for the men to sit on the earth lodges during the day and watch the people as they went about their work in the village. I sat down on a lodge with some of my friends where I could watch White Belly's lodge. I wanted to find out if she had been beaten. I saw her going toward the bank and met her between the lodges. She had been crying. She said, "He found out about last night and has been beating me. The last time he hit me on the shoulder and nearly knocked me down."

I said, "You should go to my lodge for he is angry; I do not think he will treat you kindly now that he knows I have been with you. I think I will treat you better than my clan brother, White Belly."

She replied, "I will go along to your lodge if you are not afraid of him. He told me that if he ever caught me out that way again with a man he would beat me and the man too."

I knew that some men were not very brave and would make trouble when their wives were stolen. White Belly was always cutting up in the Stone Hammer Society meetings; sometimes when the society was not meeting he would steal things; he would even carry on with others' wives but I thought he might not be brave so I said, "If we stay around here, he may catch us or do something foolish. He might treat you even worse than he has and come to my mother's lodge for you. We will run away. I will have my saddle horse hidden in the trees. We will go up to Fort Buford and stay until things quiet down."

I asked my mother to prepare me food as I was going to Fort Buford. Next day when Rubs Herself went to the place we were to meet, I came down from the earth lodge and met her there. She had a robe along and we put it on the horse and rode double, keeping to the heavier timber. She was afraid for she thought that her mother-in-law suspected something. We traveled fast and came to a place in the heavy timber where we stopped to eat. There I possessed her and then we rode along slowly. Soon someone was riding toward us and I saw that it was her husband. He pulled her off the horse, whipped her, and even knocked her down and kicked her. At first I intended to fight with him and then I thought the better of it.

She said to me, "Why don't you help me? Don't stand there and look at me." So I said to White Belly, "You came after your wife and now you want to kill her." I knew that I would never fight with him for it was not right for people, particularly those of the same clan, to fight. But she was his wife and he had the right to take her. I knew that people would say bad things of White Belly for taking back by force a wife who did not want to live with him. He put her on the horse and walked, leading the horse. I stood there after they left and did not know what to do. I wondered which of White Belly's joking relatives would say most to him. I thought that they might say too much to him and that he might even kill me. Still I kept thinking of that woman but I was consoled to know that I had not been entirely unrewarded for my trouble. Finally I mounted and galloped toward Fort Buford and Crow-Flies-High's village, arriving there the next day after sleeping out in the timber. I went to Two Bull's lodge to live, for he was a close relative of my clan.

I had not been there long when I found an eligible woman named Many Growths who was not married. Finally I saw her alone and talked to her. She said that she would marry me but I would have to give her one horse. I visited her a second time and then she wanted two horses. I decided to look for two horses but I tried to marry her without giving up horses, telling her I did not have a home and only a few relatives there. When Two Bulls heard that she wanted two horses he offered me two old ones for mine which was a good runner. I gave her Two Bull's two horses and her parents invited me to come to their lodge to live. I lived with her in Standing Bear's lodge that summer.

The people planned to go farther west to set up the winter village under the leadership of Poor Bull who had had many dreams of the buffaloes even though he had never given the big buffalo ceremonies. The people thought that he would certainly be able to call the buffaloes close to the village. Since I gave my good running horse to Two Bulls when I was married, I did not have a horse so my wife and I went back to Fishhook Village to get my gray gelding to use in the hunt. I saw White Belly who was not very friendly for a clansman since his joking relatives were still annoying him even though he then had a different wife. I was just past 30 at this time.

We went as far west as Poplar Creek and learned that there were buffaloes farther up that creek; so we went there and found a Sioux camp of 400 tipis. They invited us to join them so we traveled along to Sand Creek and finally to Wolf Mountain where there was a trading post run by Weidman, Bears Arm's brother-in-law. Buffaloes were numerous there so we stopped but the Sioux went on. The White hunters were bringing in green hides for the women to tan at $4 a robe. Our group stayed around the trading post all spring tanning and decorating robes for the trader since the council had decided to ask permission of the man in charge of the steamboat to send the old people and children back to Fort Buford with him. Those of us who went by land did not travel as fast as the older people. When I got to Fort Buford, I decided to go down to Fishhook Village to see my parents. I asked my wife to pack up some of the dry meat for them. I left my wife at Fort Buford but it was not because we did not get along well. I would have gone back to her since she did not want to live at Fishhook Village if I had not seen Coyote Woman, a Mandan.

Coyote Woman was very beautiful and I decided to marry her if I could. When I had seen her a few times she said she wanted three horses. I did not promise her at once for I wanted to marry her without putting up the horses. Finally I put up the horses anyway, but my brothers and sisters gave me most of the help. Then her father, Big-Foot-Bull, paid us to come to his lodge to live. Some of the people thought that it was wrong for me to marry her for she was of the Prairie Chicken clan. Others thought that it was all right since we came from different tribes. I got along quite well with her. She helped me in the walking ceremony and did all she could to help me buy my father's Wolf bundle rites.[19] It was not long after we were married that the people went out onto the reservation and we came up here. She died shortly afterward of tuberculosis and then Big-Foot-Bull gave me her sister named Sweetgrass Blossom who died shortly of the same disease. Then he gave me a third sister named Woman and she died.

By this time the homes were all established on individual allotments on the reservation. The agency was established at Elbowoods and Indian judges were appointed to assist the Agent. Then I married Moves Sweetgrass. She had been married to Edward Goodbird; they could not get along so they separated. She came to me and wanted to marry me so I took her. I had been told that no one could get along with her but at that time I was single and could not find anyone else. I thought, since there is no other woman available who will marry me, I will do the best I can to satisfy her. Whenever we went places I bought her nice clothes. At this time there were Squaw Dances, for the old ceremonies were not given so much, but I did not care to go myself. She liked to go and I always gave her permission to go even though I did not go along.

She complained that I was stingy. She would say, "When I go to the dances, you should have me give flour, sugar, and calicoes.[20] When I go there, I am the only one who does not give things away." She was so mean to my mothers that they stopped coming to see us and I did not like that. At this time I was caring for George Bassett, who was of my father's clan, for he was ill and poor. She refused to care for him and would not prepare my meals for me when I was working in the field.

One day she said, "I would like you if you would only give away many things at the dances. Then I would carry out your orders."

[19] See "The Wolf Ceremonies" for her contribution (pp. 392–433).
[20] Wolf Chief had a store at Independence at this time.

At that time I was afraid that she would tell lies to the Indian judges at the Agency and they would criticize me. I went to my good friend Major Clapp and said, "I am married to Moves Sweetgrass but she does not attend to my cooking She runs around all the time to the dances. I tell her you do not want the Indians to dance. She wants to give away all of our things at the dances. She dances and comes back late. You are the agent and if you say I must keep her, I will." Major Clapp asked me to bring her to the Agency for the next issue of Govern ment rations. He asked her, "Does your husband refuse to go to dances? Do you ask him to give away property? When he comes in from work, do you tell him to cook his own meals? Do you ask others to dance and to take you to dances?" Without waiting for her answers the agent said that she was wrong to demand so much and that people should not dance all the time. Then he divorced us. But the three Indian judges, Good Bear, Sitting Bear, and Black Eagle wanted me to take her back and try it again.

I said to them, "I can't. If you want to know her better, you should marry her, yourselves." Then I walked off, for I knew that the Agent was on my side. [End of Wolf Chief's narrative.]

From Wolf Chief's narrative, something of the range of marriage patterns can be observed. In some instances there were no rites whatsoever, the wife moving in with Wolf Chief. In other instances there was an exchange of horses and other property. He avoided giving horses or enlisting the assistance of his relatives in completing the marriage whenever possible, and openly boasted of his extra-marital adventures. We note that he avoided marrying those with children. He expressed sadness only when separated from Otter because of his love for his son, Standing Coyote. All through the narrative we see him referring to his dream of a long life promised him if he gave his wives four times in the "walking" ceremony to call the buffaloes. Having assisted him in the rites, his wives are cast off with little show of emotion. When he gave the "walking" ceremony with Looks-for-Sweetgrass, he concluded that his social stature was so much higher that he could get a better wife and tried to marry a woman who had never been married before, the daughter of a Mandan chief. We see that when Wolf Chief locks Looks-for-Sweetgrass out of his lodge because of an affair with White Belly, separation is accepted by both parties. A few years later, however, when Wolf Chief steals Rubs Herself, White Belly does not accept the situation and threatens to kill Wolf Chief, his own clan brother.

He also had his eyes on a captive, while with the Sioux on Sand Creek, but was unwilling to buy her from the man who had captured her because he disliked putting up horses. He did not dare steal her, for he considered that equivalent to stealing a man's horse or gun, which to Wolf Chief was different from eloping with another man's wife. In no instance did the aggrieved man's clan destroy property of Wolf Chief's household or clan, for most women with whom Wolf Chief was involved had themselves been involved in numerous marital adventures. We see that when William Bell has an affair with Bird Woman, Wolf Chief bravely moves in with Bell's wife. He is unwilling, however, to defend Rubs Herself from a beating inflicted by White Belly because of public opinion which gave a man the right to take back his wife if he was willing to face the ridicule of his joking relatives.

We must not infer that Wolf Chief's record is characteristic of his time. Wolf Chief lived in a prominent household with parents who stood high in the estimation of the tribe, for Small Ankles had not only distinguished himself in warfare but had obtained numerous sacred bundles. His wives were also prominent in various ceremonies in their own right. Small Ankles had also been honored by being selected as chief of the winter village. During his youth, Wolf Chief had older brothers and a brother-in-law who provided for the household. He usually dressed up and walked through the village when the other young men were preparing for war. His early efforts at fasting were not very ambitious. He showed so little interest that, at one time, his father criticized him sharply in public for his indifference to fasting. It was indeed an extreme measure for a father to reprimand a son. By Hidatsa standards, Wolf Chief would not be considered a good son-in-law so we see that most families did not invite him to live with them.

Further understanding of Hidatsa family relations is brought out by a study of Bear-Looks-Out's family. He was one of the "village builders" or "protectors of the people" when Fishhook Village was built in 1845. At that time he was married to Corn Woman, a Mandan, who had assisted him in purchasing the Mandan Corn Bundle years before. A few years later he married four girls who had lost their parents in the smallpox epidemic of 1837 and who had been raised as sisters by Swan. Bear-Looks-Out maintained their separate household and the five women assisted him in purchasing Old-Woman-Who-Never-Dies and other ceremonial rites. Bear-Looks-Out was a good hunter and the women were good workers. He also got many things for helping in the ceremonies. He would invite in many people to eat with him. Corn Woman died first but he preserved the Mandan Skull Bundle which had come from her father. With this background, we will examine the later family life of this household of four sisters occupying two different earth lodges, as related by Crows Heart:

People liked to go to Bear-Looks-Out's lodges for he always had good things to eat. It was not known that the women were not getting along, for their lodges were used for the White Buffalo and Goose Society dances and the women were officers. When their children were nearly grown and my mother's brother named Bears Heart had grown children, he ran away with Bear-Looks-Out's two younger wives. I can remember that Bears Heart was always chasing after women even though his own wife never divorced him for it. He was my *'ptáwada-todɛ'* and was always bossing me around, telling me just what I ought to do. He would tell me that I should stay away from the girls, for chasing girls would hinder my war record. He would tell me that girls had vaginal teeth that would bite me. He would always bring up the matter of fasting whenever he came to our lodge, and tell me to stay away from the girls and forget about them. My mothers used to tease him for he was always doing what he told me not to do.

Bears Heart was not well-to-do at the time he ran away with Different Sage and Juneberries, Bear-Looks-Out's two youngest and prettiest wives. They had to walk out west to the Crows for he had no horses and his relatives would not help. As soon as Bear-Looks-Out missed his wives, the people of his clan helped him look for them, for at first they thought something had happened to them. Bear-Looks-Out knew that sometimes they met other men, for it was hard to watch four wives, but he thought nothing of it as long as they attended to their work and did not cause too much gossip. That is why he had his clansmen watching for him. When Bears Heart, my clansman, was missing they knew that he had gone off with them.

My relatives of the Prairie Chicken clan met and put up goods to take to Bear-Looks-Out so that he would not destroy their things or shoot their horses. Several brought horses. Then they went to Bear-Looks-Out's lodge and offered to give him the things but Bear-Looks-Out refused the things saying, "What is this for?"

My mothers' brothers said, "We thought you would be angry. Don't you know that Bears Heart has taken your two younger wives?"

Bear-Looks-Out laughed and said, "Why should I get angry? I am getting old so those younger women don't want me. Take your stuff back and keep it. I am not going to do anything about it. I know those women asked Bears Heart to go away with them."

At the time they eloped, a Hidatsa hunting party was on the Missouri above Knife River. They decided to cross the Missouri well below their camp so as not to be seen by the hunters for fear that the Waterbusters in that camp would seize the women and beat Bears Heart. They made a raft of logs and put their clothing, food, and weapons on it, swimming back of the raft and pushing it across the river. In midstream the raft came apart and their things were all lost. While they were sitting on the bank naked wondering what to do, a hunter from the Hidatsa camp came along. He was one of Bears Heart's joking relatives. When Bears Heart told him what had happened, the hunter teased him about it. Bears Heart asked him to ride to the camp and ask help of the Prairie Chicken clan for himself and of the Knife clan for the women. The people of the Prairie Chicken clan sent word back that they could not help him, even while they were getting the things together for it was their duty to help their own clan members. Bears Heart was sad when he heard that his clan members, even though they were of the Hidatsa and not the Mandan Prairie Chicken clan, would not help him. He was contemplating returning to Fishhook Village with the women when things were brought down to them from the hunting camp. The people of the Prairie Chicken clan sent Bears Heart three horses, a gun with ammunition, and clothing, while the women of the Knife clan sent clothing and bedding for the women. They told Bears Heart not to come to their camp for Bear-Looks-Out's clan relatives were angry. The three went west to the Crows where shortly afterward Different Sage was captured by the Blackfeet and became the wife of a chief who appreciated her fine quillwork. Bears Heart was wounded in the battle but Bear-Looks-Out's relatives who lived with the Crow [21] would not help him so he had to walk back to the camp unassisted after the bleeding had stopped.

Some time later, a Crow who had been a good hunter but was then ill wanted raw kidneys to eat. Hearing that Bears Heart was a good hunter but had no fast horse, the Crow sent his young wife with Bears Heart to get meat. When Bears Heart saw how pretty the woman was, he thought how lucky he was; he could kill a buffalo at a distance from the other hunters and possess her while they were butchering. With this idea in mind, he sent her to a distant point near the woods and killed a buffalo there. Before he could tie up his horse and begin the butchering, the woman's father and brother joined them, never giving him a chance to be alone with her. Bears Heart suspected that a trick had been played on him so the next time the Crow offered to send his young wife with Bears Heart, he refused. The Crow men tease each other a great deal and talk about sex all the time so they would say, "The next time we go out hunting, we will let Bears Heart take our wives. Then we will get much fat meat."

Bears Heart stayed with the Crow Indians 1 year and then he brought Juneberries back to the village. When Bear-Looks-Out heard that they were back, he had his other two wives, the sisters of Juneberries, cook a big meal. Then he invited Bears Heart to come and eat with him. Some people thought that he should not go but Bears Heart said to them, "I have to go for he has invited me. I have to die sometime."

Three of his friends went with him to protect him if there was trouble. After they had smoked, one of the men said to Bear-Looks-Out, "I heard that you invited Bears Heart so I came along with him to see whether you were angry or whether you had just called him in to feed him."

Bear-Looks-Out said, "I am not angry at Bears Heart. I was angry at those women because they did not want me any longer and left me. I want you to come here, my brother,[22] whenever you want to smoke."

Bears Heart and Bear-Looks-Out were often seen together after that. Bears Heart often called on his former family but he never went there to live again for his other wife had grown children to take care of her. [End of Crows Heart's narrative.]

Reactions to the loss of a wife by elopement differed with the individuals. One should pretend disconcern, or, when the elopers had returned, invite the woman back home and there, after painting and dressing her up, put her on a good horse and take her back to her new husband. When this was done the woman would cry from shame. Should a man demand his wife back, she should return to him. It was considered cowardly to force a woman to come back against her will. Frequently a man, on discovering that a wife had eloped, would set out alone or with a small party of close friends and relatives to raid some adjacent enemy camp. However much his feelings may have been hurt, he should conceal these feelings and pretend not to care. It was believed that the woman's reputation was injured if he returned with scalps and horses because she could not partake in the victory celebration with her husband. Since families wanted to marry their daughters to men with good war records, one returning as leader

---

[21] These were people who abandoned agriculture after the smallpox epidemic of 1837 and joined the Crow.
[22] Men married to sisters are classified as "brothers."

from a successful war expedition was likely to receive many invitations to marry girls who had not been married and who had good reputations, even before the victory dances were ended.

Prominent men invariably had two or more wives. The older ones had assisted the husband in achieving his ambitions by contributing towards ceremonial purchases and formal feasts for the older men and women. As a man's social status grew, his social obligations increased. Frequently the wives encouraged their husband to get another wife to help them with their work, in which case the additional wife lived with the household. A man might bring a female prisoner to his lodge to increase the number of his wives or he could marry someone from the tribe. Not uncommonly, however, it was necessary to maintain two or more households because of the objections of the other wives to moving or abandoning their lodge. Sometimes the new wife was the chief provider for her own old people. A village leader could not risk his reputation by marrying one who had carried on numerous affairs with other men. Thus he invariably married a young girl strictly trained by her parents. Being past the age when he would be offering his wives in the walking ceremonies, he would keep close watch of her and usually enlisted his clansmen and society to do likewise. He would keep her always as his favorite wife and should a situation arise when a clansman asked for a wife to take to the "walking" ceremony, he would give him one of his first wives. Knowing that he was keeping close watch of her and had the aid of his friends and relatives as well, it was considered great sport to meet her on the sly. He would take her out on hunting trips, on visits to neighboring camps, even on war expeditions, knowing that his joking relatives would tease him if they learned of an affair going on behind his back. If her lover was one of little standing in the village or belonged to a small clan and had few relatives, he was likely to be beaten. Sometimes however, the rival was a person of considerable social stature in his own right, or even a clan brother. The Hidatsa still tell and retell the story of Two Tail's and Wolf Chief's quarrel, occurring between 1826 and 1830. Bears Arm's account is as follows:

Two Tails [23] was a great gambler. He would gamble each day at Hidatsa village on the Knife River. Wolf Chief, who was one of the principal chiefs of that village, had three wives, the youngest one being much younger and very pretty. Her parents had married her to Wolf Chief but she liked Two Tails who was younger than her husband. She would send little boys to Two Tails to tell him where he could meet her.

Two Tails was getting a good reputation as a war leader after he had given both Wolf Ceremonies, was leading successful war expeditions, and was fasting often. He would gamble all day and then go out to fast for several days. One time when he was out fasting, Sun came down and said to him, "Every morning

---

[23] The name refers to two eagle tail feathers. Two Tails was the father of Four Bears, chief at the time of the Fort Laramie Treaty of 1851.

when I come up I see you sitting there. My son, you will be a great man and a leader of your people."

One day Wolf Chief learned of the affair between Two Tails and the young woman. He became very angry but he did not let on how he felt to anyone. Instead, he organized a war party and went out against the Sioux. He stole horses and camped near Hidatsa village until morning. They painted and came into the village at daybreak, driving the horses stolen from the Sioux. Wolf Chief drove the horses directly to Two Tails' lodge and called, "Two Tails, come out and see what I brought. You go out and do the same thing right away."

Two Tails knew that the people would call him a coward if he did not go out, for everyone had heard of his affair with Wolf Chief's wife. The people knew that Wolf Chief was taking his anger out on the Sioux. Two Tails organized a war party and brought back both horses and scalps. His party went directly to Wolf Chief's lodge. Two Tails called, "Wolf Chief, come out and see what I brought back. You go out and bring in only horses; I bring horses and scalps. You go out right away; we will keep this up until the snow comes."

Wolf Chief went out again and brought in horses. Then Two Tails went out, killed the occupants of an isolated tipi and brought back scalps and horses. He stopped at Wolf Chief's lodge and called, "See what I brought. You get only horses; I get both horses and scalps. My father, the Sun, asked me to do this but I like gambling better. You have hurt my feelings so you go right out again. If you lose one of your men, we will make war right here."

Then he returned to his sister's lodge and gave her the horses. The 10 men ruling the three villages [24] met to devise a plan to prevent bloodshed in the tribe They decided to take the pipe to Two Tails and ask him to make peace. They selected a man of Two Tails' clan to carry the pipe. They found Two Tails at the head of the lodge with the scalps on sticks. When they put the pipe before him, he asked the meaning of it and his clansman said, "We want you to stop going on the warpath. It might bring trouble. We want you to smoke the pipe."

Two Tails said, "If I light it, my brother, Wolf Chief, will say that I am afraid and want to quit. Wolf Chief started this because he learned I was with his wife who likes me and sends for me. I did not want to insult her so I went out with her. Now it seems he wants to get even with me. Take the pipe to him and explain these things to him. If he takes the pipe, then you can bring it to me and I will smoke it. This trouble will then be settled."

The council picked a man of Wolf Chief's clan to carry the pipe and they went to the other man. When they went in, Wolf Chief inquired what it meant and the clan brother said, "We fear that there might be trouble, for this rivalry has gone too far. Two Tails says that you did this because he visits your wife and that it is all because of your jealousy. We 10 head men have looked into this. You must discontinue this contest or there might be trouble."

Wolf Chief replied, "It is not so; I do not care what he does to my wife; I am not jealous. I wanted him to do something for the people—be brave and do things like I do for the people. You men did right coming to me, for now you know I only wanted to make him a brave man." Wolf Chief lit the pipe and when he had finished smoking, the men went back to Two Tails.

They told him what Wolf Chief had said and added, "We know that Wolf Chief is a great leader and is brave. Now you have exceeded his war record. We now have seen what you can do. You are braver than Wolf Chief." So Two Tails built up his reputation and was a leader after that, but he no longer bothered Wolf Chief's young wife.

---

[24] Bears Arm refers here to an intervillage council that was instituted shortly before to handle problems concerning relationships between villages.

Many years later after the people moved to Fishhook Village, Two Tails' son named Four Bears also had a young wife he got after he was far along in the ceremonies. One day Bear-on-the-Water, a Mandan, stole her and took her to a Mandan hunting camp. Four Bears became very angry and threatened to kill every Mandan in the village. They fled rather than attempt to pacify him with goods and horses. He called the Black Mouth society and his clansmen to go to the Mandan camp with him for his wife. They went to the camp prepared for war. He went into the tipi where she was hiding, dragged her out by her hair, and beat her for leaving her child who was, according to Four Bears, ill at the time and had no one to care for him. He jabbed her with arrows and beat her with his bow, daring the Mandans to come to her rescue. As the party left the camp, a clansman named Poor Wolf who was also leader of the Black Mouths at the time, killed a valuable stallion belonging to Bear-on-the-Water's brother, Moves Slowly. Most of the people did not approve of Four Bear's action; they considered it unworthy of a principal chief. Poor Wolf was in an embarrassing situation, for, only a few years earlier, he had stolen a Mandan's wife and nothing was done about it. Even Four Bear's best friends thought he had given a very poor argument for taking his wife back, since the child had several mothers in the lodge to care for him. [End of Bear Arm's narrative.]

The position of the older wives in the household was quite different from that of a man's young wife. The older ones were generally the owners of the lodge and the household equipment, the associated gardens, and many of the horses which they had inherited from their mothers and grandmothers within the maternal lineage. They had assisted the husband in his ceremonial activities, prepared goods to be given away on numerous social and ceremonial occasions, had acquired much knowledge of sacred lore while assisting their husband, had borne him children, had prepared feasts for the older men on orders of the husband, and had "walked" with the husband's "fathers" during age-grade purchases or certain ceremonial performances. They had come to take each other more or less for granted.

Men were, in general, afraid to have love affairs with a woman who had participated often in the ceremonies with her husband. They were even more reluctant to marry her if the husband died. Widows frequently pledged publicly during the funeral rites not to remarry and were not asked to marry thereafter. Women who had obtained considerable knowledge of the husband's sacred rites were viewed as sacred and, therefore, potentially dangerous. This avoidance applied to all men except the deceased man's brothers or those with identical ceremonial rights. When no vow was made during the husband's funeral, some man might desire to marry her. Those not acquainted with her husband's ceremonial rights were said to be foolish to marry her. There are many traditional accounts of those violating the rule by marrying the widow of an important man, only to go insane, blind, or die soon afterward. Hence there were generally a few older widows in most households.

The younger wife rarely remained a widow very long. She had taken little or no part in her husband's ceremonial purchases and ritual activities, and it would have been considered foolish for her to vow not to remarry. The men were not afraid of her for she would have little knowledge of her deceased husband's sacred lore.

From the foregoing accounts we see that marriage was always a secular activity. The bride's household, expressing their social status by demanding horses or other property, tended to eliminate suitors who came from poor and low status households. The return to the groom's household of an equal or greater number of horses and other property expressed the bride's family's estimation of the husband and his household. Strictly speaking, marriage involved only two clans, that of the husband and that of the wife. The husband's father might speak for his wife's relatives, once they had reached a decision, but his relatives had no part in the ceremony; generally they did not attend and under no circumstances would the people of the father's clan put up horses or contribute to the feast. This attitude on the part of the people of the father's clan is consistent with a broader cultural pattern that "fathers" and "father's sisters" receive gifts and give "blessings." The Hidatsa did not consider marriages of sufficient ritualistic importance to enlist the aid of the father's relatives. The mother's relatives, the members of her clan, were a man's principal cooperators and participants. The maternal grandmothers, mothers, sisters, and brothers put up the horses and other property and welcomed the new daughter-in-law into their household. It was this group who made the arrangements with the bride's relatives. Although the bride's father might prefer a different young man and discuss the matter with his wife, the bride's mothers and brothers were the ones to approve or disapprove a proposal of marriage. In completing the marriage, they were the ones who made gifts to the bride's husband's household. The groom's economic value to the wife's household was expressed by a personal gift of a horse and weapons by the bride's household with an invitation for them to live in the bride's lodge.

Marriage within the clan was strongly disapproved of but there was nothing that could be done to prevent it other than indirect controls such as ridicule and adverse comment when the couple persisted in their plans. There was no exchange of property between households and no marriage feast. Those marrying within the clan were teased by their "joking relatives." Hidatsa thought that children suffered most because of conflicts in relationships, for a man would be both a father and an older brother. Formerly, no objection was raised to marrying one of the Mandan Prairie Chicken clan when the Mandan and Hidatsa had separate villages. After they settled together at

Fishhook in 1845, the Mandan and Hidatsa clan systems were so completely equated that marriages between them were generally disparaged. Although no objections were raised to marriage within the Three-clan moiety, the Hidatsa have recently come to disapprove, according to my genealogies and native observations, marriages between certain clans of the Four-clan moiety. It was improper for one of the Waterbuster clan to marry either a Xura or Itisuku, or for a Prairie Chicken to marry a Speckled Eagle.

Marriage of a woman to one of the father's clan was as uncommon as with one of the same clan. The genealogies show that this reluctance to marry into the father's clan was of long standing. This was in sharp contrast with the Mandan who commonly and preferably had a clansman as father-in-law with whom he talked freely and without the restraints normally shown a Hidatsa father-in-law. The genealogies show a higher frequency of marriage to men of the father's clan for the Awatixa women than for the other Hidatsa village groups. This was also the village group that transmitted some sacred bundles through the clan. In the few cases of marriage to a man of the father's clan observed by my informants, the father-in-law taboo was less rigid; they had common clan interests and the father-in-law felt obliged to assist his son-in-law in society and ritual purchases. This did not, however, in any sense alter the mother-in-law taboo relationships.

Marriage of blood brothers to women classified as sisters and of the same household must have been exceedingly uncommon although, by the extension of the kinship system, males married to sisters were classified as "brothers." Cases of the sororate were numerous. The levirate operated only when the deceased husband's family so desired, after observing that the widow had mourned long.

The basic economic unit was the household or extended matrilinear family based on matrilocal residence. The older daughters invariably brought their husbands to their lodge. If there were a number of daughters, the younger ones commonly lived with the husband's people, particularly when his services were needed at home to provide for his parents. If, however, her older sisters died, she would take her husband to her own lodge to care for her parents. If her husband died or divorced her, she would return to the mother's lodge. The household would normally consist of the old parents, old men and women of the clan, daughters with their husband or husbands, unmarried daughters and sons, and usually a few orphans belonging to the clan of the females. A few households would also have a berdache either reared in the household or brought to it by marriage. With the exception of those households where, for want of a daughter, residence was patrilocal, the unit was composed of a number of elementary families held together through the female line.

Except for certain ritualistic practices celebrated by the females and sold to the daughters, the household did not perpetuate ritual practices. A man would secure his ceremonial bundles and rites from his father living in a different lodge, and sell them to his married son residing elsewhere in the village. Thus the sacred bundle rights circulated from lodge to lodge. This was in marked contrast to the Mandan system where bundles were often retained in the same household from generation to generation.

Until the small log cabins were adopted, the lodge arrangement of families varied little between households. The section to the back of the lodge was reserved for the sacred bundles of the principal male member of the household. He lived in that section of the lodge with his wives. The right side of the lodge on entering and nearest the door was penned off for the horses. Beyond the pens were the beds for the old people and the very young children. The central section contained the firepit and seats for those of the established members of the family. A section next to the door on the left side on entering, and beyond the windbreak and area reserved for the wood, was walled off for the son-in-law and his family. As time passed and the son-in-law became permanently adjusted to the others of the household, while growing in importance in the community, he and his family moved nearer the head of the lodge and took over the favorite and honored position formerly occupied by the father-in-law and his wives. The final shift to the head of the lodge was made when the father-in-law reached old age and no longer participated actively in village matters, or at any other time when the son-in-law had attained unusual respect in the village or the father-in-law died.

The women cared for the lodge and kept it repaired. When the lodge timbers were decayed and it was necessary to rebuild it, the women provided the materials for a new roof cover. They enlisted the assistance of their related households who worked together as a team. The males living in the lodge and those belonging to the household living elsewhere raised the heavier posts, beams, and timbers. It was the duty of the clan to care for its own members. Most of the female clan members assisted in one way or another, if for only a few hours, and also brought food for the workers.

When camping away from the permanent summer village for short periods during the eagle trapping season, or on other occasions when the campsite was on the river and was to be occupied for only a few months at most, it was customary to build the small "wood lodge." These were small wood-covered tipi-shaped structures built on a four-post central platform. Being smaller than the usual earth lodge structures, two or more with entrances facing each other were usually built for each household. One lodge would then be occupied by the mothers-in-law and their husband, and the other by the younger married people. Children were quartered in either lodge. After 1860, the Hidatsa largely abandoned the large circular earth lodge for winter village use. When returning to a former winter camp, the lodges still usable were repaired as shelters for the horses, storerooms, and dancing lodges, while small rectangular log cabins were built nearby with an enclosed hallway leading into the earth lodge. Often as many as four such cabins were built adjacent to the earth lodge when the household was composed of several families.

The log cabin was in general use for winter camps by 1860, and by 1865 was replacing the large circular earth lodges of the summer village as well. In 1872 McChesney reported 35 earth lodges and 69 log cabins occupied by the Mandan and Hidatsa of Fishhook Village (Matthews, 1877, p. 4).

The household economic pattern seems to have been affected little by the adoption of the log cabin. Although two or more cabins were built to house a former earth lodge household, the lodges were built adjacent to each other or as double-roomed cabins with separate entrances and an intervening doorway. Each room had a fireplace with a plastered chimney and an opening in the roof to admit light and air. When the lodge was completed, certain women skilled in making chimneys were paid to make the fireplace and construct the chimney. This right to build chimneys and fireplaces was bought in the matrilineal line like other ceremonial rights. Each room had a cache under the earth floor. Having a separate room away from the mothers-in-law, a man felt freer to invite in his friends. The economic life of the household, however, was unaffected by the change in living quarters. The women continued to plant and harvest the crops according to the ancient system. The gardens were held by the linked households and the women worked as a group curing and storing the produce without consideration to the small family lodge units. They also shared the common stores as before. A young wife living with, or adjacent to, the husband's people continued to plant crops with her mother's group, at least until she had children and was an established member of the husband's household. The son-in-law provided meat for both his own and his wife's family.

In theory, a man provided the meat and hides for his wife and her household while the wife's household provided him with the necessary horses, weapons, and knives. For the communal trips and summer hunts, however, the Hidatsa employed a more equitable system of dividing the products of the chase. These hunts being highly organized activities, all able-bodied men could not devote equal time and effort to killing the animals. Some men, especially those of the Black Mouth police society, were continuously engaged in policing the camp or guarding the encampment to forestall a surprise attack from their enemies. Others were at a distance from the encampment serving as scouts, guarding the horses at pasture, or seeking buffaloes and planning the surround. It was customary, therefore, for those with good buffalo horses to do the killing while older men with packhorses brought the meat to the camp.

Once in camp, the meat was placed in centrally situated piles where all could help themselves, irrespective of households. Older men too feeble to engage in the heavy work of butchering and transporting the meat would assist their households in erecting drying platforms. As each platform was completed, the meat taken from the common piles was sliced in thin strips and dried by households. One was considered selfish to take meat or hides that could not be cured immediately while others were able to give these things immediate attention. From native accounts, these communal hunting expeditions were happy times. A household with many active young women, having all their meat cured, would pitch in and help the less fortunate ones. Frequently the special officers refused their extra share of hides and tongues because of the size of the kill and the limited facilities for transporting it to the village.

Animals taken in corrals were divided in a different manner. After the special awards were made to those managing the rites and directing the animals to the corral, a line was drawn through the center of the enclosure from the center of the mouth to the opposite wall. Animals lying on one side of this line went to the Three-clan moiety and those on the other side belonged to the Four-clan moiety. Employing this division in 1872, we would have found 22 households butchering on the Three-clan side and 27 on the Four-clan side. Five additional households, comprising two with Arikara female members and three represented by both moieties, would have to be taken into account. According to Bears Arm, if the households were unequal in number, mixed ones butchered on the weaker or smaller side. When butchering at the corral, each household group selected one animal until there were no longer enough animals to go around, when related households went together and shared the additional ones.

The women of the household also frequently shared certain sacred and secular rights, mythological lore, techniques of basketry and pottery decorations and manufacture, household doctoring procedures, and other activities which were transmitted through the household lineage.

Due to matrilocal residence and patrilineal inheritance of most sacred rites, sacred bundles obtained by a male usually passed out of the household in one generation. Thus a man, after he had married, would normally obtain his bundles through his father living in the younger man's maternal household but belonging to a different household lineage. Although the sacred bundle rites were not long kept within the female household, the members of the various households had certain duties and obligations whenever the transfer was made. In the purchase of the father's bundle rites, a man received assistance in the form of goods and food from his brothers and their wives, mother's brothers and their wives, his sisters, and his sisters' daughters and sons when they were old enough to assist. From his wife's household he received the assistance of his wives, his wives' sisters and their husbands, and the mothers-in-law. This group of relatives, varying in number, would occupy different households but the principal contributions came from two household groups; his mother's and his wives'. The clan and society members of both the buyer and his wife were also expected to lend assistance, but their responsibilities were not as great. These many relatives and other cooperating groups lightened the burden of ceremonial purchases and enhanced the prestige of all of them.

The household group was a stable unit for generations as long as there were daughters to inherit the lodge complex. With strong loyalties to the mother's household group, any study of a Hidatsa male or female must take these ties into account. The Hidatsa say that a person without relatives is nothing.

MATURITY AND OLD AGE

Membership in the Black Mouth society was viewed as a mark of maturity and respectability. As a man moved upward through the age-grade system, his role as buyer of ceremonial rights changed to that of seller. A man's position in the lodge also changed in time. At first, as a young married man living in his wife's lodge, his section of the lodge was that nearest the door on the left side as one entered. As the older people became aged and infirm, they slowly shifted their beds and personal equipment in a clockwise direction. The most mature and active male member of the lodge would then occupy the head of the lodge where he kept his personal property and sacred bundles, and entertained his friends.

A woman's position in the household was essentially the same as that for a man. As her parents grew older and were unable to participate actively in the affairs of the household and village, she slowly took over the roles formerly performed by her mothers and maternal grandmothers. A woman would normally be participating actively in the Goose society by this time.

The Hidatsa showed great respect for age. They recognized that each person was an individual with his or her own distinctive characteristics and achievements. The rules dealing with the care of the aged and unfortunate of the clan, and the special respect shown to people of the father's clan, largely set patterns for the care of the aged within one's own immediate family. There was no such thing as abandonment of the aged and the infirm, for young people were taught early in life to respect the aged; even the least distinguished old people ought not to be neglected. There are many references in Hidatsa mythology dealing with this matter. A prominent theme of Hidatsa mythology told how some old people with little visible evidence of wealth or supernatural powers brought misfortune upon others by magical means when they were neglected —or unusual good fortune when they were treated well. The Hidatsa associated age with wisdom. They spoke well of those middle-aged people who were caring for a number of their old relatives. People would say that those lodges were occupied by generous and wise people. There, old people of the lodge, both men and women, would tell their young grandchildren of times as they used to be, teach them the sacred and traditional myths, and advise them in various matters so that when they grew up they would be of great help to the people.

An old woman without meat would go out to the edge of the village to await the return of the hunters. It was her right to demand meat of any man, regardless of his age, if he stood in the grandson–grandmother relationship to her. By the numerous extensions of the Hidatsa kinship system, a woman would normally have many grandsons in the community and none should deny her meat or hides if she so requested. Old men would not customarily do this. Instead, an old man would attend ceremonial and social functions, sitting in the honored section of the lodge, and receive gifts of many sorts from those performing the rites. In the Northern Plains where the Hidatsa lived, largely surrounded by the nomadic tribes such as the Crow and Assiniboin, they had an opportunity to observe the care of the old people of those tribes. They were well aware that both the Crow and the Assiniboin sometimes abandoned their old people when traveling. It was possible under the semisedentary life of the Hidatsa to provide much better care for their old people than those wandering tribes living near them. The result was that Hidatsa households frequently cared for the aged, widowed mothers and very young orphans from these and other nomadic tribes which came to the villages to trade for corn. The Hidatsa never seemed to have considered caring for these unfortunate people an undue hardship and my Hidatsa informants spoke highly of people who cared for the unfortunate of other tribes.

A few old couples or a single old woman who preferred to get along alone usually were to be found in all the Hidatsa villages. In some instances they were left without younger sons, daughters, or grandchildren, or they might have been childless themselves. If the old couple or old woman, as the case might be, were the survivors of a large household once living in the usual-sized earth lodge, the task of keeping the lodge in repair would be too great for them as years passed. In this instance, when the lodge needed extensive repairs, it was customary to tear down the old lodge, preserving the stronger timbers, and erect on the same ground a much smaller one built on a four-post foundation without the peripheral posts. This lodge, when covered with earth, resembled the tipi made of hides and was identical to those constructed at the eagle trapping sites. Surface outlines of ancient villages of the Hidatsa along the Missouri River frequently reveal the location of these little lodges.

Hidatsa informants were in agreement that some older couples practicing special arts and crafts found it more convenient to live apart from their extended relatives. An example of this would be an old couple, man and wife or wives, specializing in pottery making. Pottery making for the Hidatsa was a secret and sacred activity. The old woman who had bought rights in pottery making, usually from her mother's or father's sisters, would practice her skills more energetically as she grew older. She bought this right from one having ceremonial rights coming to her from the snakes. It was believed by the Hidatsa that only the snakes made pottery in former times. One day the snakes took an old couple out on the prairie where they had been working. They showed this old couple piles of dirt scattered about and explained to them that in making pottery one must mix certain clays with sand or the grit produced by crushing certain stones long used around the fires. The husband would assist his wife in the heavier operations of pottery-making such as securing the clay and paddling out the vessel forms. There were many exposed clay banks in the neighborhood of the various Hidatsa villages. The potters would test the clay to find those deposits that had the proper qualities. Near Fishhook Village, about 4 miles to the northwest, there was an exposed vein of lignite coal. The potters of Fishhook Village secured all their pottery clay from the beds immediately above and below this coal layer. The men would sack up the clay and either carry it on their backs or pack it on horseback to the village. The old men would also gather the fired stones from about the village and take them to their lodges.

Pottery making was a secret rite and one should not visit or stand around talking with those making vessels. It was customary to perform secret rites directed to the snakes and sing the appropriate sacred songs while shaping the vessels. Women were considered more skillful in impressing into the damp walls of the vessels the various designs and patterns which they had bought the right to use either at the time when the initial rights were purchased or at a later time when a particular design owned by other women met their fancy. So they would bar the door to their lodge, pass the word about through the village that they were making pottery, and work in secret. It was necessary to keep off drafts from the wet clay and the newly shaped vessels;

Most of these finished vessels were given to their own immediate relatives as gifts, knowing that the receivers were looking after their welfare. In other instances, the vessels were traded directly with women desiring pots for those things which the family did not already have. It is not known today how many pottery makers there were in the Hidatsa villages, but informants believed that only a few families made pottery.

Another category of specialists who preferred to live alone because of the nature of their activities were those who worked with flints and other stones. The Hidatsa secured most of their flint from the higher buttes and uplands west of the Missouri River. Here, irregular layers of flint were exposed and they had a number of traditional places where they quarried the stone. The best stone was that which was covered with dirt and had to be exposed, using hardened ash poles as digging sticks to break off the layers. Working of chipped stone was a ceremonial activity, and goes back to two ancient traditional systems; one derived from the large birds, such as the eagles, hawks, owls, and thunderbirds, and the other derived from the beavers. Concerning the latter system, little is known today other than what has been passed on traditionally. The former system was connected with the sacred arrows of which there were a number of bundle owners living at the time my informants were young men. Even so, they no longer practiced their skills of stone flaking. It is said that in former times a man working at stone flaking operated in a closed lodge using the light from the fireplace and, like the potters who kept their clays stored away in cache pits or shallow pits near the inner edge of the lodge, the stoneworkers likewise kept their flints moistened and covered until used. It was believed that the stone would fracture irregularly if people stood around watching and, like pottery making, stonework was done in secret.

Another organized group was that of the berdaches. These people were men who, during their late teens and after many dreams from the Holy-Woman-Above, changed their clothing to that worn by women and assumed special roles in the community. They usually formed attachments to older men, generally men without children and having trouble keeping their wives, and set up separate households. At the time this study was made, informants could remember two such people in the generation above them, but they had heard that in former times there were sometimes as many as 15 to 25 berdaches in their villages.

Since the berdaches were viewed as mystic possessors of unique ritual instructions secured directly from the mysterious Holy Woman, they were treated as a special class of religious leaders. Although a berdache might have lived within an extended household as one of the cowives, informants thought that separate households more commonly were maintained. According to tradition, these were well-to-do households. The "man-woman" worked in the garden, did bead work, and butchered as did the women. Being stronger and more active than the women, the berdache could do many things more efficiently and was never burdened down with childbearing. Accounts we have of the berdaches tell of industrious individuals working harder than the women of the village and exceeding the women in many common activities. Informants felt that separate households established around the berdache were very often better fixed than those where the men carried on active military duties.

The berdache performed many ceremonial roles. When the Sun Dance ceremonies (Naxpike) were to be performed, it was the berdache's duty to locate the log for the central post from driftwood in the river. Whenever a major ceremony was being given, the berdache would dress like the other members of the Holy Woman Society and receive gifts as an equal member with the women of the society.

The berdaches comprised the most active ceremonial class in the village. Their roles in ceremonies were many and exceeded those of the most distinguished tribal ceremonial leaders. There was an atmosphere of mystery about them. Not being bound as firmly by traditional teachings coming down from the older generations through the ceremonies, but more as a result of their own individual and unique experiences with the supernatural, their conduct was less traditional than that of the other ceremonial leaders.

The berdache was a brother or the son of a man holding tribal ceremonial rights in the Woman Above and Holy Woman bundles. There are no known instances of exceptions to this rule and the Hidatsa believed that only persons standing in these relationships to those bundles ever assumed the woman's role. The berdache commonly adopted orphans from the village or secured young daughters and sons through the capture of prisoners by their relatives, transmitting their property and their ceremonial knowledge to their younger adopted children. Like certain male medicine men, they surrounded themselves with many individual rules of conduct for guests in the lodge. This limited the activities of people associating with them and, like several outstanding male medicine men surrounded by these many rules, people tended to fear, respect, and avoid them. In this sense they resembled in their social position males possessing unique and special mysterious supernatural powers. Berdaches tended to disappear once warfare had ceased and their ceremonial system had collapsed.

LAST ILLNESS AND DEATH

Whether a doctor was called in when a member of the household became ill was largely a family matter. When it was known that an individual possessed ceremonial rights dealing with some commonplace illness, such an individual would normally be called in and paid for his services. In general, it would seem that the household more commonly relied on the supernatural powers of its own members at first. For most illnesses, help was not solicited beyond the immediate household and other near relatives. If a doctor was called in and agreed to assist after a preliminary examination, the price for his services being already determined, and it was evident that the patient would not recover, it was customary to ask the doctor to remain until death and to give comfort to the sick person. This was especially true when the doctor belonged to the sick person's father's clan for the father's clansmen had particular roles to perform at the death of their sons and daughters. Many individuals never sought aid of a doctor as they had faith in their own ceremonial bundles to carry them through life.

Most people reaching middle age and older had the clothing they were to be put away in set aside and ready for the moment of death. Since many lived many years after initial preparation of their clothing, from time to time they would substitute new items, and either wear out or give away those which they formerly had kept. Each individual at some time also indicated the person who was to "bring the robe" and had instructed him or her on how his body was to be prepared and the manner of disposal that was to be employed. Some individuals long outlived those first selected and named new ones throughout the years.

In the event of the illness of a young married person, it was customary to return to the mother's lodge. In the case of a young married man it was rather difficult to look after him in a lodge with parents-in-law since the young man's brothers and sisters would be the ones most concerned about his welfare. Thus a young man when ill would return to his mother's lodge where those coming in to look after him would have greater freedom of action.   The same applied to a young married woman living in her husband's lodge.

The Hidatsa tried to anticipate the moment of death and to have the person painted in his distinctive designs and dressed in his burial clothing before death.   The duty of attending to this fell to the members of the father's clan.   In the case of little children, this duty usually fell to some well-known father's clans-woman selected by the child's mother.   There was a formal way of addressing the woman so selected in which the mother would go to her and say "your brother's child is about to die.   You are to bring the robe."   When this was done, no one could refuse.   It was her duty to select a robe in good repair, one of the best that she had, or go out through the village and find a well-decorated robe that she thought the child would have liked.   She would then go to the lodge, dress the child in appropriate clothing, and wrap him tightly in the robe.   Other brothers and sisters or clan brothers and sisters might bring additional robes and ask that the child be buried in them or give them to some member of the father's clan who in turn was expected to provide an additional robe.   Whether child or adult, it was customary, if possible, to bury or to place the dead on a scaffold or in a tree during the day of death.   If, however, the person died late in the day and it was not possible to complete the burial arrangements that day, it was customary to leave the corpse in the lodge overnight.   Old moccasins with hot coals in them were placed in the entrance of the lodge to keep away the evil spirits and to protect the people from the ill-effects of having a dead person in the lodge overnight.   When this happened people would stay up all night awaiting the break of day for the funeral services.

It was the duty of the people of the father's clan to take care of and handle all of the funeral arrangements.   First of all there was the preparation of the body.   The manner of disposal was largely a family custom inherited from their family lines going back to the three original village groups on the Knife River.   The Hidatsa recognized that there were a number of different traditional methods of disposing of the dead.   They were well aware of the fact that more people were buried in the ground at Hidatsa village on the Knife River than at the other villages.   This was evident to the Hidatsa themselves for, after leaving the Knife River and up until a few years ago, the Hidatsa commonly made trips downriver to their ancient villages.   They had seen the many burial mounds and depressions at Knife River, at Hidatsa village, and the few that were found around Awatixa and Awaxawi villages.   The Hidatsa-proper claimed that this difference in disposal practices dated back to their first appearance on the Missouri River and they have many traditions dealing with burial in the ground.

There were some who believed that Hidatsa earth burials were adopted from the Arikara. However, this position cannot be held in light of other evidence. In the first place, it is inconsistent with the evidence to maintain Arikara origin of earth burials since both the Hidatsa and Awatixa villages were contemporaneous and situated less than a mile apart. Further evidence is the fact that in 1837 when smallpox broke out in the Hidatsa and Mandan villages, the people of Hidatsa village moved upstream a few miles below Lucky Mound Creek and lived in the woods apart from the other people. Nevertheless the smallpox did reach them at this village known today as "Where People Died of Smallpox." Several informants mentioned this village also and the many burial pits of that date were still to be seen in 1932. Old Hidatsa informants who had been to the shoreline areas of Devils Lake to the east where they formerly lived, claimed that they had seen the burial mounds of their old people who formerly lived there.

The other method of disposal was above ground in trees, on scaffolds, or under overhanging rocks. When living in winter camps, it was common to place the dead in trees. During the summer months, while occupying the permanent villages, scaffolds were erected on a four-post frame at the edge of the village. The area might contain both burials and scaffolds. In some instances all the members of some households would be placed on scaffolds, while all the members of other households would be buried in the ground. In other instances a household might practice both scaffold disposal and interment. When a person died away from the village, it was usually impossible to bring him back. If his brothers and sisters wanted his bones brought back to the village, it was then the duty of some female standing in the relationship of father's sister to the deceased to make the arrangements for the return of the skull a year later. She would then communicate with various people going out in that direction and provide them with a bag in which to place the man's skull. When it was returned to the village, it was customary to rewrap it and place it on one of the existing scaffolds with his relatives or, in the event of interment, to bury it just below the surface, over the body of one of his close relatives.

Another closely related practice was to paint the skull and set it on a nest of soft sage in one of the skull circles near the village. These skull circles were customary fasting places for those seeking dreams. When Fishhook Village was abandoned and the Hidatsa moved out on the reservation, one such skull circle was maintained on the hills northeast of Elbowoods. People coming primarily from Awatixa and Awaxawi villages on the Knife River were wrapped and set on the ground at this place. When the wrapping had deteriorated and the flesh had decayed, close relatives would remove the skulls and set them in a rough circle surrounded by buffalo skulls. This practice was abandoned a few years prior to 1932.

Occasionally a small child was buried at the outer edge of the lodge, believing that a child would be lonely away from his close relatives. In other instances, children were placed in bundles beside their relatives on scaffolds. The Hidatsa appear to have no traditions of cache-pit burials within the village. They do, however, have references to the separation of the skull and the other bones, the skull becoming a part of a skull circle while the other bones, wrapped in a bundle, were buried in a soft place along the river bank or within the fortification. There are also traditions of earth burials made in mounds or mounds built over the burial in the outline of the individual's "spirit god."

Regardless of the method of disposal employed, the same sets of relatives participated. The principal official was the one designated to "bring the robe." Other people of the father's clan assisted in building the scaffold or digging the grave. Both men and women assisted and received generous payment for their services. They likewise were viewed as the principal mourners. When a person died, most of his personal property usually was already willed away and it was the duty of the relatives to see that those promised different things received them. A man might promise his favorite buffalo horse to his "pal" or his gun to another person. When death occurred, it was the right of the brothers and sisters and the closer members of the person's clan to come in and take possession of his unwilled personal property. They, however, were obliged to put up the goods to pay those of the father's clan who had performed various services and/or others of the father's clan and certain distinguished people of the village whom they felt were entitled to special recognition.

A man's ceremonial bundles were treated in two ways. Those that were of a personal nature and that had been established by the deceased on the basis of his dreams or as gifts from a near relative were generally wrapped in the bundle with the body or hung on one of the posts of the scaffold. In no instance were they kept around the lodge or treated lightly by the survivors. Tribal bundles associated with the long-standing ceremonies were viewed as tribal property and were kept by the nearest relative. Here two subpatterns prevailed. A widow who had participated with her husband in the initial acquiring of the bundle usually held custodianship of it until it was either sold to someone in the village standing in the "son" relationship to the deceased or it was preserved and kept until the man's own sons reached proper age.

The Hidatsa did not tend to place much personal property with the bodies; a man's favorite firearms, bow and arrows, pipe, personal sacred bundle, and paints of various colors were the most common articles. When the individual was placed on a scaffold, it was common for those having distinctive military records to request that the symbols associated with these records be painted on the posts. Food of the type a man would carry on a long journey was usually placed in a dish or bag with the body.

The mourners and the participants would meet at the deceased's lodge and move to the burial grounds in a procession. At the head would be those carrying the body, immediately followed by the nearest relatives. For a man these relatives would be his sisters, mothers and father, brothers, and wife in that order.

Prior to the removal of the body from the lodge and usually immediately after the moment of death, it was the custom for the sisters and mother to prepare their mourning clothing and hair. First of all, they would cut their hair short and jagged. Then they would cut off the lower section of some old dress and remove the sleeves. A woman was expected to cut off a section of a finger for anyone who had given her a horse on returning from a successful war expedition. Since a man normally gave horses only to mothers and sisters, these generally were the ones who cut off fingertips. Men rarely cut off the tips of their fingers in mourning; they, however, did do this when fasting for visions and supernatural powers.

For distinguished men and women, the amount of goods given to the mourners was often very great. Most of the goods was secured as gifts from members of the clan. However, a man's age-grade society would frequently contribute goods to be given to various distinguished persons. No two individuals tended to have exactly the same kinship ties and relationships. One individual, whether male or female, might during his lifetime adopt many sons and daughters and be adopted as son by many others, even of alien tribes. When such a person died, it was expected that the brothers and sisters and all these sons and daughters would present gifts to distinguished people in the deceased person's name.

My informants were all in agreement that the fires in the lodges were all extinguished on the death of a great chief. However, my informants could not agree on the particular categories of chiefs involved. All agreed that the head chief of the village, commonly known as the Village or Peace Chief, the principal War Chief, and the four men "protecting the four directions" would be so honored. It may well be that the lack of agreement after the Hidatsa moved to Fishhook Village was because there was not the same cultural unity within the village that there had formerly been when they lived in separate villages.

When it was learned in the village that someone was about to die, it was customary for those who had lost loved ones shortly before to come to him with messages to be carried to their dead in the spirit world. One about to die sometimes had many of these messages to deliver. A mother would send word to a recently deceased child, giving it instructions and advice of one sort or another.

In no area of Hidatsa culture were there so many diverse views as in that pertaining to the hereafter. All informants agreed that life in the hereafter was very much like that on earth. Murderers were excluded from the villages of the dead and became aimless wanderers much as in life when, after committing a murder, the individual, should he succeed in escaping the wrath of the victim's clansmen and sons, was excluded thereafter from the social life of his community There was disagreement among informants relative to suicides. Some informants thought that suicides never reached the land of the dead but wandered about much as murderers did. However, since most suicides were committed by females, the views of women in this matter probably more correctly reflect the views of the Hidatsa. All my female informants believed that no distinction was made between suicide and natural death; that people did not commit suicide except during epidemics; and that in those days the Hidatsa did not believe that any people would survive. Therefore, these women claimed, people committed suicide during the periods of epidemics simply to catch up with and rejoin their recently deceased relatives, at a time when the household was largely destroyed by these newly introduced diseases.

Hidatsa beliefs relative to the hereafter are based on two bodies of data, their ancient traditions and mythologies and recent dreams and visions. Numerous informants spoke of the return and reunion of their people with those who were once left behind in very early times when the Hidatsa came up out of the ground at some place to the southeast. According to this tradition, the Hidatsa and all other Indians were at that time living underground. Finding an opening reaching to the land above, the people began moving upward to the surface of the earth. One woman heavy with child broke the vine by which they were ascending, separating the people. Many people believe that on death the individual returns to this land below. It was Mrs. White Duck's opinion, given her by her father Poor Wolf, that this village of the dead was downriver and underground. Bears Arm, one of my principal informants, also believed that there was a reunion of the dead with those who were divided when the vine broke. He thought that the land below and the land above the earth constituted the first and third levels of the universe. He stated that the land below and the land above were identical to the land on which they were now living. To the west were high mountains and to the east were the woodlands.

Another view held by other informants was that many others were the descendants of the 13 initial family groups from the sky who established a village on Charred Body Creek below the present town of Washburn, N. Dak., led by Charred Body who had first discovered this land below. Mrs. Good Bear, whose husband was one of the Sun Dance makers, believed that on death they returned to the sky. This view was shared by Wolf Chief whose father held one of the Waterbuster clan bundles consisting of two human skulls believed to have once been of two eagles who transformed themselves into men; one man came from their village at the headwaters of the Missouri River, where the sky and land meet, to live in Awatixa village.

Another view, held by Four Dancers, was that the village of the dead was on the earth. He based his views on instructions and information given by the owners of the Earthnaming bundles. Other older informants believed that when they died they would return downstream to the mouth of the Knife River or to Devils Lake and join their deceased relatives there.

Another view held was that when a prominent medicine man died, his spirit father would come to meet him and escort him to the village of his spirit people. In addition to these views, there were individual views not generally shared by very many people and which were based on individual visions and dream experiences in which they had seen their deceased relatives living in earth lodges, practicing agriculture, hunting buffaloes, and conducting warfare with their enemies in much the same manner as when they lived.

THE AGE-GRADE SYSTEM

The Hidatsa placed great importance on relative age in determining behavior between individuals. The same concepts were extended to include status of the members of the organized societal and religious groups. Theoretically, the entire male and female population was arranged in a series of groupings based on age. For the greater part of the population, these groups were formally organized with names, symbols of membership, songs, and prescribed rights and rules of behavior. The system for men was more complexly developed into a series of age-graded military societies. Individuals were *not* organized into formal societies during two periods in their lives: prior to reaching the age of 12 (depending upon the village group), and after they had achieved old age and had passed through the age-grade system. The social and ceremonial system imposed so many burdens and obligations on the individual that it was practically impossible to fulfill his traditional roles and assume his customary positions in the village life except with the assistance of the organized groups to which he belonged, chief of which were his clan and the age-grade societies.

MEN'S SOCIETIES

The Hidatsa do not consider the men's societies as sacred, and speak freely of their participation in society activities or even of societies to which they never belonged—unlike the sacred ceremonies which are never discussed except under rigidly prescribed conditions. Still, the men's societies have many patterns characteristic of the sacred ceremonies. The societies have traditional and mythological origins, as do the sacred ceremonies, and when no myth was known and the symbols of the society did not conform to the general cultural patterns, the Hidatsa invariably ascribed the presence of the society to recent borrowing from alien groups.

TABLE 4.—*Age-grade societies by villages*

Society	Hidatsa	Awatixa	Awaxawi
Stone hammer	×	×	
Notched stick			×
Little dog	×	×	?
Crazy dog	×	×	?
Lumpwood	×		×
Crow imitators		×	
Kit fox			?
Half-shaved head	×	×	×
Black mouth	×	×	×
Dog	×	×	×
Old dog	?	×	?
Bull	×	×	×

The age-grade grouping seems to have been characteristic of all Hidatsa village groups for some time prior to A.D. 1800. Since most of the societies comprising the system were also represented by the Mandan village groups, there existed an area along the Missouri River from the vicinity of the Knife River to the region of the Cannonball River occupied solely by Mandan and Hidatsa village groups, comprising in all about 13 distinct and permanent village groups, in which age-grade groupings occurred. As late as 1833, Maximilian (1906) recognized slight cultural differences between these village groups, although a basic social and economic pattern prevailed which distinguished them from even the culturally related Arikara and the linguistically related Crow.

The smallpox epidemics which began in the last quarter of the 18th century sharply reduced the total population of these peoples and the number of village groups. This tended to introduce inconsistencies into the system and to introduce competition between some so-

cieties for position in the system. Since competition is not characteristic of the Hidatsa age-grade system, they temporarily reconciled
these conflicts by providing two "routes" to the Black Mouth society
until one "route" became more popular than the other, with the
resultant cessation of the unpopular societies.

There is historic and traditional evidence that not only were new
societies added to the age-grade system from time to time but that
the existing societies changed their relative positions. This is consistent with native traditions of cultural differences between independent villages. Union of two or more village groups, or the breaking up of an existing village group into two or more groups, affected
the number and order of the societies in the system. Since a member
retained his membership until bought out, any undue delay in purchase by the younger men would tend to shift the position of the
society in the age-grade sequence. It is of historic record that the
village groups bought additional dances such as the Hot Dance,
Grass Dance, Big Grass Dance, and Night Grass Dance during the
19th century. In addition, a number of societies (such as the Black
Mouth, Bull, and Kit Fox) are of traditional Mandan origin and are
not believed to have been of very great antiquity with the Hidatsa.
The preservation of Mandan origin myths for these three societies and
the absence of comparable myths for the Hidatsa further strengthens
native beliefs of their recent introduction.

Of the Hidatsa age-grade series, the Stone Hammer and the various
Dog societies are frequently mentioned in their sacred myths. In
fact, variations in the origin myths as related today suggest former
village differences or versions. The Hidatsa, informed in the sacred
myths referring to the various Dog societies, speak of the common
bond uniting these four societies: the Little Dog, Crazy Dog, Dog,
and Old Dog.

In the old villages at Knife River, the order of purchase preliminary
to entrance into the Dog societies differed. The Awaxawi, who
during the 18th century were closely associated with the northern
Mandan and the Nuptadi Mandan, had no Stone Hammer society.
Boys entered the age-grade system by joining the Notched Stick society, whereas young Mandans of the same age had a Magpie society
in some villages, while those villages having the Corn Bundle rites of
Good-Furred-Robe had a similar Notched Stick society believed to
have supernatural powers over the rains.

The Crow Imitator society, which was found only at Awatixa and
at the Mandan villages, was of late introduction, coming from the
Crow Indians. This society was never important after 1837.

The absence of an origin myth, together with native beliefs that the
Half-Shaved Heads were of Crow origin, leads me to believe that this

society was not of long standing among either the Hidatsa or Mandan village groups. During the last century (1832–1932) the society has been closely associated with the next higher society, the Black Mouths, and it acted as a check in the upward advancement of the lower age-groups to Black Mouth status.

The position of the Black Mouths just above the Half-Shaved Heads seems to have been a universal Hidatsa and Mandan characteristic prior to 1837. After that date, when the survivors of the smallpox epidemic united into a smaller number of villages, the number of societies situated in the age-grade sequence below the Black Mouth status increased and the Half-Shaved Head society became extinct. Although the role of the societies prior to attaining Black Mouth status—preparation to police and supervise—was identical for all villages, the actual order of advancement through the system varied due to a slight difference in the actual societies through which one passed. This situation seems to have introduced into the system competition not characteristic of the age-grade system, particularly for the societies characteristic of the younger men.

From what I was able to determine from genealogies and traditions, the Hidatsa-proper and the Awatixa more closely resembled each other in number and order of purchases during the first quarter of the 19th century than did the Awaxawi. This may be due, in part, to their closer residence during the preceding century in adjacent villages less than a mile apart. The Awaxawi, on the other hand, were farther removed during the last half of the 18th century, living downstream near Painted Woods where they had intimate contacts with Mandan groups.

The Notched Stick society at Awaxawi had no Hidatsa or Awatixa equivalents, but the symbols and rites closely parallel religious rites performed both by the Awaxawi and certain Mandan groups. I could find evidence at the Awaxawi village only of the Notched Stick, Kit Fox, Lumpwood, and Half-Shaved Head societies for men who had not yet reached the proper age for entering the Black Mouth society. There was no evidence of the Stone Hammer, Crazy Dog, or Crow Imitator societies. This does not mean that these societies had never been present with the Awaxawi. It is very possible that some of these, particularly the Little Dog and Crazy Dog, were formerly represented there. It is of historic record that the Awaxawi suffered extreme losses when their village was destroyed by the enemy during the last half of the 18th century. Being more sedentary than the Hidatsa-proper, they also suffered more severely from smallpox and other epidemics. Their small numbers may account for some of the differences reported by Bears Arm, whose father came from that village. On the whole, the Awaxawi show many similarities to the Mandan system.

The close similarity of the Hidatsa-proper to the Awatixa is significant in view of their traditional short residence in adjacent villages. If traditions of the long residence of the Awatixa group on the Missouri at Painted Woods and even as far south as the Heart River as an agricultural group, with their earliest contacts with the Mandan after their separation from the Mountain Crow and prior to the appearance of the Awaxawi and Hidatsa–River Crow are correct, one would expect greater similarities to the Mandan than to the Hidatsa-proper.

The order of buying and selling is nearly identical for all Mandan and Hidatsa after reaching the Half-Shaved Head and Black Mouth societies. The exceptions for the Mandan were the Black-Tail Deer society, which was represented in only the westside village groups at the Heart River prior to 1785, and the Raven society (?) for one of the Hidatsa villages. Both societies were of limited distribution even in their own tribes and died out about 1837. The order of purchase from Black Mouth to Dog to Old Dog to Bulls was characteristic of all Hidatsa and Mandan village groups and seems to have been fixed for a considerable time. Instability of purchase order was at the lower half of the series. It was also at this point that innovations crept in with supplementary purchases of new societies. Older people were probably more conservative than the younger men.

Prior to the union of the three Hidatsa groups into one village in 1845, each village endeavored to maintain an independent age-grade series and membership was regulated largely by residence. Even for those societies common to all villages, one bought and sold with his own group and membership rarely extended beyond village limits. When a society was not represented in a village, as in the case of the Stone Hammer found only at Hidatsa and Awatixa or the Notched Stick and Kit-Fox societies of Awaxawi, there was an occasional participation in society purchase with one's age group of another village. According to native informants, this was more common after the epidemic of the 1780's when the Hidatsa village groups moved into the three villages near the mouth of the Knife River. Since there was a great deal of rivalry among villages, informants did not think joining a society from a different village was a common occurrence until after the epidemic of 1837, when conditions fostered further union of village groups for mutual defense.

In the light of village traditions that the Awatixa represent the oldest Hidatsa village group on the Missouri with long residence at the mouth of the Knife River, whereas the Hidatsa-proper and River Crow were late arrivals on the Missouri, living largely upstream from the Knife River, the greater similarity of the Hidatsa–Awatixa societies suggests a recent development based on an older pattern embracing the Awatixa, Awaxawi, and the Mandan village groups. Those Hidatsa–River Crow who moved farther upstream developed a system such as was found among the Crow in the 19th century. Those who stayed on the Missouri and took over the earth lodge culture drew heavily from the Awatixa, their nearest neighbors downstream. The smallest village group, the Awaxawi, had the Half-Shaved Head, Black Mouth, Dog, Old Dog (?), and Bull societies as did the other Hidatsa and Mandan village groups. The series for younger men at Awaxawi resembled the Mandan more closely than did the other two Hidatsa villages. In light of the intermediate position of the Awatixa with both "father-son" and clan inheritance of sacred bundle rites, the former pattern being characteristic of the Hidatsa–Awaxawi and the latter pattern that of the Mandan, it would appear that the age-grade sequences as reported by my oldest informants had changed, at least for the younger men, during the last half of the 18th century.

During the 19th century, and prior to the dispersal of the native population from Fishhook Village onto the reservation, further changes occurred in the societies although the age-grade pattern persisted. The union of villages caused a bunching of societies at the bottom of the series. At the same time, societies and dances bought from the Sioux and Arikara had wide popularity because persons of both sexes were admitted without regard to age. During this period the position and importance of the Black Mouth society remained unchanged. The Notched Stick society of Awaxawi was never popular after the three village groups united. There were religious taboos associated with a rainmaking ceremony, Tying-the-Pots, that had died out with the death of the bundle owners and with their death there were none to serve as singers. Shortly after 1837 the Awaxawi abandoned their independent village and united with the Awatixa and those Hidatsa who had remained at the mouth of the Knife River. The young boys then entered the Stone Hammer society with boys from the other two villages.

Although the Hidatsa recognized the Notched Stick and Stone Hammer societies as the first ones entered by boys, there were numerous informal societies organized by older men which boys could join. Any older man, seeing a number of young boys watching the dances or remarking that they wished they had a dancing society, might organize a dancing club. He would suggest various forms of dress and serve as the singer for the boys. These informal societies usually consisted of little boys 4 to 6 or 7 years of age who usually played together. Frequently the leader was some old man of the household who was interested in the boys sufficiently to relate war accounts and show an interest in their training. If the number of boys in the household was small, boys of related households frequently were invited to participate. When my informants were children (about 1865) one group of boys dressed in small robes with magpie feathers in their hair, and were frequently nicknamed Magpies. The man who served as singer owned a sacred bundle of Woman Above who was believed to wear magpie feathers. Another group of boys dressed as buffaloes, suggested by their singer's sacred bundle. This group was frequently called Mangy Buffaloes since the youngest member of the club wore a poor robe to impersonate a mangy buffalo. The people would remark that when the buffaloes came to the river to drink, there was always among them a lean mangy buffalo calf that had wintered badly. From time to time new societies for small boys would appear. They would be invited to meet and sing in imitation of their elders. Whenever they danced, spectators were sure to appear to give them presents, to invite them in to eat, and to urge them to follow the example of their elders so that they would be brave and strike the enemy when they grew up. According to informants, the number of these small informal societies varied from time to time. Wolf Chief thought that there were probably a dozen or more of these informal dancing groups. The number was always changing according to the inclination of their leaders.

Stone Hammer Society

The Stone Hammer was the first organized society at Awatixa and Hidatsa villages, and was bought by the young boys before they were old enough to become Little Dogs. When the population of the three Hidatsa villages and the Mandan of Mitutanku built Fishhook Village, this was a popular society. There are frequent references to the society and its traditional origin in the sacred myths of Two Men and Charred Body. In these sacred myths relating to events occurring near Painted Woods, Grandson is said to have founded the society, drawing its emblems from his stock of sacred objects. The principal symbol of the society was the carved stone hammer which was designed by Grandson during mythological times. The society was psychologically associated with the Naxpike or Sun Dance which had as its principal sacred object a stone ax carried by the person impersonating Long Arm.

Boys were 12 years and older when entering the society. When the number of available boys was large enough to form a society of 30 or more members, the older people would encourage the boys to meet and plan the purchase from those who had owned the society for a few years. It was customary for young men when joining the Stone Hammer society to go together as a group to the Sun Dance shelter to fast during the next performance of the Naxpike. Purchase was by an organized group from an organized group, the relationship between the two groups being that of "father–son." The buyers were encouraged and assisted by their respective households. Not all boys joined the Stone Hammer society. Some families were not interested in assisting their sons. There was a reluctance for boys to join when the household had recently quarreled with another household or a close relative leading a war party had returned in mourning from an unsuccessful war expedition. Some boys were bashful or were reluctant to ask help of their relatives. Not uncommonly, a family would refuse to assist a close relative because people had criticized them unfairly. There was no ceremonial offering of wives for, theoretically, boys of this age had not married.

Purchase into the Stone Hammers introduced new rights and obligations. The society had the right collectively to steal food for their meetings, but they were obligated individually to appear on each ceremonial occasion providing group fasting and to make efforts to secure supernatural instructions. One gets the opinion from native informants that there were those who were indifferent to these instructions to seek visions and that others, having no particular desire to be brave, did not join the Stone Hammers. We have here the weeding out of the cowardly and indifferent individuals.

Kit Fox Society

Since 1837 the order of purchase of the Kit Fox, Crazy Dog, and Little Dog societies has not greatly concerned the Hidatsa. This is due, it seems to me, to the reconciliation of different village systems inherited from the first part of the century when three village groups were in existence. The Hidatsa interpret the societies bought and sold before reaching the status of police or Black Mouths as preparatory steps toward entrance into this important society with its many police and governing functions. The Kit Fox society, as far as I could determine, was not present at the old villages of Hidatsa and Awatixa. Mandan traditions state that this society was one of the numerous ones organized by the Mandan culture hero Good-Furred-Robe to dance whenever the corn rites associated with certain bundles were celebrated. This was also the basis for the practice of inviting one with Corn rites to officiate as one of the singers for the men of the Fox society; Moves Slowly was a singer for the Mandan and Bear-Looks-Out served as singer for the Awaxawi about A.D. 1870. Good-Furred-Robe founded two sacred bundles whose owners were singers for the Kit Foxes. In late historic times one of these bundles was sold to an Awaxawi married to a Mandan woman, at which time young men of Awaxawi bought the society from the Mandan. Bear-Looks-

Out was owner of the bundle at Awaxawi where the Kit Fox society was organized and served as one of the singers. He was the only member of the society to survive the epidemic of 1837. He sold the society to a group of young married men at Fishhook Village after the society had been inactive for a number of years. Because of the "friendship" bond between this society and the women's Goose society, owners of this society were reluctant to sell until the members of the buying group had married, since women of the Goose society were married. Instead, when the selling society thought that the prospective buyers were too young, the price was set high enough to discourage purchase. This practice tended to slow up purchase, during which time the younger groups would generally buy into either the Crazy Dog or Little Dog societies. It was customary for young men of Hidatsa and Awatixa to move from the Stone Hammer to the Little Dog while waiting to reach the age for entering either the Kit Fox or the Crazy Dog. During the 19th century, after the union of the three groups at Fishhook Village, the Little Dog and the Kit Fox were in competition for position intermediate to the Crazy Dog and Lumpwood societies. In spite of the prominent role of the dog in the sacred myths and rites, the Little Dog society lost popularity as the Kit Fox society expanded its membership with each successive sale. At present (1932), the Kit Fox society is one of the few surviving societies.

Of the entire series for the three original villages, the Notched Stick, Stone Hammer, and Crazy Dog societies were owned by boys and young men whose members were predominantly unmarried. There was no ceremonial surrender of wives even when some of the members of the purchasing group had already married. Another feature of these societies reserved to younger men was the practice of employing singers of the older age-grade societies. As a rule, the society paid its singers to officiate until either they learned the songs and dances or the singers and members tired of each other.

The purchase pattern for societies higher in the age-grade structure than the Crazy Dog society was essentially the same as for the younger men except that surrender of wives to the buyers became the rule. Those who were unmarried but otherwise qualified and accepted by the purchasing group were not, however, disqualified since it was the duty of any clansman asked to supply a wife for the occasion. The Hidatsa interpret age-grade purchase from an older age group as a means of acquiring additional supernatural powers through participation in various ceremonial activities not a part of the age-grade series. The purchase provided an opportunity for an older man to "bless" his "sons" by means of ceremonial sexual licenses with the giver's wife. This practice is not unique to age-grade transfers but is a general pattern characteristic of numerous ceremonies performed for calling the buffaloes near the village. An ambitious young man wishing to get ahead might, before undertaking a perilous mission, invite a prominent ceremonial leader to accept his wife.

Lumpwood Society

By the time young men had reached the age when they should normally purchase the Lumpwood society, they should have married and participated in several war expeditions. The Lumpwood symbols of membership, the painted and carved staffs, resemble closely those used in the Painted Red Stick ceremony performed for the calling of the buffaloes. Although decorated and carved sticks are found in the Eagle Trapping, Big Bird, and Thunder bundles, it was with the Painted Wood sacred sticks that the staffs belonging to the Lumpwood society showed closest similarity. According to tradition, the Lumpwood society was found only at Hidatsa and Awaxawi villages at the Knife River; the Awatixa did not have the associated Painted Red Stick ceremony. The Hidatsa recognized the society as one of the age-grade series but attributed to it the supernatural power of attracting the buffalo to the villages. The drum was believed to have the power to bring rains. The Awatixa had other buffalo-calling rites but no associated Lumpwood society.

Half-Shaved Head Society

The Half-Shaved Head society was closely associated with the Black Mouth society. It served as a buffer society to protect the Black Mouths from premature purchase until the younger men had sufficiently distinguished themselves in warfare, ceremonial activities and fasting, and had shown evidence of good judgment so that the group could be entrusted to fulfill the many social obligations and responsibilities of the Black Mouth society. The Half-Shaved Head society is traditionally of Crow origin. Although the same society is known to have existed at the Mandan village of Mitutanku in Maximilian's time, my Mandan informants knew of the society only from traditions, as it apparently died out there in 1837. According to the Maximilian accounts and Hidatsa informants, the society was bought immediately preceding entrance into the Black Mouths. Poor Wolf was 27 when, with other young men, he bought into the society and remained a member of it for 9 years (Lowie, 1913). One year after the purchase, the same body bought the Black Mouths. Thus, the same men held simultaneous memberships in both societies for 8 years.

BLACK MOUTH SOCIETY

Unlike some Plains tribes where the responsibilities of group management were passed around from society to society, the Hidatsa and Mandan village groups entrusted police duties to one society, the Black Mouths. Curtis (1907 a) lists two societies with police duties; the Black Mouths and the Wood-roots. The names actually refer to a single society. The name "black mouth" refers to the particular painting of the members of this society, whereas "wood-root" refers to the clubs carried by the members. The society is of Mandan traditional origin, according to the Hidatsa. My Mandan informants claimed that the society was organized by Good-Furred-Robe to protect the Corn People. For that reason, the Black Mouth society had the right to meet whenever the feasts were given for the Goose society. The Mandan claim that the society was borrowed by the various Hidatsa village groups and, in light of Hidatsa traditions that the society is of recent introduction from the Mandan, we can assume this to be the correct order of diffusion. The Mandan have sacred origin myths relative to the founding of the society, which I was unable to discover for the Hidatsa.

The Hidatsa comprehended the Black Mouth society as occupying an intermediate and transitional position between the lower societies (whose members had recently begun their first fasts, ceremonial adventures, ritualistic feasting, and participation in the war expeditions as beginners and immature men) and those older males who had attained the principal objectives prescribed by the culture. In the process of society purchases, the individuals comprising the various groups were tested. Those who failed to measure up to the highest standards of the society dropped from the system. In the process of advancing through the lower societies, recognition was given to those showing special skills when officers were selected to wear the badges of the society or to perform certain honored roles. Young men who had advanced to the point of buying into the Black Mouth society, were frequently stopped at that point for a number of years. When the Black Mouths were asked to sell by a younger group, they would invariably present the matter to the two older Dog and the Bull societies for their approval. If the older and better-informed men felt that the younger men were moving along too fast and were not ready to assume such important obligations, or if conditions in the village or relations with neighboring tribes were not right, the sale was delayed. Opposition to sale usually took the form of individual advice from one's own relatives. The Hidatsa were very sensitive to public opinion, whether in the purchase of age-grade societies, sacred bundles, or other activities. When public opinion was against a group, assistance was denied them. Occasionally, however, young men would speak of their accomplishments as collectively exceeding those of the existing Black Mouths and persist in their ambitions to complete the purchase. In such instances, exorbitant demands or downright refusal halted the negotiations. About 1872 the Crow-Flies-High band separated because sale by the Black Mouths was refused. There are numerous references to the bypassing of younger men's societies. This was impossible in the higher societies because the Dog, Old Dog, and Bull societies were reserved for older men who had had wide experiences in warfare, ceremonies, and group leadership of one form or another. The Hidatsa think of these older societies as the policy makers for the village. The Black Mouths served as executors to enforce the policies of the older men and the customs of the village.

Prior to the union of the three Hidatsa village groups when Fish-hook Village was built in 1845, each village had an independent police or Black Mouth society. Each society was organized in the same manner as the others with the same number of officers, the same symbols of authority, and the same relative position in the age-grade structure. Collectively, each society addressed the same society of the other Hidatsa or the Mandan villages as *irakúu* in Hidatsa or *kotomanaku* in Mandan, the kinship term for "pal." A society had no authority except with its own village group until after 1845 when the union of three village groups brought together three independent Black Mouth societies. The three societies functioned as one during the summer months, but during those winters when the population broke up into separate camps based on the original village lines, the police societies likewise dispersed according to former village affiliations. This was a common practice until well into the 1850's when, as a result of intermarriage, the original village lines were blurred.

The Black Mouths' duties fell into a number of categories. Invariably the group met whenever a major ceremony was performed. The Black Mouths were concerned only with those public matters which involved the entire village population and they had no authority to interfere in factional or personal matters unlikely to involve the entire population. Thus stealing, whether of meat and corn from a household or of another man's wife, were matters for the clans and households to handle. In fact, a Black Mouth might often be involved in such matters himself without materially affecting the status of his own society.

Probably the most important duty of the Black Mouths was to enforce the orders of the council of older men. Whenever any important decisions were under discussion, the Black Mouths would meet with the council. As soon as a matter had been settled, the announcer for the Black Mouths went through the village informing the people of the decision. News of important village matters quickly spread, for those of the council were widely scattered through the village and invariably discussed the matters with their own households. When people heard the announcer call through the village, they would listen. The council's duties were broad and involved matters concerning the people at large: moving the village; the time of leaving for the summer buffalo hunt and the various camping places along the way; the prohibition on leaving the village for warfare; peace treaties with neighboring tribes; and, more recently, policies with respect to the White traders and Government officials.

On other occasions, the Black Mouths enforced the regulations of other leaders such as the Winter Camp leader or the Summer Hunt leader. The Hidatsa elected each fall a Winter Chief who was responsible for the welfare of the group during the time they were organized under his leadership. It was customary for the winter leader to make frequent offerings to his sacred bundles and to seek the assistance of other distinguished sacred bundle owners for success. Should the enemy attack the camp and kill some of the people or steal horses, hunters be injured when running buffaloes, or other misfortune strike, the leader was held responsible and blamed for these misfortunes. If there were many deaths or accidents, the people would say that they made a poor selection. The Winter Camp leader selected someone as his personal announcer to keep the camp informed of his plans and to integrate the activities of the group. The Black Mouths were in continuous session during most of the winter and frequently behaved in what sometimes seemed to be a very arbitrary manner. These camps being undefended, it was necessary to send scouts out continuously to note the movements of enemy groups and to see that the horses were brought in quickly in case of an impending attack. Since the purpose of these winter camps was to move some distance from the summer village in order to conserve wood and to spare the game ranging near the summer villages, great reliance was placed on the game killed during the winter both for food at the time and for a surplus supply to be taken back to the villages in the spring when normally the herds were away from the river on the summer range. The importance of these winter herds in Hidatsa economy is indicated by the number of formal group rituals for the winter buffalo and native statements of intensive individual fasting for the return of the herds to the river bottoms during the shortest and coldest days. Boller (1868) has given us an excellent account of the role of the Black Mouths in organizing the group for the performance of winter buffalo-calling rites, the prohibitions against premature hunting, firing of guns, and noise around the village, and even the prohibition of kindling fires, when the herds were observed approaching the camp.

Frequently no leader was selected to supervise the winter camp when the people could not agree in council. In case of disagreement, the conflict was resolved by these alternatives: no leader was selected and the population was at liberty to move out in small groups under individual leaders of their own choosing, generally eagle-trapping leaders (this was the custom before enemies were numerous); the population remained in the summer villages under the existing leadership; or the Black Mouth society was selected to assume the role of Winter Camp leader and police. This latter alternative was of common occurrence when the Black Mouths had individually distinguished themselves and the people thought that one or more of their members would have good luck as Winter Camp leaders.

When the summer village had been organized by the council under the leadership of one or two outstanding chiefs for a number of years, the people frequently had relied so heavily on their good judgment that when their chiefs died or were killed, a period of disorganization followed while minor leaders competed for top positions in the council. The council then frequently found it convenient to avoid rivalry and hard feelings in selecting a Winter Camp leader by delegating the authority and responsibility to the Black Mouths at large. On such occasions, the Black Mouths selected the campsites, set the date for moving from the summer village, supervised the party when moving to camp, and kept in continuous session with a separate council lodge for their meetings during the winter. They assumed collectively the duties and responsibilities of camp leader. In case of misfortunes during the winter, the entire group was criticized but the two leaders of the society, representing the two moieties, were chiefly blamed because of their positions in the society. It was such a camp organized under the Black Mouths that Boller described.

The Black Mouths performed comparable services when, after the corn had been hoed for the last time, the village organized a summer buffalo hunt. In this instance, the council selected a leader who had taken part in numerous ceremonies, particularly those concerned with the buffalo or with sacred bundles containing buffalo skulls. He was responsible for the activities of the group; he selected the various camping points along the way and announced them in advance; he selected the scouts to travel ahead to watch for enemy war parties or camps and to keep track of the herds and note their size and general movements. These scouts were selected from organized men's societies inferior to Black Mouth status. In recent years the Kit-

Foxes were generally assigned this duty, chiefly because of the size of the society. It is said that formerly different societies for young men were selected, according to the leader's inclinations. Apparently some rivalry existed between these younger men's societies when members of more than one society were selected as scouts. This is a rather unusual situation since the societies were generally non-competitive, and suggests to me that this is a recent phenomenon arising from the union of several villages and the subsequent competition among these younger men's societies for positions and members.

The Black Mouths performed much the same roles as when moving to Winter Camp. They enforced regulations against straying away from the main body, prohibited premature attacks on the herds, and defended the group from attack. There are instances when, in spite of the widespread practice of seeking vision instructions from sacred things not believed to send dreams to those fasting at the summer villages, the Black Mouths even prohibited fasting outside of the camp when there was danger from enemy raiding parties. In all their activities, the Black Mouths worked to protect the reputation of the leader. Being on continuous watch for infractions of customs and armed to meet an attack of enemy raiding parties, the Black Mouths took no active part in the buffalo surround but depended on others to provide the meat for their households.

Occasionally some families would feel that the Black Mouths had acted in an arbitrary manner. In general, however, the people felt that the society performed a definite social function which the households and clans could not undertake. Had they acted out of revenge, the social group would not have supported them and they would have lost individual status with the village. When a man fired a gun or went hunting when the village group was ordered neither to make a noise about the village nor to hunt, the Black Mouths invariably took his weapons away from him and broke up his arrows, cut up his clothing, and even killed his horse and destroyed the meat he was bringing back. The individual's reactions to punishment largely determined the next steps taken by the police. If the man admitted his error and was repentant, he was invariably repaid for his personal loss many times over in comparable goods. If, on the other hand, he resisted the police or persisted in disregarding their prohibitions, he was severely beaten. In two instances in the memory of the older Hidatsa at the time this study was made, the violators (alien visitors) were beaten and killed without any adverse reaction by the group as a whole. In general, it can be said that the Black Mouths had definite duties to perform for mutual harmony and well-being but they were expected to use good judgment in attaining these objectives. This was the principal reason why the Hidatsa, like the

Mandan, were reluctant to permit young men to advance through the age-grade series to Black Mouth status until they had demonstrated mature judgment. Entrusting village police functions to a society of men of all ages, as observed by them when neighboring tribes visited them, was considered to be a poor way of handling people.

The Black Mouths were expected to act with discretion and not in anger. A number of years after 1845, the three Hidatsa village groups were in separate winter camps along the Missouri. At that time scouts from the most northern group discovered buffaloes approaching their village, drifting along with a strong north wind. Orders were immediately given in the village that the dogs should be tied up, woodcutting stopped, and fires extinguished. Until that time no buffalo had been on the river bottoms and the people were short of meat. While the people were awaiting the arrival of the herds and waiting for them to fan out in the timber and brush along the river bottoms, a Black Mouth was told that someone had fired a gun just below the village and around a bend in the river. Several Black Mouths ran out and found a man from the next village downstream who was just starting to butcher a buffalo which he had killed. As the Black Mouths ran up they called *UUII* and the hunter knew that the Black Mouths were angry; that call was given only when someone's actions had met with their displeasure. He looked toward the village but could not see it for the bend in the river nor could he hear the sound of barking dogs or of axes in the woodlots. He suspected then that the village was quiet because herds had been discovered approaching. When he was told that hunting was prohibited, he expressed regrets even though his weapons had already been taken from him. He explained that he had been sent up from the next village to see how the upper camp was faring, that he had seen many buffaloes as he walked along, and that he had concluded that the upper village had already been hunting. Seeing that the man meant no harm, his weapons were returned to him and the men butchered the buffalo before returning to camp. At the camp he was rewarded with goods for his "good behavior" in admitting his error and offering appropriate apologies.

In dealing with infractions, the clan had its role in the practice of using as spokesman for the Black Mouths, one of the same clan as the individual who had committed the infraction. When a conflict situation developed and the village leaders resolved to settle the matter lest permanent differences arise, the spokesman for the Black Mouths would take a pipe belonging to the moiety of the offender and ask him to smoke the pipe and forget his grievance. The same procedure was followed when addressing the leader of the opposing side. When individual Black Mouths in the performance of their duty acted with what the offender considered bad judgment, there were numerous recourses that could be used later against him. He could be denied property for use in a ceremony or be blocked in his ambitions by the aggrieved person's relatives who had social and ceremonial rights for sale. Gossip and ridicule could be employed. Women who had a grievance might withhold aid to the individual of the Black Mouths who had acted unfairly. As a joking relative, if such relationship existed between them, she might even go to considerable trouble to embarrass him publicly or dig up things in his past that he would prefer to forget. A common practice was to make him a decorated shirt for which he would be obliged to give her his favorite buffalo-hunting horse. This could be an extreme sacrifice. Although the Black Mouths collectively had such authority as the clans and households allowed them, at all times they were individuals in daily contacts with the group, and the culture provided numerous checks to their authority.

The Black Mouths of the various villages performed important roles in preserving peace and reconciling conflict situations between different Hidatsa and Mandan groups. This was an important function of the Black Mouths, for it was imperative that the various village groups live together peacefully during the past two centuries when pressure of enemy groups was great and continuous. In these early times, if native traditions are correct, the clans of different villages had not been completely equated nor had they assumed the important roles manifested in the 19th century. Each village, however, had an identical police organization believed to have been derived from a common founder, the Mandan culture hero Good-Furred-Robe. Thus, when a theft in one village was committed by a member of a different village, the Black Mouths of the former reported the matter to the Black Mouths of the latter. The suspect's lodge or person was then searched and the property, if found, was returned to the Black Mouths of the village where the theft occurred. Although thefts of small items might be easily overlooked, taking horses belonging to another person, even though they had strayed away from the rightful owner, could have had serious consequences if left to the rightful owner and his village relatives to come into another village to lay claim to his property. Village loyalty obviously was very strong at that time.

The Black Mouths had no authority over the movements and actions of neighboring village groups of their own tribe as long as their common interests did not clash. If, however, one village group had imposed restrictions on its people because of the impending approach of the winter buffalo herds, the other groups living nearby were expected to do likewise. This was, however, a matter for the intervillage council to handle and not the Black Mouths.

The Black Mouths were also responsible for the safety of the people and their good conduct whenever visiting tribes were in the village. This was an important role prior to the middle of the 19th century since many tribes came to the Hidatsa villages to trade for garden products. As soon as word reached the village by advanced runners that people were coming for the purpose of trade or to visit, the council and police met to arrange the reception. Very often those families who had recently lost members of their related households in warfare with the visiting band announced that they would not be received. This was their socially recognized right even though in the long run they could lose prestige with those families anticipating a profitable trade with the enemy. The culture, however, provided numerous methods of satisfying those who recently had lost relatives. In some instances the grievance was not actually toward the enemy but with the Hidatsa war leader who had not inflicted sufficient self-torture or had not fasted long enough after the loss of young men of his party; the relatives had thought that he had failed to show proper respect for their relatives and had treated their young men's lives lightly. Whatever the circumstances, it was the right of families in mourning to refuse to admit the enemy band even for trading purposes. This left the council one of two alternatives: buy off the mourners with horses and other valuable things, or refuse to admit the enemy band. The mourners were generally paid off unless they had very strong feelings in the matter. It was the duty of the Black Mouths to put up the goods and horses and carry the society pipe to them.

The Black Mouths met continuously when an enemy band was in the village to forestall trouble. In historic times, each visiting group had an organized police to work with the Black Mouths. Should a fight break out between two individuals of opposite groups, each policeman would seize his own tribesman but refuse to touch one of the other group. In general, unless there was a great disparity in numbers, and one group could be taken by surprise, conflicts rarely got out of hand. It was an established rule that once an outside group or an individual had been taken in and fed, peace should prevail. According to a long-standing custom, a visiting group assisted its hosts in repelling any attack from outside. Thus we find references to one Sioux band, enjoying Mandan–Hidatsa hospitality, being obliged to assist in repelling another Sioux band, their own tribesmen. We also find references in their traditions to admitting to Fishhook Village war parties of Assiniboin bent on attacking the Mandan at the Knife River. Those Mandan with lodges in the Village assumed the position of "guests" and were refused permission to make an attack on this enemy group; custom required that the Black Mouths afford the Assiniboin protection as long as they were in the village. However, in at least one case, the Hidatsa advised the Knife River Mandan of the impending attack, informed the Mandan in Fishhook Village of the enemy's proposed course, and entertained the enemy while warriors sneaked out of the village to prepare a trap for the Assiniboin.

From earliest times, the Black Mouths served an important role in preserving good feelings and relations with the White trades. Chardon (1932, p. 125) mentions that the society had found horses belonging to the traders and had offered to return them. In another instance he refers to sending tobacco to the Black Mouths and advising them to keep the village quarantined as smallpox had not broken out there (ibid., p. 129). We also find references in traders' accounts to the practice of employing a member of the Black Mouths as policeman around the trading post, serving as an intermediary between the traders and the Indians in preserving order. On the other hand, when traders went into the winter camps to live or had their trading posts near the summer villages, they were restricted in their movements just the same as the Indians were. They learned very quickly that when orders were given out that no hunting or woodcutting was permitted while the herds moved into the river bottoms, it was to their best interest to comply, and that the Indian police meant business when they said "no hunting."

From the foregoing discussion of the functions of the Black Mouth society, we see that they performed roles not characteristic of the lower societies. 1 have not indicated the roles of the Black Mouths in the ceremonies since a section of this study is concerned with Hidatsa ceremonial organization. It is needless to say that the Hidatsa, like the Mandan, were unwilling to entrust so important a matter as police functions to inexperienced youths. Instead they reserved those functions for mature men who had been to war, had participated in numerous ceremonies, had given many feasts, and understood tribal history and values. In their advancement, they had eliminated the cowardly, the lazy, and the incompetent.

The Hidatsa placed the duties of the Black Mouths in the same class as other services performed for the good of the society at large. They emphasized the importance of fasting for the younger men of the Stone Hammer and Crazy Dog societies to be followed by general participation in the buffalo-calling ceremonies or those formal rites providing group fasting and individual purchases of sacred bundles for males of the Kit Fox, Little Dog, and Lumpwood societies. In general, the Hidatsa disapproved of young men assuming the leadership of war expeditions until they had reached the Half-Shaved Head and Black Mouth societies. My case histories show numerous exceptions to this rule, however. It was one of the Black Mouth society's duties to forbid the young men to leave the village on unauthorized expeditions. In some instances, horses brought back from a successful raid were killed by the Black Mouths when they had been ordered by the council to forbid the raid. These unauthorized raids could start a great deal of trouble when the raid was made against a band with whom peace negotiations were being conducted by the council. In such instances the young men were frequently severely whipped and their weapons destroyed. On other occasions, when enemy war parties were near and the young men succeeded in getting away from the village undetected to return with war honors, victory dances were celebrated and the Black Mouths overlooked the matter.

These unauthorized war expeditions were a constant cause of friction between age-groups in the Hidatsa villages. The culture provided formal patterns whereby those showing promise as leaders could advance by steps to the status of war leaders, and shortcuts were not sanctioned. Nevertheless, there were those who took shortcuts by organizing war expeditions of their own age-group and were successful. Parents—particularly the older and more conservative people—disapproved strongly of these unauthorized expeditions and endeavored to keep their boys at home by denying them sacred objects to take along. The group feelings toward these unauthorized expeditions were reflected in the actions of the Black Mouths. Even in these conflict situations the Black Mouths preferred to avoid displays of force. Learning of some ambitious young man with ideas of organizing an expedition, a member of the Black Mouths standing in the relationship of "father" would go to the young man and talk to him, telling him of the dangers he would encounter, particularly if those he met in battle were older, skilled in warfare, and had many sacred gods protecting them. He would refer to the fasting and ceremonial participation of those in the tribe who had good reputations as war leaders. He would emphasize the self-punishment on returning from an unsuccessful expedition he must endure to regain the respect of those whose young men had been killed. He would point out men who had "kicked the stone," a term used to designate those unsuccessful leaders who had lost men and were scorned until proper restitution was made. Those who persisted in their ambitions generally met disaster sooner or later, and their military ambitions were no longer supported even by their own age-group. The unsuccessful war leader usually dropped his society membership after "kicking the stone" a second time and took little or no interest in other social or ceremonial functions.

The Hidatsa praised those who aspired to be leaders and followed the pattern set before them of rising to the top by stages. They believed that a young man should follow the prescribed course, gaining experience and supernatural powers as he went along, and that the major positions of responsibility should not be assumed until he had demonstrated ability. In the process of his training he was assisted by his relatives and his societies. Many males never aspired to top positions in either war or village matters and did not care to assume the responsibilities of leadership. Although the majority of the village leaders were in the higher societies, many of them had never personally organized and directed a war expedition, being content with striking coup, capturing horses, or giving feasts. Even among the Black Mouth membership composed of middle-aged men between 30 and 45 years of age, probably less than half had ever attained war leader status chiefly because the culture provided other and equally effective outlets for leadership.

Dog Societies

After selling out to younger men, the Black Mouths bought into the next higher society of Dogs known by both the Mandan and Hidatsa as the "Real Dogs" (pl. 3) to distinguish them from three other Dog societies; the Crazy Dogs, Little Dogs sometimes called "Dogs-Whose-Names-Are-Unknown," and the Old Dogs. The order of purchase into the Dog society was the same for all Hidatsa and Mandan villages, as far as information could determine. The members of this society were expected to be brave and to have a good reputation in warfare; those who had not shown good judgment in handling police matters or who had shown cowardice in warfare would have become the object of ridicule of their joking-relatives had they attempted to buy into the society. Thus the same screening and dropping-out characteristic of the lower societies continued.

Origin myths of the various Dog societies are numerous for both the Hidatsa and Mandan and are so interwoven into their mythology that it is to be presumed that these societies were of long standing in both tribes. The wide distribution of the Dog society in the Plains suggests considerable antiquity as well as popularity. On the basis of the integration of the Dog myths into the sacred myths of the Hidatsa, my informants and those Mandan who have lived longest with the Hidatsa believed that the Dog societies were of Hidatsa origin. However, the Mandan have identical myths interwoven in their sacred legends which suggests to the other Mandan that the societies were of Mandan origin.

The Dog myths suggest Mandan origin to me chiefly because the theme—"imprisoning the animals"—is common to Mandan sacred rites but is rarely found in Hidatsa mythology. Nor does one find frequent reference in other Hidatsa myths to the Dog Den Buttes, an important region in Mandan mythology.

In the Hidatsa myth, a beautiful young woman refused to marry or to have sexual intercourse with any man, and her people said that it was her prerogative. One hot night she could not sleep until early morning, after the lodge had cooled off. When she awoke, she saw a man put his white robe around him and leave her bed. This happened 3 nights in a row. On the fourth visit she threw red paint which hit him between the shoulders. When she looked for the paint mark among her tribesmen she found instead a white dog sleeping in her own lodge with the red paint on his shoulders. He ran out of the lodge and 2 months later she discovered that she was pregnant.

When the time came to deliver the child, she went to a washout beyond the village limits and there gave birth to nine pups. The first eight were males and the youngest was a female. The oldest was named Black Wolf or Cedar-Between-the-Eyes; the next oldest was Blows-Through-a-Hole. The youngest male was named Brisket or Last Male; the others were Little-Dogs-Whose-Names-Were-Not-Known. She left the pups in the dry washout and would return now and then to nurse them. One night there was thunder and lightning with rain. When she returned, her babies were gone. She followed them to a tipi and there found the pups with their father and was invited in by Brisket. In the morning she was alone. She followed their trail. This happened three times and on the fourth day they reached Dog Dens. Again Brisket invited her in and she went into Dog Dens which she discovered to be a large earth lodge. Last Male or Brisket warned his mother to tell her people that they should not come to Dog Dens for his brothers would cause all except dogs to freeze their feet if they came there. (From this warning those of the Dog society would afterward go around in the village without moccasins to show that they were the Real Dogs.) Brisket's brothers would also cause people to go insane; hence the name of Crazy Dogs for some people. Brisket agreed to return home with his mother, transformed into the small wood owl named Little Owl. Today the Hidatsa say the seven stars of the dipper are Little Owl's seven brothers.

At this point the Dog myth takes up the theme of the Mandan Snow Owl sacred myth. An eagle trapper imprisoned in his trapping pit, dug out and found himself at the lodge of Big Owl and his servant, Little Owl. He was sent out to capture an elk that had many guardians. He succeeded in killing the elk. Then Big Owl sent him out to get Striped Scalp and he secured the help of Old-Woman-

Who-Never-Dies, for Striped Scalp was very holy. He took the scalp to Big Owl. For helping Big Owl the young man named Black Wolf was given an owl skin to wear in the dances and 10 sacred arrows to protect him on his way home. Big Owl warned him of dangers along the way. After passing four dangerous persons, he met a young woman who lived in Dog Den with her brothers. Big Owl told him that when he told this evil woman of his exploits she would be afraid of him and her brothers would be afraid of the owl skin.

He met this Woman in Dog Den and she took him inside the butte. Here some of the dogs were foolish or crazy; they would take their feet, arms, and even their heads off when they danced. Black Wolf frightened them with the owl skin and they ran out without their limbs. Old-Woman-Who-Never-Dies used her whistle to send a blizzard, and they begged to get back into the butte. When they came in they were afraid of Black Wolf. Black Wolf married this Woman in Dog Den and he knew that she was the daughter of a Hidatsa woman and White Dog.

Some time later they returned to Black Wolf's lodge, which was in the same village where Grandson, who established the Stone Hammer society, lived. Black Wolf announced that his wife was a supernatural woman and that she forbad anyone to touch him. One day his brother's wife touched his robe and his wife became angry. Fearing that she would leave the people, they sat up watching her for 4 nights when all fell asleep. Then she returned to Dog Den. He followed her and found the entrance and smokehole had been closed over.

Later a man in the village announced that he was a dog and that his fathers were the dogs who had lived in Dog Den Butte. He told how his fathers had gone to the sky to make up the dipper. The people would see him looking toward the sky at night and talking to his fathers living above. This Yellow Dog announced that he would organize four societies: Little Dogs, Crazy Dogs, Dog, and Old Dogs. He announced that he would sing the songs that belonged to the Dog society, for they would do most of the fighting for the people in the future. He gave owl feathers to the dog societies to wear during the dances. Then he announced the decorations they should wear and sang the songs of the various dog societies. He told them that these four societies were related but that one must wait until he had reached the proper age before joining.

At this point in the sacred myths, two versions are given. In one version Grandson becomes angry because Yellow Dog has intercourse with his wife and retaliates by imprisoning the animals in Dog Den. In the other version it is the Sun who imprisoned the animals. In both versions, First Creator—the coyote—assisted in freeing the animals. In the Grandson version he returned to the sky when his efforts failed. He warned the people that, although he did many things for them and founded the Stone Hammer society while on earth, should they make offerings to him or pray to him, they would be unsuccessful. In the Sun version, the animals merely became hungry and refused to stay imprisoned in the butte. Both versions have widespread distribution among the Hidatsa but the Grandson version seems to have wider distribution since it is the only version I was able to record for the Mandan. In the Mandan version, however, there is no reference to the founding of the Stone Hammer society nor is there the prohibition of praying to Grandson.

The concept of age-grading runs through the dog myths in spite of the fact that the supernatural dogs founding the society were brothers. This is not unusual, for the Hidatsa distinguish age even in twins; the first born being older brother or sister depending on the sex. The psychological relationships between the various dog societies are based on common parents and are expressed by numerous common symbols, particularly dress and ornaments. Maximilian stated that Mandan informants said the Crazy Dogs were higher up in the series formerly, but this seems to be based on an interpretation of the myth rather than actual memory of their former higher place in the series.

We find in the myth the native beliefs about the Dog societies. The Crazy Dogs bring bad luck and insanity to those who get lost near Dog Den; the Little Dogs are an abbreviation of their full name of "Little-Dogs-Whose-Names-Are-Unknown" because in the myth only the two oldest dogs and the youngest male dog were named; the Dogs were brave and could not retreat; and finally the Old Dogs were the bravest of all and painted their bodies white to represent their father, White Dog.

The Dog society was popular in all of the Mandan and Hidatsa villages and continued so until the aboriginal culture broke down. The Old Dog society was less popular in the Hidatsa villages than with the Mandan. Maximilian does not list an Old Dog society for the Hidatsa—unless the society *Waschu'kke-Achke*, meaning Dog society but which he translates as "Old Dog," should be so considered. The Old Dog societies died out at the Mandan villages after the smallpox epidemic of 1837 and must have been even less popular with the Hidatsa for, in spite of native traditions, I could find no knowledge of the society either at Hidatsa or Awaxawi prior to 1837 although it was reported to be an important society at Awatixa. This is not unusual in view of the other cultural similarities between this village group and the Mandan.

However unimportant the Old Dog society may have been in recent time, the Dog society was an important one to which the chiefs or leaders of various subgroups of the village belonged. They were mature men who had distinguished themselves in many ways. Informants would say, "That is the society that all of the greatest leaders belonged to." When buying into the Dog society, the Black Mouths relinquished their wives as in other society purchases, but there was less inclination to avail themselves of that privilege. As a man grew older, having prayed often for younger men, it was believed that his supernatural powers given to him from time to time during his lifetime by fasting, supernatural experiences, bundle purchases, and feasts for the older people, were running low. Those who were still sexually active attributed this situation to possession still of great supernatural powers, and they sometimes availed themselves of the "son's" wife. By the time the Dog society bought out the Bulls, the latter society members rarely availed themselves of that privilege, although their "sons" still continued to go through the formality.

BULL SOCIETY

The Bull society was fast going out of existence after 1837; none of my informants had ever belonged to the society or observed its sale and transfer. After 1837, this was the highest society in both the Mandan and Hidatsa series. Traditionally it was always at or near the top by virtue of certain ceremonial attainments prerequisite to membership. The society in both the Mandan and Hidatsa villages was limited to those males who had purchased sacred bundles containing sacred buffalo skulls together with the right to instruct younger men in the ceremonial painting of these skulls. Membership in the society was a reward for village major bundle purchases. This placed a premium on ownership of hereditary bundles and bundle rites rather than on personal bundles based on vision experiences. We find that both the Mandan and Hidatsa continued to recognize the superiority of those bundles containing sacred buffalo skulls even after the Bull society died out. Whenever a ceremonial feast was given, all those having these sacred bundles were expected to attend without formal invitation.

The Bulls were expected to meet and dance in public four times each year, at which time they represented the buffaloes of the particular season and direction when the performance was being given (pl. 4). Both the Mandan and Hidatsa sacred and origin myths make common reference to the buffaloes of the four seasons and directions, so on this basis one would not be able to determine which group first organized the society. Although Lowie (1913) suggested a few minor differences in the society of the two tribes, my informants explained that these were not important. This society differed somewhat from the others of the age-grade series in the acceptance of junior members to represent mythological characters associated with the buffaloes. In this respect, the society is patterned closely after the White Buffalo society owned by the women. In both instances they dramatized the return of the buffaloes to the village to dance and visit their junior members. The Bull society also included in its membership a number of young girls whose duty it was to "bring water for the buffaloes" when the society met. Whenever the Bull society was painting its members preparatory to making a public appearance, their announcer would go through the village and call "The buffalo herds are coming to the Missouri. Everyone come out and see them drink."

The similarity of masks and the popularity of the buffalo dance in the Mandan Okipa suggest, in light of the numerous references in the Okipa rites to the buffalo dances, a greater antiquity of the Bull society for the Mandan. However, the Bull dance was of wide distribution in the Plains and may well be a cultural feature that subsequently affected the Okipa. The Bull society seems to have lost its popularity after 1837 due to a change in the Hidatsa and the Mandan system of grouping sacred bundle owners. Formerly, owing to the greater village and tribal size, it was customary to subdivide the major bundle owners possessing sacred buffalo skulls according to related ceremonies. Thus, when a rain, wolf, or other ceremony was given, only those who owned rights in the particular ceremony met to receive goods and honors. The population was so small after 1837 that, generally, all those who possessed sacred buffalo skulls came irrespective of the bundles of which the sacred skulls were a part. In this internal tribal adjustment, an organization of sacred buffalo skull owners replaced the Bull society.

WOMEN'S SOCIETIES

If one excluded those women's societies recently adopted from the Mandan, little would remain to indicate an age-grade series for females. Both the White Buffalo and Goose societies were reportedly bought from the Mandan during the early 19th century. Both groups equate the Hidatsa Enemy society with the Mandan River society, although there are features not common to both tribes. The Mandan explain the differences as due to imitation of the River society rather than actual purchase. The Hidatsa, on the other hand, consider the Enemy society one of their age-grade series. After the building of Fishhook Village there was considerable crossing of tribal lines into the lower societies of the series, but each tribe maintained separate Goose and White Buffalo societies for several years after moving out onto the reservation.

SKUNK SOCIETY

The lowest of the Hidatsa societies, the Skunks, seems to have had no Mandan equivalent. The Skunk society consisted of young women from 15 to 20 years of age and a male singer selected by the society. Their "friends" were the men's Stone Hammer society; they assisted each other on various social occasions and for society purchases. Although purchases were made collectively, each woman of the society standing in the "father's sister–daughter" or "mother–daughter" relationship, it was not considered improper for others to paint themselves in the same manner and dance when the men returned from a successful war expedition. They were entitled to presents from those who had just returned with war honors. This was not an exclusive privilege of the society; frequently on such occasions others also took the victor's weapons and required payment for their return. Individuals were taken into the society from time to time by individual purchase and were considered full-fledged members thereafter.

ENEMY SOCIETY

Lowie (1913) gives a full account of the women's Enemy society. This was second in the series of Hidatsa age-grade societies and its members were "friends" of the Foolish [Crazy] Dogs. The society was composed of young married women who met whenever the men returned from a successful war expedition and took an important part in the victory parades. Although the Mandan think of this Hidatsa society as a poor imitation of the River society, the Hidatsa ascribe its origin to First Creator who organized the society for the purpose of dancing during the victory celebrations. Singers for the society were men of "friendly" societies and held their positions on invitation of the women.

GOOSE SOCIETY

The Goose society was of Mandan origin according to all of my informants, in spite of the fact that Maximilian (1906) lists it only for the Hidatsa. According to Mandan traditions, this society was of long standing with them and even preceded their arrival upstream to the Heart River. The society was associated with agriculture and had as its principal singers men who held rights in various corn ceremonies. This society differed from the societies of younger women by being concerned exclusively with rites for insuring good crops. According to Hidatsa traditions, the Awatixa were longest to have this society and, since this Hidatsa village group has the longest traditional history on the Missouri, it would appear that as each Hidatsa group settled on the Missouri, this society became a part of their society system. In the Mandan villages, the male singers were bundle owners who managed the garden and fertility rites. These sacred bundles were of two categories: those originating with the culture hero, Good-Furred-Robe, and those originating with Old-Woman-Who-Never-Dies. There were two bundles relating to the Good-Furred-Robe: the Medicine Robe and the Skull bundles. In early historic times, at least, these bundles were kept in different villages. Villages not represented by these two bundles had Goose societies whose singers were holders of Old-Woman-Who-Never-Dies bundles. It is with the latter pattern that the Hidatsa Goose societies were associated until 1837 at which time Bear-Looks-Out, an Awaxawi and owner of an Old-Woman-Who-Never-Dies bundle, received the Skull bundle through his wife, a Mandan. Her father contemplated putting it away since his family had experienced bad luck during the smallpox epidemic. He sold the bundle to his son-in-law, a normal transfer pattern for the Mandan who practiced clan-inheritance of tribal bundles, and thus the bundle passed to the Awaxawi village of Hidatsa. At that time both the Hidatsa and Awatixa had Goose societies associated with male singers owning rights in Old-Woman-Who-Never-Dies bundles. In 1845, when the three Hidatsa villages united, the three Goose societies were united into a single organization.

The purchase of the society was a group transaction. Young women who had belonged to the Enemy society, and any others who might wish to belong to the Goose society, met with the Goose society members to obtain their permission to buy. Since the society was chiefly concerned with agricultural pursuits, those showing little interest in the gardens generally did not care to buy. Meetings were held at the principal male singer's lodge. At Fishhook Village the Hidatsa met at Bear-Looks-Out's lodge until he transferred his Sacred Skull bundle to Poor Wolf, after which the meetings were held at the latter's lodge. During this period, the Mandans met at the lodge of Moves Slowly, he being the principal singer for the Mandan Goose society and the owner of the Good-Furred-Robe bundle. When one group was buying, they brought in food for 60 consecutive nights and placed it in rows inside the lodge. Young men who had been successful in war, two from each society, were selected to run toward the meat while the women cried. Afterward food was passed around to the selling group.

Women were usually between the ages of 30 and 40 when they entered the society. In addition to this age-grade group, one young girl was selected by the principal singer to carry their pipe on certain occasions and to present the pipe and dried meat to the principal singer. The younger member represented the duck and smaller water birds while the other female members represented geese. The selling group selected "daughters"—younger clan members or "brothers' daughters"—for each of whom they prepared an ear of white or yellow corn wrapped in white sage, a headband of gooseskin with the head attached,[25] and a complete set of clothing consisting of a buffalo robe, dress, leggings, and moccasins. A woman could select as many as four women standing in the relationship of "daughter." During the 60-day period of feasting, the younger women were taught the songs and rites of the society and received instruction in the traditional origin of the society and its relationship to other corn rites. In return for this instruction and the ceremonial paraphernalia, each younger woman paid her individual "mother" or "father's sister," according to the relationship that existed between them. At the end of the period, the society was surrendered to the younger women. However, there was not the same clear-cut separation from the society by the sellers as was practiced by the men buying into the men's societies.

Members of the Goose society frequently received supernatural experiences, associated with Corn rites, in which the individual was instructed in a vision to make feasts to the society or to various sacred bundles concerned with the corn. Some women also bought the right to have "corn spirits" come up in their throats on certain public occasions. These women were retained by the buyers as honored life members of the Goose society. They met with the society of younger women and on all other occasions when public rites were being performed by bundle owners having supernatural powers over the garden crops. These women might even retain their rights in the Goose society while buying into the next higher society, the White Buffalo Cows, with their own age group.

The most important meeting of the Goose society was held in the spring when the first water birds arrived from the south. Usually someone dreamed during the winter of the return of the water birds and asked permission of the society to prepare a feast for the geese when they returned so the Goose women could pray for good crops. Frequently, several people who had dreamed of the geese would go together and give the feast, otherwise a series of ceremonies were given individually by those receiving supernatural instruction. The women would meet with their singers at the appointed time and go to a point just outside the village where the rites were performed. This was the largest and most important ceremony heralding the first arrival of the water birds and the end of winter.

During the summer, individuals would frequently prepare feasts and ask the women of the Goose society to dance. At planting time

---

[25] The Hidatsa Goose society formerly did not have the headband. See Lowie, 1913, p. 335.

the women of the village would come to the singer who was performing the "fertility" rites on his earth lodge to receive a few kernels of each variety of corn, beans, squash, and sunflowers. Moves Slowly held superior status to Bear-Looks-Out in Fertility rites. It was believed that the corn spirits went south with the water birds in the fall and were cared for by Old-Woman-Who-Never-Dies until spring when they were sent northward again. As the geese were the messengers of the Old-Woman-Who-Never-Dies, so were the women of the Goose society the messengers of the sacred bundle owners.

When droughts threatened, the people would go to the sacred corn bundle owners who would invite the Goose society to dance. If the drought was prolonged, the Goose society members would invite others having rain ceremonial rights to perform their Rainmaking rites and pay them for their services. When a rainmaker failed to bring rain within a definite number of days, he would terminate his rites and direct them to take the goods to another rainmaker. If Hidatsa interpretations of the role of the Goose society are correct, all rainmaking rites were undertaken on the initiative of this society. There were a number of bundles that could be classified primarily as rainmaking bundles, but anyone who had fasted much and had demonstrated supernatural powers might be asked.

On one occasion during the 1860's, the Goose society took their goods to various men each of whom tried for a day or two, giving up when rain did not come. At last they asked help of Broken Ax, a Mandan noted for his numerous performances of the Okipa, and the rains came, penetrating the soil to the depth of a hand's width. Broken Ax did not think it would look proper for him to keep as personal possessions all of the goods contributed by the Goose society, so he shared everything with other "holy" men who had tribal bundles and with those who had fasted much during their youth. In gratitude for services rendered, the people of the village materially thanked the Goose society.

Slightly later, grasshoppers were numerous and flew into the river valley from the adjacent prairies, attacking the corn silk as fast as it appeared. The women of the Goose society again met to select "holy men" to help drive away the insects. Crows Heart, who observed the activities of the Goose society at that time, tells us that

The women were crying, for the grasshoppers were eating up their corn plants before the kernels could form. The Goose women were invited by those who had gardens to meet and see if something could be done to drive the insects away. Each day grasshoppers flying in the air near the sun would settle in the trees as the sun went down until they were so numerous that even the leaves were nearly all gone. The Goose women went to various men to ask their help; these men tried because they were asked and goods were promised to them. But the men were soon discouraged and quit. At last the women went to Broken Ax who had brought the rain, and put things before him. Broken Ax laughed when they came to him and said, "I can't do anything; no one ever heard of holy men driving away grasshoppers. I do not think grasshoppers would listen to me. Since you brought these things, I will try."

The women placed their goods in front of his medicine bundle with the pipe on top of the goods. He lit the pipe and prayed to his gods to help the women. The day turned out very hot; the grasshoppers rose up into the air in swarms as though going towards the sun. When night came, not a grasshopper was in the gardens. All this I saw as they went up toward the sun and we never knew what became of them. The people were all happy and thought that Broken Ax was surely a great medicine man.

The fall migration of the water birds was commemorated with ceremonial offerings by the Goose society. These rites were usually performed by the Goose society on invitation of some household as thanks for a good crop. It was believed that the geese and other water birds, as they traveled southward, participated in the feast and took the spirits of the corn and other garden crops with them to the Old-Woman-Who-Never-Dies who spent the winter months in a large earth lodge on an island near the mouth of the Mississippi River. As a rule, the Goose society did not meet during the late fall and winter months although, occasionally, someone would ask that they attend a feast and pray for good crops the succeeding season.

Some women were believed to have corn spirits in their body. These women were respected members of the society, for the appearance of an ear of corn in their throats might occur at any time of the year, particularly whenever a number of hungry people were sitting around a fire waiting to be fed. On these social occasions, the woman invariably had numerous "attacks" before the corn actually appeared in her mouth. Those sitting near her were expected to give her presents so that the corn would go back down. My informants claimed that after the woman received the goods and some of the food cooking at the fire, the ear of corn went back into place and did not pain her any more.

Although there was no objection to meetings of a social nature during the winter months if someone wanted to feed the members of the society, rites practiced at that time were not considered especially effective since the corn spirits were believed to be far away in the care of Old-Woman-Who-Never-Dies. For that reason, once the fall ceremony was completed, the Goose society was normally inactive until spring approached.

White Buffalo Cow Society

Beginning with the approach of winter, the women of the next older group, the White Buffalo Cow society, would talk of meeting for the purpose of bringing the winter buffaloes to the village. This was the highest of the organized age-grade women's societies known to the Hidatsa and Mandan. The society was of Mandan origin, according to both Mandan and Hidatsa informants, and does not appear to have been of long existence with the Hidatsa. Although Maximilian did not include the society in his Hidatsa series, Matthews (1877) listed it in his Hidatsa series as of Mandan origin. Boller gave a detailed eyewitness account of the winter buffalo-calling rites belonging to this society which is essentially the same as that furnished me by the older Hidatsa who recalled the particular winter and incidents mentioned by Boller (1868).

According to traditions, a Mandan was fasting on a high hill during the shortest and coldest nights of the winter. Each night he heard a voice above the noise of the wind and drifting snow. On the fourth night the voice was so near and distinct that he could distinguish the words. The voice kept repeating, "Put a child with them."

Soon a man came carrying two children. The man said to the faster, "I am going to give you these children. Prepare a feast of corn and I will come. I am the buffalo. When the feast is ready, I will come and then you will have winter buffaloes with you always."

The faster returned to the village and told the people of his experiences. He asked that a feast be prepared, using all the different kinds of corn, and he selected two old women to care for the small children. Soon a party of strange women arrived and showed the people how to perform the dance. Then the strange women ate the food prepared for them. When these buffalo women left, the two buffalo children struggled to free themselves to accompany their mothers. One escaped and the other was raised in the village as an Indian. Each year when the women dressed up and danced, the buffaloes would come back to see the little child who danced with them. The buffalo women would bring the winter buffalo herds with them.

Women not yet through the menopause were not permitted to join the society as it was believed that menstrual blood would drive the buffaloes away. This was in direct contrast to the belief that menstrual flows were "good" for the gardens. After the existing group had owned the society for 8 or 10 years, and the membership of the society was getting small from the death of its members, women who had belonged to the Goose society and such others as wished to belong to the White Buffalo Cow society, met and organized a temporary society for the purpose of negotiating for the purchase of the society rights from the older women. All ceremonies and negotiations were conducted after the gardens had been harvested in the fall and prior to the normal time for the return of the water birds. Since even talking of the society was believed to bring cold weather, women were reluctant even to think of the society or to hum its songs during the growing season lest frosts come and destroy their crops. Even as late as 1932, Calf Women and Scattercorn, representing the Hidatsa and Mandan societies respectively, who had entered the society as representatives of the buffalo calf left with the tribe, were reluctant to relate the myth or discuss the society with me during the month of August lest frosts destroy their gardens.

The actual sale of the society occurred in the late fall after the village had gone into winter camp. The purchasing group first made their intentions known to the older group; a sale price was agreed upon; and a date for the commencement of the instructions and meetings was set. In the meantime, each older woman selected from among the buying group those whom she addressed as "daughter" and for whom she prepared the clothing and other society paraphernalia. One could select as many as four "daughters," but ordinarily fewer were selected. The women built a sweat lodge frame at their meeting place and the purchasing group provided five or six robes for the covering. Each buyer gave a wooden bowl and robes to the individual from whom instructions, paraphernalia, and rights were obtained. The buying group selected one of their number to take the white robe and to occupy the leading position during the dances. She was one whose husband had an important role in other buffalo-calling rites. The child representing the buffalo calf of the origin myth was a girl 2 to 9 years of age. It was her duty to stand in the center of the line when dancing, with the hair of her tiny robe on the outside. A woman standing at the end of the line wore the robe of a summer buffalo and was known as Summer Buffalo. A woman standing next to the child wore her robe with the hairside out and attended to the incense as waiter for the group. All the other members wore robes with the skin side out. The special officers were females who either possessed buffalo bundles in their own right or were married to men with such rights. The child representative likewise came of a household possessing buffalo-calling rights. For the Mandan, Scattercorn was selected for this office because her father was the Hoita in the Okipa and possessed one of the sacred turtle drums used in that ceremony. When the last Hidatsa group purchased the White Buffalo Cow society, Calf Woman was selected by the older Hidatsa women because her father lived in the Mandan ceremonial lodge with his Mandan wives and was custodian of the buffalo masks worn by the Mandan during their Okipa performances.

In the purchase of this society, the Hidatsa adopted many features of the Mandan ceremonial system. The male singers for the Mandan were men who possessed ceremonial rights in the Okipa. The Hidatsa, having no comparable ceremony, selected men who had rights in existing buffalo ceremonies. The same association of male sacred bundle owners and a woman's society existing for the Goose society followed for the White Buffalo Cow society. Because of this association, when one group of women sold out, the sale did not affect the male singers whose positions were held by virtue of their rights in other ceremonies. The songs and rites were identical to those of the Mandan which suggests recent adoption from the Mandan. On the other hand, the Goose society differed slightly in paraphernalia, songs, and rites from the Mandan—consistent with native traditions that this society was adopted from the Mandan long before the White Buffalo society was purchased.

According to Mandan accounts, the Bull society formerly met with the White Buffalo Cow society during the winter observances, but in later years this men's society had died out. During the 19th century the Black Mouths met with the women since one of the important duties of this society was to organize the village for fasting when the days were shortest to bring the buffalo herds to the river bottoms near the village. When it was announced that the society was to meet on the invitation of some individual—frequently the man selected as Winter Camp leader—and that goods had been put up for the rites, it was the duty of the Black Mouths to enforce the quiet order in the village. Then the dogs were taken into the lodge; premature and individual hunting was prohibited; women remained near their lodges and cut no wood; and fires were frequently extinguished unless a strong wind was blowing from the direction the animals were taking. The women met each day at the lodge selected for the rites. During this time other individuals brought goods or horses and asked the women or the singers to pray to the buffaloes, telling them that the society was dancing and that they should come to see their "child." The robes belonging to the special officers, the sacred pipe, and the white headbands were smoked in the fumes from wild peppermint stems. If the buffalo herds were late arriving, the women would sometimes meet daily for quite a while. Usually their first meeting was when large herds were observed at a distance and the storms had begun.

CHARACTERISTICS OF THE HIDATSA AGE-GRADE STRUCTURE

The Hidatsa age-grade societies were organized and named groups comprising, with a few exceptions, persons of approximately the same age and sex. The few exceptions were older men retained as singers by those recently buying a new society, young women engaged by the Bull society to bring them water during public displays, male singers for the women's societies, young girls selected to represent the water birds in the Goose society, and the buffalo calf in the White Buffalo Cow society.   These societies cut across clan and moiety lines, dividing the population of the village into a number of organized groups.   In earlier times, when the Hidatsa lived in three or more villages, the societies were limited by village bounds and membership in a society of a different village was unusual except in those instances when one having rights in a particular society married and moved to another village.   In these instances the individual sold out his rights with his own group and participated subsequently with the society of his new residence.

In organization, all societies followed a characteristic pattern. There were officers who were distinguished from the rank and file members by special paraphernalia, face painting, and duties.   These invariably had distinguished themselves in various socially approved ways.   Men were usually selected by the group for bravery or other manifestations of military skill while women were selected for industry and participation in specific ritualistic activities.   Each society had a male announcer or crier whose duty it was to inform the village at large of the activities of the society.   He could be one of the regular membership or an older and respected person selected for his kindness to certain members of the society.

With regard to origin, the Hidatsa recognized two groups or societies; those for which no tribal origin myths were known, and which are therefore presumed to be of foreign origin, and those having tribal origin myths which they believed their ancestors founded.   Each society had prescribed rites and dances which in some way distinguished it from all other societies, while those societies having similarities were believed to be "related" to each other.   Each group had periodic meetings according to the traditional customs of the group and extra meetings whenever one of its members had distinguished himself in warfare.   The men's societies all placed great emphasis on warfare but had other functions as well.   Certain societies had ritualistic aspects and conceptual ties with bundle rites.   The Notched Stick was related to Corn rites at Awaxawi and it was believed that whenever the young boys of this society danced, rains were certain to fall.   The Lumpwood society used staffs resembling those of the Painted Red Stick and Thunder rites for buffalo calling and rainmaking respectively.   The Stone Hammer society was related to the Sun, Moon, and Woman Above rites.   The Dog societies were related to Earthnaming rites due to the use of owl feathers by both groups. The Bull society dances during the four seasons were symbolic of the buffaloes of the four seasons and directions.

Although the secrecy of the sacred rites did not apply to the age-grade societies, each society was clothed in a certain amount of sacredness by virtue of individual membership in various ceremonies. Each society was thought to possess collectively more supernatural power than the preceding one because individuals continuously sought supernatural powers until past middle age. Thus Stone Hammers were not thought to have collectively very much supernatural power since they had just begun their fasting, whereas members of the higher societies had individually fasted a great deal, participated in many ceremonies, and had given many feasts to older persons recognized as holy men.

The role of the age-grade system in providing a mechanism for the acquisition of supernatural powers is indicated by the similarity of the purchase to ceremonial purchases. With a few exceptions, the ceremonial purchase was by a "son" from his "father." The same pattern prevailed for age-grade purchases. Another feature of the ritualistic quest of supernatural power was that of the relinquishment of one's wife to the ceremonial "father."

The Hidatsa do not think of the societies in themselves as sacred, and informants offered no objections to discussing details concerned exclusively with the societies. Nevertheless, the Hidatsa think of a society purchase as a mode of acquiring supernatural power. A male secured this power during the purchase from individuals standing in a "father" relationship who prayed for their "sons," "walked" with their sons' "wives," and received various goods. Although the purchase was made as a group, it was essentially an individual affair between a man and one or more "sons." Some men preferred to have the same "father" for each successive society purchase while others thought more supernatural powers would be obtained if different "fathers" were selected for successive purchases. The concept of age-grade purchases as organized activities designed to acquire supernatural power is further indicated by the reluctance of a buyer to select as "father" one who had suffered repeated misfortunes or had a poor reputation. In fact, such unfortunate individuals frequently relinquished their sacred bundles or completely dropped out of the age-grade societies. Others took no part in age-grade activities until they had overcome their bad luck by successes in warfare, rain-making, or "calling the buffaloes."

This feature of acquiring individual supernatural powers within an organized group does not seem to be characteristic of the women's groups. The societies for younger women were concerned exclusively with warfare. Each of the Goose and White Buffalo Cow societies collectively purchased rights in specific ceremonies: agricultural and winter buffalo-calling rites. Men, on the other hand, did not acquire specific ceremonial rites through purchase of an age-grade society nor did they secure the right to participate in the "father's" ceremonies. Instead, they received only such supernatural power and assurances as the "fathers" offered them.

Societies were cooperating groups. Whenever an individual suffered misfortune, his society should help him. Men would help each other in warfare, assist in the recovery of stolen horses, and put up goods if one of their number was making important ceremonial purchases. Women would assist a sick member with food and clothing, and plant or care for her gardens. If a member died, the society would supply food and gifts to the relatives of the deceased for the funeral rites. On occasions when a member of the society returned with war honors, the society would dance and put up goods for the victory rites. Other men's groups, two societies removed, would likewise assist on these occasions.

The concept of group cooperation extended to the opposite sex as well. Each men's society usually enlisted the assistance of a women's society composed of individuals of the same age and known as "friends." This "friend" relationship between societies of opposite sex does not seem to be integrated into the traditions and sacred myths of the tribe nor was there agreement among informants as to "friend" groups of the opposite sex. This suggests that, due to recent borrowing of the River, Goose, and White Buffalo Cow societies from the Mandan, the Hidatsa had not established a fixed system of correlations strengthened by custom. Informants all agreed that the Stone Hammer and Skunk societies were "friends," but this may be due to the fact that these societies are of Hidatsa origin and of long traditional existence in the tribe. The Enemy Women are usually associated with the Crazy Dogs but sometimes selected the Lumpwoods as "friends." Likewise the Goose society sometimes had either the Crazy Dogs or the Lumpwoods as "friends." But the selection was largely a matter of age. The women of the Mandan Goose society had the Fox or the Black Mouths for their "friends" because, as they said, this association was based on the creation of these three societies by Good-Furred-Robe. The White Buffalo Cow society was the "friend" of the Black Mouth society. It seems probable that they formerly were also "friends" of the Bull society, as with the Mandan for whom traditions and customs are more definite, and that the Bull society was not associated with them in later years chiefly because the Bulls died out early with the Hidatsa. The record indicates that "friends" were established societies of opposite sex based chiefly on relative age rather than on any preconceived ideas of societies belonging together.

Theoretically, everyone ought to belong to a society—in practice, many did not join in or were in and out through life. If an individual belonged to a society, both he and his society members were subject to the ridicule of his "joking relatives." The societies reached a smaller percentage of women. Although theoretically noncompetitive, some evidence of rivalry for position existed among the societies after 1845 due to the union of the remnants of three village groups with slightly different age-grade systems.

One owned rights in a society until he sold out. If regular purchases were not made, accumulation of ceremonies occurred. For instance, if the Half-Shaved Heads bought the Black Mouth society before selling their rights to the Lumpwoods, they would own two societies. Temporarily, the Half-Shaved Head dances would not be performed since a group expressed its position in the system by the highest society owned. The same situation frequently developed when the Dogs bought the Old Dog society before selling out to the Black Mouths. If a society was not bought by the younger group, ownership was retained by the existing members as long as they lived. In recent years, societies went together to purchase other dances such as the Grass and Night Grass dances brought to the tribe by the Sioux. This destroyed the age-grade character of the system and the societies quickly died out through failure of the younger men to continue the purchases.

Each village group had independent societies and, as seen in table 4 (p. 175), slight differences existed between villages because of their different histories and group contacts. Although the membership of a society was limited to the village group, a "friend" relationship existed between the same societies of different villages. There were two Hidatsa concepts of property transfer. The first, or "father–son" transfer, provided for an actual transfer and relinquishment of rights (as when one organized group sold to a group of "sons") and was the pattern of society sales within the village. The second transfer pattern was known as "taking in friends" and was the method of transferring society rights to another village or tribe without relinquishing original ownership. Thus, if a group from another village or tribe wished to buy a society owned by the Hidatsa, after the details of the purchase price and time for the sale had been arranged, the buying group was considered "friends." The buying group then selected individual "friends" of the sellers who were, in the case of two groups having common clans, individuals of the same or related clans. There was nothing unique in this system since Hidatsa commonly adopted either a "son" or a "friend" of other village or tribal groups. The buying group paid their individual "friends" for the paraphernalia and the right to own the society in the same manner as when the buying group was of the same village.

The "friend" relationship established during the sale of society rights was a permanent one between groups of individuals. While visiting neighboring villages or tribes, these "friends" treated each other as brothers or, in the case of the women's societies, as sisters. They were invited to live with a "friend," usually a clansman, for the duration of the visit. Although an individual had rights only in the particular society of the village where he bought, the concept of group assistance to an unfortunate member extended to other villages as well. When a man undertook to avenge a brother killed by the enemy, society members of other villages frequently volunteered to give military aid. In light of the wide territory occupied by the various Hidatsa village groups prior to 1785, the diffusion of many common age-grade societies to all village groups no doubt strengthened the ties between the different village groups when they moved to the Knife River region. The establishment of common societies with the Mandan likewise probably contributed much to peaceful relations with that tribe.

Although the Hidatsa think of age-grading as an institution of considerable antiquity, they think of the number of societies making up the series as increasing through the years. A parallel situation prevailed in regard to the ceremonies. They speak of ancient times when the people had few skills, few ceremonies, and much hunger. To them, their golden age was prior to the appearance of the Whites and their diseases; an age of many societies and ceremonies. Of the numerous societies found among the Hidatsa, the Stone Hammer and various Dog societies have the best claim for respectable antiquity since they are of traditional antiquity and are frequently mentioned in their origin and sacred myths. If we eliminate the women's societies of traditional Mandan origin, we have remaining nothing of a women's age-grade system. Thus, it would appear that the Hidatsa have borrowed more from the Mandan than they have given in return.

WARFARE

INTERTRIBAL RELATIONS

Military activities had social, ceremonial, and economic aspects which affected the entire population. There was scarcely any aspect of their cultural life left unaffected by the intensive warfare that ranged about them on the Plains during the period for which we have documentary accounts and traditional information of Hidatsa informants. Nor was the prehorse period one of peace between tribes; there are numerous traditional accounts of expeditions far into the eastern woods or into the valleys of the Rockies even before the horse reached them. Although the Thompson accounts speak of their former residence on the Red River and its tributaries, until driven out by the Chippewa who first obtained guns, most Hidatsa traditions refer to an even earlier residence on the Missouri by some groups. Thus, it is to be presumed that formerly, as given by the traditions, the Hidatsa and Crow groups as we know them today were scattered along the lower portion of the Yellowstone, the Little Missouri, the Missouri from the mouth of the Yellowstone to Square Buttes and then eastward into the Devils Lake, Red River, and Sheyenne River regions. Archeological evidence indicates that those groups living on the Missouri practiced agriculture and held firmly, in cooperation with the Mandan, a considerable section of the Missouri from the Knife River to the Cannonball. So far as we know today, the larger area claimed by the Hidatsa as the exclusive territory of the Crow, Hidatsa, and Mandan groups was formerly uncontested by other groups with a peripheral area into which many groups occasionally penetrated.

Numerous efforts have been made to interpret Hidatsa migrations in terms of an old Mandan tradition that tells of the first arrival of the Hidatsa-proper on the Missouri at a point a short distance above the mouth of Heart River where they were named by the Mandan who gave them their first corn. This tradition, however, is not consistent with the general traditions of the various Hidatsa groups which operated independently, nor with the archeological evidence of the area. The Mandan have made a great deal of their traditions of teaching corn growing to the Hidatsa-proper, but this is in direct contradiction to the Thompson-supported Awaxawi traditions of an agricultural economy on the tributaries of the Red River and in the Devils Lake region (Thompson, 1916, pp. 225–237) and the archeological record for the Schultz sites on the lower Sheyenne which tie up very closely with the oldest traditional Awaxawi sites on the Missouri. Although my researches do not reveal any evidence that the Awaxawi abandoned the eastern region because of the pressure of enemy groups equipped with firearms, their former residence there is indicated by traditions and the custom of the older people even within the memory of living informants to return to their later village sites around Devils Lake. Instead, the Awaxawi traditions speak of a former prehistoric agricultural life on the streams to the east and at Devils Lake prior to a "continental flood" which drove them westward onto the Missouri where they found related groups already established in earth lodge villages.

The Awatixa village group had lived so long on the Missouri that even in Lewis and Clark's time they had no traditions of residence

elsewhere.   Their large traditional village at the mouth of the Knife
River indicates a period of long residence; probably since 1550 or 1600.
Their traditions are largely concerned with the later settlement of the
other Hidatsa groups on the Missouri River, and the Crow groups on
the adjacent Plains.   Neither does the Hidatsa–River Crow migration tradition supply us with positive evidence of pressure from eastern
groups as the basis for their westward movement.   However, the
traditionally late westward movement of the Awaxawi and the
Hidatsa–River Crow indicates a general abandonment of the territory
east and northeast of the Missouri about the time firearms were first
introduced to tribes in the Winnipeg and Great Lakes area.

Except for the traditional village site of the Awatixa at the mouth
of the Knife River, none of the traditional Hidatsa-proper or Awaxawi
sites on the Missouri show evidence of great antiquity.   On the
basis of pottery types represented in these sites, it has been possible
to distinguish them from those of the adjacent Mandan and to indicate
that during their residence on the Missouri these Hidatsa village
groups were both sedentary and agricultural.   Except for short
periods, their agricultural villages were at or below the mouth of
the Knife River, although the same pottery complex is widely distributed in hunting camp sites upstream along the Missouri and the
Lower Yellowstone as well as on tributaries (such as the Little
Missouri and the Powder Rivers) wherever a quantity of wood was
available.   The basic similarity of the pottery types and frequency
of types over a wide area extending westward from the Sheyenne
and Devils Lake area to the Yellowstone suggests that there were
continuous contacts between the various Hidatsa-Crow groups and
that the abandonment of the eastern wooded section of their territory was rather late, but that it preceded the introduction of the horse.

A significant feature of the Hidatsa position upstream from the
large concentrated Mandan population below Painted Woods and the
Crow position to the west of the Mandan is the fact that they lived
here together in a weak confederation of independent village groups.
With one exception, a short war between the Hidatsa-proper living
above the Knife and the Awaxawi living farther downstream who
undertook to establish a permanent village above the Hidatsa, there
are no traditional accounts of warfare among these three tribes.
With the final abandonment of the region east of the Missouri, this
cluster of friendly tribes controlled an area from the mouth of the
Cannonball to the mouth of the Yellowstone thence upstream to the
Powder River and eastward across the Little Missouri with the
course of the Cannonball as their southern limits.   The three tribes
held a commanding position in this region until 1780, living peacefully
and assisting each other in conducting offensive warfare against those

groups which attempted to penetrate the region. Prior to 1780 the Assiniboin pressure to the north had scarcely been felt (in 1738, La Vérendrye found them living back from the Missouri farther to the northeast), but the Sioux had already moved into the Red River, James River, and Devils Lake regions. Even as late as 1797, Thompson found the Assiniboin northeast of the Hidatsa on the Mouse River, in the Turtle Mountains and northward, with the Sioux as far west as the Dog Dens and in general control of the tall grass east of the Missouri.

After 1780 the Hidatsa, together with the Mandan and Arikara, were under constant pressure from mounted nomadic groups frequently better equipped with firearms. This was also the period of devastating smallpox epidemics. Both these factors materially affected them. Before 1780, having the powerful Mandan village groups to the south in the direction of the Sioux and Arikara, the Hidatsa showed little inclination to fortify their villages or even place them for defense or the easier and safer herding of the horses. There is no archeological evidence that ditch and wall fortifications were constructed at their principal villages prior to 1780 although the Mandans to the south had been fortifying strongly since before A.D. 1500. However, the Mandan situation was somewhat different; their pressure was as great during later years from the Arikara living below them on the Missouri as from the nomadic groups, particularly the Sioux and Cheyenne.

The epidemics of the 1780's materially changed the picture on the Missouri, for the sedentary bands usually lived together in large agricultural groups during the summer and in somewhat smaller winter camps situated close to each other. The nomadic bands rarely came together as large social groups for longer than a few weeks during the summer, thus contagious diseases weakened them less than the sedentary groups. The losses of the latter are painfully evident when a comparison is made between the large Mandan village sites with European trade material near the Heart River, abandoned after this epidemic, and the two small villages of survivors reported by Lewis and Clark to be living near Fort Clark in 1804. Of the Hidatsa groups, the Awatixa and Awaxawi suffered most, probably due to their custom of going into winter camp as a village unit. In contrast, the Hidatsa-proper, then consisting of organized bands which sometimes practiced agriculture, broke up into smaller winter hunting camps much as did the Assiniboin described by Thompson in 1797.

A further factor affecting the Hidatsa village groups was their position on the Plains. To the northeast, the Assiniboin and Chippewa had permanent trading posts situated near them at a much earlier date and were better armed than their western neighbors. To the south, the Sioux (Dakota) had immediate access to trading posts on the Missouri and Mississippi and endeavored to prevent trade with the earth lodge groups. Other Siouan (Dakota) groups traded regularly with the posts in Minnesota. Even as late as 1800 traders found it difficult to reach the Missouri to trade with the Hidatsa and Mandan. On the other hand, due to their northern and eastern position in the Plains, the horse reached them rather late; raids by mounted Indians from the southwest were of common occurrence by 1780 although the Hidatsa were probably not completely mounted by that time. The first result of these factors—horses and White trade—was a concentration of the population into compact villages. Whereas their village sites of prehorse times, with the exception of the Awatixa, were composed of widely scattered lodges and small clusters of lodges (as seen at the Upper Sanger, Gaines, and Fort Clark Station sites below the Knife) or the temporary campsites (as the Energy or Stanton Ferry sites, and elsewhere to the mouth of the Yellowstone River), the population now either went into strongly fortified sites (Big Hidatsa 35, Lower Hidatsa 34, Rock Village 53, or Awaxawi 32), or completely abandoned the region above the Knife River for summer villages and united with the River Crow. Not only were the post-1780 villages reduced in size by compactly arranging the lodges, but they were very strongly fortified with ditches and walls. After one attempt to maintain a village—Rock Village—some miles north of the Knife River, the population united at the mouth of the Knife River and built the three villages observed by Lewis and Clark in 1804.

There was a comparable concentration of the Mandan population a few miles downstream from the Hidatsa villages. When the Mandan originally abandoned the Heart River region, the east side or Nuptadi Mandan sought to move above the Hidatsa on the Missouri and thus violate a long-standing arrangement of village groups. These Mandan had been intimately associated with the Awaxawi and the Mandan of Painted Woods while living farther downstream and had intermarried with them. Nevertheless, the Hidatsa refused them permission to move above the mouth of the Knife River in territory claimed as exclusive Hidatsa hunting territory. The Hidatsa welcomed the Mandans, however, as close neighbors and the entire Mandan population finally united into two village groups downstream from the Hidatsa where they were found by Lewis and Clark in 1804. A period of close cooperation between these village groups in all matters of common interest followed. They assisted each other in warfare at a time when the Crow had moved so far west as to afford little aid. Although permanent ties with the Crow were now severed, Hidatsa war parties and visiting groups often went to the Crow and assisted them in stealing horses until the aboriginal culture broke down.

Whereas during the 18th century, the Arikara were in conflict with the Mandan and Hidatsa in their northward penetration of the Missouri River valley, by the close of the century they were willing to cooperate with their northern earth lodge neighbors against a common enemy—the Sioux. Peace between the Arikara and their northern agricultural neighbors developed slowly due to old grievances—chiefly competition for agricultural grounds—and trouble frequently broke out during the period prior to 1837. As the pressure of the Sioux increased, numerous efforts were made to bring the Arikara into the earth lodge federation. In 1836, after a few years of nomadic life when their corn crops failed, the Arikara came north with the intention of rebuilding (Greenshield site) near Painted Woods. This region had been abandoned by the Hidatsa and Mandan groups in their northward migration along the Missouri and one village group of Arikara from the Grand River had, on several occasions, settled there temporarily. This arrangement was generally accepted by the Hidatsa and Mandan, now greatly reduced in numbers, for it offered protection on the south from the Sioux who had meanwhile hunted in the Heart and Cannonball River regions abandoned by the Mandan a half century earlier. So the Arikara came to the trading post at Fort Clark in the late winter of 1837 and were received by the Hidatsa and Mandan (Chardon, 1932, p. 100). During the late winter, one Arikara band went out hunting with the Hidatsa onto the Upper Missouri and the other remained with the Mandan.[26] When spring came they did not separate to build a separate village as had been planned, and when smallpox broke out that summer, the three tribes suffered so severely that the Arikara took over and occupied the Mandan village at Fort Clark. From that time on, the Arikara were accepted as friends;[27] they assisted the Hidatsa and Mandan when attacked. After 1837 there was growing evidence that, due to increased pressure by the Sioux, the Assiniboin should be included in this federation. Whereas the Arikara had carried on continuous warfare with the Crow on every occasion, with the establishment of friendly relations with the Hidatsa, warfare with the Crow was discontinued. The Hidatsa had established permanent friendly relations with a few Assiniboin bands after a century or more of conflict with them over the control of the Missouri upstream

---

[26] They probably represented the two separate village groups reported by Maximilian and others during the period 1810–34.

[27] Occasionally, quarrels occurred which demanded prompt action by the respective police and councils. For procedures in resolving these differences before the entire groups became involved, see Chardon, 1932, p. 188.

from the Knife. These cooperating groups camped together during the winter and went out on friendly hunting expeditions together. This friendship had never extended to the entire Assiniboin tribe, for the western Assiniboin were in constant conflict with the Crow and those Hidatsa living with the Crow after 1845. Likewise, there was a great deal of hard feeling toward the western Assiniboin bands for their attacks on that northernmost Hidatsa group which had attempted to establish a village above the Big Bend after the epidemic of 1837. On the other hand, marriage, adoption rites, and temporary winter residence worked to bring about a federation with friendly eastern Assiniboin bands. During the Sioux wars, the Assiniboin often left old people or widows with small children unable to travel or to stand the rigors of winter with the Hidatsa when leaving for the winter villages after coming to the Hidatsa to trade for corn. During the 19th century, a number of people were adopted into the tribe and married Hidatsas or Mandans. In addition, small children sometimes were left in alien villages—while their parents were trading for corn—to be raised by the inhabitants of that village. On a few occasions shortly after 1800, when the Assiniboin were contesting the Hidatsa for the Missouri River region, the latter destroyed Assiniboin winter hunting camps, taking the women and children as captives. Once taken into the tribe, these captives maintained a dual citizenship which was acceptable to the Hidatsa. Assiniboin coming to trade would visit their relatives in the village and, as far as can be determined, once a female had married and had children by a Hidatsa father, her position was more secure than with her own group. In several instances, however, where the Hidatsa husband had died, no objection was raised when she returned with her children to her own people. These were household decisions over which the council had no authority. Her children were related to groups of individuals in both tribes and could and did move back and forth between both tribes without risk of their lives as long as they were recognized.

The practice of intergroup visiting and "adoption" had made great progress toward terminating warfare between the Hidatsa and certain bands of Assiniboin, Chippewa, and Sioux even before the aboriginal culture broke down. These alien groups came to the Hidatsa villages for prolonged annual visits and, on several occasions, assisted the Hidatsa when attacks were made on the village. Groups of aliens sometimes went into winter camp with the Hidatsa and got along very well.

A man organizing a war party invariably avoided attacks on those bands with which he was related by blood (in much the same manner as did Medicine Bear of the Sioux, whose mother was from the Mandan village of Nuptadi).   In the case of a few alien bands of small size that had maintained frequent contacts with the Hidatsa and were known individually to all of the young Hidatsa, learning that an encampment was of their acquaintances, they went into the camp to visit rather than to steal their horses.   In one instance, a war party of young Hidatsas went to Devils Lake to steal horses from the Sioux. Discovering that the horses stolen during the night were those which their people had given to a band of Chippewas a few weeks before to send them away happy, and knowing that their relatives would disapprove of stealing horses from their friends, they drove the horses back into the Chippewa camp, telling them of their mistake.   The young men of the two tribes then organized a common raid on a distant Sioux camp.   Even as late as the 1850's, warriors of friendly bands would come to Fishhook Village to visit when on the way to the Arikara village at Fort Clark to steal horses.

TRAINING

No other aspect of the culture received as much attention as warfare. As soon as a boy was old enough to walk, he was given a bow and arrows; childhood games emphasized military adventures in imitation of their elders.   Observing the behavior of the older people as they danced and sang the victory songs when a successful war party returned, or wept when the party was unsuccessful, the small children would, with the encouragement of their elders, go on imaginary war expeditions although the enemy defeated was often only a young gopher or rabbit.   Waving the dead animal, and with their faces blackened with the dirt from a pocket gopher's mound, they would come into the village or a make-believe village consisting of old hides hung over bushes, singing the victory songs and waving their trophies.   The little girls, pretending to be the sisters or the wives of the warriors, would paint up, often with the help of their older relatives, and dance as the young women of the Enemy, River, or other societies did.

As children grew older they could observe the preparation of young men for military careers: the, at first, brief attempts to endure the tortures of the 4-day fasts during the Sun Dance or the Wolf ceremony; the prolonged fasts during the ceremonies providing opportunities for self-torture or the organized fasts under the supervision of old war leaders; and, finally, long sustained fasting either alone on the prairies, at the skull circles, or about the village when thongs were inserted into their flesh by which they were suspended or buffalo skulls were dragged.   Equally important in molding the young man's character were the visible positive awards by which the society recognized military achievements; the public parade with the victor mounted on a horse; the bestowal of a new name and the privilege of making a public display of giving away goods; the praises of the relatives; the right to wear emblems, symbolic of military accomplishments, on public occasions and particularly when visiting tribes came; or the right to assume an important role in rites reserved for the brave. Wolf Chief described the training of the young men as equivalent to a wagon drawn along a deeply rutted road; there was no way to get out of the road except by going forward in the same path as others had done before—one could make no progress backing up, and the depth of the ruts prevented one from taking a different course. A young man, according to Wolf Chief, got along very well as long as he performed in exactly the same way as his elders had; he was destined to be very unhappy if he attempted to stray the least bit from the beaten path. The only effective alternate was to become a berdache. As a boy grew up, the culture provided him with many opportunities to prepare for a military career; there were the organized footraces and military games supervised by the older men, horse racing and contests on horseback, and shooting contests of various sorts.

The ritualistic aspects of warfare were highly developed. Young people were encouraged to fast to secure supernatural powers so that their lives would be saved when they went to war or when the village was attacked. Supervision was the duty of the older members of the clan, but it was from the father and the members of the father's clan that one secured most of his ritualistic training. The older men would endeavor to prevent unauthorized war or horse raiding parties from leaving the village. The Hidatsa were realistic about military training, for they mixed a bit of both ritualistic and technical training and never confused the two. One ought to have a considerable knowledge of both. The successful war leaders would watch the young men at their games or at their fasting and encourage them to make even greater efforts with a promise that they would soon be ready for war, but the society frowned on efforts of the young men to shortcut the established procedures. An older clan member would often bring together a number of his "younger brothers" and send them out to some spot a distance from the village. There, under the supervision of a recognized war leader, the young men fasted with the promise that those who had successful dreams and fasted faithfully would be taken on the next horse-stealing expedition. This supervisor was paid for his services by the young men's households and even by those young men who had secured appropriate visions. In return for the goods, the "leader of the fast" prayed for the success of the giver.

The Hidatsa were continuously plagued with unauthorized military expeditions led by irresponsible young men. The weight of disapproval rested primarily with the "father" of the young man indicating a desire to go out, and it was his duty to cancel these socially disapproved expeditions. In these matters, the father should be obeyed. The Hidatsa villages were not so large that news of a contemplated expedition did not spread quickly. Collectively, the fathers of all of the boys carried considerable prestige. Although the Black Mouths enforced the edict against war parties leaving on occasions when the public welfare required that all remain in the village for the mutual defense of the group, such crises generally were met successfully by the prestige relatives, the "fathers." The various families, however, were greatly concerned for the safety of their untrained youths. Since a leader must have warriors to make up his party, the older people usually were successful in breaking up any plans of an ambitious but unqualified leader simply by securing invitations for their young men from recognized successful leaders leaving soon on a raid. Nevertheless, young men did, from time to time, bypass most of the requirements for military leadership.

When a competent war leader was in the territory where an unauthorized group of young men was looking for horses, it was common practice to waylay them and embarrass them before their relatives and friends at home. The most common way of doing this was to observe the young men from a distance until they had tied up their horses for the night and had put their arms aside to eat and sing about their girls. Then, during the night, one group would steal the horses while others sneaked up to the camp, rushed the unsuspecting fellows, and struck them with whips or seized them as though they were enemies, all the while calling to each other "I have struck one Sioux" or "this Sioux was not very smart; he doesn't know how to protect himself." By calling out when making the charge, the young men were informed that the attacking party was of their own tribesmen. Nevertheless, the attacking group endeavored to inflict severe beatings on the young fellows and to frighten them so that in the future they would avoid surprise attacks.

About 1872 a war party was out under the leadership of Kidney in the Devils Lake region when the scouts reported seeing two men approaching driving two horses. The leader directed the party to wait until late in the evening when the two men would be engaged preparing their meal as the best time to make the attack. Kidney's men crept in close and led the stolen horses away from the camp. One large horse was gentle and Crows Heart recognized it in the dark by its large joints as belonging to Bear Necklace. Kidney did not believe him so the horse was taken back to their camp and examined in the light of their own campfire.   Knowing then that the party was from Fishhook Village, Kidney announced that they would have some fun with them and "strike them" while they slept.   They sneaked in close and listened to the young fellows talk, not knowing that their horses had been taken from them and that "enemies" were in the neighborhood.   Kidney's party rushed them so fast that it was not possible to tell who had "struck the coups."   The boys were without food as the enemy had been close on their tracks.   Nevertheless, they had permitted their own people to sneak into their camp, steal their horses, and strike coups on them.   The boys were fed and their horses were returned to them in the morning.   Their credit for stealing two horses was somewhat dampened when Kidney's party returned and told the young men's joking relatives of striking coup on them in the night.

The Hidatsa endeavored to organize their military activities so that the warriors advanced in status by degrees in much the same manner as advancements were made through the age-grade series.   Boys 14 or 15 years of age who had done some fasting, were skilled with weapons, and were handy around horses, were selected as camp tenders as rewards for effective and faithful fasting or for caring for the older men's horses.   On these military expeditions, the boys waited on the leader and the older men of Old Wolf status, bringing wood for the fires, preparing the food, and attending to the horses.   On these trips, the boys were given few opportunities to leave the main party either to steal horses or to engage in fighting: The leader kept them near him all the time.   They assisted the leader by bringing things needed in the rites—wood, branches, or dried buffalo manure—and usually served as waiter in passing the ceremonial pipes around to the warriors. Whenever the leader called for assistance, the camp tenders were expected to jump up and perform the duty requested, even though one could do the job as well as several.   Camp tenders cared for the horses, seeing that they got water and grass, and generally made themselves useful wherever they could.   In case a member was wounded in battle, they cared for him.   The military pattern provided public recognition for their services and those who performed faithfully were praised publicly when the party returned to the village.   Even in later life, as a distinguished war leader, one would often relate publicly his exploits as a boy when he built a travois on which to bring back to the village those wounded in battle, feeding and watching over them all the time, and thus saving their lives.

Even as those who had shown interest and obedience while serving as camp tenders were praised publicly by the leader, names of those who were lazy and wanted to sleep all the time were omitted.   The tribe would listen during the Victory dances for the names of those who had distinguished themselves, and repeat the names of relatives who had contributed to the success of the military expedition. The mention of a relative's name was an occasion to bring forth presents to be given away in the name of the one so distinguishing himself. Hearing that a young man had distinguished himself as a camp tender and had shown great interest in getting a good reputation, other war leaders would compete for his services, even promising him a higher position as a scout.

OFFENSIVE WARFARE

Offensive warfare was primarily pursued as a result of a vision in which one was instructed to go out in a particular direction or to a certain spot where honors would come to the one following all the prescribed rules set down by the guardian spirit. In one instance the vision recipient would be promised a specified number of horses to be distinguished by distinctive features, such as color or the manner in which they were grazing. In other instances, a specified number of enemy lodges or households were "seen" in the vision. However, the Hidatsa did not approve of young untrained men's expeditions away from the village. When a young man reported his vision to his household, particularly the father or an older brother-in-law occupying the position of father, he was advised to accompany an older and better-trained leader in the hope that the things revealed to him in the vision would come true, or to forego taking possession of that which had been promised him in the vision until a later time. So, at any time, there would be many individuals claiming ownership of horses or scalps of which they had never been able to take possession. Frequently, in the social and ceremonial activities of the village, an older man too feeble to go out on military expeditions "gave" to a "son" his rights to certain horses encountered under the conditions described in his earlier dreams. Then, regardless of the person first seeing a peculiarly marked horse, the horse was delivered to the one having prior right to it by vision or purchase from this "father."

A young man who had given numerous feasts to the older men of the father's clan frequently had a number of these claims to complete. If one was anxious to go out to take possession of these animals, the older people of the household and of the clan benefiting most by the completion of the claim were the first to discourage individual initiative by young men, or someone of the household skilled in warfare would volunteer to serve as military leader and invite others to assist him in making up the war party. Offensive warfare was conducted entirely on the basis of vision instructions either as the result of one's own visions or the visions bought from another who had never completed his prior claims. These visions were received during the privations of one of the formal ceremonies or as a result of prolonged fasting; but, more often, after pledging to purchase the father's ceremonial rites when the young man had already distinguished himself in warfare and had consequently married.

When a person signified his intentions of leading a war party, he undertook to make up his expedition by invitation. As he went from household to household, inviting various young men to accompany him, approval or disapproval was given by the older men. If the older people thought he was not ready to go out, they would discourage their young men; if they thought the visions were genuine, they would encourage their young men by providing sacred objects to be worn during the trip. A young man leading his first military expedition invariably endeavored to give the organization dignity by inviting as coleaders individuals who had formerly distinguished themselves in warfare so that the personnel of the party would be composed of experienced persons as well as beginners. Theoretically, the party was invited to meet at a place outside the village at a certain time. In practice, however, it was not uncommon for others to go along without invitation. Those who had already distinguished themselves were welcome additions to the party while beginners were tolerated. Informants could not remember any instances when unwelcome individuals were refused permission to go along.

When the party had assembled at the predetermined meeting place, usually a day's journey from the village, the leader selected the various officers: the coleaders or Old Wolves were selected on the basis of their ceremonial membership and previous military record; the Young Wolves comprised the remainder of the party which was, in turn, subdivided into scouts, warriors, and camp tenders, depending on the size of the party. If the party was small and carefully selected, the group consisted only of Old Wolves led by the military leader and the scouts under a leader selected by the leader of the Old Wolves. The position of leader of the scouts was given to one of wide military experience, frequently one who had come up through the ranks and had been a war party leader in charge of the rites on other occasions. He organized and directed the other scouts working with him and determined whether an attack should be made in the event the enemy was found. Frequently the scouts were the only ones to meet the enemy since, once having fulfilled the objectives of the expedition without loss of men, the expedition was terminated and the party returned to the village. The Hidatsa endeavored to find the horses promised or the enemy as seen in the dream and, once these objectives had been attained, the leader's mission was completed. He had succeeded in establishing the potency of his sacred bundle.

Hidatsa offensive warfare was normally highly ritualistic in character, particularly as practiced by those who held rights in the established ceremonies. For that reason, the older people endeavored to keep their sons associated with these recognized leaders rather than with young aspiring men whose sole claim to distinction was based on personal vision experiences not immediately associated with the long-established bundle rites. Personal vision experiences were considered adequate for membership and participation in military adventures under a highly successful leader whose authority stemmed from wide participation in the tribal rites. To be successful as a war leader, however, it was believed that, in addition to property rights in well-established sacred bundles, one should fast to the limits of one's endurance, give freely to other recognized holy men, and assist a great deal in the performance of village rites, particularly those concerned with buffalo calling.

If we are to believe native traditions, there was a greater tendency among the population of Hidatsa village to organize war expeditions on the basis of supernatural experiences outside of the formalized village ceremonialism—and with public approval—than there was among the Awatixa and Awaxawi who conformed more closely to the Mandan pattern that war leadership should be restricted to those who had pledged or had performed public ceremonies. From our knowledge of the history of the Hidatsa in relation to their neighbors, this would suggest that they more closely conformed to the Crow pattern than to that of the more sedentary Awatixa, Awaxawi, and Mandan. With the union of the Hidatsa village units, this tendency of certain groups to initiate military expeditions on the basis of a personal vision, although approved by a portion of the population, was a source of friction with the more conservative Awatixa and Awaxawi. After 1860, Crow-Flies-High more or less represented the progressive element, and his unusual military successes outside of the formal pattern of the Awatixa and Awaxawi eventually lead to internal friction which was not reconciled until the progressive group broke away under his and Bobtail Bull's leadership.

Although the rituals performed while on the military expeditions vary slightly according to the rules belonging to the bundles and bundle lines, the general organization and practices were essentially the same. The following narrative by Wolf Chief indicates many of the basic features of the Hidatsa warfare pattern:

Kidney gave the Wolf Ceremony in May to buy his father's Wolf bundle. He had a dream just after giving the ceremony so he decided to go out to war to try out the powers of his new bundle. I went along with him from Fishhook Village. There were nearly 40 men and large boys selected by Kidney.

He selected a place to stop near the present town of Stanton where he said he would try that night to find out what was going to happen. In the morning he said that he was going to appoint the scouts to go out ahead on horseback. He picked up the sacred bundle and walked a few yards from us, spread it out and said, "Crows Breast, step forward; also Red Robe, Rabbit Head, Crazy Raven, Wolf Chief, Old Dog, and Good Bear. Crows Breast will be the leader of the scouts for he is already a headman. You will go over towards Wolf Den Buttes and see if there are any enemies. We will follow you over that way and build the fire and you will come back and meet us. Crows Breast, I want you to stand in front of me; I will paint you just as I saw things in my dream right after giving the Wolf Ceremony. I will paint you with white clay first, for you are the leader of the scouts; then I will paint the other scouts. I will sing a holy song."

He wet the white clay but before he painted us, he sang one of the Wolf songs. As he painted, he sang and talked to his gods saying, "You are our leaders and we want you to give us good luck."

Then he sang, "When I look for a horse, I always say this." He sang this song because he wanted to get a horse.

As he painted the foreheads of the young wolves or scouts, he said to the wolf hide, "I want you to save their lives when they strike the enemy; I want to see them all have good luck." He sang again; then he picked up the wolf hide from his sacred bundle and put it around Crows Breast's neck saying, "You men go a long distance on horseback; then if you think it best, you can go the rest of the way afoot."

Whenever the chief of the scouts or young wolves wanted us to go faster he always said *Huiiii*. We rode nearly 60 miles that day, going to the tops of the hills to look around with a telescope. By evening, since we had not seen any signs of the enemy, Crows Breast sent two young wolves out to kill antelopes for our evening meals and they brought in three while the rest of the scouts watched for the enemy.

After the scouts had been selected that morning, Kidney named four men to be his assistants or coleaders, for they were very holy and could be of much help to him. All were older men who had important sacred bundles and had lead successful war expeditions. Spotted Horn was selected because he had a Creek bundle; Loud Walker because he had fasted often in the Mandan Okipa and had many dreams from the buffaloes; Moves Slowly because he was the Hoita in the Okipa, and Porcupine Pemmican because he represented Long Arm whenever the Naxpike ceremony was given.

We scouts had just finished eating when the others reached camp. We were sitting in a circle singing about our girls and having a good time teasing each other when Kidney told us to be quiet. Then we knew that the time had come to find out what Kidney was after on this expedition.

He said, "I want to learn what is going to happen; if we are going to be successful, I want to know that beforehand. All you men sit facing the south. One of you young men go out, cut a chokecherry branch, and bring it here."

It was the custom on a trip like this for the camp tenders to be alert and to jump up whenever the Old Wolf asked for something. If one failed to do that, the older men would see it and say that he was lazy and no good. As soon as he mentioned the branch, from fear of being called worthless, several of them went, although one could have done it.

Kidney put his saddle blanket down in front of him with the sacred bundle on it. He stuck the branch in the ground in front of the bundle. He took a stuffed hawk, one of his personal sacred objects, lifted it toward the south, sang a sacred song belonging to the bird, and tossed the bird towards the branch. It stuck to the branch and hung there.

Then he took out a little black bear skin that belonged in his eagle trapping bundle and spread it out on the ground under the hawk; then he took out the wolf hide and smoked it with "sweetgrass" while he held it toward the west.

We waited to hear what would happen. He sat there for some time and then he said, "I have had a sign and I think we will be lucky. I was told by my gods that there would be a sign of the future; even though there are no clouds now, the hawk says that after sundown a small cloud will go over and it will sprinkle for a little while. Another sign tells me that tomorrow we will find a horse. The sign is that it will be a cripple. If you scouts find it, you must look for paint for the one who finds it will conquer the enemy. In the morning you scouts will go to Wolf Den Buttes (about a mile southeast of the present town of Dickinson, N. Dak.) and wait for us." So we knew now what the gods had planned for us.

Next day we went toward Wolf Den Buttes, going to the high places to look around as we traveled. We reached the buttes at noon and hid our horses while we looked around. Some killed antelopes, others of us watched for the main party, and I looked for a good place to camp. Soon the main party came along and Kidney sent us scouts on ahead toward Rainy Buttes to find a good place to camp for the night. It was hard to find a good camping place there but we finally found a good camping place and spring on the east side. We came together there late that night.

Crows Breast had had his foot injured in a former battle and the stirrup caused it to swell, so he told Kidney of it and asked that he be relieved. Kidney appointed me leader of the scouts. Kidney instructed me to take the scouts to the east side of Buffalo Home Butte. I thought that if I did not take too large a party, we could travel faster. So Old Dog, Rabbit Head, Red Robe, and I started ahead thinking that we would get there before the sun came up. We did not get there that early for on the way Rabbit Head and Red Robe wanted to stop to smoke and rest. At the same time we saw many Juneberries. There were some high rocks where we stopped and Old Dog, who was on guard while we stopped, came running howling like a coyote and we knew he had found something. He stopped and said that there was a horse not far away.

When we went toward the horse there was not much wind so we thought that it would be a good idea to burn some buffalo manure to make it easier to catch. The wind went down so we decided to surround the animal instead. I said to the others, "We have already found the horse that our leader saw in his sacred signs. Now we should try hard to catch him."

As we came close, we saw that the horse had hobbles on that had cut into its skin. We knew then that it belonged to the enemy. One said to me, "Kidney saw a crippled horse in his dream. This one is not crippled. It must be that our leader does not have a sharp eye."

There was spring water on the north side of Buffalo Home Butte so we picketed the horse there and climbed the butte to look around with the telescope. Old Dog saw something in the distance; we thought it might be a bear, elk, or buffalo and kept turning to it. At last we saw that it was a buffalo going to water. Two stayed back on the butte while the rest of us went for the buffalo. By leaving our blankets and leggings we were able to travel as fast afoot as a horse galloping. There seemed no place to approach the animal for it was flat there so I, being the leader, told the others to go to the other side of the buffalo and crawl toward it. If it came my way I would head it off so that someone would get a shot at it. This way we killed it but we teased one warrior because he jumped up when a cactus stuck into his leg. This was the best time for hunting buffalo for they are fat in the summer. We took the best meat and piled it to one side. We took the paunch for a bucket, cleaned out the inwards, and drank the blood that accumulated on the inside for we were hungry. Then we went back to our camp with meat for the others.

When almost to the butte, the rain predicted by Kidney came and we were soaked. It was dark so I called like a coyote and the others answered so we went to the east side where the leader told us we would meet. When we went down to the foot of the hill, we heard them singing and knew that they had arrived. We saw their fire and called like the coyote and they answered. They had found the horse that we had left picketed. That made Kidney happy, even though the horse was not a very good one, for it proved that Kidney's bundle had great powers.

We had gone a long distance from home and I did not know the country but the older men like Kidney did. He said, "I think we will move tomorrow to the place where you killed the buffalo and stored the meat, for there is a stream at that place that flows towards Powder River."

After supper Hard Horn said to me, "Wolf Chief, my father, I want you to cut my skin; there is a hawk's nest here; I want to fast near it tonight. I have a horse and some blankets at home that I will give you for doing this."

When he said that, I did not know what to do for I did not have much to pray to. Even Hard Horn had more bundles than I did and had often been out to war. I thought that it would be better to ask one of my older clan brothers named Dancing Flag.[28] I went to Dancing Flag and said, "My brother, our son wants me to cut his skin but you are older and have more gods and power than I have. He is going to give a horse and blankets. I will return the arrow to him."

Dancing Flag said, "That is right; you are younger than I am. Since you want me to, I will take the arrow."

Hard Horn furnished two sharpened sticks and three or four heavy stakes to fasten into the bank. It was too steep where the nest was and there was no place to drive in the stakes for it was too rocky. Dancing Flag found a place where he could drive the stakes in the ground nearby. Dancing Flag put the sticks through Hard Horn's skin and let him down. We had an extra rope fastened to him lest the sticks pull out of his flesh allowing him to fall and be killed. About midnight we thought he would be exhausted so Dancing Flag and I went back, pulled him up, and took the sticks out.

Next morning I thought that by custom I really owned the horse because I was leader of the scouts when it was found, but others thought it belonged to Kidney because he had actually seen it first when he had his bundle predict the future. Kidney was happy when I said to him "You should take the horse, for you saw it when you sang the holy song."

We moved to the place where we had killed the buffalo and had the meat piled with our shirts arranged around it to keep the wolves and coyotes away. We stayed there several days enjoying ourselves and examining the butte from which the buffaloes were said to come. While we were there two other war parties of our people arrived looking for the enemy. Hairy Coat was one leader who had with him Scattered Village and Takes-the-Gun. Shortly afterward, Iron Eyes came with Big Bull, Bears Teeth, Red Leaf, Wolf Ghost, High Eagle, Bear Chief, and Coyote Necklace. We stayed together for a few days and then decided to unite and go west in search of the enemy.

The three war parties united and then we had three leaders, Kidney, Hairy Coat, and Iron Eyes. We traveled as before with the scouts out to the front. The

---

[28] Dancing Flag was a Mandan of the Speckled Eagle clan; Wolf Chief was of the Hidatsa Prairie Chicken clan.

first day we found some old horse tracks and came back in the middle of the day to eat and to report. Kidney had selected a good place to camp in high cotton-woods for we were now in enemy territory.

After we ate we talked to our gods, asking for good luck and advised the younger fellows to do likewise. Each war party had its separate fire about 100 feet apart so that each group could hold its separate ceremonies. Kidney instructed our group to cut some cottonwoods and construct a lodge tipi with the door facing the southeast. It did not take us long to stand the logs up like a tipi for it was really a corral of posts standing upright. When Kindey completed building it, we saw that it was a symbol of the Walking-with-Woman [Painted Red Stick ceremony, see pp. 451–463] that the people gave for the buffaloes back at the village. Then Kidney told us to scrape the ground smooth, leaving no grass standing on the floor, and we did.

When the lodge was ready, Kidney went inside with his sacred bundles and began to sing. He asked us to bring him a cottonwood branch sharpened so that he could stick it into the ground. The leader stuck the branch into the ground in front of his sacred bundles. Then he called for us to bring some coals and place them in front of his bundles. He was then ready to perform the rites so he called to us "Come in and gather around me; sit in a circle and be quiet. One of you draw a human foot on the ground and have the tracks reach up to my bundles; draw a bear's foot on top of the human tracks. Each of you others draw a bear's foot on each side of the human foot. The last one will draw a mark of a bear seizing a human."

He had the painted hawk on the stick, the bear skin beneath it, and the wolf hide lying on the ground nearby. He said, "My gods, this will be the last chance you will have to tell us whether we are going to discover anything or not."

He picked up the painted hawk and lifted it toward the south, sang the holy songs belonging to the hawk, and said, "Everything is all right for us." Then he picked up the bear and pointed it to the south and said that it was going to be all right.

Then he picked up the wolf hide and said, "It is all right; it will be ready tomorrow. While I was singing these holy songs, I saw off in the distance on Powder River a flat place and on it was a dead human. The wolves and ravens were eating the body; all that will be happening tomorrow. As its head was to the east and the animals were eating, it means that it will be tomorrow. Get ready, for tomorrow you will need to be prepared. Take your paint along."

Kidney stood up and called to Hairy Coat and Iron Eyes who were at their fires and when they answered he said, "There will be the three of us leaders. The leader of the man who kills the enemy, will get the credit. All you scouts do the best you can to discover this enemy tomorrow and don't miss the place I described to you."

By this time Crows Breast's foot was well again so he took his place as head of the scouts. Crows Breast said, "Do the best you can to kill that enemy given to Kidney but if you can't, we will all have to go together and kill him."

Before daylight we scouts went out. We climbed each high butte we came to and looked around. At last we saw the place Kidney spoke of and from a dis-tance it looked just like the place he had described to us. The others came up and we stopped to eat. Porcupine Pemmican had walked off a short distance. He saw a rider coming towards him. He ran back to us and reported. We stopped eating and prepared to attack but when we went out, the enemy had run away. We should not have gone into the low place but should have stayed on the high ridges. We had been in too great a hurry to eat.

Kidney told us that he was picking out five men to go out and see if there were any more. When the five scouts left, the rest of us rode on. Soon we saw one rider but when we looked in the opposite direction we saw a number of riders coming toward us. We fought them while the five scouts went after the lone man whom they killed. So the five scouts got the best of us. Before they left that morning, Flying Eagle asked Crows Breast to pray for him so that he would be successful when he met the enemy. Crows Breast sang his holy songs and said, "My son will get the best of the enemy" and he let Flying Eagle carry his medicine bundle.

In the battle, Flying Eagle was ahead, carrying Crows Breast's sacred bundle, so he killed the enemy and was first to strike him. Then came One Wing and after him came Red Robe. The other scouts rushed in; Hard Horn claimed he hit with his gun on the man's head and Good Bear claimed that place too so no honors were given for the fourth coup since none could be certain.

While the scouts were killing and striking the single enemy, the rest of us fought with the other enemies. There were about 30 of them. We shouted, sang our medicine songs, and rattled our tongues so that the enemy could not shoot straight and they did the same. When they heard our scouts singing the victory songs, the enemy rode away. We came together singing and all had a good time, for we knew what Crows Breast had promised before the battle had come true. When Hard Horn fasted by the hawk's nest, Dancing Flag and I prayed for him; nevertheless, he did not get the best record. He struck fourth with others, however, so we did not get credit for our prayers in his behalf.

The credit went to Kidney for one of his men killed the enemy. These enemies were Hunkpapa; afterwards we used to visit them often. Shortly afterward we discovered 20 tipis and farther on there were hundreds of tipis. We knew that we had been reported so our leader thought that we should go west as the enemy would think that we had left for home. We learned afterwards that the Sioux thought that we were Crows and that it would do no good to follow us, not knowing that we were Mandans and Hidatsas.

We traveled long hours until we reached the Little Missouri west of the Killdeer Mountains where it is rough. We found a good place to rest the horses. While we camped there, Kidney fixed the scalp; he cleaned the flesh off it, stretched it on a circular stick, and dried it over the fire. The hair was long; it was divided between Kidney and the four leaders he appointed to assist him when we camped the first day. We were tired so we stopped to hunt while the older men sang their victory songs at the camp.

When we got back to the village, we painted our faces black, and ran between the lodges shouting and firing our guns. Then the people brought out the big drums and all the people danced. Everyone was happy, for Kidney had proved that the ceremony that he had just performed had great supernatural powers.

The above narrative by Wolf Chief brings out numerous significant behavior patterns. Wolf Chief first emphasized that Kidney was instructed to organize a military expedition in a dream he had shortly after he bought rights in the Wolf ceremony owned by his father. We see that the expedition was socially approved by the acceptance of invitations by numerous individuals highly respected for their own military achievements; in fact, Kidney's status at that time was not as high as several of his party. When the party first left, it was not known whether he would select coleaders or assume the responsibilities himself nor were there any understandings with others that they would assist him. He recognized the good reputation of others by selecting four of them as coleaders and Crows Breast as leader of the scouts although, at this time, Crows Breast held the highest military position in the village, being the village war chief. We see that one ritual activity after another was performed while out from the village. At first the party knew nothing about his plans other than that he had a dream shortly after giving the Wolf ceremony. Their confidence in his leadership and supernatural powers was indicated by the size of the party. Although the others assumed that the purpose of the expedition was to test the supernatural powers of his recently acquired bundle, in his first ritualistic performance, we find him first employing the painted hawk, then the little black bear belonging to his eagle trapping bundle before introducing the wolf hide to the party gathered around him. Thus, he expressed his wealth of supernatural property which should collectively add to his supernatural powers. We see that the scouts have the most difficult duty, traveling far out ahead of the main party, but that they have prior claim to all the horses they first see. In this case, however, the scouts interpret Kidney's "sign" in which he saw a crippled horse as a prior claim. In this connection also, it would be well to note that very specific rules defined ownership of horses taken on these raids. The horses belonged to the first person seeing them, irrespective of the persons executing the capture of them. This was an incentive to those who were active in getting about and finding horses. Occasionally this rule did not work; one might have discovered fresh tracks and be following them only to meet one of the party in actual possession of the horses. It was then necessary for the leader to decide whether the man finding the horses had seen them before the other had discovered their tracks, for the discovery of fresh tracks was equivalent to seeing the horses. On one occasion, the possessor of the horse proved that the tracks were not made by the horses he brought back because one of them had a broken hoof which did not show in the tracks the other was following.

Note that Hard Horn called on Wolf Chief to supply thongs so that he might be tortured near a hawk's nest, hoping that he would get a vision from that bird. We have here a case of deliberate effort to acquire this particular bird as a guardian spirit. By the clan kinship extension, Wolf Chief was Hard Horn's "father." Wolf Chief, due to closer relationships with the Mandan, considered Dancing Flag of the Mandan Speckled Eagle clan, which was at this time being absorbed by the larger Mandan Prairie Chicken clan, his "brother." So he invites Dancing Flag, an older person, to assist him. The two men assisted Hard Horn in his self-torturing and prayed for him, but we see that Hard Horn got only a questionable fourth coup when the enemy was killed. Therefore, Wolf Chief and Dancing Flag did not get credit for their prayers and could not enumerate this honor on public occasions at home.

We saw the partial union of three war parties because of the danger that one group would reach the enemy first and thus cause the others risk of detection when they arrived. So the leaders of the three groups planned for the future by agreeing on the division of the honors. Each group had its own campfire and performed its own rituals independently of the other. When they stopped in the timber before reaching the enemy, Kidney introduced a new ceremonial feature; the temporary shelter erected in the village when he formerly had given the Painted Red Stick ceremony and had called the old buffalo impersonators in to exercise ceremonial sexual license with his wives.

Crows Breast succeeded in demonstrating his supernatural powers by praying for a "son," Flying Eagle, who killed one enemy and was first to strike coup on the body. By doing this, Crows Breast came out ahead of Wolf Chief and Dancing Flag. Although Wolf Chief did not say so in the narrative, other "sons" would thereafter pay Crows Breast to pray for them whenever they undertook dangerous missions.

It is important for an understanding of Plains warfare to note that, although the enemy was greatly outnumbered and there was a fine opportunity to kill a great many of them, the battle was stopped and both groups retired once the scouts had killed one man separated from his group. Kidney had fulfilled his mission—to possess one crippled horse and one enemy who would be found on a flat near Powder River. Since his honors were expressed in the number of his successful military expeditions without loss or injury to his party, nothing further was to be gained by continuing the battle.

This military expedition led by Kidney was only one of a number of successful ones which he directed. He provided an opportunity for various households to obtain horses and for the young men to win military honors. In time, as he supplemented his military activities with frequent feasts for the older people, he grew in social stature. The older people subsequently met to reorganize the village leadership and he was selected as "protector of the people" to represent one of the cardinal points.

Although the Hidatsa had a rather clear-cut dual division of village leadership into war and peace or village roles, some military honors were expected of the peace or village chief. The village functions for the Hidatsa-proper and Awaxawi were normally inherited with Earthnaming bundle ownership and as long as the village groups were independent it made little difference what the military record of the village chief was as long as he gave an adequate performance of this rite. If he were successful in warfare, that was so much to the good. When the Hidatsa-proper and Awaxawi united with the Awatixa to build Fishhook Village, we find duplicate and competing bundles and chieftainship. Guts represented the Hidatsa-proper and Poor Wolf the Awaxawi. They were equally proficient in the performance of the rites. Poor Wolf had a good military record but Guts was accused of bringing endless misfortune to any war party that he accompanied.

Four Dancers supplied the following account of his paternal grandfather, Guts, which is reproduced here in condensed form to show the group attitude toward one who was entitled to a high position in the ceremonial life of the people but who had suffered considerable embarrassment because of his bad luck in warfare.

My grandfather, Guts, inherited the Earthnaming bundle while he was living in Hidatsa village on the Knife River before the smallpox of 1837. Because he got the bundle of his parents, he had the right to pray to all of the living things on the earth. He was taught that in the beginning all the gods would meet at the hole on top of Killdeer Mountains to sing. But he was never lucky in warfare; nine times he went out and succeeded in killing the enemy but nine times when he was out, someone was killed by the enemies. It was not that he did not try. During his earlier years he was one who wanted to succeed but later when his son, Bobtail Bull, was old enough he sold his rights to my father for my father was lucky at everything he did even though he followed the same rules my grandfather gave him. Then the people looked to my father, for he could pray to all the living things, and did not pay so much attention to Guts when he talked for he had been unlucky. The people respected my father because he could pray to all the living things. Poor Wolf was jealous and tried to find something wrong with my father's record. The only thing he could find wrong with my father was that he was younger than Poor Wolf. I think it would have been better if there had been two villages; then there would not have been this trouble between the two Earthnaming bundle owners. At last there was so much jealousy that some of the people told my father that they would follow him if he would find a new place to build. That was when we went to Fort Buford about 1870.

Guts liked to go on war expeditions, but it was strange—every time he went out with a bunch, they always had bad luck. The others were afraid to go out if he came along. So he would not be invited but he would wait 2 or 3 days after the others had left and then he would join them. The others would not like that but each time they would think that his bad luck must surely come to an end sometime.

One time 10 men went out with Big Bull as leader; this was from Knife River. They went west and crossed the Badlands and Yellowstone River. They had a good time eating the meat the scouts brought in. One day the scouts saw two riders and came back to report. They painted up, fixed their sacred objects, and then killed the two enemies. Eight men struck honors on the two enemies. Big Bull was very happy and as they rode along, coming home, they sang the victory songs.

They had killed the enemies early in the morning; at noon they stopped to fix the scalps and eat. While the leader fixed the scalps on long poles, singing the victory songs, he called the names of those who had struck the enemy and said that they would be chiefs. He said to the young men when they stopped to camp that evening, "About this time at the village the young women are out playing games."

They camped in the timber on the Yellowstone. They built two fires, one for the leader and his assistants and the other for the younger men. They surrounded the old men's fire with a fort made of logs. Guts was at the shelter set up for the young men for it had begun to rain. The young men were sitting around the fire with their robes over each other and their guns between them when someone fired a shot into the camp. All the young men ran and jumped into the river except Guts, whose finger was caught in his robe. While shaking loose of his robe he aimed quickly towards a flash from a gun, calling to his friends, "I am the only one who came to fight; you should come back and fight too."

By that time the Old Wolves came running over to the young men's camp, firing their guns, so the Cheyenne ran away. Guts found that the two who lay next to him had been killed; there were three others dead near the fire; one was missing and none knew what had happened to him. At last they found the body of the missing man who had run in the wrong direction and had been caught and mutilated by the Cheyenne. The dead man was Guts' "friend's" brother-in-law. The "friend" wanted to take the body back to the place where the other five were but he was afraid, so Guts carried the body while the other brought the gun that the enemy had missed in the night. Guts did two honorable things: he carried the dead man that the other should have since they were brothers-in-law; he stopped to shoot at the enemy when the others ran away. They piled the six bodies together and covered them with their robes and sticks. Then the party started for home.

They ran afoot all night toward home. The leader had been nicely dressed before but in the night as they ran, the others did not know what he was doing for in the morning they found that he had cut his hair all off; he had taken off his leggings and moccasins and was running bare naked he was so sad; he had cut himself in many places with his knife and had cut off the ends of two fingers. The others begged him at least to wear moccasins but he refused, he was so sad. The others begged him again as they ran along crying, and at last he consented to put on moccasins and a shirt.

They came to Hidatsa village on the Knife River but he refused to go into the village. He was so sad because he had lost six men. So Big Bull stayed outside fasting and crying, thinking that he would be paid back in the future. For a year he would fast for a few days; then he would rest a few days before fasting again.

While he fasted he thought that he would go back in 1 year to see the young men who had been killed. He thought that this time he would take along the greatest medicine men of the five villages of Hidatsa and Mandan. He went through the other four villages thinking of the different men he could ask until he came to the south village of the Mandans where the highest war record was held by Four Bears.

When he came to that village he saw Four Bears sitting on his earth lodge. Four Bears came down and they went into his lodge, for he saw that Big Bull was carrying his medicine pipe. He set the pipe before Four Bears and, tapping him on the head, said, "I am looking for my gods; I want to get even with the Cheyenne who killed my six young men; I have thought of all of the great men and my thoughts always come back to you. I have decided that you are the one who can help me do it."

Then Four Bears said, "What do you want to do?"

Big Bull said, "I want to go out to see my six young men and to kill the enemy and even things up. I want you to go as leader of the scouts to be out in front to find the enemy."

Four Bears agreed and they set the date to leave 4 days later. This time Guts went along. Some did not like it but they said nothing for Four Bears, the greatest war chief of that time, was along. As they went along Four Bears served as leader of the scouts, going out each morning before daylight ahead of the main party. At last they came to the bones of the six men where Big Bull cried for a long time. Then they went on. Evenings they would stop to eat and sing the war songs. Everyone had a good time.

One morning Four Bears was out with his scouts. When the sun was up to the height of a man, a small cloud came over and it rained. They came to a gumbo flat and the buffalo wallows were full of water. This was a good sign, for Four Bears' god was the medicine robe with a rainbow painted on it. He got this sacred robe at the time he fasted beneath an oak tree in which a large hawk had its nest after his brother had been killed by the Arikara several years before. Four Bears opened his sacred bundle and unwrapped the robe; he placed it before his scouts and asked someone to volunteer to make a mark on it. One young man volunteered and asked what he should paint on it. Four Bears told the young man to paint a rainbow on it.

When the young man painted the rainbow on the robe, Four Bears looked at the signs on the robe, thought of the shower that had just come because he had wanted such a sign as an indication of the time when the enemy would be found, and said, "I do not think we will be going very much farther for my gods have sent the shower to tell me they are thinking of us just as they do in the village when the weather is too dry for the corn. I think we will find what we are looking for today."

When they finished the painting of the robe, Four Bears put the robe around his shoulders and they went on into hilly country. They discovered seven horsemen and met them on top of a high hill. One enemy was dressed in a fine red shirt and beautiful leggings; he was carrying a good gun. This enemy was killed even though he was very brave; then the others ran away. Four Bear's party took his fine clothing, his scalp, and gun. No Tears was first to strike the enemy. The second honors went to a Mandan who was with the party. I forgot who hit third and fourth.

They returned to the main party, running in single file and howling like the coyote. The main party put a robe down for them to jump over and they came into camp howling. Four Bears gave the scalp and other things taken from the enemy to Big Bull. Four Bears announced, "The man we killed was the leader when you lost the six men a year ago."

Big Bull was even, for he had now succeeded in killing the one who had brought bad luck to him a year before. Guts also got credit for he had lost his friend a year before.

Big Bull was one who fasted much. Formerly he had been lucky in stealing horses and killing the enemy. Now he had overcome the handicap of losing six men by fasting long and then going out to prove that his sacred powers had been restored to him. His god was the Prairie Wolf that he saw in a dream but he never put up the village ceremony for his bundle. Instead he made it up himself from what he had dreamed.

The above narrative brings out some additional behavior patterns not indicated by the Wolf Chief account. He speaks as a relative of one who should have had good luck by virtue of the Earthnaming bundle from Hidatsa village, which he had acquired by normal tribal inheritance from his father. Having fulfilled all the obligations to acquire the bundle, he should have, according to the previous records of former bundle holders, been highly esteemed by his village group. His principal duty as bundle owner was to organize the various Buffalo Calling rites and to serve as the authority in matters involving village traditional actions. As long as he performed these duties well and showed bravery about the village, the group did not expect more. Nevertheless, he liked to go out to war. So far as we know, he never acted as leader himself; this was not expected of the Earth-naming bundle owner. Still, he would accompany others on what generally proved to be unsuccessful expeditions until he had the reputation of being unlucky for any group he accompanied. A sequel to this narrative is indicated by Four Dancers' statement that Poor Wolf got ahead of Guts. Here we have a conflicting situation involving village bundles. Prior to 1845 there was one Earthnaming bundle for the Hidatsa village group and another for the Awaxawi, but in 1845, when the Hidatsa village groups united, two separate and competing bundle lines existed. Poor Wolf, in addition to in-heriting the Earthnaming and several other village bundles, also found time to accompany or lead numerous war parties without suffering the embarrassments of bad luck. Thus, Poor Wolf occupied a higher status than Guts who, when his son named Bobtail Bull grew up, passed the bundle on to him in an effort to reestablish the family's rightful position. Four Dancers volunteered the opinion that his grandfather's reputation was beyond repair by that time. Bobtail Bull proved a worthy competitor to Poor Wolf. Four Dancers brought out the point that the people took sides according to previous village affiliation, and that this division continued until the building of a Government fort at Fort Buford provided an outlet for one group by separation which was otherwise impossible due to the pressure of the Sioux.

In describing the organization of the war party under Big Bull, we see no essential difference from that of the previous account. Formal rites as practiced by Kidney were simpler because One Bull's authority was based on the personal vision patterns. Even though Guts shot only because he was tangled in his robe and could not escape quickly, it was a recognized form of bravery; and even though the Cheyenne had the advantage of surprising their adversaries, still they did not press the attack, being content to kill six men in the initial attack and to scalp one. Here we find the same pattern as in the Wolf Chief account where the fight was terminated when one enemy fell. Four Dancers brought out the point that it was obligatory for one to look after his brother-in-law since they were related through the wife and sister. Since a man brought the horses taken to his sisters whose husband was the principal benefactor, so must he in return look after his wife's brother even as he would protect his own wife. In fact, the brother-in-law was often jokingly referred to as "my wife."

The self-inflicted torture and behavior of Big Bull was normal and customary. We find that members of his party think he is undertaking too severe punishment and interfere, insisting that he wear moccasins and a shirt. Here we have an example of interference by his kin groups, his father's clansmen, and his society members. We are told that he refused to go back into the village. Instead he fasted and continued self-torture. Although Four Dancers did not say so, in other comparable situations he and other informants emphasized that Big Bull was watched by his society members. Seeing that he was endangering his life, they went to the relatives of those killed and asked them to take the pipe to Big Bull and beg him to terminate his suffering. The "long period" of mourning, in contrast to the 4-day period, was normal when one had "kicked the stone" as the Hidatsa say of a leader who has returned from an unsuccessful military adventure. Big Bull dressed in mourning and fasted frequently for 1 year, during which time he received a new personal guardian spirit— but Four Dancers knew few details about it for, in contrast to a sacred bundle acquired by formal public purchase, personal supernatual experiences tended to be forgotten.

Four Dancers indicated the degree of cooperation that existed at this time between the various earth lodge village groups living near Knife River by relating how Big Bull walked through the other four villages with his sacred pipe searching for some distinguished warrior leader who was willing to serve as "chief of the scouts" on the contemplated expedition to see the bodies of those who were killed a year earlier. Having enlisted the most distinguished Mandan chief[29] of that time, the narrative from that point on is chiefly an account of Four Bears' role. The situation in which Four Bears served under another of recognized inferior status is not unusual, but it does throw a great deal of light on the widely diffused character of the social control mechanism of an earth lodge village population.

Four Dancers had a considerable knowledge of Four Bear's sacred bundle rites, for this bundle, although obtained after fasting beneath an oak tree at the time his brother was killed by the Arikara, had been assembled by his elders according to established tribal custom and publicly transferred to Four Bears at a ceremonial feast. Four Dancers knew little about Big Bull's bundle which had been made up personally without the formality of a ceremonial feast. It was

---

[29] When Four Bears died of smallpox, Guts married the widow and reared Four Bears' son, Charging Eagle.

widely known that Four Bears' bundle was primarily connected with rain calling; hence, when a shower fell, it was thought that the bundle had not lost its "powers." Four Bears read the "signs" when the robe was painted, just as Kidney did in the previous narrative, but nowhere do we find reference to rites by Big Bull.

Four Bears' scouts concentrated their attack on the best-dressed enemy who was assumed to be the chief of the party. Still there was no inclination to continue the engagement once one enemy had been killed and struck coup upon. The manner of approaching the main party after a successful engagement was the same as in the Kidney account. (Note that the traditional accounts of the behavior of the scouts when approaching the main party after striking the enemy belong to the Hidatsa Wolf ceremony while the same procedure was followed in this instance by the Mandan scout leader, even though that tribe had no known comparable tribal Wolf rites.)

The killing of one enemy was considered adequate compensation for the six of their own men killed a year before; numbers apparently did not count. The object of an expedition was to strike the enemy without loss to one's own group. Four Dancers shows awareness of the conflict of opinion in the village as to whether military leadership should be sanctioned by virtue of vision or vision plus formal purchase of the bundle:

It was strange that Guts had so much bad luck. While living at Knife River he went out again with Three Coyotes as leader. Three Coyotes had the coyote as his god. I think what one dreams is more important than what one buys through his fathers, even though he dreams of it first, because after our group moved to Fort Buford, we did not have many of the ceremonies that the others had at Fishhook, still our men had good luck. Crow-Flies-High did not buy his father's gods until he was old—still, he was a very successful leader.

When Three Coyotes went out, there were 32 men in his party. They did not want Guts along but he went anyway. He was tall and strong; he liked to go on these trips. They traveled to the southwest until they had passed the Black Hills. All the time the scouts were out ahead looking around but the enemy saw them before the scouts did. There was a large camp and soon the enemy drove them into a washout. The enemy came in great numbers on horseback so that the Hidatsa were unable to run away. When the enemy attacked, one Hidatsa took a red shirt out of a bundle and Guts said to him, "You should not put it on or they will see you. I will put it on. I always seem to bring bad luck. If they kill me they will think that I am a great chief. Then they may stop fighting and let the rest of you go away."

The Sioux did not start the fight right away. First they surrounded the Hidatsa so they could not get away and then the women and children came along bringing their tipis and setting them up nearby where they could watch the fight. They must have sent messages out for soon another large group came up and began setting up their tipis too. While this was going on, the Hidatsa painted up and put on their sacred objects. The Sioux did likewise. The young Sioux boys rode back and forth practicing with their horses, riding so that their bodies did not show, stopping their horses quickly and pretending that they were fighting the enemy. This they did to frighten the Hidatsa boys so that they would not be brave. The Hidatsa all thought that they would surely not be able to save their lives.

When the Sioux were all properly painted to show their honors and medicines, the battle began. Three Coyotes picked out his two best men to be at the corners. One was Black Shield; he was a good shot. His medicine was the gun and whenever he fired it, he was sure to get something. The arrows flew toward the washout in great curves like grasshoppers dropping into the grass.

Before the battle, Black Shield wet some gunpowder and painted his face; he put white cloth on his head and white paint on his lips and eyes just as he had seen these things in his dream. He had a young man beside him who loaded the gun each time. They agreed to make a great noise each time an enemy was killed so that the enemy would be afraid to come into the fort. Each time Black Shield shot, an enemy was killed; then they came closer to get their dead for fear the Hidatsa would go out and scalp them. After a while, one of the Hidatsa would go out of the fort, shoot an enemy, and run back. Just as he went out, a Prairie Dog Owl flew above him and the others knew that he was not shot because this bird was his god.

When the dead were taken back to camp, the Hidatsa could hear the relatives crying. All the while the older Hidatsa would repeat to the young men who had not been out before, "They will cut your scalps off, but be brave and do not cry."

While the Sioux were taking back their dead, the Hidatsa painted themselves anew for they knew that the enemy were not done fighting. They could not leave the fort or the Sioux would run them down. During the lull in the fighting, Guts said to a friend, "Let's go up on top of the hill and sing our war songs. I think there are some Sioux women who can hear us from there."

So they went up on the hill and sang their war songs and when they had finished, the Sioux howled in recognition of their bravery. Then the Sioux sang their war songs for the Hidatsa who were showing such bravery.

Then the two Sioux bands went together. They knew then that their enemy was brave so the Sioux selected a man who impersonated a bear, and could not be shot through, to lead for he was so brave. He was their greatest medicine man. The Bear man was ahead and Black Shield would shoot at him but he would not fall down. Then Black Shield knew that the Bear man really had great supernatural powers. When Black Shield had dreamed of the gun, his gods had told him if his life was ever in extreme danger he should hold the gun to the north, pour powder from his left ear, shot from the right ear, and put the powder and shot in the gun while he sang the song that should be used only in extremely critical situations.

So Black Shield did. He shot at the Bear medicine man who fell down. Black Shield shouted so the enemy could hear, "You were foolish; you didn't have any power. You should have known that mine was greater."

When the Bear man fell, the Sioux stopped fighting and took his body away, for they did not want to give the Hidatsa the honor of scalping their holiest man. Then the Sioux set the prairie on fire so that the smoke would cover their advance. Some of the enemy went onto the hill where Guts had sung the war songs. They hit the sickly young man who had been filling Black Shield's gun and one other but the Sioux would not attack the fort. Again the fighting stopped. The Sioux dragged their dead away so that they could not be scalped and as word got around in their camp, the women set up a loud howl as they cried for their dead relatives.

The Hidatsa were tired and thought that they would surely lose their lives the next time. There was brush about a mile away. Some thought they could run for it, but others thought that it was too far. Three Coyotes and his coleaders decided to run for the brush, fighting their way through the Sioux lines. He selected Guts, who was a great medicine man, and Black Shield, who was a good shot, to take the two ends while the others sneaked out, following a narrow coulee part of the way. The two went onto the hill to attract the Sioux's attention and when the others were on the flat, they ran too. When all were near the brush, the Sioux rode in front of them but they were not prepared for the attack and were easily driven out of the way. When they got into the brush, the Sioux returned to their camp and did not try to follow them further.

The two on the corners were the ones who saved them, one a great medicine man, the other a good shot. The sickly one had been killed at the fort and one other was lost running towards the brush.

Because they lost two, even though killing many of the enemy that they could not strike, the party came back in mourning. But the Sioux kept Three Coyotes from dancing the victory dances for they kept their dead out of reach of the Hidatsa. It was too bad that he could not possess any of them for the Sioux camp was in mourning when they left from losing so many young men. If Three Coyotes had taken even one scalp, the relatives of the two dead men would have called for the victory dances after a period of mourning.

The above narrative by Four Dancers of the Three Coyote military expedition imparts a number of factors not included in previous accounts. He emphasized that what one dreamed was more important than what one got through public purchase from the father. He rationalized the war record of Crow-Flies-High who did not, even though receiving the appropriate dreams, buy his deceased father's ceremonial bundle rites until he was along in years. Instead, he made up personal bundles based on vision experiences without the benefit of public performances. He stated that the people who split away did not have as many tribal ceremonies but that their men were just as successful as those who stayed in Fishhook because they fasted to compensate for ceremonies which the Fort Buford group did not own. In this respect, the Crow-Flies-High band showed strong similarity to the Crow religious pattern. By contrast, the other Hidatsa groups preserved more of the formal pattern of ceremonial transfer whereby vision experiences were organized and classified in terms of existing tribal rites.

We note that Guts showed his bravery by asking to wear a red shirt so that the enemy would think he was chief and that by killing him, the enemy might call off the attack. One often wonders to what extent behavior is affected by confidence in supernatural powers. Here we have an instance in which, in selecting the men to occupy the end positions in the line, Guts was selected for his supernatural powers while Black Shield was selected because he was a good shot. When this narrative was recorded, after hearing of Black Shield's rites of "pouring powder and shot" out of his ears, I presumed that Four Dancers was referring to him as the possessor of great supernatural powers. He explained, however, that it was Guts who was selected as the great medicine man in spite of his repeated military reverses because the Earthnaming bundle had great potential powers even though Guts had not heretofore been able to manipulate them. Nevertheless, the powers were there according to tribal traditions.

We find the leaders instructing the younger men to make trilling noises, whenever an enemy was killed, to prove their bravery. The Gun rites performed by Black Shield are interesting because the same rites were frequently practiced in exactly the same manner by others as a result of identical vision experiences and were bought and sold in a "father–son" relationship as were the long-established tribal rites. The only reference Four Dancers makes to "signs" is in the case of one man who, when he saw a prairie dog owl flying over him, was prompted to manifest unusual bravery since the bird was his god. We are told something of the formal character of Plains warfare expressed in the desire of Guts and his friend to sing their war songs for the benefit of the Sioux women and the prompt response by the Sioux women who sang their victory songs for the Hidatsa because of their bravery.

A significant role of Hidatsa offensive warfare was expressed by the reaction of the Hidatsa to the appearance of the Bear medicine man. Here we find revealed the concept of the measurability of supernatural power. Each side believed its supernatural power to be greater and endeavored to test this power by a contest. One wonders if the Bear impersonator was actually the Bear medicine man or some young man selected to play the role. If the same pattern prevailed as with the Hidatsa, we would more likely find the Bear bundle owner dressing some young man, addressed as "son," in the paraphernalia, singing the sacred songs for the young man, and sending him forward with the assurance that when the battle was over his honors would elevate him to chief. We see the demoralization of the Sioux when their Bear impersonator was killed and their unwillingness to engage in hand-to-hand combat by overrunning the Hidatsa defenses in a gully. Four Dancers expressed regrets that no scalps were taken as proof of an engagement with the enemy and symbols to be carried during the victory dances. He indicated that even when a war leader lost a man, the victory dance was sometimes performed after an appropriate period of mourning. He does not say so, but we know from other case histories that the relatives were compensated with property and other valuables, after which the dances were given. In this instance it was not possible because no scalps were taken and no coups were struck.

Even though Guts was believed to possess potential supernatural powers by virtue of his inheritance of the Earthnaming bundle, bad luck continued to plague him. In his village duties he showed "power" to bring the buffalo herds near the village but he liked to fight so he taught his sons that warfare was an honorable life. In the following narrative, Four Dancers traces out his grandfather's later activities relative to the training of his sons and his eventual relinquishment of the bundle when two of his sons are killed while following his instructions.

Guts got his Earthnaming rites from his parents and had the right to pray to all of the gods. Guts would say to his sons, "When you are out looking for the enemy, you must be brave. Fast often and buy many gods; they will assist you when you are out against the enemy. If you have something to worship in the ceremonies, then you will be a head man and the people will look up to you. If there is a fight and the enemy surrounds any of your relatives, do not be afraid to go to their help. Then you will have a good record. If you don't do that, your misfortunes will reflect unfavorably against me for I am expected to give you all of these instructions."

His son, Never-Runs-Away, was one who liked to put on the ceremonies for the buffalo so he had his wives "walk" four times with the old men. Charging Eagle's real father was the Mandan Four Bears but Guts adopted him as his son when he married Four Bear's widow after the smallpox. Charging Eagle fasted much like his father, Four Bears, did and got the medicine robe like his father had in a public ceremony. Sitting Owl was one who fasted much but he never got to 7 days. The youngest was Bobtail Bull, my father. He dreamed of the "walking ceremony" just as Never-Runs-Away did.

At the winter camp called Killed-the-Bent-Enemy [1854], Never-Runs-Away and Sitting Owl followed two enemies who had stolen horses and struck an enemy first and second. Guts followed behind because he was interested in seeing what his sons would do when they first met the enemy. When he found that his sons were ahead of the others tracking the enemy, he was proud of his sons. Back at the camp when the victory dances were held, Guts took out his large rattles for the Earthnaming ceremony and sang publicly, "My sons said they would be brave in the future and it is so."

Then the two sons were recognized as leaders and the people began to respect them. Then they got new names.

Another time the enemy came and stole horses but the people crowded them so hard that they went into the brush. Wolf Eyes told the younger men not to go into the brush or some would be killed. Just at that time a Mandan named Three Rabbits came up and said, "What are you people waiting for? You Hidatsas are always going far down the river looking for your enemies but now they have come to you. When you are around in the village you are always showing off before the women pretending you are brave."

The enemy had already shot a Hidatsa in the mouth and the others had withdrawn. The Mandan went in and was killed. Sitting Owl, Bobtail Bull, Never-Runs-Away, and Guts came along at this time and announced that they were going to jump into the fort while the others rattled their tongues to confuse the enemy, but the enemy ran away instead and jumped into the river. The people praised the brothers because they had volunteered to go into the brush.

Shortly afterward, the Sioux attacked the village of Fishhook and the men got ready to fight. The Sioux ran to save their lives when the Hidatsa came out. Bobtail Bull said to his brothers while they were painting for the battle, "Let's each catch a Sioux." They came to a creek where there was a large bunch of

Sioux and one shot down Sitting Owl; Never-Runs-Away thought he would get ahold of one but when he crossed the creek, the enemy knocked him down also.

Someone asked Sitting Owl how he was and he said, "I am not suffering." His father came up and Sitting Owl said, "You have always told us to be brave and now I am all in. I am going now and I think my brother, Never-Runs-Away, is on the way and waiting for me. I do not want any doctor. Cover up my face with my robe." And when they took it off again, he was dead.

At the village, Guts tore his mouth in mourning for his two sons who were so brave that they did not have long to live. He took off his clothing and threw it away. He cut deep gashes in his body and cut out pieces of flesh. He cut off his hair and went about through the village in mourning for a year. He would go out onto the hills or near the graves and scaffolds to cry and fast. Their brothers did the same. Guts would go out at night in the winter and cry through the village. One night when he was crying that way Different Wolf called him in and told him that he had fasted long enough.

Different Wolf said, "You will get even. I have been fasting because I have felt so sorry for you. My gods called me Medicine Chief and offered me five squash to eat. When I had finished eating, they had turned into five enemy skulls. That means that you will get five enemies for the two sons you have lost. I dreamt that while you were mourning, so you should stop now. You have been sad long enough. When you get the five enemies, you will enjoy yourself again. I have had this dream for you."

About a month later he still had not stopped crying when some men saw the tracks of five men. The enemy had come to the outskirts of the village looking for horses. Crow-Flies-High was first to find the tracks. The men all went after the enemy and camped out on the prairies. When morning came they saw the enemy. The men painted and put on their holy things before fighting them. Four of the enemy were killed. The fifth enemy had a beautiful necklace that a Crow Indian wanted. In the battle he struck the enemy in the eye with his hand for he was very brave. Then the enemy ran. Ten "brothers" ran after the enemy and cut his head off and broke it up with their axes.

Guts was very happy for now he was even with the enemy for killing his two sons. No longer did he fast. He painted his body black and rubbed off the white paint. He brought out the large rattles belonging to his Earthnaming bundle and sang the victory songs for Different Wolf saying "What Different Wolf said was right; what he promised to give he has given."

Because Crow-Flies-High found the tracks and was always to the front where he struck the enemy, the people praised him and gave him a new name.

Then Bobtail Bull, whose two brothers had been revenged, began to plan his life. He fasted 4 nights in the Naxpikᴇ and did not eat. He dreamed of Guts' Earthnaming bundle and that he was out to war and was bringing back the scalps from two men. He notified his "fathers" of his dream and they said that the bundle was instructing him to take over his father's place. So the young men he invited to go out with him came to his father's lodge, and there Guts opened and hung up the sacred bundle before them and prayed that they would have good luck. Guts promised that they would strike three enemies. The men went out and found two enemies and killed them without losing any of their own. Because Bobtail Bull was the leader he got credit for the two men and now the people said he was on the right path; he had revenged his older brothers' deaths and he was a war leader.

Because they honored him, the old men came often to his lodge to eat and smoke. There were old people there eating and smoking all the time. Bobtail Bull said to them, "I claim nothing for myself; it was my father's gods who did it."

But the people did not pay so much attention to Guts any longer for so often he had brought bad luck. Guts told the old men that since his son had dreamed of the Earthnaming bundle, he should put on the ceremony and possess it since he was now a head man. So Bobtail Bull pledged the ceremony and right away he dreamed of one tipi and the old men told him that one enemy family was given to him by his gods. He gave the four day ceremony of the Red Sticks to bring the buffaloes and the old men "walked" with his wives. Then he went out and took possession of the family, killing all of them and taking their horses.

The old men came as before and said that since he had killed a whole family and had possessed their horses, he was even a greater chief. All the time there were old men at his lodge eating, for they liked to eat with and help an ambitious and lucky man. His wives worked hard preparing nice things for the old men. The old men told him many things he should know to be a great chief of the village because this knowledge was expected of him. Now Bobtail Bull thought he would surely get ahead of Poor Wolf who had the reputation of knowing many sacred traditions and stories of the olden times. So he invited the old men in often and gave them good meals and the old men would tell him of the olden times even back when the people first came on the earth. At this time one of his wives went off with another man and he found out about it. He was very angry at her, for she did not take care of their children. He sent two old men to bring her back.

The two men went to her and said, "Your husband is calling for you."

They took her back to her husband's lodge and Bobtail Bull sat down beside her; he painted her face black as she would have had the right to do if she had been beside him when he came back from a successful war expedition. He dressed her in good leggings, moccasins, dress, and robe, and put her on his best horse and told the two men to take her to her new husband saying, "Take her away from here."

Not long afterward the other wife ran away with another man and her children were going about through the village looking for their mother. The children were having a hard time, for they had no mother to take care of them. Bobtail Bull was angry because his wife had left him and he could no longer invite in the older men. So he resolved to go to war again. His younger brother, Charging Eagle, offered to help him for that was much better than fighting with one's own people. His clansmen and friends volunteered to help him when they learned he was going to war again. Not far from the village they found an enemy with one foot and killed him. Now Bobtail Bull was a bigger chief, the others in the party said. Then they found an enemy going along a dry creek and Charging Eagle killed him. The people praised Bobtail Bull and Charging Eagle when they came back into the village with the two scalps and the horses.

Bobtail Bull had done this because another had gone off with his wife. He sent two men to bring his second wife back and when she was with him again she began to cry but he painted her up, dressed her in good things, mounted her on his best horse, and sent her back to her husband. All this he did because he was a chief. Then his brother-in-law gave Bobtail Bull a different sister for the one who ran away. This was good, for then he had his children with him and the old men were welcomed once more.

Again he gave the Walking ceremony and the old men "walked" with his new wife. Then he went out to war again and his young men killed and struck three enemies. Soon the younger men were giving him presents in the ceremonies and he was living a good life. Others asked him to assist when the buffaloes were called to the village.[30]   One day a Crow Indian visiting at the village wanted Bobtail Bull as his father and he went west to the Crow to adopt his "son." While they were there, the "son" asked Bobtail Bull to go with him on the warpath and to carry the medicine pipe. They went west as far as the Rocky Mountains and had a good time, for there were many buffaloes farther west. Bobtail Bull and his "son" were the leaders, for he was training his "son" to be a great war leader. One day the scouts came back howling and Bobtail Bull put the robe out for them to jump over. The scouts reported three enemies at a distance shooting buffaloes.

Everyone painted up and took out his medicines to wear during the battle. Because Bobtail Bull carried the pipe, the three enemies were killed. When they returned to the Crow camp, they painted their faces black and rode in between the lodges firing off their guns and making a great noise. The Crows honored Bobtail Bull shouting, "What he said is true; his arrows are holy; his gods, the swallow and the hawk [31] have supernatural powers."

Then the people gave him horses and many other valuable things. When he returned to Fishhook with the scalps and the fine things, the people saw them and knew that what he said was true. He gave the goods and horses to his brothers and sisters and they helped him put up feasts for the old men. Poor Wolf and Crows Paunch did not say much, but Bobtail Bull knew they were jealous because he was coming along so fast.

Bobtail Bull and Crow-Flies-High were younger than the other chiefs but they had done more in battle than Crows Paunch and Poor Wolf who then selected four assistants (village protectors) and left Bobtail Bull and Crow-Flies-High out because they were younger.

One day Bobtail Bull and Crow-Flies-High came back from hunting to learn that their friends did not approve of the way Government rations were being distributed. Crow-Flies-High was angry and mounted his pink horse. He rode through the village with a war bonnet on his head following the interpreter wherever he went, telling him that the old chiefs were selfish, that the people needed new chiefs who would look out for them. The young men whose old people had been accused of selfishness were angry and threatened to kill Crow-Flies-High if he did not stop, for quarrels would bring bad luck to the village.

It was at this time that my father, Bobtail Bull, was sent for by his friends and the pipe belonging to the Earthnaming bundle was lit. Then Bobtail Bull took the pipe to Crow-Flies-High and told him to go back to his lodge. Crow-Flies-High was very angry at first and threatened to kill the first person who attempted to interfere with his division of the 50 cattle the Government was furnishing for rations. He was telling the interpreter how selfish the chiefs were and that he was going to see that the people got a fair division when Bobtail Bull put the pipe before him. Because Bobtail Bull was his "friend" and they worked together, he lit the pipe and announced that he was leaving. That night the people met in two different earth lodges. Those who followed Bobtail Bull met in his lodge and Guts, my grandfather, was there, for he was an older man and could talk better for the Earthnaming bundle. Most of the people in that lodge were those who had formerly lived at Hidatsa village on the Knife but there were a few others from the other villages because they too were not satisfied with the chiefs. The others met at Poor Wolf's lodge. Most of those were from Awaxawi and Awatixa and from the Mandan villages.

Even the Black Mouths split up according to the way their relatives went. During the night the two groups discussed their grievances separately while some

---

[30] See the "Earthnaming Ceremony," pp. 433–438.
[31] See the myths of Woman Above (pp. 323–333) and Earthnaming sacred rites (pp. 433–438).

of the older men who were respected by both groups went back and forth between the groups trying to work out a solution. The young men of Bobtail Bull's group thought that the other chiefs kept them back, even though they had more horses and war honors than the others who were always giving medicine feasts. They thought that it would be better to live by themselves.

During the night, Bobtail Bull agreed to be their chief in another village if they would move peacefully, but he would not serve as their leader if any fights broke out to discredit his Earthnaming bundle or the other tribal bundles containing the sacred objects. He told the people that once before in their history most of the people were destroyed by fire when two brothers quarreled [32] and that there was no place that he could take them safely if war broke out, for it would be like brothers fighting since the clans were all mixed up in the village.

That night he walked through the village with his medicine pipe and reassured the people. When morning came the people packed their things and prepared for the long march to the mouth of the Yellowstone. Those who had more things than they could carry left them in the care of their relatives. Even the lodges were given to their relatives. Some even borrowed horses of relatives at Fishhook.

When the time came to leave, some families decided to remain at Fishhook while others decided at the last minute to go along. Those who went west lived well, for there were many buffaloes and the young men were hired by the Army to be scouts. The two village groups visited back and forth a great deal and helped each other in the ceremonies. Some families would live in one village for a while and then they would go back to the other one to live. They got along well together. Even today we live on this end of the reservation apart from the others but we visit back and forth and our young people marry into the other group. Still we think of ourselves as a separate group and have our own leaders.

When we left the old village, we did not have so many of the old ceremonies, for most of the people with the rights stayed back. The old people thought we would have bad luck. The young men fasted much and had their own bundles. Some would go back to the old village to buy bundles. But, in time, we thought that the gods one got fasting were as powerful as those one bought through the fathers, for our young men got more horses and war honors than the young men of the other village. Then we would tease our joking relatives in the other village.

Crow-Flies-High became the head war chief without owning any of the tribal bundles. His father owned an Old-Woman-Who-Never-Dies bundle at Hidatsa but the bundle was put away when he died of smallpox in 1837. Crow-Flies-High was reared by relatives but he never undertook to take up his father's gods until he was an old man and after he had won his position. As a young man he fasted one night at Short Missouri where he dreamed of the eastern Old-Woman-Who-Never-Dies. His clan fathers told him that she was instructing him to give the 4-day rites to take up his father's gods but he did not follow their instructions for he was poor and did not have many relatives to assist him. Instead he made up a personal bundle of the things he saw in his dream.

Another time during the winter he fasted at Sack Butte on the Big Bend. At that time some buffaloes were crossing the Missouri with their calves following behind. In his dreams he saw that the calves could not get up onto the bank so he went to help. At first the calves were afraid of him. He pushed each one up over the bank out of the water and then he went back to his fasting. Then the buffaloes came and took him to Porcupine Butte on the Little Missouri near

---

[32] See "The Legendary Period" (pp. 297-308) for this incident.

Medora and taught him how to bring the rain.   Later, when the gardens dried up, he brought rains for the women at Fort Buford.

Another time he fasted above the spring near Percy Baker's place at the grave of a Crow Indian.   Whenever anyone went there, this Crow would send a high wind and frighten the faster away.   This time the wind came but he was not afraid.   Then the wind went down and someone stood on the hill and sang a sacred song.   He had never seen the Crow but he thought the person standing there must have been the Crow whose grave was nearby.

He would stay out fasting for 7 days at a time but he did not put on the public ceremonies.   In his sacred bundle he had two dresses made of hides and painted yellow.   This was what he saw when the buffaloes took him to Porcupine Butte.   When he was old he gave them to his sons to use for calling the rains.

He was always successful in leading war parties; that is the way he became the war chief and the people respected him.

The above narrative further elucidates the relationship of military adventures to village behavior.   Although Four Dancers spoke of the right of the owner of the Earthnaming bundle to pray to all of the gods collectively, there were specific gods and associated rites over which the bundle owner had no definite authority.   In the ritual, the gods were believed to assemble and come to the village as a group to bring good luck to the giver of the ceremony.   One should note that while Guts' own sons performed those rites controlled by their father, Charging Eagle, the stepson, received visions of the Mandan Four Bear's, his own father's bundle even though the father had died nearly a quarter of a century earlier.

We see Guts checking up on his sons to see if they had performed bravely and urging them to participate in the battles.   When they perform bravely, he brings out his rattles from the Earthnaming bundle and sings the victory songs, thus identifying their bravery with his sacred bundle.   Again the sons show bravery, when the enemy build a fort in the heavy timber to protect themselves, by volunteering to go into the brush when others have had bad luck.   Associating their good fortune on numerous occasions with the supernatural powers of the bundle, we find them daring each other to "catch a Sioux" and, while distinguishing themselves for unusual bravery, they are killed.   Had they succeeded in their mission, not only would Sitting Owl and Never-Runs-Away have been highly respected, but Guts would have succeeded in removing much of the mistrust and lack of confidence the people had for him.   His reputation would then have been as great as Poor Wolf's, the rival bundle owner from Awaxawi village.

Guts' self-torture was greater than that normally practiced by a war leader losing young men in battle, but this was probably due to both the loss of prestige and of his sons; normally a war leader did not take his own sons to war.   The dream by Different Wolf, in which five squash change into five enemy heads, is interpreted to mean that his "brother," Guts, will get even. Here Different Wolf thinks of Guts as a brother although actually the relationship is quite extended: Man-With-Long-Hair and Different Wolf belong to the same clan, the Prairie Chickens, and both came from Hidatsa village while Man-With-Long-Hair and Guts had the same father; therefore they are brothers, although Guts belonged to the Maxoxati clan. At any rate, however extended the relation may be, an "older brother" comes to the aid of Guts and directs him to stop his mourning, saying that he has suffered long enough. Note that the obligations of brothers to avenge the death of one of their number is expressed by cutting off the head of one enemy and breaking it up. Four Dancers uses the kinship term here in its broader meaning to include clan members and others so classified.

Four Dancers introduces the concept that, at this point, Bobtail Bull begins to plan his life. This is not a unique situation, for, in recording the biographies of various Hidatsas, the informant invariably stated that "it was at this time he began to plan his life." We see that he initiated his plan by fasting during the Sun Dance while another was buying the rights from a father, but that the vision he received was of his own father's Earthnaming bundle. Here we see unfolding the tribal bundle purchase pattern: regardless of the ceremony being performed during fasting, it is of one's father's bundle rites that one normally dreams. When he tells the "fathers," including his biological father, that when dreaming of the bundle, he was also promised two enemies, Guts says that he will get three. His reputation is not improved when Bobtail Bull successfully kills two instead of the three enemies his father predicted he would get.

We see that as Bobtail Bull's reputation grew, the number of older men who came to his lodge to eat and smoke increased. Guts then realized that although the bundle has supernatural powers, he has not succeeded in controlling this power and is, therefore, avoided. At this point he decides to relinquish the bundle to his son although it was customary for one to keep this bundle until his death. Closely associated with his initiation into the bundle rites were his performances of the "Walking" ceremonies when his wives were ceremonially "given" to the fathers. But the path to eminence was not an easy one. While the old men were instructing Bobtail Bull in tribal lore, the wives worked hard preparing feasts for the old men. It was during this instruction that the first wife eloped with another man, abandoning her children to the other women of the lodge. The husband had the legal right to take her back or to destroy his rival's or the rival's relatives' property, but to do that would bring the ridicule of his joking relatives upon him. Although he could take her back, the honorable thing to do was to pay no attention to the matter or he could go further by using the occasion to embarrass both the wife and her eloper by casting her off with an elaborate public display of gifts. This Bobtail Bull does to the embarrassment of the elopers and the ridicule of their joking relatives who tease the eloper by saying that his new wife is so poor "that he has been paid to take her." When a second wife elopes, Bobtail Bull was frustrated in his chiefly ambitions; no longer could he invite the old men to his lodge, for he has only his mother-in-law and a young unmarried sister-in-law in the lodge. By this time it is evident that a conspiracy exists to hold him back by depriving him of the assistance of his wives. He resolves to take out his anger on the tribe's enemies rather than on his own group, and at the same time humiliate the elopers by adding further military honors. We see that his brothers, clansmen, and friends volunteer to assist him. Returning with military honors, he sends for his second wife and again embarrasses her and her new husband by dressing her in good clothing and sending her back with a good horse. The only thing that the wife's brother could do to resolve the situation was to provide another wife. In this case another sister was substituted; the children remained in the household under the care of their grandmother and the new mother.

Village cleavage was then complete; those who had come from Hidatsa village and a few Mandan families looked to Bobtail Bull, owner of the Earthnaming bundle from Hidatsa village; the Awaxawi and Awatixa were represented by Poor Wolf, the bundle owner from Awaxawi. There was little that the former could do to extend his authority within the village. Poor Wolf's faction held intact. It was at this time that a Crow Indian visiting at the village indicated a desire to become Bobtail Bull's "son" through the medium of the medicine pipe. To complete the ceremony, Bobtail Bull and a few of his friends went to the Crow camp where his "son" indicated a desire to go on the warpath with Bobtail Bull as leader. Again he won military honors, extended his kin to include many Crows, and returned to Fishhook with scalps, fine goods, and many horses. At this point Four Dancers remarks that Bobtail Bull does not keep the things he received of the Crows. Instead, he passes the things on to his "brothers and sisters" as payment for past help and future assistance when he gives further feasts to the older men. This point brings out the advantage one with many brothers and sisters and membership in a large clan enjoys. Here we have one of the factors giving rise to the rapid reduction and assimilation of clans occurring among the Mandan and Hidatsa during the 19th century.

Probably the most significant feature of this conflict was the opposition of the next older age-group headed by Poor Wolf which should have been a respect group according to traditional behavior. In this crisis situation, Bobtail Bull alines with Crow-Flies-High who, although entitled to enter the fraternity of traditional bundle owners by virture of descent from one owning rights in the Old-Woman-Who-Never-Dies rites, flaunts tradition and establishes a personal bundle without the benefit of public ceremonies. Orphaned by the smallpox epidemic of 1837 and poor in his youth, he followed a different course from that of most of the other young men; when his age-grade group fasted during the organized rites, having no close relative to put up goods, he could not compete with the larger households. He avoided fasting on these occasions to seek visions alone on the prairies. But he often went out with others on the war path, winning more honors than those who had followed the traditional course. Like others of his age-grade group who had won honors without the benefit of public rites and many who had come from Hidatsa village and had been in closer contacts with the River Crow from whom they were recently separated, they shared the belief that personal and individual fasting was as effective in bringing good luck as fasting during the formalized rites or the purchase of tribal bundles.

Crow-Flies-High's action in assuming authority against the respected older age-grade group was equivalent to overthrowing the entire traditional system, and has been largely explained by the more conservative element as ignorance due to his early training without the benefit of close relatives to advise him. However, the conflict as I see it was more deep-seated than that; the village group from which he came traditionally conformed more closely to the Crow pattern, being more closely associated physically with that group. His actions on the occasion of the division of the 50 cattle would have been normal for the Crow but were outside the pattern of group behavior for either of the other two Hidatsa village groups or the Mandan.

A significant aspect of the conflict was the new role that Bobtail Bull assumed as Earthnaming bundle owner and symbol of the traditional peace role of this bundle owner. Note how he first ordered Crow-Flies-High to return to his lodge; this is indeed a demonstration of authority rarely manifested. We see the authority and symbolic significance of the bundles manifested in the orientation of the population according to allegiance to one or the other of the two competing Earthnaming bundles. Even the police authority was immobilized because the Black Mouths membership took sides individually.

At this time, Bobtail Bull and Crow-Flies-High both belonged to the police society while the chiefs whom they wished to replace were in the next older age-group. This was a distinct revolt against the established age-grade structure. The instructions in traditional lore, which Bobtail Bull had previously received from the old men, proved timely. We find him referring to the Creation Myth in which most of the tribe was once destroyed by fire because Hungry Wolf and High Bird, brothers having the same mother and father, once quarreled.[33]

The establishment of an Army post at Fort Buford provided a ready outlet and easy solution to the problem. Since 1837, the combined numbers of the three villages had barely been able to defend themselves from the Sioux. Now it was possible for a faction to break away much as must have been the case in earlier times, if I correctly interpret the archeological evidence of the numerous small village settlements in their traditional territory, and without the danger of destruction by overwhelming attacks from their nomadic neighbors. Bobtail Bull agrees to be their leader provided there is no bloodshed, for he was unwilling to assume the responsibility for the group if brothers fought. So he walked through the village throughout the night in his peace role, just as Poor Wolf as owner of the other bundle did, to see that no quarrels occurred. It is significant to note that when a crisis arose, these two bundle owners stood as the top authority and the customary police authority was missing.

The division was a peaceful one; most families had made a decision long before the final crisis occurred. Those who were remaining behind assisted their relatives who were leaving, even providing them with extra horses for the trip. Arrangements were made for the use of abandoned lodges by relatives and clan members. There was never a thought of continuing the conflict once the issue was decided and the separation was completed. The two populations visited back and forth even though they lived 150 miles apart; each group assisted the other in the performance of ceremonies and rejoiced when the other had won military honors; individuals moved from one group to the other to live without discrimination. Fewer tribal bundle rites were owned by those moving away, and the ceremonial life suffered by comparison with the Fishhook Village group. In time, the Fort Buford group came to look to Crow-Flies-High as the leader and less was heard of Bobtail Bull, chiefly because of the shift in emphasis from the formal ceremonies to individual fasting. With these comments we close the Four Dancers' narrative.

It was customary for one to enumerate his military honors and the details of his various military exploits on numerous social and ceremonial occasions and to depict them by dress and painting. For many individuals, and on most public occasions, one's status

---

[33] See "The Legendary Period" (pp. 297–308) for details of this incident.

could be determined largely by his display of these honors. It was customary for the younger married men to invite those possessing good military records to eat with them and to relate their military achievements. This had become a ritual with the Hidatsa and followed a set pattern; one would select a "father" or a group of "fathers" to come eat with him when he had enjoyed good luck in hunting and had an abundant supply of fresh meat. Usually the "fathers" received a few presents consisting of new robes on which they were invited to sit while partaking of the meal. On approaching the lodge where the feast had been prepared, the fathers would invariably indicate how much they had craved fresh meat and now thanked their "son" for thinking of them. As they ate, the young man would ask them to tell stories of the olden times or of their military adventures. The old men would tell a younger man that this was the way to get ahead and then pray to their sacred bundles for the "son's" success.

These feasts to the older men provided one mechanism for the perpetuation of the military record of many individuals. Sometimes a young man wanted to learn more of his own father who had died years before; these feasts provided a means of acquiring this information. For the acquisition of knowledge about one's own clan members there was less formality; older brothers as disciplinary officers usually provided that information as a part of the training of the younger brothers. Older clan members belonging to the household would, from time to time, undertake to transmit their knowledge of the clan informally while assembled around the lodge fire during long evenings. This was done without thought of pay, since one enjoyed rights in the property of his clan members. The personal achievements of those who attained universal respect of the entire group became a part of the traditions of the group long after their deaths.

The Hidatsa had produced a number of leaders during the last century whose record has become a part of the traditional lore of the people and is repeated to the young and discussed among the old whenever a few gather for a feast or to smoke. Four Bears, son of Two Tails who was one of the war chiefs at Knife River, rose to eminence as one of the war chiefs after 1837 and is distinguished principally for his part in signing the Fort Laramie Treaty in 1851. Bears Arm supplies the following narratives of Four Bears' life, securing the information from his father, Old-Woman-Crawling, who at one time served as an Old Wolf on one of the military expeditions undertaken by Four Bears.

When Four Bears was giving the Wolf Ceremony to get his father's rights, while the people were still living at Knife River, he dreamed that he was going out to the northwest to get six men and one white horse. He thought that he was well paid for his efforts in putting on the ceremony. Then he went to several holy men who had gods that had come down to them generation by generation from the olden times and asked them to be his helpers. There were eight of these holy men who were to help him: Raven Bear had the Big Bird bundle; Crows Paunch had a Long Arm bundle; Bears Heart, Old-Woman-Crawling, Marries-by-Carrying-Water, and Edge-of-Stone had Grizzly Bear bundles; Red-Buffalo-Cow had a People Above (Mandan) bundle; and Boy had a Hawk (Arikara) bundle.

He invited these and enough young men to make up a party of about 40. As was the custom, he did not announce what he was looking for until they went into camp 1 day's distance from the villages. Then he told them that he was out looking for the six men and a white horse promised by the Wolves. They went on and passed the mouth of the Yellowstone, traveling westward. Raven Bear and Marries-by-Carrying-Water were appointed leaders of the scouts to take young men and go ahead to look for the enemies. Just before they came to their trail, they camped, and Raven Bear stood up with the sword that belonged to the Big Bird ceremony and began to cry. He said to the Big Birds, "Have pity on me. When we surround an enemy, I want to strike one."

The scouts went ahead and saw the trail which the Assiniboin had followed. They reported to Four Bears and the next day the party followed the trail until they came to a post with a sign carved on it. There was a picture of the Rocky Mountains with an arrow showing that they were going there; Sitting Wolf as leader with the pipe was shown; the moon with 15 cuts below it showed that they had left on the 15th day after the new moon; the human head with 100 gashes told that there were 100 in the party. Four Bears came to the post and saw that it had been put there by the Assiniboin. They followed the trail, watching both ways, for they knew that the sign had been put there so another band of Assiniboin would know where to find the head band. In 3 days, the scouts reported that they had found the camp. Seeing the scouts coming back howling, the Old Wolves put out a robe for them to jump over. Sometimes they put up a mound of dirt, buffalo manure, or a robe to jump over. When they had done this and then kicked the mound down, it was a sign that they would overcome their enemies.

Then Four Bears stood, holding the wolf hide which he had given to the leader of the scouts to carry, saying, "My father's gods, when I had your ceremony, I stood before the four holy women of the four winds [34] suffering while thinking that someday I would meet my enemies. I became dizzy and fell to the ground; then I saw a trail leading westward and I saw six persons and a white horse at the end of that trail. For that reason, the scouts have seen the camp and I want to take what has been promised me. I want you to lead off six men from that camp so my men can get them without any bad luck coming to us. I want that white horse you promised me too."

Raven Bear stood up and told what he had seen in his dreams. He said, "My gods, the eagles, the big birds, and thunder, you came to me from my father and I have taken good care of you. When we have those enemies surrounded, I want you to help me to be the first to strike one of them. I have come to the enemy this day and I want to hit that man you promised me."

Bears Heart stood up and said, "My god, the yellow grizzly bear, I got you from my father. I got the arrow that came from Two Men back at the beginning

---

[34] See "Wolf Ceremonies," given below, for their role in this ceremony.

of times. I want to hit one enemy with that holy arrow and I want to strike one enemy myself."

Then Married-by-Carrying-Water took out his sacred lance and addressing the silver grizzly bear, told the men that he was supposed to cut 3 inches from the end of the lance each time he struck an enemy. One time he had been walking along the edge of the timber at Shell Creek when a bear attacked him. They were so close together that there was not room to use an arrow so he took up his stone ax. When the bear was about to seize him, he hit the bear on the head and the Bear said, "Don't hit me again," so he drew back the stone ax. The bear reached over back of his head and took out a red feather, handed it to the man and said, "Whenever you meet an enemy, put this on your head. Make a long lance and paint it red; when you meet the enemy, take out the stick and hit the enemy with it. Even if they are aiming their guns at you, they will not be able to hit you. Whenever anyone asks for the stick to strike the enemy, give him both the stick and the feather for he will be successful. When you strike the enemy, cut off a piece of the stick and take it to the west side of the camp and point to the west as an offering to me." [35]

Boy was the next to get up. His god was the hawk that he got from his Arikara father. He had the tail feathers and a red feather that he held up as he called his son, Bear-Comes-Out, to stand before him. Boy prayed, "I want my boy to be one of the first to strike one of the enemies."

Raven Paunch had the Long Arm bundle but he prayed to the horse instead. He told how he had fasted 4 days and nights out on the prairies with his horse which he led during the daytime by means of thongs in the arms. The fourth night he had a dream in which he saw the horse decorated with grass on top of the head. The horse said, "Do like that with me when you go out against the enemy; whether you take me or some other horse, paint us with white clay on the shoulders in four places. The four white spots represent the 4 days you fasted with the horse; it also represents the four legs I run with, for the four spots will give my legs strength so that I can run without stumbling." He was riding that horse then.

Each of the other Old Wolves told of their dreams and ambitions. Four Bears said to the scouts, "Go out and see if the six men and the white horse have left the camp."

The scouts crept close to the camp and saw the six men and the white horse leave the camp with dogs trailing along, so they came back and reported to Four Bears. When the enemy was some distance from the camp, Four Bears' men surrounded and closed in on them. Bear-Comes-Out was first to strike the enemy that his father had asked the hawk to give him. They killed the six men and took the white horse, giving the scalps and horse to Four Bears who had a prior claim to them since he had seen them in his dream. Then they hurried back to the villages to dance the Victory dances. Four Bears called out the names of those who had struck the enemy so that all would hear.

Again Four Bears had a dream from the Wolves who gave him one enemy so he organized a party to go out for that which had been promised him. This man was an Assiniboin who would be found alone far to the north. They traveled north until they came to the lake region. There was a lone tree by a lake and Bluestone asked Four Bears to camp there as he wanted to fast under the nest occupied by young eagles. Four Bears thought that it was a good idea. Bluestone's chest skin was cut and he was hung from a limb so that his feet could scarcely touch the ground.

---

[35] The west side of the eagle trapping lodge is holy.

In the morning, Four Bears inquired if Bluestone had been given a dream and he said that he had the same dream as his clan brother, Four Bears, except that it was the eagle in the tree that told him instead of the wolves. In the dream he saw an old man standing by the tree with an eagle feather in his hair and this old man told him that they would see one enemy and that Bluestone would be the first one to strike this enemy.

When Bluestone said that he would be the first to strike the enemy, there were faster young men in the party who did not believe that. They went on until they found an old Assiniboin man picking up duck eggs near a lake. Bluestone was next to the lead but when the Assiniboin was about to shoot, the front man stumbled and fell so Bluestone struck the enemy someone farther back had shot. The second man to strike was the one who had shot the enemy.

Four Bears went out again along the White Earth Creek looking for the two enemies he had been promised. He got both of them, women this time, making nine enemies in all that his sacred bundles had "given" him. The people said that if he could go to four times without "kicking the stone" he would be a great man, so he fasted much and gave liberally to the older people.

One time shortly afterward, the enemy came to the village and stole horses. One Buffalo, who also had a Wolf bundle, organized a party to go after them. When they were a short distance from the village, One Buffalo stopped to select the scouts. He selected, in this order, Raven Bear as leader, Owns-Many-Spotted Horses, and Lifts Heart. When the leader saw Four Bears get up, he named him to be fourth. Four Bears said, "I was expecting to be called first."

The scouts went out and Four Bears got ahead of the others, finding an Assiniboin sleeping. He had not found any horses. Four Bears killed and scalped him before the others came, but the other scouts went to the place and struck him second, third, and fourth. The war expedition was called off and they went back to the village to dance.

Four Bears decided to go out again soon afterward to get one enemy and a horse. Since he had been out so often, he thought that his supernatural power might be running out, so he decided to enlist the assistance of some other holy men. Finally he selected his clan brother, One Buffalo, who agreed to help him. They made up a party of 32 men. They traveled southwestward until they came to Buffalo Lodge (Home) Butte. Since it was quite a large party and the hunting was poor, they were soon out of food. Usually buffaloes could be found around this butte, for that was a home of the buffalo spirits. The young men thought they would surely starve and the older men thought they might die, too.

Two scouts went out ahead and soon afterward the others saw a buffalo running about 2 miles away. One Buffalo said to the others, "We are all in; we can't run that far. We will have to find some other way to get that buffalo."

One Buffalo seated his party in a row. Then he held his braid to one side and hit his head; powder came out of the ear; from the other ear he took a bullet. He put the powder in the gun, using soft sage as the wad; then he put in the bullet with sage on top of that. All the while he sang a holy song. He directed Four Bears to fill the pipe and start it at the opposite end saying, "As soon as I see smoke coming out of the pipe, I am going to fire the gun."

They lit the pipe and began to smoke. One of the Old Wolves said, "They are smoking now," so he fired the gun. They continued to smoke and pass the pipe along the line. There were 30 men in the row and when the pipe was to the middle of the line, some claimed a little further, they saw the buffalo fall over nearly 2 miles away.

After they had enough to eat, the party decided to turn back towards the Missouri at the mouth of Heart River. One day the scouts found a horse, so the two leaders rode double.　One day they found two women and a berdache digging wild turnips on the prairie.　Until they were near they thought they were women, for all three Sioux were dressed alike.　Before making the attack, Four Bears told his party that they would strike coups on the women but spare their lives.　Four Bears got ahead of the others and struck both but the berdache was brave, saying, "You can't kill me for I am holy.　I will strike coups on you with my digging stick."

Then the berdache sang a sacred song and chased them.　Four Bears shot an arrow at the berdache but it would not penetrate the robe.　Then he knew that the berdache had great supernatural powers.　Since he had been successful on all other military expeditions and did not want to spoil his luck, he called his party back.　The expedition was successful, for they got the horse.　Four Bears used good judgment, for it was hard to kill a berdache since they were holy. Later Poor Wolf bought his clan brother's Bullet rites.

Later the Assiniboin learned from the Whites that the Hidatsa were dying of smallpox and decided to come and kill off the Hidatsa, for then they would have a large territory on the Missouri River.　At that time the Awatixa and Awaxawi were at Snake Creek on the bend above the mouth of Knife River and many of the Hidatsa-proper were around Sanish where they went to escape the smallpox. The head men selected Raven Paunch as chief of the scouts to locate and watch the movements of the Assiniboin camp, for they had their women and children along.　He found the Assiniboin on Stevenson Flats.　The police were on guard all night, and in the morning the men, numbering about 50 and constituting all who had survived the smallpox, hid near the trail the Assiniboin would take.

Seven Bears told the men that they should kill all the Assiniboin men and older boys they could, but to spare the women and children for many of the Awaxawi and Awatixa had lost their wives and families with smallpox.　If they could take the women prisoners, there would soon be many children in the tribe again.　In the battle, taking the Assiniboin by surprise, the men were all killed off and about 50 women and children were taken.　They were taken back to the village and traded around so that all the single men had wives.　Some escaped from time to time but the people never looked for them, thinking that they had children at home they wanted to see.　Many of the people in the tribe today are the descendants of these women and children taken at that time, but the people never tell if a person is the descendant of a captive for it would hurt his record in the tribe. In this way, young male descendants of captives and Hidatsa fathers have the same chance as the other boys.

When they got back to camp, they found that Four Bears had been shot through the body.　His clan brother, One Buffalo, went among his clans-people asking assistance so they could engage a doctor.　They gave robes, war bonnets, guns, and one horse.　Then One Buffalo went to Cherry Necklace with the pipe and asked him to doctor Four Bears.　Cherry Necklace instructed One Buffalo to bring in four of the round hand-drums.　Then he dressed in his medicine objects, the otter, and went to Four Bear's lodge where all the people were gathered.　He said to the people, "Do not let any dogs into the lodge for that is a rule when I doctor.　If a dog gets in, my patient will die.　The Waterbusters selected one of their members to sit at the door and keep the dogs out.

Four young men were selected to use the round hand-drums and sing the holy songs with Cherry Necklace.　Then he said to the people, "Go over to the river bank and see how I am going to do this."

Cherry Necklace and Four Bears were naked with only an otter skin on Cherry Necklace's head.　They went to the river where Four Bears was led into the water until they were in the water to the depth of Four Bear's belt where he was wounded.

Cherry Necklace took down the otter skin and wet it all over and said to the people, "I am not holy at all; I can't do anything by myself. But the otter is the one I get my powers from."

Cherry Necklace spoke to the otter saying, "It is you who has the powers. You should cure this man so the people can see with their own eyes what you can do." Then he sang the Otter songs.

He dipped the otter skin under the water and when he took his hand away the second time the otter came up on the other side of Cherry Necklace and swam over to Four Bears, touching the spot where he was wounded. When the otter backed away from the wound, blood came out. Then the otter swam to Four Bear's back and did the same thing. The otter did that four times and then Cherry Necklace said, "I am glad that this wounded man is going to be healed."

Cherry Necklace instructed Four Bears to wash his head in the river and drink a little water. Then the clansmen helped him back to his lodge where Cherry Necklace continued to sing the holy songs. It was not long until he was walking about again. Cherry Necklace was highly respected, for he had succeeded in saving the life of a great war leader.

Four Bears was consulted when the people were looking for a new village site and because the people were accustomed to put up offerings for the buffaloes at Fishhook Bend, he thought it would be a good place to build, but he did not take part in the ceremonies when the village was built.

The above describes warfare of the first half of the 19th century. Unlike the Four Dancers narratives of his own father, in which he explains each event in terms of his father's ambitions to eminence traditionally enjoyed by the owner of the Earthnaming bundle, Bears Arm relates the principal military adventures of one who was destined to attain top rank as war chief during the critical years of village disorganization following the smallpox epidemic of 1837. While Four Dancers belabors the misfortunes of his grandfather, Guts, who eventually relinquished the bundle to his son, Bobtail Bull, he says little of other ceremonial roles which the bundle owner traditionally enjoyed. Perhaps initial interest in the Poor Wolf bundle stems from the fact that, during the period of village disorganization between 1837 and 1845, the Hidatsa-proper had indicated the intention of rejoining the River Crow from whom they had separated not long before. In fact, many Hidatsa families had actually gone west and were encouraging the rest of the village to join them. At this time the Awatixa and Awaxawi, whose separation from the western Crow had occurred long before, decided to remain on the Missouri and live much as they had before the epidemic.

In the Bears Arm narrative of Four Bears, we are concerned with the life history of one who, through inheritance of Wolf bundles from his father, Two Tails, received his principal distinctions as a military leader rather than as the director and supervisor of certain aspects of the village ceremonial life. We find that after giving the Wolf ceremony to acquire his father's bundle rights, he dreamed of six enemies and a white horse, thus establishing prior rights to them. Bears Arm lists the Old Wolves whom Four Bears invited to assist him. They are selected entirely from his own, the Four-clan moiety, and hold rights in several of the tribal bundles. By means of drawings on a post, the Hidatsa learn that one band of Assiniboin under Sitting Wolf has gone farther west.

The purpose of the expedition, as explained by Four Bears after the party has left the village, was to take possession of the six enemies and the white horse which his gods had promised him. Had he failed to take possession of his rightful property at that time, we learn from other case histories that his claim still stood. Should he have been unable on this or subsequent trips to have taken possession of them he could have sold or given his rights to another as in the following narrative by Wolf Chief.

The recitation of one's bundle rights before going into battle has been described before. It served a useful purpose in stimulating young men to buy their fathers' bundles and to give them courage in the immediate battle. In this instance, the Old Wolves reciting their ritualistic rites are of both the Mandan and Hidatsa villages, although at this time the union of the population into a single village had not occurred. In selecting coleaders, he has selected from the equivalent moiety as well.

In this instance we find a group of "brothers" cooperating to bring honor to one of their number. Four Bears took possession of the six scalps and white horse for which he received credit, while the others shared the 24 honors of striking coup. This raises the question of the disposal of other honors, had the group been able to kill and strike additional enemies or possess additional horses. By the rules, Four Bears would have taken only those horses which he saw first, since additional horses went to those first seeing them. As leader of the war party, he would have received credit for all additional enemies killed and struck, with the right to show this accomplishment on his clothing. Those who struck the enemy could wear feathers. One seeing a number of horses rarely took possession of them, for he was expected to make gifts according to the membership of the group.

Four Bears' second expedition to the north for one enemy promised to him brings out the point that the Hidatsa fasted in many situations. Here a clan brother assisting him finds an eagle nest under which he decides to fast. Some of the young men think it very funny when Bluestone tells how in his dream he has been promised the first honor of striking the enemy Four Bears is seeking, since Bluestone was not a fast runner. One wonders if fear caused the one in the lead to stumble, permitting Bluestone to strike first. Crows Heart told the writer of an instance when young men going into battle found it convenient to get off to fix their saddles, thus permitting others to do the actual fighting.

We see that after Four Bears has been out several times, the old men tell him that if he can go out as leader four times without "kicking the stone" he will be a great man. This imparts that even the greatest military leaders gave but a small amount of time to actual military campaigns of their own. When the men go out to look for their horses stolen by the Assiniboin, we see a war party being organized sometime after leaving the village and Four Bears is not pleased because he is not selected to be the leader of the scouts. Why? The informant did not know what One Buffalo had in mind but, in any case, he was shown to be in error since Four Bears was first to win the honors. We see in this account how quickly the Hidatsa terminated a military expedition once they had the better of the enemy. Once an enemy is killed and coups struck on his body, the search for the horses is called off.

When Four Bears planned a fourth expedition, he acknowledged that his sacred bundles had brought him good luck to that time and wondered if they had begun to lose their supernatural powers. Thus, he selects a clan brother, One Buffalo, to be his assistant and they strike out afoot toward the Black Hills until they come to Buffalo Lodge (Home) Butte, the home of the buffalo spirits. We see that when the young men complain of being hungry, the Old Wolves seem to agree with them, thus setting the stage for the magical Bullet rites by One Buffalo. Here we have a variant of a ritual which Four Dancers described above when his grandfather accompanied Three Coyotes. In the former case, a similar ritual was employed to kill the Sioux Bear medicine man. The two scouts were out when the buffalo was seen about 2 miles ahead, so the reader must suspect that, since guns did not shoot 2 miles at that time, the appearance of the two scouts on the scene at the time the buffalo was killed was scarcely accidental.

The encounter with the two Sioux women and a berdache discloses interesting reactions by the party. In the first place, Four Bears was not looking for women, so they are content to strike coup on them and let them go. This was commonly done and is not unique in itself, but the recognition of one as a berdache altered the situation. The Hidatsa berdaches, although considered to be somewhat queer, were also possessed of great supernatural powers and customarily carried digging sticks as a part of their ritualistic paraphernalia during certain tribal rites. Here they encounter a Sioux berdache carrying a digging stick which was being used for digging wild turnips. When the berdache said, "You can't kill me for I am holy. I will strike you with my digging stick," he was repeating a ritual similar to one used in the Hidatsa rite in which the berdache said, "I am holy; I can do anything." When the arrow Four Bears shot at the berdache bounced off the robe, they were convinced of his supernatural powers and called off the fight. Having been successful on all other military expeditions, he was not taking chances. Although his vision had only been fulfilled in part, this was accomplished without the loss of any members of his party. His claim to the enemy remained; he could go out again or transfer this claim to another, preferably a "son." In the sale of the Bullet rites to Poor Wolf, a younger clan brother, One Buffalo follows an inheritance pattern not so common with the Hidatsa but highly developed with the Mandan.

In the final account of the slaughter of the men and the capture of the women and smaller children, the arguments offered for waylaying this party of Assiniboin are scarcely convincing. In the first place, a small party of Assiniboin would never have attempted to storm these strongly fortified Awatixa and Awaxawi villages, and, in the second place, it was not customary to take women and children out on military expeditions. The argument served a useful purpose, however, in justifying their actions in the face of White critics, although we know that at this time there was a high degree of cooperation with the Mandan and Arikara who would have come quickly to their assistance. The Hidatsa had customarily raided small hunting bands, going to the Rocky Mountains even before the advent of the horse. That this attack provided an opportunity to replenish the population cannot be denied, and the people quickly took advantage of this small band to take possession of the women and small children. In the Hidatsa society, a man who had many "children" lived materially better than one with few or no children.

Since this event occurred after 1837, one would expect genealogies of the tribe to show many of these captives, which is not the case. Actually, these captives were quickly integrated into the household and clan system and are rarely mentioned as captives. Although genealogies supplied by one person for other family lines do not reveal this Assiniboin blood, I did not find the Hidatsas reluctant to speak of their own foreign blood, although they would not freely reveal such information about others. Bears Arm speaks of the escape of captive women and relates that nothing was done about it when it was known that they had children with the Assiniboin. I found numerous instances when the Hidatsa provided captives with opportunities to return to their tribes because they had small children living there, as well as instances in which members of neighboring tribes came to the Hidatsa and claimed their families taken captive.

The curing rites for Four Bears followed a common pattern when a doctor outside of the family was employed. Note that the clan took the initiative; they collected the goods and selected the doctor. When the doctor saw that the case was not hopeless, he dressed in his ceremonial garb and took over the curing. Although the supernatural depicted in the rites did not always "come to life," this was believed to be a common experience when the greater doctors performed. We see the employment of sacred songs, the public display, and river bathing.[36] This curing rite expresses significant societal values; in spite of all of the fanfare when the military leader returned successfully, or the deep sorrow and loud wailing when he "kicked the stone," the real authority and confidence rested with a restricted number of village sacred bundle owners whose authority came to them out of the traditions and sacred rites of the past. Although the highest acclaim and respect was shown those who pursued a military career, in crisis situations, such as the doctoring of the military leaders or the establishment of a new village, the people looked to the older men whose sacred bundle rites were of traditional great antiquity, and the military leaders played no significant role. A review of the first building of Fishhook Village will show that in the rites on this important occasion, Four Bears, who then occupied the top military position, was not mentioned.

We close these case histories of military and related activities with a summary of Wolf Chief's experiences. Born in 1850 into one of the respected households, he well represents the culture of his generation (pl. 5). His father, Small Ankles, was the owner of Woman Above, Waterbuster Clan Skulls, Eagle Trapping, and Wolf Ceremony village sacred bundles. Rarely were so many sacred bundles owned by one man. In Wolf Chief, we have an individual who lived an easy life; the father was a distinguished bundle owner and Wolf Chief had several brothers who were good hunters. Wolf Chief's interest in the opposite sex was of wide knowledge in the tribe and his love affairs are given in detail under "The Life Cycle."

The following abbreviated narrative covers the significant points in his preparation for a military career:

My father was one of the real medicine men and fasted often. My maternal grandfather, Big Cloud, was also a great medicine man and gave me much advice. He had cut off his fingers in the Mandan Okipa and I saw the wounds on his chest and arms. Even my older brothers talked to me often and told me that I should take fasting seriously. When I was young I got most of my advice from Big Cloud, for he was getting along in years and was around the village more than my brothers and father who were busy hunting and working for a living. Big Cloud told me how after the smallpox only 10 families stayed at Hidatsa village on Knife River, so they went out west and camped on Rose Creek with the Crows for a while. He went out with another to fast on a high hill; during the day they would stand on the

---

[36] River bathing was universally associated with those bundles containing objects from creatures commonly inhabiting the streams and lakes.

hill and cry and stay in a cave nearby at night.   A rain came and they went under the rocks; it turned hot as though they were near a fire.   They saw a bird as large as a bullboat with the head as large as a human's; something shiny-looking like silk was hanging down from the bill.

Because they were frightened, they ran back into camp and the people closed the tent flaps.   When I was born, he gave me a name and said that I would live to old age.   He called me He Comes, for when the clouds and thunder come from the west, they make a loud noise.

When I was 7 or 8 years old, Big Cloud made up a cloth of this big bird with a round clamshell bead and said that if I wore it, I would live to be an old man.   I was 15 when he was taken ill; I stayed near him because he had been so good to me. One day he asked me to sit by him and he said, "My grandson, I am getting old and I think it is the best time to go.   When I die, you will know where they bury me; you come there to fast.   If I remember, I will give you a holy song or mention something so that your wishes will come true.   If I can't do it, it will still be all right."

They buried him where some others were buried.   I remembered how he had treated me and was crying.   My father said to me "Don't forget what your grandfather said to you before he died.   He was a great man and struck many enemies; he fasted much; you must do the same.   You should go out there where he is buried; he may be able to help you.   You could go out there evenings for 30 days. If you do not get a dream, you might try another 30 days."

Because my father asked me to go out, I went out there for part of the night for 1 month.   I rested and then went out 30 nights again.   I would cry and say that I was poor and wanted a god so that I would have a good living.   I tried it 30 days but no dream came.   I went to 90 nights when the weather was getting cold so I gave it up.

The next spring I tried it again.   My father talked to me and said, "If you go out again, you should stick to it.   There are some bodies on scaffolds out there. You might go to those scaffolds and hold onto the posts while fasting.   Perhaps that will help you."

I was a little frightened out there with the human bones scattered around from the fallen scaffolds, the circles of skulls, and the skulls and other bones sticking out of the sunken graves.   I thought, too, of our enemies who might come and attack me.   I would stay around there until late in the night and then go back home. Once the men told of seeing enemies about but I went out to fast.   One night I had the sensation that something was seizing me and at the same time I heard a "woosh" from my grandfather's grave.   Then all the bodies made the same noise; I was so frightened that I nearly ran away.

That night when I came back and went to bed, my grandfather came back.   I saw my grandfather standing on a high hill about 30 miles downstream from Fishhook.   His hair was white and he was smiling.

The next year my father went out west to Shot in Nose Creek.   There were many young men fasting on the side of a high hill with sticks put through their skin.   Because I was not among them, my father's joking relatives teased him about his worthless son who did nothing but eat and chase the girls.   This made my father very angry so he came to me while other men in the camp were crying to their gods to send their sons good dreams, saying, "You should not sit around here and do nothing but eat all the time.   You should follow the example of the other young men and fast for a god so that you will be successful."

Takes-the-Gun [Three-clan moiety] and Moccasin Carrier [Waterbuster clan] came to take me out without asking if I wanted to go and said, "We are glad that you are going to do this so that you will get a god."

They made two thongs from a Juneberry branch; by this time it was so dark that they lit a fire to see to insert the sticks. First they told what they had seen when they suffered, and then they put the sticks through. It felt as though I was burning in the fire. They tied me to an overhanging tree and I could hardly breathe. They noticed my trouble and said, "He has had enough; we better take him down."

All this time my father had been shaking his medicine rattles, praying, and singing the holy songs of the eagle-trapping rites. But I did not get a dream for my breath would not come when they tortured me.

The next summer, when I was 17, the people went to Bear Den Creek hunting. There were many high rocks and two hawks were flying about above the cliffs. We were enjoying ourselves, for the buffaloes were plentiful. I thought of the things people had said about me and resolved to fast in the rocks near those hawks. I went to Wolf Grass and Coyote, who belonged to my fathers' clan, and asked them to help me. Because the bank was so steep at the place I wanted to hang, they put an extra rope around me so that I would not be killed if the thongs pulled out of the flesh. All the time my two fathers were praying to the hawks to send me a dream. I stayed there until after sundown and then my fathers came for me.

That night I dreamt of a man who came and asked me to stand beside him on the right side saying, "Look to the west."

I looked and saw a thunder cloud coming. He was carrying burning cedar on a plate. He said, "See how I burn this cedar while facing the west and the rain comes. Someday you will do the same as I am."

Then he sang this sacred song, "Birds are coming from the clouds; they bring rain." He told me that when I wanted to bring the rain I should do as he had done, but I never did try it.

When I was 18, my father was appointed to lead the winter camp. That winter we went to Blue Buttes just above Independence in the deep timber. I had often seen the dark spot on the moon and the old people had told me that the moon was a human. I went out every night to cry, asking the moon to help me. After the 120th night I had a dream again, hearing someone speaking from the sky, "Look to the east; there is a boat coming."

In my dream I wished for a cord of wood. I saw a log house here where I later built and a steamboat near Lucky Mound Creek. I saw a large stone on a hill and then I walked into a log house. I awoke and thought of my silly dream and of the silly dreams the other young men often told of getting. Then I went to sleep again and a man came, saying, "They want you over there."

I came to a high hill and saw a man sitting facing the north. He had his face painted below the nose; he had an eagle feather in his hair and scalps hanging on his leggings. He asked me to sit on his right side. He had a pile of buffalo manure before him and a pipe. While he smoked I thought, "Anytime I go out for the enemy I am supposed to go against the wind for he is facing the wind."

He handed me the pipe to smoke and said, "Son, look towards the south." I saw great mountains and large herds of horses; I thought that it meant that I was to own many horses.

That year I also had a dream of four frames surrounding my father's sacred bundles, the outer one being old and broken down. My father interpreted this dream to mean that I would give the Walking ceremony four times and make my wives "granddaughters of the buffaloes," and that I would live to be an old man. Shortly afterward the enemy came to fight near the village and, being brave, I was to the front chasing them. One man turned and shot my horse, killing it. My fathers of the Waterbuster clan sang the Victory songs for me. When I returned to our lodge, Different Snake was at our lodge and wanted to marry me, for it was the custom to marry when one had received first war honors. I did not keep her but I married another shortly afterward.

When I was 21 I killed a fat deer while we were in winter camp and called in two of my "fathers," Poor Wolf and Sack who belonged to my father's clan. Poor Wolf asked Sack to speak to me and he said, "There are many ways to become a chief; some spend most of their time fasting and striking the enemy. When I was a young man after the smallpox I went out fasting often. Once in my dreams I saw a man so old that he could hardly get up and I expected to get that old. Now that you have fed me, I would rather that you would be the old man instead of me."

I thanked him saying that I hoped I would be a lucky man, have a good home, and live to become an old man.

When I was just past 22 I thought that since I had seen the man with the scalps on his leggings, I ought to go out to war and get the horses I had seen, but my father tried to discourage me. He said, "I do not see any wounds where you have been fasting much; I think you ought to do a great deal more fasting and torturing of your body before you go out after those horses."

He urged me not to take young men out but I was insistent. I said, "I think I have done enough fasting and suffering. When I was 18, I dreamt of a man with scalps on his legs and he was smoking and facing the wind. I think I have the power now to succeed. I fasted at different places; one time I went out 120 nights to cry."

He was not convinced but I went anyway. I picked young fellows of my age, but a number of them could not go as their fathers did not like the idea. I took 12 young men my age and appointed Son-of-Star the chief of the scouts and Wolf Ghost, Dog Bear, and Bluebird scouts. We followed the east bank of the Missouri going downstream. North of Washburn the scouts found some horses and colts, and a mule. Wolf Ghost and Bluebird both claimed the horses and they disputed each other's claim to the first discovery so I said to them, "You are trying to get ahead of each other; do not do that; in the future you will discover more horses."

We went on, and opposite Standing Rock we found a horse grazing, so I sent the scouts to take possession. They crossed to the west side where the enemy discovered them so they brought in only one horse. I kept the horse that had been taken from the camp because the scouts did not see it first; by that time the two men had agreed on the division of the other horses.

Not long afterwards I decided to go out for more of the horses that I had been promised in my dreams. This time my father approved and said to me, "I think you will be successful for on your last trip you showed that you have powers from your dreams. Do not take too many along, for some of them might be careless. If you had to hide from the enemy, a large party would be a handicap. This time take some of my Wolf medicines. Before sending your scouts out, pray to the Wolf to help you."

Before I left, my father took down his sacred Wolf bundle, tied it on a long pole, and hung it up outside. [37] He wanted to find out what was going to happen. He did this so he would get a dream that night. He burned some sweetgrass and put the wolf hide in the smoke, singing this sacred Song of the Wolves, "Whenever I need anything, I always say this."

He said to Sunrise Wolf, "I want you to lead my son who is going out after the enemies," and he sang a second holy song, "You are the holy ones; that is why I say so."

---

[37] See myth of the Wolf Woman (pp. 412–415) for native beliefs that wolves talk to the bundle owners.

Then he instructed me, saying, "Start tomorrow evening; have your bullboats ready. When you select the scouts, rub dirt on their legs just as Wolf instructed and tell them not to touch each other or their legs will get weak. Sing these two sacred songs before you send the scouts out. Do not travel until it is dark."

Next morning my father said, "I had a dream of a man coming towards us with a mule and a bay horse with a bald face. He had some meat, too. I am not sure whether you killed him or not.

When it was getting dark, my father took his medicines all down and stood before us, for we were meeting at my father's lodge. He was praying to his bundles when Poor Wolf, my father's clansman, came in. My father asked him to pray for me, his son, who was going out to seek the enemy.

Poor Wolf said, "I know that you have had pity on me and fed me when I was short of meat; you are my son, too. In my early days I dreamed that I was to get a roan horse but I never was able to take possession of it. Now I am getting old so I will relinquish it to you."

Then he prayed for me and told how he used to fast and pray in his younger days.

My father said, "I am going to have my son take my wolf hide along. He will see a rabbit run ahead of him. It will stop. That is the sign that they will meet their enemies the same day."

It was close to midnight when we got into our bullboats and started downstream. At noon we stopped to select the scouts. I took out my father's sacred bundle, prayed to it, and selected Wolf Ghost, One Buffalo, and Lean Bull to be the scouts. I rubbed the dirt from the pocket gopher mound on their legs and ordered them not to rub their legs together. Wolf Ghost carried the wolf hide. I asked them to go along the rim of the valley not far from the river and we would meet them farther down.

Before they discovered the horse, a jackrabbit jumped up in front of them and they knew that something would happen that day. They went in the direction the rabbit went and there found the horse. It was the roan horse that had been given to me by Poor Wolf before we left. Wolf Ghost who found the animal brought it down to the riverbank and said, "I have the horse that was already given to you before this happened."

I wondered how we would manage to float down the river and at the same time look after the horse. I thought that Crows Breast, who had a bad foot, might find it hard to travel if we did not find more horses farther on, so I gave him the horse and told him to go back.

Our next stop was the big Mandan village ruins north of Bismarck. Then I sent the scouts over to the other bank as we floated down to Bird Bill Butte. The scouts came back and reported seeing three men riding north. They went out again and found a man butchering an elk. He had a bald-faced horse and a mule. They decided to wait until he had butchered before killing him, but, in the meantime, two more came along on horseback so my scouts decided a camp was nearby. They decided not to make the attack even though they had found the bald-faced horse and mule that Small Ankles had seen in his dream.

Coming back to camp they found a horse which later fell into a ditch and was killed. When they reported, I knew the enemy would learn we were out. Since it was not possible to get the horse and mule, we cut up our bullboats and sank them in the river, returning home afoot.

Another year passed and I was 24. I told my father that I was going to try it again.

He replied, "You have enough of it. If you try again, some of your men might be killed; that way you would 'kick the stone' and undo all of your good luck.

It takes a man who does much fasting and buys many gods to go to war often without losing his luck."

I replied, "I had a dream from the time Sitting Elk gave the Naxpike and I believe that I will have good luck. In my dream I and one other went out looking for the enemy. I killed one enemy but as we were coming back the enemy attacked us and shot my partner through the bowels so that blood was flowing. At that time a doctor came along and said, 'It will not take long to cure that man' so I think it is all right for me to follow my dream."

My father replied, "I do not think that was a very good dream. You say that one was shot while still another came to do the doctoring. There are so many instructions and you have to rely on so many others, I am afraid that you will not be successful."

After that I did not lead any war parties, for my father was skillful in those things. "I do not want you to stop your fasting; you might get a dream. Then when the enemies attack the village, you might win over one of them," he said.

When I was 28 or 29 my clan brother, Corn Smut, was giving the Naxpike [Sun Dance] so I fasted to help him out. When the third day was over nearly all the fasters were gone, for it was hard to do. Two Bulls was hanging from the buffalo hide tied at the top of the post and I thought what a hard thing it was to suffer that way. All this time the older men were telling the young men to stick to it and not leave until the ceremony was over, that it was their own fault if they gave up and so were always poor. The old men would say, "Those who fast much and are patient while they suffer are the ones who will be successful and respected by the people. When you move to the winter camp you can see many poor people walking and carrying their things on their backs; their children are barefooted. We do not like to see that. If you young fellows stick to your torturing, you will be successful, have many good horses, and plenty of food. You will not have to suffer like those who have nothing and do nothing for the people. You can tell those who have most patience by their property, fine wives and healthy children, and their nice clothing."

On the fourth day, Spotted Bear was to be tortured but when his fathers cut the skin, he was afraid and in pain so they took the thongs out and sent him home. Only Corn Smut, who was giving the ceremony, and I were left fasting. Two of my fathers were singers so I went to them—Red Basket and Walking Chief of the Waterbuster clan—and asked them to cut my skin. Red Basket said, "That is the way to have a god. Run as fast as you can and pull hard on the rope."

He sang his holy songs of the Spotted Eagle, praying all the time that I would be successful. He said to his gods, "I want you to give my son, Wolf Chief, a good dream tonight." Then they put the thongs through my flesh. My clan relatives paid him for his prayers.

Older men standing around said, "Put your head back and do not be afraid." Then the different men began to sing their sacred songs.

Then the singers for the Naxpike sang the first song while I put my head back. I pulled as hard as I could while I looked up at the buffalo head in the fork of the post. At first it was hard to do; I had nothing in my stomach; I was dizzy. They told me to get up and walk around while they sang the second song so I got up from my hands and knees and began running around the pole. It seemed that my throat was going to close and I could not walk I was so weak. I could hear the holy songs but I could not distinguish one person from another. I sat still for a while until I was able to breathe normally when my fathers came to me to remove the sticks but I said to them, "I am going to try once more to go around that post."

The singers said, "We will go down to the river for a drink and a bath and leave him until he is done suffering and has rested." After a while they came back to take the sticks out. They sang one sacred song but I could not jump for my legs were too numb. Then they took the sticks out. Porcupine Pemmican, who represented Long Arm, sprinkled Corn Smut and me with water, using sage to cleanse us.

When I reached my father's lodge he said, "I am glad that Red Basket used those particular songs for you when he cut your flesh, for the sacred songs he sang have always been lucky in conquering the enemy. Now you will surely have good luck." After a while I went to the river and bathed. When I got back, I ate a little too much and had terrible pains from it.

My father had been offering smoke to all of his medicines while I fasted and he said to me when I came back from the river, "Put these sacred things beside you when you go to bed. I have asked my gods to send you good dreams." But my wounds had swollen and my insides hurt from the food I had eaten after fasting so long so that I was not able to go to sleep right away.

Toward daylight I went to sleep. I heard someone singing a song and saw a man coming from the west. He was singing a new song in the Crow Indian language. He sang, "There is plenty; I am satisfied."

I could not understand what it meant, for in the earlier days when going for the enemies, I had the best of success. I thought that since there were now no enemies, it meant that I would have plenty of property. It seems that I was right, for since that time I have had much property, once shipping 50 cattle in a single year.

A few years before fasting in the Naxpike, I missed an opportunity to get a dream. Kidney was giving the Wolf ceremony and since he was a clan brother I was fasting to help him. I asked the same fathers I used in the Naxpike fasting, to put thongs through my back so I could lead my horse. Because the horse was so high-lifed, they were afraid that the horse would drag and kill me. I said, "It does not make any difference whether it kills me or not. I am not afraid. I want to try to get a dream from the horse."

They begged me not to do it, but when they saw how determined I was they put a bridle on the horse and tied the reins to the sticks so that I could stop the horse. I walked around between the earth lodges; once in a while the horse would knock me down. When the young men came out from fasting, I went among them leading the horse, while the old men sang the medicine songs. But I did not have any dream.

I often think how important it was in the olden days to do the same as the others did and there was no way to get out of it.[38] We fasted and we went to war because our fathers did. The fathers took their "son's" wives in the ceremonies. It was like a deep trail; one had to follow the same path the others before had made and deepened.

When I was 30 I dreamt of my father's gods and I knew that the time had come to put on the ceremonies to possess them. So I bought the Wolf and my brother, Red Basket, bought the Old-Woman-Above. It was hard to do for the game was scarce but our relatives helped us. But there were no enemies then so I never tried it out as war leader as Kidney had done a few years earlier.

In the Wolf Chief narrative we have accounts of experiences during that period between 1865 and 1880 when warfare rose to its highest crescendo and then stopped abruptly with the establishment of military posts, the building of railroads, successful military campaigns

---

[38] The berdache was one outlet.

against the powerful Sioux, and the establishment of reservations. Here and there in the narrative he refers to the older pattern and new interpretations that were creeping in. No longer was fasting endured or bundles purchased to lend supernatural assistance in overcoming the enemy or capturing horses. The buffaloes were gone and concern for the future was emphasized. So, we find his dreams later interpreted as assurances from the supernatural that he would have plenty of food and a good home.

In the narrative he begins with an enumeration of his vision and military experiences by referring affectionately to his step-grandfather, Big Cloud, who had been kind to him and had awed him with numerous marks of bravery on chest and arms. Big Cloud, being too old to hunt, sets the stage for Wolf Chief's fasting by providing the appropriate atmosphere: he tells of his people's misfortunes from smallpox; how the people feared the supernatural and closed their tipis; and how the big bird came during a shower. Wolf Chief reviews his experiences with the supernatural when Big Cloud made up a bundle representing this bird, tied a clamshell to it, and gave it to him to wear as assurance of a long life.

The indifference to death shown by Big Cloud was characteristic of a brave man, but his death, as related by Wolf Chief, was not taken lightly by his relatives. We see that at the age of 15, Wolf Chief had not, yet, taken fasting seriously. Small Ankles reminds Wolf Chief of the promises Big Cloud had made to him. This is a rather extreme measure for a father to take, but he had been teased by his joking relatives, other informants told me, because Wolf Chief's training had been neglected.[39] There was a saying that a chief's sons were often spoiled. It was the clan's duty, and particularly that of the older brothers, to attend to such matters and to see that the fasting was conducted faithfully. So we find Wolf Chief, at the request of his father, undertaking to fast near the grandfather's grave. What he does not tell us is that during this time he met various girls whom he took into the brush when his father presumed that he was crying to the gods; that Wolf Chief's clansmen discovered him and whipped him for deceiving his father; and that Small Ankles' joking relatives teased him for staying in his lodge singing his sacred songs to bring a good dream to his son presumed to be fasting. These are the things that Wolf Chief's joking relatives told me at the time this study was made. So we find that when Wolf Chief went out during the succeeding spring to fast near his grandfather's grave, Small Ankles was prompted to say to his son, "If you go out again, you

---

[39] Wolf Chief's earlier indifference must have been the subject of widespread comment, for old people mentioned the matter often when I made this study and would inquire whether Wolf Chief had mentioned it to me.

should stick to it.   There are some bodies on scaffolds out there. You might go to those scaffolds and hold onto the posts while fasting. Perhaps that will help you."

As far as Wolf Chief could recall, the dream of Big Cloud standing on a hill downstream from the village was the first that he associated with the supernatural.   It is interesting to observe that in the dream Wolf Chief saw his grandfather to the southeast, the direction of the spirit villages.

The incident at Shot in Nose Creek during the following summer brings out the role of the joking relatives in group behavior.   Here we have a boy of 16 who has made little progress in fasting at a time when his age-group was seen making serious efforts to secure desirable visions, with the result that the father was being severely criticized by certain relatives.   While other boys were fasting or serving as camp-tenders during military adventures, Wolf Chief slept late, dressed well, and kept his eyes on the girls.   Even his brothers who normally should have disciplined him could do nothing with him. If they tried to shame him, he merely smiled; if they ducked him in the river, he laughed about it.   But the father's moral weight, though slow in being asserted, finally broke down his son's indifference. Both father and son felt the sting of their joking relatives.   When other young men were fasting while their fathers were singing their sacred songs, Small Ankles could take no more criticism.   Then he scolded his son, saying, "You should not sit around here and do nothing but eat all the time.   You should follow the example of the other young men and fast for a god so that you will be successful."

Wolf Chief does not tell us what prompted Takes-the-Gun and Moccasin Carrier, the father's clansmen, to come for him.   His joking relatives know, and it was from them that the writer secured the information, that Wolf Chief's older brothers took robes to the two "fathers" and informed them that they should take their younger brother out.   We see that they supervised his suffering, inserted the thongs, and repeated their vision experiences while Small Ankles remained in camp, opened his bundle, and sang his sacred songs. We note that once the thongs were inserted, Wolf Chief was immediately overcome with pain and that they removed the thongs at once.   Nevertheless, a beginning was made; frequently this was as far as the "fathers" could go when the first suffering was undertaken.

Even Wolf Chief was conscious of the fact that his record was inferior to that of his brother, Red Basket, 6 years younger.   While recording the Wolf rites, he said of Red Basket, "He had been around our father a great deal and knew many songs and stories about the eagles.   He was more interested in those things and braver than I was, for he had struck the enemy, had fasted much, and had cut his own fingers off."

We find the weight of tradition and public opinion bearing so heavily on Wolf Chief that on the following year at the age of 17, while the village was on the summer hunt and camping near Bear Den Creek, he took the initiative and asked two of his father's clansmen to officiate so that he could suffer near two hawks. His display of bravery was commendable and the vision is understandable in terms of native concepts of the rain-making role of the large birds of prey. It is significant that under no situation did Wolf Chief request assistance from his own father in inflicting self-torture. Assumedly, one never tortured one's own son.

The selection of Small Ankles as leader of the winter camp was an important event for the Wolf Chief household. It was his father's reward for living a good life, fasting, bundle purchases, and generosity. At the time of his selection, the households paid him to lead them. In this position, his pay for past services came back to him. Again Wolf Chief fasted, not from direct compulsion, but from "proof" that it paid good dividends; his father was even living a better life now that he was leader of the winter camp.

We find Wolf Chief addressing appeals to the moon because the moon is one of the above-world spirits associated with the big birds and the thunderbird appealed to on a former occasion when fasting at Bear Den Creek. All of these spirits were associated with warfare through the sacred arrows and rainmaking rites associated with thunder and lightning. Due to the severity of winter fasting, a 4-month period of vision seeking at that time represented great self-denial. Coming at a time when the father was winter camp leader, he contributed immensely to his father's status; still he could not remember that his father had assisted him in interpreting his dreams. We find his dreams reflecting his personal ambitions to own many horses and to be a war leader. Without the aid of others, he interpreted the vision of a man with feathers and scalps to signify that he would strike his enemies (from the presence of the feathers), and that he would be a war leader (because he had seen scalps).

The next year Wolf Chief dreamed, without fasting, of four concentric frames surrounding his father's sacred bundles. At a loss to understand the dream's meaning, although he believed there was some sacred significance attached to it, he called on his father for an interpretation. Although Wolf Chief described the wooden fence as similar to the enclosure for the fishtrap, his father interpreted the fence to be that of the temporary enclosure erected for the "walking" ceremony. This dream greatly influenced Wolf Chief's later behavior, for Small Ankles further interpreted the dream as meaning that Wolf

Chief would give the "walking" ceremony four times with the promise of a long life. No doubt the promise of a long life in return for a pledge to give the "walking" ceremony greatly encouraged Wolf Chief when the village was attacked—he fought at the front of the line where his horse was shot from under him, and his life was saved only because others rode between him and the enemy. To be wounded or to have a horse killed or wounded was recognized by certain symbols of dress and painting, and by public acclaim during the victory dances.

After this public acclaim, a young woman, formerly married, moves into the lodge with him without a formal ceremony. From other studies we find that an individual did not long remain single once he had won war honors, but to marry earlier was the grounds for considerable teasing by the couple's joking relatives. A young man without war honors would be teased as though he were a small boy who had married his grandmother; the woman would be teased by her joking relatives for marrying a baby so she would have a husband when he grew up "because she was so homely none of the men would have her." Thus, a young man arrived at the marrying age when he had won first war honors. Nevertheless, the Hidatsa were realists in the matter of selecting mates for their children, and the concept of first marrying age was modified by other factors such as industry. A young man who was a good hunter and provided well for his parents was in great demand as a son-in-law. One who was a good hunter and provider, while at the same time winning military honors—if no more than striking fourth or assisting around camp—was likely to have offers of marriage from the best families of the village. Wolf Chief, who was shiftless and lazy, was able to capitalize on a first military honor and the respect that the village had for his parents. Whereas prior to winning first war honors Wolf Chief had had many clandestine love affairs by his own admission—some even during his presumed fasting periods—and had caused his father's joking relatives to criticize him, he could now marry without fear of his own joking relatives. Thus he accepted Different Snake for a few days immediately after winning first military honors for it made him feel grown up, but she was not the woman of his choice and he cast her off shortly afterward for another.

We see that at the age of 21 and married, Wolf Chief killed a fat deer in order to invite in two members of his father's clan for a feast. On such occasions the "fathers" were expected to contribute important advice or to pray to their gods for their son's well-being. In this instance a "father" told Wolf Chief that he wanted to share the promise of a long life with him. As far as we know, Wolf Chief never invited in a "father" for ceremonial sexual intercourse with his wife. Wolf Chief preferred to offer his wives publicly during the formal ceremonies according to the pattern indicated by his father when interpreting the dream of the wood frames. Others under similar circumstances regularly sent their wives to a "father" during the feast and asked that he have intercourse with one of them. Under these circumstances, the "father" was not permitted to buy himself out by praying to his bundles.

Wolf Chief, at the age of 22, organized a war party to go out and take possession of the horses claimed by virtue of an earlier dream. He did not mention former expeditions which he accompanied as a camp tender. From other informants it was learned that he had been criticized for laziness, staying around camp, eating, and loafing all the time. Late arrivals joining the war party on another occasion teased him by saying that his girl was seen with another man, causing him to sneak away and return home. His father knew all these things and attempted to discourage his son, but we find no evidence of repression by the police society; instead, the various households imposed their own controls when the fathers stepped in and checked their sons. He was able, however, to get together a small war party from which he selected scouts who had a considerable knowledge of warfare. It is interesting to note that, in spite of the higher military status of his scouts, when a dispute developed over the division of the horses, they accepted Wolf Chief's advice. The expedition was considered successful when the objectives of the trip were attained without the loss of any men. Wolf Chief had established the reality of his dream.

When Wolf Chief announced his intentions of going out a second time for horses, we find complete acceptance of the plan by his own household; his father lent ritual assistance and advice. Anticipating that his approval would be reflected in the number of young men seeking permission to attend, he advised his son not to take too many along. For the first time, Wolf Chief was permitted to use his father's bundles as a recognized war leader and to perform rites for the success of the undertaking. We find that the "signs" predicted by the father—the appearance of a rabbit—were followed and the roan horse "given" to Wolf Chief by Poor Wolf was captured. Although the scouts found the horse, it was delivered to Wolf Chief who had a prior claim by virtue of Poor Wolf's assignment of his original rights to Wolf Chief. The immediate disposal of the horse by gift to Crows Breast, an older man of the opposite moiety, emphasizes quite definitely the fact that the rewards of warfare were not measured in material property values; a man's status was measured by his generosity. In this instance Wolf Chief established the potency of his dream and his ability to conduct successful military expeditions which, in itself, enhanced his standing with the people. He could have kept the horse and nothing would have been thought of it; by relinquishing his horse, he indicated that his acts were for the welfare of the group and not for personal gain.

When the party found the mule and bay horse "seen" by Small Ankles when he hung the Wolf bundle outside his lodge in the evening, it was decided not to attack the enemy. This indicated the nature of Plains warfare; do not expose yourself or your party to unnecessary risks. Since Wolf Chief could not take possession of the property "given" to him by the father, his claim still stood. Wolf Chief often spoke of the mule and roan horse as his legitimate property which he was never able to possess because warfare terminated shortly thereafter.

We see from the narrative that, when Wolf Chief had reached 24 years of age, he indicated his intention of going out again. On the former expedition he had the ritual assistance of his father's Wolf bundle. Although Wolf Chief does not say so, from other and similar case studies we learn that having returned from a successful military expedition in which the father's bundle was used, the son invariably had a vision to buy rights in the bundle. He was then expected to go out on subsequent occasions as the full owner of a bundle, but during the intervening year Wolf Chief took no steps to perform the rites and secure a bundle. Now the father said, "You have enough of it. If you try again, some of your men might be killed; that way you would 'kick the stone' and undo all of your good luck. It takes a man who does much fasting and buys many gods to go to war often without losing his luck."

Small Ankles discounted the value of a dream because too many persons were depended upon; if one participant failed in his role, the entire venture failed. Moreover, paying these assistants was costly. It is important for an understanding of village organization and policing to note that restraints were imposed by selected individuals of the household rather than the police. In a former situation we found that numerous households denied their young men permission to accompany Wolf Chief. We must assume that on neither occasion was the village in danger of attack, otherwise the older men would have forbidden war parties the right to go out. Restraints would have come first from the household itself, as in the case of Small Ankles' denial of permission, and then from the police, in situations where the households failed in their role.

In 1876 the Government undertook to enlist scouts from the village for the Custer campaign. The councils of the Arikara, Hidatsa, and Mandan met separately to discuss the matter since many families disapproved of the idea, feeling that the young people were needed to protect the village and the horses. The Arikara decided not to impose restrictions, but the Hidatsa and Mandan, weakened by the removal of the Bobtail Bull band to Fort Buford, voted to impose restrictions on leaving the village. During the late winter and early spring of 1876 the Hidatsa and Mandan Black Mouth societies were in continuous session to see that none went with Custer. The real and effective sanctions were imposed, however, by the households. The older men of the households advised their young men that they should not go with Custer because of their small numbers and the risk that those Sioux not participating in the campaign might attack the village and murder the women and children, leaving no one to perform the Victory dances if the young men did return successful. I was unable to find a single instance of physical restraint by the Black Mouths—the households had performed their roles effectively.

In spite of his early indifference to fasting, we find Wolf Chief as clan assistant to Corn Smuts performing an honorable role by staying near his clan brother to the end of the Naxpike ceremony and submitting to final torture after all others had terminated their fasting. He cites the indoctrination of the young with promises of a good life and wealth in contrast to those about them who were poor. The reference to Spotted Bear's inability to endure the ordeal brings out the point that, in status seeking, the torture feature was an effective screen to eliminate some aspirants to high positions; by displaying fear and pain, Spotted Bear unquestionably eliminated himself as a war leader, irrespective of the dream he might have obtained during the ceremony. We see Wolf Chief's "fathers" at this point praying to their own sacred bundles, not to the Naxpike bundle. Wolf Chief's description of the ordeal, the weakness of the faster after 4 days without food and water during the hottest part of the summer, and the role of his ceremonial fathers might well apply to any other Hidatsa ceremony during which fasting was customary. Obviously, Small Ankles did not at this time realize the extent of changed conditions when he said, "I am glad that Red Basket used those ... songs for you when he cut your flesh, for the sacred songs he sang have always been lucky in conquering the enemy. Now you will surely have good luck." By this time (1879) there was little warfare. It appears that Wolf Chief was aware of the changing times for he interpreted the dream to mean that he would have much property. We find that later events were interpreted as being predicted by previous dreams; as he accumulated more property, particularly cattle, he believed that his future had been previously revealed to him.

Had aboriginal warfare continued, Wolf Chief's bravery in requesting that his fathers tie him to a horse would have provided him great prestige in military and social activities. Unfortunately for him, it was not long after this that warfare was suppressed by the Government and the buffaloes were exterminated. The old values were no longer recognized. He was 30 years of age before buying his father's Wolf bundle.[40] There was no attempt to lead a war party as Kidney had done a few years earlier when he purchased his father's bundle.

DEFENSIVE WARFARE

Defensive warfare introduced a different set of responsibilities. The basic concepts of village protection were symbolized by the four "protectors of the people" representing the four sacred directions. These spiritual defenders of the people represented symbolic defenses established during the mythological period to protect the people from the attacks of various evil spirits who conspired to destroy the villages. Their role in the physical defense of a village, however, was of importance only to inspire confidence in the defenders. When a new village was built, the "Protectors" selected the sites for their four lodges first and conducted the appropriate ceremonies at each spot, after which the other households selected lodge sites within a prescribed area according to household, kinship, and other ties.

When Fishhook Village was built, new "protectors of the people" were selected by the council from the survivors of the three independent Knife River village groups who were joining together for common defense. The Awatixa and Awaxawi assumed the principal ceremonial role as builders of the site since the Hidatsa-proper were at that time contemplating reunion with the River Crow. In fact, a number of the Hidatsa households had already moved to Crow territory when the site was laid out. These "protectors of the people" were males past middle age who already occupied eminent positions in the hierarchy of traditional bundle owners. In a society organized for both offensive and defensive warfare, living in an area where pacifism meant quick extermination, consideration was also given to one's position with respect to established ceremonies, generosity and personal qualities, and knowledge of tribal sacred and secular lore.

The physical defense of the village was entrusted to the police society which received its instructions from the council composed of an indefinite number of members representing the various households. The war chief was the principal military executive while some highly respected older man was his announcer. Whenever reports of impending enemy attacks reached the village, the older men distinguished either as warriors or ritual leaders, assembled to discuss the situation and to define group action. The first concern was to protect the women and children inside the stockade. The horses were brought

---

[40] This purchase is detailed under "Wolf Ceremonies."

in from pasture immediately upon word that strangers were approaching. Herders and hunters kept an eye out for strange movements on the prairie or reported signs of enemies lurking in the neighborhood. Fishhook Village was protected by a wall with a gate until the later years of its occupation. A bell signaled the opening of the gate in the morning, after which the horses were taken to pasture and the people went about their duties in the gardens and on the prairie. One of the important duties of the announcer was to ring the bell to indicate the time for opening and closing the gate and to warn the people whenever scouts or herders signaled the presence of potential enemies.

Direct attacks on the village were few indeed, chiefly because of the character of Plains warfare; one gained little by killing and striking the enemy if he, in turn, lost several of his own party. But there were several instances of attacks in which efforts were made to burn the village. Lewis and Clark report the near extinction of the Awaxawi prior to 1804 when a surprise attack was made by the Assiniboin. Henry speaks of an attack made on one of the Knife River villages about 1790 in which 600 tents of Sioux cut off the village from water and besieged it for 15 days. In this attack, the Mandan and Awaxawi remained neutral. The village was able to supply itself with water during the night, so the Sioux, after losing 300 men in the various engagements and seeing that the population could not be driven from the village, called off the seige (Henry, 1897, pp. 358–359).

When Fishhook Village was built, large mounted war parties frequently attacked the village from the north or land side which was protected by a wall. When these failed, as all attacks did due to the strength of the wall, the Sioux tried various devices to entice the Hidatsa from the village to fight in the open. Whether or not the enemy was engaged outside of the village was a matter to be decided by the council and war chief. During the deliberations and, in fact, whenever war parties were near the village or the village was under attack, it was the duty of the "protectors of the village" to open their respective sacred bundles and perform magical acts designed to give the Hidatsa mastery over the enemy. When the council of older men decided that the group would remain within the village lest the enemy have a trap set for them outside, it was the Black Mouths' duty to see that all obeyed. Disobedience could have led to extreme measures, even the clubbing or killing of an offender. Nor were war honors accumulated when disobeying council orders publicly recognized.

In later years, with improved guns, the Sioux would often appear on the opposite bank of the Missouri and fire into the village in an effort to entice the Hidatsa to cross in their bullboats. These invitations were usually rejected or the Hidatsa went out and, in a roundabout way, crossed the river unobserved by the enemy.   The head chief and council seemingly were in no way held responsible for losses suffered in defensive warfare to the extent of extreme personal torture such as the leader of an offensive war party inflicted on himself. Such loss of prestige as did occur was individual in character; a father would urge his son to go out with those pursuing the enemy and pray for his son's success.   If his son was killed or severely injured, the prestige the father enjoyed, by virtue of the possession of presumed important bundles, was lowered.

Alien groups frequently were visiting at the Hidatsa villages when an attack was made on the village by one of their own bands.   On such occasions, visiting groups invariably assisted in the defense of the village, even against their own poeple.   In recent years, the Sioux conducted warfare against all of the other tribal groups who normally came to the Hidatsa to trade and visit or to assist in ritual practices.   Keen rivalry often developed between the Hidasta and their visitors for principal war honors in battles fought near Fishhook Village.   They fought together and afterward danced together when war honors were won; they even mourned for each other's dead, made offerings to the mourners, and exchanged names.

CANNIBALISM

Although the Hidatsa claim never to have eaten the flesh of their enemies, they did mutilate them, and they carried scalps, hands, feet, and skulls during the Sun Dance.   By contrast, informants frequently mentioned the practice of cannibalism by the Chippewa and Cree after assisting them in warfare near the village.   Palliser (1853, p. 286) wrote of cannibalism at Fishhook Village:

The skirmish now terminated; the Sioux retired, and the Minitarees returned to their village in triumph, dragging the body of their unfortunate victim along with them.   Then commenced a truly disgusting sight; the boys shot arrows into the carcass of their fallen enemy while their women with knives cut out pieces of the flesh, which they broiled and ate.

The Hidatsa claim that this battle occurred during a visit of the Chippewa.

Several informants referred to cannibalistic practices by the Chippewa and Cree although they had no knowledge of its practice by other Plains groups.   Concerning an incident that occurred at Fishhook Village a few years before Crows Heart's birth, and was related to him by his relatives, he said:

The Sioux attacked the village and the men went out to chase the Sioux away. Some Chippewas were at the village visiting and their men came out to help. Some of the Sioux were killed near the present Nishu School and the others jumped into the river.   Our men took their clothes off, held their knives in their mouths;

and went into the water after them.   They would stab them in the back or cut the cord on the heel.   One Sioux, a good swimmer, got across and Young Eagle overtook him in a mudhole.   When they came back, they found the Chippewas had lit a fire and were roasting the meat of their enemies.   They had taken the flesh from the legs and the heel cords, for that gave one the power to run fast, they said.   They had cut the ears off, which they roasted and ate.   Our people were afraid and stood back at a distance.

In another instance, Crows Heart mentioned a personal experience near Devils Lake at the scaffold of a Sioux who had just died.   During one of his horse-stealing raids, Crows Heart looked for food around the body during the night, thinking that the Sioux relatives might have put out something edible when the body was disposed of.   Even the thought of eating a piece of the Sioux was revolting to him, although in his famished situation and far from home, he was willing to partake of the dead Sioux's funeral feast had he been able to find any. I doubt that the Hidatsa practiced cannibalism, at least during the 19th century, although Wolf Chief thought that a number of young men visiting the Chippewa would probably have eaten enemy flesh had they been asked to, and if none of the older people were around.

MILITARY HONORS

When an attack was made on the village, any military honors were individual in character.   Unlike the organized military expeditions in which the leader afterward wore scalps on his clothing to indicate that men under him had distinguished themselves, there was no leadership recognition other than social approval of the top village authority.   Individual awards were the same as for offensive warfare. However, a defensive organization often quickly changed into an offensive one.   Someone would announce, as soon as the enemy moved off, that he was organizing a party to meet them farther away from the village at a time and place when they could be taken by surprise.   In this event, the leader took the same risks as on other offensive expeditions and enjoyed the same honors if they returned successfully.   To succeed in offensive warfare, one needed a great deal of skill, familiarity with the country, and leisure from other activities.   Some young men, particularly those training for a career in the tribal ceremonies, rarely went out with war parties, for their time and interests were directed toward village matters.   It is suggested that this selective factor contributed, in part, to the cleavage of the male population into two overlapping groups; the warriors and the village leaders.   This does not mean that each group did not participate in the activities of the other.   In general, however, most of the military honors of the village leaders were acquired as a result of skirmishes at or near the village.

The Hidatsa and Mandan recognized the same military honors. The highest honors were shown to one who went out alone far from home to kill and scalp an enemy unassisted. This honor was chiefly reserved for those who went out to avenge a sibling or clan member, particularly a blood brother. One was not made ineligible for the honor when a group of friends went along, provided the individual who had vowed to revenge the brother's death did the actual killing and scalping unassisted. In such cases, others of the party also were not near enough to strike coup. According to native accounts, the honors were sometimes won by going undetected into the enemy camp at night to kill a particular person known to be the brother's slayer. A variant to this form of brother-revenge occurred when one who had recently had his wife stolen from him by a tribesman went out unobserved by his tribesmen to vent his anger on the enemy. Usually one announced his plans to a brother or sister but, not uncommonly, he just disappeared and the group speculated on his whereabouts. When one wished to embarrass his rival or his wife's people suspected of encouraging the elopement, he often went alone far from the village, even in the dead of winter, to kill and scalp an enemy. Sometimes a man would announce his decision to his closest male friend or siblings, saying that if he stayed around the village, he might do something foolish—that it would be better to take out his anger on their enemies. One showed these honors by painting one legging and the corresponding side of the shirt and sleeve black, and the other side yellow or white. He wore a coyote tail at each ankle to show that he saw the enemy first and struck him and wore one eagle tail feather. He was expected to dress in this manner whenever leading the fasters during ceremonies.

When several went out and participated in the killing and striking of the coups, the first to strike painted one side of his shirt and leggings black, wore one coyote tail, and one eagle tail feather. The second, dressed and painted in the same manner except that he painted one red band on the eagle tail. The third and fourth to strike painted only the leggings black; the third wore a feather with two stripes and the fourth wore a feather with three stripes. For the first time on an expedition, when only one enemy was seen and has coups struck on him, each warrior counting coup put two X's on one of his leggings. For the second such honor, one put another pair of X's either on a shirt sleeve or the other legging. If one struck four times when only one enemy was seen, he put X's on both sleeves and leggings.

The coyote tail was worn if one struck an enemy far from home. Two tails were worn if one struck an enemy on two different trips or on one enemy when one went out alone. The feather of a crow or raven worn in the hair signified that one was first to see the enemy while serving as scout. The leader of a war party was entitled to carry a scalp stick with as many scalp segments as scalps taken by the men under his leadership. The war leader could also wear as many scalp segments on his shirt or leggings as enemies scalped by warriors under his leadership. These scalp segments were bunched and placed on different parts of the clothing. One scalp on each legging and sleeve signified that the wearer had been out as leader on four occasions when an enemy was scalped. The war leader did not wear feathers or paint his leggings and shirt unless he participated in the killing and striking of the enemies on his own or others' expeditions. For being first to strike three enemies, one painted the entire left legging red; one who struck three enemies, second in order of coup counting, painted the left legging red above the knee; the third to strike painted three stripes on the left legging and the fourth to strike painted four stripes.

The first to strike the enemy in a battle during which several enemies were killed, painted three black stripes on one legging; the next three to strike the same enemy painted three red stripes. It was considered an even higher honor to strike coup on the last enemy killed. The first to strike coup wore black double stripes the full length of the legging and four pairs of equally spaced horizontal stripes. The second, third, and fourth to strike coup wore only the four pairs of black stripes.

The four striking a slain woman or one whose life was spared, as in the case of women found out on the prairie away from camp, wore a short carved stick decorated with porcupine quills and feathers. The legging or shirt decorations were not employed; the leader was entitled to carry a scalp.

Striking a live enemy was considered a higher honor than striking one who had been killed. One could paint two hands on one side of the chest to show that a live enemy had been struck or one could have two hands tattooed on his chest. If the horse had participated in striking the live enemy by hitting him with the legs or body, one could likewise paint two hands on the horse for each enemy so struck. One who had been shot could wear a stick painted red with a knot carved on it; if one's horse was shot and wounded, the carved stick could be tied to the horse's mane or foretop. One who had been stabbed by a knife or spear could wear as a hair ornament a stick carved to resemble a knife. The one reporting the first tipi when on a war expedition was entitled to wear a white swan feather in his hair. One hit by a bullet was entitled to paint a red spot on the shirt with lines running down from it to represent blood. One could exhibit his successes on horse-stealing raids by painting horse tracks on his robe, bunching the tracks to represent separate raids which he had directed.

These honors, together with other visual representations of sacred bundle rights, gifts, and ceremonial participations, expressed one's age-group status when displayed on important social and ceremonial occasions. Since no two individuals participated equally in recognized status-building activities, rarely was the social personality of two males identical. In a tribe actively engaged in both offensive and defensive warfare, and in a region where social values were primarily determined by military accomplishments, it is somewhat surprising to discover that other values played an important part in the makeup of the social personality and status of many Hidatsas whose military contributions were not significant. In spite of the military "veneer," there existed a central core of societal values based on other significant aspects of their culture. In this respect, it appears that the Hidatsa and their neighbors, the Mandan and Arikara, differed from the nomadic groups of the Plains who, in the years preceding the Reservation Period, measured social status largely on military records.

HIDATSA CEREMONIAL ORGANIZATION

The Individual and the Supernatural

Hidatsa ceremonial organization was highly formalized and exceedingly complex. In theory, all supernatural powers have their origin at the beginning of time when the earth or "in between" land was made over by the mythological beings for man's occupation. At that time First Creator, with the assistance of other mysterious persons, created numerous gods from whom the Hidatsa could acquire supernatural powers and thus survive by performing various rites. In the beginning all of nature was created for the benefit of the people but certain rules were laid down which the people must obey if they were to survive. The society theoretically survived by virtue of the supernatural powers acquired by various means: fasting; ritual performances; feasts; ceremonial purchases from other tribes; and rigid conformance to the tribal rules of individual and group conduct. At the base of all Hidatsa religious activities and concepts is the belief in individual and group-owned supernatural powers which are controlled according to long-standing rules.

Supernatural power was thought of as a "force" above and beyond the physical capacities of man. When a man lost his supernatural powers, death occurred; contests were won by those with the greatest supernatural powers. All death, however, was not the result of such loss. In the beginning of time, when the land was first created by virtue of a contest between Lone Man and the First Creator and the latter established his immortality for all time, it was decreed that in the future people would live no more than one hundred years after which they would leave for the Village of the Dead where they would live the same life and with the same status and honors as when they died. So we observe, as I have on a number of occasions, old people still able to get around quite well praying to their sacred bundles that the long life promised them be given to younger people, and accepting approaching death calmly, their chief concern being that their bodies be properly dressed and painted, and that adequate goods and food be collected for the funeral feast.

The death of younger males actively engaged in military or economic pursuits, or of younger females occupied with the rearing of little children or providing for the wants of their old people, had a more

282

disruptive effect on the social order. Although people felt badly and mourned their deaths, there was always the tendency to ascribe death to supernatural causes and to look into their record and to interpret events in terms of the supernatural. Convenient excuses were to say that: he must have fasted wrong; his dream instructions either must not have been genuine or were improperly interpreted by the older people; he must have violated some tribal rule; he must have spoken unkindly to or mistreated someone possessing unrevealed supernatural powers; or his supernatural guardian must have subsequently blessed the enemy and he had not reestablished his priority with the same supernatural being by medicine feasts and renewal rites. Even minor accidents were interpreted either in terms of loss or lack of supernatural power.

Ridicule or question of the potency of ritual acts was liable to result in minor injury—at least to the disbeliever. On one occasion, not long before the old village life was abandoned, a Crow Indian observing a Thunder rite expressed doubt that thunder was a large bird. A few hours later, while sitting on an earth lodge, he was hit and severely burned by lightning although none of the other young men sitting nearby were injured.

An individual should perform any rites for which he was otherwise qualified by inheritance, or at least pledge the ceremony when he received repeated vision instructions. On one occasion a Hidatsa had received numerous visions instructing him to perform the Horse ceremony, but he never got around to making the pledge to perform the rites. One day while he sat talking with some of his friends, a horse strayed by and kicked him, severely injuring him. Since his father owned a Horse sacred bundle, the others inquired whether he had ever had visions sent by the horse and, being answered in the affirmative, it was concluded that the kicking was merely another effort by the supernatual acting through the horse to induce him to purchase a Horse sacred bundle. On still another occasion, about 1878, a party of Mandan and Hidatsa were traveling to the Crow to sell them one of the Grass Dances. In the party were some young Crow Indians. As they passed the scaffold on which a Sioux had been placed, the young Crow men shook the bones from the scaffold, rolled the skull down the bank into the Yellowstone River, and appropriated the pipe for their own use. The older Mandan and Hidatsa called their young men back, saying that once bodies had been put away that way, they should not be disturbed. While cooking their evening meal that day, the women accidentally set fire to the prairie and the fine ceremonial paraphernalia they were taking to the Crow Indians were burned.

Native concepts of supernatural power affected and shaped their behavior. A child normally had no supernatural power except as a member of a household whose members provided both physical and supernatural protection. Women had less supernatural powers than men because they needed less in their daily activities than did men who were always facing danger in hunting or in military engagements. Men were not normally born with supernatural powers. Until they were old enough to seek visions and to obtain supernatural powers by other means, the supernatural powers of their relatives' sacred bundles protected them. Children were given some sacred objects when 5 or 6 years of age and were taught how to perform simple rites for their own protection. This instruction was usually given by some older male of the household other than the father, who contributed ritualistic training only when the child was old enough to seek actively a sacred bundle or dream of his own.

Ordinarily, the older brothers took the younger ones to the fasting centers when rites including fasting and personal torture were practiced—but the members of the father's clan inflicted the actual cutting for the torture ordeal. At least in later times it was not customary to inflict tortures except at the request of the individual desiring that it be done to him. On some occasions, when the child was very young and not well acquainted with the males of the father's clan, he might ask one of his own clansmen or his own father to perform the act. I found no evidence that one was ever forcibly tortured and the thought of physical compulsion was contrary to native beliefs that vision quests should be sought voluntarily. Informants were in agreement that men formerly submitted to physical torture more frequently and began at an earlier age, citing the greater number of weals observed on their older relatives.

While living at Fishhook Village, small children not more than 5 or 6 years of age were taken to the fasting rites with older brothers and looked after until hunger and thirst could no longer be endured. Rivalry between age-groups was encouraged but one was free to abandon fasting whenever he so desired. Usually first fasting was for a day or two. When one was able to fast for 3 days, he was considered qualified to endure further personal torture. It appears from accounts that a century ago physical torture was inflicted at an earlier age. Maximilian (1906, vol. 23, p. 378), in speaking of the Hidatsa Naxpikᴇ ceremony (Sun Dance), advises us that—

None but the candidates dance, and the only music is striking a dried buffalo's hide with willow rods. There have been instances of fathers subjecting their children, only six or seven years of age to these tortures. We ourselves saw one suspended by the muscles of the back, after having been compelled to fast four days. No application whatever is subsequently made for the cure of the wounds, which leave large swollen weals, and are much more conspicuous among the Manitaries than the Mandans. Most of the Manitaries have three or four of these weals, in parallel semicircular lines, almost an inch thick, which cover the entire breast. Similar transverse and longitudinal lines, arising from the same cause, are seen upon the arms, nay, the whole length of the limb is often disfigured by them.

Although supernatural power was usually manifested by visions, it was believed that those who fasted often or performed other power-seeking activities without the benefit of visions also were possessors of this power even though they had no symbols to show for their efforts. Thus a child who fasted often without having visions was believed to possess more powers than one who had not fasted at all. Supernatural power was viewed as variable and measurable but the limits were defined in terms of ultimate success; results were what counted. One who purposely sought supernatural power and later performed dangerous acts without injury to himself or those under him was believed to have found a genuine guardian. One would rarely entrust his welfare to those who had shown little interest in obtaining supernatural power.

Since the vision quest was a common way of obtaining super-natural power, the novice had little capacity for interpreting dreams. Instead, the Hidatsa pattern provided for organized fasting and the quest of visions under the supervision of a ceremonial "father." The young were encouraged to relate their dreams to their "fathers."

The formal character of Hidatsa fasting resembled closely the Mandan pattern and differed sharply from that of the Crow where fasting was largely an individual matter. Hidatsa fasting efforts were constantly being channeled into formalized and preexisting ceremonial patterns, most of which they believed had existed since the beginning of time. It was thought that a male child eventually ought to receive vision instructions to take over his father's cere-monial bundles and rites. Living in the atmosphere of the father's sacred bundles, it was believed inevitable that what one saw and heard in the lodge would eventually affect his dreams. Nevertheless it was impossible to learn of a single instance where a youth's first vision was interpreted by his elders as an instruction to perform his father's rites. Those case histories which I recorded indicated that the first dreams of the very young never became an important part of an individual's sacred lore. At the time they were considered valued property but as one pursued further fasting under more severe conditions with greater knowledge of ritual seeking, the early visions were generally forgotten or disregarded as more specific instructions were received.

The concept of quantitative supernatural power, capable of being added to or subtracted from, was indicated by numerous social practices; one should not undertake many military adventures unless he fasted frequently or continued to add to his supernatural powers by ritual purchases, informal feasts, bundle renewals, or other power-seeking activities; one who had been leader of the summer buffalo hunt or the winter camp should not accept another similar appointment too soon as such responsibilities drew heavily on one's supernatural powers. Here we see this concept of the variability of supernatural power expressed in social behavior, that is, the rotation of the personnel entrusted to group leadership. As another example, because the same bundle is used for fish trapping and eagle trapping and because a great deal of supernatural power is necessary to catch fish, the manager of a fishtrap during the summer should not supervise the fall eagle traps—he would bring poor luck to his eagle trappers. Similarly, one should not too frequently accept invitations for sex expression in the "walking" ceremonies. The custom of inviting other recognized possessors of great supernatural powers to assist as coleaders on hazardous military expeditions further expressed native concepts of the quantitative character of supernatural powers.

Similar grading of the supernatural existed in the sacred myths: Packs Antelope, although having great supernatural powers as a hunter by virtue of the powers given him by the Eagles, is drawn under the Missouri waters by Grandfather Snake who once was one of the Sacred Arrows; Two Men are made to suffer hunger because, during the ceremonies at Old-Woman-Who-Never-Dies' lodge, Grandson selects the arrows having the greatest supernatural powers and thus secures for himself the supernatural powers formerly possessed only by Two Men. The same concepts are expressed in other instances. The Woman Above blesses a Hidatsa and promises him seven enemies; before he can take possession of them, however, the enemy makes greater sacrifices to her and she gives him even stronger supernatural powers so that he is able to overcome and kill seven Hidatsa men instead.

According to Hidatsa concepts, all of the supernatural has existed from the beginning of time and various aspects of the supernatural have been revealed to them from time to time during the history of the tribe. As new revelations were revealed in visions, "seeing with their own eyes," purchases from other tribes who had similar revelations, or the appearance of certain culture heroes who came to live with them, the people were given instructions in the establishment and performance of the various formal ceremonies. Thus, the existing ceremonial structure continued only as long as the younger generation was given appropriate visions to continue the various rites. This is somewhat at variance with the Mandan pattern where one bought because he was the proper relative to inherit the bundle and to perform the rites, and vision instructions were not necessarily prerequisite to all bundle purchases. In fact, as often as not, when a Mandan grew old and feeble, he would request that the proper relative learn the rites and accomplish the transfer. Hidatsa vision experiences provided the sole motive for bundle transfer or, if not eligible according to "father-son" inheritance, provided appropriate substitutes such as feasts to existing bundles.

The Hidatsa ceremonial system was "open at the top," my informants would say, to provide for the occasional introduction of new bundle rites. The Hidatsa were reluctant to accept vision experiences as ends in themselves but rather as the first steps toward tribal bundle rites. They were equally reluctant to elevate to a high position any individual who had not been active in the long established rites or had not been closely associated with someone who held important tribal ceremonial functions. Many of my informants were aware of the greater informality of the vision experiences of their close associates, the River Crows. The Awatixa and Awaxawi seem to have been conservative, like the Mandan, and to have interpreted vision experiences in terms of existing tribal rites. The Hidatsa-proper were intermediate between the other two Hidatsa village groups and the Crow. This intermediate cultural position was also indicated by their frequent abandonment of agriculture for a few seasons at a time to go out onto the Plains as true nomads. They were away on one of these periodic migrations in 1837, thus partially avoiding the devastating smallpox losses suffered by the other two village groups and the Mandan.

The extent to which Hidatsa concepts of supernatural powers had been institutionalized and channeled into fixed patterns is indicated by the custom of explaining most institutions and behavior, as well as the natural environment, by means of origin myths. Even such recent events as the first introduction of the horse is now a part of the magical practices and mythology relating to the Earthnaming ceremony. Concepts of the role of visions have influenced cultural borrowing. Recently a Horse ceremony was introduced into the tribe by individuals who had adopted Assiniboin "fathers" who practiced the Horse rites. Afterward these Hidatsa buyers' "sons" dreamed of their "fathers," Horse bundles and purchased the ceremonial bundles and rites of them.

The Hidatsa reconize two general groups of sacred bundles: the tribal bundles acquired by vision and subsequent purchase, and personal bundles acquired by vision. Those in the latter group are informally prepared without the benefit of group participation and the incidents relative to their preparation are not widely known except as the individual owners choose to speak of them during social or ceremonial gatherings. The bundle was prepared in the manner prescribed by the supernatural spirit and the songs and ritual were privately owned. The guardian spirit could be any creature in nature not specifically associated with a particular tribal bundle as long as the proper name of a spirit of one of the established bundles was not used nor the songs recognized to be identical or similar to existing sacred songs.

When the similarities in the vision experiences were so great that people associated them with existing rites, one making up a personal bundle was in danger of public condemnation, not for stealing another's ceremony, but for failing to call on his "fathers" for an interpretation which would have led to a medicine feast and public approval of his association with existing ceremonies. But all personal vision rites were not sufficiently similar to be associated with existing ceremonies. The owner would include the various personal bundles in his total repertoire of sacred objects, periodically "feed" the objects of the various bundles, and even mention them as contributors to his numerous successes whenever called upon to assume various roles on social and ceremonial occasions. The bundles were personal in character and acquired privately, so they had no important rites or traditions associated with them. They were symbols of the individual's social personality during his life and usually were placed with his body when he died.

Occasionally a grandfather would make up a separate bundle for a grandchild, or an elder would buy the right to doctor minor ailments, but the real authority for various tribal practices was derived from the sacred tribal myths. No doubt most personal bundle rites were conditioned by the culture of the group, but the Hidatsa do not admit that; instead they say that one dreams as he does because particular gods have selected him. It was considered good luck to dream of spirits or incidents from the sacred traditions. Nowhere do they admit that one's visions were conditioned by the culture. Nevertheless, we find "father-to-son" inheritance of tribal bundles and rites occurring generation after generation.

A common belief of the social effect of possessing great supernatural powers was expressed by native utterances such as "because he was now a holy man he conducted himself with dignity, and people, watching him as he went about the village discussing matters and advising younger 'brothers,' could see that a great change had come over him. He dressed well and gave more attentiom to his appearance. He had an air of confidence that people liked to see, for all this had come from his suffering." By contrast, one who believed that he had lost his supernatural powers went about dejectedly and was the object of pity by all he met. Some who had never partaken of rites to obtain good dreams or had no important dreams to show for their efforts often, as in the case of Old-White-Man, accepted the situation with indifference or a happy-go-lucky attitude. They rarely offered advice or imposed their opinions on other people, particularly outside their own households. Even as a man was expected to behave in such a manner as to reflect his group's estimation of him, the "joking relatives" were first to criticize one whom they believed was carrying things too far.

One was never measured by his wealth in personal property; those highest in the regard of the group were likely to be relatively poor because of their numerous social obligations. A man's position in the tribe could also be measured by the amount of goods that he had given away publicly and privately as well as the amount that he had received as gifts from others in similar situations. All through life there were important formal events when one was expected to give property to one's older tribesmen, those who possessed superior supernatural powers, and those who were objects of pity—particularly of the father's and of one's own clan. Otherwise most gifts were to persons, both male and female, of the father's clan from whom most supernatural powers and authority were derived. On the occasions of birth, vision experiences, first military successes, and ceremonial purchases, one presented valued things to the members of the tribe, especially the members of the father's clan—and occasionally to the entire membership of the father's moiety when the father and son were of opposite moieties. Even as one worked hard with the assistance of the household and clan to accumulate goods and horses to use during the various crisis periods of youth to middle age, so did one who had advanced in status in this way get it all back several times over in the years after middle age.

So we find older men advising their "sons" to fast often and to buy many ceremonial rites in order to live a good life in their later years. But one's position as the receiver of honors from the younger men also imposed restrictions; one would have quickly lost prestige had he, in the position of ceremonial father, kept for himself all the goods presented to him on such occasions. While a man endeavored to show his status among his cooperating relatives by providing great quantities of valuable things for disposal on the occasion of the purchase of the father's bundle rites, hoarding of the goods so received would have brought forth criticism from the whole tribe but more particularly the joking relatives. As ceremonial father he might keep only what he needed for his own use and distribute the surplus to his friends and old people in need. He benefited both by receiving and giving. He could enumerate publicly the goods and horses he had received from others as symbols of their estimation of his eminence; he could, by means of certain designs worn on his clothing, show people the extent of his ceremonial giving. Social values did not sanction the accumulation of wealth for wealth's sake. Except that the household was well organized and neat because people came there a great deal to eat and discuss group matters, a chief's lodge differed not at all from that of his neighbors.

A woman's position was somewhat different. There was no organized fasting at puberty and rarely did a woman seek to build up personal vision bundles. They were never tortured during ceremonies by having thongs inserted in their flesh although they might fast and cry to seek certain ends such as good health, successful return of a close relative from war, or the avenging of an enemy. Women aided their brothers in the purchase of sacred bundles, held rights in certain bundles, and participated in the "walking rites" of the husband's Buffalo Calling ceremonies and age-grade purchases.

Hidatsa concepts of the supernatural are highly formalized and institutionalized, and are drawn chiefly from two sacred narratives which deal with (1) the creation of the earth by First Creator and Lone Man for man's occupation and (2) the exploits of the Sacred Arrows.

The Creation myth is concerned chiefly with the accounts of the making of the land from bogs and swamps by First Creator and Lone Man. This myth relates the details of the shaping of the land and three river systems, the Missouri, Red, and the Mississippi; the creation of both animate and inanimate things and various sacred beings whom the people learned to worship to obtain supernatural powers; the bringing of the people to the surface of the earth, where they were to live, and their final separation from those living below; the dispersal of the population all over the lands; the separation into diverse tribes and related bands based on language; the independent movements of different Hidatsa–Crow bands; the conflict between brothers for which the people are punished by a great celestial fire; the early separation of the Hidatsa-proper and River Crow from the Awaxawi somewhere to the east of the Missouri; the preservation of corn by the Awaxawi who escape to the Missouri and its loss by the Hidatsa–River Crow when they go north to the land of the moose and polar climate to escape the flood; the return of the Hidatsa–River Crow to the south where they build at Devils Lake and discover that the Mandan are living on the Heart River; the appearance of Two Men with elements of the Sacred Arrow rites at the villages on the southern shore of Devils Lake; the migration of the Hidatsa–River Crow to the Missouri where they quarrel and separate, with the River Crow taking the Tobacco rites away with them; and finally, the recovery of the corn from the Mandan and the ensuing close relations of the Hidatsa-proper and the other Hidatsa groups and Mandan villages. It is from this sacred tradition that the Hidatsa have drawn in the reconstruction of the early history of two groups: the Hidatsa-proper and the Awaxawi. The myth also provides the basis for the meaning of numerous customs, ceremonials, and features of the natural environment.

In contrast to the traditional experiences of the Hidatsa–River Crow and Awaxawi, part of which can be substantiated with archeological evidence on the Missouri River and elsewhere, the myths of the Sacred Arrows provide quite contradictory accounts of the creation of the earth and its occupation by certain Hidatsa groups. In this myth, which provides traditional accounts of the origin of most formal tribal bundle rites, the earth was prepared for occupation by First Creator and other supernatural beings for the future home of the Hidatsa but the details of its creation are generally passed over lightly. Instead, the people later making up the 13 clans resided in the sky in earth lodge villages extending from the zenith to each horizon and lived much as those who came down to the earth did in later years except that the society above was better regulated with no death or evil spirits to bother the people. Charred Body discovered this land below and came down from the sky as an arrow, for the people above were "at heart" arrows because of their methods of travel. He found the earth occupied by many evil spirits who resisted intruders from above. Recognizing that life below would be difficult, he selected 13 young married couples to accompany him below where each established a separate household from which the 13 clans were ultimately derived. Each household was symbolically represented by some part of the arrow (fig. 1).

They reached the earth at Charred Body Creek, a few miles downstream from the present town of Washburn, N. Dak., where they immediately encountered numerous evil beings who resisted their efforts to settle there. Because Charred Body had the spirit of the Sacred Arrows with which to protect the people, the population increased and 13 villages representing the 13 clans were later established from the descendants of the 13 unnamed household groups.

Meanwhile, unborn twins were torn from their mother by an evil monster who threw one into a spring nearby and the other to the inner edge of her earth lodge. With the help of First Creator and Charred Body, the two boys, now named Spring Boy and Lodge Boy, grew quickly and undertook to annihilate the evil spirits which surrounded them. Since Spring Boy was the leader in destroying these evil spirits, he was captured and taken above to be tortured by Long Arm—at this point the Sun Dance (Naxpike) began. The

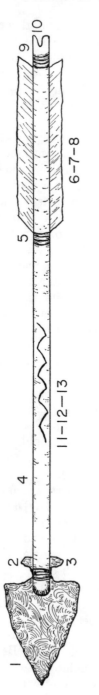

1	Tip
2-3	Tang
4	Shaft
5	Sinews
6-7-8	Feathers
9	Sinews
10	Notch
11-12-13	Groove

FIGURE 1.—The 13 parts of the sacred arrow. (Drawn by Bears Arm.)

myth then went on to explain the origin of Holy Women participation in the various ceremonies, certain Buffalo Calling rites, Snake Curing rites, Black Medicine rites with the red baneberry root, and the institution of village police.

At this point in the sacred narrative Moon caused an Awatixa village woman to follow a porcupine into a high cottonwood tree. She found herself on the land above where she married Moon for whom she bore his son, later to be named Grandson. Because Grandson was the son of one of the sky people he was very holy even as a small child. When his mother was killed by a stone thrown down as she attempted to escape from Moon, Grandson fell into Old-Woman-Who-Never-Dies' garden. [41]

The exploits of Grandson form the basis for the introduction of additional sacred rites and practices, chief of which are the Old-Woman-Who-Never-Dies rites, Snake Curing rites, altar rites of Eagle Trapping, Sacred Arrow rites, Bear with Arrow rites, Eagle Trapping rites, Fish Trapping rites, Buffalo Corral rites, the Stone Hammer society, and Star Bundle rites.

Grandson's quarrel with Yellow Dog also laid the traditional foundation for the origin of the four Dog Societies. Then, in anger towards the people for whom he had done so much but from whom he had received so little, he returned to the sky after announcing that he would destroy any village that thereafter made sacred offerings to him.

After the return of Grandson to the sky, the two myths converge into a single one involving the more recent traditional and mythological history of the three village groups still recognized. The various gods formerly living with the people are believed to have then moved to various places in the universe to assume protective roles for the people by means of the many major and minor rites and ceremonies.

In native theory, all of the Hidatsa village groups had by then taken their relative positions on the Missouri; the former village groups originating with Charred Body had been named and, through intermixture in a reduced number of villages, had become the clans. Six clans later went back to the sky to become one of the constellations, leaving seven clans and one lineage of the Xura at the Awatixa villages. When the Hidatsa-proper and Awaxawi came to the Missouri to live, they traditionally adopted the seven clans of the Awatixa.

According to native concepts, the two principal sacred narratives were associated with two different ethnic groups of the Hidatsa and Crow: (1) the Awatixa and Crow, who represented an early popu-

---

[41] This garden and lodge were situated near the Holding Eagle home in the southeastern edge of the Fort Berthold Reservation. For an archeological study of the lodge, see Woolworth, 1956.

lation on the Missouri above the Heart River and on the tributary
streams to the southwest and who had enjoyed a long period of
friendship with some Mandan groups; and (2) the eastern Hidatsa–
Crow groups who lived on the Sheyenne River, other western tributaries of the Red River northward, and across into southern Canada
until late in the prehistoric period when they moved onto the Missouri
as the Awaxawi, Hidatsa, and River Crow. That these native
concepts of migrations and ethnic relationships may have some authen-
ticity is suggested by the archeological situation in these traditional
regions: At Lower Hidatsa site 34, the traditional home of the Awatixa
at the mouth of Knife River, the deep refuse accumulations indicate
a long occupation.

The Hidatsa think of the ceremonies deriving from the two sacred
myths as knots on a string. The string represents a sequence of
events and the knots, the various ceremonies. No individual or small
group of individuals knew all of the parts of either the myths or the
ceremonies deriving from them. Instead, a bundle owner would know
all of the details of the particular ceremony in which he held rights
and its position in the series with respect to the ceremonies immediately preceding and succeeding his own. Thus, the entire sacred
myth was divided into segments which were entrusted for preservation
to various individuals of the group. Those ceremonies which were
derived from the same sacred myth or similar situations involving
the same culture heroes or mythological characters were felt to belong
together. The authority for certain individuals to attend whenever
a related ceremony was being performed was derived from these
relationships. It is usually difficult to understand by what right
certain individuals were permitted or expected to attend ceremonies
until one knows the details of the sacred myth from which each
authority was derived.

We find the two sacred myths merging at the point where the
Thunderbird bundles were founded and Grandson returned to the
sky. Two Men, the founders of the Sun Dance, traveled out from
the Missouri and found other Hidatsa–River Crow living at Devils
Lake. Thereafter we see an intermixture of scenes, both on the
Missouri and at Devils Lake, after which the population gathers along
the Missouri, the River Crows move away and take with them the
Tobacco rites, and a new series of rites is founded by some village
groups and borrowed by the others.

According to native beliefs, the ceremonial life continued to be
enriched until about A.D. 1875. The older rites of this series had
been integrated into the culture pattern so effectively that if they
were borrowed from other tribes this fact was no longer recognized by
my informants. There is an intermediate series, however, repre-

sented by the Sunrise Wolf, Wolf Woman, and certain Eagle Trapping rites, that suggests borrowing from the Mandan during the 18th century; the Goose Society is of traditional Mandan origin; the White-Buffalo-Cow and Adoption Pipe rites were borrowed during the first part of the 19th century; and, during the 19th century and within the memory of living informants, the Horse rites were bought from the Assiniboin.

We have seen that the Hidatsa ceremonial system is based on a series of segmented rites originating through time. Each segment was preserved by formal instructions to those making the ceremonial purchase. Those who had completed the preliminaries to ceremonial participation and were admitted as legitimate custodians of various segments of the ceremony were entrusted with the responsibility of correct interpretation and performance of their parts. To deviate from the ways laid down by the culture heroes was to invite bad luck and to undo all of the promises the gods had made. The Hidatsa speak freely of the virtues of seeking supernatural guidance but the details of specific rites, practices, and songs are not freely given even to individuals of their own household or village. It was believed that one ought to be in a proper receptive mood to learn all of the details correctly and to be able to repeat and interpret them accurately before they were given. For that reason, the Hidatsa treated all rites as sacred matter to be discussed only under prescribed situations. Variation from the traditional lines was to invite trouble.

One should not be entrusted with great supernatural powers unless he knew the proper techniques for their control. Those who had gone to great efforts to obtain important sacred bundles, only to be plagued with bad luck, were believed to have somehow deviated from custom even though the details of their errors were unknown. But an individual owning rights and possessing precise information pertaining to a particular ceremony did divulge a great deal of his knowledge from time to time so that the rites were never entirely secret. There were other situations, such as ceremonial feasts to which one interested in segments of the sacred lore closely related to his own bundles was invited, that provided formal transmission of the sacred lore.

A man was expected to become informed in tribal lore as he advanced in status. Beyond what he knew of tribal lore from the sacred bundles he had bought, he was expected to give feasts frequently to those possessing other important sacred lore and to have these myths related. A few individuals who were unusually ambitious and possessed good memories frequently knew most of the sacred myths of the village. This knowledge was, in turn, expressed in social behavior and recognition as councilmen or peace chiefs. One did not buy myths belonging to another in order to sell them; one bought as a guide in offering wise judgment to younger people.

In addition to the central sacred myths which related ceremonies to each other in time and space and provided a rudimentary history of the various village groups, there were many myths of a semisacred or sacred character which occupied an indefinite position; some were freely told as good entertainment and often with a moral exalting generosity, others were related to certain bundle rites without actually comprising the central core of the rites.

First Creator stories were told freely by both men and women and his magical acts were a constant source of entertainment. However important First Creator was in organizing the habitat for man's first existence, he was represented in certain rites only as the waiter. In spite of his traditional role of creating many things, there was no ceremony in which he occupied the principal position. Instead, he is the trickster who entertained the people while those spirits he created provided the psychological basis for the performance of the various rites.

Bundle inheritance was by two distinct patterns. Most sacred bundles were transmitted from father to son with wide leeway to provide for "father and son" inheritance by clan as well as blood relationships. This pattern included rites from both of the sacred myth series. There were, however, a number of sacred bundles formerly kept at Awatixa village which were transmitted within the clan. These were the Waterbuster bundle of human skulls said to represent two eagles; the Knife bundle of two eagles; and the Holy Robe of the Prairie Chicken clan. The other sacred bundles from Awatixa were inherited in a father-to-son pattern as were all bundles at Hidatsa and Awaxawi, so far as informants knew.[42] This deviation from the normal pattern at Awatixa is significant since this group with its long traditional residence on the Missouri River shows many features of the Mandan clan-inheritance pattern not clearly indicated for the other two Hidatsa groups who traditionally arrived much later on the river.

Details of the Hidatsa ceremonial organization are given in the chapters that follow. In organizing the great mass of materials at my disposal, I have presented the material roughly in the order in which my informants believed the sacred beliefs and rites were introduced into the tribe. I could have presented the Buffalo Calling rites in conjunction with the Rain rites but many natives think of them as having separate origins. Some ceremonies are viewed by the natives as of multiple origins and, in those cases, I have presented them with closely related rites.

---

[42] Genealogies, however, suggest possible clan inheritance for some of the Awaxawi Snake ceremonies.

The Legendary Period

The Hidatsa legends of the creation of the earth as told today differ somewhat in detail from those recorded by Henry in 1806 and Maximilian in 1833, resembling in most details the Mandan myth, whereas the older legends show greater similarities to the Crow creation myths (Lowie, 1918). In the older myths, the creation of the earth was chiefly the work of First Creator who secured the mud from a diving bird. In the Mandan creation myth, through which runs the moiety theme, the earth was made by two culture heroes working on opposite sides of the Missouri. Further evidence that the older creation myth has been modified by Mandan influence is indicated by the general indifference the Hidatsa give to details of man's earlier existence. In the more recent accounts, the Hidatsa myths state quite definitely that the people on the land below were agriculturalists who brought corn and the other garden plants up with them. The Hidatsa had not, however, gone as far as the Mandan in founding sacred bundles and rites associated with the principal leadership of those coming from the land below, although they had made rapid changes in that direction during the 19th century through marriage and sale, whereby the Mandan Corn Skull bundle got into Awaxawi hands.

FIRST CREATOR MYTH

It would appear that the sacred myth of the creation of the earth by First Creator, Coyote, from mud brought up by a diving bird represented the older and more widespread version which the Mandan had modified to fit their concepts of moiety or dual organization. Further evidence that the Hidatsa creation myth was probably modified through contacts with the Mandan is suggested by the fact that, in the recent versions, the Hidatsa assign a significant role in creation to Lone Man. He is not mentioned in any of the earlier Hidatsa versions although with the Mandan he is considered one of the principal deities who founded the Okipa, sacred cedar, sacred turtles, and many other sacred objects and practices.

Matthews likewise assigned great prominence to the First Creator as the maker of all things without mentioning Lone Man as the comaker of the earth. My studies of many Hidatsa myths and ceremonies did not confirm Matthews' accounts that First Creator created everything; there are many myths about spirits of the "sky world" and the "underworld" that were in no way related to the creation of the earth by First Creator. It would appear, instead, that the beliefs relative to First Creator involve only the creation of the "in between" land now known as the earth. Matthews (1877, p. 47) wrote:

The object of their greatest reverence is, perhaps, Itsikamahidiś, the *First Made*, or First in Existence. They sometimes designate him as Itakatétaś, or *Old Man Immortal*. Some Indians say that itsikamahidiś means *he who first made*, but such a rendering is not in accordance with the present etymology of the language. They assert that he made all things, the stars, the sun, the earth, and the first representatives of each species of animals and plants, but that no one made him.

The following abbreviated account provides the essential features of the creation myth. My observations and analyses are given in brackets.

The land was then chiefly under water. First Creator was alone and wandering about by himself. He thought that he was the only one when he met another person named Lone Man. They discussed their origin. Lone Man concluded that he came from the western wheat grass, for in tracing his tracks he saw blood on the grass, and that his father was the Stone Buffalo, an earth-colored wingless grasshopper, for he saw its tracks near where he was born. First Creator did not know who his father and mother were but he thought that he had come from the water. The two men undertook to learn who was the older; Lone Man stuck his staff in the ground while First Creator lay down as a coyote. Years later Lone Man returned to the place where coyote was lying and, seeing the bones scattered about, took up the staff, whereupon First Creator came back to life and was declared the older.

First Creator and Lone Man decided to make the land inhabitable and, seeing a goose, mallard, teal, and red-eyed mudhen, they asked the birds to lend assistance by diving below for mud. [Note that there is no reference here to First Creator's creation of these water birds. Matthews is evidently in error in ascribing the creation of all life to First Creator.] Goose, mallard, and teal failed; only the mudhen succeeded in bringing earth from below. Lone Man divided the earth and gave half to First Creator.

First Creator made the lands on the west side of the Missouri from the Rockies to the ocean while Lone Man made the land on the other or east side, each using half of the mud brought up by the mudhen. First Creator made many living things later occupying the land and from the mud left over he made Heart Butte. Lone Man made his side flat and with the mud left over he made Hill, a small butte north of the present town of Bismarck, North Dakota. He made the spotted cattle with long horns and the wolves.

First Creator caused the people who were living below to come above, bringing with them their garden produce. The people continued to come up, following a vine, until one woman heavy in pregnancy broke the vine.

When first encountered, Lone Man carried a wooden pipe but he did not know what it was used for. First Creator then ordered Male Buffalo to produce tobacco for Lone Man's pipe. [This act explains the use of pipes in the various ceremonies, which later were introduced, and the concept of tobacco as being sacred.]

First Creator decreed that people in seeking a living would scatter into small groups all over the land and would fight. [This decree established the various bands and linguistic groups.]

Because the spotted cattle could not stand the cold winters and the wolves sometimes went mad, First Creator did not think they should be kept. So the spotted cattle and the maggots around a dead wolf representing the White people were thrown eastward across the waters until a later time when they would return as the White men and their cattle. Finding the land to the east too level for shelter from storms, they roughened it with their heels to form the land as it is seen today. The people dispersed over the land into tribes and the two men visited them in their villages and camps. At this time the people, called Mirokac whom we know as River Crow, Hidatsa, and Awaxawi, moved northward toward Devils Lake and lived together as a single group. There were many lakes where they lived at that time.

Hungry Wolf of good reputation lived in the village with a younger brother named High Bird. Young men would line up along the path taken by the young women getting water to ask for a drink. When water was offered one, it indicated that she was fond of him. High Bird's friend, an orphan, lived with him. Hungry Wolf's wife offered High Bird water; he refused it because she was his brother's wife and she became angry. She told her husband that High Bird had attacked her. Although witnesses denied the charge, Hungry Wolf did not believe them. He announced that he was organizing a war party and High Bird and the orphan decided to go along. To cross a large lake, 40 bullboats were made to carry the 80 men. They traveled 4 days by water. High Bird as scout brought in an enemy's scalp for his brother but Hungry Wolf ordered his party to leave quietly by water while his brother slept, leaving him no means of reaching the mainland.

Hungry Wolf called back to his brother that the Water Buffalo, his "father," had ordered him to do this. High Bird was protected by his gods who ate those who assisted Hungry Wolf. [The narrative here introduces the sun as a supernatural guardian and also as a cannibal. The concept of the sun as a cannibal appears throughout Hidatsa sacred mythology. See Woman Above rites for additional references to Sun as a cannibal who causes bad luck so that he can feast on the bodies.]

Hungry Wolf called back that if High Bird crossed the water, the Sharp Noses would kill him so High Bird matched the supernatural powers of the Sharp Noses with that of the Thunderbird, his supernatural father. [This conflict provides the setting for at least one of the Thunderbird ceremonies performed by the Hidatsa in recent years. When this study was made, White Fingernails had a Thunder sacred bundle traditionally originating with High Bird. For the rites, see pp. 358–363 which deal with the Thunder Ceremonies.]

Before the war party was out of sight, Hungry Wolf threatened that Owns-Many-Dogs' dogs would eat High Bird. [The narrative at this point describes the penalties to the social group when brothers quarreled. Bears Arm said that people were quick to put brothers aright if they showed a tendency to quarrel or fight. This applied also to clan brothers. He explained that as a result of the destruction of a large part of the population, people learned that brothers must always aid and support each other, revenge the other's death by the enemy, and provide for those the brother loved and respected while he lived.]

Thunderbird came down from the sky, learned from High Bird the cause of the quarrel, and gave High Bird advice on escaping from the island. High Bird learned from Thunderbird that the water buffalo was in reality a large snake living in the lake. [We find here introduced the conflict between the sky gods represented by the big birds and the water gods represented by the snakes. This conflict runs all through Hidatsa mythology.]

High Bird fed the large snake four corn balls to reach shore where the snake was killed by Thunderbird. High Bird cut up the snake and Thunderbird called the other large birds to a feast. [This feast is reenacted by those performing rites to White Fingernails' bundle.] These big birds then gave High Bird advice on overcoming the magical powers of Owns-Many-Dogs and the Sharp Noses. Thunderbird decreed that the village where the two young brothers lived would be destroyed unless Hungry Wolf gave High Bird enough tobacco for one pipe's filling. Then High Bird started for home.

Northeast of Devils Lake he overcame the Sharp Noses and when he was nearer to Devils Lake he encountered Owns-Many-Dogs and sent her northward beyond the great fire which was to destroy the village. Far to the east, where the rivers flow southward, High Bird heard a man weeping and discovered that it was his friend, the orphan. They reached home and found that a Mourners Camp has been set up, for his relatives had concluded that he was dead. Each day the people from the other camp came there to mimic them by singing victory songs. [The Mourners Camp was often set up by the Hidatsa and Awaxawi. It was not customary for either the Mandan or Awatixa to establish a separate camp of hide tipis as did the other village groups.]

High Bird sent his mother to Hungry Wolf four times for tobacco and each time he refused so the people of the Mourners Camp dug deep holes in which to protect themselves from the celestial flames. Each day the mourners would go to Hungry Wolf's camp to sing under the direction of seven singers. They sang the Tobacco songs. [Here we find the first reference to an institution highly developed with the Crows which also was traditionally a part of the original Hidatsa and Awaxawi culture.]

One day a fire came down from the sky. High Bird's people were in deep cellars and were saved. All of the others were destroyed except Hungry Wolf's wife who was the cause of the quarrel. She was given the name Calf Woman after the fire. She described the destruction by the fire and it was then decreed that from this time there would always be women who would make trouble between married couples. Because the seven Tobacco singers were with the mourners, the Tobacco rites were saved. Even today one sees the results of this fire, for there are no trees to the east except along the Red River and its tributaries where the fire could not burn.

After this fire the survivors separated, the Awaxawi lived to the south of Devils Lake where they planted corn while the Hidatsa and the Crow with their Tobacco rites stayed farther north near the large lakes. There Magpie discovered an approaching flood, the penalty for sticking a feather through Fat Bird's nostrils and ordering a buffalo calf to carry its mother's entrails. Those Awaxawi who believed Magpie escaped to Square Buttes on the Missouri River where they were joined by Magpie, his mother named Yellow Woman who represented corn, and Spring Buffalo. The buffaloes of the other three seasons drowned on the way to establishing three important hunting areas between the Missouri and Devils Lake. [Bears Arm explained that the linguistic differences between the Hidatsa–River Crow and the Awaxawi developed as a result of the separation after the celestial fire. He interpreted this flight from Devils Lake as evidence that the Awaxawi brought gardening to the Missouri and did not adopt the practice from the Mandan. He believed the flight northward to avoid destruction from the flood involved only the Hidatsa and River Crow. We see that the traditional migrations are intimately associated with magical beliefs. It would appear from the accounts of David Thompson that these migration myths have at least some historic validity.[43]

These people who came to the Missouri in advance of the flood were the Awaxawi who had separated sometime before from the Hidatsa and River Crow while still living northeast of Devils Lake; those who were on lowlands were destroyed by the flood.   After the waters had subsided, the Awatixa were found living on the Missouri also.   [This is the first reference in this important sacred myth to the Awatixa whose large village at the mouth of Knife River shows evidence of longer occupation than the traditional villages of the Hidatsa and Awaxawi of the same area.]

When the waters subsided, there were lakes and sloughs to the northeast where First Creator and Lone Man had roughened the earth with their heels.   Fish became abundant in all of the lakes.

---

[43] Manoah, who had lived in an Awaxawi-Mandan village after the smallpox epidemic of 1782, supplied David Thompson with considerable information on the Awaxawi.   In the following quotations, my comments and notes are within parentheses; brackets are in accordance with the source.   Thompson writes that—

"The inhabitants of these Villages (obviously referring to the Awaxawi only), have not been many years on the banks of the Missisourie River: their former residence was on the head waters of the southern branches of the Red River; and also along its banks; where the soil is fertile and easily worked, with their simple tools.   Southward of them were the Villages of the Pawnees, with whom they were at peace, except [for] occasional quarrels; south eastward of them were the Sioux Indians, although numerous, their stone headed arrows could do little injury; on the north east were the Chippeways in possession of the Forests; but equally weak until armed with Guns, iron headed arrows and spears: The Chippaways silently collected in the Forests; and made war on the nearest Village, destroying it with fire, when the greater part of the Men were hunting at some distance, or attacking the Men when hunting; and thus harassing them when ever they thought proper.   The mischief done, they retreated into the forests, where it was too dangerous to search for them.   The Chippaways had the policy to harrass and destroy the Villages nearest to them, leaving the others in security.   The people of this Village removed westward from them, and from stream to stream, the Villages in succession, until they gained the banks of the Missisourie; where they have built their Villages and remain in peace from the Chippaways, the open Plains being their defence."   (Thompson, 1916, pp. 225-226.)

". . . . As Manoah was as a Native with them I enquired if they had any traditions of ancient times; he said, he knew of none beyond the days of their great, great Grandfathers, who formerly possessed all the Streams of the Red River, and head of the Mississippe, where the Wild Rice, and the Deer were plenty, but then the Bison and the Horse were not known to them: On all these streams they had Villages and cultivated the ground as now; they lived many years this way how many they do not know, at length the Indians of the Woods armed with guns which killed and frightened them, and iron weapons, frequently attacked them, and against these they had no defence; . . . ." (ibid., pp. 230-231.)

David Thompson provides further information on the Hidatsa earth lodge village group and the Crow, all of whom he calls Fall Indians:

"Fall Indians who also have Villages, are strictly confederate with the Mandanes, they speak a distinct language; (This seems to be the first reference in the literature to earth lodge groups other than the Mandan in this area.) . . . . The Fall Indians are now removed far from their original country, which was the Rapids of the Saskatchewan river, northward of the Eagle Hill; A feud arose between them, and their then neighbors, the Nahathaways (Crees) and the Stone Indians confederates (Assiniboin), and [they were] too powerful for them, they then lived wholly in tents, and removed across the Plains to the Missisourie; became confederate with the Mandanes, and from them have learned to build houses, form villages and cultivate the ground. (Note that this is a contradiction of his earlier statement that the Falls were formerly agricultural on the Red River and its tributaries.   Obviously he is here referring to a southern group of Falls who were agricultural and a northern nomadic group which he identifies with both Hidatsa and Crow bands.   This is in agreement with the sacred myth of both nomadic and agricultural groups of Hidatsa moving westward and southwestward to the Missouri.)   The architecture of their houses is in every respect the same as that of the Mandanes, and their cultivation is the same: Some of them continue to live in tents and are in friendship with the Cheyenne Indians, whose village was lately destroyed, and now live in tents to the westward of them.   Another band of these people now dwell in tents near the head of this River (Missouri ?) in alliance with the Peeagans and their allies; . . . ." (ibid., pp. 235-236.)

Note that Thompson refers to two distinct groups of Crows; one living farther west who are allied with the Piegan, and another group to the west of the Missouri and nearer the Hidatsa villages who are allied with the Cheyenne.   The Hidatsa consider the more western one to be an early offshoot of the Awatixa and the group allied to the Cheyenne as an offshoot of the Hidatsa-proper.   It is the latter that is called by the Hidatsa *kixaicas* which refers to "Separation due to a Quarrel."

The Hidatsa and River Crow [collectively they are addressed by the term *mirokac* which does not include the other Hidatsa–Crow groups as far as I was able to determine; at least it refers to the population prior to the separation of the two groups after which separate names were applied to each group], who had gone far north to escape the flood, eventually returned southward to Devils Lake and, finding the region uninhabited, concluded that the others had been destroyed by the flood. [Note that by this time the original Hidatsa–Crow population extended east and west from Devils Lake to the Missouri upstream from the Mandan villages and onto the Plains west of the Missouri. Only the agricultural groups were on the Missouri; the nomadic ones lived adjacent to the Missouri.]

A hunting party from the camp at Devils Lake discovered Mandan villages near the Heart River and, because the Mandans could not understand exactly what was said to them across the river from the opposite bank, they called them *Minitari* by which name the people of Hidatsa village are known from that time. [The older Mandan still used the same term in historic times. The Awaxawi are called *maxaxa* and the Awatixa *mitixata*.] The hunters returned to Devils Lake, after promising that they would return with their people in 4 days. But the 4 days became 4 years when the Hidatsa–River Crow appeared on the opposite bank after abandoning the Devils Lake region.[44]

A quarrel developed over the division of a buffalo and one group moved farther west, taking with them the seven Tobacco singers. The group leaving comprised the *kixaicas* and those who remained behind to take up agriculture became the Hidatsa. [Note that the Hidatsa account for the absence of the Tobacco rites by the fact that the seven men possessing the rights in the ceremony happened to be camped on the side which moved away.]

The Hidatsa were living in tipis near the Heart River when they became frightened by two owl spirits held sacred by the Mandan so they moved upstream to build north of the Knife River. Before they left, the Mandan gave them corn and taught them the Corn rites which they had lost while in the northland.

This completes the first segment of the Hidatsa sacred narrative and is concerned chiefly with the migration of the Hidatsa-proper, River Crow, and the Awaxawi. We see that by 1932—the date of this study—events such as warfare with armed tribes are not mentioned; instead, the incidents have been completely reinterpreted in terms of the supernatural.

The Hidatsa, however, do not ascribe the foregoing legendary history to the Awatixa who had separate traditions of long residence on the Missouri. This is not a new native interpretation for, as early as 1804, two distinct traditions were recorded by Lewis and Clark although they failed to recognize the independent and separate histories of the various Hidatsa villages. They recognized dialectic differences between the Awaxawi and the other two Hidatsa villages and spoke of the Awaxawi as an independent "nation," a difference indicated by my informants in speaking of the separation of the Awaxawi from the Hidatsa–River Crow while living east of the

---

[44] For a similar account supplied by the Mandan in 1833, see Maximilian, 1906, vol. 23, pp. 315–317.

Missouri. Speaking of the village groups of Hidatsa and Awatixa, Lewis and Clark wrote, on November 21, 1804:

The Mandans say that this people came out of the water to the east and settled near them in their former establishment in nine villages; . . . The Minnetarees [Awatixa] proper assert, on the contrary, that they grew where they now live. . . . They also say that . . . the Minnetarees of the Willows [Hidatsa], whose language with very little variation is their own, came many years ago from the plains and settled near them. Perhaps the two traditions may be reconciled by the natural presumption that these Minnetarees [Hidatsa] were the tribes known to the Mandans below, and that they ascended the river for the purpose of rejoining the Minnetarees proper. . . . [Lewis, 1893, vol. 1, pp. 198–199.]

These two traditions recorded by Lewis and Clark are essentially the same as those which Hidatsa informants gave in 1932. For our study it is important to note that the Hidatsa-proper–Awaxawi sacred myth, although providing the traditional basis for numerous simple household rites and beliefs, did not account for more than a few of the formal tribal ceremonies. Corn was considered sacred because it was brought above ground by the performance of certain magical acts; corn was lost to the Hidatsa while escaping the flood; thunder and snakes are mentioned and one bundle is believed to be derived from the Thunderbirds at that time; the four buffaloes provided traditional hunting grounds east of the Missouri; Buffalo was considered holy but none of the specific rites originated during that time; tobacco and pipes were introduced for rituals.

SACRED ARROWS MYTH

The myth given above records traditional Hidatsa-proper and Awaxawi legends of an Eastern origin. The second legend, accounting for most of the formal rites, enumerates incidents on the Missouri River, chiefly upstream from the mouth of the Heart River. This myth is identified with the earliest Hidatsa population on the Missouri, the Awatixa, who traditionally were agriculturalists during their entire residence there. According to the myth, they were formerly most closely related to a group of Crow Indians who separated at an early time to become nomadic hunters west of the Missouri, and to the Awaxawi, Hidatsa, and River Crow because of linguistic ties.

The second sacred myth complex could more properly be called the "Myths of the Sacred Arrows" since culture heroes possessing the power of flight like the arrow are so prominently mentioned. This complex accounts for the origin of many ceremonies, most of which began on the Missouri in a restricted area between the Knife and Heart Rivers. Informants compare the ceremonies to knots on a string; all are independent ceremonies just as each knot is independent of the other knots but, at the same time, they are connected and related in the same way that knots are related to each other by their order on the string. The myth as summarized in this study has been assembled from many informants. It has been rechecked with several informants and represents, in my opinion, the best that can be done at this time to organize and relate the various ceremonies. In only a few instances were there disagreements between informants as to the order of origin. No single individual ever held ceremonial rights in more than a few of the formal rites of the series; nevertheless, each bundle owner knew where his sacred myth and rights began and another's terminated. Likewise each individual would know whose sacred rites began where his terminated. Generally, several individuals would own the preceding "knot" and so on. The formal ceremonial pattern was symbolized by strings with knots.

Bears Arm provided a unique design, an inverted Y, to illustrate the pattern both in respect to time and space. The two forks of the Y constituted: (1) the making of the earth, the creation of the living things, and the exodus of the people from the underworld; and (2) the sacred arrow legends of the settlement of the lands by people from the sky. The convergence of the two lines represented the convergence of the various Hidatsa village groups onto the Missouri River after the Crow had moved away. The continuation of the base of the Y as a single line represented the period of intervillage cooperation during which a new series of ceremonies developed. He then proceeded to make "knots" on the string to represent the points in the traditional history of the tribe when the various ceremonies originated. A summary of the events of Myth of the Sacred Arrows of Awatixa village follows:

Charred Body lived in a large village in the sky. All the people there were living in four large earth lodge villages a day's journey from each other. Charred Body was a sacred arrow and, hearing the bellowing of the buffaloes which he did not understand, he looked through a hole in the sky and found that a new land existed below on which many buffaloes were walking. He liked the appearance of this new land so he changed himself into an arrow and descended to the earth near the present site of Washburn. The spirit people living below immediately attempted to destroy him. A man named Fire-Around-his-Ankles encircled Charred Body and burned the feathers from his arrow.

Charred Body made 13 earth lodges on a high bench overlooking a creek now bearing his name and returned to the sky where he selected 13 young couples to occupy the lodges he had made. Since they possessed the spirits of arrows, all flew down to the new land. These 13 households increased to 13 village groups, for this was a rich land to which they had come. [These household groups are named later and become the clans.]

First Creator found the village, visited Charred Body, and was invited to come to the village to smoke with the men. Surrounded by various evil spirits who were always attempting to drive them out, the people of Charred Body's village accepted First Creator's offer of assistance. First Creator and Charred Body went to the east to another village to see the chief's daughter, thinking that if she would marry Charred Body, her village group would come back with them and help them repel the enemies. The chief's daughter rejected him and insulted him so Charred Body killed her. The chief called on Bear, Buffalo Bull, Man-with-No-Head, Man-with-Fire-Around-his-Ankles, Old-Woman-with-Basket, White Beaver, and all living things on the earth to assist him in destroying the village and all agreed to assist him. [Wolf Chief explained that this fight between villages was equivalent to interclan quarrels after these small village groups united into large villages. The narrative illustrates the penalty for murder to be the destruction of the group. Note above that a village group was also destroyed when Hungry Wolf and his brother, High Bird, quarreled.]

First Creator visited the enemy village, learned their plans, and sent the meadow-lark back with instructions. The chief's gods, however, caused Charred Body to forget what he had been told. Yellow Weasel decoyed Charred Body from the village and First Creator concealed Charred Body's sister in a corn chamber before the attack on the village was to be made. The village was burned and the people were killed.

After the battle, Charred Body rebuilt a lodge and the sister was called from the corn chamber. The two men hunted game for her and discovered that the enemy had stationed four spirit people, Man-with-Fire-Around-his-Ankles, Man-with-No-Head, Old-Woman-with-Basket, and White Beaver, around the lodge to destroy them.

Charred Body built a sweat lodge and decreed that in the future the people should use the sweatbaths when returning from hunting and they would keep in good health. [Sweat lodge origin is at this time.]

The sister was told not to admit any strangers who might come to the lodge when the two men were out hunting. Man-with-No-Head came to the lodge while the men were away and she prepared roast meat for him. He declared that he ate only when the meat was placed on the abdomen of a pregnant woman. Since she was pregnant, she permitted him to eat from her abdomen; he used his long nails to rip open her abdomen and pull out a baby which he cast towards a pile of old moccasins near the edge of the lodge, giving the child to "edge of the lodge" as his servant. He became known as Lodge Boy. A second child was ripped out and given to a spring near the lodge as the spring's servant and became known as Spring Boy. The mother was suspended between two forked poles and made to appear to be laughing.

Charred Body returned and found his sister's body, which he placed on a scaffold, and Lodge Boy who was hiding in the dark under the inner edge of the lodge. The two men performed rites and Lodge Boy grew to the size of a young man. He asked for gambling sticks and a stone and First Creator made a set for him. Returning from the hunt, First Creator discovered strange tooth marks in a buffalo tongue and Lodge Boy admitted that he had been playing with a strange fellow who lived in the spring. Spring Boy was captured and, after rites were performed over him, he vomited out the shells of the clams he had been eating and was made to look and behave like other Indians.

Since the mother came from the sky, the two boys had the supernatural powers of the arrows. Spring Boy performed rites over the mother with his arrows and she was brought back to life. In later times when these powers were transmitted to the people, the Arrow ceremonies began. [Arrow rites began at this point.]

The mother warned the two boys not to go near Man-with-Fire-Around-his-Ankles but they visited him, borrowed his moccasins, ran around him, and thus destroyed him with his own moccasins. They burned his lodge as was customary after a successful battle.

The mother warned them of Old-Woman-With-Basket so they visited her, borrowed her basket, pointed it at her, and destroyed her with fire. They gave their mother the basket and she danced while singing the victory songs, instituting the custom of dancing and singing when the enemy had been defeated. [The previous myth claimed that the custom was instituted by Hungry Wolf who sang victory songs at the Mourners Camp.]

When she warned them to stay away from No Head he insulted them by telling them how he killed their mother and disposed of the two babies. Then the boys killed him also by magical means. Then they killed the White Beaver.

Having killed one enemy each time out to war, they were now known as Two Men. [The Hidatsa respected highly one who had led four successful war parties even though only one enemy was killed each time out. One who had led four successful expeditions, killing and scalping one man each time, was more highly regarded than one who had led only one war party which had killed four enemies. Also, higher honors were bestowed on one who had led four successive successful expeditions than one who had gone out a greater number of times in order to win four records. Because they had gone out only four times and were successful each time, Two Men had attained the highest honors recognized.]

Charred Body warned Two Men always to be on their guard, using the sacred arrows for protection, for the gods were all angry because of the holy things that had been destroyed by them. When out hunting, Two Men would stick their sacred arrows into the ground while sleeping and the arrows would fall over and awaken them when in danger. One day the arrows did not warn them. Long Arm had overcome the supernatural powers of the arrows, for he was the leader of the People Above. He found the boys while they slept and took Spring Boy, who was the principal offender, above for punishment. The people prepared a forked post on which to torture Spring Boy. A brush shelter was built around the post and the people came to sing and watch while Spring Boy died. Ten songs were sung over and over while the men danced. Two mounds were built from earth brought in from outside, between which Spring Boy would be placed and covered with this earth when he died. All through the ceremony Long Arm stood watching, holding a stone ax.

Lodge Boy awoke, missed his brother, and traveled over all of the earth as an arrow looking for Spring Boy. Returning to the place where they separated, he discovered a hole in the sky above him. He changed into a sacred arrow and went through the hole in the sky to the land above. There, changing himself into a small boy, he was taken into the lodge of a very old woman living alone and fed. She informed him that Spring Boy was being tortured in the brush shelter and took him to see the ceremonies. He was recognized by Spring Boy and was obliged to leave quickly when Long Arm suspected that Lodge Boy had come.

During the night, Lodge Boy freed his brother and they escaped towards the hole in the sky, taking with them Long Arm's ax with the watching eyes. Long Arm awoke, discovered Spring Boy and his sacred ax with the watching eyes gone, and ran to the hole in the sky. There he put his hands over the hole to prevent Two Men from escaping to the land below. Now that they had Long Arm's sacred ax, which was his chief source of supernatural powers, they threatened to cut off Long Arm's hand if he attempted to prevent their return home. He agreed to free them providing they performed rites on the earth in the same manner as they had observed in the sky. Then he explained the ceremonial significance of each article and rite of the Hidebeating ceremony which he was sending to the land below.

Later, Two Men traveled over the earth and came to a village where rites were being performed and decided to have a "son." They caused a virgin to become pregnant without intercourse and instructed the virgin's mother to name the child Unknown Man. The child's mother died and he was cared for by his mother's brother and maternal grandmother. [Note how the pattern develops: Two Men now have the supernatural powers and knowledge formerly possessed by Long Arm. To transmit this power, they select a "son" thus establishing the rule that rights in the ceremony are to be transmitted through "father-to-son" relationships.]

As a young man he was a good hunter for, in spirit, he was an arrow because Two Men had taken him as their "son." Upon leaving for the winter camp, he went out ahead and found that game was scarce so he returned to the summer village with his grandmother. They learned that one family did not go along because the husband, a gambler, was too lame to travel. The old couple had a daughter who went out a great deal with Unknown Man hunting and butchering so the old people asked them to marry. [One of the requirements for tribal ceremonial purchases is that one must be married.]

While out hunting shortly afterwards, Unknown Man met Two Men and invited them to his camp where they promised him supernatural powers in hunting. [Here the informants interpreted unusual skills in hunting as evidence that some supernatural being was assisting him.]

Two Men doctored Unknown Man's father-in-law for his lameness, using the Black Medicine [red baneberry] root. They took out a bullsnake from each of his legs, and instructed Unknown Man and his wife in doctoring. [Here again we find the transfer of curing rites transmitted to a son and daughter-in-law. Many of the snake curing rites went back to this incident; others owe their origin to different traditional incidents. In either case, Black Medicine was used and the methods differed little between bundle lines.]

Two Men sent the buffalo herds to the village, as they had promised, in return for the feast which Unknown Man and his wife had prepared for them. The Holy Women butchered and hung the meat on corn scaffolds during a fog. [Here the narrative introduces the Holy Women, an organized group of individual bundle owners who met on most ceremonial occasions. See the accounts below for further references to this group.]

Scouts returned from the winter camp for corn since hunting was poor. They discovered the meat on the various scaffolds of the village. They returned to the winter camp and the people returned to the summer village. Sometime afterward, Unknown Man was sitting on his lodge when he was enticed from the village by a buffalo which he followed. Each time he shot, the arrow was deflected magically until he was taken into a large earth lodge occupied by a man, a large snake, and the buffalo.

Unknown Man lost his memory and was forced to hunt and wait on the mysterious man. While hunting one day he remembered who he was and called for Two Men, his "fathers," and they came immediately to help him. [This pattern of action, calling for assistance of one's supernatural "fathers" was the basis of Hidatsa rites.]

They killed the snake and mysterious man, and were about to kill Buffalo when he said, "I am also a prisoner; I am the one who brought the buffaloes that the Holy Women butchered for the village. If my life is spared there will always be buffaloes."

Buffalo then gave instructions in making offerings to the buffaloes. [This instruction by the buffalo was considered the traditional basis for the widespread practices of offering sage and speckled eagle feathers to buffalo skulls, both at household shrines or out on the prairies even far from the villages, whenever one wished to secure supernatural assistance.]

Now Unknown Man was ready to give the Hidebeating Ceremony for he was mature, had a good record, and had a wife to help him. Then Two Men came to the village and directed him in the performance of the rites as Long Arm had instructed them when they brought the sacred ax with the watching eyes down from the land above.

HIDEBEATING CEREMONY

This ceremony, performed in order to acquire the father's ceremonial rights, is called *Nax'pikɛ'* by the Hidatsa. This is an abbreviation of *nax'pi* meaning 'hide,' *ni'ki* which means to strike, and *hɛ* meaning 'this act or event.' The ceremony generally has been known and described as the Sun Dance. The Hidatsa think of these rites as directed to the "people above" but more particularly to the Moon, since a different ceremony with a different set of officers was performed to the Sun. The rites were theoretically a dramatization of Spring Boy's suffering when he was taken above and tortured under the supervision of Long Arm. At this time, Long Arm instructed Two Men to have the ceremony performed by their son in order that the supernatural powers for success in hunting and warfare possessed by Two Men would be transmitted to the Hidatsa by means of the sacred arrows and sacred ax.

The bundle rights were transmitted from father to son, all bundles originating traditionally with Unknown Man who first bought from his ceremonial fathers, Spring Boy and Lodge Boy. A father could sell his rights in the ceremony four times. However, there was no evidence that more than one sale had been made within the memory of the oldest informants nor could any informant recall an instance of multiple sales. It made no difference whether the father was living or not when the ceremony was pledged since a member of the father's clan prepared duplicate bundles for all except the fourth sale. Performance was not limited by clan membership although, because of the small number of bundle lines in existence, all clans were not represented. Since the father and son were of different clans, clan membership of bundles changed with each succeeding sale. Due to the predominantly matrilocal residence custom, new bundles were continually being established in different households. In addition to the Naxpikɛ sacred bundles owned by the givers of the ceremony, persons ineligible to perform the rites, due to inheritance, would frequently make up somewhat similar personal bundles according to visions received.

There is no evidence that the performance of the rite was an annual event. It was probably held most years prior to the epidemic of 1837. Its occurrence, however, was based on bundle purchases of which there were only seven lines after 1837: four from Hidatsa village and three from Awatixa. Due to the limited number of bundle lines after the epidemic, there usually were intervals of from 2 to 4 years between successive performances. Good Bear was the last to perform the ceremony in 1879.

Good Bear, Waterbuster clan, bought from his father, No Milk of the AwaxEnawita clan from Hidatsa village; Rabbit Head, Prairie Chicken clan, bought a year earlier from his stepfather Snake Cane, AwaxEnawita clan, of Hidatsa village (Rabbit Head's own father was a Mandan); Sitting Elk, Itisuku clan, bought a few years earlier from his father, Narrow Nose of the AwaxEnawita clan of Hidatsa village; Puts-Away-his-Hair, Itisuku clan, bought from his father, Owns-Many-Spotted-Horses, Knife clan of Hidatsa village; Crows Paunch, Prairie Chicken clan, bought from his father, Twisted Wood, Knife clan of Awatixa village; Crying Dog, AwaxEnawita clan of Awatixa, bought from his deceased father but the line died out when his descendants did not keep up the rites; and Knife of the Prairie Chicken clan bought rights from his classificatory father, Porcupine Pemmican, AwaxEnawita clan of Awatixa village.

Except for the last bundle line, all sacred bundles were of equal status. Since one relinquished his own rights only when the fourth sale was made, there were 10 equal bundles at Fishhook. Porcupine Pemmican's bundle was superior in status to the other for, in addition to having rights in Two Men by virtue of performing the NaxpikE, he had bought the sacred ax symbolic of Long Arm whom he impersonated each time the rites were performed. The Long Arm rights were purchased separately by means of a medicine feast to the NaxpikE bundle owners to give the purchase social recognition. In theory Long Arm rites could likewise have been sold four times with a new ax prepared each time but there is no evidence that there was ever more than the one bundle which was kept at Awatixa, the group which traditionally founded the ceremony. Whenever the ceremony was performed in other villages, the Long Arm impersonator from Awatixa officiated. During the years preceding the abandonment of the three independent villages on the Knife River, the Awaxawi occupied an intermediate position between the Hidatsa-proper– Awatixa and the Mandan, both territorially and ceremonially. Awaxawi informants had no knowledge that the NaxpikE was ever given at their village although they recalled that their young men participated actively in the Okipa due to intermarriage with the Mandan after 1782, when they united for about 20 years with one Mandan village group. The Awaxawi had other summer ceremonies, concerned chiefly with agriculture, that were not celebrated by the other Hidatsa village groups.

Theoretically, one could give the ceremony only when his father had also, but native informants believed that should one receive repeated dreams relating to the ceremony, he should not be denied the right to give the ceremony. Such was the case whereby Knife bought the Long Arm rights from Porcupine Pemmican, his classificatory father. A man volunteered to perform the ceremony after receiving a vision interpreted by the older men of the father's clan as an instruction from the gods above. Actually, young men often had visions relating to the gods above which were never interpreted as signifying instructions to perform the ceremony because their fathers did not possess rights in the Naxpike. Likewise, young men eligible by inheritance frequently did not experience appropriate dreams. When Wolf Chief dreamed of Charred Body, his father's clansmen interpreted the dream as an instruction that he would be a successful eagle trapper since his father had rights in those ceremonies. When Crows Heart dreamed of the big birds of the sky possessing the supernatural powers of the arrows, the "fathers" interpreted the dream to mean that he was to buy Big Black's Thunder rites.

However, such was not the case when Good Bear reported a vision he received during a performance of the Naxpike. His widow, Mrs. Good Bear, provided the following information concerning the preliminaries to pledging the ceremony:

Sitting Elk was giving the Naxpike and Good Bear was fasting in the lodge with the other young men. He would get up and dance each time with the other young men. During the second and third days while the torturing was on, young men who wanted sticks through their skin paid with calicoes and other valuable things to have their "fathers" pray for them and put the sticks through. Good Bear was poor and had nothing to pay with for his mother was dead. When his father remarried, the new wife did not want him so he was taken by Poor Wolf, his mother's brother, to raise.

Poor Wolf came to him and said, "You should go up to the post and have your breast cut; that is the way to have good dreams."

Good Bear said, "I would like to but I have nothing to pay with for I am poor." Poor Wolf said that all clan brothers should help each other so he went for cooked corn and calicoes.

He said, "Go to Porcupine Pemmican who belongs to your father's clan and say 'I want to run around the post and suffer like Spring Boy did up in the sky.'"

Porcupine Pemmican took the cooked corn to the singers and kept the calicoes. He said, "My son, come and sit against the post in the center."

Good Bear was painted white with clay brought from Knife River. Porcupine Pemmican sang his sacred songs while he painted Good Bear again with the clay. Good Bear shivered as though he were cold. Then Porcupine Pemmican called two young men to do the actual cutting for him and gave each of them a piece of the calico. Porcupine Pemmican said, "Good luck will come to you, my son. The first fight you are in, you will strike a Sioux," and the two men pierced the flesh when Porcupine Pemmican said "Sioux." The sticks were tied to the hide hanging down from the post and he was given a whistle. All the fasters stood up and danced through four songs. He ran and swung around the post, sometimes swinging nearly to the roof. When he was exhausted, Porcupine Pemmican pulled the sticks out and pressed down the swellings, putting white clay on the cuts to heal them and to keep the swellings down.

That night Good Bear left the lodge and went north about 3 miles onto the hills out of sight of the village to cry. He was in great pain and very tired. In his dream he was walking south on a beautiful flat when something very bright and shiny came down from the sky. He thought it would surely hit him but it missed him, coming down just in front of him. A cross was on this bright object. When he saw all this he thought that it was an instruction for him to give the NaxpikE. He thought that the hoop was the sun or the moon when it was full and that the cross represented the laces on the hoop.

He awoke, thought of his dream, and again went to sleep. Again he was walking along on a large flat; he saw two bulls belonging to White men and stopped to look at them. There was a voice and then a man dressed in fine clothing and a white collar drove up in a light wagon. The man saw him admiring the two bulls and inquired if he liked them. Since he thought the bulls were pretty, the White man told him he could have them. Then Good Bear awoke, returned to the ceremonial grounds for a short time, and went to his lodge to eat.

That night he again had a vision that he was traveling south on the prairie until he came to some White men's houses. There was one long house with a fence in front of it and many boxes of goods piled near it. He awoke and wondered what it all meant, the White man, the cattle, the White man's long house, the goods, and the shiny thing that came down from the sky. He talked to his mother's brother, Poor Wolf, about it and inquired what it all meant.

Poor Wolf studied a long time and at last he said, "I think the gods above want you to take your father's bundle; that shining object that came down from above was the Sun. I think the gods want you to give the NaxpikE."

Then the two went to Good Bear's own father and told him of the dream. No Milk said, "In the evening, before dark, cry from the top of an earth lodge so all can hear, 'Next year when the leaves are full grown I will build a house for you; I will hunt up all the bedding you will want; I want to get good luck for my people, make all of us free of diseases, and bring happiness to all of us.' When you have made the pledge all the people will hear you. It will take a year before you can give the ceremony. In the meanwhile you must get all the goods that you can, buffalo robes, blankets, and calicoes. You will need 50 robes so you will have to go out often looking for buffaloes to get the hides. It will be hard to give the ceremony but the gods above will repay you well for your trouble."

Ordinarily, one was about 30 years old before giving the ceremony since one must have demonstrated responsibility before undertaking so important a step. Dreams were carefully screened and the qualifications of eligible candidates were carefully examined. Permission was given by an older and eminent member of the father's clan— not necessarily one's own father, who was frequently dead—who would have lost status had he sanctioned making the vow by one whom he knew to be cowardly either in battle or in the protection of the village.

One should have already demonstrated by previous participation in fasting and personal torture that he was able to endure the privations of 4 days of fasting. He must also be sufficiently intelligent to be able to follow instructions in minute detail. Since the wife assisted in certain rites as well as in supervising the preparation of the goods, one must be married to a person who was unlikely to run away during the period of preparation or performance of the rites. If, in the opinion of the father's clansmen, the prospective candidate might not be able to go through with his pledges, he was usually advised to withhold making the pledge until he could "build himself up." They would tell him that because of his vision, he would have good luck in everything that he did just the same as though he had given the ceremony. This seems to have been a common practice whenever someone else was giving the ceremony during the coming summer, in order to avoid repetition of the ceremony during the same summer period, and to discourage an individual from making the vow until he had demonstrated his qualifications for enduring the ordeals. It was not necessary for one so seek advice again since it was the duty of the "fathers" to notify the young man when the time had come to make the vow if, in the meantime, he had distinguished himself in warfare or had enjoyed other good fortune indicating that he had been blessed by the gods above.

The principal officer of the Naxpike was the Long Arm impersonator, represented by Porcupine Pemmican during the period when the ceremony was performed at Fishhook Village. This Long Arm bundle was formerly kept at Awatixa village and traditionally originated with this village group. For that reason, the Hidatsa believe that the Sacred Arrow rites were originally instituted by this village group first to settle on the Missouri as a part of the western Crow and that the ceremony was adopted by the Hidatsa-proper, River Crow, and Awaxawi [45] when they came to the Missouri. As further evidence that the Awatixa were the originators of the ceremony, native informants cite the fact that they had seen a great many more Sun Dance circles on the prairie adjacent to the old and new Awatixa villages than at the villages of Hidatsa and Awaxawi. In any event, there is no traditional knowledge that the ceremony was performed prior to their arrival on the Missouri from the east. While at the Knife River, each village depended on Awatixa for top leadership by virtue of its possession of the Long Arm bundle. The ceremony was always performed at the outskirts of the summer village and never while away on the summer buffalo hunt.

The preliminary preparations and the performance of the ceremony brought together a great many people, some of whom had conventional duties and obligations. When permission was given to perform the Naxpike, or any other established formal ceremony, the pledger was always reminded by a father's clansman of the warning given to

---

[45] I found no evidence of bundle lines at Awaxawi.

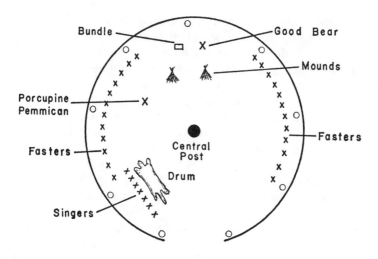

Plan of Naxpike Lodge (Sun Dance)

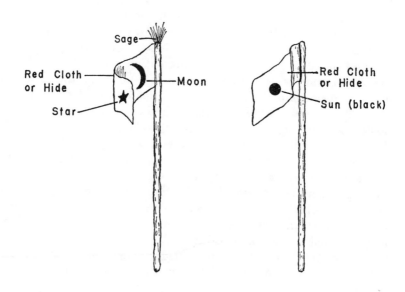

Offerings to Naxpike Bundle

FIGURE 2.—Plan of the Naxpike lodge and offerings to the Naxpike bundle.   (Both drawn by Mrs. Good Bear.)

Spring Boy and Lodge Boy by Buffalo when he was freed by Two Men in which he said, "If any human being promises me anything and does not do it, I will destroy that person." Such was the penalty for failing to fulfill a pledge involving those sacred bundles that included a buffalo skull. Another group of relatives was expected to lend assistance in accumulating the goods for the payment of the officers. One's clan was expected to contribute generously since a successful ceremony brought credit to the entire group. All those whose fathers were of the same clan were also expected to assist. Since the wife secured benefits from the performance of the ceremony, all her brothers and sisters and clan members were likewise called on for assistance. The man's age-grade society was expected to meet and to put up goods for the occasion. A similar responsibility prevailed with respect to the age-grade society to which the wife belonged. In the interim, the pledger was expected to hunt often in order to get an abundance of hides for tanning. Whereas on other occasions he customarily shared the raw hides and meat with other households due to numerous obligations to his relatives, it was understood that once he had pledged a ceremony he should not be asked to part with these things.

The pledger selected a member of his father's clan as supervisor and instructor shortly after making the vow. It was the supervisor's duty to secure information on all details of the ceremony from the one best qualified to supply that information. When the father was living, this information was provided by him and the Long Arm bundle impersonator, otherwise it was usually provided by the Long Arm impersonator to the instructor who in turn passed this information on to the pledger of the ceremony. The instructor was one outside the Naxpike ceremonial fraternity and therefore initially uninformed in the rites and the significance of various elements of the ceremony. Once the ceremony was given, his knowledge of the rites was as great or even greater than his pupil, still he acquired no permanent rights whatsoever in the ceremony, his sole reward being the property which he received for his services and the distinction of being selected as "ceremonial father." It was also the instructor's duty to see that the goods were kept dry and in good condition, and to burn incense of pine spills on four separate occasions during the preparatory period.

Regardless of the amount of goods already accumulated or pledged, when the time approached for the performance of the ceremony, the instructor carried the red tubular pipe the pledger was to receive during the rites and stopped at each lodge where young men of the pledger's clan lived to cry, "This is a great thing your brother is doing for his people. You should help him now. He has worked hard to bring credit to your clan. He will soon be suffering where Spring Boy suffered. Then you can come and suffer too; perhaps you too will get a good dream and become a leader among your people."

Final preparations were completed when the leaves were full grown and the days were hot. The instructor would invite the pledger and his wife to his lodge to outline the final steps preparatory to the erection of the ceremonial shelter. The Holy Women's society was invited in at the same time and feasted. From the society eight women who had passed the menopause were selected to prepare the ceremonial grounds. Those berdaches who were to assist in digging the hole for the central post were taken in with the Holy Women with whom they cooperated in various ceremonies. When Good Bear performed the ceremony, a Sioux named Twelve was selected as, shortly before, the Mandan berdache had been killed by the Sioux and the only Hidatsa berdache had fled to the Crow Agency when the Government agent forcibly stripped him of his feminine attire, dressed him in men's clothing, and cut off his braids. The berdache selected the central post, which was of cottonwood from driftwood in the Missouri, and received his instructions from the instructor. When a log apparently suitable for the central post was discovered, the berdache called for the instructor to inspect it. If suitable, and the log was floating in the river, rawhide thongs were attached to it, and it was staked down to prevent the current from carrying it away. Aid was then asked of the young men in carrying it to high ground.

On the day when the central log was to be brought in, the Long Arm impersonator took charge. He would instruct his announcer to call through the village, "This morning is the time to get the big post. Fix up in your best clothing; get on your best horses; bring your lariats with you."

Young and middle-aged men would respond and form a line. Long Arm impersonator called for the pledger's wife and she walked in front of him to the place where the ceremony at the post was to be held. He would point his eagle wingbone whistle toward the sky and blow it; this was the signal for the young men to charge the post as though it were an enemy. The young man striking first was believed to have received the supernatural powers to strike an enemy. Four men took credit for striking the post. Then the men gathered around the log, where each sang his own personal sacred songs, prayed for supernatural powers, attached their lariats under the log, and proceeded to carry it between them to the ceremonial grounds.

When they started with the log, Long Arm impersonator advanced toward them, pointing his whistle alternately toward the sky and ground. They stopped four times in bringing the log to the ceremonial grounds, each time on a signal of Long Arm impersonator. The fourth stop was at the shelter.[46] The pledger's wife, eight Holy Women, and the berdache [47] must be on the grounds when the log arrived. The instructor delivered a buffalo head with a strip of hide along the back and the tail to the berdache who fastened the head to the fork in the log and then tied sandbar willow brush and buckbrush to the head. Young men raised the post into place and the berdache tamped the soil around it. The eight Holy Women meanwhile put the side posts in place and tamped them securely. The young men then cut and brought in the roof poles. There was rivalry between the young men to see which side would be first to complete its section with cottonwood branches. Unlike the Mandan in similar competitive situations, moiety division was not employed. They would say that the first person to reach the central post would be lucky. The lodge was completed that day before sunset.

Long Arm impersonator would devote the next day to arranging things in the lodge. First he would mark the location of the doorway to the west of south. Then he erected two small mounds, north of the central post and near the edge of the lodge, from earth already brought in. A bundle of buckbrush was placed upright on each mound. During the ceremony, Long Arm impersonator's place was to the west of these mounds. While Long Arm impersonator was fixing the lodge, the pledger brought in bedding and arranged his bed behind the two mounds, placing buckbrush under his robes.

The ceremony began that evening with "Cuts Hole in the Mouth" dance. Four young men who had struck first coup on the enemy and were noted for their bravery were selected by Long Arm impersonator to be the first to enter the lodge. Meanwhile, Long Arm impersonator had erected a small post and dressed it to make it appear like an enemy standing there. The clothing, which had been provided by the pledger and his wife, consisted of a man's complete outfit and fine robe decorated with porcupine quillwork. The four warriors went to the two mounds and sang, dancing back and forth toward the small post dressed as an enemy. The fourth time they rushed the "enemy," striking him. The first to strike took the robe while the three other performers divided the remaining goods between them. This completed the Cuts Hole in the Mouth ceremony. As the dancers left the lodge, they gave the clothing stripped from the post to old men standing outside the door. The pledger paid the eight Holy Women and the berdache in robes for their services and the ceremonial shelter was ready for the fasters.

---

[46] This approach by four stages was a common pattern for Hidatsa ceremonies.

[47] Formerly all berdaches participated.

Long Arm impersonator and the pledger were first to enter, followed by the fasters. Usually all clans were represented but younger clan brothers of the pledger were usually best represented since a certain obligation was felt to help clansmen. There was no dancing the first night, only the cries of the fasters seeking visions. Each had an object from his father's sacred bundle, hoping that his father's gods would send an appropriate dream. Younger fasters imitated their older clansmen. Crying continued all night. Some would go outside beyond the limits of the village to cry, hoping to experience visions there, and return to the ceremonial lodge in the morning.

First day.—Although 1 day had been devoted to rites of erecting the lodge and another to preparing the altar and performing the "Cuts Hole in the Mouth" dance, this was all considered preliminary to the main performance. The ceremony began with the arrival of the 10 to 12 singers who were to direct the singing. Individuals desiring to qualify as singers received prior instructions and training from the Long Arm impersonator whom they paid for their rights to direct the singing and to receive pay from those fasting during the ceremony. The recognized singers performed each time the ceremony was performed. Long Arm impersonator, the pledger, and the fasters remained at the shelter during the night. As soon as the people saw the singers leaving for the shelter, they knew that the ceremony was about to begin. The entire population gathered and stood around the lodge to observe the practices; only menstruating women were barred.

As soon as the singers arrived, the Long Arm impersonator dressed the pledger to represent Spring Boy. He led the pledger to the front of the mounds where white clay which had been previously mixed with water was ready for use.[48] Using dark sage as a brush, Long Arm impersonator painted the pledger's entire body white, singing the Painting song as he worked. Black paint was used to draw a new moon on the forehead with the "horns" extending onto the cheeks. The nose was painted black. A tanned leather apron was tied around the pledger's waist and extended to his knees. Then his wrists were painted black, an enemy's scalp was tied to his left wrist and a dried human hand to his right. He wore a jackrabbit skin cap. A hoop of willow wrapped with otterskin to look ornamental was tied on his back; this hoop represented the Moon. Then his ankles were painted black. All the equipment was prepared beforehand by the instructor with the assistance of the Long Arm impersonator. Each faster received an eagle wingbone whistle.

---

[48] The white clay was secured from hills on the Knife River near the present town of Golden Valley. Long Arm sent some young man out for the clay and gave him authority to use the clay for doctoring. It was considered a high honor to be so selected.

When the pledger was properly painted and decorated, he approached the central post. This was the signal for all fasters to stand and blow their whistles. This provided the fasters with an opportunity to observe the pledger dressed and painted as Spring Boy had been prepared according to tradition when he was taken into the shelter to suffer during the first performance of the ceremony in the sky. The ceremony was directed by the Long Arm impersonator just as the original ceremony in the sky was supervised by Long Arm. The pledger danced back and forth between the two mounds and the central post where the buffalo head and hide hung. The hide and head also represented Spring Boy. In the mythology, Buffalo volunteered to take the place of Spring Boy who was tied to the forks of the post during the original ceremony at which time Lodge Boy came to free him.[49]

The parents of those fasting during the ceremony were expected to feed the singers. Whenever relatives observed that one of their young men was tired from dancing, it was customary to bring food for the singers who would then halt the rites to eat. Fasters were required to get up and dance each time the singing commenced, but the pledger was expected to dance more energetically than the others. It was customary for a clan brother fasting during the ceremony to assist the pledger, whenever the latter appeared exhausted, by assuming his place. Then the Long Arm impersonator painted and dressed the assisting clan brother in the pledger's outfit for several dances. Dancing and singing ended shortly before sunset.

Second day.—The preliminaries to the dancing were essentially the same as for the preceding day. Usually most of the young boys who had not terminated their fasts the preceding evening were no longer able to endure hunger and left during the forenoon of the second day, leaving only those who seriously sought visions. The Long Arm impersonator painted and dressed the pledger as on the previous day. Then the singers arrived and the dancing began. One wishing to endure the torture feature would go to his parents and announce his desire. They would say, "That is the way to be successful and prominent. If you do that you will have a good reputation and the people will listen when you have something to say. Perhaps you will be lucky and get the many fine horses and other things that you want. In warfare you will be lucky and strike the enemy."

In other cases an older brother discussed the matter of "running around the post" prior to the ceremony and urged him to take these steps to become lucky. In a few instances older brothers had been known to be exceedingly abusive with one showing little inclination

---

[49] The word for buffalo is *mit*E an abbreviation of *mit*Ec meaning 'I die.' It was believed that the buffalo was called *mit*E because he volunteered his body for use in the ceremony.

to undertake personal privations, but fathers usually did not speak sharply to sons unless driven to such extreme measures by their joking relatives. When a young man announced that he wished to be tortured at the post, the parents sang their sacred songs and praised their son publicly before bringing the food, calicoes, robes, and horses which were to be given to the "father" inserting the thongs. The "father" selected—always an eminent man with a good war record—would go to the young man and lead him to the post, all the while singing his sacred songs and relating the successes that his "son" too would achieve. He would say, "My son, this is a great thing you are undertaking. You will be lucky. This will make your people lucky too."

The "father" would then select two men to do the actual flesh-cutting for the insertion of the sticks. When the Long Arm impersonator was selected as "father," it was customary to name two men who had the high military honor of striking and killing a single enemy when out alone. When such individuals were not available, men with the next higher honors were selected. The "father" would pay his assistants with part of the goods, give the food to the singers, and keep the balance of the goods. The man was tied to the rawhide strip by means of the thongs and left to run and swing around the post while the relatives cried and prayed for him. When he was exhausted, he was untied from the hide; the thongs were removed by the Long Arm impersonator who pressed the flesh down and covered the cuts with white clay. Then another candidate submitted to the torture ordeal. As each candidate completed the torture ordeal, he picked up his sacred bundle and robe and left the ceremonial grounds to eat, bathe, and rest. He frequently sought a quiet place beyond the village limits to rest in the hope that he would receive a good dream.

Third day.—This day was a repetition of the second. Long Arm impersonator painted and dressed the pledger as before. This was the principal torture day and the activities began as soon as the singers arrived. Each candidate selected a "father" to conduct the rites at the post. Large crowds would gather to see what goods each faster gave to his "father" and to observe the responses each faster made to the infliction of pain. The parents would cry as their sons ran around the post. Sometimes the sticks would tear out and the candidate would be thrown across the shed or even fly through the wall. Since a young man was not freed until he was exhausted or showed fear, it was frequently impossible to accommodate all candidates.

Fourth day.—The pledger was painted as before. Normally there was no torturing on this day but Wolf Chief submitted to torture and recalled that it was not unusual. The dancing continued all day. Fasters could leave any time they wished. As before, the parents brought food for the singers whenever their boys appeared tired. Some fasters would leave for the hills to continue the fast, others would break the fast but retire to isolated spots to sleep in the hope of receiving good dreams. By this time there were usually only a few fasters left. A fasting clansman was expected to stay until the ceremony terminated in order to take the pledger's place should the latter become totally exhausted. The singers and remaining fasters left the lodge at sunset. Long Arm impersonator delivered to the pledger all the things he had worn while impersonating Spring Boy. These items became his personal property and were made into a ceremonial bundle which he cared for during his lifetime and which was placed at his grave or scaffold when he died.

The ceremony was concluded with sweat lodge rites attended by the pledger, his wife or wives, and the Long Arm impersonator at the latter's lodge. The instructor usually attended, since he had handled the sacred objects too. Special cleansing songs were sung by Long Arm impersonator while rubbing the occupants with a switch made of the dark sage. The sweat lodge participants then partook of food prepared by the wives of the Long Arm impersonator. While participating in the cleansing rites at the termination of the Naxpike, the Long Arm impersonator gave the pledger the right to doctor injuries from falling limbs or trees. This right to doctor could be sold four times independently of Naxpike performances. The lodge was left standing until it fell down. When the ceremony was next performed, a new site was selected.

We see that a Naxpike performance provided a formal institution for the transfer of bundle rights from a father to his son. In addition, it provided an opportunity for others to fast and thereby receive vision instructions to purchase their own fathers' bundle rights to this and other ceremonies. The ceremony also provided the public with an opportunity to observe young men's abilities to endure the torture features of the ceremony. Having performed the Naxpike did not entitle one to take the part of the Long Arm. This bundle right was sold independently to a son or sons who had formerly performed the Naxpike, but, in historic times at least, there seems to have been no inclination to maintain more than the one bundle line originating at Awatixa village.

There was reluctance on the part of men to marry widows who had participated in the ceremony with their late husbands and it was said that the decision whether or not to marry largely rested with the man. This was in line with native concepts that supernatural powers were controlled by certain rules which the uninformed would not know. Women of bundle owners frequently made a public vow during the husband's funeral rites that they would not remarry.   There was one important exception to this rule; the widow could marry the deceased husband's brother or one who owned the same bundle rights without bringing bad luck to the husband since they were familiar with, and had participated in, the ceremony. Since this rarely happened, widows of bundle owners generally remained unmarried as in the case of Mrs. Good Bear who took the vow when her husband died and was never asked to marry thereafter.[50]

The ceremony has frequently been compared with the Mandan *Okipa* as though the two ceremonies were identical.   This is not the case.   The entire drama involved quite different culture heroes and settings.   By comparison with the complex Mandan *Okipa*, the Hidatsa *Naxpike* is a very simple rite.   Maximilian wrote:

They likewise celebrate the Okippe (which they call Akupehri), but with several deviations.   Thus, instead of the so-called ark, a kind of high pole, with a fork on the summit, is planted in the centre of the open circle.   [Natives insist that this is not true; that the ceremony was always performed at the edge of the village.   These dancing spots can still be identified at several of the old village sites.]   When the partisans of the war parties intend to go on some enterprise in May or June, the preparations are combined with the Okippe of several young men, who wish to obtain the rank of the brave, or men.[51] . . .   The partisan [pledger] is bound to build the medicine lodge.   During the ceremony the spectators eat and smoke; the candidates take nothing, and, like the partisans, are covered all over with white clay.   The latter, when they dance during the ceremony, remain near their pits, and then move on the same spot, holding in their hands their medicines, a buffalo's tail, a feather, or the like.   None but the candidates dance, and the only music is striking a dried buffalo's hide with willow rods.   There have been instances of fathers subjecting their children, only six or seven years of age, to these tortures.   We ourselves saw one suspended by the muscles of the back, after having been compelled to fast four days.   [Maximilian, 1906, vol. 23, pp. 377–378.]

I doubt that the ceremony was called *Akuperi* since that is the term by which the Mandan Okipa ceremony is known today.   His description of the Naxpike ceremony, which is the only one employing the forked post, is essentially the same as described to me except that, in later years, the principal torture feature was performed on the third day and fathers did not subject their sons to torture unless requested by the son (and then at an older age).

The Charles McKenzie account of 1805 (McKenzie, 1889, vol. 1, pp. 354–357) from his observations of a performance at Hidatsa village indicates that the torture feature was more severe at that time than in 1879 when Good Bear performed the ceremony.   He mentions simultaneous "assembly line" piercing of the flesh of a number of

---

[50] I asked several men why they did not marry her and each said that she was holy and they would have bad luck.

[51] Maximilian is correct that the rites stimulated military activities; those who had good dreams were always quick to test the potency of their dreams by going out to take possession of the property promised them by the supernatural.

candidates and the fastening of the thongs of different candidates to buffalo heads, the number to which the candidate was tied depending upon his military reputation. Although Mrs. Good Bear did not observe anyone so tortured when her husband performed the rites, an individual frequently requested a "father" to pierce his skin so that he might drag buffalo heads through the village on other occasions. Perhaps the fact that the population was so much smaller in her time provided time for all who wished to receive torture at the post. McKenzie mentions those warriors who had killed the enemy as wearing skulls and scalps while fasting. This was not a practice unique to Naxpike; fasters frequently wore human bones on other occasions or fasted near the scaffolds and graves of their own people or near heaps of bones belonging to the enemy. The practice of throwing the buffalo heads over a beam in order to suspend the candidates was not employed in later years at Fishhook.

In former times, according to Mrs. Good Bear, it was customary for the pledger to offer flesh and fingers to the gods above during the performance of the ceremony, but in her time this was not done; in fact, it was optional to the pledger whether he submitted to personal torture. Rabbit Head did, but her husband did not. In McKenzie's time old women of the Holy Women society who prepared the grounds also chewed Black Medicine root which they spat on the wounds. In Mrs. Good Bear's time, although she knew of the above practice, the Long Arm impersonator provided white clay for cleansing the wounds.

McKenzie correctly describes the practice of taking the finger tips and flesh to the edge of the village as an offering to the Sun since the Sun and his sister were cannibals who ate human flesh and decoyed people into battles so that they could eat. Although the Hidatsa Naxpike has undergone numerous changes since first described in 1805, the same changes were being made in other ceremonies also.

As the Hidatsa culture changed under the impact of White culture, the Naxpike was no longer considered a means chiefly of attaining supernatural powers through the medium of the sacred arrows to become skilled hunters and warriors with the arrow as a weapon. Mrs. Good Bear interpreted her husband's dreams preliminary to performing the ceremony in terms of existing values as of 1879:

All of the things that Good Bear saw in his dreams or was promised by Porcupine Pemmican and the other men came true. The first time he was away to war he struck a Sioux. He afterward learned that the man in the white collar and dressed in fine clothing was the Roman Catholic priest. And the shiny thing that he saw coming down from above that he thought at the time was the hoop used in the Naxpike he learned after he joined the Church was the Holy Ghost coming down from Heaven. Because he saw the two bulls that belonged to the White man, he had many cattle. The boxes of goods stacked in front of the long house he afterward learned represented the store that he had for a number of years. Porcupine Pemmican promised him during the ceremony that he would be a leader among his people and the Government named him a judge to try Indian cases and he was judge until he died.

Expressed in social status, one giving the ceremony—although highly respected—did not otherwise enjoy a higher position than those who had performed other socially recognized rites.

WOMAN ABOVE AND HOLY WOMEN CEREMONIES

According to native traditions, shortly after First Creator and Lone Man had created the earth and the male animals, a mysterious or holy woman named Village-Old-Woman living in the southland learned of this new land. She resolved to create females of each species created by First Creator and Lone Man in order to perpetuate life, and to give the people female creatures to worship. For each species of living males created by the other two culture heroes, she created females to serve as gods as well as food for the people who were to inhabit the earth. Long after she had done this, she heard of the people living near the Knife River and followed the Missouri River underground to its source in the Rocky Mountains, failing to find the village. In her searches for the people she dug deep trenches, producing the valley in which the stream and its tributaries flow.

She returned underground to Knife River where she entered the womb of a young woman and thus was born into the village. When she grew to maturity she created the "Holy Women in the groves of the four directions," Woman Above, and all other female deities. From time to time she introduced new ceremonies and practices which the people adopted. Because she created both the Holy Women and Woman Above, she introduced many common sacred objects for these sacred bundles and ruled that whenever a ceremony was performed, rites should also be performed for the Holy Women whom she had created.

According to native belief the two ceremonies—Holy Women and Woman Above—did not begin at the same time. The Holy Women are mentioned in the myths of Unknown Man prior to the founding of the Naxpike rites and it is believed that rites to these women go back to the beginning of time when the two sexes were created and Village-Old-Woman was born into the tribe, bringing to the people her supernatural powers. In the Unknown Man myth the Holy Women bring meat and cover the scaffolds during a fog sent to the village by Two Men (see p. 307). Reference to the Holy Women is made in most of the ceremonies.

In historic times the Holy Women religious society was composed of aged females who had bought their rights individually from their

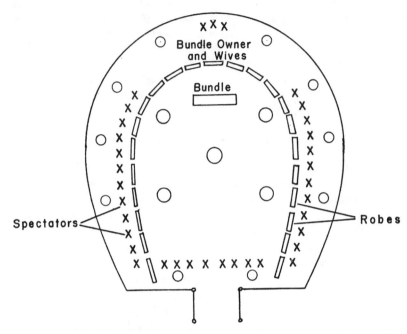

FIGURE 3.—Ceremony to the Sun, Moon, and Woman Above. (Drawn by Wolf Chief.)

mothers after dreaming of the Holy Women. In this sense the organization differed from the White Buffalo Cow and Goose societies which, although religious in character, were group-purchased. Membership was composed chiefly of daughters of women possessing rights in the Holy Women organization and wives or sisters of Woman Above bundle owners. All individuals meeting these requirements did not, at least in early historic times, seek membership. This was due, according to native interpretations, to the failure to obtain appropriate dreams or the inability to amass the required property to complete the purchase. There was, however, an increase in popularity of the White Buffalo Cow society, the members of which were women of about the same age; it is possible that the Holy Women organization suffered from this competing society.

The leader of the society was the Village-Old-Woman impersonator and the other members represented Holy Women of the groves of the four sacred directions. They selected a male singer who met with them. In historic times Cherry Necklace was singer until his death. When no one offered to buy his rights, the women performed without a male singer. The singer bought his rights from the society but particularly from the Village-Old-Woman impersonator. Since Village-Old-Woman created all of the other female deities, the singer occupied a ceremonial position superior to all male owners of Woman

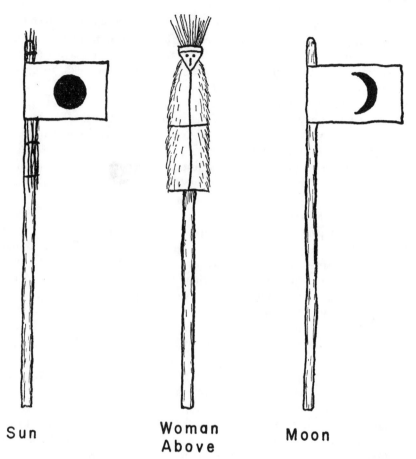

Sun   Woman   Moon
             Above

FIGURE 4.—Ceremonial appointments for Woman Above ceremony. (Drawn by Bears Arm.)

Above bundles. Each village had Holy Woman representatives; in fact, they were represented in the Mandan villages also. The Mandan had even gone one step further and had named one of their clans, the *Managoctadomak* or "People in a Grove" from these Holy Women. The organization was composed of about 20 members, including the village berdaches, according to the recollection of my informants, but new members were not taken in during later years and the number never increased.

These spirit women were identified with the magpies that lived in the ash and oak groves. All dressed alike in mountain sheep dresses painted white. Each woman wore two magpie feathers in her hair and a braid of sweetgrass on her left shoulder. Each painted a red oval on each cheek and sometimes on the forehead. Each carried a stick, made of ash and decorated with white sage, about 4 feet long in her right hand, using it as a cane. Their red-painted robes were rolled up and carried under the left arm. The singer carried a similarly painted robe under his left arm and red drumsticks, using his robe as a drum whenever the group sang. Although the four directions were represented in the total membership, no distinctive dress or painting distinguished members of the various directions. The mother sold rights only in the direction which she represented and could sell four times before relinquishing her rights. In the purchase of singer rights, males seeking to join the organization secured the assistance of a clan father as instructor, following the same pattern indicated for the purchase of Naxpike rights.

The organization met whenever a tribal ceremony was being performed; their role differed between ceremonies. They also met and danced whenever a successful war party returned. In aboriginal times they represented an important group, in fact, the only group that could claim some rights of participation in every ceremony. This was by virtue of the fact that the organization was associated with every ceremony that involved deities created by the Village-Old-Woman impersonator. Of all the ceremonies, the Holy Women were considered to be related most closely to the Woman Above rites although, according to native concepts, this ceremony was established very late after Grandson had founded the Stone Hammer society and some time before the first horses were acquired.

The customs of the berdache were based on native concepts that for a man to dream of Village-Old-Woman or a loop of sweetgrass was an instruction to dress as a woman and to behave as a special class of "females." It was believed that when a man saw a coil of sweetgrass in the brush he should look away, otherwise the Village-Old-Woman or the female deities whom she created would cause his mind to weaken so that he would have no relief until he "changed his sex." Often a man would tell of his experiences, how everywhere he looked he would see the coiled sweetgrass and how hard he was trying to keep from changing over. Those who made the change and assumed feminine attire and activities were pitied by others. The people would say that he had been claimed by a Holy Woman and therefore nothing could be done about it. They were treated, until recently, as mysterious and holy. Since they had been "claimed" by a Holy Woman, they met with the organization and performed many tasks otherwise too difficult for the women, such as raising the posts for the Naxpike ceremony. They dressed and painted in the same way as the Holy Women for ceremonial occasions. Inasmuch as the organization of Holy Women was considered to be a benevolent group, doing much to assist the people in time of starvation, berdaches were well thought of, although pitied. Young men going to war would ask supernatural aid of the Holy Women, receive a sacred object to wear, and, if successful, prepare feasts for them.

According to native beliefs, the Woman Above ceremony did not reach the tribe from "above" until very late in Hidatsa history.[52] Only three bundle lines were unbroken by the epidemic of 1837: Twisted Wood of Awatixa sold to Crows Paunch; Seven Dogs of Awatixa sold to two sons, No Tears and Dogs Urine; No Tears sold to Hairy Coat; and Small Ankles sold to Red Basket, brother of Wolf Chief. It is not certain whether the rights came to Small Ankles from his stepfather, a Mandan, or Old-Man-Shoots-With, his own father. It is suggested by Wolf Chief that it came from the Mandan stepfather. If that is the case, organized bundles existed only at Awatixa. In the case of the Seven Dogs bundle line, only No Tears sold to his sons for Dogs Urine later showed cowardice by pushing his daughter from his horse when they were pursued by the Sioux. After she was killed, he dropped all of his rites, put all of his bundles away on the prairie, and no longer participated in any social or ceremonial activities. He entertained no friends and avoided meeting people. Although his son, Sitting Bear, tried to get ahead, he was ashamed of his father and would have nothing to do with his father's rites.

By contrast with the Hidatsa village groups, seven distinct bundle lines were preserved by the Mandan with whom the rites were highly developed with numerous sacred myths and skull circle shrines on the adjacent prairie. The bundle rites were practically identical for the two tribes and those having rights in the ceremony met together irrespective of tribe, a practice which it is said they followed even before the two tribes united at Fishhook. The poor representation of bundle lineages for Hidatsa and Awaxawi village groups and the highly developed rites and practices of the Mandan indicate that the beliefs had been formalized into ritual performances for the Mandan somewhat earlier, and that the Awatixa, who have the longest traditional residence on the Missouri, had the highest development of the rites and beliefs. The Hidatsa-proper and the Awaxawi, who were traditionally last to take up residence on the Missouri, had not gone very far in establishing these bundles.

According to native conceptions, the following sacred tradition, given in condensed form, provided the basis for the establishment of rites to Woman Above:

There were great and powerful spirits above. One household up there consisted of a man and his wife, one daughter, and two sons. The older son observed the Hidatsa below and, liking their habits, indicated a desire to go down there to live.

---

[52] For matters of organization of the data, I have recorded it at this point because of its close psychological ties with the Holy Women rites. For an actual bundle purchase, see pp. 405–409.

His father said that it was a hard thing to do and gave him instructions in getting into a young woman's body so that he could be born into the tribe. The father sent him down that evening when the stars came out, warning him not to forget who he was.

The young man walked into an earth lodge and turned himself into a kernel of yellow corn. He was eaten with the mush. In time he was born. His father's sister wrapped him in a hide tanned at the smokehole and he forgot himself.

He grew to be a large boy and, one evening while playing with burning corncobs on arrows, his father from above came down to refreshen his memory but the boy became angry and ordered him away. The old man and his wife above called the boy back and he died to return to the sky.

The younger brother asked to go down to the earth and promised that he would not forget his true identity. He, too, was wrapped in the smoke-tanned hide and lost his memory. When he was 18 years old, his older brother living in the lodge told him that it was now time to begin fasting so that he would become a prominent man in the village like those he saw about him. While the young man was fasting on the third night, a stranger appeared and the boy then remembered himself. He was told to go to war, that he would get one enemy on the first trip, two on the second, three on the third, and four on the fourth trip.

The young man returned to his parent's lodge and was taken to the head of the lodge near the sacred objects where he continued to fast, but he received no additional dreams. He made three trips out for the enemies promised him and everything happened just as he was promised.

Meanwhile his sister up in the sky received no offerings from him, only his father, and she became jealous. Because he did not make offerings to her also, she blessed a warrior of an enemy tribe who made offerings to her and adopted him as her "son," promising him that he would overcome seven of the Hidatsas.

When the young man went out the fourth time, the expedition was unsuccessful and seven of his party were killed by an enemy painted red and wielding a club of burnt ash wood. The young man fasted seven nights for seven different times. Each time as he came back after fasting seven nights, the other young men would come out to meet him to cry also. The seventh time during his fasting, four old women with their robes tied at the breast came from the four directions to inform him that his sister in the sky had blessed the enemy and had adopted a "son" there, protecting him with a string reaching down from the sky. They informed him that this enemy could only be killed if this young man performed rites for the Holy Women and Village-Old-Woman who created all of them, including this "sister" living above.

He returned from his fast and prepared the sweat lodge as instructed by the four holy women and they flew in from the roof through the smokehole. Since none of the women assembled there felt capable of carrying the pipe to the holy women in the sky, they sent for Village-Old-Woman who created all of them and she, too, flew into the lodge through the smokehole.

Village-Old-Woman did not believe that the Woman Above would take the pipe since she had already adopted a young man living with the enemy and had already promised him that he would be victorious over the Hidatsas. Nevertheless, she agreed to go above to secure a hair from Woman Above's necklace to put in the sweat lodge with the stones. She promised that, if successful in getting the hair, the young man giving the ceremony would not destroy 30 but 400 lodges.

Village-Old-Woman left for "above land" with the pipe, asking the Holy Women to come out and wave their robes at noon when Sun stopped to smoke. Woman Above refused to smoke for she had blessed an enemy and had taken him as her "son." Village-Old-Woman threw a louse onto Woman Above's head and the Holy Women below waved their robes. Woman Above became drowsy and permitted Village-Old-Woman to touch the necklace with her pipe.

Woman Above ate the corn balls, smoked the pipe, and then went to sleep. Village-Old-Woman stole the necklace, sang the victory songs, and flew down to the village where the ceremony was being performed, again entering the lodge through the smokehole.

The Holy Women placed the image in the sweat lodge pit, put the hot stones on it, poured in the water, heard the image burst, and then announced that the young man had conquered his enemies. With this assurance, the young man led a war party toward Mouse River and built two mounds [53] as Holy Women directed.

Hearing young men singing, he found that they were being led by Swallow and Hawk who were teaching them the Stone Hammer society songs.[54]

The young man selected Swallow and Hawk to kill the enemy who had been adopted as Woman Above's son and gave them instructions in cutting off the head so that it would not come back to life again.

During the fight, the leader of the enemies was seen coming into the conflict, painted red on the forehead and cheeks with a robe of calfskin and wearing magpie feathers in his hair. All the time he was protected by a string reaching down from a small cloud overhead.[55]

Swallow and Hawk cut the string, causing their enemy to lose his supernatural powers originating with Woman Above. Woman Above came down from the sky, carrying her ashwood stick in her right hand and wearing her robe with a coil of sweetgrass. She was painted red on the forehead and cheeks. She demanded the head which Swallow and Hawk had taken but they took it to their leader instead. He extended his pipe toward the head, which died. Then the eyes closed.

After removing the scalp, he gave Woman Above the head which she failed to bring to life again. The war party returned to the village where the Holy Women danced the scalp dances and received many presents. They sewed scalps to the young man's shirt, for he was now a chief, and gave him the name Young-Man-Chief. Whenever the warriors returned successfully from war the Holy Women would dance. When times were hard, they would butcher animals and put the meat on the scaffolds for the people. The rites were passed down from generation to generation. Because Young-Man-Chief did not make offerings to his sister above, the people learned that she was holy so they prayed to her too. Village-Old-Woman was represented recently by Fast Dog's grandmother and Cherry Necklace was the singer for the Holy Women.

---

[53] Similar mounds pertaining to these beliefs together with medicine poles are erected adjacent to the villages as shrines for the arrangement of skull circles: see Catlin, 1841, vol. 1, pp. 89–91, pl. 48; and Maximilian, 1906, vol. 23, p. 340.

[54] This incident dates the sacred myth as subsequent to Grandson's residence with the people since Grandson founded the Stone Hammer society. According to native concepts, the sacred myth is interpreted to relate incidents that occurred prior to the founding of the Earthnaming rites and the first introduction of the horse—Swallow and Hawk, who are mentioned in this rite, had died and were spirits when the Earthnaming rites were established. By relating incidents of this kind, native informants determine the relative chronological position of the various rites. For further information concerning Swallow and Hawk, see the Earthnaming rites, pp. 434–436.

[55] This description of Woman Above's "son" provides the basis for subsequent dress and painting for those Hidatsa who owned rights in Woman Above bundles. Note the close similarity of dress and painting to the Holy Women; the basis for native concepts that the Holy Women and Women Above bundle owners should meet together on ceremonial occasions.

Woman Above rites began much later than the Holy Women rites because the Holy Women were represented by Village-Old-Woman who went back to the beginning of time, while all the others were created by her.

In the mythology, Woman Above is usually associated with her brother the Sun because both were believed to be vindictive and jealous, sending good luck to the enemy when offerings were not made to them; both were cannibals and arranged battles in order to eat the victims; both consumed the flesh of dead animals; and both were responsible for hot winds that destroyed the crops. For this reason, when offerings are made at the mounds adjacent to the scaffolds and graves, both Sun and Woman Above were usually represented by poles and offerings.

The Woman Above was considered opposite in character to the Holy Women. Whereas the Holy Women were thought of as benevolent spirits, the Woman Above was thought of as an evil-dispositioned spirit to whom curing rites with Woman Above bundles were directed chiefly to avoid misfortunes such as miscarriages, premature births, insanity, and paralysis. Men dressed in women's clothing and "renounced their sex" as a result of frequent visions sent by her and coils of sweetgrass placed in their paths by this mysterious woman or one of the Holy Women. Of the four berdaches remembered by Hidatsa informants all were sons either of a Woman Above Bundle owner or of a member of the Holy Woman fraternity. For that reason, the berdache was considered holy because Woman Above had "captured" him. He was considered a "prisoner" of the Woman Above and was authorized to participate in all ceremonies pertaining to the Holy Women with whom he was classified. Since women were barred from actual participation in certain rites, he was their representative when heavy work was required.

In view of the apparent absence of Woman Above rites or, at most, their slight formal organization in Hidatsa village on Knife River, it would appear that the berdache had there a ritualistic role stemming from the Holy Women rather than with Woman Above. The Awatixa group, however, with both Holy Women and Woman Above ceremonies, was organized in the same manner as the Mandan where many formal bundle lines and rites survived to the present day. In detail, the Mandan and Awatixa rites are so similar as to indicate the diffusion of the complete complex from one tribe to the other even to the skull circles which were ceremonial grounds established by the Woman Above bundle owners. Apparently, only the Awatixa of the three Hidatsa village groups on the Missouri had definite Woman Above bundle lines although the Small Ankles-Wolf Chief line may have come from Hidatsa through Small Ankles' own father. In any event, there is little evidence that the

Hidatsa-proper and Awaxawi gave the rites to Woman Above as much emphasis as did the other village group, the Awatixa. The Holy Women, however, are mentioned in both Hidatsa creation myths and seem to represent very old rites which had a wide distribution within the Mandan–Hidatsa groups. The Woman Above myth is considered to be a segment of the Sacred Arrow myth thought to be connected with the older Awatixa agricultural group on the Missouri.

At this point it is noteworthy to observe that the Woman Above rites were associated with certain beliefs and practices relating to the human body after death and that there seems to be a relationship between the development of Woman Above rites and the disposal of the dead. There are numerous references in the literature dealing with the Mandan concerning "skull circles," mounds, and posts with offerings which informants readily recognized as part of the beliefs and rites performed to Woman Above. She and the other gods above were believed to consume the flesh of those placed on scaffolds, after which the skulls were placed near one of these Woman Above or Sun shrines as a fasting ground for those seeking supernatural powers.

These beliefs seem to have been deeply rooted in Mandan culture. Primary earth burials, except in or adjacent to the lodge, have been exceedingly rare at all of the long-occupied Mandan villages. Instead, we commonly find secondary bundle burials of adults without the skull in all of their Heart River villages which indicate that the body had been exposed to the air, probably until the flesh had all decayed, when the skulls were taken to these skull shrines. The other bones were wrapped in hide and buried in a shallow grave adjacent to the village or within the refuse accumulation of the village itself; apparently without ceremony. Of the two large Hidatsa groups, the Hidatsa-proper and the Awatixa, it is worth noting that the latter group, whose villages on the south bank of the Knife River show occupation for two centuries or more, have scarcely a grave adjacent to the village, a situation such as is encountered at the old Mandan villages. The Hidatsa-proper, whose village ruins indicate a much shorter period of occupation, have a large and extensive burial area extending for more than a half mile to the west.

Further evidence that cultural differences existed in native beliefs concerning cannibalism by Woman Above is indicated by the fact that both the Mandan and Awatixa had several sacred bundles containing human skulls, whereas none have been reported or are known of for the other two Hidatsa villages. The high development of Awatixa beliefs and practices concerning the Woman Above rites, although never as highly formalized as with the Mandan, indicates that native traditions of separate migrations of Hidatsa groups to the Missouri over a period of years are valid, and that of all these groups, the Awatixa are probably the original Hidatsa group to reach the Missouri.

The bundles were identical as to content. In fact, most Mandan bundles contained essentially the same articles and the songs and rites were identical. A complete bundle contained 1 large gourd rattle, 12 short ashwood sticks decorated with white sage, braided sweetgrass, an enemy's scalp, a jackrabbitskin, magpie feathers, white down from an eagle, a bundle of white sage, and a buffalo skull. Bundle purchase followed the tribal pattern in that sons bought their rights from their fathers after receiving visions interpreted as instructions to make the purchase. Usually one first made offerings through renewal feasts for the father's bundle after winning war honors while wearing some object, usually a magpie feather supplied by the father who had prayed that his son would be successful. It was customary for a son to put up feasts to his father's bundle even though not contemplating the purchase of the rites, and to receive some object from the bundle as recognition of his efforts.

New bundles were assembled when a complete purchase was to be made. On selling the fourth time, the original bundle was relinquished. A clan "father" was selected as instructor to assemble the articles, direct all preliminaries, and arrange for a bundle owner with singer rights to officiate during the bundle transfer. The ceremony was of 1 night's duration.[56] When the purchaser wished to have singer rights, it was necessary to get extra instructions from one having those rights. The seller prepared an extra rattle or purchased one from one who was too old to officiate or from the widow of a former singer. The rights to the rattle and to be singer were transferred at a feast for those holding rights in Woman Above bundles. In recent years those Mandans having rights in Woman Above and other female deities also met with them.

Bundle renewal was an important responsibility of a bundle owner. It was customary for the bundle owner and his family to perform a renewal rite occasionally, at which time they were assisted by their clans in accumulating the goods. At the termination of the rites, the family would be nearly propertyless but it served a useful purpose in demonstrating that "supernatural possessions were to be preferred to material wealth." Their relatives usually replenished their material needs. Individuals, particularly those whose fathers belonged to the bundle owner's clan, often pledged feasts to the bundle if they returned from a successful military expedition. Other "sons" and "daughters" sometimes pledged feasts before a military adventure was undertaken. All the leading bundle owners of the tribe, those

---

[56] See pp. 405–409 below on the Sunrise Wolf rites for a detailed account of a bundle transfer.

whose sacred bundles contained buffalo skulls, were invited to feast and to receive gifts. The sacred songs were sung and each gift recipient prayed for the success of the giver. At the close of the feast three ash poles were set in the ground outside of the village to represent Sun, Moon, and Woman Above. Two mounds were constructed with sage at the top and human skulls were placed in circles surrounding the image of Woman Above. Fasters frequently went to these shrines to fast.

Since Sun and Woman Above were believed to be cannibals, offerings of flesh and the tips of fingers were often made to them. There were doctoring rites to cure those manifesting mental disorders, also rites to cause an enemy to "lose his mind" so that he wandered about aimlessly on the prairies to be killed by Hidatsa war parties and to be "eaten" by Woman Above. Since the ashwood stick was a part of the sacred equipment, those who suffered injuries from falling trees called in a bundle owner to set broken bones and repair their injuries.

Old-Woman-Who-Never-Dies and Related Ceremonies

After providing the traditional setting for the Naxpike ceremony (Sun Dance) and the Holy Women society, the Sacred Arrows myth introduces incidents leading to the adoption of another group of other closely related ceremonies. Because Grandson or Old-Woman-Who-Never-Dies, or both, participated in certain supernatural events during the sacred mythological period, the rites having traditional origins at that time are believed to be related. Thus, individuals possessing sacred bundles representing these experiences were entitled to attend rites performed for one of the related bundles. No individual owned complete rights in all of the related bundles.

The Sacred Arrow myth, which provides the mythological and traditional origin of the bundle rites of the complex, begins at the point where Two Men terminate their instructions to Unknown Man in the Naxpike rites and inform him that he is the first to make the Sun Dance brought down from above. The Sacred Arrow myth in abbreviated form from that point follows:

Three young women out in the trees gathering wood discover a porcupine. They select the youngest one to climb the tree and shake the animal down. The tree grows as she climbs until she reaches the world above when she is taken to Woman Above's lodge where two sons, Sun and Moon, live.[57]

Moon is in the lodge with his mother for he was the one who had decided to marry the girl. Sun comes in at sunset and announces that he has married a Toad Woman. Toad fastens herself to Moon's back when he teases her, a right he has since he is her brother-in-law.

---

[57] This Woman Above is not to be confused with her daughter also named Woman Above to whom rites were performed.

A son is born to Moon and the girl from below. Meadowlark tells the son he does not belong up there. Moon forbids his wife to dig "wild turnip's sister" and in digging one she finds the hole in the sky. Moon's wife makes a rope of the sinews from one buffalo but Moon did not include all of them so the rope reaches only to the tree tops. Moon's wife and son attempt to escape down the rope and Moon discovers them hanging at the end of the rope at the level of the treetops. He drops a stone, directing it to kill the woman but to spare his son.[58]

The son remains around his mother's body which falls near a large garden cared for by Old-Woman-Who-Never-Dies. Discovering a child's tracks in her garden, she wonders whether they are by a boy or a girl. She makes a bow and arrows which will be taken if it is a boy and a ball if it is a girl. Finding the bow and arrows taken, she knows that the tracks have been made by a boy so she looks for him and takes him to her lodge near by.

She forbids him to roast the red corn, giving him permission to use any other variety. He roasts red kernels; they turn into blackbirds which he kills. She appears pleased but she takes them outside and frees them for they are her helpers in the gardens.

She forbids him to go into a certain thicket but he goes there and finds a large grizzly bear who does not kill him for the bear is afraid of the boy's father, the Moon. So he takes the bear to his grandmother to serve instead of a dog. [This act introduces the Bear rites and relates them to the Old-Woman-Who-Never-Dies rites.]

During the evening he hears Two Men singing love songs to Old-Woman-Who-Never-Dies from a village on the north side of the river.[59] Meanwhile he observes that his grandmother feeds someone who is staying under her bed and behind the curtains.

The grandmother forbids him to go to Red Hills but when she was not in sight he goes there and finds that the hill is full of snakes. The snakes tell the boy that they are eagle trappers and that the lodge arrangement is for the ceremonial capture of eagles. [The myth at this point describes the lodge arrangement for the rites of eagle trapping and explains that the snakes were the first eagle trappers to set up the altar.]

The snakes bite into a paunch, leaving their teeth there, and offer it to the boy who roasts the paunch. This burns their teeth and they all run out. The snakes address him as "Grandson," for they and all other snakes represent the husbands of Old-Woman-Who-Never-Dies.

The snakes ask him to tell them a story. Grandson tells how the buttes make a noise like the wind and then it is quiet again; part of the snakes go to sleep. The streams make a noise like the wind and then it is quiet again; half of the snakes are asleep. The large trees make a loud noise in the wind and then it is quiet again; only a few snakes are still awake. The wind blows hard and then it dies down; all of the snakes are asleep.

Grandson kills all of the snakes except the last one which goes into a hole. This snake warns Grandson never to lie on his stomach to drink. [This red hill provides the name for one of the Mandan clans, the MasƐdomak or "Red Hilled People," receiving the name from Clay-on-the-Face who provided the names of the seven clans making up one moiety. I could find no evidence that the Hidatsa clan names were in any way associated with this hill situated less

---

[58] For a picture of this stone, now a shrine to Old-Woman-Who-Never-Dies, and another version of this myth, see Beckwith, 1938.

[59] This site was excavated by the Smithsonian Institution in 1952. The artifacts—particularly pottery— observed by this writer, appear to give the site a date of late prehistoric period, Heart River Focus.

than a mile southeast of the Holding Eagle home in the Fort Berthold Reservation.]

Grandson learns that it is a large snake, Old-Woman-Who-Never-Dies' husband, who consumes the food placed back of the curtains, so he kills him. The large snake is placed in Short Missouri which from that time on, though it had no inlet or outlet, never went dry.[60]

One day Grandson observes that his grandmother is bathing in the river. Each time she submerges and comes up again she is a little younger. The fourth time she comes up as a young woman. This way she never grows old and dies. Then he knows that she is the one who has control of the vegetation, causing it to grow each year when the water birds come north and the snakes appear.[61]

She comes to fear her grandson for he has killed her husband. Grandson drinks water while lying on his stomach and the snake from Red Hill enters his body, going up into his head. Moon asks Thunderbird, Wolf, and Sun to assist him in freeing their son from the snake.[62] Grandson is freed from the snake and punishes him by rubbing his nose with a sandstone until Snake agrees to be harmless and never to disturb people again if the rest of his face is spared.[63]

Two Men come along and butcher a buffalo for Old-Woman-Who-Never-Dies but Grandson, who is helping them butcher, sees a foetus in the buffalo which frightens him so he climbs into a tree. Long after this Two Men discover Grandson dead in the tree and restore him to life.

Two Men ask Grandson to inform his grandmother that they will bring supernatural powers to Grandson by "walking" with the grandmother. Grandmother tells her grandson that Two Men have endeavored to marry her but she has always refused them for they travel around all the time as the arrows. She, however, can't do that for she is the custodian of the gardens and must stay in one place.

She informs her grandson that Two Men are bringing the Sacred Arrow ceremony and that during the ceremony he must select the oldest bow and arrows if he wants the ones with the greatest supernatural powers. [This section of the myth provides the setting for the origin of the Arrow rites as well as relating them to Old-Woman-Who-Never-Dies rites.]

Grandmother dresses one of her helpers, a white-tailed deer, to impersonate her, putting two small pumpkins in the dress to provide the form of the breasts. Then Old-Woman-Who-Never-Dies hides until the ceremony ends.

Grandson calls for all the gods to come and they appear. First Creator agrees to be Waiter if Two Men will invite him. During the rites, each of the gods takes the deer outside for intercourse but First Creator, who is last, is suspicious and does not think he had intercourse with the real Old-Woman-Who-Never-Dies. Grandson takes the oldest bow and arrow which is the holiest one so Two Men are not so lucky afterward in hunting.

Grandmother is angry at Two Men because they asked to "walk" with her. She has a sacred whistle which she uses to bring rain for her gardens but which brings storms and snow if blown at other times.[64] Since the whistle, when blown

---

[60] This body of water within the valley of the Missouri rises and falls according to the level of the Missouri. It was a sacred shrine for both the Mandan and Hidatsa, particularly those who sought supernatural assistance in growing gardens. Both men and women fasted there. Crow Indians also fasted and made offerings here when passing through.

[61] She is one of the original characters who, like First Creator and Village Old Woman, were not created by any other god but who were in existence at the first creation. She occupies the same position as "goddess" of vegetation that Village Old Woman did as "goddess" of the females of the animal species.

[62] Note that the four are considered brothers, and fathers to Grandson.

[63] He is also introduced into numerous medicine bundles to the Snakes.

[64] This whistle from the sunflower stalk is a part of all Old-Woman-Who-Never-Dies bundles and was used to bring rains while the crops were growing.

during the winter, brings the cold and drives the game away, she instructs Grandson to fly into the air and blow the whistle, driving the animals off. Two Men are starving and promise to give a medicine feast if Grandson will come down and stop blowing his whistle.

Two Men send Grandson for the hide of the Chief of the Antelopes to be used in the rites. Grandmother prepares the antelope's hide for covering the basket used in the ceremony. Two Men, First Creator, and all of the gods come to the ceremony during which Grandson permits Two Men to hold the sacred bow and arrows until their supernatural powers have in part been returned to them. [The narrative here accounts for the sacred basket covered with antelope hide which was a part of the Old-Woman-Who-Never-Dies bundle.]

Old-Woman-Who-Never-Dies continues to live near Short Missouri with her Grandson and both are very holy. All this time Two Men travel around a great deal for they are in reality arrows. Long after the Chief of the Antelopes was killed, the Hidatsa–River Crow come to the Heart River and cross there onto the west side. One young man goes up the Heart River to fast, thinking that some new spirits might reveal themselves and he receives a vision from Sunrise Wolf who instructs him to go on the warpath. [This dates the origin of the Sunrise Wolf rites.]

This Village-Young-Man comes upstream to Short Missouri where his party is fed by their "grandmother." She feeds them in clay pots and instructs them to stir the food when it is low and the pots fill again. She promises them success if they go to the west, saying that they will find seven enemies wearing wolf hides around their bodies and carrying bows without bark. She asks for one of the scalps to hang on the side of her basket. The war party finds the seven enemies (pl.9), kills them, and brings a scalp to their grandmother. She tells them that whenever they want to get the best of their enemies, they should promise her something. [This incident is used to explain the presence of scalps in a sacred bundle primarily concerned with agriculture.]

By this time the people learn where she has her lodge and come there frequently to eat. Heretofore, as she caused her gardens to thrive, the gardens of those she blessed also thrived but she was annoyed by their frequent visits. So she instructs the people through visions how to perform the rites and hunters discover that she has disappeared and abandoned her lodge and gardens. The hunters see a ring of stones to the southwest where her tipi had stood. Long after this Two Men discover that she has taken up residence far to the south on a large island where she cares for her gardens and is guarded by four water monsters. They learn that the spirits of vegetation, particularly the corn and other garden things, spend the winter with her, coming south with the waterbirds in the fall and returning with them in the spring.[65]

One day Grandson returns to the earth lodge at Short Missouri to discover that his grandmother is gone and her lodge and gardens are deserted (see also Woolworth, 1956). He goes south to a village downstream from Knife River to live with Water Grass whom he adopts as "friend." Grandson has the sacred whistle which brings rains for the crops if used during the summer but which drives away the animals when used at other times.

Grandson does not reveal his identity, but First Creator comes to the village and tells the people that the stranger is Grandson who came down from above.

Grandson informs Water Grass that they will found the Stone Hammer society and he gives his friend instructions in the rites and meanings of the objects used. He tells Water Grass that the pole across the smoke hole represents the pole his mother put across the hole in the sky when they came down, that the string used for the necklace represents the sinew his mother used to come down from above, that the red side of the hammer represents the sun and the black side the moon, and that the road followed by Sun and Moon in their travels across the sky will be represented by two lines. Grandson rules that those who buy will later sell to those they call "sons." He rules that it is proper for them to steal food during the nights when the ceremony is being performed.

Water Grass forgets and blows the whistle during the cold weather and a severe storm drives the game away. Grandson leaves the village with his wife and pitches a tipi where he performs rites which bring the stars down carrying buffalo meat which they place around those lodges that have a pipe set out for the stars to smoke. After that the people would put a pipe by Grandson's lodge and the stars would come down to eat and smoke, bringing buffalo meat with them.

But Yellow Dog, the founder of the four Dog societies, has designs on Grandson's wife. [The myth has now dated the mythological origin of the Stone Hammer, Little Dog, Foolish Dog, Dog, and Old Dog societies.] Yellow Dog takes liberties with Grandson's wife. Grandson and the gods from above are bringing meat to the village when he discovers her unfaithfulness and attempts to leave. His wife steps in front of him and attempts to stop him with the pipe. He makes a zigzag path where he steps around the pipe and announces that those who follow this track in the future without falling will live to be old.[66] Then Grandson and the gods return to the sky.

The people are angry at Yellow Dog and will not feed him. The people move to new hunting grounds upstream but Yellow Dog is so weak that he cannot travel. Grandson imprisons all game in Dog Den.[67]

Grandson's wife assists Yellow Dog and marries him. First Creator discovers the condition of the people and assists Yellow Dog in rites to save the people from starvation.[68]

First Creator advises Yellow Dog to throw turtle fat into the fire and the "Leader of the Wolves" will help bring the game.[69]

First Creator turns into a young buffalo bull and brings a herd of buffaloes near the village, is shot in the thigh, and runs to Dog Den where Grandson removes the arrow. Then First Creator asks Grandson to stop punishing the people as the people are not starving. Grandson sends Fox to Yellow Dog's camp to learn the news. Fox is taken in a deadfall, fed by the people, and returns to report that Yellow Dog's people are not in want.

First Creator goes out and brings another herd of buffaloes to Yellow Dog's camp. Grandson sends Chickadee to Yellow Dog's camp; he, too, is trapped, taken to the camp, and fed. He returns and reports that the people are not starving. Again First Creator begs Grandson to free the animals.

---

[66] This happens about 1 mile south of Sanger, N. D.

[67] In the Mandan sacred myths it is the Hoita of the Okipa rites who imprisons all the animals. The Hidatsa seem to have no organized rites to dramatize this imprisonment of the animals.

[68] Note that First Creator holds supernatural powers superior to Grandson, for the former represents one of the original characters who created the lands. Still, as far as it was possible to determine, there was no First Creator ceremony although he assisted in many rites. There seem to be no tribal rites originating from the "freeing of the animals" other than references to the incident in the Dog society songs of the age-grade system.

[69] The turtle is also associated with the buffalo on other occasions. Throughout Hidatsa hunting territory are numerous turtle effigies arranged from boulders and situated on high hills with the head pointed toward the river (pl. 6). Nearby are piles of stones on which individual offerings were made to clear the fogs so that the buffalo herds could be found.

First Creator brings Yellow Dog's people another herd of buffaloes; Grandson sends out the Red Fox and he reports the people are not starving. Again First Creator asks Grandson to free the animals.

First Creator brings Yellow Dog's people a fourth herd of buffaloes and shortly afterward Grandson sends out Mousehawk who is captured, fed, and freed to return to Dog Den where he reports to Grandson that the people are not starving. Again First Creator asks Grandson to free the animals.

Grandson sees that he is defeated. He enumerates the many things he did for the people while he was on the earth for which, never once, did he ever receive any offerings or pay. He now rules that since he never once received an offering, if people of any village ever make an offering to him hereafter, that village will be destroyed.[70]

Then Grandson returned to the sky for all time. He is one of the large stars [Venus] and never is seen in the sky during the summer while the buffaloes are calving for he is afraid of a foetus or a newborn calf. Neither does he, in his travels across the sky, appear near the Moon, his father, for his father was instrumental in causing the death of his mother when she attempted to escape from above.

The myth of Old-Woman-Who-Never-Dies provided the basis for native beliefs and practices for the propagation of the cultivated crops and she was considered the "goddess" of all vegetation. It was probably with this latter belief that she was associated by non-agricultural groups in the area such as the Crow and Cheyenne. The Hidatsa thought of her as the custodian of all vegetation that ripens or sheds its leaves in the fall and is "rejuvenated" in the spring with the northern flights of the waterbirds which she accompanied. She was equally regarded as the "producer" of wild fruit crops; occasionally, offerings of calicoes and meat were offered to the shrubs and bushes. Many of the unorganized household rites relating to her showed considerable variability.

In light of the universal distribution of Old-Woman-Who-Never-Dies rites in the Mandan and Hidatsa villages, the existence of Corn rites among those groups such as the Cheyenne who no longer practiced agriculture during the 19th century, and similar myths for the Crow where there were no organized Corn rites, it would appear that the native view of Old-Woman-Who-Never-Dies as "goddess" of vegetation was an early belief that preceded agriculture. Only in the earth lodge villages of the Mandan and Hidatsa do we find these myths organized into formal rituals. For the Mandan we find that the Corn rites have been associated with the Women's Goose society (Densmore, 1923, pp. 183–205) which was organized by Good-Furred-Robe to dance during the northern and southern flights of the water birds and whenever the gardens suffered from drought. Nowhere in the Hidatsa sacred myths do we find reference to the origin of the Goose society. Consistent with Hidatsa concepts that those institutions

---

[70] I found no evidence that offerings were made to Grandson.

and customs for which there is no origin myth were recently borrowed from other tribes, we find them explaining the presence of Women's Goose societies in the three Hidatsa villages as recent adoptions from the Mandan.

The unequal development of Corn rites between the Hidatsa and the Mandan seems to have a direct relationship to the relative importance of agriculture to the two tribal groups. The Mandan and Awaxawi were considered more stationary than the Hidatsa by most early explorers. Henry (1897, p. 338) wrote in 1805 that—

> The Mandanes and Saulteurs (Awaxawi) are a stationary people who never leave their villages except to go hunting or on a war expedition. They are much more agricultural than their neighbors, the Big Bellies (Hidatsas), raising an immense quantity of corn, beans, squashes, tobacco.

Of the Mandan and Hidatsa village groups on the Missouri, the Mandan seem to have gone farther than their Hidatsa neighbors in the development of Corn rites. Their exodus myth from underground was ritually expressed through Corn and Fertility rites associated with Good-Furred-Robe, Cornhusk Earrings, and Uses-His-Head-for-a-Rattle, and their sister, Corn Silk, who taught that gardens were sacred. The exodus of the Corn spirits and their migrations were symbolically represented by the objects in the Sacred Robe bundle. The Goose society, likewise, was definitely integrated into these Corn rites. The Old-Woman-Who-Never-Dies as "goddess" of fertility, on the other hand, was represented both by independent rites closely resembling those practiced by the Hidatsa groups and as fused or composite bundle rites associated with the myths of the exodus from the ground.

The Mandan believe that the Old-Woman-Who-Never-Dies rites and bundles represent the older rites of the Heart River area as practiced there by the earliest population, the Nuitadi. They also feel that the Good-Furred-Robe and Skull bundle rites reached the region much later by migration of southern Mandan groups, the Nuptadi and Awigaxa. The concept of the settlement of the Heart River and Sanger region by successive migrations is substantiated by the archeology of their traditional sites. (The outline of the Old-Woman-Who-Never-Dies lodge is rectangular, similar to those found at the Huff and Clark's Creek sites of early Mandan who have traditions of former rectangular lodges, but the Hidatsa have no such traditions.) This concept seems reasonable in light of the fact that there were traditionally never more than two of the Sacred Robe and Skull bundles, both of which are still preserved, whereas the number of Old-Woman-Who-Never-Dies bundles was sufficiently great to be represented in each aboriginal village.

According to Hidatsa traditions, however, the Goose society was bought from the Mandan shortly before 1800 and the Skull bundle reached the Awaxawi through intermarriage after 1837. According to the Mandan, this society and bundle both are late additions to their rites by migration of southern groups out of the Grand River to the region intermediate to the mouth of the Knife and Heart Rivers. If we eliminate these two additions to the Hidatsa Corn rites, the Old-Woman-Who-Never-Dies rites would be common to both tribes and represent the most popular Corn rites before the last Mandan migration northward. The Old-Woman-Who-Never-Dies myth as related by people of the two tribes, shows only a few insignificant differences dealing chiefly with Grandson who, in the Hidatsa myth, founded the Stone Hammer society.

Probably no Mandan or Hidatsa myth is as widely related and discussed as that of the Old-Woman-Who-Never-Dies. Most of my informants had performed rites of one kind or another to this "Old Woman," ranging from simple household cleansing rites after a day in the fields to the major bundle transfer rites when buying from their fathers. Likewise, the varieties of ritual forms within one village were greater than for any of the other ceremonies. The simplest and most universal rites were performed by women as individuals or household groups of females and consisted primarily of simple offerings of meat and pieces of hide placed on sticks in the garden during the northward or southward flights of the water birds. This was often done without benefit of public gatherings or payments to bundle owners. On other occasions a woman, while working in the garden, often dreamed of those spirits associated with the gardens and set up within her garden a high post on which a newly composed personal sacred bundle was hung as a "protector" of the garden. It was customary to bring these sacred bundles to the lodge when the crop had been gathered and to return them to the gardens again in the spring at the time of cultivation.

A woman who allowed her sacred bundle to hang in the garden all winter, however, would have bad luck. The story is told of a woman of the Prairie Chicken clan who dreamed that the Wolf Woman would work in her gardens all day and appear at the camp of warriors far from the village when the ribs were cooking.[71] She forgot to bring in her bundle and during the winter a wolf came into camp and bit her on the nose while she slept. When the men came, hearing her cry, they killed the wolf and found that it was so old that its teeth were worn down to the gums. After that the name Bites-in-Nose was given to young men of both the Mandan and Hidatsa tribes.

---

[71] See Wolf rites, below, for an account of this woman.

In addition to the simple ritual practices involving only the females of a household, there were those practices which centered around the Old-Woman-Who-Never-Dies sacred bundles of which there was one major bundle in each of the three Hidatsa villages of the Knife River prior to 1837. These bundle owners organized and managed the village rites during the period of the spring northward and fall southward flights of the waterbirds. Prior to planting the crop, individuals would pledge to have the rites performed if the crop was bountiful or the household enjoyed good health. After the pledge was made, there followed a period of preparation. At the appointed time a ceremonial feast was given, during which those possessing rights in the Old-Woman-Who-Never-Dies bundles, the animals and birds mentioned in the sacred myths associated with the bundle, and all others who had secondary rights in associated bundles, were authorized to attend. Each received goods and prayed for the giver's success.[72]

There were three bundle lines at the time of the smallpox epidemic of 1837: Hidatsa village represented by Bears Heart's bundle; Awaxawi village represented by Bear-Looks-Out's bundle; and Awatixa represented by Crow-Flies-High's father's bundle. Each bundle was equal to the others in status. At this time the Mandan had two types of Corn ceremony bundles; those which were concerned chiefly with rites to Old-Woman-Who-Never-Dies as described in the sacred myths, and a second bundle complex of two bundles which additionally represented dramatizations of the myth of the exodus of the people as corn spirits from the ground and their various experiences until reaching the Heart River. Mandan informants state that since there were only two Good-Furred-Robe bundles, several villages had only Old-Woman-Who-Never-Dies bundles while others had both kinds.

The final diffusion of the Women's Goose society to all Hidatsa village groups appears to have taken place during the early part of the 19th century. Nowhere in the Old-Woman-Who-Never-Dies sacred myth is there reference to this society. Nevertheless, the Old-Woman-Who-Never-Dies bundle owners were, in all villages, the singers for this society during the entire period of recorded history. According to Hidatsa traditions, the society was bought from the Mandan who have a tradition of its founding by Good-Furred-Robe to dance whenever the gardens needed rains. At first the Hidatsa society did not wear the duckskin or gooseskin headbands, only carrying bundles of sage in their arms. But, since the recent union of the Hidatsa and Mandan societies, even that distinction no longer exists (Lowie, 1913).

---

[72] These rites are described in considerable detail by Curtis, 1907 a, pp. 148–152.

According to Hidatsa traditions, the three village groups did not simultaneously adopt the Goose society to assist the Old-Woman-Who-Never-Dies bundle owners. The society was first to reach the Awaxawi through the Mandan living near Painted Woods; the Awatixa were second, and the Hidatsa were last. This would seem to confirm beliefs that the Hidatsa-proper were relatively late to adopt agriculture while the other two village groups had a relatively long history of agriculture, the Awatixa on the Missouri above the Mandan villages and the Awaxawi on the stream courses to the east.

Recent changes in the culture patterns resulting from bundle buying would indicate that the Hidatsa have greatly enriched their Corn rites chiefly as a result of Mandan contacts. Immediately after the smallpox epidemic of 1837 Bear-Looks-Out, Old-Woman-Who-Never-Dies bundle owner of Awaxawi, married into the Mandan family owning the Skull bundle of the three culture heroes who led the corn spirit people from the ground. His Mandan father-in-law, Red Bird (also known as Different Pipe), had been a leader in the Mandan Corn rites and was singer for the Goose society. Red Bird was discouraged when his only son died after the epidemic had run its course and then indicated a desire to dispose of the bundle which, in spite of the high price he had paid for it, had not brought his family good luck during the epidemic. Bear-Looks-Out indicated a desire to buy the bundle with his wife, Corn Woman of the Mandan Prairie Chicken clan, and the sale was made with the approval of the Mandan of the Mitutanku village group.   The bundle is popularly known as the Good-Furred-Robe Skull bundle. Sale by a man to his son-in-law was a common Mandan pattern.

The bundle represents the three brothers and their sister, children of Corn Father. The children are believed to have been separated from their father during the exodus from the ground at a point downstream near the mouth of the Mississippi when the vine was broken by a pregnant woman who attempted to come to the surface. The bundle contains the skulls of the three brothers, Good-Furred-Robe, Cornhusk Earrings, and Uses-His-Head-for-a-Rattle; white sage; corn silk; a headdress of foxskins; and a wooden pipe (Bowers, 1950, p. 186, fig. 24).

The Skull bundle was obtained by the Awaxawi at the time of the union of the Hidatsa and Mitutanku Mandans for the building of Fishhook Village. Although Bear-Looks-Out kept the two bundles separate, both were taken to ceremonial functions, thus providing a situation wherein both the Mandan and Hidatsa groups were entitled to meet collectively for Corn rites. As singer to two Goose societies, it proved more convenient for the two societies to meet simultaneously with both the Mandan and Hidatsa singers. This arrangement was followed as long as the Nuptadi Mandan remained below the Knife River. The great prestige of the Mandan Corn rites is indicated by the fact that Bear-Looks-Out was selected over all other Corn bundle owners to represent the southern direction when Fishhook Village was built. Concerning this event Curtis (1907 a, p. 138) wrote, quoting Bear-Looks-Around (Out), "My lodge shall represent the lodge of Old-Woman-Who-Never-Dies. It shall stand to the south whence the warm winds come that they may cause the plants to grow. As her garden prospered so shall it be with my people."

As long as the Mandans remained divided into two groups, those of Nuptadi living below the Knife River and the Nuitadi at Fishhook Village with the survivors of the Hidatsa villages, only two Goose societies existed. The Hidatsa and Mandan at Fishhook had a single society whose singers were the Mandan and Hidatsa Old-Woman-Who-Never-Dies bundle owners and the Skull bundle owner. At Nuptadi village, the singers for the society were the Robe bundle owner and Old-Woman-Who-Never-Dies bundle owners. When the final union of the Mandans at Fishhook occurred around 1860, a reorganization of the membership of the Goose societies occurred. The Mandan formed a single society with the Robe bundle owner as the principal singer while the three Hidatsa village groups met independently with the Skull bundle owner as principal singer. This situation continued until part of the Hidatsa separated under Bobtail Bull and Crow-Flies-High to build near Fort Buford. Those women who had rights in the Goose society organized anew at Fort Buford, but for a number of years had no singer. Then Crow-Flies-High "took up" his father's rites in the Old-Woman-Who-Never-Dies, which had died out at his death in 1837 from smallpox, and the women then invited him to become their singer. Fishhook Village continued to support two Goose societies; a Hidatsa society with Bear-Looks-Around (Out) and later Poor Wolf the principal singer, and a Mandan society with Moves Slowly the principal singer. Bear-Looks-Around had the Mandan Skull bundle and Moves Slowly had the Robe bundle. Only at Fort Buford was the Goose society organization not associated with a Mandan Corn bundle.

Although the Goose society, Old-Woman-Who-Never-Dies, the Skull, and the Robe rites tended to fuse into a single ritual containing features of all four ceremonies during the 19th century, complete union of the four ceremonies had not been achieved when the aboriginal societies collapsed. Each bundle ceremony had its separate songs and rites which were still recognized by the older informants at the time this study was made. The singer, when performing at the request of the Goose society, sang only the society songs unless paid to enrich the ritual by singing the Old-Woman-Who-Never-Dies, the Skull, or the Robe songs.

Individuals receiving dreams associated with the Old Woman, the Skull, or the Robe bundles could bypass the Goose society members in performing rites and frequently did. And female membership of the Goose society was of unequal status in respect to their relationships to the male bundle owners. Some women had put up goods collectively to purchase the society and held their rights in the society until a younger group bought them out. On the other hand, there were numerous women who had dreamed of the sacred bundles relating to agriculture or had assisted their husbands or brothers or both in performing rites to the Old-Woman-Who-Never-Dies, Skull, and Robe bundles as well as buying with their group into the Goose society. These women retained rights to meet even after they had sold rights in the Goose society to "daughters." This special group also included the wives and sisters of Old-Woman-Who-Never-Dies, Skull, and Robe bundle owners.

The Goose society, although associated with Old-Woman-Who-Never-Dies, had all the characteristics of a separate ceremony. These women kept their own pipe, drums, and sacred paraphernalia when the society was not performing and did their own singing and conducted all of the ritual acts when no singer was available. The Hidatsa thought of the society as an addition to the long-established groups.

The Old-Woman-Who-Never-Dies rites are a dramatization of the sacred myths, and the bundle was associated with these plants, animals, and birds mentioned in the myth:

corn	elk	blackbirds
beans	deer	geese
pumpkins	bear	ducks
sunflowers	dogs	cranes

Bundle purchase was a 4-night ceremony attended by all those whose sacred bundles contained buffalo skulls. Traditionally, only those with rights in Old-Woman-Who-Never-Dies bundles and those ceremonies mentioned in the myth attended prior to the epidemic of 1837. The number of legitimate owners was so small after that date, however, that the category of those invited to attend and to pray for the success of the bundle buyer was increased to include the principal bundle owners for the other tribal rites. Purchase was from the father, and a father's clansman was selected to make up the new bundle and give ritual training. The father's clansman also selected the singer for the rites. The singer approached the ceremonial lodge by the usual four steps, singing a different sacred song belonging to the ceremony at each of these stations where the buyer and his wife met him to deliver the sacred wooden pipe and a robe. It was customary for the same group of relatives to assist in putting up the goods as when any other tribal ceremony was being performed. The Goose society did not meet as a group but individuals who had qualified formerly by giving ceremonial feasts to the Old-Woman-Who-Never-Dies could attend. During the bundle transfer, the buyer fed the participants and spectators, received the blessings of the sacred bundle owners, and paid those who were entitled to attend and to participate.

The contents of a principal or complete sacred bundle varied slightly between village groups, whether Hidatsa or Mandan. There was, first and foremost, a corn basket covered with a tanned antelope hide from which the hair had been removed. The corn basket frame represented Old-Woman-Who-Never-Dies and the antelope hide represented Chief-of-the-Antelopes who was killed by Grandson on orders of this old woman. The Sacred Arrows referred to the visit of Two Men to her lodge when they gave Grandson his choice of arrows in return for "walking" with the grandmother. The human scalp referred to her assistance to Village-Young-Man who once came to her lodge to eat and rest before going to the west to get the seven enemies she had promised him. A wooden pipe with the carving of a goosehead on the stem represented the goose as the harbinger of spring and the termination of the growing period in autumn. Two clay pots represented the sacred pots which were once placed on the shore by the Snake people and which were used to feed visitors.[73] By stirring the contents of the pots, the vessels could not be emptied. The headdress of foxskin represented the fox who served as messenger for Grandson when he imprisoned the animals in Dog Dens. White sage was used to cleanse people; it was kept in all households, and after the women returned from working in the gardens they used it to cleanse their bodies from the corn spirits and to remove insects picked up in their work. The gourd rattle represented one of the garden plants. A piece of elkskin was included since the elk assisted her in the gardens; a deer skull and horns were included also, for the deer, too, were her servants. A piece of bearskin was included because Grandson once tamed the grizzly bear to become her helper in place of dogs which she formerly worked. Blackbird heads were included, for they were her helpers—eating the insects in the gardens—and are also mentioned in the myth. A circular drum decorated with goose tracks was sometimes also included. Corn, particularly yellow corn, beans, pumpkins, and sunflowers, and a whistle made of the stalk of the sunflower, representing the whistle used by Grand-

---

[73] Pottery is generally associated with the snakes and water. It was customary when making pots to shape them in a secluded and dark place, as in an earth lodge with the entrance and part of the smoke hole covered.

son to drive away the animals and punish Two Men, were also included. When blown in summer the whistle brought rains; in the winter it brought blizzards. These were the primary sacred objects of a principal bundle, according to Mrs. White Duck whose father, Poor Wolf, owned the Awaxawi principal bundle. She thought that there had formerly been a snakeskin in the bundle also but that he had sold this to a "son" who had dreamed of the snake belonging to the bundle and that it had never been replaced. Old-Woman-Who-Never-Dies' husband at Short Missouri was a large snake, and, in her southern home, Two Men once discovered that four large "grandfather" snakes associated with water guarded her island home from trespassers.

The list of objects contained in Bobtail Bull's Mandan bundle, according to Mrs. Owen Baker, was the same as reported by Mrs. White Duck.[74] This would indicate that even for the Mandan before their union with the Hidatsa, two almost identical Corn ceremonies were celebrated. By contrast, the Robe bundle owned by Moves Slowly had these objects: a buffalo robe said to have been worn by Good-Furred-Robe, on which was painted a map of the world showing the Missouri River as a huge snake and the hole through which the people were believed to have passed in reaching the earth; a carved wooden pipe showing the head of a goose; headdress of fox-skins; white sage; buffalo hide moccasins with hair to the inside; clay pot (it had been broken and was never replaced); a piece of elk hide; gourd rattle; corn silk; three ears of corn (white flint, yellow, white soft); strip of badger skin; several blackbirds and one green-head duck's head; a deer skull to rest the bundle on; three dried squash; a sunflower head; and a robe made of kit fox hides.

The ceremonies were restricted entirely to the period from the first appearance of the waterbirds in the spring to their fall flight southward. The principal rites were performed at the beginning and end of the period. It was customary also for the Goose women to meet at these times whether paid to do so or not. Until the old culture broke down, there were usually several meetings in the spring and again in the fall, and at other times when invited to dance.[75] Usually a number of people pledged to have the Goose society dance and put up goods and meat for the spring dances. The fall dances, by contrast, ushered out the summer garden period. Dances at that time were said to please the water birds which, as messengers of the Old-Woman-Who-Never-Dies, upon reaching their winter homes with

---

[74] This Bobtail Bull was killed July 13, 1851, and should not be confused with the Bobtail Bull who led the Hidatsa to Fort Buford.

[75] See Lowie, 1913, vol. 11, pp. 330-338, for a description of their rites; Boller, 1868, pp. 147-149; Curtis, 1907 a, pp. 148-152.

the corn spirits whom they guided south, reported the various offerings that had been made to her. As a token of her thanks for these offerings, it was believed she would send the winter buffaloes near the village so that the people could live well until the next crop could be planted and harvested. Certain women claimed to have corn spirits in their body. Occasionally, especially during corn rites, this spirit would appear in the woman's mouth, and payments were made to her to "make the spirits go back down." Women sold these mysteries to "daughters" independently of the other corn rites.

Curtis (1907 a, p. 134) describes an instance in which the Goose society was bypassed in securing supernatural powers directly from the Old-Woman-Who-Never-Dies:

> During the growing season the owner of the field took a buffalo robe as a gift to one of the Corn Priests, asking him to pray to Old-Woman-Who-Never-Dies and to the spirits that controlled the weather, that the corn might thrive to ripeness. The priest returned with the husbandman to his lodge, and there burned incense and held a stalk of corn in the sacred smoke, praying that the crop might prosper, and be plentiful. He then passed the stalk to the owner of the field, saying, "Keep this," and it was hung in the sacred place of the lodge as a token of a bountiful harvest.

It frequently happened that one made the request before the gardens were planted. In this instance a young shoot of the cottonwood was substituted for the corn plant. Others, however, made requests for supernatural assistance to win over their enemies in battle. A young man would go to a bundle owner who stood in the "father-son" relationship and pledge that he would give a feast for the Old-Woman-Who-Never-Dies and decorate her basket with a scalp if he won over the enemy. If successful, after the scalp dances had been celebrated, a date was set for the decoration of the basket. Food was prepared. As many robes and other things as possible were collected from his household and other cooperating relatives. Then the bundle owner was invited in with his sacred bundle. Prayers were offered to the "son" and some object from the bundle was given him for his personal use. In general, however, the bundle rites were concerned chiefly with garden crops.

Maximilian (1906, pp. 372–373) writes of the sacred pots used in connection with rainmaking rites as follows:

> She gave the Minitaries [Hidatsa] a couple of pots, which they still preserve as a sacred treasure, and employ as medicines, or charms, on certain occasions. She directed the ancestors of these Indians to preserve the pots, and to remember the great waters, from which all animals came cheerful, or, as my old narrator expressed it, dancing. The red-shouldered oriole came, at that time, out of the water, as well as all the other birds which still sing on the banks of the rivers. The Minitaries, therefore, look on all these birds as medicine for their plantations of maize, and attend to their song. At the time when these birds sing, they were directed by the old woman to fill these pots with water, to be merry, to dance and

bathe, in order to put them in mind of the great flood. When their fields are threatened with a great drought they are to celebrate a medicine feast with the old grandmother's pots, in order to beg for rain: this is, properly, the destination of the pots. The medicine men are still paid, on such occasions, to sing for 4 days together in the huts, while the pots remain filled with water.

Native informants were in general agreement as to the Old-Woman-Who-Never-Dies' beliefs contained in the above statement by Maximilian, but none could recall a ceremony in which clay pots were filled with water. Within their memory clay pots were used to hold coals with which to incense the objects in the bundles. When these pots were broken, in recent years, large sherds were used. When dramatizing the visit of Village-Young-Man to Old-Woman-Who-Never-Dies' lodge, when clay pots were in general use, it was customary to stir the contents of the pots and to say that the food renewed itself. The participants would leave a portion of the food in the vessel for the snakes.

Closely associated with the Old-Woman-Who-Never-Dies' rites were the Tying-the-Pots rites. Informants insisted that this ceremony, practiced only at Awaxawi, had quite a different traditional origin and was established after reaching the Missouri River.

Grizzly Bear Ceremony

This ceremony was performed to the grizzly bear and the sacred arrows and should not be confused with a small black bear ritual for eagle trapping. The Hidatsa recognize two classes of Grizzly Bear bundles; the hereditary bundles which have their traditional origin from the bear captured by Grandson to serve as his grandmother's [76] servant, and personal bundles obtained by vision. The latter class was based on visions, often obtained as the result of being mauled by bears as in the recent cases of Old-White-Man and Foolish Head. These bundles have no long history of inheritance and no traditional sacred myths. The rites were simple and often had only one or two wordless songs. They were the personal property of the vision recipient; feasts were rarely given to the bundle. When the owner of the bundle died, the bundle was put away and, unless sold to a close relative, the songs were soon forgotten. In spite of the personal character of these bundles, we find the vision recipient receiving directions to doctor; the principal role of the hereditary bundle rites. In many respects the personal bundle rites and beliefs partake of the hereditary bear rites without the restrictions imposed by tradition. Not uncommonly, a personal bundle temporarily occupied a relatively high status due to the personality of its owner.

---

[76] She is the Old-Woman-Who-Never-Dies.

Another closely related bundle was the Bear Bullet bundle rites originally instituted as a result of a vision. These rites also took on a hereditary character; those Bullet rites which were instituted as substitutes for the Sacred Arrows of the Bear bundles assumed the hereditary character of the bundles, while those Bullet rites which were instituted by visions independent of hereditary bundles tended to die out.

The data on this ceremony were contributed chiefly by Bears Arm, the hereditary owner of the principal bundle of Awaxawi (frontispiece). The relationship of the bundle and the rites to other hereditary bundles is indicated by the sacred myth and his interpretations of the pattern of the rituals. A condensed account of the sacred myth by Bears Arm follows:

Charred Body, a holy arrow, found a hole in the sky and looking down, saw a new world much like that above. He came down as an arrow and established a village of 13 households representing the 13 parts of an arrow. (See fig. 1.) He returned to the sky and invited 13 different family groups to come down and occupy the lodges previously constructed.[77] From the beginning, life on the earth was difficult as there were many evil spirits bent on exterminating the village. First Creator came along and volunteered to be the waiter whenever a ceremony was given.

Charred Body's sister, while alone, had a visitor who forcibly removed her unborn twins which he named Spring Boy and Lodge Boy but who, when they grew up, were known as Two Men. They were very holy and destroyed many of the gods residing in that neighborhood. Of the two, Spring Boy was considered the more offensive and he was taken back into the sky to suffer ceremonially, which deed led to the establishment of the Naxpike ceremony. The two boys returned to the earth, grew to maturity, adopted a son named Unknown Man, and taught their son the Naxpike ceremony. They also taught the Arrow ceremony.

One time they prevailed on Moon's son, named Grandson, to have his grandmother, Old-Woman-Who-Never-Dies, put on a ceremony to which were invited all the sacred beings who agreed to "adopt" sons in the tribe for the future, thus helping their sons to get ahead. By doing that, they expected these sons to make offerings to them according to the particular tastes of the various spirits.

The Grizzly Bear, who was one of Old-Woman-Who-Never-Dies' helpers, took as "son" a young man named Brave-While-Young who became a successful hunter and eagle trapper after that.[78] He went out for four successive seasons hunting and trapping eagles, and each year he was very successful. He failed to make an offering to the grizzly bears and, whenever the gods met at medicine feasts after that, they teased Grizzly Bear about his selfish son who never gave him anything and seemed to have entirely forgotten his "father."

Grizzly Bear resolved to punish his son, so on Brave-While-Young's fourth hunting and trapping expedition, Grizzly Bear stole the young man's wife and two children, taking them to his lodge in a dense cedar thicket. A year later when the young man returned, he was alone. He cried for his wife. Grizzly Bear directed

[77] This traditional site is situated on the east bank of the Missouri River a few miles below Washburn, N. Dak.

[78] In historic times grizzly bear bundles did not carry eagle trapping rights. These rights went with the small black bear.

the young man to the lodge where the family lived and informed Brave-While-Young that he should perform the Bear ceremony the following year when all the holy people would attend.

Brave-While-Young worked 1 year preparing for the ceremony. Twenty robes and twenty pairs of moccasins were needed, for the bear has ten fingers and ten toes. Spring Boy and Lodge Boy were to bring their holy bow and arrows to present to Brave-While-Young. All the animals would be there and the buffalo, bear, elk, deer, and dog would have special parts. Two Men would make the rattle, cover it with an owl's skin, and decorate it with raven feathers; First Creator would provide a snare with which to catch the enemies. The gods would bless the young man and wish him success. The buffaloes would stay near the village. He would be able to doctor the sick with the bear and remove arrow points or other foreign objects from the body with the aid of the sacred arrows.

When the appointed time came, the gods arrived and the ceremony was performed as outlined by the grizzly bear. All the Grizzly Bear bundles began with that ceremony although variations occur in some family lines because of subsequent visions.

Bears Arm traced his Bear bundle rites back patrilineally to his great grandfather, Crow Bull, of Awaxawi village. He believed, however, that there was an unbroken patrilineal line from Two Men and Brave-While-Young to Crow Bull even though he did not know and had never heard the names of the intermediate bundle owners. There were hereditary bundle owners in each of the three former Hidatsa villages where ritualistic differences between villages were assumedly no greater than between individual bundle lines within the same village. Only two hereditary bundle lines were unbroken as a result of smallpox deaths in 1837. Cherry Necklace held the bundle from Hidatsa and Bears Arm's father, Old-Woman-Crawling, from Awaxawi. Purchase was inspired by repeated visions of the father's bundle or characters and events associated with the bundle. While inheritance was traditionally from father to son, one exception was made for Black Shield who, as a result of repeated dreams, bought from Cherry Necklace, his maternal grandmother's brother.[79] Later, Cherry Necklace also sold to a son, High Hump. It appears from native analyses that one not of the patrilineal line would not be denied the right to purchase a new bundle should he have appropriate reappearing visions. The first step was to put on a medicine feast to the family's bundle; then, if the visions persisted, the Bear bundle owners met and consented to a bundle purchase ceremony.

Bears Arm provided the following narrative relative to the ceremony:

Crow Bull went out fasting on the hills called Rainy Buttes for 7 days and nights at a time. Each time he fasted he had a good dream, but none of them satisfied

---

[79] Mandan inheritance from the mother's brother or the maternal grandmother's brother was a normal occurrence. Bears Arm (Awaxawi) considered Black Shield's case rather exceptional, although he could recall other purchases made through the mother line at Awaxawi village.

him. He thought that if he fasted more he would see something with his own eyes without having to dream about it. On the seventh day of the seventh time out, during the middle of the forenoon, he cut off the first finger next to the thumb. He cut all the flesh off with a piece of sharp flint and the blood spurted out.

He cried from the top of the butte. Soon he heard someone back of him singing, "He is the one I can depend on."

He looked up as a small cloud passed over the butte. There was a large bear standing on the butte, also, trying to look over the rim to see who was doing the singing. All this time Crow Bull could hear the singing at his back. The singer said, "When he (meaning the grizzly bear) does that, he always overcomes what he has in mind."

Then the cloud over the butte passed on. The voice said, "You have always wanted to see these things with your own eyes and not in a dream; now you have seen them."

Every time they passed the medicine down from father to son, there was a sacred bow and arrows with it. After Crow Bull was through with his fasting and crying, he thought he should go up the Little Missouri River where the railroad now crosses near Sentinel Butte for the enemy who had been promised to him in his dream. The Grizzly Bear had said, "Be there and though some of your men will be wounded, none will be killed for you can doctor them now."

He went to the place where he was instructed to go and sent out scouts to look around. The scouts returned to tell him that they saw the enemies coming. They waited for the enemies until they were nearer. When the enemies saw them, they climbed one of the high buttes. The men with shields were told to go ahead and all the others would follow closely behind them in a compact group. Each man, using his bow and arrows, was supported by a shield carrier who walked in front to deflect the arrows with his shield, thus protecting the man in back of him. In this way the shields protected them and in a short time they had killed all 30 of the enemies. At that time there were a few horses but no guns. These people were the Snake Indians so after the battle the people named the butte Snake Indian Butte.

Crow Bull's father had the Bear rites and when Crow Bull saw the bear on a cloud, his father thought that the bear wanted him to get the rights too. Crow Bull gathered 20 robes and 20 pairs of moccasins that he needed for the ceremony and his wife was expected to become the daughter-in-law of the bears. When she did that, she could not remarry. If she should remarry again after her husband died, both she and her second husband would have bad luck.[80]

Crow Bull gave the ceremony and was a successful leader both in warfare and doctoring, for the bears had instructed him through his father.

Crow Bull's son, Breathing, went out to the hills fasting and often dreamed of the bears. Even at home sleeping, he dreamed of the bears and that was why he took over his father's rites.

Old-Woman-Crawling, my father and son of Breathing, was married and living at Awaxawi village when the smallpox came. Even before he was married, he dreamed of the bears several times. In one dream the bear was chasing the men who were shooting at him, but the bullets would not penetrate. He had this experience several times in his dreams. He thought that he would not have the bear yet since he was not married. Once when he dreamed of the bear, he decided to get the bear's ear. Each time he had a dream from the bear, he would take

---

[80] This does not seem to apply if she married one with rights in a similar Bear bundle, particularly the husband's brother.

the ear down from the wall. There would be a bullet inside. Each time he would take the bullet to the edge of the village and put it away. Six times he had a dream and found a bullet in the ear the next day; yet he did not want to have the bear for he was still single. It was almost impossible for a single person to perform the ceremony and get the Bear rites. The Bears told him that if he took the Bullet medicines, the bullets would not go through him; still he did not want it yet. After that he did not dream of the Bear Bullet rites again.[81]

The next dream he had was of the Bear ceremony. He went into the lodge and made the pledge as a father's clansman instructed him. In the ceremony there was to be a waiter (*ixtakis*) representing First Creator. It was his duty to keep up the fires. Then there were the Two Men, Spring Boy, and Lodge Boy. Spring Boy had a bow and two arrows, one red and one black; Lodge Boy had only the two arrows, one red and the other black. Old-Woman-Crawling went out for the bear and his father's clansmen prepared the hide for the ceremony.

Bears Arm was assistant to his father, the singer, when Black Shield purchased the rights. He was the only male informant acquainted, from observation and instruction, with the details of the rites and their meaning. He never bought a complete bundle nor killed a grizzly bear ceremonially because the aboriginal culture had broken down before he had attained the proper age and had married. He supplied the following eyewitness account of a bundle purchase in which he assisted and which he believes was conducted in the traditional manner:

Black Shield dreamed of the bears several times and his mother thought that the bears wanted him to put on the ceremony for her mother's brother's bundle. Black Shield made the vow to perform the ceremony. He selected a man of his father's clan, the Low Caps, to supervise collection of materials to go into the bundle and the persons to officiate. Purchase was from Cherry Necklace who was then dead. The portions of his bundle which had not been sold had been put away. He had been wrapped in the bear hide for it was believed that when one died, he and the bear went away together.

Black Shield shot a grizzly bear to get the hide since it was required that the purchaser kill the bear whose hide was to be used during the ceremony. This was to become the principal article in the bundle. As soon as the bear was killed, a father's clansman was called to take off the skin for the purchaser was not permitted to butcher or skin the bear.

The killing of the bear was considered a ceremonial act and he said before killing the animal, "My father, I have come for you. I have a feast prepared and I need you. You will come and live with me now and when I die, we will go away together."

Then the animal was killed. The father's clansman skinned the animal and delivered the hide to the father's clansman in charge of collecting the materials for the bundle.

Twenty robes and twenty pairs of moccasins were required, together with enough corn balls and meat to feed the participants. In this case the ceremony was held in Black Shield's lodge although it was customary at Fishhook Village to use the large Okipa lodge belonging to the Mandan on similar occasions.

---

[81] For additional information on beliefs and practices relating to bullets, see "Warfare."

When the ceremony was about to begin, the First Creator impersonator carried the bear hide into Black Shield's lodge and spread it out on the right side of the lodge, placing a buffalo robe under it. The head faced the entrance to the sweat lodge which was on the opposite side of the lodge. First Creator was addressed by the name of *ixtakis*, a term of address also employed for the waiter in the eagle trapping lodges. First Creator impersonator then carried in a buffalo bull's skull. Old-Woman-Crawling was the singer for the ceremony for, in addition to buying the Bear bundle, he had also bought singer rights at an additional ceremony to the Bears. All those with Bear bundles, whether hereditary and acquired by purchase or individual ones built up as the result of dreams, assisted him with the singing.

Bear bundle owners met at Old-Woman-Crawling's lodge beforehand and advanced as a group to Black Shield's lodge. There were four stops to sing the Bear songs as they approached the ceremonial lodge.

At the first stop they sang, "I want to eat cherries," for the grizzly bears were often seen in the chokecherry thickets eating cherries.

They advanced another quarter of the distance and sang, "It is a pile of goods, I think. The gourd I will take to it."

At the third station they sang, "I want to eat cherries."

The fourth station was the entrance to the earth lodge where they sang, "It is a pile of goods, I think. The gourd I will take to it."

The four stops represented the distance from the home of the spirits to the home of the Hidatsa. In all of the ceremonies, this distance is represented by the four stops to sing and dance.

Then Old-Woman-Crawling led the way into the entrance where they sang, "I want to eat cherries."

He entered the lodge and took his place back of the bearskin, followed by the owners of Bear and other major bundles which included a buffalo skull. Black Shield and his wife took their places at the head of the lodge. The other participants took places as indicated in figure 5. Although the First Creator impersonator was assigned a place at the first central post on the right when entering, he did not sit down much since his duties kept him on the move.

Spring Boy was represented by No Milk who had given the Naxpike; Lodge Boy was represented by Frosty Mouth who was the owner of a Sacred Arrow bundle. Old Mouse made the sweat lodge in return for permission to be tortured there. He also heated the rocks and kept the fire burning. Otherwise it would have been Black Shield's duty to build the sweat lodge and heat the stones. Old Mouse called Black Shield a brother although they had different mothers. This was the reason he did it.

Old-Women-Crawling asked Black Shield to fill the pipe and have it ready. Black Shield filled the pipe and placed it in front of the bearskin. Then First Creator impersonator carried coals to the front of the bearskin and burned sweetgrass after holding the grass to the west, north, east, south, the sky, and the ground. This was an offering to the spirits of those directions. He then carried the pipe to the buffalo skull and burned incense of pine spills. The pine was offered only to the four directions, meaning that the buffaloes live only on the land. The man who burned incense before the buffalo skull lit the pipe which had been placed there, after which all the sacred-bundle owners lit their own pipes and smoked.

Old-Woman-Crawling asked the holy men to go to the buffalo skull, light the pipe, and smoke to the skull. One man lit the pipe, offered the smoke to the skull, and took goods placed on the skull. Old-Woman-Crawling produced a snare such as was used in Eagle Trapping rites, tied it to his robe, and fastened some Black

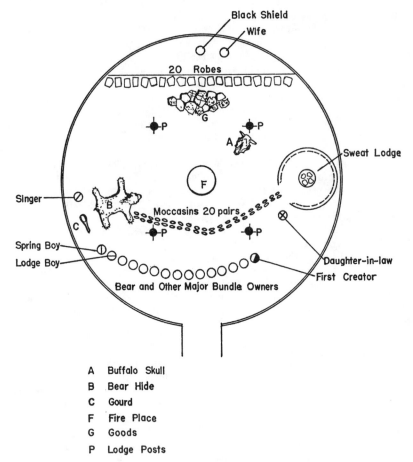

FIGURE 5.—Diagram of Bear ceremonial lodge. (Drawn by Bears Arm.)

Medicine root to the snare. This root represented Two Men and was used in the ceremony to ward off bad luck. It was also believed that the snare would capture any evil spirits that came to the ceremony.

When the snare and Black Medicine were tied to the robe, the Buffalo Song was sung four times. Each time the song was completed, First Creator impersonator added wood to the fire in the center of the lodge where the stones for the sweat lodge were heating.

According to the mythology, when this ceremony was first being given by Brave-While-Young, First Creator went to the buffaloes and told them that they should be represented in the ceremony. They selected their oldest bull to attend. As he approached the village where the Bear ceremony was to be held, he sang the Buffalo song, which became a part of the Bear ceremony, and constantly hooked his head from side to side. He appeared angry as he came into the village. First Creator saw him coming and told Buffalo that he would have to sit by himself. This accounts for the buffalo skull being placed apart from the other ceremonial paraphernalia.

While the Buffalo song was being sung, First Creator picked up the skull and hooked it from side to side in imitation of the bull's approach to the village for the first ceremony.

A male and female elk, a male and female beaver, a male and female otter, and a dog, traditionally attended the first ceremony but in succeeding ceremonies they were represented by persons owning bundles in which these animals were the principal characters. During the feast, a piece of dried meat was fed to the giver's dog. The dog was represented, as dogs were believed to be related to the bears. The bat was represented because it was believed to protect bear-bundle owners during the night. The elk was said to have been the first to arrive when Brave-While-Young gave the ceremony. Elk told Two Men that if they would permit him to attend, the people could kill the elk on slippery ice to get their teeth. Beaver came and promised the people long lives if they would drink water and vomit out the bitter things in their stomach each morning while bathing. Otter promised easy delivery for women at childbirth.

The singer was assisted by the other sacred-bundle owners. The order of singing was: Song to the male elk; song to the female elk; song to the male otter; song to the female otter; song to the male beaver; song to the female beaver; song to the buffalo bull.

Whenever the Buffalo Bull song was being sung, one of the sacred-bundle owners would pick up the buffalo skull and hook it from side to side and take the goods piled on it for his pay. A whistle had been made from willow bark and painted with alternating red and yellow stripes. This whistle was associated with the elk and one owning one of these whistles was believed to have the supernatural power to possess many wives. The clan father preparing the bundle was expected to provide one of these whistles. Black Shield received his whistle when the seven songs listed above were to be sung.

After the songs to the elk, otter, beaver, and buffalo bull were sung, the singing stopped for the feast consisting of meat and corn balls. First Creator impersonator was the waiter. He offered food to the buffalo skull and bearskin first, then passed food to the singer and bundle owners. Black Shield, his wife, and the spectators were fed last. Old Mouse and a number of clan brothers who were fasting for dreams did not eat.

The Dance of the Female Bear came next. First Creator impersonator announced, "We are going to sing the Female Bear song. Any of you women who know the Female Bear dance should get up and dance."

Black Shield stood in front of the bearskin and each time a dancer passed him, he gave her a corn ball until each dancer had four. Then the singing and dancing stopped.

First Creator impersonator put down a buffalo robe in front of the sweat lodge and my father, Old-Woman-Crawling, placed the bearskin on it. Then the waiter said to Black Shield's wife, "Come over and sit on the robe."

She walked over, removed her dress, and pressed the bearskin to her naked breast. This was known as becoming "granddaughter" to the bears. This she did through her husband who was taking the bears as his gods. If he died, only those with bear rights could take his place between the widow and the bear gods. For that reason, unless a younger brother took up the Bear ceremonies, the widows could not marry, for other men would be afraid of them.

Then my father, Old-Woman-Crawling, and I went into the sweat lodge. My father called, "We are ready now. Any of you who wish to may come in."

The waiter carried the hide back to the west wall and took corn balls over to the sweat lodge and set them down at the entrance. Old-Woman-Crawling broke up a corn ball and gave a piece to each person in the sweat lodge. He directed

Black Shield to draw an image of an enemy on the bottom of the sweat lodge pit. When the first stone was placed in the pit, each man struck the stone as though it were an enemy. Each of the first four stones was struck in that manner. Then the waiter carried in the remaining stones, the bearskin, and the buffalo skull. Old-Woman-Crawling dipped sweetgrass in water from a wooden bowl and sprinkled the bearskin and buffalo skull. All those, including even little children who did not go into the sweat lodge, came to the sweat lodge entrance and were sprinkled.

Before water was added to the hot rocks, Old Mouse, who was to fast in the sweat lodge, asked two men of his father's clan to put thongs through his wrists and both sides of his chest so that he could be hung above the heated rocks in the sweat lodge. He came to the door of the sweat lodge and said, "There are many bears and other gods gathered here. I asked Black Shield, when he was getting up this ceremony, for permission to heat the rocks because I wanted to be pierced. I am poor. I want to do this so some god may take pity on me and send me good luck."

The sweat lodge was large and Old Mouse had put up extra posts strong enough to hold him. When he was fasting at the posts, Old-Woman-Crawling said, "It is the rule that we must pour 20 buffalo horns full of water on the stones. But I do not think Old Mouse can stand that much heat. When it is hot enough, anyone can call, 'That is 20 already!' I will sing the four Bear sweat lodge songs. There are four of them. When I sing the fourth song, you will all seize the sweat lodge frame and shake it like bears shaking plum bushes to get the fruit."

He poured two horns full of water onto the hot stones. The men called, "That is 20 already," and Old-Woman-Crawling called to the waiter to lift up the cover.

They found Old Mouse hanging there unconscious; he appeared to be dead. First Creator impersonator poured water on him. Old Mouse regained consciousness and was sent home. Afterward Old Mouse said that while he was lying there he saw the bearskin in its place at the head of the lodge and thought this ample reward for his efforts. Afterward he killed two enemies, stole some very good spotted horses, and lived a better life. The sweat lodge rites completed the ceremony. Black Shield got all the things which his manager had provided for him.

Some Bear bundles included the Sacred Arrows while others did not. Buyers whose fathers held these dual bundles could buy either the Bear or the Sacred Arrow portions of the bundle or both, depending on the nature of the vision instructions. Likewise, purchase could be made separately or at the same time. If complete purchase was made with one ceremony, two clan fathers were selected, one to secure the articles for the Bear bundle and the other to provide the Sacred Arrows. There was one principal tribal Sacred Arrow bundle kept, formerly, at Awatixa village. It was kept in the Porcupine Head household, Frosty Mouth having the principal rights in this bundle at this time and passing it on to Robert Lincoln who was living when this study was made. The bundle had its traditional origin with the sacred rites at Old-Woman-Who-Never-Dies' lodge at Short Missouri and did not include Bear bundle rights. Distinctive songs and rituals were employed whenever individuals bought from their fathers or whenever Sacred Arrows were to be incorporated into other bundles. It was customary, also, for those desiring to make and use arrows for daily use to present simple offerings to an Arrow bundle owner to enhance the arrow's efficiency. Those leaving for war customarily made offerings to a bundle owner who would add arrows to be used against the enemy.

Bear bundles were primarily for doctoring. Bears were considered to be the great doctors because they cared for their own young and because of their great strength. The beaver and otter were also included in the bundle, for they too were considered to be great doctors.[82] The arrows were used to bleed patients who had swellings and infection. The bundle was also used in warfare. Bears Arm explained that only very brave men ever owned Bear bundles before guns came, for the purchaser, having made his vow, was required to kill a grizzly bear unassisted. He considered killing a bear a most dangerous undertaking since a wounded grizzly was more dangerous than any other animal the Hidatsa knew. The bundles acquired through inheritance were considered major bundles because of the possession of the buffalo skull, and owners were rated of sufficient distinction to be placed in charge of winter villages and even, as in the case of Bad Horn, to be selected as "protector of the north direction" at Fishhook Village. It would appear that this concept had universal acceptance, for Wilson secured information from Wolf Chief in 1911 which the latter restated for me when I made this study. Wilson (1934, pp. 351–353) wrote concerning the ceremonial arrangement of lodges and the selection of "village protectors" during the initial building of Fishhook Village in 1845:

> Then the medicinemen addressed Bad-horn. "You stand up and choose a place for your lodge!" "My gods are the (grizzly) bears," said Bad-horn. "The mouths of bears' dens always face the north. Therefore I want my lodge to open towards the north; my bear gods will remember them and I will wish this village to stand a long time." What Bad-horn said of (grizzly) bears is true; they always have the mouths of their dens toward the north.

Ownership of these bundles did not include the rights to eagle trapping but there were certain practices and beliefs common to both the Grizzly Bear bundle rites and the Acira or Little Black Bear rites of eagle and fish trapping. Both bundles had sacred snares made of the fiber of the "snare vine." Bear bundle snares were used ceremonially for ensnaring the enemy, while Acira bundle snares were believed to possess supernatural powers for "pulling" the eagles down out of the air to the trapping pits. White eagle down was used as a ceremonial offering to the bearskins of both bundles. The altars for both bundles were set up on the west, i.e., sacred, side of the lodge. The waiter in both ceremonies was called *ixtakis*. Beyond these common elements, the ceremonial similarities were no greater than between other major

---

[82] For additional beliefs regarding the beaver and otter, see Creek rites, pp. 380–389.

bundles.   There were no songs common to both bundles.   In spite of the fact that in the sacred mythology, Grizzly Bear was angered at Brave-While-Young for failing to make suitable offerings while eagle trapping, there is no evidence that eagle trapping was ever associated with the Grizzly Bear bundles.   Both bundle groups met when the purchase of an Acira bundle was being made and, because one dreamed frequently of bears, purchases commonly were made into both ceremonies.

THUNDER CEREMONIES

The Thunder ceremonies comprise a closely related group of separate rites performed to those supernatural beings believed to "possess the power" of producing thunder and lightning.   These supernatural beings comprise two groups, the sky gods and the water gods, between whom there were endless conflicts during the mythological period.   The welfare of the Hidatsa was generally believed to be dependent on the outcome of these contests.   There was a wide range of contests between the supernatural, chiefly involving Old-Woman-Who-Never-Dies, Two Men, Packs Antelope, Eagle People, and various water spirits such as large snakes, toads, turtles, mink, beavers, otters, and muskrats.

The Thunder rites showed a wider variation in supernatural experiences during the sacred past than other rites and, in general, the territorial settings for the incidents leading to the establishment of the rites ranged over a large area of the Northern Plains in contrast with the local character of most ceremonial origins.   According to native concepts, rites relating to thunder were established from time to time.   The oldest of these formal rites now identified by informants are concerned with the High Bird–Hungry Wolf conflict which occurred at a large lake to the northeast, generally identified today with Devils Lake, prior to the arrival of the Hidatsa-River Crow (Mirokac) on the Missouri.   In a quarrel between two brothers, Sun and Thunderbird protected High Bird from Hungry Wolf's gods.   This supernatural experience provided the traditional setting for the origin of the Thunder bundle owned by Raving Bear (AwaxEnawita clan) of Hidatsa village who sold to his son, Smells, of the Low Cap clan.   He in turn sold to his son, White Fingernails, of the Knife clan, bundle owner at the time this study was made.   In native concept, this bundle represented the oldest and came down through the years by father-to-son inheritance from the time of the residence of the Hidatsa far to the east.   Smells believed that the rites had originated on the banks of Devils Lake and, during war expeditions to that region, usually stopped on the banks of that lake to perform rites and to make offerings to his sacred bundle.   Those in his party claimed that when the wind was not blowing during the evening and there were no clouds in the sky, they could hear the large snake in Devils Lake breathing as the water lapped the shores. The Thunder bundle owned by Smells seems to have been the only one originating from supernatural experiences relating to the Exodus myth. (See pp. 298–299 for this myth.)

The Sacred Arrow myths relate the supernatural settings on the Missouri for a number of other Thunder rites believed to have originated with the original "Missouri River" peoples. The myth is one segment of the exploits of Two Men. To place this sacred myth in its proper chronological position in the system, it was customary for the narrator to relate the preceding section of the myth. This Wolf Chief did while relating the sacred Thunder myth, which, in condensed form, follows:

A village of Hidatsa live at Devils Lake; there are no clans.[83]

Two Men are living there; they are Big Medicine (Lodge Boy) and Black Medicine (Spring Boy). Because Two Men are actually arrows, they travel all over and are protected by the arrows when they sleep. Black Medicine is taken above to be tortured for killing the sacred things below. Big Medicine finds the hole and goes above. He travels from the zenith westward and reaches the village of the speckled eagles; the next day he reaches the village of eagles with white heads and tail feathers (bald eagle); the third day he reaches the village of eagles with white bars and speckles (old calumet); the fourth and last village is of the young calumet. There he finds an old woman living alone and learns that Black Medicine is there and is being tortured by Long Arm.[84]

Big Medicine learns that his brother is to be killed on the pole and buried between two mounds. Big Medicine frees his brother and Long Arm attempts to prevent their return. When they fail to cut off the [Long Arm's] hand they declare that this job is to be left for succeeding generations. Two Men return to Devils Lake where the chief is named Horn-Between-the-Water.[85]

Two Men travel to the east and shoot at a white object flying by, tie themselves together, are carried far to the southeast by a strong wind, and land on an island. They meet Old-Woman-Who-Never-Dies who formerly lived farther upstream at Short Missouri. She has her servants about her and is guarded by four large snakes living in the water surrounding her island. They hunt for her but she frees the deer they bring in for the deer are her servants. Being homesick, they ask her help to get home. She directs them to the grandfather snakes. One snake carries them on his back and is fed four corn balls; so he reaches the shore. There he swallows Black Medicine.

Big Medicine cries and Thunderbird, a white hawk, comes along. There is a dual between the bird and the snake, each sending out lightning, but the snake is killed.[86]

---

[83] This reference to the absence of clans before reaching the Missouri is commonly made. Clans traditionally originate from events or incidents relating to residence along the Missouri River.

[84] Narrator introduces listener to concepts of four eagle villages 1 day apart extending from the zenith to the horizon. It is from this fourth village, believed to be in the Rocky Mountains where the earth and sky meet, that eagles left to establish the Waterbuster Skull bundle described below.

[85] This is the first reference to Two Men in association with Devils Lake. From this point, the Exodus and Sacred Arrow narratives unite and are concerned with events on the Missouri River.

[86] This is an example of the conflicts between the sky gods and the water gods.

Black Medicine is given medicine and he vomits up the small fish and shells he had eaten while in the snake's mouth.[87]

Two Men travel on and reach a wood lodge (eagle trapping lodge) occupied by eagle people. They learn that one of the eagle children is ill because a mysterious elk stuck his horn in the boy's leg and the birds know of no way to get it out. Black Medicine uses black medicine to remove the horn and pus. [Myth here provides the supernatural basis for doctoring with black medicine, a root of the red baneberry, and lancing with an arrowpoint.] Two Men stay with the eagles through the winter until the bald eagles, the scouts for the other big birds, come north in the early spring. Bald Eagle stops and sings a sacred song belonging to the Big Bird bundle rites.

Bald Eagle states that there are many people around Devils Lake while the people living along the Missouri have many offerings out also in anticipation of the return of the big birds from the south. Offerings consisting of food and pieces of hide on sticks are placed at the edge of the villages. The eagles travel northward to receive their offerings and Two Men travel afoot.

Two Men find a large snake with a head on each end. Finding no way to get around the snake, they burn a hole through it. Black Medicine eats some of the meat and slowly turns into a similar snake. He is carried westward overland and put into the Missouri River at Bird Bill Butte. Black Medicine announces that in the future he is to be known as Grandfather. One head is at Bird Bill Butte, the other at Thunder Creek.

Grandfather announces through his brother that people may make offerings to him and the other six holy people of the Missouri River by placing objects on the river bank and they will have a long life. [This transformation provides the supernatural setting for the origin of the Missouri River rites, also for certain beliefs and practices relating to the Big Bird rites.]

Grandfather announces that he cannot return with his brother because the big snake in the river wants him. He teaches him the Missouri River songs and the rites which are to be performed, and tells his brother to inform the people that when a man braids his hair and ties it up in a knot, that will be the sign he is to have a long life. He tells his brother that all offerings to the Missouri River must be made when there is no ice on the river, announces that he will be seen for the last time the next year at Thunder Creek [on the west bank of the Missouri a few miles below the present town of Sanish, N. Dak.] when the Juneberries are ripe, and asks that their parents come to see him.

He promises to help the people when crossing the Missouri and to notify the other six gods living in the river to do likewise. [This provides the origin of rites at the time of making a bullboat to insure good luck to those using it.] He says that he eats the large intestines and that anyone can make offerings of dried intestines, call him Grandfather, and ask for good luck when crossing the river.

Black Medicine gives his sweetheart to his brother to marry and they go upstream to see him when the Juneberries are ripe. They offer him and the other six gods seven cornballs and then return to the village at sunset after the large snake has appeared for the last time.

It was about this time that the people began to leave Painted Woods and Charred Body Creek to settle at Knife River. The Hidatsa now had left Devils Lake, settled with the Mandans, and had been frightened away by two owls. Then they moved northward to Knife River also.

Packs Antelope was a great hunter because he had the medicines of the Sacred Arrows which came from Two Men. The arrows would protect him if he went to

---

[87] He vomited out the same things when Charred Body and First Creator freed him from the spring.

sleep while out hunting.   Two Thunderbirds take Packs Antelope to their nest on Thunder Buttes while he sleeps.[88]

He awakens to learn that he is on a high butte with no way of escaping.   The Thunderbird children tell him that he has been brought there by their parents to protect the children during molting time from the double-headed snake that lives in the lake on the west side of the buttes.   The Thunderbirds feed Packs Antelope meat cut from deer they have butchered.

When the Thunderbird children shake themselves, their down floats out onto the lake and the snake knows that they are now defenseless and ready to eat. The snake's two heads appear on opposite sides of the butte and Packs Antelope shoots sacred arrows into both heads, killing the snake.

The Thunderbird children instruct Packs Antelope in the rites for calling the large birds to the feast at which the snake will be eaten.   These songs were later used when announcing that a ceremonial feast for the big birds was ready.   The big birds, while assembled, change Packs Antelope into a big bird to hunt for them and he is given a wooden sword to kill with.[89]   Thunderbird's daughter teaches Packs Antelope the special song the big birds use for killing and they know, when they hear him singing this song, that he is now as powerful as they.

Packs Antelope hunts snakes for the big birds for 4 years, during which time the Grandfather in the Missouri is angry because all of the snakes are being killed off. Grandfather prepares a sweat lodge.   Then he entices Packs Antelope to come near, seizes him and pulls him under the water.   Packs Antelope is carried into the sweat lodge and caused to vomit out the snakes; he is fanned with sage until he regains consciousness.   Then Packs Antelope becomes a human again.

Packs Antelope looks up and lightning flashes from his eyes.   Grandfather gives him a low cap to wear over his eyes and tells him that from this time on he and his brothers, mother, and sisters will wear low caps and will be called Low Cap people [clan] by the other groups.

Grandfather instructs Packs Antelope to give the Big Bird sweat lodge ceremony and says that the Grandfather will be in it as the principal one.   [This explains rites both to snakes and the big birds in the Thunder ceremonies.]   Grandfather announces that he is more powerful than the eagles, for he was able to capture Packs Antelope.   [This provides the basis for snake poles and rites in the trapping lodge when out trapping eagles in the fall.]

Packs Antelope goes back to his own people south of the Knife River—the Awatixa village with which the rites of the Sacred Arrow are generally associated. He announces that he is going to give the ceremony for the big birds and notifies the people that the weather in early spring will be cloudy and rainy for 4 days, after which the birds will arrive in groups from the south.   Packs Antelope places meat on sticks and, as the birds arrive, they take the meat, return the sticks, and promise Packs Antelope success in war. [90]

The Eagles instruct Buffalo Skull to promise Packs Antelope good dreams so that he will be successful in hunting.   After this, the buffalo skull was a part of the altar.

The Eagles take Packs Antelope to the sweat lodge and promise him good health and the power to doctor; they teach him the holy songs and instruct him to keep his holy bow and arrows since that is the most important part of the bundle; they give him the sword with the marks of lightning on the side.

---

[88] These buttes are southwest of Sanish, N. Dak., and west of the Missouri.

[89] This sword was a common object in these sacred bundles.

[90] These sticks are known as Bird Sticks.   Eagles taken during the trapping period were also fed meat by means of these sticks.

The Eagles inform him that another eagle, his father, never comes that way and that meat should be put on the right side of the lodge for him when the ceremony is being performed.   This is an offering to the Low Caps.

Before dying, Packs Antelope tells the people that when he dies, he will return to the sky with his father and mother, the Thunderbirds.   A gentle rain with no lightning for the growing crops is a sign that he has returned unseen.

He tells the people that if offerings are made to the eagles, the givers will be successful; that people will no longer have the power to go around and make deep holes in the ground as he did looking for snakes; that the sight of a dead log or tree breaking down is a sign that a snake once lived there.

These myths provide the supernatural setting for, and the meaning of, the various rites and practices whereby the supernatural powers promised the people reached individuals of the tribe.   With few exceptions (such as the exploits of High Bird and Hungry Wolf associated with an earlier eastern residence, and the more recent exploits of Packs Antelope which take place along the Missouri River) the rites and traditions were also shared by the Mandan who, in recent years, usually attended all Hidatsa performances.   Although the Hidatsa recognize differences in ritual practices and beliefs said to arise from different group histories—no doubt more apparent in earlier times when the three village groups first came together near the Knife River—the Hidatsa system of bundle transfer tends to erase these differences and to unite variants of the same rites into a single complex by the custom of engaging a father's distant clansman as instructor once geographical distance between village groups was reduced.   One was usually informed of all details of the father's rites beforehand through living together in the same household.   The instructor, however, rarely drew on the giver's father's lore for his learning but rather from another who held singer rights or broader knowledge than his clan brother could have provided.

Often, by the time one got around to meeting all the prerequisites to bundle purchase, the father was dead.   The father played a minor role in the actual transfer.   This practice provided for wider contacts when making a ceremonial purchase, for it gave the instructor wide leeway in choosing his assistants from whom he obtained the knowledge, interpretations, and practices transmitted to the buyer.   In cases where slight cultural differences existed between bundle lines, whether within the same village or between villages brought together by pressure from alien tribes, the instructor played an important role in erasing ideological and ritualistic differences between bundle lines. By contrast, the Mandan system of individual-to-individual sale provided for exact duplication of bundles for seller and buyer, tending to preserve the individual character of the bundle lines.

Closely paralleling the hereditary bundle rituals were the personal bundles set up as a result of vision experiences.   Like other personal bundles, these tended to die out with the death of their owners and were disposed of by placing them at the grave of their owners. These supernatural experiences were of a wide variety but, in the final analysis, show rigid conditioning induced by the general knowledge the people had relative to the big birds.

BIG BIRD

The most important ceremonial periods were during the spring at the time of the northwestward flight of the big birds—eagles, hawks, ravens, and crows—to their summer nesting grounds along the streams, in the badlands, and on the high peaks of the Rocky Mountains. At this time of the year the bundle owners and others who had received individual dreams would place meat and pieces of hide on short "bird sticks" which were stuck into the ground on high hills adjacent to the villages. It was believed that these offerings would cause the birds to pass near the village and bring rains for the gardens. It was customary to have these offerings out prior to the first spring thunder. On the day following the first thunder, each bundle owner would take his sacred bundle to some isolated spot near the village, there to offer incense to the sacred objects and to pray for good crops. Similar rites of making offerings placed on "bird sticks" out on the prairie were performed during the autumn when the leaves began to fall. The spring rites were performed somewhat later than the Old-Woman-Who-Never-Dies rites; the water birds normally came north while some snow was on the ground but the eagles and other large birds arrived afterward. The fall rites were likewise performed somewhat earlier since the big birds were believed to fly leisurely southward along the Missouri, hunting as they went, while the water birds remained north until driven out by cold weather.

Although there is a close psychological association between the Big Bird rites and those of eagle trapping, the bundle lines were entirely independent and originated traditionally from quite different mythological experiences.

Seven recognized bundle lines survived the smallpox epidemic of 1837: two from Hidatsa (Smells and Big Coat); three from Awatixa (Big Black, Young-Man-Chief, and Bobtail Wolf); and two from Awaxawi (Negro and Dry Squash–Wolf Eyes). The greater number of bundle lines from Awatixa, even though the population surviving the epidemic was less than half that of the Hidatsa village, indicates the traditionally greater importance of the Packs Antelope rites at this village. The prior rights of those of the Low Cap clan, due to the important role of Packs Antelope in founding the rites, is expressed ritually by placing meat and other offerings on the right side of the lodge for the people of the clan. The rites provided the supernatural sanctions for chipping flint and it is said that in former times those who wished to make flint objects received their "authority" from those having rights in the Big Bird ceremony. Doctoring authority by cutting with a flint knife also came from these rites. The use of black medicine root in curing came from Two Men and the sword carried ceremonially in war was believed to have originated with the female eagle.

The bundles were of major status and differed only in rank according to the presence or absence of Singer rights. In 1845, when Fishhook Village was built, Bobtail Wolf, owner of a Big Bird bundle, took the western direction or that "from which the rains came." During dry periods, it was customary for groups, individuals, or the Goose society to pay a Big Bird bundle owner to perform Rain rites. He would then take up his position on an earth lodge, there to sing the sacred songs and perform such additional rites as appertained to the bundle.

A complete bundle contained these objects: "Sleep feather" of the eagle; white feather from near the tail feathers of the eagle; feather from the eagle's head; feather from left side of the eagle's claw; 12 bird sticks painted red; bullsnake skin representing the Grandfather in the Missouri River; a turtle shell; an otter skin; a ferret skin; sage; a wooden sword with an image of lightning on each side; a flint knife; rattles; and a wooden pipe.

Wolf Chief, who served as instructor (ceremonial father) when Hard Horn bought rights in the Big Bird ceremony, supplied the following account of a bundle purchase:

I remembered that Wolf Eyes of the Prairie Chicken clan had put on the Big Bird ceremony long before. His son, Hard Horn, was now going to put on the ceremony because he had dreams of the Big Birds. He asked me to be his "father" in preparing the articles for I was of the Prairie Chicken clan. After making the vow he started to save goods for the ceremony and planned to go up to Fort Buford to hunt for there were still many buffaloes and other large animals up there.

I did not know the rules of this ceremony so I called on Smells who also owned this ceremony. Because I did not know the rules I was afraid. So I was careful to learn them correctly as Smells related them to me. He was a leader in the ceremony for he had the big rattles and knew all of the songs, but he told me that it was hard to remember all the parts even for one knowing and performing the ceremony often. He volunteered to help me since, at that time, I had several gods and had bought the buffalo skull and the right to paint it in two ceremonies. He thought that I had made sufficient progress to show that I could learn things correctly.

He said, "When your son, Hard Horn, stands in front of you, you can promise him that he will be successful in all that he does."

When Hard Horn came to my lodge to ask me to be his "father" he brought a pipe and left it in front of me while his relatives brought in goods. Smells told me that I should give the pipe back to him when I talked to him during the feast.

I had been worshiping the eagles and other gods that I saw in my dreams and had given many feasts to my father's gods. So I prayed to my gods, saying, "I have worshiped you and fed you and shown you every respect. Now my 'son' has come to me. I want him to be lucky when he goes out to kill buffaloes. If the enemy attacks, I want him always to be on the safe side."

When I finished praying, I lit the pipe and smoked it, pointing it in all four directions and to all of my gods. Then I returned the pipe to him. This time Smells was with us and I said to him, "You have more powers than I have and you should pick out the best corn balls and articles."

He took out the best ones, for he knew all of the rules. After he finished selecting them, Hard Horn said that he was glad. He thought he would be lucky and that there would be plenty of buffaloes for all the people.

As Smells left, he said to me, "I will be back again and teach you the rules."

He came back later and said, "These objects are holy but I will explain the rules to you so you will not have bad luck. This pipe is holy; we use it when we put up the sweat lodge. I have this pipe that I got from Dry Squash but I will let you use it. I will lend you this ferret hide. When Hard Horn puts on the sweat ceremony, he should return it to me."

I said, "You bring the pipe, for I want to learn to use the pipe and to sing the songs."

Smells went back to his lodge. While he was away, I looked for some tobacco and calicoes. When he came in, I spread out the calicoes on the floor and he put the pipe and small ferret hide down. He was happy when he saw the blankets, calicoes, and roast corn before him for that was his pay for helping me. He said, "You will need some red paint."

There was plenty, for my father always kept much on hand. He had many bundle rites that required it. Smells took some and painted the pipe, praying and talking to the pipe and ferret skin as he painted. He asked me to hold out my hand. He was chewing the black root that came from Two Men. He spit some in my hand, telling me to rub it all over my body, and I did. He did the same. Then he sang the song. The ferret was about worn out with no hair on it. He gave me the pipe and ferret, instructing me to paint them as he had. Then I put them back on the robes again. The pipe was a wooden one like in my father's Waterbuster Skull bundle.

When he had finished singing the songs and painting the pipe and hide, he called for roasted corn. I took some with dry meat, setting it before him. He selected a few pieces and said to the pipe and ferret, "I want you to eat. I always took good care of you. Now I am going to give you to Wolf Chief to give to his son, Hard Horn. I do not want to have any bad luck." Then turning to me he said, "I am well paid for this. Wrap the pipe and skin with a nice calico or hide and put it away for your son." Then he ate the rest of the food.

Before Smells left, he directed me to look for one feather from under the left side of the wing of the eagle and called the sleep feather, one on the left side of the claw, a white feather on the tail, and a fourth one from the head. I was to save these feathers and take good care of them. I was to make 12 "bird sticks" and paint them red, representing the eagle's 12 tail feathers and also the 12 sticks for the moccasin game.

Smells said that I could tell my son to take these sticks when he went to war and paint them while saying, "I am painting you and I do not want to be killed."

Then there were the bullsnake, turtle, and otter to go into the bundle to represent the Missouri River and Two Men who were the great doctors. He asked me to look for all these and I did. I found them but before I even touched them, I chewed black medicine and rubbed it over me for Smells told me to do that or I might lose my life.

Before the feast was ready, Smells came and said that he had had a good dream in which he saw the pipe painted nicely. He thought that it was a good sign.

That fall some people came to the village to steal horses. The people shot at them and they went off without the horses. Our people went after them with Old-White-Man in the lead. He got off and was near the enemies when they threw their guns away and motioned him to come. He went towards one enemy and hit him in the face with his shield. The enemy said, "I will give you my necklace; we did not come to kill you."

They discovered that this enemy had a ferret skin on his neck, just like the one that was to be used in the ceremony. I tell this because they took it away from him. Hard Horn had promised to put on this ceremony and that is the reason why they got the horses back and found the ferret on the man. Smells had dreamed that there would be good luck; if it had not been for his dream, it would have been hard for me to find one of these ferrets to use in this ceremony.

After Hard Horn had left for Fort Buford to get the hides and food for the ceremony, I heard how he was getting along. He hunted and got many buffaloes that winter. Because he had promised to put up a sweat lodge ceremony, the enemies came to his camp and stole horses. The young men went out to get the horses back. Hard Horn went along. He thought he might kill some of the enemies since he had promised his gods that he would give the ceremony. They found the enemies hidden in the brush where they were eating, and surrounded them. One of the enemies ran towards Two Bulls and shot Two Bulls through the chest, killing him. Bird Bear was shot through the skin but did not fall; he shot the enemy and Hard Horn's brother struck coup on him. Even though one of our men was killed, the three enemies were killed. Hard Horn and his brothers succeeded in striking coups; it showed that his luck was good because he had made this promise even though one man was killed.[91]

Smells heard about it and said, "It is all right; Hard Horn was the one who made the pledge. He and his brother were successful so he is going to become a chief."

When the grass began to turn green in the spring, Hard Horn and all his brothers and sisters came back from Fort Buford in bullboats, bringing the things he was to use. He selected the large lodge occupied by Never-Eats-Marrow, where the Mandan Okipa ceremony was held, for his ceremony and paid the family for its use. He cleaned out the lodge and told me that he would be ready the next day. I was expected to go there when it was dark. When I came in, I saw that they had a line stretched all the way around the lodge. There were robes hanging on it, all the way around. There were also three sticks at the head of the lodge to show that I was to receive three horses also.

He called me over and said, "There are 60 hides and some of them are well tanned and decorated. Three sticks go with them; it is up to you to decide how they are to be divided.[92] Get a man, who has more power and more songs, to eat and sing the holy songs; then pay him part of the things I have gathered here." [93]

---

[91] Presumably Hard Horn did not "kick the stone" because he was not personally in charge as in the case of organized military expeditions.

[92] This is not entirely true. Each ceremony provided rules for the division of the goods put up as payment for the various performers. There seems to have been no rule outlining the precise number of robes and horses required. In this case it was largely determined by their success in hunting. For the minimum amount of goods for the Bear ceremony, see p. 352.

[93] Hard Horn seems to have assumed a rather dictatorial attitude not characteristic of buyers; it may be because of Wolf Chief's youth. This is the only instance I encountered in which the buyer undertook to advise his ceremonial "father" in the management of a ceremony.

All along Smells knew that he was to sing the holy songs so he had been repeating them over to himself before he went to the lodge, thinking that he might have forgotten some of them.

The next morning I was called over to the lodge and found that Smells had already selected the 12 men who would get the bird sticks to show that they were to attend. Smells got 12 good men who had important sacred bundles with buffalo skulls, for these men added prestige to the buyer. He selected: Small Ankles, my father (Eagle Trapping, Wolf, and Holy-Woman-Above bundles); Different Wolf (Buffalo Skull bundle); Belly Up (Eagle Trapping bundle); Bear-Looks-Out, (Old-Woman-Who-Never-Dies and the Mandan Skull bundles); Bears Heart (Bear bundle); Poor Wolf (Earthmaking bundle); Crows Breast (Eagle Trapping and Naxpike bundles); Red Tail (Wolf bundle); Son-of-Star (Wolf bundle); Wolf eyes (Eagle Trapping and Thunder bundles); Hairy Coat (Holy-Woman-Above bundle); and Chippewa (Thunder bundle).

In addition to these, all those who had other bundles containing buffalo skulls were expected to attend and to receive presents. Hard Horn had gone out when Smells and the 12 men carrying the bird sticks were heard singing. They stopped four times as they came towards the lodge and each time Hard Horn was expected to give some article.

They had reached the lodge and were in their places when I was called in. Smells was in the center of the circle of old men, painted up with zigzag marks on his body to look like lightning; his entire body was red with blue paint on the nose and the marks of lightning all over his face. He had two rattles of buffalo hide with stones inside. From his wrists hung eagle claws.

Smells stood up and said, "Bring one of the robes before me; spread it out in front of the sweat lodge; pile up the corn balls there. When you put them there, I am going to walk around them and sing a holy song. That dried meat should be put in one pile together with the bird sticks. When I sing the song, distribute the meat to each of these medicine men. Use these bird sticks." [94]

Then he began the song, using the rattles. Hard Horn, his brothers and their wives, and his sisters passed the dry meat to the 12 men. There was a buffalo skull inside the sweat lodge and Smells said, "Put some of the dry meat in front of the skull; I will appoint different holy men to take the meat from the skull. They will each pray for you."

Hard Horn spoke up, saying, "Of course, these robes belong to Wolf Chief and he is the one to do with them as he wishes. There are a few additional articles that I will do with as I please. It is up to him how he disposes of the robes for I have promised them to him already." [95]

I stood up and said, "I am glad you spoke that way. I prefer that you use these articles to cover the sweat lodge. I am glad that all of you people who own powerful bundles are here. I can see that there are plenty of articles. I know that Hard Horn wants to succeed, have a good home, and bring the people good luck. In the beginning you made the pledge; at first I thought that it would be a hard thing to do. I had no power but I took it up with an old man who has more gods than I and he helped me. Now I see that this ceremony will be successful. Everything will turn out well. Smells will carry out everything that you wanted me to do. I was looking for your medicines all this time; we have succeeded, even though I knew it was going to be hard to find them. Smells had a good dream and our enemies came. He brought one of the ferrets which are

---

[94] This act was symbolic of the spring and fall feeding of the big birds during their flights past the villages, at which time offerings of foods and hides were placed on bird sticks outside the village.

[95] That is true—but it is also Wolf Chief's duty to see that all those who pray for Hard Horn receive adequate reward.

hard to find. We had one that was nearly worn out and I am glad that we found this new one. I am glad that you are a leader and that after you made your pledge, you went up to Fort Buford where your brothers struck the enemy. Now they call you a chief; you are successful and have a good name. I am supposed to have these 60 robes but in the beginning I asked Smells to come over and help me. I am giving him 10 of them." I thought I would keep 40 of them, and I did.[96]

Smells began to sing the holy songs while Hard Horn and his brothers passed the meat around on sticks for the old men. Each man would pray for them before handing the stick back. Then Smells sent the holy men to the buffalo skull, saying, "There are many articles in front of the skull; go there and pray for Hard Horn." Each prayed and then took the article that Hard Horn gave him.

Smells announced that he was going into the sweat lodge and invited those who wished to do so also. He wore a robe that was painted red and a cap down over his eyes like Packs Antelope wore his, for he also belonged to the Low Cap clan. He sang this song four times, "He almost reached the sky."

As he approached the sweat lodge, singing this song, Hard Horn and his relatives put down a robe, then another at the entrance where he stood. He sang the same song again while facing the west. While he was singing the fourth time, he turned toward the entrance to the sweat lodge but he did not take his rattles with him. He had something in his hand; it was covered with sage. In those days they carried a flint knife which was the sign of an eagle claw. That was what he had concealed in the sage. There were many corn balls in front of the sweat lodge, for the family had worked hard. He sang the same song and said, "hoo hoo" and stuck the flint knife into the corn balls four times.

The sweat lodge was covered and he went in saying, "You old men have some of your number come in here."

The older men went in around the side with their clothing on. Smells said, "Bring that skull, otter, snake, and all the other holy things and put them on top of the sweat lodge."

Then he asked me to bring sage and I did. He put it in my mouth and pulled it out again, directing me to spit onto the stones. We repeated that four times. Then he directed me to call Hard Horn and his brothers with their wives and the three sisters. I called them to come into the sweat lodge. He dipped the sage into the water and sprinkled the sacred objects and all of the buyers. He said to them, "Now you will feel as though you have new life. You will have good homes. This is a rule that was established a long time ago and it holds now."

At this time they were sitting before the sweat lodge while some of the old men were inside. He sprinkled all those attending the ceremony if they requested it.

Then Smells said to me, "Take those sacred objects back and call your son, Hard Horn; tell him to keep these things. He must always keep them in good order."

I took the skull back to its place. Then I put the otter, the pipe given me by Smells, the ferret, the eagle feathers, and the other things in their places, saying to them, "I am poor myself and have no powers except what my gods have given me. I hope that when I give you to Hard Horn you will take good care of him and obey what I am now asking of you."

Then I called Hard Horn over and handed them to him. After I had finished the transfer, Smells called from the sweat lodge, "Come over, all you men and sit

---

[96] This was a selfish act that brought down severe criticism from Wolf Chief's elders, including his own parents. He afterward employed these articles to buy back good will by inviting in various old men and providing them with robes and food. It would have been more appropriate to have disposed of them publicly at the ceremony.

beside the sweat lodge; I will sprinkle water over you for there is much sickness among us. Then you will have new life and be healthy. You women come over too."

Each time he sang, he would dip the sage in the water and sprinkle the water over them. He would say, "My Grandfather, I want my people to be well, lucky, and free of sickness." [97]

Even the children came over to the sweat lodge and were sprinkled. They liked it and believed in it, thinking they would be lucky. They would crowd to get ahead and be the first. While this was going on, there were only four stones in the sweat lodge, all the others being left outside.

When he had finished, he called three old men, Hairy Coat and two others whom I do not remember, and instructed them to distribute the dry meat and corn balls saying, "We are eating before our gods and I hope there will be no bad luck. Try to distribute the food so that all will have an equal share." After eating, the rites in the sweat lodge began.

Smells called Small Ankles to break a stick and throw it into the sweat lodge pit. They usually picked a man who was brave when he met the enemy to do that. This act meant that Hard Horn would overcome the enemy. When this was done, Smells said to Hard Horn, "When you put a stone in the sweat lodge, you should call the name of some enemy you want to kill saying, 'I killed ———' and hit the stone as though you were striking the enemy. Whoever carries the stone in will allow you to hit it. That is the sign that you will overcome your enemy."

They did that and four men would hit each stone. After putting the four stones in that way, they threw the rest in without striking them. Then they covered the lodge and poured water on them.

After the sweat bath was over, Smells said again, "What are we going to do with the cover? There are many articles making up the cover."

I said, "You do as you wish. I have my share for I have 3 horses and 40 robes. There are many holy men here; you can do as you wish."

The robes were distributed and it seemed that everyone was well satisfied with the distribution. When the ceremony was over I took my share and the three sticks representing the horses. All this goods was the reason I always thought that I had a good protector in early times. It was proof that I was well protected. If old times were back, I would give others the same advice if they wanted to become lucky and strike their enemies.

When away from the village, bundle owners of Big Bird, Missouri River, and Creek rites also performed hunting rites at the various stone effigies of animals associated with these bundles—for the purpose of clearing fogs. These effigies have been observed by the writer on Mount Nebo (sec. 29, T. 143, R. 83) west of Price, N. Dak. (sec. 17, T. 141, R. 82) (pl. 6), and 4 miles northwest of Golden Valley, N. Dak. An effigy situated about 2 miles southwest of the Upper Sanger site was removed to Bismarck and set up on the Statehouse lawn. Will (1909) reports an effigy outline near Ludlow Caves in northwestern South Dakota, one of the Buffalo Home Buttes of the Mandan. With the exception of the latter, all effigies are situated in the historic and late prehistoric hunting range of

---

[97] "Grandfather" refers to one of the Two Men who was changed into a snake.

the Hidatsa. My Hidatsa informants had observed a turtle effigy on the north bank of the Missouri near Williston to which they went to perform rites while hunting in that area. A large snake effigy of glacial boulders west of Independence was frequently visited for the performance of similar rites. In view of their peculiar distribution near the Missouri, it would appear that these known effigies were largely Hidatsa–Mandan shrines. However, the Mandan had similar bundle ceremonies which suggests that comparable practices were observed while they lived near the Heart River even though the actual shrines have not been identified; in the late 1860's, while on a hunting expedition near Williston, Clam Necklace, a Mandan owning a Big Bird bundle performed rites both at the turtle effigy and later elsewhere on the prairie. Concerning these practices, Crows Heart related to me that—

The next night we camped by a circle of stones in the form of a turtle. The gods had arranged these stones, the older men said, for none living had ever seen one of these effigies made. There was a hill nearby and on it was a pile of rocks. The turtle's head was pointed to the river because the turtles stay in the water so the gods must have arranged all the turtle outlines in that direction. This is the only effigy I ever saw but I heard that the old people knew of many others down the river near their old villages and would go there to make offerings. Anyone could make offerings of knives, pieces of hides, or dry meat and other things to eat when asking for rain or other good luck such as living to be old. If they had children, they would ask the gods that go with the turtle to send good luck. To give to the turtle was the same as giving to all the other gods that went with the bundle.

While we stopped near the turtle, people made offerings to the turtle and the other gods that went with it. Some left knives but in the olden times the flint knife was given, for the flint was a sign of the big birds who go with the turtle and the other gods in the Missouri and the creeks around.

After we moved on from this turtle it was so foggy one day that the leader could hardly find his way. The hunters had to hold each other's hands to keep from getting lost. An Arikara brought a knife and gave it to Clam Necklace (Mandan with a Thunder or Big Bird bundle) and asked him to try to clear the fog. Clam Necklace took the knife and marked out the shape of a turtle in the ground. When he finished shaping the turtle, he prayed to the turtle, telling him that the people could not go any farther and asked the turtle to clear the fog away. Then he stuck the knife in front of the turtle image, saying that the knife belonged to the turtle and the other six things in the water. It was not long afterwards, and while the men were standing around the image, that the fog cleared away from where the turtle lay. Then it cleared out in a circle around the turtle, growing larger and larger, until the fog entirely disappeared. Those who were connected with the big birds and the snakes of the Okipa were the ones to pray.[98]

---

[98] Mandan major bundle status was expressed by participation rights on Everything-Comes-Back day of the Okipa ceremony.

MISSOURI RIVER

These rites are nearly identical conceptually and ritually with the Grandfather Snake rites of the Mandan. Their traditional origin relates to the eating of a snake by one of the Two Men who afterward was transformed into a large double-headed snake and put into the river by his twin brother. Before taking up his eternal residence there, he instructed his brother in the rites to the Missouri River and explained that although he was formerly a Sacred Arrow, he would thenceforth be chief over all the water spirits, the various snakes, the otter, beaver, turtle, mink, muskrat, and frog. In a sense, the sacred bundle was almost an exact duplicate of the Big Bird bundles, the essential difference being that the latter had additional objects representing the big birds. Natives explain the presence of objects representing the water spirits by saying that the grandfather snake who became the "chief of the river spirits" was himself formerly a big bird identified with the Sacred Arrows. The bundles were of major status with buffalo skulls and were held in high regard because one of the Two Men who is represented in the bundle possessed such great supernatural powers that he was able to draw Packs Antelope under the waters even though he had been blessed by the eagles, had learned their sacred songs, and carried their sword.

There were three complete bundles after the smallpox epidemic of 1837: Man-With-Long-Hair, Prairie Chicken clan, from Hidatsa village; Missouri River, Waterbuster clan, of Awatixa village; and Roadmaker, Waterbuster clan of Awaxawi village. Similar bundles and rites were possessed by the Mandans. The Hidatsa bundle line was broken when heirs did not buy the rights of Man-With-Long-Hair. The Awaxawi bundle line became inferior to that of Awatixa chiefly, I believe, because Poor Wolf was involved in too many ceremonies and could not make appropriate feasts to maintain its status. Missouri River's bundle line was perpetuated by his son, Women-in-Water of the Awaxenawita clan, who took an active part in preserving the rites and beliefs concerning the Grandfather and other water gods.

Although the principal bundle line was maintained by father-to-son inheritance, minor bundles were frequently established through vision experiences of individuals of more distant relationships. Even these minor bundles frequently were sold from generation to generation with the ceremonial sanction and assistance of the principal bundle owners serving as singers. The pattern of River bundle relationships with major bundles is characteristically Mandan rather than Hidatsa; complete rights in all of the seven animals of the River together with their songs and sacred myths, and the recognition of minor rights related to segments of the complex. A complete bundle carried rights in several ceremonies. The owner possessed Sacred Arrow rights since the Grandfather snake was formerly one of the Two Men. He could doctor, using the sacred arrows for opening wounds, and he could remove arrows. He derived his authority to use black medicine for doctoring from Two Men who were represented in the bundle by the snakeskin.

Bullboat-making rites were inherited with the bundle, and those desiring to make bullboats paid the bundle owner for these rights. When the sale was made, the bundle owner sang the sacred song "belonging to the bullboat" for safe passage on the water. Thereafter, whenever a new bullboat was completed, the song was sung and prayers were directed to Grandfather and the other six water gods.

Important rainmaking rites were performed with the bundle. These rites stem from native beliefs that moisture for the native vegetation and the gardens comes both from the sky and the streams and lakes. Likewise, the sky and the water gods both possess lightning. Snakes are generally associated with precipitation: One of Old-Woman-Who-Never-Dies' husbands, a giant snake, was put into Short Missouri and maintains the water level of that pond; Grandfather snake maintains the level of the Missouri; another large snake associated with the Little Missouri maintains the flow of that stream and, by means of his supernatural powers, provided good hunting along its banks. Other traditional snakes maintain the lakes of the area and when a lake dried it was said that either the snake died or had moved away. And, of course, Old-Woman-Who-Never-Dies is protected by four large snakes on her island in the southland. The same concepts are extended to include small streams, many of which are thought to be the particular home of the seven water spirits. In other instances, men have been known to fast at certain small springs or streams in an effort to learn which spirit made his home there. When one of the seven spirits "revealed" itself, this knowledge often became a part of the sacred lore of the group. It has been "revealed" through fasting that a giant frog lives in the spring near Tom Smith's home. The large spring on the Little Knife Creek is the home of an otter which was "revealed" to Crow-Flies-High.

It was believed that on cloudy days during the hot weather of the summer, the Big Birds produced clouds as they flew about looking for snakes and other spirits inhabiting the various bodies of water situated on the land. Then occurred the contests such as transpired at intervals throughout the mythological period. Natives have observed that lightning is sent down on these occasions by the Big Birds and is returned by the snakes and the six other animals who make their home in the water.

Bundle owners were authorized to doctor for rheumatism and stiffness and had the power to remove snakes, usually occurring as short worms, from their patients' bodies or their joints; these rights stemmed from Two Men who doctored Unknown Man's father-in-law in mythological times. They were also called in when parturition was difficult. The patient was given the otterskin to hold and to rub, the smoothness of the otter and its ability to slide through narrow openings being thus transmitted to the child; or the patient was given a concoction of black root and the scrapings from a turtle's shell in water. When a male doctor was called, it was customary for his wife or a sister having similar rights to assist in the physical care of the mother and her infant while the male directed the rites.

Anyone could make offerings to the Grandfather and the other six gods of the River and it was customary for those who were on the river a great deal to make these offerings regularly. Women also made offerings regularly and placed the objects near the river's edge in order to have plenty of moisture for their gardens. It was not necessary for the major bundle owner to attend and he rarely did unless his presence was requested. The snake's favorite food was large intestines, a section of which from a buffalo was usually placed on a stake or thrown into the river. The remainder of the offering consisted of seven corn balls which were thrown into the water. When additional offerings of greater value were to be given, it was customary to invite a bundle owner to pray for the success of the giver and receive the goods for his own use. Offerings were first given when the ice went out in the spring and might be given at any time until the river froze over in the fall.

According to tradition, the potters were formerly owners of rights in the Big Bird, River, and other Snake bundles. Pottery was made in a darkened place; usually the earth lodge with the entrance blocked and the smoke hole partially covered. The potters impersonated the snakes who were believed to inhabit dark places away from the big birds who preyed on them. Although rights to make pottery were inherited and purchased through females, these lines paralleled the male bundle lines. The rites were secret and defined the meaning of each step in terms of the supernatural. For that reason, individuals not possessing rights to make pottery were not permitted to sit around and watch. There was a limited number of households possessing rights to make pottery, and the other households bought their pottery in exchange for decorated robes, clothing, and other property. There were sacred songs used during the mixing of the ingredients, the shaping of the vessel, and the application of the decorations.

When the vessels had been completed except for the firing, they were covered with damp hides until the clay had set. Should an individual come into the lodge unexpectedly or should the vessels be uncovered by an unauthorized person, it was believed that the big birds who were always flying about looking for snakes would cause lightning-shaped cracks to appear in the vessels either before or during firing. This would also cause the vessels to become weak and break easily while in use. Thus, the making of a pot was a contest between the big birds and the snakes. The designs are said to represent the snakes, lightning, clouds, water birds, and rain, but it was impossible to secure precise interpretations of the various patterns impressed into the surface of the vessels, since pottery has not been made for many years and none of the old potters were still living. There was general agreement that the zigzag lines were lightning since similar designs still appear on arrows; others associated a curved design on the rim with clouds or rainbows, horizontal lines around the rim with snakes entwining the pot, and herringbone designs with tracks of the wading birds—snipes, heron, and cranes.

Men and women cooperated in making the vessels; men brought in the clays from selected veins and assisted their relatives in making the pots after they had advanced in age and were no longer able to take an active part in hunting. Big Black from Awatixa, owner of a Big Bird bundle, and his two wives, Red Blossom from Awatixa and Buffalo Woman, a Mandan, were the last to make a business of pottery making when my informants were young. He would ride northwest of Fishhook Village to a bank which had been deeply undercut by those removing clay from beneath the overhanging cliff. He shaped the pots with a cottonwood paddle while the two women applied the designs they had the purchased right to reproduce. He assisted them further by bringing the wood for the firing. At this time he was too crippled from a hunting accident, when his leg was crushed by a buffalo, to assist in hunting so he traded the pots around through the village. He also made and decorated a few pots which were used in the various ceremonies but informants acknowledged that the vessels were not very good for they broke easily. Nevertheless, out of respect for these old people, and in order to have around these reminders of olden times, people would buy their pots even though recognizing the superiority of the metal vessels. Big Black also had rights in the sacred arrows by virtue of his rights in the Big Bird ceremony and would work hard making arrows to sell and trade.

One's ritual possessions were so much a part of his daily life that whenever someone is mentioned, people today recall both his ritual rights and other records (as illustrated by Bears Arm's account of Roadmaker). In time, each personal achievement was expressed in terms of the supernatural. These personal records are repeated over and over until they become stylized and differ no more, as told by different individuals, than do the sacred myths relating to the various ceremonies.

Roadmaker was one of the members of the tribal council during the first half of the 19th century and is still recognized as one of the outstanding Awaxawi leaders. Bodmer, who painted his picture in 1833, lists him as a Mandan (pl. 7). This error is probably due to the close cultural ties which the Awaxawi maintained with the Mandan of Painted Woods prior to the removal of the Hidatsa and Mandan village groups to Knife River. The name is readily recognized from the Bodmer spelling of the name, *Addih-Haddisch*. Bears Arm's account of Roadmaker follows:

Roadmaker (*ari hiris*), who lived in the village of Awaxawi, had a full sister and she had a son, Poor Wolf, who told me these things. When Roadmaker was a young man he joined the Stone Hammer and other societies. In the lodge where the men met he said, "Now that I have joined the Wood Rattler society, I want to fast and seek visions from the spirits."

The old men said, "That is a wise decision; that is the way to become famous."

They were making the ceremony called "Tying-the-Pots" in which one of the pots was a man and the other a woman. These pots were given to the Awaxawi by the watersnakes. These large pots were dressed up like a man and a woman with war bonnets on both of them. The headman who had charge of the pots would burn incense over them and ask for rain, good crops, and other things the people wanted. Then they would remove the clothing from the pots and a drumhead from the lining of a buffalo paunch was put over them and tied down securely to make drums of them. This putting on of the drumheads was called "Tying-the-Pots." Then the singers would take sticks bent in a loop to beat the drums with.[99]

This ceremony required 4 nights to perform. Roadmaker fasted 4 days and nights during the ceremony; then the ceremony broke up and the whole population went out on the summer buffalo hunt to the neighborhood of Rainy Buttes.[1]

The camp moved farther west, but Roadmaker stopped at the buttes and fasted 7 days and nights. When he finished, he lay down to sleep. In his dreams he saw black clouds coming from the west and in the clouds he saw a large bird with huge claws coming down. As the bird approached the butte, it closed it claws and a voice from above said, "These claws which you see never fail to catch something."

Then he awoke and knew that it was the Thunderbird he had seen and heard talking to him. Later he fasted 4 days again in the Tying-the-Pots ceremony.

There was a battle with the Assiniboin near the village and Roadmaker was in it. They killed many of the enemies. When night came, Roadmaker went to the place where the dead and scalped Assiniboins lay. He carried some of the bodies to one spot and lay between them with their heads on his arms, crying. Roadmaker afterwards said, "I do not know if I was awake or asleep. I heard voices from the west; I thought that it might be the friends of the dead Assiniboins returning and that I would surely be killed. However, it was only the wind and in it were voices. The voices came back a second time with the wind and I could hear them say, 'Take this bead; when you have taken a scalp, put the bead on the

---

[99] See the Tying-the-Pots ceremony below for the details.

[1] This ceremony seems to have occupied the position of the Naxpike of the other two villages. I found no evidence that any of the older people of this village had ever given the Naxpike.

end of the scalp. When you have done this, you will be victorious in all of your undertakings. We are your enemies but you honored us because you fasted and lay here with us. You will always have your own way.' "

Shortly after this dream, the enemy came and stole 10 horses. Those who had lost their horses were sad. Roadmaker said that he would go out and look for the animals, for the other young men had not been able to find them. Others volunteered to go with him. The scouts found the enemy camp of four men far to the west, nearly to the headwaters of Knife River.

Roadmaker said, "We will sneak up on them and then wait until they eat. Then they will put their bows and arrows down."

Some had muzzle-loaders too but all of the enemies were killed before they could get to their weapons. The scalps were given to Roadmaker since he was the leader. He said, "We will now take the horses back to the village. You will be required to return them to their former owners if they pay us for our efforts. They were taken by the enemy and became the property of the enemy and now we have taken them back."

They started for home but it took them several days, for it was slow traveling with the horses as they had to keep scouts out ahead all the time so they would not lose the horses to the enemy again. When they came near the village, they painted [themselves] to show that they had struck the enemy, tied the horses together, and drove them through the village so that all the people could see that they had been successful.

Roadmaker sent an announcer through the village calling that the former owners could have their horses back providing they paid the warriors for their services. The people who had lost these horses were glad to get them back and made payments in dresses made of mountain sheep, robes, and moccasins.[2]

Several years later Roadmaker awoke one morning and said, "Three tipis have been promised to me," meaning that if he organized a war expedition, he would kill off three households. He called for volunteers and 79 men volunteered. Some came from the Mandan villages too. They went to the north to a place east of the present town of Minot where a small stream enters the Mouse River. Beyond this point the scouts discovered three tipis and returned to report. Roadmaker directed the men to wait until the camp moved and then he would not lose any of his men.

His men hid themselves in the path of the three families and when the enemies were close, he gave the order to attack. Roadmaker's party had good horses at that time and, the enemy being taken by surprise while they were spread out, it did not take long to wipe out the entire party. He made a staff to which he tied one scalp at the top, one in the middle, and a third at the bottom to represent the three households he had been promised.

One day another man named Yellow Hawk went out and took many warriors with him. They found the enemy on the flats and there was a battle. Yellow Hawk's men were outnumbered; one young man was wounded and could not travel. The young man said, "Here is where I am going to have my eagle trapping pit," meaning that he was going to die and the others would bury him there. A young man named On Buffalo, who belonged to the Little Dog society, had his staff painted black and white with four black marks and with many feathers along its length.

---

[2] Note that the payments were in things the women wore. This was to compensate the female relatives since a man gave most horses stolen to his sisters and mothers.

On Buffalo sang his songs and said, "You have heard this man speaking. When you get back tell my people that I died bravely while defending this wounded man."

He stuck his society staff in the ground and made his stand there. He wounded some of the enemies but they were too numerous. He pulled up his staff and carried the wounded man back, but the enemies rushed him and finally shot and killed him. Many others were killed in Yellow Hawk's party and when he reached the village the people said that he had "kicked the stone."

When On Buffalo's relatives heard of his bravery, the father wept, cut his hair off, stuck arrows through his flesh, and went through the village singing. The mother cut herself and wore short dresses. Many others mourned, for On Buffalo was so brave. Even the dogs howled.

Roadmaker became angry and said, "The people up at Hidatsa village may be wondering what I am going to do about it." The man defended by On Buffalo was named Young Buffalo and belonged to the same clan, the Waterbusters, as did Roadmaker. Roadmaker announced that he was going out to war and that he would destroy 15 tipis.

He went north with a large force. Before leaving, he talked to the Grandfather snake who lived in the Missouri River saying, "Grandfather, I am going out into enemy territory. I am angry for they killed my brother; I want to kill the enemy and I want your help. When I come back I will have a scalp for you."

The large snake promised him success, saying, "When you get to the enemy and have killed them, an otter skin will be found and presented to you. It will be a large tanned one. Take it and wear it as a cap with the tail to the side. Use it in saving the people when they are sick. Then you will become a great doctor. When you get back to the village you must pledge the 'Ceremony to the Water People.' "

Roadmaker and his party set out. The first night in camp a count was made and it was found that there were 452 warriors. They represented the five Hidatsa and Mandan villages. Among them was a man who wore tanned bangs from the buffalo which he used as a cap. This man, named Foolish Eagle, would say, "When you find the enemy, I will be the first to strike him" and when the men were roasting ribs he would say the same and strike the ribs. Then the camp tenders would give him the ribs. At other times he would say, "Those enemies must have guns, bows, and arrows to fight with. If I am killed, I will be home before you are."

The next day the war party went on. Roadmaker belonged to the Waterbuster clan so he selected a crier from this clan. He instructed the crier to line up the 40 scouts and selected the best as the number was too large. The 40 ran and the first 20 to reach the line were selected to serve with Bull Looks, a Waterbuster clansman, who had been appointed by Roadmaker before they left home. This leader ran with them and called out "hoo" four times to make them run faster.

Roadmaker moved his party at night and traveled that way four times. On the next morning his scouts came back and reported that they had found 15 tipis and that it looked as though the people were preparing to move camp.

Roadmaker said, "We will form here and, when they are opposite us, we will make the charge."

Foolish Eagle was on the left side with his group from Hidatsa, Stirrup was on the right with his group from Awatixa, and a Mandan named Whistling Ghost who had married an Awaxawi woman and was living at Awaxawi took the central position.[3] When the enemy was opposite them, Roadmaker gave the signal. Foolish Eagle was first to strike an enemy, Whistling Ghost was first for the central group, and Stirrup was first of his group. They killed all the enemies and took their horses and other property.

Roadmaker moved his camp and they stopped for the noon meal and to rest. He called his criers and said, "There was an otter skin that was promised me by 'Grandfather' and I need that."

The criers went through the camp telling all that they must look for an otter skin because Roadmaker wanted it to wear on his head while he sang the Victory songs.

There were two young boys who were taken prisoners in the fight and the older men met and decided that the boys were old enough to remember what had happened to their people and that it would not be wise to take them into the villages. When they grew up they might do damage or run away with horses and return to their own people. The old men decided to turn them over to the Black Mouths. Since it was not customary to kill a person who had been taken into camp, the Black Mouths went to the boys and told them to go back to their own country. The boys started out and, when they were some distance from the camp, the Black Mouths pursued and killed them.

The camp moved again, and the next day at noon Roadmaker said, "I have prayed to 'Grandfather' that none of my people would be shot or killed. As you all know, I have not lost a man. My 'Grandfather' promised me the otter skin saying, 'It will be the largest one with beaver claws sewed on the mouth.' That skin must be in this camp somewhere and the person having it should have given it to me. The criers announced this yesterday. It has not been found. Whoever has that skin can keep it now for it is a good skin. Whoever he is, he will not live very long. We will take his body out and place it on some of these hills here in enemy territory where he will be lonely. We will put the otter skin beside his body and leave him alone with his skin."

When this information was announced through the camp, and while the Old Wolves were gathered smoking, a man stepped forward and threw the skin before the men saying, "There is the skin."

Roadmaker opened the bundle and found that it was the skin he had been promised. It was the largest one he had ever seen. It had large beaver claws fastened to the mouth so that when it was shaken, they rattled. He had bluffed the man and thus secured his skin. He put it on his head as a cap with the tail hanging to one side over his shoulder, blackened his staff, and tied to it the three scalps taken by Foolish Eagle, Whistling Ghost, and Stirrup.

He sang his Victory songs, calling the names of those who had struck the enemy. Because there were so many, he called out only their names and the villages they came from. He mounted his horse and rode through the camp calling the names of those who had been bravest. Then the party started for home. On the way home they killed buffaloes and all were happy.

They had guns at this time. Most of the guns were brought in by the Chippewa from the northeast and traded for robes and corn. These people would come down to the villages with dog teams and sleds, rarely with horses, as they did not have many and were afraid of having them taken away from them by their enemies along the way.

The party traveled all night in order to reach the opposite bank of the Missouri near the villages where they howled so all could hear them. When it was daylight, the people could see them waving the scalps. They brought bullboats across to

---

[3] Note the division of warriors based on villages.

take the men back. Those anxious to get home drifted over on rafts. It took much of the day to cross the 452 warriors and their equipment.

When they had reached the village, Roadmaker said, "I am tired now and need to rest. I will rest today and tomorrow I will sing the Victory songs with my men."

It was the custom for people to go around singing, and those seeing that would give them presents. Roadmaker announced that On Buffalo's parents should be invited to his lodge and that those who had won war honors should come and give the old couple presents during the victory dances.

Next morning the warriors painted their bodies and faces black and danced, singing the Victory songs. Many other groups danced too. On Buffalo's father and mother went to Roadmaker's lodge and sang this song, "Just a little while ago you did this and now you have done it again. Roadmaker went out and found three tipis and killed all the people. He went out again and found 15 tipis and killed all the people."

Roadmaker came out of his lodge and placed his finest war bonnet on the old man's head. He gave him a new gun with powder horn and said, "You can use this gun for a cane, my father."

The old man went from lodge to lodge singing the same song; all gave him presents of fine things. This made the old man and woman very happy.

Then he made the ceremony to the "Grandfather" in the Missouri River who had promised the otter skin, for Roadmaker had been told that he must do that as the price for success. He took the scalp to the spot where the Knife River empties into the Missouri, at which place there was a deep pool formed by the swirling water. He gave it to the Grandfather. In the dream his Grandfather had said, "You must make the sweat lodge and give the ceremonies to the River; you will become a great doctor; the people will recognize your powers and call you in to doctor them. When you treat a patient, give him two or three pillows placed under his back; raise the head, and he will breathe easier. Scrape the small turtle and put some of the scrapings in a horn spoon full of water from the Missouri. Make the patient drink all of it whether he wants to or not. When you have done that, take grease and rub on the patient's chest and abdomen. Then rub wild sage on your hands and knead the sick man's abdomen, for that is where the pain all lies and gathers. By kneading the stomach after greasing the patient, this grease goes through the skin and eases the pain so that things will work right inside. The blood will circulate. In 4 days you can stop doctoring. However, if it is a severe case, you will need to doctor for 8 days, but the patient will recover."

These were the instructions that the grandfather gave to Roadmaker.[4] He became a great doctor and leader of war parties. Three years later Roadmaker put on ceremonies to buy the bundle during the winter. He went out for the enemy six times and never lost a man in war so he was famous both as a warrior and doctor. Men of the three villages would come to him and volunteer to go along.

The Awaxawi would say, "If you are in the age-grade societies, get up and tell what you did and it will be sure to come true." The men would get up in the dance and tell how brave they were and the number of times they had struck the enemy and made wishes that came true. So it was that the people of Awatixa and Hidatsa, when hearing something funny, would say that it sounds just like an Awaxawi talking.

Roadmaker said, "When any of you have a dream that you are being killed by the enemy, you can always avoid that by dressing up in your best clothing, going

---

[4] These are general beliefs associated with all Missouri River bundles

out, and having some of your friends chase you. They will pretend that they are killing you and take your clothing, bow and arrows, knife, or whatever weapons you are accustomed to carry. It will be a sham battle. You will come back naked and by doing that you will avoid bad luck."

Poor Wolf dreamed the enemy came upon him and killed him, so the next day he told his friends of his dream. Roadmaker, his mother's brother, advised him to dress up in his best, have the people come out imitating the enemy, knock him down, and strip him. Poor Wolf did, and the warriors took after him. He stopped to fight back and the men struck him down, took the horsehair that he wore as a scarf, and went back to the village. About that time he heard an uproar on the south side of the village where men were running their horses and shooting as they rode about. Poor Wolf heard one of them cry "The enemy has killed one of us" and he ran over there to see if he could get into the fight, only to learn that they were referring to the sham battle in which he had been "killed."

When Seven Bears (Awaxawi) had a similar dream he put on a sham battle and said, "This is the time that I cheated my body" meaning that he had used his sacred bundles to ward off arrows.[5]

Poor Wolf told of a man from Awaxawi who pretended to be lame and would limp during all of the ceremonies. He unbraided one side of his hair and let it fall over the eye. He would say, "My left eye socket is hollow for the eye has broken and is all white."

The people would say to him, "One should not wish for evil, only the good things in life," but the man would only reply, "I do not believe in those things; I want to see if there is any truth to them. That is why I am doing this."

In time he had a sore eye. It broke open and then it was hollow. He would take his hair down to cover it. Poor Wolf said to him "You were always telling us you had a bad eye with cataracts and now you have what you have been wishing for. Why don't you put your hair up so we can see your eye?"

Seven Bears would not, for he was ashamed of it. The enemy came and he was far back in the line but a bullet glanced and hit him in the thigh, breaking the bone. When he was well again, he had trouble getting around.

Roadmaker had the right to wear everything that a chief wore and died at Awaxawi village after the smallpox epidemic was over.

CREEK

These sacred bundles and their associated rites were closely related to the Missouri River bundles and rites. There were two bundles after 1837 but both were considered subdivisions of a sacred bundle and rites originating at Awatixa. Both bundles can be traced back to Missouri River bundle owners; Missouri River for the Awatixa, and Poor Wolf (an older Poor Wolf who died about 1840) of Awaxawi. The bundle rites were associated with certain spirits believed to reside in the small tributaries of the Missouri River, the chief god being a large snake who resided in the Little Missouri and assured good hunting along that stream. A complete bundle contained beaver fur and claws, otter skin, turtle shell, buffalo skull, mink skin, dried frog, black root or medicine, peppermint, sage, cedar, muskrat skin (option-

---

[5] I did not find reference to this practice for the other Hidatsa groups, but the Mandan made comparable references to sham battles for warding off misfortunes.

al), and water snake skin (optional). The contents in the bundle closely approximated those of the Thunder and Missouri River bundles. Nethertheless, the rites and songs associated with the bundle are distinctive and in no way duplicate those for the other bundles. The following, an abbreviated account of the origin myth, was related by Wolf Chief:

Beaver, Otter, and Turtle who lived in the northland made plans to come to the village to teach the people to doctor and to care for the sick. They discussed taking black medicine along to aid them in their doctoring. They decided to take big medicine along also. Then they decided to take peppermint and sand-bar willows. They decided to use a dipper from the left horn of the buffalo, too. They selected a special song which was to be taught to those doctoring one who has been sick a long while. They also agreed that fat from around the buffalo's heart should be used when doctoring those who have been sick long.

They agreed on a special song for those who were sick in the stomach and had an evil spirit with a long tail in there. There was another song to be used while doctoring should a woman with monthlies come into the lodge, otherwise the sick person would get worse.

Beaver, Otter, and Turtle talked about all these things. They invited Buffalo Skull, who had a holy song, to be their leader and asked him to shake himself. This was to be the sign that any sick person who stood up and shook himself would recover.

They traveled southward until they came to a creek. Mink was there; he threw water on dead brush, while singing, and green leaves came out. They reached the Missouri; again Mink sang while sprinkling the dead branches, and green leaves appeared.

They reached Knife River on the fourth day and Mink called for poles to make the sweat lodge. He taught the people the Sweat Lodge songs, telling them that earth, wood, stones, and water went together in doctoring. [This combination provides the sacred origin of Earth Lodge rites given whenever a new lodge is being erected.]

Frog announced that he also belonged in the creeks, so he taught the people his doctoring song.

Mink then instructed the people in the meaning of the various rites: Use black medicine for those who are sick or have been poisoned; use the scrapings from the clamshell for those who are nearly dead; use the turtle shell to learn whether the patient will recover; use fat from around the buffalo's heart for those who have been ill a long time; use the buffalo skull for those who seek protection from their enemies.

Inheritance has followed a consistent pattern for the last three transfers: a group of siblings, male and female, bought from their mother or mothers, and sold to the children of the female siblings. The purchasing group customarily indicated which articles of the bundle were to be kept individually during their lifetime. Then, when the younger generation indicated a desire to purchase, those of the original group of buyers met to complete the sale. All features of the bundle and its transfer are characteristic of the Mandan and do not conform to the Hidatsa bundle transfer pattern. During its entire recorded period, the bundle has been associated with the Xura branch of the Waterbuster clan at Awatixa and the closely related Prairie Chicken clan at Awaxawi. It was also customary for individuals dreaming of the animals associated with the bundle to make offerings to the bundle and to secure pledges from the bundle owners that contemplated military and other undertakings would be successful.

In addition to the doctoring rites, there were earth-lodge-making rites which enjoyed some small measure of popularity. Whenever a new earth lodge was being built, or new central posts were to be erected, the household sought the assistance of someone owning rights in a Creek bundle. While she trimmed and shaped the forks of the four central posts, she addressed the sacred objects, saying, "These people are building their new earth lodge; I ask you not to fail them. They want to have good luck and no sickness. I ask you, my gods, to send them good luck. These articles they have given you, I will keep."

The restricted distribution of earth lodge building rites is significant when examined in the light of traditional residence on the Missouri. The Mandan had a well-developed system of earth-lodge-making rites which was intimately interwoven into the Okipa and Corn sacred myths. This system had no equivalent in the Hidatsa groups. Traditionally, all Hidatsa Earth Lodge rites are based on the supernatural teachings of Mink who, while singing the Sweat Lodge songs, explained that "earth, wood, stones, and water go together." Although the rites were a part of the sacred lore of the Creek bundles, females frequently purchased Earth Lodge rites independently of the other Creek bundle roles. These rites, however, seem not to have been renewed by subsequent sales; instead, new buyers preferred to purchase directly from the original Creek bundle owners. Creek bundles were traditionally of Awatixa village origin from whence they spread to Awaxawi village in recent times, and never reached Hidatsa village. The similarity of the rites to those of the Mandan is further evidence substantiating native belief that the Awatixa represent the first Hidatsa agricultural group to join the Mandan on the Missouri River.

Wolf Chief's following narrative provides pertinent data on the beliefs and habits relating to this sacred bundle:

My maternal grandmother's name was Otter Woman, for she was named from the bundle. My mother's name was Strikes-Many-Woman. Otter Woman put on the rites to get the bundle when my mother was about 10 years old. She often told her how she put on the ceremony. She made the vow just like the men did and then put up many buffalo robes and a big feast. In that way she bought the medicines that her mother and brothers had. She used to put on the sweat ceremonies for the bundle even though she owned the bundles. Sometimes she would also put on a feast and call in all those who had rights in the various animals that lived in the creeks.[6]

My mother was taught to doctor and most of the time when she did the doctoring, she cured the sick persons. Only a few of them died during my time. While she kept this bundle, she would call me to make offerings to the mink, otters, and turtles; I would give my robes to the bundle for they belonged to my mother. She often told me that this Creek bundle was almost like Missouri River bundles as they were of the otters, mink, and turtles also, so I would sometimes make offerings to the Missouri River as well.

One time we were downstream below Fishhook Village on the west side. I killed a buffalo and cut the lower part of the leg off and offered it to the "Grandfather" in the Missouri. I had heard that it was customary to put meat and calicoes on the bank for the Grandfather, a large snake. I took the ankle and fastened it to a stick and dropped it into the river, saying, "My Grandfather, I am giving you this meat." [7]

I was 10 years old when my mother taught me how to pray to these sacred things. She would say, "If you make offerings often and say, 'I want to save my life,' when you come to the enemies, you can pray to the bundle."

My mother gave me an otter skin to keep. When I went out to attack the enemy, I put it over my head; I was always lucky and did not lose my life. I did not put on the ceremony to own the bundle, for my mother owned it and prayed whenever I was to war. About 1882 my two brothers, Spotted Bird and Two Teeth, and my sister named Brown Woman went together and bought my mother's bundle rights. They made the vow and then went up the Missouri hunting to get the meat. While they were out hunting, they came to the Crow-Flies-High's village and their clans-people up there put in some goods for the ceremony.[8] A dance was given there also, during which time "sons and daughters" of the people of the Prairie Chicken clan gave many fine things, knowing that their "fathers and mothers" would need these things for the ceremony. They stayed up at Fort Buford until spring when the cherries were in bloom.

When they gave the ceremony, they called in the holy men; they were the people who had buffalo skulls in their sacred bundles. They really did not have to be invited, for it was expected of them. These people represented the holy men: Smells (Big Bird rights); Chippewa (Big Bird rights); Hairy Coat (Woman Above rights); Son of Star (Wolf rights); Bear-Looks-Out (Old-Woman-Who-Never-Dies rights); Bear Heart (Bear rights); Wolf Eyes (Wolf rights); Crows Breast (Naxpike rights); Red Tail (Wolf rights); Different Wolf (Buffalo rights); Woman-in-Water (Missouri River rights); No Milk (Missouri River and Naxpike rights); Poor Wolf (Missouri River rights); and Small Ankles (Waterbuster skull rights).

Poor Wolf was the leader of the singers, getting his rights both from the Creek bundle and the sacred buffalo skull through the Imitating Buffalo ceremony. He invited the Holy Women society to come to the feast. They used the Mandan Okipa lodge for the ceremony. Anyone who prayed to even a small part of the Creek bundle was expected to attend. When the procession reached the lodge, my brothers filled the pipe and gave it to one of the Waterbuster clan "fathers." During this time my mother was using the rattles and singing the holy songs.

---

[6] Bundle renewal feasts. When none pledged these feasts, it was customary for a bundle owner to perform these Renewal Feasts.

[7] This was also a popular food for Old-Woman-Who-Never-Dies.

[8] Although this group had separated a few years before, the bond between clan relatives remained strong.

As the pipe passed around, the holy men would say, "You are going to have a long life and a good home," speaking to my brothers and sister. My brothers and sister would give my mother a valuable article each time she finished one of the sacred songs. There were many plates for the roast corn and a large pile of corn balls in the center of the lodge. She would sing four songs and get a pile of robes; again she sang four songs and got another pile of robes. There was a sweat bath ready and they used only the finest robes to cover it. Many of the robes were fancy ones worked in quills.

Then she went into the sweat lodge, saying "Any of you old men, who wish to, may come into the sweat lodge.[9] After you have been cleansed, they will distribute the corn balls and other articles. All you old men walk towards the sweat lodge and stand at the door. I will sprinkle you with water and give you new life."

She directed Spotted Bird to bring the sacred objects and place them on robes in front of the sweat lodge. She also directed him to sit beside her at the entrance to the sweat lodge saying, "I will sing the holy songs. You wanted to get these gods so listen carefully. Do not forget them."

Then she repeated all of the holy songs that came down to us from the beginning of time. When she finished, she sprinkled all of the old men and called for the women and children to come. They were sprinkled also.

When she finished, she called Spotted Bird, Two Teeth, Brown Woman, and myself to sit down near her. She sang the holy songs again in the order that they were given to the people long ago and sprinkled water over us. Brown Woman's husband did not take part even though he hunted for her, but he could have bought in with his wife if he had given his mother-in-law a scalp. Then she called my two brothers and their wives and Brown Woman to sit in front of her at the entrance of the sweat lodge. There she repeated the same sacred songs. Then they took all of the sacred objects from the top of the sweat lodge.

They had a stone ready to put into the pit. My mother said, "Those of you who wish may break up a chokecherry stick and throw it inside where the stones are. It will signify that you will kill an enemy. My son, break the stick into four pieces and throw them in one at a time. Each time mention the name of an enemy you want to kill."

Spotted Bird mentioned a Sioux named Two Bears that he wanted to kill and threw in a stick; with the second stick, Beads-Stick-Out-of-His-Side, a Sioux, was mentioned; with the third stick he called Medicine Bear,[10] a Sioux; with the fourth stick he called the name of Red Spear, a Sioux. He had heard of these enemies by name only, for they were holy men of the Sioux tribe. When he finished, the other stones were put into the pit and the sweat was ready.

Before putting water on the stones, my mother said, "You men here in the sweat lodge who wish to fast may do so, for you have many enemies. I am ready to pour the water. If you fast, you may have good dreams to bring good luck."

The men in the sweat were crying, for they wanted to be great chiefs. They were people who already had sacred buffalo skulls. I heard them saying in there, "I want to kill my enemy; our enemies we have thrown into the pit, and we want to kill them. We are poor and we beg you to help us."[11]

Then the sweat lodge rites were over. She said to the older people who owned sacred buffalo skulls, "You bring me a stick so I can feed these gods first" and

---

[9] She used the familiar term "old man" as used commonly for a husband.

[10] Medicine Bear's mother was a Mandan taken prisoner as a little girl when Nuptadi village north of Bismarck was destroyed by the Sioux prior to 1800.

[11] The man in the lodge at this time represented the most distinguished males of the tribe.

then she fed them. She continued, "My sons and daughter, you are the ones who put on this ceremony and you should pray to your new gods. Also, all you men who own rights in black medicine and peppermint should give them some to make them lucky."

Then she addressed the bundle, saying, "You are passing out of my hands now; you will be in Spotted Bird's keeping. I have always treated you well and I hope that while these people keep you, there will be no trouble."

She touched the different kinds of food—the corn balls and the meat—with the stick, and then she touched the sacred objects, saying, "You eat this. Your son has given this to you and you can see what he has done. Perhaps there are some holy spirits standing outside that we do not know about" so she made a motion with her stick as of feeding them also. She touched the food and pointed the stick to the different creeks and rivers, saying, "Your grandsons are giving you this. They want to be lucky and have a long life. Sometime they may want to cross over you so you should look out for them while they are crossing."

She called Two Teeth, Spotted Bird, their wives, and our sister, saying, "I am going to sing a holy song that belongs to the Frog and that will be the end. When I sing that song, it will mean that you will have a good living and many children." Finishing the singing she said, "I have received many benefits from owning these gods. Now I have received good things for them and am ready to give them up. I will heap these robes and the food into two piles before my children distribute them to you old people. Each of you older people pray for my children and promise them good luck so that they will conquer their enemies and become chiefs."

There was so much to divide that it took a long time. When this was done, my mother said, "We have finished eating and we are all happy that our children have done this for us. You spirits should now go back to the places that you came from; the creeks, the Missouri River, and the four directions." [12]

Formerly we did not get pay for doctoring unless the patient lived. If the patient died, the doctor was afraid to take what had been promised him. In the last 40 years [40 years prior to 1933] the younger people have been taking the pay.

When I was about 12 years old [1863] four sisters, Juneberries, Bird Woman, Different Sage, and Roots, the mothers-in-law of Percy Rush, came to her. [13] One of their daughters was ill and different doctors had tried to cure her. They came with a red pipe and walked up to my mother's sacred bundle and said, "We have come for you. We want you to come over and doctor our daughter."

One had a robe and some calicoes with her. My mother inquired of my father whether she should go there to doctor, for he had told her that she ought not go out doctoring too often or she might lose her powers. Then her own children might catch a serious disease. This time he said, "I think they need you badly so you should go over there and find out if you can help. You know how to tell if the patient is going to die by feeling the stomach. If it is a hopeless case, you do not have to stay." [14]

They offered to pay three horses and several robes to have the girl cured. Before they left, they put the pipe in front of my mother's bundle and she smoked it while talking to the bundle. Then she went to the sick girl's lodge.

My mother came back and said that the girl was very skinny and that the people had given her two sets of eagle feathers; 24 tail feathers. My father

---

[12] Note that Strikes-Many-Woman was more generous than Wolf Chief, who kept for himself a large share of the goods put up by the buyers. Note also that food and goods were taken from two piles by the moieties.

[13] Bear-Looks-Out's wives; see Old-Woman-Who-Never-Dies rites.

[14] Since the four sisters and other doctors had tried and failed, Strikes-Many-Woman could enhance her bundle's status if she succeeded.

promised to lend assistance. The parents wanted my mother to stay in the lodge overnight for it was then that she got frightened, thinking she would die, and got worse. My mother said, "I gave the girl some water. She swallowed some of it so I think I will stay over there tonight. I can tell better in the morning whether she will recover."

I did not see how she doctored for I was not there. Next day my mother came back and said "I felt of her stomach and I could tell that there was a pulse toward the back of the stomach on both sides. I kneaded the stomach and it seemed that one side is getting better. If it improves, I think she will recover."

She came back the second day and my father inquired if the girl had eaten anything and my mother said, "She would not eat yesterday, but today she wanted roasted corn and I gave her some."

Small Ankles, my father, was also a good doctor for he had a dream from the bear and buffalo but he could not doctor for his neighbors, only his own children. He did not like to doctor others, for in his dream he was doctoring his own children. Since he and Bear-Looks-Out both belonged to the Waterbuster clan, the sick girl was also Small Ankles "daughter" so he thought it would be all right since Strikes-Many-Woman thought she would recover.

He said, "I will go along with you this time and help you a little."

She said, "Yes, you come along and help me for I think I can cure her. I felt of her stomach near the backbone and it seems that it is getting soft on one side."

My father went to his bundles and I heard him praying to them. Then my parents went off together. When they got there my father said, "I am not a regular doctor but I will help, for in my dream I saw myself doctoring. If I see that she is going to get well, I will stay with her and help her along."

Bear-Looks-Out's family was glad and promised a good horse. He began doctoring by telling what he had seen in his dream from the bear. He sang the holy song the bear had sung and blew water over the girl. He did this four times and the sick girl sat up, saying, "I am well now and can eat. I would like to have some chokecherries."

It was hard to find the cherries for this happened just before the cherries were ripe. The women went out through the village and found some dried cherries from the preceding year's crop. They left the berries near his sacred bundle.

Small Ankles talked to the bundle, saying, "I saw you in my dream and you taught me how to doctor and I am doing that now. You showed me how to doctor with the chokecherries."

He sent some young men who had come in to go out and bring in some branches with the cherries and leaves on, for he was going to mix these cherries and leaves into a mash, cook it, and feed her. While the cherries were cooking, he burned an incense from cedar for that went with the bears who live in the cedar thickets. He chewed up the cherries and leaves while singing the bear song and, addressing the bear, he said, "I would like to see this sick girl lie down stretched out on her back."

He stood at her feet, sang the holy song, and, directing her to open her mouth, put the mixture on her tongue.

She chewed it and said, "I am eating fresh chokecherries."

Small Ankles said, "That is fine. You are going to get well because you have eaten the new chokecherries. How do you feel?"

She said, "It seems that I have new life and can carry myself around."

Small Ankles told the women that they should give her some food and that her mother should feed her. She began to feed herself shortly afterward while, before that time, she could not lift her hands. She sat up and ate the food by herself.

Small Ankles said to my mother, "Now it is your turn. I know you have some medicines to doctor her with. You should use some of the peppermint to cleanse her with. You have many kinds; use all at the same time so she will recover the faster." Then he teased my mother, saying, "You see how I doctored her. You are supposed to be the real doctor for you have the things that came from early times. I am not supposed to be a great doctor for I only dreamed of mine. Still you have seen how I did it. So you should not sit there all the time but do something."

My mother used a plate to dip the peppermint in, and, sprinkling the girl, she said, "I would like to see this girl recover; I want to get these horses; I do not want to stay here too long."

Then she said to my father, "You did not say whether the sick girl would recover or die. I think you ought to tell me." But he would not make a prediction.

She doctored a second time, greasing the girl with fat taken from around the buffalo's heart and singing the song that went with the use of the fat. When she had finished rubbing the fat into the girl's skin, the girl said, "Now I feel like a different person."

My mother had a turtle shell in her sacred bundle. She said, "I am going to find out if she will recover; it is time to find out now."

She burned some of the peppermint before the girl, took up the small turtle and sang the sacred song, "Mink is holy; he came; he is here" and chewed peppermint and spit it on the turtle singing, "Peppermint is holy; he came; he is here."

While she sang, she held the turtle shell in her hand, motioned with it three times and said, "When I throw the turtle on her, she will recover if it stops on her; if it drops down, she will die."

She threw the turtle towards the girl and it stopped on her abdomen so she said to my father, "Take a stick and tap the turtle lightly."

He took the stick and tapped the turtle with it and the turtle slid down slowly and fell off the girl.

My mother said, "I promise that the girl will get better and walk around within 3 days."

They came back to see the girl after that and my father said that he could see that she would recover by her eyes. Within 10 days the girl was walking around again. My mother came back then to cleanse her. She gave the girl a small piece of mink hide to wear around her neck whenever she walked for she was still quite weak and thin.

When she came home my father said, "It is all right; it was just like winning a game. We heard that many doctors had tried and then we succeeded. We have many children of our own so you should not go out doctoring often. If someone calls you again, you should not go."

Another time Picture came and said that her boy was very sick. It was the custom when they begged, saying, "I know you love your children and do not want to have any bad luck" that one could not refuse. Mother went over to see what ailed the boy and came back to tell my father.

She said, "You stopped me from going out to doctor. This woman came over and begged through our own children, saying that we honored our children. I do not have to go if you do not want me to. You must decide."

He said, "Since that old woman came here and begged, honoring our children, I do not see how we can refuse. You could go without taking your sacred bundle, feel of his insides, and see if you can cure him."

She felt of his stomach and then ordered the people to prepare the sweat lodge. She took him inside and sang the songs of the Creek bundle. When he came out he felt better and begged for food. I heard her telling my father that she thought he would recover for his eyes were bright.

My father said, "Since you think it is all right and they have promised two horses, I think it is better that I go over too and help you. It will be all right for you to stay there 1 night."

She tried hard to cure the boy; she examined the stomach and found a hard place there next to the backbone. She thought it was the place where the sickness was centered. She kneaded the stomach every few hours. She pressed the abdomen and then she felt a movement inside. She came home and said that she had been up nearly all night pressing the stomach. She begged help of Small Ankles, saying, "I think the boy is going to get over his sickness. I think you should go along with me and help the boy."

He said, "You can go in the morning and I will be over there at night. If I think he is going to get well, we will go together. Then I am sure we can work a cure."

She came back before sundown and said, "I had a hard time today. Red Head came in and just as soon as she left, the boy lost consciousness. I heard that this woman had her monthlies. I used the medicines that I am supposed to use when this happens but it seems that the boy is worse. I think you ought to go along as you have medicines when a woman with monthlies comes around."[15]

My mother's rites consisted of a song, "That woman came to the lodge door; she is holy; she goes out." [16]

The two went back. The boy was still unconscious. They took their sacred bundles this time. They blew peppermint over him and sang the sacred songs. Towards morning it seemed that the boy was a little better.

Small Ankles said, "I have been using the powers that I got from the bears; now I am going to use my Buffalo Spirit rites."

Before doctoring the boy, Small Ankles stood and addressed all in the room, "I tried to have a god of my own; I found a place where there were many buffalo skulls and bones. I piled them together and built a little lodge a short distance away. In the daytime I stood by the pile of bones, and at night I stayed in the lodge for this was during the winter. On the fourth day I cut skin from my leg and offered it to the gods so that I would be successful in all that I undertook. I want to remind you, my gods, that I did all this and now I want to cure this boy. I am going to sing the songs you taught me. You told me you were the Buffalo Spirits and you gave me these two buffalo teeth and hair. In my dreams you showed me all this so I am going to try to cure this boy and get the two horses. I will sing the sacred songs."

He sang the songs twice. He shook the boy and inquired how he felt and the boy said that he was feeling better already. Right afterward, the boy went to sleep.

Next day Small Ankles inquired how he felt and the boy said, "I feel much better; it seems that I can feel my body now. I want something to eat."

They doctored for about 14 days and then they had the boy up. They cleansed the boy in the sweat lodge and brought back with them all the things promised except the horses, which the people brought in from grazing and delivered the next morning.

---

[15] That is, she is menstruating.

[16] Small Ankles' rites were concerned with eagle trapping. There were particular menstruation rites which were performed to prevent bad luck to the eagle trappers.

When I was 9 years old, the people went out hunting and ran nine Santee Sioux into a pocket where they built a fort. There was a fight and four of our men were killed. A man named Little Bear was in the fight and he would say, "If we stay around here we will all be killed; we should jump into the hole and drive them out."

He tried and was killed. Then Bluestone went toward them with his sacred spear but he was killed before he reached the fort. Cedar was next; he jumped into the fort killed one enemy, and then he was killed. By that time six of our people were killed and we had only one of theirs.

Chokecherry said, "Wait until I can see how to get rid of those eight enemies. Bear Necklace, my son-in-law, stand in front of me. All you young men stand with him. Each time I sing, you make a noise. When I have sung the fourth time, run over there, jump into that hole and kill them. Bear Necklace will take my shield and bear bundle. You will never get killed so long as I sing my song. The song I will sing is the one I was taught by the grizzly bears in my dream. Do not be afraid."

Each time he sang, he shook the chokecherry brush in imitation of the bears. When the song was sung the fourth time, the young men jumped into the fort, killed all of the enemies, and butchered them with their knives.

In the fight, Bear Heart was shot between the two bones of the lower arm. It was only a flesh wound but he came to my mother to cure him for she had the right to doctor the wounded from a dream she had from the mink in her Creek bundle. She sang "It is badly smashed by the bullet but he will recover."

When she sold her bundle, she passed the New Mink song on to her children.[17]

When her grandchildren had high fevers, she would doctor them. She would not take pay from her own children as she had in mind being of assistance to her own children when she bought the ceremony. Outsiders were required to pay well before she would doctor.

TYING-THE-POTS

This ceremony, performed at Awaxawi village, had no precise equivalent at any other Mandan or Hidatsa villages. It was, according to traditions, a popular rainmaking ceremony at Awaxawi and was performed annually during the hottest part of the summer. This important summer ceremony occupied the same prominent position at Awaxawi that the Naxpike or Sun Dance did at the other two villages.

It was not possible to identify any survivor or older descendant of that village who had ever participated in the Naxpike as bundle purchaser. This would indicate recent union with the other two groups, too short a time for complete intergroup borrowing of their respective ceremonial bundles. Informants recalled, however, several of their older relatives who had participated in the summer Tying-the-Pots or the Mandan Okipa ceremonies.[18]

Like other native traditions concerning clay pots, the sacred origin myth for the ceremony relates the experiences of the snake people.

---

[17] Here we find an instance of ritual enrichment.

[18] This group has traditions of residence on the tributaries of the Red River until early historic times.

The following abbreviated account by Bears Arm comes from Poor Wolf and Old-Woman-Crawling who lived at Awaxawi village until its abandonment after the smallpox epidemic.

A very handsome young man living at Awaxawi village seldom went arouud with the girls because he thought that most of them were foolish.   One morning he awakened to see a young woman leaving his bed.   She came for 4 nights and he resolved to follow her and learn who she was.   When she left the last time, he followed her and she led him northward until, when evening came, a killdeer bird was frightened up and she knew the bird was scout for the Big Birds.

The young woman requested her companion to cut a chokecherry branch to represent a snake, which they put near the entrance to a cave situated on the river bank near Mannhaven.   In the night they heard the thunder and knew that the big birds were attacking the branch.

After the storm passed, they traveled northeastward and came to a large lake. He followed her into the water where he found a new land and saw that the people were snakes.   The young woman was the daughter of Chief-of-the-Snakes.

One day he heard thunder and saw lightning.   The people said that the thunderbirds were trying to kill them, but the lightning could not penetrate through the water.

After a while the young man became homesick and longed to see his people again.   The young woman being married to him, she agreed to return with him. Although she went about a great deal in the village under the lake, she remained at home all the time in her husband's village.   Snake Woman would stay in the lodge seated on a buffalo hide from which the hair had been removed; she was afraid of thunder.   She worked all the time decorating robes, leggings, and moccasins with porcupine quills but she never went outside to get wood and water, or to work in the gardens.

She ordered that no woman must ever touch her husband and he had this information announced through the village.   One day his sister-in-law touched the corner of his robe while teasing him.   He cut out the spot in the robe where it was touched but his wife detected it and disappeared shortly afterwards.

He returned to the lake and tried to go to the land beneath the lake but each time he dived down, he came back up again.   He cried long and his wife appeared out of the water with two pots, one large one and one small one.   She explained that the large one was a man and the small one a woman, and stated that they were to be used as drums for bringing rain.   She instructed him in dressing the pots with clothing and in making the snake poles.   She taught the songs that went with the rites.

She warned that the pots should not be carried about from place to place but must be stored in a deep hole with a strong roof over them when not in use, as protection from the thunder.

The ceremony was an annual affair and was celebrated during the hottest days for the purpose of bringing rain.   Both men and women pledged to perform the rites but women were excluded from the lodge where the rites were performed as was customary whenever fasting was practiced.   The person pledging the ceremony was assisted by his relatives in the same manner as in the Naxpike or the Wolf rites but the costs in goods were not as great as when buying a bundle.   The one bearing the expenses of the ceremony was expected to provide fancy clothing, for the decoration of the pots, and robes for the singers.

The principal ceremonial equipment consisted of two very large clay pots decorated to represent the water snakes from whom it was believed they were obtained.   One was slightly larger than the other and represented the male and the smaller one represented the female. It is said that the decorations on the body of these vessels represented the snakes.   However, no one living at the time this study was made could provide a precise description of the decorations.   The two vessels were kept in a corn chamber in a bed of soft sage [19] and covered with a strong roof of ash poles and earth.   They were taken from the pit only on ceremonial occasions.   They were never exposed to direct sunlight and were kept in the earth lodge while the ceremony was performed.

This apparently was the only rainmaking rite which provided opportunities for formal fasting and torturing.   Young men conducted themselves in essentially the same manner as when fasting during the NaxpikE, the Wolf, or the Mandan Okipa ceremonies, calling on members of their father's clan to insert the sticks for the suspension or dragging of buffalo skulls.   The use of a carved log to represent a snake with eyes, mouth, and nostrils at one end and carved notches along the back was unique to this ceremony.   During the performance of the ceremony, the leaders ran back and forth beside the log dragging a vibrator over the notches.   The resulting noise was believed to represent the sounds made by the snakes when "bringing the rains." On other occasions during the performance of the rites, drumheads made from the buffalo's paunch were tied tightly over the two clay pots and allowed to dry.   The drumsticks consisted of curved willows with a crosshatching of sinews.   There were special songs for "Tying-the-Pots," referring to the tying of drumheads over the pots, which is the name by which the ceremony is known today.

Those who fasted during the ceremony were provided with small notched sticks or carved ribs which they rubbed together whenever the singers caused the large vibrator to be sounded.   It is suggested that these small individual vibrators are the numerous notched ribs found frequently in all of the Hidatsa and Mandan village sites of the Heart River focus or culture.   When the ceremony was completed, the pots were returned to the cache and protected by a pole and earth cover.   Informants thought those giving the ceremony also received rights to make pottery with certain designs.

The ceremony had many features in common with the men's Notched Stick age-grade society of Awaxawi village.   It appears that

---

[19] Called "different sage" by the Hidatsa.

the ceremony was an expression of the greater emphasis placed on agriculture by the Awaxawi.[20]

The rites were abandoned a few years after moving to Fishhook Village when the principal sacred bundle owner died. The people at first returned to Awaxawi during the summer for the annual performance, but the rituals never became popular at Fishhook when the three village groups united there. Due to the prohibition against moving the pots, they were never taken from Awaxawi. The exact spot where they are buried is unknown; the last person to possess that information died a few years prior to the time of this study. According to native concepts, the Tying-the-Pots ceremony originated after this village group reached the Missouri, this belief being based on incidents that occurred on or near the Missouri.

WOLF CEREMONIES

The Hidatsa recognized three distinct hereditary Wolf ceremonial complexes, Wolf Woman, Sunrise Wolf, and Sunset Wolf. Each ceremony was transmitted independently of the others through established hereditary lines although the Wolf Woman impersonator officiated also during all performances of the Sunrise and Sunset Wolf ceremonies. Traditionally, the three ceremonies were founded rather late. The Wolf Woman is conceptualized to be one of the females created by Village-Old-Woman during earliest times. Nevertheless, the sacred origin myths related by the Wolf Woman bundle owners and the Holy Women attribute the origin of this specific Wolf Ceremony to incidents occurring after 1800 when a small group of Hidatsa quarreled and moved onto the Little Missouri to build a village near the mouth of Cherry Creek.[21] The Hidatsa consider the recency of the events leading to the establishment of these bundle rites merely as the recognition of a supernatural being who was with the people for a long time, gave them personal dreams and sacred bundles, but was not recognized by formal tribal ceremonies until recently.

The Hidatsa date the establishment of the Sunrise Wolf ceremony by the fact that it was instituted by Village-Young-Man from visions experienced while living at the mouth of Heart River [22] subsequent to residence at Devils Lake and to the fact that his war party found Old-Woman-Who-Never-Dies still living on the Upper Missouri. The Sunset Wolf rites were believed to have been established after the

---

[20] "The Mandanes and Saulteurs (Awaxawi) are a stationary people who never leave their villages except to go hunting or on a war excursion. They are much more agricultural than their neighbors, the Big Bellies (Hidatsa and Awatixa), raising an immense quantity of corn, beans, squashes, tobacco" (Henry, 1897, p. 338).

[21] George F. Will dates this settlement as about 1811. See Will, 1946, pp. 16–17.

[22] These rites also bear close similarity to Mandan practices and may well have been borrowed from the Mandan while at Heart River.

Hidatsa had moved northward to the mouth of Knife River and subsequent to the removal of Old-Woman-Who-Never-Dies to her permanent home in the south. Traditionally, then, the order of adoption of the various formal Wolf ceremonies was: (1) Sunrise Wolf; (2) Sunset Wolf; (3) Wolf Woman.

The Wolf rites are distinctive in that their principal emphasis was on warfare and their ritual training consisted primarily of teaching the formal offensive warfare patterns. Offensive warfare with the Hidatsa was a highly ritualistic activity in which the participants, irrespective of the sacred bundles carried by the leaders, impersonated the wolves and coyotes. The leaders themselves were known as the Old Wolves, the scouts were the Coyotes, and the other members of the party were Young Wolves. The great florescence of rites emphasizing warfare was traditionally of recent occurrence. The elements comprising these rites, however, were plucked from the long-standing cultural traditions and seemingly do not represent many features new to the Hidatsa groups. The ritual attitude toward the wolf is not unlike that of the Mandan, who had gone even farther than the Hidatsa in the development of hereditary bundle rites, or the Crow, Sioux, Cheyenne, and their other neighbors; but the form taken was quite different. Mandan Wolf rites were intimately integrated into both the ceremonial and clan systems while we find no evidence that Hidatsa Wolf rites followed any particular clan pattern.

In the Mandan sacred myths, Clay-on-the-Face, a wolf impersonator, regretted that only the moiety representing the buffaloes and founded by Lone Man had a leader, and he pledged that, should the war expedition which he was planning return successfully, he would give names to the people of the opposite moiety. So, when he met the enemy and overcame them in battle, he thought of his vow. As he returned toward the village he observed the prairie chickens, the speckled eagles, the bears, the badgers, the snakes living in the red hills, the crows, and the people in a clump of woods, so he gave these names to the people of the opposite moiety as clan names, designating those of the numerically superior Prairie Chicken clan to be the "carriers" of the Wolf rites. The clan inheritance feature was preserved by transmission from "mother's brother to sister's son" or "father-in-law to son-in-law" inheritance, both being aspects of clan inheritance. These Mandan beliefs and practices were entirely lacking with the Hidatsa. Transmission was from father to son, thus cutting across clan lines, and Wolf Woman rites were transferred from a female to one she addressed as "daughter"—father's sister to brother's daughter, or mother to daughter.

SUNRISE WOLF

Wolf Chief, who bought full ceremonial rights in this ceremony, provided a detailed account of the sacred origin myth and his bundle purchase efforts. The following is a condensed account of this myth:

When the Hidatsa, the people who afterward lived on the north bank of Knife River, reached the Missouri they first crossed and settled near Heart River. The people would see the high buttes around there and think that some great spirits surely lived in them. A young man though the would try to learn which spirits were in these buttes so he walked far up the Heart River and fasted at one of the highest buttes. He fasted from time to time for 4-day periods until one morning just before sunrise he heard someone singing Wolf songs and talking from afar.

The voice said, "I take their part going out against the enemies and now my son here will do the same." Then the wolves ran, singing, "You will take the part I used to take. I used to go out against the enemies and take their scalps. Now you will do the same as I did."

They ran a third time but he could not see the people who were running. Each time they stopped they sang a holy song. They said, "My son, you should do as we did and go out and overcome your enemies." They ran again and stopped to dance. They said, "It is easy for us to do that and, you being our son now, we give you the power to do it also."

The wolves came into view and he saw nearly 30 of them. He heard the songs but he did not understand them. He went home and in his dreams he saw wolf hides over the wolves' shoulders and caps of wolf hide, to which the ears were attached, on their heads.

The Wolves said, "You have been suffering so long to get a god of your own. We knew that you were fasting and we have come to instruct you to put on the Wolf ceremony so that you can carry on these rites that we want your people to have. This is a good thing we have brought to you. There are many enemies to the south and they will come against you. You will need this power. In the future you will pass the ceremony on to others but, before they put up the ceremony, they must first go out and kill their enemy. You see how we said 'We have been victorious over our enemies.' You repeat that to your sons, too. There will be another wolf, the Wolf of the Sunset. Tell your people that you want to put on the ceremony for the Flatland Wolf. When you do this, we are going to sing a holy song and change you into a wolf. You do not have to go out and kill an enemy afterwards but pretend that you do. Then the people will make fun of you and give you a funny name. Whenever you sing this holy song you will change into a wolf. We will show you how to get more strength and power so that you will never become exhausted no matter how far you travel. Do not show off too soon. It may be that some enemies will attack and surround you and then we will instruct you further."

The Wolves showed him how to use the sacred things—Black Medicine, Sweetgrass, White Clay, and Earth—so that he and later generations would know what to do when tired, saying, "You should inform the people that there are songs to go with each of these four things. When you pass them on to the younger generation, you should teach them when to use the songs."

Then the Wolves sang, "This earth is holy; sweetgrass is holy; black medicine is holy; water is holy. All these things are holy; they will give you back your strength again."

The Wolves said, "There will be a buffalo skull too and a song to go with it and they sang, "He came to the lodge; he is coming."

The Wolves added, "In the future you will want to reveal all this supernatural power we have given you, but do not tell them anything until they make fun of you. When you are out against the enemy, and the scouts report the enemy near, there is a holy song that the scouts should use. Tell them that when they run back to report, they should pretend to be coyotes. Then the others should stand in a row. The warriors will sing and the scouts will tell where they saw the enemies. There is also a holy song that belongs to a very old female wolf: at the end there is a howl.[23] Anyone who sings this song and makes a wish will be unusually successful in getting what he asks. Whenever the warriors come back with success over their enemies, they should put red paint under their noses; this is a sign of success. It may be that in the future other generations will want additional dreams. Then they, too, may get additional holy songs from us."

So ended the Wolves' instructions.

Each time the warriors went out to kill their enemies, this young man would say that he was going along and that he was the one who would do the actual killing. When the party returned, he would put marks on his leggings. The people thought this was funny for he had not been out to war. His pal would tell him what the people said.

One time the warriors, including the pal, were out and they made up a war song giving him a name, singing, "The Man-who-Stays-at-Home-Smoking-and-Jealous, he pretends to be brave; still he has not done anything. He is just fooling himself."

So the people called him Village-Young-Man. He told his pal of his experiences with the wolves and which he had now passed on to the others to make them successful. He announced that he was really going out to reveal his supernatural powers. There were 12 in the party which included himself and his pal. They came to the lodge of Old-Woman-Who-Never-Dies and she brought out bowls of roasted corn for her "grandchildren." The men thought the pots were very small indeed and she sensed their thought, saying, "Those are indeed small vessels. When the vessels are nearly empty, stir them and they will fill again. When you go out, go to the west. There are seven men whom you will meet.[24] You can kill them all off. They will have wolf hides around their bodies and carry bows without bark. When you kill those seven enemies, I wish you would bring me one of the scalps to hang on the side of my basket." [25]

They went west to an oak grove, killed the seven warriors, and gave the old woman the scalp. She said, "Whenever you want to get the best of your enemies, you should promise me something."

At home the people danced and Village-Young-Man decorated his spear and wore feathers to show what he had done.

Black Hawk organized a war party and the pal thought they should go along so further demonstrations of his supernatural powers could be revealed. Village-Young-Man went to his fasting grounds to get further instructions from the wolves. Then he saw the tipis far to the north so he asked his wife to prepare his moccasins. She did not believe he would go out for he was always promising and never went out.

---

[23] This reference is to the Wolf Woman of the Wolf Woman ceremony.

[24] These seven warriors were turned to stone (pl. 9).

[25] It was customary for young men going to war to seek supernatural assistance of the Old-Woman-Who Never-Dies bundle owner and to promise a scalp for the ceremonial basket when successful in striking the enemy.

The next day he instructed his wife to go to the river bank and hide. He walked by her and swam the river. There he howled like a wolf and when she uncovered her head, she saw a wolf on the opposite bank. He called to her, "Now you see that I am holy" and he ran over the hills towards the north.

Before the party left, he told his pal that he would join them on the fourth night while the others were singing derisive songs about him and that when they heard a wolf howl he should bring roasted shoulder meat to the edge of the camp and leave it. Then on the next day Village-Young-Man would be far to the front and coming from the enemy's village when the others first saw the camp. All these things came true. Village-Young-Man and the other scouts returned to their camp where he reported that he saw the lodges and they were as thick as the spots in the buffalo's mouth and informed the scouts that in the future scouts must repeat the same information.

The leader did not believe what Village-Young-Man said so he went out to see for himself. Village-Young-Man went into the enemy camp. There he waited until daybreak so his party could see him. Then he killed a woman, scalped her, and ran away slowly so that the enemy would follow. He ran back to the scouts who had not yet reached the enemy camp, instructed them as the Wolves had taught him in running so as not to tire, and led them into battle against the scouts which the enemy had sent out. While instructing the scouts, he demonstrated his new supernatural powers by knocking down four enemies with the assistance of his pal.

While returning to Black Hawk's camp, he instructed the scouts in the use of white clay to make them light on their feet so they could run faster. The main party stood in a line when they heard the scouts coming and Village-Young-Man gave the scalp and elk-horn scraper to Black Hawk's wife, addressing her as sister-in-law. Black Hawk was not sure that they might not be old lovers and Village-Young-Man criticized him for acting unchieftainlike. The scouts told Black Hawk of Village-Young-Man's skill and supernatural powers and they danced the scalp dances.

Village-Young-Man said to Black Wolf, "I am going back home and will be there before sunrise for I am not really human any more. I will transform myself into a wolf and be there when the sun rises."

He crossed the river at daybreak and went into his lodge. Since he returned so soon, his wife thought he had been lost. He told of turning himself into a wolf and she was happy. But he said nothing to her of his part in the battle. He dressed up and put marks on his leggings to show that he had killed the enemies and he wore scalps and feathers too. The people thought he must be insane and laughed at him.

On the fourth morning home he saw an old man walking through the village and he asked him to be announcer to tell the people that the war party would arrive that day and to use the word *sakucha* which in the future would signify that the party had been successful. The old man made the announcement even though he thought the young man was insane.

Soon the people saw the war party on the opposite bank singing an Honor song and each time they sang they mentioned Village-Young-Man. It was customary for the relatives of those who had killed the enemy to give out food and goods. His parents hesitated for they did not believe their son had accomplished these things and were crying for shame.

Village-Young-Man came off of his lodge and said to his wife and parents, "I am the one who killed all the enemies they mention. Now they are asking for articles and you should give them some. Paint your faces black and dance for I did all that they tell you I have done."

His wife stood in front of their lodge with her face painted and was happy because her husband had been successful.

Village-Young-Man instructed the people that the war leaders should not look into holes in the ground nor eat meat from the buffalo's hocks. Village-Young-Man taught the ceremony to those who came to him and wanted to give a feast to the wolves.

The Wolf rites differ from most other ceremonies in several respects: (1) the sacred myths were more widely known than those for other ceremonies, due in part it seems, to the training young men received prior to and during their first military expeditions; and (2) there were no special singers for the rites whose status during ritual performances exceeded that of other comparable bundle owners.

Items in a Wolf bundle were: a wolf hide; a braid of sweetgrass; black medicine root; cap of wolf hide with the ears attached; any fox or coyote—Wolf Chief's being a gray fox—to represent the scouts; a buffalo skull; and 12 sticks. Four bundle lines represented by Two Tails, Yellow Shoulder, Red Basket, and Small Ankles survived the smallpox epidemic of 1837. During the succeeding years the number of bundles doubled but at no time were the sales sufficiently numerous to become an annual event.

Wolf Chief was one of the last to buy a bundle during which the full ceremony was performed. This ceremony was performed in 1880 or 1882 in conjunction with his brother who was buying their father's Woman Above rites. Since that time, due to the termination of Plains warfare, interest in the bundles died out. Most of the bundles have since been put away.

Wolf Chief provided the following account of the purchase of a Sunrise Wolf bundle. In this joint purchase his brother assisted him and received their father's Woman Above bundle.[26] The details of the purchase preliminaries and the final transfer are given essentially as related by Wolf Chief. This narrative is especially valuable in illustrating simultaneous purchase of two distinct bundles, a practice characteristic of the later years when the aboriginal culture was breaking down rapidly. Of the purchase, Wolf Chief said:

This Wolf rite, before my time, belonged to my father, Small Ankles. One day my brother, Red Basket, came to me and said, "I dreamed about our father's Wolf bundle."

That was when I was 30 and my brother was 24.

I said to him, "I had such a dream, too. Now you are trying to do the same thing but it is very difficult to do. Let's think it over a while and not make any promises we cannot fulfill. In your mind you have it already for you have seen it in your dream. I do not want to refuse you for we might get into trouble and have serious misfortunes. You did not say a certain bundle. You said that you want to own all the bundles that our father has. You know that he has many other ceremonies which makes it all the harder. Our father owns the Wolf of the

---

[26] For the myths and additional information on the Woman Above ceremony see pp. 323–333.

Sunrise, but he has the Black Bear for eagle trapping. Then he also owns the Old-Woman-Above and the Waterbuster Eagles. It would be easier if you mentioned a certain one. We should pick out certain ones to use. I think you should pick out the Old-Woman-Above ceremony and I will take the Sunrise Wolf for that would be easier."

We informed out father about our plans and he said, "It is going to be hard for you because the buffalo are nearly gone. The only way you will be able to do it will be to ask the different societies. It may be that they will give you enough valuable things such as robes, horses, and clothing to make up the ceremony."

Then he taught us how to say we wanted to own our father's gods. He told Red Basket to say to Old-Woman-Above, "I want to own you and I promise to build a sweat lodge for you. I will have enough articles. My father's god, I want to own you."

He said to me, "You should say, 'I want to own you, Wolf of the Daybreak. I want to own you, my father's god.' After you make your promise, you will have to look for another 'father' who will repeat the holy songs belonging to the Wolf and the Old Woman Above. Since the songs for the two bundles will be mixed, you should pick two 'fathers' but you could have one sweat lodge. Select Hairy Coat (Waterbuster clan) to do the singing in the ceremony as he has the Old-Woman-Above rights."

We decided to appoint Lying Chicken [27] as our ceremonial father for we had heard much about how he had fasted. Even in war, although he had been wounded, he was able to save his life. We thought he would be a pretty good man to ask. Before we went to see him to tell him of our plans, we got several fine blankets and robes. Our father told us we should take the pipe along when we spoke to him of helping us get the bundles.

He was not at home when we called but we saw his sacred bundle hanging there. His wife saw us carrying the pipe and inquired what we wanted and we said, "Mother, where did our father go?"

She said that he had gone out visiting somewhere and we said, "We wish that you would go out and look for him as we come for a great purpose." She went out and in a short time she came back with him.

As soon as he came in, he inquired what we wanted and we said, "We want to own a god so we selected you as our 'father.' My brother wants to own the Old-Woman-Above and give that ceremony while I want to own the Sunrise Wolf. We want to go together and get these bundles from our own father who owns them both."

Lying Chicken said to us, "It is a hard thing to do but it will be all the better for you when you are through. When the time comes, I will be ready to take the things over, my sons."

At the time we took the pipe over, we left it in front of his bundles. When he finished speaking, he went to the bundles and lit the pipe saying, "I want my sons to be successful."

When we came back home our father, Small Ankles, said, "I think it is going to be pretty hard to get a wolf for they are nearly extinct. You will have to get one. I have an extra hide here that I can fix up and repaint. I think it will be just as good as a new one. I will look for the ash stick and make it up into shape for the Old-Woman-Above. I will have to get some braided sweet-grass and buffalo hair to wrap around it for the Old-Woman-Above always used

---

[27] Lying Chicken belonged to the Itisuku clan which was, at this time, being incorporated into the Waterbuster clan as was the Xura clan. He had taken an active part in the various Buffalo Calling ceremonies and had fasted on the hills during the coldest part of the winter to bring the winter herds.

that. I think those things will not be hard to find. Then we will need a scalp from the enemy but I am afraid that will be even harder to find. The important thing for her real powers is the jackrabbit. You find one and skin it. Tie a piece of buffalo tail to the hide. That is very important for when she goes after anything she always has that. Then there must be a magpie to go with the rest of the Old Woman's sacred bundle and that is very important. Pull two or three of the long tail feathers of the magpie and get eagle down from the calumet eagle; you will need two of those feathers. Someday you may go out to attack your enemy and then you can wear these down feathers. We will have to bring the sweetgrass in and have it braided nicely and then folded into a circle for the Old-Woman-Above used that on her breast. There will be 12 sticks (about 6 inches long) made of 6 sticks split into 12 and painted red. You will also be given a buffalo skull."

We pledged to give the feast at the time when the chokecherries were ripe. I said to my brother, "We will have to go out southwestward to hunt buffaloes. There might be a few even though the hides will not be very good now. By fall they will be better. By the time we get back we should have plenty of meat. Then we can invite in the different societies to donate various articles for our use."

We went out and passed Dickinson. There were my brother and myself together with our wives, four of us in one wagon. When we came to the Little Missouri west of Dickinson, there were many tents. White men were living there. They were killing all the buffaloes and we saw the meat and hides. I was angry but I did not say anything even though they were leaving most of the meat to rot and were just taking the hides. Many places we saw the dead animals and the hides spread out. They were killing the best ones and leaving those that were too poor and shaggy. We went up the Little Missouri until we came to high mountains at the head of the river where there were many small branches to the stream. We crossed and went west again, killing many fat deer and antelopes. We dried the meat whenever we stopped. We continued west but we could not find any fat buffaloes for the hunters were leaving only the shaggy ones, so we turned back toward the Little Missouri again.

We decided to stop there to hunt deer and trap eagles. My brother did not have complete rights in eagle trapping but my father had been teaching him a little at a time, for which my brother had paid him. He thought we should try to trap anyway and I thought it would be all right. We stopped in a place where there was plenty of wood and good water. We saw a high butte and thought that the pits should be near its base. He sang and prayed, and then we dug the holes. When the pits were ready, we killed a jackrabbit, cleaned it, and filled it with grass so that it looked alive.

My brother said, "If it is good weather tomorrow I will go into my pit. If the wind is not from the west, we will fix another pit for you."

The next day was a fine one for trapping eagles so he went out before sunrise without eating breakfast, for one was expected to fast while in the pits. I stayed around camp looking after the horses, thinking that some stranger might come along and get them or bother the women. After dinner my brother came back with a fine eagle. When he brought the bird into camp, there was no place to put it as we did not have a lodge built for the eagles. He tied the bird to our tipi and pulled the 12 tail feathers out.

I said to him, "We should have a lodge for the eagle as we have no right to do this to the birds. We have plenty of time to make a lodge. I found a beaver dam and we could take that wood."

We brought the wood and made a lodge in a short time. Then we lived separate from our wives.

We tied the bird back of the lodge. Then there followed 2 poor days for trapping. While looking around, we found holes that were formerly used. We saw many birds in the air and thought that this must be an old eagle trail that other trappers had found. I selected an old pit and my brother cleaned it out while I stayed in camp in case strange men came along.

I said to my brother, "I will have to pay you for praying for me for I want to be lucky."[28]

I told my wife to pick out some fat meat and a hide to give to my brother for fixing the trap. He thanked me and said that he would do the best he could. He came back in the evening and said that he had it ready and that it was well concealed. I thought it looked like a good location.

Next day the wind was from the wrong direction and I decided to hunt for blacktail deer. I killed one buck and a doe. I fixed some of the meat for my bait, using a piece that was fat and bloody. I gave it to my brother to pray to and fix as our father had taught him. I gave him one side of the ribs roasted for his pay.

He said, "I am satisfied with my pay. I am not supposed to own the whole ceremony, only the part that was taught me by my father. He taught me how to dig the holes and tie the bait. He taught me the songs that go with that and I am going to sing one of them before we go further."

He sang the song that he had learned and said, "Now you sing it with me" and we sang, "The bait you carry on your shoulder; the bait you carry on your shoulder; the bait you carry on your shoulder; the bait you carry on your shoulder; black bear is fixing his lodge. What will be the best bait to draw birds to it? The best part for bait is the breast."

Next day the wind was from the southwest. We could not go out trapping when the wind was from the east. We knew the birds would be moving with the westerly wind so I thought it would be all right for us to go out since our wives were not afraid to stay alone. We should not stay too long here trapping eagles as it was nearly time for cold weather. We went out without eating. I went into my pit and pretended to be fasting and crying, but I did not let my voice out loud. After a while I saw a black spot in the air. My pit was near a sharp bank. Suddenly the eagle came up from below and onto the bank. My father had often told me how to seize them for, should I miss, I might push the bird over and lose it. I took a careful aim, pulled his legs together, scraped the feathers, and pulled them out. Then I tied the bird up and went back into the hole again.

I saw another black spot in the air. I had been told that when one comes, the other will come from the same direction. It sat on my bait and I pulled it in also. I pulled the feathers out and said to the eagles, "I wish I could get some more and I would make a warbonnet."

Being late, I started back to camp. Not having a rope, I tied one eagle to my belt and carried the other under my arm. When I got back I saw two eagles behind the lodge for my brother had caught another, a spotted eagle.

I thought, "We are supposed to put up a big ceremony; that is why we are so lucky" for I had always heard that when one pledged a ceremony, he would be lucky at everything he undertook while getting the things together.

Next day the wind was not in the right direction so I said, "We should go out for deer. We should go in different directions. The deer will be fat by this time."

I killed a blacktail deer. It was fat even for this time of year. I took off all the meat over the ribs in one piece for it would make good dry meat for the feast

---

[28] Wolf Chief, though older than his brother, had not bought Eagle Trapping rights of his father as Red Basket had.

that we were to give later.   At that time it seemed that the wind was changing to the southwest so I hurried with my butchering and got ready to trap eagles.

I used my brother's rabbit for bait as my meat had turned black, and I tied some fat to it also.   Many magpies came around to eat the fat.   I would punch them but they would come right back again.   After a while an eagle came down and I caught it.   It was getting cold and it seemed that there were many eagles flying so we went into our pits the next day.   In a short time I saw a black spot in the same direction as before.   It disappeared before coming up over the bank and onto the bait.   I pulled in another fine calumet eagle and took the 12 tail feathers out.   I was crying for I wanted to catch another calumet.   It was not long until my prayers were answered and I pulled it in.

It was getting cold and uncomfortable so I left early.   I took the two birds and went back to camp.   I tied the two eagles at the back of the lodge with the others. My brother came in late with a "soft small" eagle.   He had been around our father a good deal and knew many songs and stories about eagles.   He was more interested in it and braver than I for he had struck the enemy and had cut his fingers off and fasted much.   He was cold when he came in and I thought that we might have a blizzard.

I said to him, "I have often heard the rule that when it gets cold and the edges of the rivers are frozen, we are not supposed to go out any more.   It seems that it is going to freeze up.   If the birds get their feet cold, it means that the people will get into trouble.   I think the time for trapping is over and that we should stop before going any further.   We have enough eagles now."

We did not go through the regular ritual here for we did not have a qualified leader who knew all the rules for cleansing out the spirits.   Then there is a regular order with a head man to pray when the birds are killed so they will go back where they came from.   We did the best we could and turned them loose the next day to fly away after feeding them fresh meat during which time my brother prayed to them saying, "I did not have the regular right to do this.   I had only the right to dig the holes which my father taught me.   I have no way of sending you back but I ask you, Little-Black-Bears,[20] to help me send them back.   I do not want any trouble.   I want you to carry out anything I do not know and excuse me."

We had a big load on for the women who had worked hard drying the meat and hides. We had a wagonload of dry meat piled up high and we tied some poles to the back of the wagon on which we piled about 60 deer hides.   We came back through Dickinson where we sold 10 hides to buy coffee and sugar.   There we found fresh tracks and soon overtook Spotted Bear and his party to learn White men had come to the village while we were away and had stolen most of our horses. We hurried home when we learned that.   The river was carrying a great deal of ice but we crossed our stuff in bullboats, even taking the wagon apart and crossing the parts in boats.   My brother went back to his wife's parents and I went to my wife's parents' lodge.

Our wives did not give away all the hides for I had a good wife.   I wanted to sell many of them and turn them into other articles.   I belonged to the Grass Dance as did my brother.   Wolf Eyes (Sunset Wolf bundle owner) came in and I told him that I was going to feed my society for I wanted them to put in some articles to help us fulfill our promise.   He thought that it was the right thing to do for it was hard to get the articles together.   He thought that it would be a good idea to pass through another year before fulfilling the promise as it was so hard then for the people were so poor.

---

[20] The traditional custodians of the Eagle Trapping rites.

Wolf Eyes went back to his lodge. He belonged to the Big Grass society and he told his young men about it. He was one of the real chiefs in a way for he was usually selected "Leader of the Warriors" in the Sunset Wolf performances. He said to the members of his society, "Wolf Chief has undertaken a great thing for it will bring rain for the crops; food will be abundant and our people will increase.[30] I think all of you should put in some things for Wolf Chief."

I heard afterwards that they were having meetings and would notify me when they met. I belonged during this time to the Night Grass Dance and my brother was a member also.[31] We heard that they were going to dance. I had already sent word to them. Big Bull, their announcer, went through the village telling the people that we were going to meet that night. I told my wife to have meat, corn, and coffee ready. They prepared several pails of food.

The meeting was to be in the Mandan Okipa lodge.[32]

My wife and I dressed and she took the food to the lodge. All the people of the society came in and danced. I told my society that I was in need of their help. When I mentioned it, they did not say anything for a while.

Then Red Wing who was highly respected said, "Wolf Chief is doing this for the good of all the people. He wants to have a good home and fine gardens; he wants our people to increase; he wants no sickness among us. It is hard for him to get all the articles so I advise you young men to help him along, even with small things that he can use."

The people met in small groups and talked it over. Sitting Owl said, "It is all true; it is a good thing for us. We should help him. When we pass the barrel around, each person should put up something. I am going to put up a 2-year old colt for the Wolf Ceremony." They had two wooden barrels and stopped at each end to sing the society songs. As they went along with the barrels, the people put in things.

There were 50 members in the society and they gave freely. Cherries-in-the-Mouth gave a red pipe. On the other end of the line someone gave me a blanket. We would get an article and then they would sing. Nearly everyone there gave us a fine blanket, robe, calicoes, quilts, or other things. When the barrel came to Rabbit Head, he got up to dance and gave a mare and 2-year old colt, saying that it was for the benefit of all.

The barrel came to Long Bear, Old Dog's father, and he told how he had fought the enemy. He began to tease some of the members of the Dog society sitting there. They were there and had to hear it. He told how he ran the enemy into the creek. I thought he was very brave by the way he was dressed. Old Dog was there and he had his father give an eagle tail of 12 feathers and a good spotted horse for he was proud of his father the way he talked.

Eventually the barrel came to Bears Heart and he danced. He was in the same age-grade society as Long Bear. He showed how he seized the enemy, making many humorous movements that amused the people immensely. He said, "I do not see why those of my age and society do not get wounded. They must be cowards or they always manage to be somewhere else when the enemy is around. Right after the smallpox we were few, still we were always after the enemy. A bullet hit me and that is what I represented just now. Another time we went

---

[30] Note the shift in emphasis to other societal values with the abolition of warfare by the U.S. Government.

[31] These Grass Dances were of late introduction from the Sioux and were rapidly replacing the older age-grade military societies.

[32] Note the many references to the use of this ceremonial lodge by the Hidatsa for the performance of various social and ceremonial functions. Formerly the Hidatsa met in the various lodges but there was a gradual increase in the use of this lodge for their public meetings until, just prior to the abandonment of the village around 1889, the Mandan ceremonial lodge was used interchangeably by the two tribal groups.

to the north and they shot me in the back but it did not go through. Another time near Knife River the enemy attacked and went ahead. Before I got to them they shot me in the flesh of the arm. That was why I held up my arm. But these, my friends, must stand a long ways back from the enemy for they never get hit. But I go up close and that is why I was wounded four times. Another time nine enemies made a fort and I got wounded for I was up close to the fort but this man here must have been far back for he never got any wounds. I had used all my bullets so I had only my ax. I jumped into the fort and they shot into my hand between my fingers. Still my friends here did not get any wounds. I am old and my horse is old too but you can get something out of him. The horse is my donation."

All the people laughed but some of them felt a little hurt, for he criticized them in public where they had to sit and listen.

In all there were four horses donated to us in addition to dry goods, blankets, guns, and eagle feathers. We called our wives to help us take the things back to our father's lodge and put them away there for the future.

Two days later we heard that another society, the Big Grass society, was going to have a feast and dance to help us. We saved the best foods, as much as we could, for our use in the ceremony when the time came so this time we mixed the dried meat, cut into pieces, and corn which together made enough to feed all.

When we heard the drums beating, I told my wife and my brother's wife to take the food over. They left it on the floor. Then I said, "I need help of this society; I would like some things to help me as I am trying to own a god."

This time Wolf Eyes who was leader of the society said, "It is for your benefit. What Wolf Chief is doing is for all the people."

Then Lucky stood up and said, "It is a good thing for all of us and we should all help him; it is a great thing that he is looking to our future and the increase of our numbers. It may be hard for some to give anything but give a little dry meat or goods, even a pair or two of moccasins. All this will help him out."

At that time I did not dance with them but sat between two older men who were my clan brothers and belonged to the society. Representatives of the society came together to talk the matter over and then they went back to their seats.

Spotted Horn stood up and said, "There is no way for us to get buffalo hides for we are poor. We should try to do the best we can for he is looking to our benefit. My son, White Bird, will give Wolf Chief a war bonnet." Spotted Horn was the announcer for the group.

They started a barrel on each end of the line. The drums were beaten. The older people were dressed in headdresses and feathers to show their war records. Others wore scalps on their leggings or other signs of success in warfare. Big Coat's wife [33] had her husband give a stick to indicate that she was donating a horse. In all there were only three valuable things, a war bonnet and two horses. Others gave moccasins, shirts, and many knives.

These were not the only times we got donations as my age-grade group helped me and individuals came in with things.

We kept all the goods at my father's lodge and my wives could not give any of them away for the things were given to use in the ceremony. My father told Two Teeth that he could help us, his brothers, in getting goods and participate in the ceremony to get some of the rights.

---

[33] A member of the Maxoxati clan, the same clan as Small Ankles' first wife and Wolf Chief's half brothers and sisters.

When the days were shortest, our dry meat was getting low, for we had been giving so many feasts. There were many deer at that time so my brothers and I went out hunting a great deal. Then we would put on a feast and invite in clan brothers and sisters and they would give us things for the ceremony.

There was a dance of the Night Grass society towards spring and Young Wolf donated a horse. There were many other dances of the Grass society through the winter and the pile of articles continued to grow. All this time our sister, Brown Woman, continued to help us. Wolf Eyes, whom we appointed to help us and to look after the articles, would come over once in a while. We heard that he had been looking for a wolf hide.

One day he called us over to his lodge. There we found Hairy Coat, who was the leader for the Woman Above rites, and my father. Wolf Eyes' sacred bundle was on a four-post platform. I saw some fox and coyote hides but I could not see a wolf hide. I thought it would be hard to get one for wolves were scarce.

Wolf Eyes said to Hairy Coat, "You are the man who is leading and will sing the holy songs. I am supposed to get the wolf hide and the other things for Wolf Chief but it is pretty hard to get the scalp and wolf hide but otherwise I think I have all the things that I should get for them."

Hairy Coat said, "Since they made the promise, I thought we might have an enemy come so that we could get a scalp. We should be able to get a wolf but I see now that we may have trouble. Of course in the early days I promised a ceremony to the Woman Above, but in those days there were many enemies. One of our people went out and killed one enemy. He gave the scalp to my 'father' to use and I have that in my bundle. If they will pay enough, they can have that scalp."

When we heard that we were glad. I was 13 years old when this attack was made on the village and they gave Hairy Coat the scalp when he put on the Old-Woman-Above ceremony.

Small Ankles said, "I am glad they have promised to give the ceremony. Up to this time they have had no bad luck. It shows that their wish is coming true and yours, Wolf Eyes, and yours, too, Hairy Coat. All this makes me very happy."

Wolf Eyes was the one to get the scalp from Hairy Coat and pay for it.[34]

Small Ankles said, "I understand that you did not get a wolf hide but I gave the ceremony when I was young. My 'father' gave me a hide and I had good luck in war. Now I see that you do not have one for your 'son' and I will let you have mine, only you will have to pay me."

Hairy Coat said, "I am glad that all the articles that our sons are supposed to have are at hand. We are to begin tonight for these two ceremonies are to be held together. This is to be a practice meeting tonight but tomorrow we will put on the regular ceremony. Each time I sing a song, you must pay a little."

The men sang and when our fathers brought the holy things in and laid them on the ground, we were supposed to give some articles. We knew there was plenty.

After they finished talking we went back and roasted the corn and cooked the dry meat ready for the feast. While they were together, the three "fathers" selected Different Wolf to be the announcer for he belonged to my clan and would see that the ceremony was well advertised. He went out through the village calling, "Wolf Chief asks all those with the Old-Woman-Above and the Sunrise Wolf to come. He has a big sweatbath ready and he wants you to come. Whoever owns the Buffalo Skulls come too."

---

[34] Wolf Eyes occupied an important position in the Wolf ceremonies at this time because of his military record.

When evening came, we took the meat in.   There were already many people there who owned the different bundles such as Wolf and Buffalo Skulls.   Even some old women had the right for they had put up feasts to the bundles although they had not put on the big feasts or ceremonies to buy the whole rights.   By that time Lying Chicken, our ceremonial father, came in with a buffalo skull and put it at the head of the lodge.

My father, Small Ankles, said to us, "Hairy Coat was supposed to sing the holy songs but he forgot one place where he was to instruct you young men for he is young.[35]   When they take the skull in, you are supposed to put the pipe and an article in front of the skull.   Hairy Coat is supposed to call an old man to take the pipe and article, and pray for you but he forgot to tell you that for he is young and has not gone through the ceremonies many times."

When we came in, the buffalo skull was in its place.   Hairy Coat said, "You are to bring me some articles and I will begin the holy songs.   Bring me a little fire."

My brother took some.   Hairy Coat smoked the skull and rattles with sweetgrass.   He began to sing a holy song of Woman Above.   While he was singing we distributed food to the older men.   He sang a song that I do not remember, something about 'calling the enemy.'   When he finished he said, "Whoever has the rites of the Sunrise Wolf should take the pipe before the Buffalo Skull.

Kidney (Bull Buffalo is his other name) went over and sat by the skull.   He called me and my two brothers to come to him and he said, "Buffalo Skull, these are your sons; they want long lives.   You can see what they have done for you, bringing all these fine articles.   They wish to be successful and have plenty of food for all the people."   We brought articles and placed them before the skull for Kidney.

Hairy Coat called for some more articles and another small fire to burn sweetgrass, and then he sang.   Again the pipe was placed in front of the skull and we carried articles there.   Another man prayed and asked the buffalo skull to send their "sons" good luck.

We passed the food around then, feeding all those who had the right to attend.   Even the old women with Wolf Woman bundles and rights, by virtue of feasts they had given, were fed.

When the people had eaten, Hairy Coat called for more coals and the filled pipe to be placed before Buffalo Skull with some articles.   He asked if there was any food left and we told him that it was all gone.   He said that it would be all right for it was nearly daybreak by that time.   He told the old men to get up and pretend to be holy men, impersonating their gods, and to go back to their lodges.

So ended the practice performance.

During the day we prepared for the final performance.   We took all the articles and the sticks to represent the horses to the Mandan Okipa lodge and hung them up.   Our "fathers" were in one of the lodges and they came out with their sacred bundles.   We had had the lodge swept out and cleaned out nicely by the Holy Women owners, and a new sweat lodge was built inside ready for use.

Small Ankles had instructed us how we were to do, saying, "Before they peek in the door, have the articles and horses they are to get ready for them.   These men will leave their lodge and sing the holy songs at four different stations on the way to the lodge.   When they sing the fourth time they will come in and distribute the articles among themselves.   Before they come in, you are ex-

---

[35] Note how one bundle owner checks up on another to see that performances are conducted strictly according to custom.

pected to have most of the articles spread before the buffalo skull; also have some near the sweat lodge. When they bring in the sacred bundles that you are to get, such as the wolf hide and scalp, they will leave them on top of the articles that you have heaped there."

We had the sweat lodge covered with dry goods and many fine articles, also the sticks representing the horses. It was evening. We had given only a few articles on the previous evening for this was the important meeting.

My father said, "Whenever Hairy Coat calls for some articles, take our four and give them to him for he is the leader. Whatever he asks for will come true."

My brother brought coals as Hairy Coat had directed. Hairy Coat burned some sweetgrass and smoked the rattles before beginning the songs. He was painted with red paint over his body and face and wore magpie tail feathers in his hair. He wore only his breechcloth. When he finished singing he said, "Whoever owns the Old-Woman-Above bundle step forward to the Buffalo Skull and pray for your son. When you have prayed for your son, you may take the articles on the skull. Pray that he will be successful."

Big-Foot-Bull, a Mandan who owned the Sacred Shell Robe of the Mandans and Awatixa, stepped forward and prayed, "My god, Woman in the sky Above,[36] I wish that you would see that my 'sons' here have long lives for they want to be successful in all that they do." Then he smoked the pipe before the skull and took the goods.

Again Hairy Coat called for a fire and sweetgrass. I put goods before the skull and another man prayed for us. Then we would distribute corn and meat to the people and my sister would give the food to the old women who had rights in Wolf ceremonies. Sometimes the songs belonged to the Old-Woman-Above and other times the songs were to the Sunrise Wolf.

Then he called for other old men to go the the skull and pray. Short Bull went there and prayed, "Up in the sky, holy Old Woman, I beg of you to help these sons enjoy a long life; you are the one who has the power. These articles that are given to you I am going to use."[37] Then he asked Red Basket[38] to come forward, saying, "Whoever owns the bundle for the Sunrise Wolf step forward and take the articles and pray for your sons."

Then Hairy Coat stopped singing and there was a short rest.

Small Ankles came to us and said, "Your 'father' did not tell you about this but there are some old women who own the ceremony of the Holy Woman. These women always meet separately when a ceremony is in progress. They are together now so you should save some of the articles for them. They represent the very early days before this ceremony was founded. Besides the Old-Woman-Above there were these other women in those times."[39]

Hairy Coat called for coals again for he was going to sing the Invitation song again. The Wolves sang this song whenever they wanted the gods to come to the feast, so we passed the food around again in imitation of the Wolves.

Again Hairy Coat invited someone with Sunrise Wolf rights to step forward and take the things at the skull. This time Wolf Eyes did, saying, "Stand by me, my sons. In the early days I tried to own this god. I had a hard time so I know

---

[36] He belonged to the Waxikεna clan and moiety opposite that of Wolf Chief who was a Prairie Chicken; hence, Wolf Chief was a "son."

[37] Short Bull, a Mandan, had an equivalent Mandan Old-Woman-Above bundle and was of Wolf Chief's opposite moiety.

[38] Waterbuster clan, so a father to Wolf Chief; he had rights in the Sunrise Wolf and his wife was one of the Wolf Woman owners.

[39] Note here how the Hidatsa relate two ceremonies in time.

what a difficult thing it is.   I ask the Wolf, my father, that my 'sons' here have good homes and become leaders among their people.   May they have many children to increase our population."

Hairy Coat said to our ceremonial father, Lying Chicken, "You are the main one who was going to give the bundles to your sons.   There are many things under the bundles, but you did not furnish all the articles.   Small Ankles gave the wolf hide and I furnished the scalp.   You have to pay us for those things for you have many articles.   You do not have to worry about your pay."

Lying Chicken came forward, picked up the bundles, and put them on the buffalo skull.   He put the articles in a heap saying, "I am glad our sons promised to give the ceremony for, since they promised, there has been no bad luck.   I have listened to the old men praying to their gods and I can tell from this lack of sickness and death among our people that it is because they promised to put on this ceremony."   He divided the goods into two piles and put two sticks on each pile.

He continued, "Hairy Coat is the singer and he took a greater part in singing the songs.   He can have one part of the articles and that stick which is the spotted horse given by Old Dog, for it is a good horse.   Small Ankles furnished a wolf hide.   I can see that it is very holy.   We know he got good results from it and now his sons want to own this wolf hide.   Now I am glad that his sons are going to own his gods so I give Small Ankles this pile of goods for there are many fine things in the pile, as well as a good horse."

Small Ankles took the horse and articles.   Again Hairy Coat called that he wanted his pay and we put 12 articles consisting of blankets and robes in a pile.   But he called for more so we brought more.   By that time the stones for the sweat lodge were heated.   Hairy Coat said, "There are many articles left.   After we come out of the sweat bath, our sons will distribute them among the old people."

When the things were distributed, Hairy Coat said, "I think Lying Chicken has his share.   Before I deliver these bundles to our 'sons' they should bring up their wives if they want to become 'granddaughters' to these bundles."

He walked towards the sweat lodge while singing another holy song and shaking the rattles used by the singer of the Woman Above songs.   He said to the old men, "Those of you who wish may come into the sweat lodge.   Act like the god that you represent."

The song he was using was one which called for sweetgrass.   He sang the song and made the request four times.   When he was inside the sweat lodge, my brother took in the stones.   Those whose bundles included buffalo skulls went to the entrance but there was not room for all to go in.   There were other young men, mostly Prairie Chicken clansmen, in the lodge crying and begging for a good living and success.   When the old men came out of the sweatlodge, Hairy Coat said, "I want the first chance.   Then the rest of the goods will go to those who own a branch of the Wolf and Woman Above ceremonies.   Then the people with Buffalo Skulls and other bundles can have the rest."

Hairy Coat stood in front of Buffalo Bull Skull and said, "My granddaughters,[40] you must take your leggings and moccasins off.   Leave one dress on.   If you want to, you can step forward and call this skull your grandfather.   If you want to keep your grandfather as your protector, do not be foolish; keep yourself clean and do not run after other men; then I will sing a holy song.   If you think you will be tempted and can't do it, I will not sing that holy song for you here."

At that time my wife was Big-Foot-Bull's daughter, Coyote Woman, who was a Mandan.   Hairy Coat called for some coals as he wanted to smoke the bundles

---

[40] Note a change in kinship; heretofore they were daughters-in-law.

in front of the buffalo skull. He held up the sacred bundles and said "You women who respect your 'grandfather' and will obey his rules, come to me. If your are not sure of yourself, I will not sing it."

My wife stood up and said, "Sing the holy song."

Then Red Basket's wife, Skunk Woman, said, "Sing the holy song."

He sang the song and said to the women and the sacred bundles, "Now these are your granddaughters and they expect to look after you. They want long lives. Hold out your hands. I am going to give you a grandfather."

They held the bundles up for a while. Then he picked up the buffalo skull and incensed it a little, saying to Coyote Woman, "If you are going to respect this grandfather, rub the skull against your breast. Promise that you are not going to think of any other man no matter how good looking he is. Then your grandfather, the Buffalo Skull, will look to your benefit."

There was a certain man who always painted the buffalo skull for my father. Afterwards my father always had good luck. So I wanted Small Ankles to paint the skull for me but I had to pay him extra. I thought I might use the skull some day when I was attacking my enemies. At this time I took the red paint and left it by the buffalo skull and said, "My father, I would like to own the right to paint the buffalo skull. I want you to show me so that I will know."

He stepped forward and said, "I see that my son wants to own the painted skull but of course he spoke to me before. I want all you older people to hear what I say. I used to pray to the skull, cut myself, and go out to hunt my enemies; I used to paint the skull on the tipis and it was easy then for me to get my enemy. My father, Buffalo, I want to show my son how to paint you. I want to turn you over to him and I wish that you would give him strength and a long life."

I was sitting behind him all that time; he had water to mix with the red paint. He said, "If I mention any words in the song, you should pick up the skull and scratch the ground with it as hard as you can."

During the first song he was singing, I was painting the skull and was ready but in the first song there were no words so I finished the painting. In the second one there were words and I scratched the ground. The older men were happy and shouted, "aho! aho!"

After we finished he said, "Up-in-the-Sky-Holy-Woman, you taught me the things you taught in the very early days. You taught us to use the skull and I am teaching its use now. When I owned this skull, I kept it in good order and now I am giving it to my own son here." Then he said to me, "In the future you might attack the enemy or come to a tipi where there are many buffalo skulls on the ground protecting its owner. You will then know how I sing the songs. You sing the song, pick up one of the skulls, and lay it back on the ground. Then you can call your men and attack the tipi for they will get the best of your enemy."

Then he said to me, "You have already learned how to do it from me and it is the same now except that you will own the buffalo skull. Distribute what is left to these Holy Men for some of them came from the big timber and far away. They represent the Holy-Women-of-the-Timber around here and the woods to the north."

Meanwhile our mother was in her lodge preparing for us to invite in the Holy Women so I took my bundle and the buffalo skull to my father's lodge where I put them with my father's bundles. The Holy Women had a leader named Cherry Necklace who was already there. He was dressed with a mink hide, I think, around his head and a robe upside down. He had a few magpie feathers scattered over his robe. He was there but a short time when my mother looked out and said that all the old Holy Women were coming, about 10 of them in all. Red Head, Roots, and Goes Around were all I remember.

They came in rapidly with face and foreheads painted red. Each had a digging stick made of ash. They announced, "We have come from the brush, the heavens, and the north but we can't be seen."

They pretended to be foolish women of the woods. They ran around in the lodge and bumped into each other. We sat back in the lodge where we could watch them perform. Cherry Necklace was carrying his rattle and, walking around between them, he sang, "I am the Old Woman; I am the genuine Old Woman. I would rather be the Old Woman to have great powers."

When he finished, the women pretended to be like the old women and then one said, "I have come for the things you promised me but I am a spirit and can't be seen."

They stopped jumping around and formed a circle, when one said, "Bring the pay I am promised for this."

My father said, "You should take those articles and distribute them."

I said, "My mother, here is an article."

She said, "I came from far away in the heavy timber and brought this medicine for you. Open your mouth." Then she put black medicine on my tongue.

Each one told where she came from. Some said, "There may be illness in your family so you can use this black medicine to doctor with."

After they finished, Cherry Necklace said to the women, "Go back to the different directions where you belong." They ran out fast carrying the goods, and scattered in all directions.

That was the end of the ceremony. After receiving all these bundles, we fixed a place for them beside our father's bundles and on the same platform. My father spoke to the bundles saying, "They own you now and you should send your sons good dreams."

Night came and I had a dream. I heard many wolves singing but I could not tell if they were inside the lodge or outside. When they finished singing, I memorized the song at once. It was a long one without words. I had never heard it before. Then I dreamed again. I saw where we had the ceremony in the big lodge. There was a hide rope around the lodge and the wolf hide given to me was there. The hide was painted red in the middle and it looked like a new hide. In the morning when I awoke, I was happy for I thought from the freshness of the wolf hide, the red paint, and the Wolf song that I would be successful when attacking my enemies. As soon as I arose I told my father about it.

He said, "It is good that you saw red paint for that is a sign that you are going to kill the enemy and have a long life." I was happy about this dream.

At the same time, Red Basket told us that he had a dream also. My father said, "Let me hear what you learned. Don't be afraid to tell me for your brother has already told his." I told my brother how I had seen the wolf hide and that when he was out hunting he should take a piece of wolf hide and put it around his head. Then he would be successful.

Red Basket sang the song he had heard. When he finished my father was happy and said, "In your dream you had a song from the Woman Above. I am glad for it means that you are going to have a good life. You will become a leader of your people."

The song was, "My son, my son, from up in heaven above you."

SUNSET WOLF

These Sunset rites, which also included ceremonial participation of certain females possessing rights in the Wolf Woman bundles, were considered to be independent of the Sunrise Wolf rites in spite of the fact that bundle owners of both rites had important ceremonial duties whenever this ceremony was performed. Each of the ceremonies, the Sunrise Wolf, the Sunset Wolf, and the Wolf Woman, has a separate origin myth. Although wolves are represented in many of the origin myths relating to very early times, the Hidatsa village groups do not consider the Sunset Wolf rites in their later forms to be very old. This ceremony is considered more recent than the Sunrise rites since it traditionally was founded after the Hidatsa-proper had moved from the Heart River where the Sunrise Wolf rites were instituted. Since the Hidatsa-proper think of the Knife River villages as quite late in tribal history and the Cheyenne as late arrivals on the Plains, they consider the ceremony one of the last major ceremonies to be founded by the gods.

Bears Arm and Joe Ward provided most of the data on this ceremony. The origin myth, summarized by the writer to include the principal points stressed by both informants, was as follows:

A young man, later to be named Hungry Wolf, was out eagle trapping with his wife to the west. He had his pit which he would go into when the winds were right; at other times he would hunt mountain sheep and other game. When he had caught four eagles and they had all the meat the dogs could bring back, he notified his wife that he would go out for fresh meat while she packed the things. When he returned his wife and the dogs were gone. He found the tracks of seven men who had taken his wife and dogs away. At last, near the headwaters of Knife River, he saw the enemy camp of many lodges.

When night came he found one path leading to a waterhole where the Cheyenne women were accustomed to get their water. He hid near the path and watched for his wife, telling her that he would take her away during the night. Instead of going away with him, she notified the Cheyenne who captured him. Some of these enemies struck coups on him and one man cut a small piece of scalp from Hungry Wolf's head.

They decided to kill him so they brought two large ash poles and drove them into the ground. Instead of killing him outright, they decided to torture him first. They ran knives through his ankles between the bone and large cord and did the same with his wrists. They brought rawhide ropes and fastened them through the holes in the legs and arms. They tied him to the posts so that he hung there, and they brought wood for a fire. The women danced around him, among them Hungry Wolf's wife.

At last the Cheyenne broke camp, leaving him fastened to the posts. Magpies, ravens, foxes, and coyotes came to the campgrounds to eat the scraps thrown out. He hung there 3 days unable to free himself. On the fourth day the raven flew back toward the "spot where the sun sets." He told the Chief of the Wolves that a young man was being tortured in the abandoned camp.

The wolf called all the other wolves and they met.   They resolved to go to the camp and free the young man.   They traveled as wolves and changed themselves into humans as they approached the deserted camp.

Chief of the Wolves said, "We heard about you and we came over here to help you."   They cut the rawhide cords and doctored him until he was well again.

The leader said, "This is a Wolf ceremony.   You have seen how we paint our bodies and wear caps made of coyote skins.   There are raven feathers on our heads.   There is only one kind of white clay to use.   We will go west to the place where this clay falls down from the sky.   Use that for paint when performing the ceremony."

They took the young man west with them.   On their way the young man heard something roaring as it came down from the sky.

The leader said, "When giving the ceremony, someone must come here to get the white clay to paint their bodies with.   You will be retu rning home now but in a year come out this way with your warriors.   You will fi nd a camp and your wife will be among them.   I will give you 100 enemies to destroy.   You will take your wife but you do not have to keep her.   When you perform these ceremonies, there must be two brothers dressed alike."

"You will have coyote skins tied around your wrists.   Use the head from a coyote skin for your cap; wear split raven feathers on top of your   head; sew a coyote tail on the cap so that it will hang down the back of your neck.   You will carry two canes and on them there will be four marks.   Pain t your body with the clay we showed you.   When you are having these ce remonies, have a bowl of clean water and red grass from the hills ready.   Dip the grass in the water.   The water is sacred.   The grass is sacred too.   You will use that for the ceremonies as well as for doctoring.   There is also a song to the old female wolf."

Then the wolf showed him the canes saying, "These canes will represent the two posts set in the ground where you hung, and the fo ur marks will indicate the four days that you suffered.   Tie a coyote tail to the top of each cane.   You will have a mound formed to represent yourself and the people will dance around the mound just as they danced around you.   These canes will be used by old people and they will live long because they will use them to brace themselves."

"On the last day the Holy Woman society will clean the dance grounds and dig out the little cacti for the fasters are hungry on the last day and may fall down.   You must sing the song 100 times on the last day.   Since we promised you 100 enemies you must select one man to sit in the middle and keep track of the singing.   When the song has been sung 100 times, he will say 'stop.'   While the men are dancing and running around the mound the women must stand around waving their robes as though driving the enemy away.   You can go out with us and we will have a feast before you go back, for you have been fasting now for 4 days."

The Wolves went out and killed a buffalo.   This was the beginning of the ceremony.   He reached his home at Knife River.   During the winter he made arrows all the time and gave them to the old men who trimmed them and passed them on either to their sons or sons-in-law living with them for these younger people were the ones who would use them.   When the arrows were all completed, his helper gave them back to him.   He blessed them and made arrow ceremonies for them.   He gave them to the brave warriors and they in turn gave them to their sons or sons-in-law.

He married one of the best young women in the village.   Then he was ready to give the Wolf ceremony.   When the ceremony had ended he told the people that the next time they went out on the buffalo hunt they should kill many old buffalo bulls to get their hides from the shoulder and neck for shields.   He directed them to cut out round pieces from the hides, spread them on the ground, put hot stones on them, and roll these hot stones over the hides until the hides were charred.   When a hide was dry, they should cut the edges again until the hide was round.   Tanned buckskin should be fastened over the hide.   Then when the tanned buckskin was painted with pictures of the young men's gods, these shields would protect them when attacking their enemies.   All the men did that and the arrows would not penetrate the shields.   The other tribes saw these shields and copied them.   Hungry Wolf also had the power to bring rains.

The war party moved camp, going toward the southwest.   When they reached Like-a-Prairie-Chicken-Tail Butte they found red paint inside stone balls and took all they needed.   Scouts returned to report a large camp   They charged and the enemy ran.   They killed 100 and allowed the others to escape.   His former wife and another old Hidatsa woman were in this camp.   The old woman told how she had been taken captive by the Cheyenne when a little girl and had raised a family there so she did not want to return to the Hidatsa.   Many women and children were taken prisoners and kept at the Knife River villages.   When Hungry Wolf was old, he sold his ceremonies to his sons and so they passed down to present times.

In spite of the fact that women with Wolf Woman rights participated in this ceremony, only one brief reference is made in the myth to the Wolf Woman bundle and that is to the effect that there is another song without words that belongs to a very old female wolf. A summary of the sacred myth which the Hidatsa claim to account for the origin of the Wolf Woman bundle is supplied at this point since the bundle owner had an important role in the performance of the Sunset Wolf rites.

The myth has its origin with the Hidatsa who were living at the mouth of Knife River on the north bank.   A very holy man named Strong Jaws lived in this village.   He had grown holy because he fasted 9 days and nights and had dreamed of all the different kinds of wolves.[41]

The wolves told Strong Jaw to stuff a wolf hide with sage and to take it outside of the lodge whenever the wolves howled and they would reveal what news they were sending him.   Because he could predict the future this way with the help of the wolves, he was of great assistance to the village.

The other holy men were jealous of Strong Jaw's supernatural powers and a friend warned him that it would be best to leave the village and take the friendly families with him.[42]

Thirty-five families broke away and traveled westward towards the Killdeer Mountains until they reached a place on the Little Missouri where they built a new village.   They hunted afoot for there were few horses in those days.   They lived there 3 years.   Strong Jaw had a son named Walks-at-Dusk and a daughter who was 8 years of age.

Farther west the Snake Indians lived.   One of their men was very holy so he was looking around to find someone suitable to buy his sacred rites.   His power was a sacred hoop through which he could look and see every tribe on the earth.

---

[41] The informant, Joe Ward, interpreted this to mean that, in addition, he had given public performances so that the people knew and approved Strong Jaw's beliefs of his supernatural powers and that he had further distinguished himself in battle.

[42] Traditionally this village group displayed less unity than the other two Hidatsa groups, the Awatixa and Awaxawi, and is said to have forsaken agriculture from time to time, living nomadically for several years at a time.

He would take up his hoop and point it towards tribe after tribe, looking for the right man but he could not find anyone who was as strong as he was. He looked through all the tribes until he saw Strong Jaw and his party traveling towards the Killdeer Mountains. He saw a man in the camp with something powerful looking back at him.

The Snake Indian called the people together and announced that he was getting old and wanted someone to take over his medicine powers. The only one fit to do so was Strong Jaw's son, Walks-at-Dusk. The Snake Indians did not approve the idea but agreed to assist in the transfer.

His tribesmen inquired how he would handle it and the Snake holy man said, "We will go after that little boy in the middle of the summer. I do not know whether we can get him or not for his father keeps a pack of wolves watching over him all the time. The only way I can get them off their guard is to feed them something. We will drive a large herd of buffaloes into their camp. When they go out to hunt them, we will have our chance. The men will be out hunting, leaving the women and children alone in camp. Do not kill any of the children."

The Snakes, 200 in number, started for the Hidatsa village, driving the buffaloes before them. One night the leader announced that he was to pray to his hoop that evening and then camp four times before reaching the Hidatsa.

They moved one more camp towards the village. Strong Jaw's daughter had a dream which she related to her parents in the morning saying, "I saw a big smoke in my dream. I was carrying my little brother on my back and did not know where to go." The old people said it was surely a bad dream but did nothing about it.

The second morning she told the same story saying that things were so clear she could not get it out of her mind. She shook from fright all day.

The third night her dream was even more vivid. Strong Jaw's wife said to her husband, "You should pay attention to what she is saying." He thought it was only a child's dream for no enemies were near or the wolves would have told him.

She had a fourth dream. By that time the Snake Indians were on the opposite side of the hills. Again she said, "I had my little brother, Walks-at-Dusk, on my back. The lodges were burning and all the dogs were howling."

This time Strong Jaw's wife convinced him that something should be done. He brought out his sacred pipe and the wolf skin. He burned sage before the skin and it turned into a live wolf. When the wolf went out of the door, the dogs rushed at him and drove him back into the lodge, just as the Snake holy man had planned it. The people told of a large buffalo herd near the village; Strong Jaw was uneasy and could not decide at first what to do. At last he decided to go after the herd and the men were soon killing the buffaloes. The Snake Indians killed the women, captured the children, and burned the lodges.

Four days later the Snake holy man took the little girl and boy, giving the other children to his tribesmen to raise. He said of the little boy, "This is the young man who will some day be your strong man."

When they reached the main camp, the little girl was given to another woman who was very kind. One day this old woman said, "I pity you. Do you think you could reach home if I showed you the way? I will take you away from the camp."

She drew a map of the Missouri and Little Missouri Rivers on the ground and showed her where the Knife River villages were situated. She said to the girl, "We will start tomorrow evening. I will take you part way. Tell your people what happened but do not urge your brother to go for he has a good home here. Some day when he is strong enough, he may come back to visit you."

Before leaving the girl, the old woman gave her advice on conserving the food and warned her not to travel during the daytime. She traveled night after night until her food was gone. She was very hungry but still she traveled. One moonlight night she saw something ahead of her. At first she thought it was a white rock but when she was nearer, she saw that it was a large wolf. The wolf wagged its tail like a friendly dog and walked up to her. Then the wolf walked on, showing her the way. When it was daylight she stopped and the wolf brought her a buffalo leg bone with some meat on it. She broke the bone and ate the marrow. That night the wolf came again to lead her and when she was hungry, the wolf brought her tallow from around the buffalo's kidneys.

The fourth night the Wolf said, "I know all about you. I did not come to you until you lost your way. When we get to Butte-with-Grass I will call all the wolves to you and they will tell you what to do when you get home."

They walked all night until light appeared in the east. Then the wolf said, "This is the place."

Wolf faced towards the south and howled. Soon wolves were coming from that direction. Then she faced the west and howled and the west wolves came. Then she faced to the north and to the east to howl and the wolves of those directions came also. She listened to their conversation and could understand everything they said. The "leader of the wolves" kept repeating, "We must finish what we have to say before sunrise."

The wolves selected the north wolves to speak to her as that was the most numerous group. Their leader said, "Whenever she goes anywhere alone, she will turn into a wolf and have powers like we have. And one thing more, she must make a ceremony to the wolves. When making the ceremony, you should give offerings and call the name 'prairie people' because the wolves are the people of the flats."

The wolves decided that the wolf who had taken her this far should lead her to the village. The wolf led her to a high hill back of the village and then said, "Your fathers will come to look for you because they know you are coming toward the village. You stay here until they find you."

While she sat there, it became light and she could see people walking in the distance. They were her father and his brothers. She scolded them saying, "Look at all the trouble we have had just because you would not listen to my dreams. My brother is with the Snake people whose holy man gives him good care. The older women were killed. I promised the wolves to give their ceremony as soon as I reached home." Her father knew what she meant. Soon the criers were calling that Strong Jaw's daughter had returned from the enemy and that the wolves had led her all the way back.

A few days later she resolved to give the ceremony to the Wolves. She carried robes and corn balls onto the earth lodge and wore ceremonial clothing such as the wolves told her she must wear. The Wolves had said, "Take the skin off of a wolf's head with the head and nose on to make the headdress of. Wear 12 eagle tails fastened to a band made of porcupine quills. Wear wolf claws around your ankles and wrists."

Then she went onto the lodge and called, "People of the Prairies."

Since she was too young to fast, her father and his seven brothers fasted and performed the dances for her as the wolves had instructed her. Each called for arrows to record his exploits in warfare. In this way the men tried to outdo each other. Afterwards others wanted to perform the ceremony and she would tell them when the proper time had come to give it again.

She grew up like other girls only all knew her to be holy. She learned to plant and harvest corn like the other women. People praised her for discovering the

Wolf dance and said that it was good for the tribe. When men wanted to go on the warpath, they would give her elkskin dresses, robes, and moccasins to bring them good luck and she would say, "I will pray for you to get many horses without being seen."

Everything would happen just as she predicted. One time a large war party was going out and the leader came to her and asked for good luck. She said, "Go on your way. Start tonight. On the fourth night I will come to you. Have a fat cow butchered, and camp in the timber near good water. Roast the ribs and at sundown I will be there. Just on the other side of the hill you will hear a wolf howl so you will know I have come."

They did what she said. Just as the full moon was coming up she howled and the leader said, "The Wolf Woman is here."

She had been working in her gardens for 4 days but on the last day she sang the war party songs saying, "I will be there when the ribs are cooked." Suddenly she changed into a wolf and all the people of the village saw her run away. She reached the war party that night and asked for the short ribs. Others brought her roasted ribs, asking for luck.

She said to the leader, "I told you I would be here to tell you what to do. Move your camp three times. The fourth time you will be near your enemies. Run a little and they will chase you; turn and you will kill many. Doing that several times you can take the whole camp. You will find the chief's lodge in the middle of the camp. Save everything in that lodge for those things belong to me. Now I am going home." They did as she instructed. They killed the men and took the women and children prisoners.

Meanwhile her brother, Walks-at-Dusk, had grown up and was quite prominent for he had a full knowledge of the Snake Indian medicine rites but he often dreamed of his own father's Wolf bundle. He was the leader of many war expeditions. In his dreams the wolves told him to go east towards the Killdeer Mountains where he could kill seven men. He knew he was Hidatsa so he was afraid they might be his own people. The Wolves sent him dreams every night until he decided to go. Each time he dreamed of seven men and one spotted horse. At the same time a Hidatsa living on the Knife River dreamed that he should go toward the Killdeer Mountains where he would find seven men and a spotted horse.

The Knife River party started out with seven men and a pinto horse at the same time Walks-at-Dusk came east with six men and a pinto. The Hidatsa sent two men ahead as scouts and the Snakes did likewise. The Snake Indians were run onto a high butte and were surrounded. One Hidatsa was sent back on the spotted horse to bring warriors from the village. Before the warriors arrived, one of the Hidatsa said, "I am going to talk to them and see if they know what I say. Are you up there, Walks-at-Dusk? If you are, you better be brave because we sent for a large force. We are about to kill all of you."

Walks-at-Dusk replied, "Come along" and he sang the Wolf songs. The Hidatsa heard a wolf howling to the west. That night the Snake Indians went out between the Hidatsa sentinels but they were not seen.

The war party arrived from Knife River the next day but none of the enemies could be found. When Walks-at-Dusk returned he told how he had nearly lost his life because of the great supernatural powers of the Hidatsa wolf leaders. After that the Snake Indians never led war parties against the Hidatsa.

Sunset bundle rites were transmitted from father to son. As was the case for other bundle transfers, it was not necessary for the father to be living. Since some bundle owners had rights in both the Sunrise

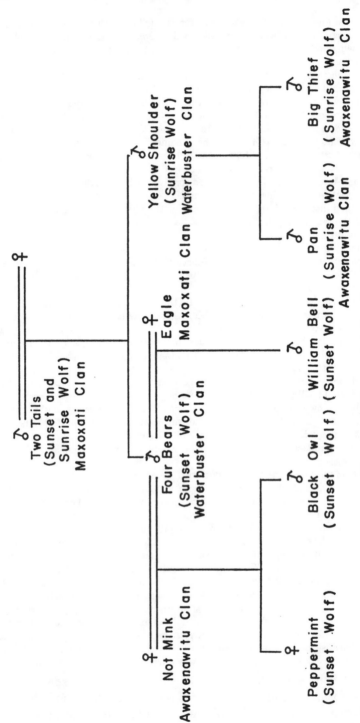

CHART 14.—Wolf ceremonies in Four Bears line.

and Sunset ceremonies, analysis of the visions usually was necessary in order to determine which rites were to be performed.   There are instances of indecision on the part of the older men, the "fathers," when vision recipients came to them for advice, and additional fasting was recommended to learn which ceremony was to be performed.   The Hidatsa reluctantly approved the performance of the rites by one whose father or a close relative standing in that relationship had not performed the rites.   When, however, the father owned rights in both ceremonies and the initial visions were not sufficiently clear to indicate which performance was to be given, individual feasts were generally given to the father's bundle or additional fasting was endured to secure additional instructions.   When the father owned rights in only one ceremony, either the Sunrise or the Sunset Wolf, mere dreaming of the wolves was considered sufficient.

Efforts to secure authority to perform the rites was further contingent on the vision recipient's capacity to secure the necessary goods and endure the traditional inconveniences and ordeals of fasting during the performance of the ceremony.   Since the performance demanded intimate cooperation between the giver, his family, clansmen, and age-grade group, as well as the confidence of the older people, individuals rarely undertook to have the rites performed until they were married and had shown some military distinction under recognized war leaders.   Once a man pledged the performance, he was accepted as a potential military leader.   It was customary for one, immediately after making the vow, to undertake a small-scale military mission to steal horses.   It would appear that not a great deal was expected at first.   Informants thought the mere fact that the leader had not lost any men, even though he had won no significant military honors, was adequate proof that the young leader had already acquired supernatural powers.

No vow was made until approval was given by someone whose bundle included a buffalo skull.   There seems to have been no special effort to select a Wolf bundle owner.   Rather, he might consult any man of the father's clan to whom he had gone for advice on other occasions.   Black Owl, son of Four Bears whose father owned rights in both the Sunrise and Sunset Wolf, gave Bears Arm this account of his instructions to perform the vow:

Black Owl said that he had been sick in bed for quite a while and was still very weak.   There were many people at his lodge.   They made so much noise that he decided to move to his brother's [William Bell] lodge while he was ill.   Black Owl wanted his "mother," Eagle,[43] to doctor him while he was there by pressing his bowels, which she did.   Black Owl's own mother was Not Mink; Eagle was Four Bear's young wife.

---

[43] His mother's "sister" by extension of the kinship system.

After 8 days, Black Owl heard a group of people singing and as they sang, they came nearer. He could hear them at the back or head of the lodge near where the ceremonial things were kept. He knew the songs to be those of the Sunset Wolf ceremony and he wondered how that could be as he had not heard that anyone was to give the ceremony at that time. It was the rule to make it known a year in advance and he could not remember hearing of anyone making the promise. He called Eagle to his bedside and inquired who was putting on the ceremony. When she said that there was no ceremony going on, he insisted that there must be since he could hear them singing at the back of the lodge.

She continued, "You must be out of your mind for there is no ceremony outside or we would all know about it."

He insisted, "There must be a ceremony for I could hear them singing and dancing outside. First they were on the other side of the village. After each song, they came nearer until they were back of the lodge."

Eagle said, "That was your father's god when he was living. It may be that you saw it before but made no promise to perform the ceremony, so you have been made sick."

Black Owl said, "I saw that once before, but it takes 1 year to get all the things together and I did not think I could complete all the preparations for the ceremony."

She said, "Go ahead now and make your vow to give the ceremony. You might get well by doing that."

A few days later he went to Poor Wolf who belonged to the same clan as his father and Poor Wolf instructed him further. So he stood on the roof of the Mandan Okipa lodge and addressed the Sunset Wolf, "Sunset Wolf, I will get you a robe. I want to get well and strong again. I want my people to be lucky and increase in numbers. I want no hardships for them."

When he made his vow, all the people heard what he promised and knew what would happen in a year. This was in the fall of the year and boys were playing around the Okipa lodge. They looked up and one of them said, "There are no buffaloes around close. How can you get a robe?"

When William Bell came home in the evening, Black Owl told him that he was going to perform the Sunset Wolf ceremony. Bell thought it would be all right and offered to help all he could. He was well a month after making the vow and set out first on the warpath. He did not lose a man. Then he began collecting buffalo robes and went out hunting often.

Rites were performed only during the three warmest months and after approximately 1 year of preliminary preparation. One of the Wolf bundle owners' most distinguished members was appointed to direct the ceremony and to see that it was performed according to custom. This position was in later years occupied by Wolf Eyes who served on several occasions, he being well liked for his generosity, respected for his intimate knowledge of these rites, and renowned for his military achievements. Custom decreed that he was to sit near the first central post on the left side when entering the lodge.

After making the vow, the bundle buyer selected a father's clansman as bundle maker. It was his duty to prepare the new bundle and other ceremonial paraphernalia for the occasion and to act as advisor to the buyer during the period of preparation.[44] A woman owning rights by public purchase in the Wolf Woman rites was likewise selected to impersonate the Wolf Woman. Since there were usually several women possessing these rights, it was customary to select an individual of the same clan or moiety as the buyer. Informants believed there were several "wolf women" for each of the clans prior to 1837. Bears Arm explained that young men preferred a "wolf woman" of the same clan where possible as it would "raise the record of the clan to perform a successful ceremony." First Creator, the waiter, was represented by one of the buffalo skull owners who selected one from their members. His place in the ceremonial lodge was next to the director of the ceremony.

Singer rights were not limited to Wolf Bundle owners. Instead, the major bundle owners—those who had the tribal bundles containing sacred buffalo skulls—took turns singing and drumming. When the last rites were performed, Bears Arm counted 42 of these bundle owners and thought there must have been a number of others who were not represented. Fasters lined the wall to the head and sides of the lodge with neither clan nor moiety arrangement (fig. 6).

Bears Arm explained that a young man's father never strongly urged him to fast on these occasions but would often, in a roundabout way, hint that it was an honorable thing to do. Older brothers, on the other hand were more direct. Distinguished clansmen were often quite severe in their criticism of younger members who showed indifference to fasting for it was both their right and duty to speak sharply to younger clansmen. Bears Arm remembered one older clan brother saying to another, "By all means don't fast or make yourself uncomfortable. You have so little time to live, you should enjoy life. And when you die we will put you on a scaffold. Then it won't be long until the ravens and buzzards will have your eyes picked out. While you lie there thinking of the good times you had, those young men who are going in to fast now will be striking the enemy; all you will be able to do about it will be to feed the birds and give off foul odors." Bears Arm added, "Nobody spoke to me about going in to fast. I was 16 years old and saw how the others were doing. I wanted to go in, thinking I might get a good dream."

After settling at Fishhook Village, the Mandan erected a ceremonial lodge for their Okipa and other ceremonies. The Hidatsa then paid to use this lodge for the ceremony. Formerly the Hidatsa rites were performed in any large lodge since it was considered a great honor to have one's lodge selected. No ceremonial lodge having been built by those Mandans who accompanied the Hidatsa to Fort

---

[44] A woman might assist her brother and get minor rights in a bundle.

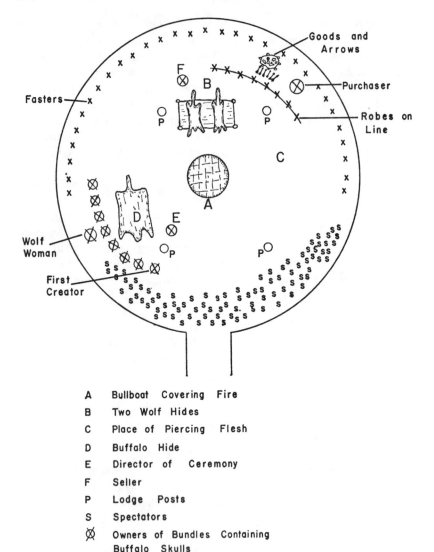

FIGURE 6.—Lodge arrangements for Sunset Wolf ceremony.

A   Bullboat Covering Fire
B   Two Wolf Hides
C   Place of Piercing Flesh
D   Buffalo Hide
E   Director of Ceremony
F   Seller
P   Lodge Posts
S   Spectators
⊗   Owners of Bundles Containing
     Buffalo Skulls

Buford about 1870, the system in vogue there was that followed in
the Knife River villages prior to 1845.

It was the bundle maker's duty to assemble the objects for the
sacred bundle. He could either kill a wolf for its hide or purchase one.
He sent some young man familiar with the country for the white
clay and gave him the right to use this clay in doctoring as the reward for his efforts. Although similar white clay was found at a

number of places west of the Missouri, only white clay from the hill designated by the wolves in the traditional origin myth of the ceremony was used.

The bundle buyer, bundle maker, director of the ceremony, and the fasters entered the lodge during the evening preceding the commencement of the ceremony and took their traditional places. The fasters would cry all night.

First day.—The older men with good military records and owning bundles including buffalo skulls dressed as though going to war. Each employed his distinctive painting and wore some article designating his ceremonial bundle rights. These men met at the lodge of the member selected by them to wear the wolfskin. The leader of the warriors and the buyer entered the ceremonial lodge; each carried a pipe and wore a wolfskin. The buyer approached the new ceremonial bundle and placed his pipe in front of the bundle, saying to the Wolves, "I promised to perform this ceremony for you a year ago. I have gathered all the things that are needed. Now, this day, I am prepared to stand up and come to you. By making this promise I wish to have my people free of sickness and lucky in everything they do. I pray that we may get the advantage of our enemies every time they attack us."

The leader of the warriors picked up the bundle buyer's pipe and, while lighting it, said to the Wolves, "You heard what your son said to you. He expects you to bring his people good luck and no sickness. He is going to suffer now for 4 days. He will take no food and water for 4 days and nights, hoping to realize all that he has asked of you. He believes all this will be given to him because of this ceremony." Then he lit the pipe and returned it to the bundle buyer.

While the leader of the warriors and the bundle buyer performed this rite before the bundle at the altar, the other warriors stood outside the lodge in a row with the Wolf Woman impersonator standing just back of them. In a roll across her back she carried an untanned buffalo hide from which the hair had been removed. She sang whenever the men sang. This untanned hide which she carried was kept as a permanent part of her sacred bundle to be used especially for this ceremony. They stood in a row and sang one particular wordless song belonging to the ceremony and known as the "Invitation song." When sung preceding the ceremony, it was an invitation for all major bundle owners to participate. A man with a Wolf bundle might, on other occasions, have food prepared for a feast and invite in the people with Wolf bundles by singing the song from his earth lodge roof. When out from the village in small parties, singing the song was interpreted as an invitation for all to attend a feast.[45]

The Invitation song was sung through four times as the warriors approached the ceremonial lodge, the fourth stop being at the entrance to the lodge. They stood in a line before the lodge. The man in front carried the wolf hide and the man on the end was expected to relate one of his military achievements. The director of the ceremony, the bundle maker, and the bundle buyer all had to be at their places in the lodge as the warriors approached.

The bundle maker supplied the arrows used in the ceremony. As the warriors approached the lodge singing and dancing, the buyer sent First Creator impersonator out four times with an arrow to give to one of them. The instant the warrior accepted the arrow, the director of the ceremony shouted, "Stop," without waiting for the singing and dancing to end. Bears Arm explained that interrupting the singing for the man receiving an arrow (which he would take the next time he went out searching for enemies) was to indicate to the young men that when on the warpath, if lucky along the way, they could turn back and not finish their trip.

Four Dancers provided a detailed account of the sending out of the arrows at each of the four stops. When Appearing Coyote, Good Bird's father, gave the ceremony at Fort Buford, the rites were held in Bobtail Bull's lodge. At the first stop No Milk received an arrow and said, "We went on the warpath towards the south. I was a scout then and found one tipi."

Porcupine Pemmican stepped forward at the second stop, took the arrow, and said, "We went out looking for our enemies and I saw a lone man on a black horse."

At the third stop, Bears Heart took the arrow and said, "We were out looking for our enemies and I found the man who was given to Bluestone the time he fasted under the eagle's nest."

---

[45] Bear-on-the-Flat explained that this was the song the wolves used after making a kill to call the other wolves, coyotes, foxes, and magpies to the feast. One time he was out eagle trapping with Iron Eyes, the only Mandan known to have performed the Sunset Wolf ceremony and then, he was permitted to do so only after dreaming of the wolves many times. One day when the trappers were in their pits, they heard Iron Eyes singing the "Invitation song."

Bear-on-the-Flat said to the younger men, "That is an invitation for us to go into camp." As each approached the lodge where the feast was to be given, he recited one of his war records. Bear-on-the-Flat said, "We were out to war and found one tipi. While we were running towards it, I struck one of the enemies." Then Bear-on-the-Flat went into Iron Eyes' lodge.

Bears Arm said, "Wolf Eyes was the leader and we went to the north against the Chippewas. When we came to the enemy, there was a battle and some of our men were wounded. I was a camp tender for I was only a boy. As we came towards home, I helped the wounded men by carrying water and cooking meat for them. I did all this until we reached home." Then Bears Arm went into Iron Eyes' eagle trapping lodge.

Iron Eyes picked up a small piece of roasted rib and dipped it into coffee; then he held it in the air and prayed to the Wolves saying, "Sunset Wolf, when you find something good, you call all the wolves, coyotes, foxes, and magpies to congregate and eat. I offer this to all of you. Eat this first. You will have the pipe to smoke also. You eat first and we will take the scraps." Then he took pieces of meat outside and placed them on the west side of the lodge for the animals.

Raven Paunch stepped forward at the last stop, took the arrow, and said, "I was one of the scouts. I saw the enemy making camp and building their fire. This was just west of the Killdeer Mountains. There were six enemies in the party; Bear-on-the-Water saw them after I saw them."

The warriors entered, followed by additional fasters carrying articles from their fathers' bundles.

When the warriors were ready to leave for the ceremonial lodge to dance, painting of the bundle buyer was started and timed so as to be completed when the warriors finished their last song. The bundle maker did the painting, using white clay moistened with water to form a thick paste. The paint was applied to the entire body; then he used his fingers to remove strips of paint from the arms and legs as well as from across the forehead. Beforehand, the bundle buyer selected a clan brother to stand with him before the wolf hides and to be painted in the same manner. Both were dressed in coyote-head caps with raven feathers sticking up at the top and a coyote tail sewed at the back so as to hang down at the back of the neck. They were given two canes each, representing the two poles on which Hungry Wolf suffered. The canes were partly peeled so as to leave four strips with bark on. The canes were peeled at the top and bottom. The four strips of bark represented the 4 nights of the ceremony and the four divisions of life; childhood, youth, maturity, and old age. The canes were used during the ceremony to bend forward on and to keep time with during the singing. A piece of wolf mane with a foot attached was tied to their wrists and ankles. The clan brother selected was one who had given much assistance in accumulating the goods necessary to pay the performers. The bundle maker then dipped red grass into the water and white clay and sprinkled the two wolf hides before placing one around the waist of the bundle buyer and the other around the clan brother.

Dancing in the lodge stopped when the warriors arrived. The four men who had recited their war records while approaching the ceremonial lodge were expected to relate additional war deeds in the same order while running toward the edge of the village. The bundle buyer and his clan brother led the way, trotting like wolves, followed by the fasters. Women desiring to fast followed the male fasters. Some fasters dragged buffalo skulls fastened to their backs by means of thongs inserted through the skin. Clan fathers had done the piercing and were individually paid by the fasters' parents for this service. The director of the ceremony and the bundle maker remained at their places in the lodge while the fasters were outside dancing.

Bears Arm remembered the following major bundle owners as representing the warriors when Appearing Coyote bought his Wolf bundle: Weasel-Blackens-Himself, Thunder and Big Bird bundles; No Milk, Naxpike bundle; His-Horse-Smells-Him, Thunder and Big Bird bundles; Porcupine Pemmican, Naxpike bundle; Bears Heart, Grizzly Bear bundle; Black Horn, Wolf bundle; Crows Breast, Woman Above bundle; Lying Chicken, Imitating Buffalo bundle; Hits-on-Back, Eagle Trapping bundle; Hairy Coat, Woman Above bundle; Dog Bear, Imitating Buffalo bundle; Plain Tail, Big Bird bundle; Marries-by-Carrying-Water, Grizzly Bear bundle; Holding Eagle, Eagle Trapping bundle; Iron Eyes, Wolf bundle; Bobtail Bull, Earthnaming bundle.

After the fasters had danced at the edge of the village, the warriors proceeded toward the lodge, again stopping four times to receive arrows and to dance and sing. The same four men related additional war records, after which all went into the lodge. The fasters were brought out four times each day. Each faster carried an eagle wingbone whistle supplied by his father and, while dancing, was expected to look toward the sky and whistle.

When all were in their places in the lodge, the "fasters song" was sung 100 times to represent the 100 Cheyenne Indians the Wolves gave to Hungry Wolf. The major bundle owners took turns singing, using the buffalo hide drum which Wolf Woman provided when the ceremony began. All fasters were expected to dance through the entire singing. A bullboat was kept over the fire so that exhausted fasters would not fall into the fire. The director of the ceremony kept track of the singing by means of 100 sticks. After each song he removed a stick from the pile until all were taken; then he would shout, "Stop." Then the singing and dancing stopped. The bundle buyer and his clan brother were required to wear the wolf hides during the dancing, so the young men could "look at the wolf as they danced and cried."

Other fasters would select clan fathers to pierce them for drawing buffalo heads while dancing went on outside at the edge of the village. Occasionally one chose to be lowered through the smoke hole by means of rawhide ropes fastened to the thongs. This was the exceptional case and seems never to have been universally practiced as it was among the Mandan in their Okipa ceremony. The fasters went out to the edge of the village in the early forenoon, just before noon, during the middle of the afternoon, and early in the evening. Between times, the major bundle owners sang and one of their number danced. The dancer would call for a specified number of arrows and the bundle buyer would carry them to him. The director of the ceremony would stop the singing the instant the arrows were delivered.

On one occasion Poor Wolf danced and called for three arrows. When the singing stopped he said,

"We were out to war against our enemy, the Sioux. We went to the south. Four Bears was the leader. When we found them, they were making their fire at the edge of the brush on a hillside. I took aim at the man making the fire and killed him. I rushed in and struck him first; a Mandan named Red Leaf struck him next. When we returned to our party, Four Bears said 'We ought to get the scalp as proof that we killed our enemy.' When he said that, it meant that any man who brought in the scalp could keep it. The rest of the party went into the brush and we thought they might be planning to kill anyone who returned to get the scalp. Nevertheless, I went out and brought in the scalp. I killed the enemy, struck the enemy, and got the scalp. Those are my three deeds for the three arrows."

The major bundle owners sang again and Bluestone danced. He called for two arrows and said, "I went out with Four Bears when he went against the Assiniboin. We found an enemy and I was the first to strike him. Another time I went out with Knotted as leader and I struck the enemy."

Red Basket danced and Appearing Coyote was directed to bring five arrows. He said, "One time the Assiniboin came in large numbers to wipe out our people because they heard that we were few in numbers after the smallpox. There was a big battle and they wounded our chief, Four Bears. I went out and struck five enemies that day."

Then Iron Eyes danced. He said, "I was leader and took my pipe along. I got one man on a black horse. Flying Eagle struck this enemy while he was riding away."

The same men would dance on successive days and call for arrows, but each time a different war record was related. There frequently were so many attending that it was not possible for a man to relate more than one record. At the close of the day's dancing, the spectators, warriors, and Wolf Woman impersonator returned to their lodges for the night leaving the director of the ceremony, bundle maker, bundle buyer, clan brother, and the fasters at the ceremonial lodge. Any fasters desiring to do so could go out beyond the village limits to cry or drag buffalo skulls through the village. In the latter case, relatives usually accompanied them to give away property in the name of the ones manifesting outstanding bravery. Fasters might go outside for personal duties anytime except when the song was being sung 100 times. The bundle buyer and his clan brother could go out anytime when not wearing the wolf hides. The wolf hides were worn only when the 100 songs were being sung.

As stated above, the warriors selected one of their number to be the First Creator impersonator and to serve as waiter. In eating, the order of serving food was: (1) Wolf Woman; (2) director of the ceremony; (3) warriors; and (4) bundle maker. The bundle buyer and his clan brother, together with the fasters, abstained from eating or drinking while participating in the ceremony. The bundle buyer was responsible for feeding the participants and was assisted by parents of those fasting. As was the case when performing the NaxpikE, clan brothers felt obligated to come and fast to bring credit to the clan. Fasting was an individual matter and one remained only so long as he wished to. Most of the younger boys dropped out after the second night. When a faster had a vision, he often thought he should fast longer in the hope of getting fuller instructions.

Second and third days.—The first day's performances were repeated on the second and third days. Only those intending to submit to severe torture remained beyond the third day.

Fourth day.—Several new features characterized the fourth and last day of the ceremony. The warriors came in as previously and took their places, making four stops on the way to relate war records as they approached the ceremonial lodge. Parents brought goods for their fasting sons to give away; some brought in much, others only small amounts, depending on the family's means. Those unable to contribute other items of value brought food.

When the warriors were seated, the bundle maker instructed the buyer and his assistant to stand in front of him before the Wolf Altar in order to be painted and dressed. He picked up his brush of red grass, dipped it into the water, and sprinkled the wolf hides, singing, "This water is holy; this water is holy; this water is holy; this water is holy. This earth is holy. This clay is holy." The two were painted and dressed as before. When the buyer and his clan brother were ready, each faster went about through the assembled crowd calling on a member of the father's clan to pray for him and wish him good luck. This took most of the day.

Bears Arm, who was 16 years of age when he fasted in the Sunset Wolf ceremony, selected Porcupine Pemmican, a clan brother of Bears Arm's father. His parents brought in his gray horse and gave it to Porcupine Pemmican who arose and said, "Come over here and stand in front of me, my son."

When Bears Arm was in front of him, Porcupine Pemmican said,

I dragged two buffalo heads at the same time. All the skin and tongues were on them; all the hide along the back and the tail was on them. They were heavy but I dragged them by means of the sticks through my skin. I had a hard time of it and suffered much, but I was well paid for my suffering. I saw in my vision that I would not get wounded even when close to the enemy in battle: It would not make any difference whether they shot with bullets or arrows. My son, I suffered for what I have told you. You have given me a fine horse and now I bless you and pray that you may live to be an old man. If there is war, do not be afraid to go in close for the enemy will not be able to harm you. If there are many hardships, do not let them worry you, for you are on the safe path.

Each faster was expected to give something to a male of the father's clan and to receive his blessing. These activities occupied much of the day. It was felt that the success of any ceremony was, in part, measured by the degree of cooperation between the fasters, the clansmen, and the age-grade society of the buyer in furnishing valuable property to be given to clan fathers of the various fasters. There was a feeling that all of the major bundle owners participating should have an opportunity to bless at least one "son." Some fasters even went beyond the clan and sought the "blessings" of males of the opposite moiety who had not been called upon to receive goods. When situations, due to the limitations of clan membership, arose in which one had few or no opportunities to pray for a son because none of the fasters' fathers belonged to his clan, there was a property transfer within the group itself or one being called on to pray for a "son" relinquished his right publicly to another of good or superior reputation. Nor did the goods received long remain in the hands of the major bundle owners. They shared on the spot with others who stood in a father-son relationship to them and it was customary to share liberally with the feeble men and women, addressed as grandfather or grandmother, who gathered near the door of the ceremonial lodge on these occasions.[46] There was a rapid exchange of property during and immediately following the celebration of all major ceremonies; in this respect the Sunset Wolf ceremony was no exception. Hoarding goods in excess of one's neighbors was frowned upon.

Meanwhile, the Holy Women and berdaches erected a mound at the outskirts of the village and removed the cacti and grass around it for the "last dance" (fig. 7). These women—and men clothed as women—wore their low-necked ceremonial dresses with a braid of sweetgrass tied at the shoulder and magpie feathers fastened in their hair. They carried bone hoes and wooden digging sticks slung over their shoulders. When the giving of property to clan fathers was ended, the bundle maker sent the director of the ceremony to the lodge where the Holy Women and berdaches had congregated, after erecting the mound, to clean up and paint themselves for the "last dance."[47]

When the Holy Women were ready, they sent word to the bundle maker. These women, together with their singer, made the traditional four stops to sing as they went along and reached the dancing grounds first, led by the Wolf Woman impersonator. They stood on the east side of the cleared space. Then the bundle owners went out followed

---

[46] See the kinship system for application of grandparent terms.

[47] Cherry Necklace was singer for these women in more recent times and they met at his lodge. After he died, no new singer bought into the society so the women did their own singing.

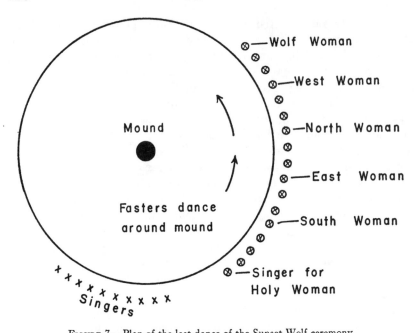

FIGURE 7.—Plan of the last dance of the Sunset Wolf ceremony.

in turn by the bundle buyer, his assistant, and the remaining fasters. A rapid pace was set; all trotted in imitation of the wolves while many of them dragged buffalo skulls. They sang the "fasting song" 100 times but at an accelerated tempo. For the fasters, this was the final dance after 4 days and nights of fasting (see fig. 7).

The mound represented the place where Hungry Wolf suffered. When a faster fell, others would stumble and fall over him. Then the dance would stop long enough for the exhausted man to recover sufficiently to get to his feet again. The bundle maker would dip sage in water and cleanse him. Seeing a son or brother fall exhausted, the relatives would return home and select a good robe, war bonnet, or other article to place on the ground near the exhausted man showing such bravery and fortitude. The Wolf Woman impersonator—running like a wolf—would pick up these articles and stack them in a pile in front of the Holy Women. Later in the day these articles were taken to the lodge where these old women met; each would take one article from the pile until all the goods were distributed. This was their pay for participating in the ceremony.

When a faster fell exhausted, the dancing stopped until he had recovered. He was then cleansed with water from the red grass bundle sprinkled on him by the bundle maker and cut free from the buffalo skulls by those "fathers" who had inserted the thongs. All the fasters were without clothing and moccasins, wearing only the breechcloth for the last dance.   The dance consumed much time since it stopped whenever a man fell unconscious.   At the end of 100 songs, the director of the ceremony stopped the dancing.

Usually only a few fasters could hold out to the end and the bundle buyer was expected to be among them.   For this reason, the older men never authorized one to perform the rites until they were assured, on the basis of previous instances of fasting and torturing, that the candidate could endure through to the end of the ceremony.   His torturing was not as severe as that inflicted on the other fasters since he was not obliged to drag buffalo skulls and rarely did so.   Moreover, the clan brother, dressed and painted in the same manner as the bundle buyer, substituted in many of the dances, thus giving the buyer an opportunity to conserve his strength for the last dance.

When the song had been sung through 100 times, the cleansing rites terminated the ceremony.   First the fasters were sprinkled, followed by those who had participated as singers, the director of the ceremony using the red grass and water for this rite.   Then the director of the ceremony, the bundle maker, bundle buyer, and the clan brother assistant returned to the ceremonial lodge to be cleansed either with the grass or by a sweat lodge rite.   When the latter method was used, these four people, together with the latter two officers' wives, met at the bundle maker's lodge where he took them into his sweat lodge, cleansed them, fitted them out with new clothes and then set food before them.

The bundle buyer and the assisting clan brother received identical bundles.   Articles in the bundle were: A coyote cap decorated with two raven feathers; four coyote manes with feet attached, to be worn around the ankles and wrists; a wolf hide; two canes with four dark strips, and made of chokecherry limbs; white clay; red grass; and a buffalo skull.   Bundles were somewhat more numerous at Hidatsa than at Awatixa and none were reported for the survivors of the Awaxawi village.   There is no evidence that the ceremony was performed in the Mandan villages prior to 1845 although the Mandan did have rites resembling those of the Sunrise Wolf described above. After 1845 Iron Eyes, a Mandan, was permitted to perform the Sunset rites at Fishhook Village when he had dreamed repeatedly of the Sunset Wolves.   This was an exceptional case and his sons did not buy to perpetuate the line.

The rites were important since they provided the Hidatsa with a second major outlet [48] for group fasting during the summer.   The Mandans, on the other hand, had only one outlet for formal group fasting—the medium of the Okipa ceremony.   For Awaxawi village

---

[48] The Naxpike being the first outlet.

there was no evidence that either a Sunset Wolf or NaxpikE bundle line survived the epidemic of 1837 and, in light of the high development of the Tying-the-Pots ceremony which was performed during the summer months as rain-making rites, some question is raised as to whether this village group ever performed these ceremonies. In historic times, this small Awaxawi group were reported to have placed greater emphasis on agriculture due, no doubt, to their small numbers and the greater danger of extermination by their nomadic neighbors. It is of traditional record of this and the Mandan groups that the Awaxawi lent considerable assistance to the Mandan in the performance of their summer ceremony, the Okipa. This is no doubt correct in light of the fact that in the period prior to 1785 the Awaxawi were closely associated with the Mandan first in the Painted Woods region and later at the Knife River.

The Hidatsa and Awatixa claim that the Sunset rites were of late establishment, although immediately prior to the first appearance of the horse. Features of the ceremony are of such widespread distribution in the Plains and even in the ceremonial structure of the Hidatsa themselves, however, as to indicate considerable antiquity for Wolf rites although probably not in the precise form taken in later years. This is indicated by the military pattern running through the other sacred rites believed to be of greater antiquity.

WOLF WOMAN

The Walks-at-Dusk sacred myth, given above as a part of the sacred beliefs and habits relating to the Sunset Wolf, provides the mythological and traditional setting for the rites associated with Wolf Woman. This female wolf who led the girl home after the burning of Strong Jaw's village on the Little Missouri was believed to be a holy woman who formerly lived at Hidatsa village on the north bank of the Knife River. She would often transform herself into a female wolf and travel out on the prairies far from the village. She lived in the village as any other old and wise woman, caring for her gardens, tanning hides, and looking after her lodge. But she would often sing her holy song for war parties leaving the village and predict good luck for their undertakings. Transforming herself into a wolf on the fourth day, she would join them at dusk. Thus it was considered a very good omen when the members of a war party heard the wolves howling on the fourth evening after leaving home. There was only one song belonging to the rites: "Friends, I tell you that dusk when the campfire glows is a good time if you are discouraged. When you have put the ribs to roasting and they are ready to be eaten, I will join you."

The Wolf Woman bundle owners were classified as members of the Holy Women and Woman Above groups because, according to traditions of the various bundle lines, all were created by a very wise old woman—Village-Old-Woman—who created the females of the species in very early times. According to present-day tradition, she created the female wolf woman who, in turn, assisted Strong Jaw and his daughter when the latter performed the rites after returning safely to the village. On the basis of these supernatural experiences, Hidatsa women established these sacred bundles.

Traditionally, there was one Wolf Bundle for each of the seven clans prior to the epidemic of 1837. Of these, only two bundles survived; one held by Yellow Head of the Maxoxati clan of Hidatsa village, and the other held by Yellow Husk of the Prairie Chicken clan of Awatixa village. This distribution provided one bundle for each moiety.

It is difficult to reconcile the traditional late establishment of these bundle rites with the widespread references to the role of Wolf Woman in the other ceremonies. The site on the Little Missouri referred to in the myth is obviously of recent occupation. The Hidatsa date the site as after the introduction of horses and near the end of the period of contacts with the Shoshonean peoples to the west. Warfare with this group was being actively pursued in 1804 (Lewis, 1893). It seems unlikely that these bundle rites should have been first instituted about 1800, spread within the Hidatsa and Awatixa villages to each clan in a matter of a few years, and died out to two bundle lines, all within a matter of less than 40 years. If the Hidatsa had preserved the belief that each clan should have a bundle and ceremonial rights, enough females should have survived to preserve the bundle lines. Bundles were regularly inherited from persons long dead. A more logical interpretation of the data would be that the moiety bundles met the new ceremonial requirements for participation in the Sunset Wolf rites and that the incidents of a historic event—the destruction of Strong Jaw's village—took precedence over the earlier Wolf sacred myths and beliefs referred to in the other bundle complexes.

The rites were of major bundle status since each contained a buffalo skull—the badge of major status—and the presence of sweetgrass and the robe in the bundle related the bundle and the rites to those of the Holy Women. One having repeated dreams about the wolves customarily went to a "wolf woman" of the same clan (or moiety) to request permission to give a feast to her bundle. Essentially the same sequence was followed as when making offerings to other bundles concerned with calling the buffaloes or bringing rain. A date was set for the feast, people with related bundles attended, each giver was "blessed" and promised success in his various undertakings, and each received some object for his sacred bundle.

When the bundle was to be transferred to one standing in the relationship of "daughter," the bundle owner's children and the younger people of the clan and household cooperated to acquire the necessary goods for the transfer feast. The transfer was a direct one to the children, one of whom held prior interest.[49] Sons were assisted by their wives, but the daughters' husbands took no part in the transfer except when a new and permanent relationship had been established with the mother-in-law by prior removal of the mother-in-law taboo. The sale was direct from mother to daughter. If the mother was dead at the time the transfer was to be made, an older woman of the mother's clan was selected to prepare the bundle and to receive instructions for the purchaser. Those owning rights in the Wolf, Holy Woman, and Old-Woman-Above bundles were expected to attend and to pray for the success of the buyers. There was a payment in robes and other goods to the legitimate participants who, in return, publicly sanctioned the bundle transfer.

The Wolf Woman being conceptually one of the Holy Women, any man with singer rights in a Woman Above or Holy Woman bundle could lead the singing. The articles for the bundle were received, in part, from Sunset Wolf and Old-Woman-Above bundles. The former supplied the wolf hide, wolf-hide cap decorated with 12 eagle tails, and the wolf claws and mane for the wrists and ankles. The Old-Woman-Above owner supplied the buffalo hide with hair removed, braided sweetgrass, and an enemy's scalp. Either bundle owner could supply the buffalo skull.

The husband, when he had not removed the mother-in-law taboo, took no active part in the amassing of the goods other than his traditional role as hunter for his wife's people and did not attend the transfer rites or claim any rights in the bundle. Neither is there evidence that the husbands of Wolf Woman bundle owners were necessarily owners of other Wolf bundles. Should a situation have arisen in which the husband and wife were Wolf bundle owners, by the customary inheritance rules, separation would have occurred in the next generation. The husband's rights would go to his son, who would be living in a different lodge by the rules of matrilocal residence, and the wife's bundle would be retained in the lodge by her daughter.

Articles in the bundle included a wolf hide, a buffalo hide from which the hair had been removed, a wolf-hide cap with 12 eagle tails attached by means of a porcupine quill decorated band, wolf claws and mane to be worn on the wrists and ankles, a braid of sweetgrass in the form of the sun, an enemy's scalp, a buffalo skull, and white clay.

---

[49] See the Creek ceremony given above for another case of transfer of a bundle through the female line.

There was one principal song belonging to the bundle. It referred to Wolf Woman's ability to transform herself into a female wolf and reach a war party out 4 days. The other songs were the customary War songs, the common property of all Wolf bundles. Bundle owners would dress in their ceremonial outfits and dance whenever scalp dances were celebrated. They were believed to get dreams from the wolves whenever their enemies were lurking about the villages. Whenever these women failed to predict the presence of enemies, it was believed that these enemies had appealed to their own supernatural guardians to bewilder and confuse the wolves so that they forgot to warn the Wolf Woman impersonators. Although the Wolf Woman impersonator had a definite part to perform in the Sunset Wolf ceremonies, independent rites were performed on other occasions. This was primarily a war bundle and little emphasis was given to other village activities. The right to use white clay for doctoring was optional.

Buffalo Calling Ceremonies

These rites constitute a series related by virtue of common beliefs and practices believed to increase the buffalo herds and bring them near the villages. These rites represent but a part of those in which the buffalo is included, but they had become recently incorporated into a related series in which the singers selected from the Earthnaming bundle owners play a dominant performing role. There is both historic and traditional evidence that this integration has occurred recently (probably since 1800) and that the pattern has changed to one approximating the Mandan as practiced through the medium of the Okipa summer ceremony although the specific origin myths for the two tribes are entirely different.

EARTHNAMING

Of the rites in this series, the Hidatsa believed that the Earthnaming ceremony was the last to reach the form as practiced until the final extermination of the buffalo. The ceremonies were based on the belief that certain spirits, including the buffalo, were residents of the various buttes of the adjacent prairies. A line drawn between those buttes situated on the farthest periphery constituted native concepts of the limits of tribal territory; it was with these limits, as defined by the bundle owners, that the Hidatsa have been chiefly concerned recently in all tribal claim negotiations with the Government. Conceptually, these buttes were the homes of various spirits whose leader was a large owl living inside the Killdeer Mountains. Each butte had a spirit and each spirit a sacred myth, ritual, and songs. These spirits would meet periodically at the Killdeer Mountains, known as Singer Butte, where rites were performed under the direction of a large owl who resided in a deep cave there. Each butte was further symbolically represented by a buffalo skull in essentially the same manner; each sacred bundle of major or tribal importance in the various villages included sacred buffalo skulls (map 1 and pl. 10).

There were two sacred bundles after 1837; one was owned by Guts and came from Hidatsa village and the other was owned by Poor Wolf and came from Awaxawi. There is no traditional evidence that Awatixa ever had one of the bundles. The two bundles and rites were identical and have provided the basis for considerable conflict due to the competitive position for peace-chief status which the bundles carried. According to traditions related by Four Dancers, grandson of Guts, and Mrs. White Duck, daughter of Poor Wolf, the Earthnaming bundle rites began with Raven Necklace. Briefly, the sacred myth is as follows:

An Assiniboin boy taken prisoner by the Hidatsa wore a raven skin as a necklace when captured and was named Raven Necklace. A few years later the Hidatsa went into winter camp on the Missouri above the mouth of the Little Missouri River (pl. 11) During the winter, the Assiniboin attacked the village and Raven Necklace undertook to protect three women of his adopted tribe. Two of the Assiniboins who attacked the women were recognized as his Assiniboin brothers. He wounded both brothers but did not kill them. After the battle it was learned that 30 young Hidatsa women were missing, among them Raven Necklace's adopted sister.

Raven Necklace traveled northward to the Assiniboin camp, looking for the Hidatsa women, and visited with his Assiniboin family. They discussed the battle and then he inquired about his adopted sister. During the night he freed the 30 women but his sister was not among them. He killed one enemy who was out as scout and then they traveled toward the Missouri, reaching a timbered coulee north of the spot where Fishhook Village later stood. Raven Necklace was about to push over a dead tree when a voice said, "Raven Necklace, leave that tree alone, for it is my home. I have my young ones here and I do not want my home destroyed."

Looking up he saw that Owl was speaking. Owl said, "This valley is known as Owl Valley. You can make a buffalo corral here.[50] I will give you a ceremony called Earthnaming. When you perform the rites the other spirits will teach you the songs and what things to use with the Earth medicines. When you call them together, they will tell you the names of these high hills. There will be a great deal of memorizing."

The 30 women helped him build the buffalo corral and they took many buffaloes, tanning the hides and curing the meat. Then they went upstream and joined the others at the winter camp, waving the scalp to show that they had overcome one enemy. All this time the spirits living in the various buttes came to him in his dreams and taught him the songs and rites.

The people went back to Knife River in the spring where many people helped him put up the goods to buy the ceremony. Among the buttes represented

---

[50] This owl was the singer whenever the spirits of the buttes met at Killdeer Mountains.

were: Killdeer Mountains, the singer; Ghost Singing Butte situated northwest of the Killdeer Mountains, so named because Swallow and Hawk were buried there; Crow Butte; Singing Butte; Heart Singing Butte; Little Heart Singing Butte; Fox Singing Butte; Rosebud Butte; White Butte; Opposite Butte; Buffalo Home Buttes; and others not now remembered by Hidatsa informants. The spirits came and established the ceremony. [See map 1 for location of these buttes.]

The precise beliefs associated with many of these buttes are no longer known. Poor Wolf had no sons and refused to instruct his daughter. Bobtail Bull had not completed the training of his son, Four Dancers, when he died, for the rites were no longer practiced and the rewards for learning the rites seemed insignificant to Four Dancers once the buffaloes had ceased to exist. Theoretically, each butte had independent rites which collectively comprised the Earth-naming ceremony. One of these, Ghost Singing Butte, was of special importance since the spirits of Swallow and Hawk lived there and were believed to have introduced horses into the tribe. Both informants supplied the sacred myth which was briefly as follows:

The people were traveling upstream from Hidatsa village on the Knife River to go into winter camps. Swallow and Hawk, who had died and whose spirits resided in Ghost Singing Butte, exerted supernatural influences on a poor young man and his wife, causing them to leave the main party at the mouth of the Little Missouri and to go up this stream where they found a washout in which they made their camp for the winter.

Swallow and Hawk who, while living, had helped Young-Man-Chief [51] came as spirits and visited the young man and his wife during the winter telling them how they happened to be buried at this butte. Swallow told how he had been out with a war party against the Blackfeet and had died of his wounds while returning to Knife River. Hawk told how he had gone out later with a hunting party, had died away from the village, and had been buried beside his friend.

Swallow and Hawk ate and smoked with the poor young man and sent him good hunting. They informed him that they would bring horses down from the heavy timber to replace the dogs; they described horses which the people had never seen before, and gave instructions as to their care and use. They told the young man not to place moccasins on the ground with the toes pointed to the east or the spirits would call the owners back.

While the poor young man and his wife lived well from the game sent them by Swallow and Hawk, the winter village was without meat and had resorted to snaring cottontail rabbits. Swallow and Hawk secured the aid of the Holy Women to cure meat for the poor young man. The people from the winter village discovered this meat and learned that the poor young man was now holy. Swallow and Hawk had given him instructions in the Bird ceremony of Swallow and Hawk who resided in one of the Earthnaming Buttes.

When the chief learned that the poor young man had become holy, he instructed his son to marry his two sisters to the poor man since the two women belonged to the same clan as the poor man's other wife. The oldest sister had a white buffalo robe and the younger one had a calfskin robe which they gave for the ceremony.

---

[51] See Woman Above rites, given above, for an account of the role of these two in protecting Village-Young-Man from the enemy who had been blessed by Woman Above.

When the time for the ceremony had come, the people went out onto the prairies near Ghost Singing Butte to await the horses which Swallow and Hawk promised. They were camped in a circle when Swallow and Hawk arrived with a gray stallion, a bay mare, and her three bay colts. The people examined the horses and said that they looked much like dogs except that they were much larger and stronger.

Speaking of the mare and her colts, the people said, "The hair is red. They are not buffaloes or bears. They are holy animals of some kind. They are red-haired-dogs." And so they were called *icuwasuka.*

The people said, "We suffered from hunger and this young man stayed here and had everything provided for us. Now we have these horses and the corn scaffolds are built and loaded with buffalo meat. We are not in need of anything. We are at the end of the world, for it is like finding a new world to find these horses which will be so useful to our people. Now we will be able to do almost anything."

Then the rites to Swallow and Hawk were performed, after which the people returned to the Knife River.

According to Four Dancers, sacred myths were likewise associated with the other buttes mentioned in the rites. Whereas offerings to the characters represented in sacred bundles were ordinarily placed on poles within or adjacent to the summer villages, offerings made to the Earthnaming bundle were placed near the various buttes while out from the villages on summer buffalo hunts. Of these buttes, four were known as the "Buffalo Spirit Places": Buffalo Comes Out Butte; Singer Butte (Killdeer Mountains); Buffalo Home Butte; and Rosebud Butte. At each of these buttes, offerings of feathers from the speckled eagle were made to increase the buffalo herds. The feathers were tied in bundles to buffalo skulls placed near caves situated under the overhanging cliffs.

The sacred bundle belonging at Hidatsa village was owned by Guts who, due to loss of prestige from bad luck in war, passed it on to his young son, Bobtail Bull. The other bundle, kept at Awaxawi, was held by Half-Smoked-Tipi in 1837, he having bought the bundle from his father, Raven Necklace.[52] He sold it to Poor Wolf, his son, shortly after 1837. The bundle rites exceeded all other tribal rites in complexity and had integrated into a related complex most buffalo rites when the aboriginal culture broke down. Inheritance was from father to son, but, unlike most other ceremonies, training, instructions, and participation in the various rituals were begun at an early age in order to become qualified to assume the father's role later. It was customary for a man to train several sons simultaneously for bundle ownership, and instruction was continued for several years. In this sense the preliminaries closely resembled the practices of the Mandan who taught the lore and rituals of their various tribal rites by sections or segments until the entire ceremonial complex was mastered. Poor Wolf and Bobtail Bull often remarked to their children that they

---

[52] He was named after the bundle.

grew up with their fathers' bundles and learned the rites a little at a time. They assisted their fathers each time rites were performed until each was fully acquainted with the rites, even before the bundle transfer was completed. The bundle owner's position as singer and director of the rites was comparable to that held by the Lone Man impersonator in the Mandan Okipa and their buffalo rites.

The final transfer of the bundle and ritual leadership was made at a public feast attended by all persons having major bundle status; that is, persons having ceremonial rights which included sacred buffalo skulls. Transfer was authorized by a man of the father's clan who interpreted the vision experience to signify that the purchase of the father's bundle was indicated. There was the usual year's preparation during which time it was necessary to acquire 100 buffalo robes, 100 pairs of moccasins, and sufficient food to feed every man possessing a sacred buffalo skull during the 4 days of the transfer rites. Conceptually, the cost of the ceremonial transfer exceeded that of all bundles and was expressed in terms of village status, the bundle owner being the leading peace chief of the village group. His status, expressed in terms of the goods mustered, indicated the importance of the buffalo in the economic life of the people.

For this study it is important to note that Earthnaming bundle ownership gave one paramount status in terms of village and ceremonial organization. He was the titular head of the rites to propagate the buffalo herds and, as such, occupied highest status in the ceremonial life. Whenever one dreamed of the buffaloes and wished to perform a feast for them, the bundle owner was ex officio singer for the ceremonies. As a symbol of the buffalo which he represented, he acted as singer for the Imitating Buffalo and Red Stick ceremonies by virtue of Earthnaming bundle status.

Although the Hidatsa did not customarily perform village rites when out on summer buffalo hunts, it was customary for one having Earthnaming rights to retire to pray at those buttes mentioned in his sacred myths and to place offerings near them according to the habits practiced at the various buttes. On one occasion, when the Hidatsa were camped near the Killdeer Mountains, Poor Wolf and his daughter climbed the cliff to the deep hole in the top believed to be the home of the speckled owl, singer for the rites performed at that hole periodically by the spirits of the buttes, and placed old robes near the cave, saying, "Buffaloes, we have brought you your old robes and put them here for you. You don't come out of this butte very often now and we are hungry."

Then they cried. As they walked back toward the camp, they saw a small herd of buffaloes and the young men killed some of them. When they cut the paunches open they found no grass, only balls of clay [hair balls] in there, and according to Mrs. White Duck, Poor Wolf said, "They must have just come out of the cave for they have only clay in their stomachs. Their hoofs are sharp too, but they would have been dull if they had been on the prairies very long."

A sacred bundle contained two very large rattles made of buffalo hide; the head, two wings, and two claws of the speckled owl; red and black clay; white sage; and a buffalo skull. Swallow and Hawk were represented by feathers from these birds. During a bundle transfer, young men paid to fast and to be tortured as it was believed easy to get dreams from the buffaloes. The Holy Women met at a separate lodge on the last day to receive their pay for the part the Holy Women performed in butchering and curing meat for Raven Necklace when the speckled owl taught him the ceremony during mythological times. The Holy Women and berdaches also prepared the dancing grounds at the edge of the village where the fasters congregated daily, dragging the buffalo skulls.

The presence of two bundle owners when the three Hidatsa village groups united to build Fishhook Village after the epidemic of 1837, whereas heretofore there had been only one bundle owner in the same village with peace chief status, resulted in endless rivalries between the two factions. This competition was settled only when one group under the leadership of Bobtail Bull, successor to Guts, left the area and built a new village near Fort Buford.

IMITATING BUFFALO

These rites, although traditionally of an independent origin, were integrated with the Earthnaming and Painted Red Stick rites in recent times by virtue of common singers. The sacred myths explaining the origin of the rites introduces two characters, Blood (Clot) Man and Buffalo Woman, who worked together to provide buffalo meat for the starving people. Theoretically, both characters went back to the origin of the land when Buffalo (male) was found on the earth by First Creator and Lone Man who concluded that Buffalo, like other things on the earth, came out of caves from the land below. Buffalo Woman was created later by Village-Old-Woman who introduced the female opposites of male living things. There are two important sacred myths to explain the roles of Blood Man and Buffalo Woman in the performance of the Imitating Buffalo rites. One deals with Buffalo Woman's experiences leading to her transformation from a buffalo cow to a Hidatsa woman after which she took up residence in the villages and assisted them in various Buffalo ceremonies, particularly the Imitating Buffalo and Painted Red Stick ceremonies.

Briefly, the Buffalo Woman sacred myth was as follows:

One winter the people came up from Knife River to build a winter camp in the timber below Elbowoods. Game was scarce and the people were obliged to bring garden produce from their summer village. Scouts could not find buffaloes anywhere. The children had caves where they played at keeping house and a strange boy who was rather dark-skinned with curly black hair invited his play wife to go home with him.

The girl went along to learn that the boy was in reality a buffalo named Calf Wedge. He was living with his mother in a hide tipi in the heavy timber. They had not been able to travel north with the herd for the mother had injured her foot on a snag. The buffalo cow gave the girl meat to take to her parents and they, in turn, made corn balls for the two buffaloes. The buffalo woman asked to move to the girl's camp and her parents invited them in secretly and pulled out the snag, for human beings could do almost anything. Buffalo woman described the rites of building the temporary lodge for the Painted Red Stick ceremony. Four days later the buffaloes appeared in great numbers. The people appointed leaders who had the right to pray to the buffalo skulls and then the kill was made.

The girl married the Buffalo Boy by rubbing her body with a buffalo skull and in the spring Buffalo Woman and her son returned north with the other buffaloes, leaving the girl with her own people. During the summer she gave birth to a child in a buffalo wallow but her mother took her back to the village without permitting her to see her child. Buffalo bulls came to the wallow, caused the baby calf to grow to maturity by rolling him, and then took him to his father to the north. He was called Spotted Calf because he was half human and half buffalo.

Four years later Spotted Calf was homesick for his mother's people so his father, Calf Wedge, and his grandmother, Buffalo Woman, agreed to return with him to help the people call the buffaloes. The three changed into humans, entered the village, and built a lodge of their own on the south side of the village, for buffaloes like ground corn.[53] Spotted Calf's mother joined them in the lodge. After that, whenever the people were in want, Buffalo Woman or her descendants would call the buffaloes, for they were buffaloes in spirit.

The myth given above explains the origin of Buffalo Women impersonators in the buffalo rites. While Buffalo Woman lived in the village the following incidents traditionally occurred and led to the establishment of the Imitating Buffalo ceremony:

An old man named Grey-Old-Man, his wife named Red-Corn-Woman, and their daughter lived in one lodge at Knife River with a rather poor young man who was hunter for the family. Since the young man had no close relatives and went around from lodge to lodge, he was taken in and treated kindly. He requested one of the older women where he had formerly lived to take meat to Red-Corn-Woman and inform her that he wanted to marry her daughter, White-Corn-Woman. Grey-Old-Man thought that it would be a fine thing to have such a good hunter as son-in-law, so the marriage was completed.

The young man and his wife decided not to accompany the others into winter camp farther upstream so he built two small eagle-trapping-type lodges facing each other in the nearby timber so each couple would have its own lodge.

Game became scarce during the winter and the young man ordered his wife not to feed her parents. He also ordered her not to return to the summer village

---

[53] Corn is associated with the southern part of the village.

for corn. The magpies went to a valley where the buffaloes were grazing and told how an old couple was starving because their son-in-law refused to help them. The buffalo bulls came together in council and decided to help this couple, selecting one of their number to be with the Hidatsa forever and to help them whenever they needed buffalo meat.

One day Grey-Old-Man walked to the river bank where he saw a buffalo standing. When the buffalo went on, he found a clot of blood where the animal had been standing. He pulled sandgrass and put the clot on it, wrapped the clot in more grass, and took it to his lodge. When he unwrapped the bundle, he found a baby boy with dark hair and strong muscles and bones. The baby asked Grey-Old-Man to name him and he was given the name Blood Man.

Grey-Old-Man performed rites over the baby four times and the child grew from a baby to a mature young man. Then he remembered that he had been sent to live with the people to prevent them from starving. Blood Man produced a fat buffalo by magical means and the old people ate without divulging their secret to the daughter and son-in-law. Next day when the son-in-law left to hunt, Blood Man informed White-Corn-Woman that he was sent to kill her husband. She agreed that it was the correct thing to do.

Blood Man went out to where the son-in-law had wounded an elk and killed the young man. When the old people learned that Blood Man had killed their son-in-law, they approved his action, for they saw that the young man's bad behavior was due to the fact that he was an orphan and had no people to teach him respect for the elderly.

Blood Man married White-Corn-Woman and went out each day hunting for the old people. The Holy Women came to Blood Man and volunteered to help him when he brought the buffalo herds to the village, saying, "When one person undertakes to do something, he should have help. We will come to help you and bring the other gods with us. Instruct your wife and her people to take wood and ice into the lodge, enough to last 4 days. During the time that the buffaloes are coming to the village, they must not come outside."

The Holy Women brought the meat from the buffaloes and a mysterious woman named Buffalo Woman looked after it, seeing that it was properly arranged on the corn scaffolds. When the old people went out, they found the scaffolds loaded with meat and a white buffalo robe on their own scaffold.

The winter camp being without meat, scouts returned to get produce from the cache pits, saw the scaffolds loaded with meat, and were invited by Grey-Old-Man to eat in his lodge. He invited the people to return from the winter camp and soon the various families began to arrive from upstream. Even after all the people had reached the village, there were many buffaloes near. From that time there was no end to the buffaloes because Buffalo-Blood-Man was a buffalo in spirit.

Several years later Blood Man said, "We should have a ceremony to the oldest buffalo bull, one who is so old that the body seems small in proportion to the size of the head. When you kill one, save the hide."

Before planting the gardens, someone who did not belong to the village was invited to wear the hide. Evergreen was put on his back, wrists, and ankles for the dances. He represented old age and the dance was called "imitating the buffalo." Everyone was asked to make pemmican to give to the dancers. Blood Man called the person dancing in imitation of the old buffalo his father and Blood Man's wife stood when the man danced and she moved as he moved. The old men cried and praised Blood Man. When a young man went to the dancer with a robe, he received a bowl of pemmican to give to his sweetheart.

People would see that and know that the couple would be happy when they married.

The people said that Blood Man did right when he killed the foolish young man for, long before, Two Men had come to save their son, Unknown Man. At that time the buffaloes had taken Unknown Man far to the north where evil spirits lived, but Two Men killed the evil spirits, sparing the buffalo's life when the buffalo promised to come whenever the people ran out of food. At that time Buffalo said to Two Men, "If a human being promises me anything and does not do it, I will destroy that person."

That was why the buffaloes came and caused the foolish young man to be killed by Blood Man. The ceremony passed down from father to son, all rights in the ceremony coming from Blood Man. Blood Man grew to old age and died in the village. By that time sons had taken over his rights.

The Imitating Buffalo rites were believed to have originated at Knife River with the Awatixa group, according to some informants. This belief is founded on the concepts that: (1) The ceremony fulfilled the same function as the Painted Red Stick ceremony which was not celebrated at Awatixa, only at the other two villages; and (2) Blood Man was a contemporary to Black Wolf who founded the eagle-trapping rites which were not celebrated by the Awaxawi and Hidatsa until they had left the eastern lake region for the Missouri when they acquired the rites and skills from the Awatixa and Mandan. Whatever may have been the development and diffusion of this ceremony, during the past century individuals inherited bundle rites through their fathers at each of the three villages. Four bundle lines were from Hidatsa, three from Awatixa, and one from Awaxawi. That the Hidatsa survivors of the epidemic of 1837 outnumbered those from Awatixa by a ratio of more than 2 to 1 suggests a greater popularity of the rites at the latter village.

The Hidatsa do not consider the ceremony to be as ancient as those relating to either the Sacred Arrow or Exodus myths although they recognize characters represented in the rites as very ancient. Of the eight bundle lines surviving the smallpox epidemics, individuals performing these rites had, in addition to rights in the Imitating Buffalo ceremony, other important tribal bundle possessions. There were many individuals possessing various tribal hereditary bundles who had never performed this specific ceremony. It is important to recognize that, while all sacred bundles belonging to the traditional hereditary group had buffalo skulls, few had bought rights in the Imitating Buffalo ceremony. This is due, it would appear, to several buffalo ritual traditions which existed as independent units or as segments of other rituals. We find the Calf Wedge myth defining the practice of arranging buffalo skulls in groups of four, thus relating this feature to the Imitating Buffalo and Red Stick ceremonies, while similar shrines arranged by other bundle owners were symbolic of the buffaloes of the four seasons.

The ceremony was traditionally an annual event at each of the villages until 1837. It was held during the late winter until, with the near extinction of the buffaloes, the herds no longer came to the river bottoms near the winter villages. Then the ceremony was shifted to the summer and became rites to the summer herds which were found farther to the west. Dog Bear, son of Missouri River who was one of the "builders" of Fishhook Village, was the last to perform the ceremony. According to a dozen or more witnesses to the ceremony, it was performed in the traditional manner with the exception that it was held during the summer instead of the winter, the shift being made because it was only during the summer that the people then hunted buffaloes. Although Dog Bear was buying rights through his father who came from Awatixa village, informants recognized no differences in village bundle line rites.

The following account of this ceremony was supplied by Bears Arm and Rattles Medicine, the latter an officer in the ceremony and the daughter of Poor Wolf who was principal singer at that time:

Dog Bear gave the ceremony to get the Imitation Buffalo rights from his father, Missouri River. He made the vow so all could hear while the Hidatsa and Mandan were on the summer buffalo hunt. Kidney had been selected as leader of the summer hunt that year and had taken the people to the southwest where scouts had reported buffaloes. While near the Rainy Buttes, Kidney named Dog Bear to be the leader of the hunters, for he had prayed often to the buffaloes because Missouri River had those rights. At first Dog Bear was afraid to accept the risk for his hunters. Then he remembered that he had once dreamed of his father's old buffalo bull so he decided that should he make the vow it would be just the same as having already performed the ceremony.

He went to Poor Wolf's lodge and talked to them about it for Poor Wolf was a "father," being of the same clan as Missouri River, and Poor Wolf's wife would be a "mother." They agreed that it was the proper thing to do and that it was wise to decide to give it, for it would give Poor Wolf an opportunity to find the oldest buffalo bull from which to get the skull and hide. This duty fell to Poor Wolf or Guts, the singers and Earthnaming bundle owners, whenever the ceremony was to be performed.

Dog Bear then made the vow, standing in the center of the camp circle, so all could hear him. Poor Wolf selected Coyote Head to be announcer and to instruct the hunters to watch for an old buffalo grazing alone. When a buffalo grew old, it was customary for the young bulls to drive him out of the herd. They had some difficulty finding an old animal and moved camp several times until they reached Buffalo Home Butte where one was found. The people remarked that because Dog Bear had been unable to find one, Blood Man had sent one out of the butte in which resided the spirits of the buffaloes.

Poor Wolf took charge of the buffalo. He skinned and cleaned the head and neck for the costume to be worn by some visitor during the ceremony. Then he cleaned off the flesh so that the skull could be used as a part of Dog Bear's Imitating Buffalo bundle when the ceremony was given.

The ceremony was given 1 year later. In the meantime, Dog Bear and his relatives collected goods and horses. Officers for the ceremony were: Poor Wolf, the singer and Blood Man impersonator; Dog Bear, buyer of his father's bundle; Bug Woman, Dog Bear's wife, impersonator of Calf Wedge's wife and daughter-in-law of the buffaloes; Iron Eyes, carrier of the Eagle Trapping snare and owner of the principal Mandan Eagle Trapping bundle; File, an Arikara, the dancer and wearer of the buffalo robe; Coyote Head, the announcer for Poor Wolf; Rattles Medicine (Mrs. White Duck, daughter of Poor Wolf) the waiter; the Black Mouth men's society; the Holy Women's society.

During the period of preparation, it was necessary to get the wife's approval since a vow to live with her husband was made during the rites. At this time she was told that should her husband die, she could make a vow not to remarry, which the men would respect. In return for this vow, she was pledged good health and a long life. If, however, she eloped or went around with other men, the promise made by the bulls would be revoked.

A runner was sent to the badlands for the creeping cedar. He received the right to use this cedar for doctoring as compensation for his assistance.

The rites were usually performed in the Mandan Okipa lodge but in this instance they were held in Dog Bear's lodge. The approach to the lodge was made by four stops, at which time Dog Bear brought the pipe to Poor Wolf who used the large hide rattles from the Earthnaming bundle for the songs. The participants followed in groups back of Poor Wolf and occupied places as indicated by the floor plan (fig. 8).

Dog Bear filled the pipe and carried it to Poor Wolf who smoked, sang the sacred songs, and prayed for Dog Bear's success. The night was divided into four periods of singing, a practice characteristic of the Mandan Okipa ceremony, representative of the four groups of buffaloes. The people fasted during the night, symbolically representing the old man and his wife who were starving when Blood Man came to kill their selfish son-in-law and to rescue them. About midnight, the Holy Women and Black Mouth societies, together with the spectators, left the lodge, leaving Dog Bear, Bug Woman, File, Poor Wolf, Iron Eyes, and Rattles Medicine to fast until morning.

Shortly after daybreak, those who had left earlier, returned bringing sacks of pemmican; all ate, dramatizing the feeding of the old people after Blood Man had killed the buffalo. Poor Wolf's wife painted the dancer, having bought the right to paint the dancer from Missouri River's wife, Root. File, the dancer, was painted with red paint; the old buffalo head and neck hide with hair on was hung over his head reaching down his back. The creeping cedar was tied to the hide. His moccasins were made from the old buffalo's hide with the hair inside and turned down at the top. These moccasins were called "straight toe." Then Bug Woman's face and arms were painted red.

The spectators arrived with the two societies and occupied places at the door, males on the same side as the Black Mouths and the females on the opposite side of the lodge. The front row was reserved for holy men who had sacred bundles containing buffalo skulls and who were not performing any specific parts in the ceremony. People came in anticipation of a feast. Corn balls were mixed with the pemmican and served with a ceremonial wooden spoon belonging to Rattles Medicine. She had bought the right from her mother who had bought it from Root. She had given her mother a horse to own the spoon and the right to use it during the ceremony.

When the food was ready to be served, Poor Wolf sang the Thanks song, holding some of the food up to the four directions and thanking Blood Man for the buffaloes. Then Rattles Medicine served the food. Poor Wolf received a small coil-basket full; the dancer received a wooden bowl full; all the others received a handful, except Dog Bear who was fasting.

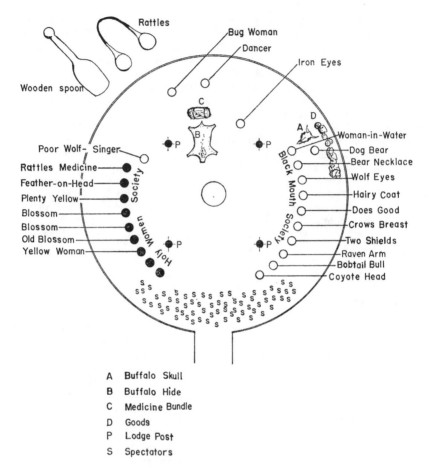

A   Buffalo Skull
B   Buffalo Hide
C   Medicine Bundle
D   Goods
P   Lodge Post
S   Spectators

FIGURE 8.—Floor plan of the Imitating Buffalo ceremony.   (Drawn by Bears Arm and Mrs. White Duck (Rattles Medicine).)

Each member of the Black Mouths and Holy Women societies took a branch of creeping cedar to carry or to wear in the belt.   Bug Woman wore a buffalo robe with the hair-side out and fastened with a waistband.   She received a small bag of Dog Medicine to which were fastened hawk or owl claws.   There were sage leaves in the bag and a song belonged to the bundle to be used in curing bites of mad dogs and rattlesnakes, or injuries from buffaloes.   Dogs were represented because the people used dogs in bringing the meat back to camp; rattlesnakes, because the hunters were sometimes bitten while chasing buffaloes; and injuries from buffaloes because they frequently attacked the hunters or their horses.

Rattles Medicine wore a stuffed owl and branch of evergreen fastened to her belt.   This was put there by the head war chief, Crows Breast, who prayed that she be given a long life and good luck.   For the dances, Bug Woman led the procession followed by File, the dancer, and the others succeeded them in no set order.   The Holy Women all carried sacks (made of the buffalo paunch) of pemmican to symbolize the scaffolds which they loaded with meat when Blood

Man "called" the buffaloes in mythological times. Iron Eyes did not leave the lodge but remained seated in his place making signs with the loop as if snaring buffaloes and drawing them magically into the corral. He sang the Snare songs belonging to Eagle Trapping rites.

Poor Wolf wore a buffalo robe with the hair side out. He had a piece of white buffalo hide about 12 inches wide around his head. A raven feather, to represent Raven Necklace of the Earthnaming bundle, was in his hair.

Bug Woman stopped at some point in the village and all would call out at once, "Come out and chase this buffalo."

Poor Wolf sang one sacred song and, when he finished, the dancer got down on his knees. The people came and asked to buy the pemmican. They received as many bowls of pemmican as they offered articles in exchange. A person who gave a horse received a bag full of pemmican. Only young men bought and they gave the meat to prospective wives. It was proper and customary for a man to give pemmican to two or three girls, providing they were not of his clan, for he had the right to marry several girls, but girls were criticized who accepted meat from more than one. It was understood that a girl accepting pemmican was willing to take the buffalo as her god and to assist her future husband in the buffalo ceremonies.

The procession moved through the village, singing and dancing. The number of times they danced depended on the supply of pemmican. When all was disposed of except what Feather-on-head, leader of the Holy Women, had in her calfskin bag, Rattles Medicine ran to Bug Woman and shook her, this being the signal for the participants to return to the ceremonial lodge. When the ceremony ended, the pemmican carried by Feather-on-head was given to Dog Bear and his wife. It was Poor Wolf's duty to supply the pemmican carried in this bag. This pemmican was made from the old buffalo whose hide and skull were used in the ceremony. The other pemmican was contributed by Dog Bear and his relatives.

On the second and third days, the ceremony was conducted the same as on the first. The ceremony broke up during the fourth night. When the pemmican had been consumed, the spectators left. Sandgrass was used to sprinkle the participants during the final cleansing rites. This was the grass on which the people believed the old man found the blood which later became Blood Man. Then Poor Wolf made up the Imitation Buffalo bundle for Dog Bear. It consisted of the buffalo hide worn by the dancer, creeping cedar, and sandgrass, together with the buffalo skull used in the ceremony.

Because Dog Bear did not want restrictions placed on him in entertaining his friends, such as the number that should be in attendance when smoking, he said, "Do not have any rules."

Poor Wolf placed a portion of pemmican on the buffalo skull, saying, "You will get this skull without any rules."

Dog Bear now had the right to pray to Blood Man and the buffaloes. He received the right to call the buffaloes to the village, doctor the sick and injured, and lead war parties. The people praised him for his sacrifices in performing the rites to insure an abundance of buffaloes.

In dividing the robes and blankets, Poor Wolf instructed the dancer to take his pick. The dancer had kept track of the number of times they had stopped outside to dance and selected an article for each stop. Iron Eyes, who had carried the sacred snare, was given four articles for remaining inside with the snare and singing the Snare song of eagle, fish, and buffalo trapping while the others were outside dancing. The Black Mouths and Holy Women each received one article. The remainder belonged to Poor Wolf. If he thought his share was too great, he must divide it with the societies represented, otherwise people would criticize him for being selfish.

In this instance, since Poor Wolf and Dog Bear's father belonged to the same clan, Poor Wolf was both ceremonial father for making up the new bundle and singer, otherwise Dog Bear would have selected a different man to make up the bundle. When Dog Bear's father died, his wife made a vow on the buffalo skull not to remarry and remained the "daughter-in-law" of the buffaloes the rest of her life.

Guts' singer rights were identical to Poor Wolf's. It was the duty of the pledger's father and ceremonial father to decide which man would serve as singer. Since these two singers came from different villages, the old people usually made their selection on the basis of the village from which they came.

BUFFALO CORRAL

The rites of corralling buffaloes were drawn from the Eagle Trapping and Imitating Buffalo ceremonies. The sacred snare was also a part of the eagle and fish trapping rites while Blood Man officiated as director of the buffalo drive by virtue of his authority to pray to them. Black Wolf secured his sacred snare for catching eagles from the Black Bears.

The following is a summary of the sacred myth on which the origin of corralling buffaloes was founded:

Blood Man was a great chief living in the village when Black Wolf returned from the Black Bears who had taught him the Eagle Trapping rites. Blood Man thought that since the buffaloes were quite scarce, he would ask Black Wolf to assist him in getting them together into larger herds.

He said, "The way it is now the young men go out and get the buffaloes but the old men can't. I want to plan things so that all get a more equal share. I know that you went over to the eagle trappers, the Black Bears, and saw it all with your own eyes. You got your supernatural powers from them and that is the reason why I need your help for what I have in mind. You have the sacred snare. You should arrange things so that we can get the buffaloes into a corral with the power of the snare."

Blood Man selected nine men to assist him and an eagle trapper to stand on the hill and use the snare. Black Wolf stood on the hill with his snare when the runners were out bringing in the buffaloes. He would paint the snare red and sing the Song of the Snare. In the meanwhile the holy men and Blood Man were concealed in the trees.

The eagle trapper stood on the high hill making motions as though catching the buffaloes with his snare. He had four motions to use: When the buffaloes were to the neck of the corral, he held his blanket to the side; when they were a little farther in, he folded his blanket; the third time he wrapped it around him; the last time he threw the robe and dirt into the air four times, signifying that the animals were corralled and the people could come. The right to impersonate Blood Man was bought by one of the Imitating Buffalo bundle owners from his father. Each village had one Blood Man representative until the smallpox epidemic of 1837, Black Shield who lived at Awaxawi being the only one to survive. When the people went to Fishhook Village, he directed the rites.

According to traditions, corrals were widely used in earlier times and, prior to the adoption of horses, each village group had one or more corrals situated near both the summer and the winter villages (see fig. 9).   If corralling buffaloes during the summer, the corrals were usually built near the Missouri at those points where the herds usually crossed from the eastern range to the west banks during the late summers when the waterholes and sloughs had dried up.   For winter corralling, the pens were situated near the winter villages on tributary streams.   Each corral was individually owned by one possessing rights in Imitating Buffalo ceremonies, but the building and repairing was a group activity under the bundle owner.   As the horse population increased and the buffalo herds became smaller due to excessive slaughtering by White hunters, corrals were less commonly used. The last corral, built north of Fishhook Village on a tributary to the Missouri, was operated under the direction of Black Shield who had inherited his rights from his father while still living at Awaxawi village.

The topography along the Missouri and Little Missouri Rivers was well suited for corrals.   Any sharp bank with a flat area extending back from the cliff made a suitable spot for the corral, particularly when the flatland narrowed toward the river bank.   This made easier the convergence of the buffalo into a compact herd at the entrance.   It was important that the cliff over which the animals were run was precipitous enough to prevent the animals from climbing back out.   It was also necessary to have these corrals near the village or winter camp to reduce the work of bringing in the meat.   The Hidatsa seemingly did not depend on the steep banks to kill the animals as did other tribes farther west, although some Mandan and Hidatsa informants had participated in cliff-killing when visiting the Crow on Powder River.   Instead, the corral was constructed beneath a lower bank 10 to 15 feet high.   From my observations of "kills" situated on Powder River in the vicinity of Broadus, Mont., it would appear that corrals were not employed there due to the scarcity of wood at many of those sites.   On the Missouri River in the territory occupied by the Hidatsa, the terrain is not so deeply eroded and fewer spots were suitable for killing buffaloes by driving them over steep banks.

Construction and repair of the corral were supervised by the owner of the site; one who had either bought the corral and the associated rites directly from his father or had built one of his own after observing the movement of the herds and the suitability of the terrain. However much one desired to build and operate a corral for its prestige value, social recognition and support of the people was essential since the work was exceedingly hazardous and involved the organized activities of many people.   The whole population assisted in making the corral.   Men and women went into the woods to cut and trim posts and rails. When constructing the corral, men of the four-clan moiety dug the postholes and brought in the posts and rails for the right half of the enclosure looking into the corral from the cliff while the three-clan moiety constructed the other half. Large trees with forked limbs were used as posts. About 2 feet of each fork were retained and the forked end was set into the ground to give the posts strength and stability so that pressure from the animals against the wall would not draw the posts out of the ground. The rails were fastened to the posts with strips of green buffalo hide which contracted when dry. Eight piles of stones were placed in a funnel-shaped arrangement reaching up to the entrance to the corral.

Eight young men, selected for their skill and bravery, stood behind these rockpiles and jumped up at the proper moment to drive the animals over the cliff. Three men, wearing wolf hides to conceal their identity, were selected to move the animals off of the range to the funnel-shaped entrance. When the animals did not move in the proper direction, smoke from small fires was used.

The eagle trapper with his snare stood on a high hill in full view of the activities and out of the path of the buffaloes. The impersonator of Blood Man and the other nine headmen kept out of sight in the trees with the rest of the people. The man with the snare made movements as though snaring the animals, singing the Snare song and praying to the Black Bears to bring the buffaloes into the corral without injury to the young men.

The speed of the animals accelerated as they approached the corral. Once the herd was past the outer stones, the men concealed there stood up and waved their robes and the animals broke into a gallop. When they were a little farther into the funnel the next opposing pair jumped up. The most hazardous positions were occupied by the last men on each side of the entrance to the corral. They could not stand until the front of the herd was even with them or the animals might turn, double back, mill around, or break away. When properly timed, the front of the herd was moving rapidly and directly toward the opening of the corral, at the instant that the animals in front sighted the corral and sharp cliff. Then the pressure of those to the rear forced the vanguard over the cliff, and the dust from the first animals concealed their descent into the corral.

Crows Heart told of the time Black Shield had a corral. Then the animals were wedged in so closely that a stray yearling that had broken away from the herd came over the cliff while the people were gathered around the corral, fell onto the backs of the other buffaloes wedged in there, climbed from the buffaloes' backs over the corral wall, and ran away. This caused everyone to laugh heartily.

The man with the snare signaled the progress of the herd with his robe as indicated in the sacred myth.

The division of the animals after they had been shot was as follows: (1) The tongues belonged to the 3 men who brought the herd to the corral; (2) the man with the snare received one buffalo; (3) the 10 men overseeing the corral each got one buffalo; (4) the 8 men stationed at the rockpiles each received a buffalo; and (5) each moiety got half of the remaining buffaloes. After the officers had made their selections, the rawhides holding the lower rails were cut and the rails were removed so that the animals could be dragged out. In dividing the buffaloes, an imaginary line was drawn through the middle of the corral as illustrated in the accompanying diagram (fig. 9). The first buffalo on the median line belonged to the four-clan moiety and the next to the three-clan moiety and so forth, alternating to the opposite end of the corral. Each moiety then took all the buffaloes on its side of this line.

A moiety selected beforehand one of its number to divide the animals among households. Each man knew the number of households in his moiety. The division went by men of the moiety, the wife butchering with her husband on his side of the corral. They tried to give one buffalo to each family when enough buffaloes came into the corral, otherwise one buffalo was given to two related households, such as to two brothers. A widow with children got her meat from the moiety to which she belonged. It was her brother's duty to see that she received her share in proportion to her needs. Officers listed above received their share as heads of families in addition to the tongues and animals which they received as their pay for bringing the animals to the corral. When the corral was only partially filled, it was considered bad taste for the officers to keep too much while other families had little. And it was considered foolish to quarrel over the division of meat which all should enjoy. Thus, the households having plenty of help pitched in to assist those in which there were many small children, few men to take hold and direct the butchering, or in which the people were old and feeble.

Once a corral was built, it was necessary only to replace the lower rails when it was ready to be used again.

The Hidatsa also captured antelopes, but the animals' great speed demanded corrals with walls less substantial but far higher than were necessary for capturing buffaloes. The rites, too, differed. Blood Man and his nine helpers were symbolic only of the buffaloes and thus were not represented. Rather, the rites were under the direction of one possessing a sacred snare. The corral was built at a point where a stream undercut a high bank. When a drive was to be made, the able-bodied men usually went out onto the adjacent prairie and drove

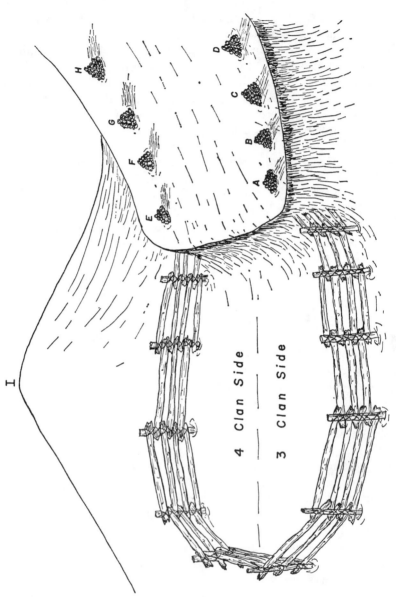

FIGURE 9.—Plan of the buffalo corral. (Drawn by Bears Arm.)

the animals together and turned them toward the river valley and wide bottoms with the corral at one end. The women and children formed a line along the edge of the timber where they concealed themselves until the animals had run down from the high hills. As soon as the herds came down from the hills and attempted to go through the trees the people stood up and shouted to turn them. In the meantime, the faster runners who had brought up the rear turned them away from the hills. The only open area was at the wide neck to the corral concealed below the bank. Antelopes traveled so rapidly that careful timing by the large number of concealed people stationed in long lines was necessary. There was not, however, the danger of accident attendant with the buffalo corral. Once driven into the corral, the animals were clubbed. There was no division within the corral by moieties. Instead, a headman for each moiety took charge and divided the animals according to the number of families and the animals captured.

PAINTED RED STICK

This ceremony was observed by Lewis and Clark. It was described in detail 28 years later by Maximilian (1906, vol. 23, p. 334) who wrote that—

Another very remarkable medicine festival is that for attracting the herds of buffaloes, which is usually celebrated in the autumn, or winter. I shall describe this festival, as an eye-witness among the Manitaries, where it is observed precisely in the same manner as among the Mandans. At this festival they leave their wives to the older men, and individual Indians do the same on certain occasions, when they desire to ask good wishes for the attainment of some object they have in view. A man, in such a case, goes, with his pipe, and accompanied by his wife, who wears no clothes except her buffalo robe, to another hut. The wife carries a dish of boiled maize, which she sets down before a third person, and the man does the same with his pipe. The woman then passes the palm of her hand down the whole arm of the person favoured in this manner, takes him by the hand, and he must follow her to a retired spot, generally to the forest surrounding the huts in the winter time; after which she returns and repeats the same process, often with eight or ten men. As soon as the man so favoured has resumed his seat, the person who asks his good wishes presents his pipe to him that he may smoke; whereupon he expresses his best wishes for the success of the undertaking or project in hand. By way of returning thanks, his arm is again stroked.

The rites as described by Maximilian applied to later times when my informants were young. This ceremony was often spoken of as the "Walking with the Daughters-in-law" ceremony from the practice of sending one's wife to an older man of the father's clan and inviting him outside for ceremonial sexual intercourse. In historic times there were two active Singer bundles for the ceremony owned by Bobtail Bull and Poor Wolf. The former traced his rights back to Hidatsa village through his father, Guts, and the latter bought from Face, an older clansman who lived at Awaxawi. There was no knowledge of a bundle at Awatixa, the people of this village customarily going to Hidatsa when the rites were performed. Although two distinct origin myths are related, one for the Hidatsa and Awatixa, and the other for the Awaxawi, the rites were performed in the same manner at all villages. In fact, with few variations, the same rites were performed in the Mandan villages. According to traditions, the rites were instituted late in Hidatsa history since all incidents are associated with the Missouri River and its environs.

The Hidatsa version as related by Wolf Chief from information secured of Bobtail Bull was briefly as follows:

Buffalo Bulls came out of the north led by one old bull who carried a red stick. He was the guide and selected the places to stop. The bulls decided to come to the village to help the people so they went there, carrying a buffalo skull with them. The club that the leader carried had buffalo hoofs tied in a row and two long wing feathers at the end.

The leader said to the other buffaloes, "We are taking much food to the people. When we reach the village we should get corn balls and a chance to have intercourse with our daughters-in-law. When we start traveling, I am not going to touch you with this club or you will not be able to carry yourselves along."

As the bulls walked along, the leader sang, "If I want to walk, I walk; when I walk I always say this."

They stopped three times and then they were at the village. The leader said to the people, "We are bringing you something holy. You will have to furnish us corn balls; we want to walk with our daughters-in-law. In return, we will send the buffalo herds to the village."

First Creator arrived and announced that he was the one who always instructed these people and served as their waiter. The leader distributed the red sticks to the other bulls and instructed the people in the Painted Red Stick ceremony. All the other spirits learned of the ceremony and came to eat and walk with their daughters-in-law while the bulls danced for the people.

The leader of the bulls announced that the one giving the ceremony would be a chief and leader, for he would be able to protect the people from starvation while one who dreamed of the drum used for the dances would strike his enemies. The leader of the bulls announced to the people that they would not come and bring the buffalo herds unless the people offered their wives to the buffalo bulls. Those men who offered their wives would have long and successful lives.

The oldest buffalo directed the youngest buffalo to dance, while the bull with the drum sang several times so all could memorize this song, "When I want to walk towards the village I say this; when I want tobacco I always say this; when I want to walk towards the corn balls I say this; when I want to walk toward my daughter-in-law I always say this. Dogs will be among them."

The Awaxawi version was as follows:

Twelve (six) buffalo bulls—men with the spirits of the buffalo bulls—lived together and painted themselves only in red, never white or black. These men were known as *wirukusi* for they carried red sticks. In this village the people gambled. A short, fat, and rather ill-looking stranger came to the village and won consistently. He would win all the property the people would put up.

Buffalo Woman, who was living in the village, predicted that because of the stranger's gambling successes, the village was in danger of starvation. She informed the people that the gambler was Sun who planned to kill off the people. If he won the arrows with bark on, he would win half of the village. If he won the peeled arrows, he would get the other half. She told one of the buffalo bulls that Moon was trying to help the people while Sun kept promising Moon a share of the bodies when the village was destroyed.

Buffalo Woman announced, "There is only one way to save the village. You buffalo holy men should select four young men to put on the 'Walking with the Daughter-in-law ceremony.' If they refuse, the village will be destroyed. Of course, when you ask them, they will not know what it is and will hesitate. You can tell them that I know how to perform the rites and will help them."

At first the young men refused but at last one agreed, saying, "Since Sun is trying to destroy the village, I will volunteer."

Buffalo Woman replied, "You have made a wise decision. This is the only way that we can win this game with Sun and save the people. You should have the man with the arrows here. Sun has already won the first 10 arrows. Do not let him out or he will gamble again and lose the last of his arrows. Then there is no chance of saving the village." Then she taught the young men how to make the vow, saying, "I am giving the ceremony for the Sun and all the different gods of the universe. I will give a big feast and call you, my gods. I will let you take my wives out."

Buffalo Woman taught the young men how to erect the lodge with the door to the south, saying, "Perhaps Sun won't come in right away. That will be my chance to get him in for I will be at the side of the door. It may be that it will take more than 4 days to get him in. When he steps in, I will seize him by the ankles and say 'I want you, my grandfather' and then we will win the game. Announce through the village that the people must build the lodge, for the warriors from those 12 villages are on their way here to destroy our village. Have plenty of dry sticks and three places for fires so the light will show over the entire world. When the lights are bright, the old buffalo bull men will begin to take out the women and Sun from outside will see what is going on. Have plenty of roasted corn and other corn products. Then the gods will come from all directions to eat, even though you cannot see them. When you want the women to walk with your gods, the gods will not be seen but they will be there. There is another way that I can help you. Moon will be there and I will ask him to invite Sun to the feast so that he can walk with his daughter-in-law. I think Moon will do that. When you are ready, have the older men go inside while the younger men stand around outside. Distribute the food which will signify that you are feeding the spirits from all directions."

When night came, they took the food to the shelter. They had the feast and the older men walked with their daughters-in-law. Moon tried to fool Sun, saying, "Our son has promised us a big feast and we should be there" but Sun held back and the ceremony broke up in the morning.

The ceremony continued for another night. Sun and Moon came towards the village where the ceremony was being held. Moon said, "All the different gods were there last night. They had a good time eating and walking with their daughters-in-law for I heard them talking about it" but Sun would not go beyond the edge of the village that night.

On the third night, Buffalo Woman went to Moon and said, "You should tell Sun that his lover might go out with someone else if he is not here." This time Sun came into the village and stood near the ceremonial lodge.

On the fourth night Buffalo Woman noticed that Sun and Moon were near the entrance. As soon as Sun stepped inside, Buffalo Woman said to him, "I am your granddaughter. Why didn't you come before, you are the greatest god. We will go outside, for you are my grandfather."

Sun did not want intercourse with her, claiming that she was already his "granddaughter" but he could not refuse in such situations when the daughter-in-law insisted. Males have less will power than females in sexual matters. So Buffalo Woman became Sun's "granddaughter" again.

When Sun was ready to leave her, she seized him and said, "You are the greatest god. I will not let you go unless you promise me that you will deliver those 12 villages for us." Sun hesitated and she continued, "Why don't you say something; you are my grandfather now and have had advantage of me."

Sun was sad, saying, "I will promise you those villages but I do not like to see you kill off those people for my 'son' is there. Since you are now my 'granddaughter,' I must promise you the villages." As they walked back toward the village Sun added, "I adopted a son in one of those villages and now I will have to eat him along with the other people."

When they returned to the lodge, the holy people placed Sun on the west side of the door which was the weakest side. They had pemmican hanging over Sun's head. When Buffalo Woman told the people that Sun was eating, the people struck coups on him with sticks just as they did to their enemies, for Sun had lost his supernatural powers to Buffalo Woman when he had intercourse with her. Then the people set fire to the ceremonial lodge at many points so that the light shone over the whole world.

Next day Buffalo Woman announced, "It will be either tomorrow or the next day that you will kill them, for Sun has promised me those 12 villages." She painted all the buffalo skulls red and faced them towards the south. While she painted, she sang her holy song, saying, "I do not think any of you will be killed, but you will kill all of your enemies." She used the song that kept the buffaloes near the village.

When the 12 villages of enemies came, the people saw that Sun's "son" was the leader. He was painted red over his entire body; he wore a piece of rawhide around his head and light sage in his hair. The enemy were all killed back to the leader. When the leader was killed, they found that his spinal cord was chokecherry wood. They had difficulty cutting the head off. One man promised that he would take the head to the Missouri as an offering to the Grandfather snake, who once was one of the Two Men, if 100 enemies had been killed. The leader was the 100th killed, so the head was offered to the snake at a point where the Knife River entered the Missouri. Sun came down from the sky and demanded the head but Grandfather snake refused for he could not give back what had been promised him. Sun found a puffball and white sage to use for head and hair. His son stood up four times but fell to the ground each time. Then Sun went off crying. The people had won their game.

The rites as performed by Wolf Chief about 1870 differed slightly from performances witnessed by Maximilian prior to the epidemic of 1837. The number of red sticks had been increased from 6 to 12 due to the union of two identical bundles, one from Hidatsa and the other from Awaxawi. Also, informants sometimes spoke of 6 bulls carrying red sticks but on other occasions even the same informants mentioned 12. It would appear that the sacred myth originally mentioned 6 bull participants but that after the villages united both bundles were used during the rites and the number of bull impersonators was increased to 12. The rites were performed under the direction of an Earthnaming bundle owner who served as singer.

The Hidatsa believed it was easy to get dreams from the buffaloes, so young ambitious men sought their supernatural assistance through the media of the various buffalo rites and age-grade purchases. The Painted Red Stick ceremony and most age-grade purchases practiced the rites of sexual license between females and males possessing rights to own and to pray to the buffalo bulls. The sexual act constituted a relinquishment of supernatural powers from the buffalo impersonator to a "son" through the "son's wife" who, prior to the sex act, was a "daughter-in-law" to the buffalo impersonator and afterward was addressed as "granddaughter." Through the medium of the sex act, the older men's supernatural powers to call the buffaloes were transmitted to the younger generation. Since the chief role of the sexual act was the transfer of supernatural powers, only men whose record demonstrated possession of these qualities were selected to carry the red sticks. The same situation prevailed in buying and selling age-grade societies. Those who lost status as a result of indifference to ritual responsibilities, evidence of cowardice or laziness, and unwillingness to assist their kinsmen in social and ceremonial activities, were weeded out of the age-grade societies, leaving only those who conformed to the highest traditional standards. Although the same concepts of supernatural power transfers regulated the sexual license of "fathers" with their "son's wives" during age-grade society sales, the rites were not practiced at the lowest level in the system because the "sons" had not married and the next higher group had not as yet secured important sacred bundles containing buffalo skulls.

Wolf Chief provided the following data on his personal experiences and beliefs as a result of performing the ceremony on the advice of his father:

Parents would advise their sons to seek gods while they were young so that they would have guardian spirits and not have to rely entirely on their fathers' gods. My father often told me that it was easy to get a dream from the buffaloes, especially if I gave the Painted Red Stick ceremony for calling the buffaloes. Before I was married, I had a dream in which I saw four frameworks of branches surrounding my father's sacred bundles and the outer framework was old and broken-down.

I described my dream to my father, Small Ankles, saying, "I had a dream last night; it seemed strange to me. I saw willows in a circle like the fishtrap. In all there were four circles of willows and the outside one was broken-down. I do not know what it means."

My father gave this explanation, saying, "I often think of the way you and your friends play around here in front of these skulls (Waterbuster clan bundle).

Now this dream has been given to you by your grandfathers, the skulls. That dream means that you are going to give the 'walking ceremony' four times and your wives will walk with your 'fathers.' You are going to live to be an old man for the last circle of sticks is old and broken-down."

I thought I would give the ceremony as soon as I married. When I was 19 years old, the Sioux attacked the village and my horse was shot. After the battle, the men of the Waterbuster clan, my "fathers," sang the honor songs because I was brave. Several girls tried to marry me but I married a Mandan girl I had been watching.

I did not know the best way to bring up the matter with her since my wife was quite young so I went to my father for advice. My father thought that we should consult my mother. She talked to the girl and the girl's mother and they agreed, saying that it would make me a better husband and we would be together always.

The girl's brother said, "It is a great thing for it is hard to do. If he puts you in the ceremonies that way, it will be all the better for you since it is like giving you to the gods to care for."

My wife thought that by helping in the ceremony, I showed affection for her and would not divorce her.

Small Ankles instructed me that in making the vow publicly, I should say, "I am promising to kindle the fire and give you the light. I will make feasts for my fathers all over the world. I want to see my people provided with enough food for a good living."

He instructed me to go to Bobtail Bull, carrying a tubular red pipe and to say, "My father, I want to put up the lodge for all the gods and send the light out for all the gods." [54]

Bobtail Bull replied, "It is a hard thing to do. Only a few men can do it. I did not do much fasting but I made up for it by giving my wives. Now I am a chief and every time I go out, I win over my enemies because I have given the ceremony. You are going to have a good home and plenty to eat. I will have my announcer give the news to the village. In the evening I will call the men who have the right to attend and give each a red stick."

Bobtail Bull selected the following men, all members of the Black Mouth society to which he also belonged: Hairy Coat; Crows Breast; Wolf Eyes; Crows Arm; Son-of-Star; Lean Bull; Two Shields; Red Feather; Bear Necklace; Wolf Grass; and Walking Chief. He selected the following individuals as officers: Guts, the announcer; [55] Bobtail Bull, the singer; Wolf Chief, the pledger of rites to the buffalo bulls; Wolf Chief's wife, the Buffalo Woman; Small Ankles, interpreter of the dream; Poor Wolf, bad luck as symbolized by the Sun impersonator; clan sisters to Wolf Chief, wood carriers; Two Shields, the First Creator impersonator.

We made the lodge of cottonwood trunks and branches with the opening to the south and within the open circle of the village where the Mandans held their Okipa and other summer ceremonies. The lodge consisted only of a wall with posts dug into the ground and the spaces between filled with small branches. There was no roof.

---

[54] He could have gone to Poor Wolf who was also singer for the ceremony. Both Bobtail Bull and Poor Wolf were "fathers"; Bobtail Bull because he belonged to the opposite moiety from Wolf Chief who belonged to the Prairie Chicken clan, and Poor Wolf who belonged to the same clan as Wolf Chief's father. Small Ankles sent him to Bobtail Bull because both belonged originally at Hidatsa village before the union of villages.

[55] Father of Bobtail Bull and former owner of the Earthnaming bundle which he relinquished to his son after suffering numerous misfortunes.

My parents gave me most of the instructions, for they had both participated in former rites, and Bobtail Bull merely outlined the events as they would occur. Since I was not buying the bundle, only giving the feast to the buffaloes, I did not have to wait so long. My clan and society, the Kit Foxes, helped me get the food, especially the roasted corn that the buffaloes preferred.

On the morning of the evening that the ceremony was to begin, Bobtail Bull's father, Guts, went through the village and called that all the young men and women should go to the forest and bring in cottonwood branches and poles for the lodge. I appointed 10 clan sisters to bring in the dry wood for the fires. Those who were to carry the red sticks to represent the buffaloes dug the holes for the lodge posts and set the posts. The lodge was built just south of the Mandan Sacred Cedar with the entrance to the south. It was roughly circular in outline and was not completed until late afternoon.

All the officers met at Bobtail Bull's lodge and I was instructed to listen for them when they came out singing just after sundown and to bring the pipe.

I heard singing and went out to meet them in the village. They sang, "The land belongs to us; we are walking along."

This meant that the buffaloes had the right to walk on their own land. At the end of the song, Bobtail Bull prayed for me and handed the pipe back to me.

At the second stop the carriers of the red sticks again sang one of the buffalo songs, "Whenever I want to walk, I always walk."

This song meant that whenever the buffaloes wanted to "walk" [have intercourse] with their daughters-in-law, there were always some who wanted to walk with them. I took the pipe to Bobtail Bull and he prayed for me again.

The third stop was at the northeast side of the open circle where they sang, "The land belongs to us; we are walking along." Again I offered Bobtail Bull the pipe and he prayed to the buffaloes to send me good luck.

The fourth stop was at the lodge entrance. Poor Wolf, representing the Sun and bad luck, entered the lodge alone and sang the song. He did not come to the lodge with the others as he was the "enemy" to be overcome. He sang, "When I want to walk, I always walk."

The holders of the red sticks occupied places along the east side of the lodge, while those who were offering their wives occupied places at the head of the lodge along the north side. Poor Wolf sat just west of the entrance with the bull skull and folded buffalo robe in front of him. The "drum of protection" was on the east side of the entrance with the 12 red sticks placed in front of it. Originally only one fire was used, and that was near the head of the lodge, but later two additional fires were built; one on the east side and the other on the west side [fig. 10].

It was customary for clan brothers of the same age as the giver to bring their wives. It was also the practice for the Kit Fox Society men to bring their wives when a member of that society was giving the ceremony. Poor Wolf, representing bad luck or the Sun, sat on the west side of the door with the announcer [fig. 1].[56]

Poor Wolf entered first. He was known as *patuki* or "savior of the village." [57] He would pray for success over the enemies and for protection for the people. He would say, "If any are to be killed, I turn the matter over to my enemies; they are the ones who should be killed." Then he prayed at four points outside the ceremonial lodge in this order: north; east; south; west. He was painted

---

[56] Figures 10 and 11 illustrate the ground plans of the two variations of the ceremony. Plan One was followed when the giver had little assistance except from a few clan brothers; Plan Two was followed when a member of the Kit Fox society gave the ceremony to the Black Mouths.

[57] Bears Arm explained that it also meant "closed" and referred to the custom of Sun impersonator to return to the ceremonial lodge late in the night, when all were supposed to be asleep, to pray that the population might increase rapidly.

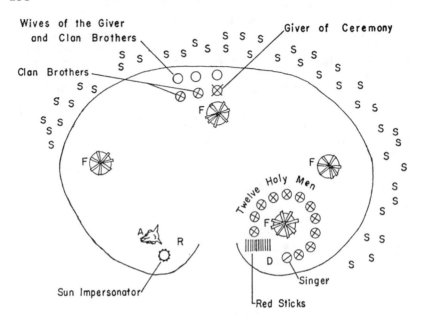

A   Buffalo Bull Skull
D   Protector Drum
F   Fire
R   Protector Robe
S   Spectators

Figure 10.—Painted Red Stick ceremony, plan one.

red over his entire body, had a piece of rawhide tied around his head, and had dark sage stuck in his hair.

The Black Mouth society entered next, when the Kit Fox society was assisting one of its members, otherwise there were 12 carriers of red sticks who followed the Sun impersonator. The men whose wives were to be offered to the holy men came in last, accompanied by their wives who were dressed only in their robes. When the Kit Foxes were assisting a member, it was necessary to bring a wife. Single members could come if they borrowed a wife of one of their clansmen. My Mandan wife helped me 2 nights and then she ran away and hid. I did not know what to do so I went to my clansman named Knife and asked for his wife for the next 2 nights.

Knife said, "My brother, you do not need to stop the ceremony. All the women married to us Prairie Chickens [clan] are eligible to go with you and help you out. You can use my wife for the next 2 nights." And I did.

The holy men who represented all the gods, and especially the buffaloes, carried the red sticks with them to the lodge. When they had taken their places, the First Creator impersonator collected the red sticks and placed them in a pile near the singer.

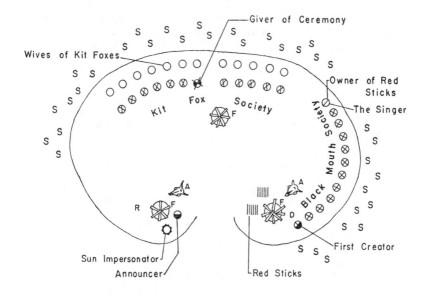

A   Buffalo Bull Skull
D   Protector Drum
F   Fire
R   Protector Robe
S   Spectators

FIGURE 11.—Plan of Painted Red Stick ceremony, plan two.

Bobtail Bull said, "Your 'fathers' have come from far away and are tired. You should give them a smoke." It was believed that these 12 holy men came from a buffalo village in the north. The giver of the ceremony and all others who had brought their wives filled pipes and offered them to the holy men. First Creator impersonator was always first to receive the pipe and each holy man, when handing the pipe back, prayed for the success of the giver.

After the pipes were passed around, Bobtail Bull said, "Your 'fathers' have come a long distance and are hungry. You should distribute your corn balls among them." Again I was assisted by those who had brought their wives.

When they were fed, Bobtail Bull said, "If you men have enough food, it would be well to give food to those spirits outside for they have come a long distance and are hungry too." Then the corn balls were passed out to the spectators standing around on the outside, the plates and bowls being taken back with a pulling motion downward from the shoulder.

The fires were replenished and First Creator held the red sticks in smoke from creeping cedar before distributing them to the holy men. Bobtail Bull sang and First Creator impersonator danced. This was followed by a song called "The Two Young Ones" while the 12 holy men rubbed each other in imitation of buffalo bulls.

Then Bobtail Bull said, "My son, have my daughter-in-law step forward."

I said to my wife, "You should walk over to Two Shields."

She wore no dress, only her robe. She said to him, "I will take you out."

Two Shields said, "This painted red stick is my power; it is as good as going out." So he handed her the red stick and prayed for her while she rubbed the red stick against her bare breast.

Then she went to the next man and offered to take him out. She went to several men who gave her the red stick to press to her chest. Before the ceremony, my father had said to me, "Do not think about it when she goes to the holy men. If you think of your wife at that time, you will not be successful. When I was putting on the ceremony, sometimes my wives went out and other times they rubbed the clubs on their chests. Afterwards I could always tell the difference for they seemed to have new life."

After a while I saw her going out with Walking Chief who belonged to my father's clan. He was the only one to have intercourse with her. Whenever the men with the red sticks prayed, they asked aid only for me and my wife. Then I sent her to Poor Wolf who represented bad luck or the Sun.

Concerning Poor Wolf's role, Bears Arm, who witnessed the ceremony performed by Wolf Chief, added:

When Wolf Chief took the pipe to Poor Wolf, he not only prayed for Wolf Chief and his wife but for the people in the ceremony and the whole tribe. His prayers were supposed to show that by giving the ceremony he was responsible for the welfare of all the people. Poor Wolf remained at the shelter to pray after the ceremony broke up each evening. At that time he prayed at the four directions, asking help for all the people. He was required to remain in his place during the ceremony.

Should any young man come to him at that time and ask Poor Wolf to move over so he could sit in Sun's place, it meant "I promise to make this ceremony in 1 year." Next day the young man would stand on his earth lodge and make the vow. Sometimes a young man wanting to give the ceremony would be away from the village when the ceremony was being given. He could wait until he found Poor Wolf or Bobtail Bull [formerly Guts] with the Sun rights seated with other older men and say "Move over. I want to sit in your place." Then all would know that he was going to make the vow. When he made the vow, the young men of his clan would hear it and know that they must help him get the goods and food ready.

Concerning his further participation in the ceremony Wolf Chief added:

When I stood before Poor Wolf he said to the red stick carriers, "I am going to sing a song that belongs to your son, Wolf Chief. I want him to have a long life and to be successful. I want him to have a large family and become one of the leaders of our people."

He asked me to face the west and he sang, "A man came, he says; Wolf Chief came too."

Lean Bull led the 12 holy men representing the buffalo bulls from the lodge, followed by all the others except Poor Wolf who remained until the village was quiet. Then he prayed for the village.

They performed the ceremony in exactly the same way on the second and third nights except that I took Knife's wife the third and fourth nights. On the fourth night there was the usual advance of the holy men through the four stations with stops for smoking and singing. Poor Wolf came to the lodge in advance of the others and sang the fourth song from inside the lodge as before. The holy men entered, followed by the young men who were bringing their wives. The pipes were passed; corn balls were given out; the dances were held; lastly, the young men's wives walked with or received the blessing of the holy men.

Near the end of the ceremony Poor Wolf stood up and announced that I would win the game; I would be successful; the village would be saved. Then he called me and Knife's wife to stand in front of him. He had a chokecherry branch sticking in the ground in front of the buffalo skull, a black-tipped eagle tail feather, a tip of a buffalo's tail, and a branch of creeping cedar. He said that they should be used for doctoring my children and some of the people laughed for I didn't even have a wife since mine had run away 2 days before and none knew where she was hiding.

As he passed the articles to me he sang, "A man came and left again; these people live to the east; Wolf Chief kills them; Wolf Chief brings the buffaloes; Wolf Chief will call the rain; Wolf Chief will bring the fruits and plants; the people will have plenty to eat." These were the things that Poor Wolf had the right to promise on the part of Sun whom he represented.

A large sack of dried buffalo meat hung on the wall back of the Sun impersonator. As soon as he left the lodge, followed by the holy men, those who had brought their wives took the sack down and divided the meat between the women who, during the ceremony, had represented the Buffalo Women. Then their husbands burned the lodge, setting fire to it at many points to make the flames leap high and throw the light far.

The Holy Women society met on the last evening at their singer's lodge. These women met during the ceremony because, when Buffalo Woman prevailed upon Sun to destroy his own warriors, these Holy Women came out and helped the Hidatsa during the battle. All of us who had brought our wives to the ceremony went to the Holy Women's lodge with our wives. Each Holy Woman stated the direction she came from, danced in her ceremonial outfit, and then demanded her pay. Each received a robe and corn balls and gave in return Black Medicine roots to use in doctoring. Then the participants were sprinkled with water, using the creeping cedar to terminate the ceremony.

The rites were performed primarily to bring the buffalo herds near the villages. In this sense, the giver performed an act of great value to the group. In return for his and his wife's part, supernatural powers were passed down from the top by the buffaloes and all the gods to the red stick and other officers. They, in turn, transmitted these supernatural powers to the women and their husbands through the medium of the sexual act, pressing of the sacred red sticks to their naked chests, prayers by the old men, gifts of food, and the presentation of pipes. There was no formal bundle transfer and once having performed the rites one did not possess the authority to serve as singer, these rights being reserved for Poor Wolf and Bobtail Bull who held equal rights by virtue of Earthnaming bundle possessions. The rites were comparable to those performed during the summer by those making the vow in order to insure good growing conditions for the crops. Nevertheless, one who performed the rites did have the authority to pray to the buffaloes and, in that sense, occupied a high status inferior only to tribal bundle owners and singers. One obtained the authority to learn and to relate the sacred myths belonging to the ceremony and to speak with added authority when disciplining younger clansmen.

The rites as performed by the Mandan and Hidatsa show close similarities that point to a common development from a single source. Each employed the sacred red sticks, but the Mandan exacted a virginity test that seems to be entirely lacking with the Hidatsa. Although the rites for both tribes are theoretically for the attraction of buffaloes to the villages and the increase of the calf crop by bringing the animals out of the various Buffalo Home Buttes (a symbolic fertility rite), each tribe had its characteristic sacred myths and rituals.[58]

Ceremonial sexual license was not limited solely to performances of this ceremony and age-grade society transfers but was individually practiced on the initiative both of young ambitious men and old widowers. A young man desiring to undertake some extremely hazardous undertaking, such as a military expedition far from home to avenge the death of a brother or other clansman, with the consent of his wife, often sought supernatural powers of an old man standing in the relation of "father" to obtain his supernatural powers to supplement his own. In this case, the old man was taken to the young man's lodge and fed, after which the young man and his family retired to another lodge until morning, leaving the "father" with one young wife. Irrespective of the sacred bundles which the old man possessed on these occasions, he impersonated one of the 12 buffalo bulls as represented by the bull skulls in all major tribal bundles. They were left together during the night with the doors barred. Although it was not uncommon for one of the red stick carriers to refuse intercourse during the ceremonies in fear of exhausting his supply of supernatural powers—preferring instead to relinquish the red sticks—it was not considered proper to refuse when invited to a young man's lodge. The young man returned to the lodge in the morning and ordered food, fine clothing, and horses for the ceremonial father who, in return, prayed for his son to be successful in his undertakings. This practice was so widespread with the Hidatsa and Mandan as to be viewed as a universal pattern. Whites were believed to possess greater supernatural powers than Indians because of their richer material culture and technology, and visitors to the villages were often given the same courtesies, both publicly during the performance of the rites and privately in the homes. Many a trader who called at the villages soon learned the cultural pattern of praying for their "sons" whenever some young woman met his fancy. Many traders, therefore, not only spent pleasant nights

---

[58] For the Mandan version see Bowers, 1950, ch. 14.

with young women, but also received rich rewards in robes and even horses from the husband in return for promises of success to the young man.

Often a small group of three or four clansmen, widowers who no longer participated in the active events of the day, would send for a distant "son" whose young wife met their fancy and offer to bring the young man good luck if he would leave his wife to them. Informants thought that this practice was more common among the Hidatsa and Crow than with the other two Hidatsa village groups, the Awatixa and Awaxawi, or the Mandan. My Mandan informants considered the practice improper, since one should not offer to part with his supernatural powers. This seemed to be the case also with many of the Hidatsa who had been in closest association with the Mandan. Many informants questioned the sincerity of those who sought intercourse with some young woman on the pretense of sending her husband good luck. Nevertheless, it was widely practiced, especially by those whose wives were dead or had left them. Informants jokingly remarked that it was sometimes necessary to send invitations to a number of young men before one agreeable to the proposition could be found. If the old men had not distinguished themselves during their younger days, owned no rights in important ceremonies, or were not generally well thought of, the matter was usually taken lightly. Since, however, the sacred myths refer frequently to supernatural manifestations by old and poor men not thought to possess any supernatural powers, unless overdone, the old men were likely to find some young man who was willing to take a chance of obtaining supernatural powers by offering his wife or wives. After settling at Fishhook Village the community was divided in its views with respect to supernatural power transfer on the initiative of the old men but took no action other than public disapproval, leaving the matter largely to the parties involved.

BUFFALO NECKBONE

This ceremony died out shortly after the epidemic of 1837, but the localities considered sacred in the ceremony continued to be so regarded until the aboriginal culture broke down. Crows Heart, whose father was Hidatsa and whose mother was Mandan, thought that both the Mandan and Hidatsa had the ceremony. When the author was conducting archeological work in ancient Mandan villages upstream from the mouth of the Heart River, for Beloit College in 1929, burials were discovered at the Larson site with articulated buffalo cervical vertebrae in such close association with the human bones in cache pits as to indicate simultaneous burial.   Maximilian (1906, vol. 23, p. 375) also refers to a ceremony in which buffalo neckbones were used:

The Manitaries [Hidatsa] are as superstitious, and have as much faith in their medicines, or charms, as the Mandans. . . . Buffaloes' heads are likewise medicine. In one of their villages they preserve the neck bones of a buffalo, as the Crows also are said to do; and this is done with a view to prevent the buffalo herds from removing to too great a distance from them.   At times they perform the following ceremony with these bones: they take a potsherd with live coals, throw sweet-smelling grass upon it, and fumigate the bones with the smoke.

After the epidemic in which the greater portion of the population succumbed, some buffalo ceremonies no doubt died out or were changed in outward ritual form since a number of the legitimate officers died without providing for successors.   Persons who could not have been legitimate purchasers of bundles, because of the laws of inheritance or transmission, purchased the right to own and relate the ceremonial myths.   In that way, some myths continued to be vital parts of the total religious beliefs of the tribe long after the related ceremonies became extinct.

Actually, the site for the last Hidatsa village (Fishhook) was selected because it was the locality where the Buffalo Neckbone ceremony had its traditional origin.   There is no evidence, however, that the ceremony was celebrated after the village was built in 1845. All that can be learned from informants is that this was a winter buffalo calling ceremony of 4 nights' duration; that two posts were set up, one dressed as a man, the other as a woman; that it was in some way related to the Holy Woman and People Above; that feasts were made to the bundle; and that the principal items in the bundle were vertebrae from the buffalo.

It is to be presumed that the rules of inheritance from father to son were followed.   There is no evidence that Four Bears was an owner of one of the bundles even though he recommended that the new village be built at this traditional shrine.   Placing of ash posts on the prairie and making up of images of a sacred character were common ceremonial practices.   The songs died out chiefly because they were ritual songs and would not be sung except during bundle purchases and renewals.

Bears Arm provided the following sacred origin myth:

The people came up the Missouri from Knife River to go into winter camp. At that time the people used dogs, for horses had not come yet.   As they traveled along, they would take the loads from the dogs when they camped and use the poles as frames for their lodges.   At last they reached timber a short distance below the Like-a-Fish-Hook Bend, where they built small earth lodges for the winter. At first there were a few buffaloes around but these soon became scarce and it would take the men 2 days to reach the herds.

Finally the buffaloes were still farther away and the people had only the things from their gardens to live on. Time passed and even the garden products were consumed. There was one man in the camp with many children, all of whom were hungry. This young man was a good hunter and the old men had often been invited in to eat and smoke with him. He respected the old men and they liked him.

One evening he said to his wife, "Fix up my moccasins. I am going to cross the river [where Fishhook Village was built many years later] and see if there is any game. Fix me a bag." [59]

Next morning he crossed the river immediately west of where the Fishhook Village later stood. He was looking for roseberries for his children but he saw that someone had been there ahead of him. At last he found some and made balls of the berries for his wife and children. As he was crossing the river, he saw a person standing on the river bank he had just left. He wondered who it was since he could not remember having seen anyone go out ahead of him.

Soon he saw two persons coming nearer. He did not know who they were and, thinking they might be enemies, he ran faster. At Like-a-Fish-Hook Bend they caught up with him. They stood in front of him and he stopped. The man was on his right side and the woman on his left.

The man said, "The buffaloes are far off and it is hard for your people to get meat. Although it will be hard for you to do this, when you get home, secure full outfits of new clothing for both a man and a woman. Bring them up here, put up two ash poles, and hang the clothing on them. Bring someone along with you. I know that your children are hungry for you have been picking berries. When you put the clothing on the poles, the buffaloes will come to your winter camp."

The young man observed that the two people were carrying clubs—painted red—in their belts. The man said, "You will kill the buffaloes and get all the meat you want. Each time you kill the buffaloes, new ones will come to take their places. In the spring you will have so much meat that many families will take their meat down the river in bullboats while the others will go overland with the dogs. You saw us far off and coming towards you. When we travel, we do not have to walk."

They did not say who they were but they flew instead of walking and were human. They flew even though they had no wings. Long afterwards Four Bears thought that the place where they walked was holy because these people had blessed the man, so we founded a village there.

When he reached camp he directed his wife to build up the fire and prepare such food as they had for he was inviting some of the old men in. She had a few corn balls and she made the rose balls into soup. When the old men had eaten, he told them what he had seen.

He said, "I saw some holy persons who were strangers to me. They told of many good things I should do and promised that I would be a chief some day. I am depending on you, for I am poor and can't do all those things without help. I have been asked to get full-dress outfits for a man and a woman."

Between them and their wives, the old men had all the things that the young man needed. They secured two ash poles; they took the white sage and made it in the form of a head; they put two magpie tail feathers in the hair. He asked

---

[59] Bags made of the paunch and used by the Holy Women in the Imitating Buffalo ceremony

one man to fix up the hair and put the robes over the poles. They painted the sage for the cheeks and forehead, using red paint.

When taking the clothing to the place where the posts were to be erected, they saw the young man's tracks and the spot where the others had traveled, the distance of their tracks being the range of the arrow. They cleared off the snow and built a fire to thaw the ground so that the posts could be set up. The posts were set up facing the south for that was the direction the two people faced to return to the sky.

The young man smoked sweetgrass and said, "I have the clothing that you wanted; there are two complete outfits. I have put them up as you wanted me to do, begging that the buffaloes will come soon." Then he used the smoke from the sweetgrass as incense for the clothing.

He said to the 10 men standing there, "I will have the buffaloes come soon. In the future our people can go through this territory after game. In the spring we will have rains for our crops. If our enemies come, we will get the advantage of them. There will be no sickness among our children and we will have many children." Then he directed the 10 men to go home saying, "I am going to cry here around these posts. I may get a dream. Announce in the village that 4 nights from now, all the people must tie up their dogs."

He cried all night and returned to his lodge in the morning. He did that for 3 nights. On the fourth night he told the old men to stay in their lodges.

Late in the night one man looked outside and said, "It is snowing hard but I heard a noise outside."

Another went out and came back saying, "There is a buffalo just outside; he chased me into the entrance."

They took up their bows and arrows, killed the buffalo, butchered it right there and had a feast even though it was not very fat, for the buffaloes breed until late in the fall and are not very fat in winter.

After that the people put up offerings at this point regularly and the place was known as "Place Where they Put Offerings for the Buffalo."

The young man was called Holy-Young-Man after meeting the two spirits. When he was old, they called him Holy Man. The reason the spirits told him to watch until they went out of sight was that if he did that he would have a long life. After that the buffaloes came into the camp and the people cured much meat to take back to the Knife River villages. Before the enemies came, the young man foretold that they were coming. Fifteen enemies were killed and he was a chief after that.

He kept buffalo skulls and bones of the neck which he would smoke with sweetgrass if the buffaloes went far off and they would come back. The people would come up from Knife River often to renew the shrine whenever someone dreamed of it.

After the smallpox of 1837, the people of Hidatsa village on the Knife River wandered around for 7 years looking for a place to have a village. Some thought they should reunite with the River Crows, but the Awatixa and Awaxawi did not want to leave their villages and abandon their gardens.

Four Bears said at that time, "Since these holy people came to this place, it should be a lucky place. The people have been putting up offerings there for a long time. I think we should take the people up there and put up a new village where we [the three Hidatsa village groups] can live together."

So the people moved to the place and built Fishhook Village on the spot where the two spirits were seen and the people were lucky in driving off their enemies.

CLAN BUNDLE CEREMONIES

WATERBUSTER CLAN BUNDLE

There was only one sacred bundle (pl. 12) for these rites and it was kept by a male of the Waterbuster clan at Awatixa village on the Knife River where, according to traditions, the bundle rites were instituted by two Eagle Men who came from a spring at the source of the Missouri River. Pepper and Wilson (1908) recorded the complete origin myth as related by Wolf Chief, son of the last holder of the bundle. In this study of the same rites, the writer endeavored to relate the bundle to the total tribal pattern. Hence, several points not brought out by Pepper and Wilson are given in order to show the position of the rites in the total ceremonial structure. (Fig. 12.)

The following is a condensed account of the origin myth as related by Wolf Chief:

Up in the sky there are four eagle villages which were seen by Lodge Boy and Spring Boy when Spring Boy was taken above to be tortured, and by Charred Body who once lived above before he came down to found the village at Charred Body Creek. They told the people that there was a hole in the sky immediately above them; that 1 day's march to the west up there in the sky was the village of the Speckled Eagle; the second village was of Bald Eagles; the third was of the Barred-speckled Eagles; the last village was of the Calumet or Black-tipped Eagles who lived 1 day's march west of the Barred-speckled Eagles and were the children of the third village group. At the place where the Calumet Eagles lived, the sky dipped down and met the earth at the highest points in the Rocky Mountains. It was from this village that the Eagles who founded this ceremony came.

When Spring Boy was taken above to be tortured, Long Arm carried him westward through the other three villages of eagles until he reached the village of the eagles whose tail feathers were white with black tips. There the people tortured Spring Boy.[60]

Long after Spring Boy was tortured and the Awatixa had moved to the Knife River from farther downstream in the Painted Woods region, two eagles came out of the spring where the sky and earth meet and talked of going to live with the Indians. One eagle liked the Awatixa and decided to live in that village while the other decided to go farther south and be born among the Siwaxuwa. No one knows today who the Siwaxuwa were but they were nomads and did not stay in one place very long.

The two eagles selected villages to live in where they could be of great help to the people. The eagle who wanted to live with the Awatixa came downstream to the mouth of Knife River and entered the body of a woman where he knew everything that happened even before he was born. It was not long after he was born that he remembered his mission was to help the people by being their leader so he carved out a wooden pipe. He thought that the people should have something to use when they became ill so he selected the peppermint.[61]

---

[60] See "The Naxpike ceremony," for the details of Spring Boy's suffering.

[61] This is the native interpretation of the plant. Pepper and Wilson identify it as one of the pennyroyals that grow in moist places.

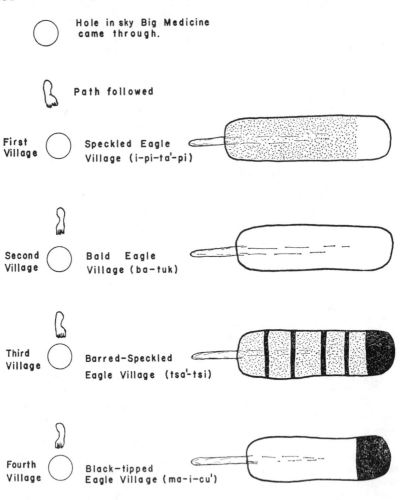

Hole in sky Big Medicine came through.

Path followed

First Village — Speckled Eagle Village (i-pi-ta'-pi)

Second Village — Bald Eagle Village (ba-tuk)

Third Village — Barred-Speckled Eagle Village (tsa'-tsi)

Fourth Village — Black-tipped Eagle Village (ma-i-cu')

(Village origin of W.Buster and Knife Bundles)

FIGURE 12.—Plan of eagle villages in the sky.   (Drawn by Wolf Chief.)

He thought the people should have something to give them good luck when their enemies attacked so he made up a corn ball to go with the pipe. He thought that he would bring his friend who had gone to the enemy and that he would use corn balls and pemmican to do this. He thought he would call the rain. The people would have plenty of food so he decided to have a turtle on which to place the peppermint when rain was wanted. He would have the buffalo skull in his lodge and that would keep the animals near the village. All these things he thought about and all these things he undertook to do.

When the year was dry he would use the turtles and sing the sacred song. Then the rains came. Sometimes the buffaloes would stray far away and he would build a small fire under the buffalo skull while he sang. Then the buffaloes would come nearer and the people lived well.

One day he told the people that it would be better to move farther upstream so they settled at a place below Shell Creek where Henry Bad Gun lives today. This must have been before the Hidatsa came for there is no mention of them in the myth for the Hidatsa, when they came, did not like to have others build in that territory. They stayed there 2 years and everything they did was successful for this Holy Man was with them and protecting them. After 2 years, many people called "People Who Live in the Woods to the East" came out of a ravine to the east and attacked the village.

The Eagle Man saw many enemies coming and said, "Wait a little before you go out against them." He took his pipe out and pointed towards the enemies four times and said, "You warriors can go out now and attack them."

While his people were fighting, he held the pipe out while singing the holy songs and lightning came out of his eyes and broke a piece of the bowl from the pipe. After the battle the Awatixa returned to their old village at the mouth of Knife River. Many enemies came but each time he would take out the pipe and his people would win.

He thought that he would give out corn balls and the peppermint to those who made offerings to the pipe when seeking good health.

He thought of his friend with the Siwaxuwa for he knew everything that happened there. His friend decided to come with his followers to kill off the Awatixa so he would have his friend with him. The Eagle Man at Awatixa knew all this and thought that it was a foolish idea to think of killing off all the Awatixa. His friend had seven different tribes come together to help him and he was the leader. The seven tribes were so far away that it would take them 4 days to come to Awatixa. The Eagle Man of Siwaxuwa started out ahead saying that he would reach Awatixa first.

When he reached Awatixa, the other Eagle Man knew that his friend was at the door. He had the pipe and corn balls ready beforehand and called his friend in. The Eagle Man from Siwaxuwa said, "I have come for a great purpose. You live here and drink this dirty Missouri River water. You have no opportunity to get around and breathe the fresh prairie air. When it rains, it is muddy here. I think this is a bad place to live. I have a better place there with plenty of buffaloes. We stop at nice springs of good water; everything is pleasant there."

The Eagle Man from Awatixa said, "You are mistaken. We were eagles before we came out of that spring. We were to live in the different tribes and be of help to the people. I am lucky; I have a pipe to bring the buffaloes. Our warriors are lucky too. We have all our own corn. I do not think this is a bad place at all. I do not think you are doing well. You said when we left the spring that you were to be the chief but I know that some of your people are not contented. The water is dirty and brown and it tastes salty. Your people are suffering from so much traveling. I prefer to have you here with me where you will have a comfortable home and plenty of food. Then you would be here forever. I told you that I have good water. I have the water right here and I want you to try it."

He gave his friend some of the water with the peppermint in it. He drank and said that it was true. He began to shake.

He gave his friend corn balls and pemmican but his friend continued to shake so he filled the pipe and gave it to him to smoke.

Eagle Man from Siwaxuwa bit the pipe and said, "Take good care of me, my partner. I would rather stay here than come here to destroy your people. My seven tribes will come in 4 days to attack you. Your men will kill them all up to me. Hurry out then with your pipe and offer me a smoke. I will die after

I finish smoking. I want you out there for some of the others might shoot me with arrows. Then there would be too much suffering."

On the fourth day the attack was made and the Eagle Man hurried out with his pipe. There were many arrows flying around and some were sticking in his friend's body. He said, "I told you to hurry; I am suffering a little now." He smoked the pipe and died.

When his friend was dead, he cut the other's head off, breaking the Juneberry stick inside.[62] All the others at Awatixa fought long and killed off nearly all the enemies. The people gave Knife River the name Walking-in-Water Creek by which it is still known because the enemy were driven across the water. He took his friend's head home and put it in an anthill for the ants to clean the flesh from the bones.

In 10 days the bones were cleaned of flesh so he fixed a platform on four posts on which the skull rested. While he was doing this, the skull said, "Do not let my head touch the ground. Put it on a soft place." He fixed a place for it on soft hides, painted it red, and left it on the platform he had prepared for it.

After that the people thought the Eagle Man from Siwaxuwa was very holy so they often made offerings of corn mush to the skull. He could not eat it but his friend sat beside him. He would offer a little to the skull and then eat the rest himself. If he could not eat all of it, the Skull would say, "Don't give any of it to another; if you can't eat it all, put it in the fire" and the other would do that. Whoever made an offering to the skull always got a small bunch of the peppermint to rub on his body. Then he would get his strength back again.

The Eagle Man said, "The supernatural powers I have made and given to the Awatixa will last forever; we will use these things for sickness and they will make you strong." After that they made offerings to the bundle and called the Eagle Man "grandfather." [63]

Whenever the people wanted good luck, they made a sweat lodge, brought in robes for payment to the bundle owner, and had the hot stones put in. The Eagle Man would say, "You will be lucky and prosper." While he was living, he would roll the pipe towards the enemy and the Awatixa would have no bad luck.

One day Eagle Man said, "Before long I am going back to the eagles" and the people wept. The people were sitting in a circle when he told them of his plans. He added, "I belong to the Waterbuster clan. I am leaving so listen to what I have to say. After I die, take my head out and put it in an anthill until it is clean of flesh. Then wrap it in a soft hide and place it beside my brother, the other Eagle.[64] Though my body is gone, my spirit will be here to look after you and see that you have plenty of food. It may be that sometime you will need rain; have both of our skulls placed on the ground with a hide under us; sprinkle water with the peppermint on us and it will not be long until the clouds will come from all directions. Since you have seen how I did it, anytime the enemy comes, take out my skull and place it on the ground, and take the pipe out and roll it on the ground. Then you will not have any difficulty killing off the enemy just as I did. When you want the buffaloes, take our skulls and the buffalo skull out and lift the pipe up. The buffaloes will come near the village. Any of you who wish to, may make an offering of corn balls before I leave. I have always eaten what my friend did not. Speak to us as though we were alive and

---

[62] Pepper and Wilson said "chokecherry." Wolf Chief corrected this to read "Juneberry," as he claimed the spinal cord was of the same wood as the arrows.

[63] All the people so address the skulls. Those of the Four-clan moiety classify Eagle Man as a paternal grandfather. This is consistent with the kinship system.

[64] Note here Wolf Chief changes the kinship relationship between the two Eagle Men.

tell us what you want. After you have made the offering of food, you can eat the remainder. Throw what is left in the fire. When one wishes to make a feast for us, he must prepare the sweat lodge. One will pour water on the stones and tell what he wants. After my body is gone, the one who takes care of us must be of the Waterbuster clan because we call ourselves holy.[65] Whoever takes care of us will live to old age."

"Don't permit running around on top of the lodge you keep us in. Whoever takes care of us must keep it clean where we are kept. Then I will make a rule that whoever takes care of us must not give any fire to any of the other lodge groups who come asking for it. If they do not ask for fire but walk in quietly and take some out carefully, do not say anything. If they ask for coals, do not give it to them. No matter where you are, do not walk around in front of us raising the dust."

When he finished talking to his people, he covered his face with his robe and died. The people of his clan did as requested; they put his head in the anthill to clean the skull and then it was kept by a man of the Waterbuster clan. How many kept these skulls no one knows, but there must have been many for the people lived long in this village without being wiped out by their enemies. They followed the rules carefully. When the buffaloes were far away, the bundle owner took the skulls onto the lodge and the buffaloes returned. When there was no rain, he took the skulls onto the roof and the rains came. When he came to old age and died, another member of his clan took care of them and followed the same rules.

Wolf Chief supplied additional information on the beliefs and practices in his time, saying—

When I was a boy I knew Missouri River who took care of the bundle. He belonged to the Waterbuster clan and came from Awatixa village, the new village closer to the riverbank. He bought from Blackens-His-Moccasin who was chief there. When Missouri River was getting old, my father gathered together all the goods that he could and took the things to Missouri River, asking for the right to hold them. At that time there were many Waterbusters and they agreed that it would be a good thing, for my father already had many holy things which he had paid well for and had taken good care of. Right after he got the skulls, the people appointed him leader of the winter village. This camp was on the river bottoms near Blue Buttes. The people thought he would be lucky so they appointed him leader. They went into the winter camp and were lucky all winter with plenty to eat. Whenever there were hard times in the camp, he would pray to the skulls and the game would come. Then in the spring they went back to Fishhook Village.

Once the weather was dry and the crops were suffering. The people brought in war bonnets and blankets to get my father to take the skulls out and pray for rain. There was a feast and sweat lodge. Two days after that the rains came and soaked the ground. I saw him do that myself. After he had called the rain and it had cleared again, he called in all the older men. He told them that he had a message from the skulls that something would happen during the summer to give all the Indians glad hearts so that they would be enjoying themselves. Shortly afterwards, the enemy came out in great numbers. I was 19 then and was in the fight. We were not very numerous but the enemy numbered over 200. All the while my father prayed to the skulls so we had good luck and drove the enemies

---

[65] The meaning of this statement was not clear to Wolf Chief; perhaps it means that one must follow instructions laid down by the gods and must not vary from the rules. During early historic times very few clan bundles existed.

back. I had a fast horse and went ahead trying to catch up with them. When I was close, they turned and shot. My horse dropped and Wolf Ghost ran in front of me so I had no trouble saving myself. It was because my father was praying to the skulls while the battle was in progress that I was able to do that.

Before my time, Missouri River was owner. He was holy because he kept holy things. The Indians met and paid him many valuable things to be their winter camp leader and he prayed to the skulls, "My people want me to be their leader and to select the place for the winter camp. While I am the leader, I want enough to eat and, should the enemy come, I want good luck for my people.'

Soon after going into camp, heavy snows came and lay deep on the ground. Then the scouts reported many buffaloes coming toward the village. During the winter some Sioux came with their pipe and a buffalo skull. It was the rule to bring these things when seeking peace. Missouri River called all the older men in and asked what should be done, whether to kill them off or not, since the Sioux had brought in the pipe. They discussed the matter between themselves and left the matter for Missouri River to decide saying, "Because you are leader, we want you to decide for you have been successful in bringing the game and all of us are happy."

Missouri River said, "I see now that you people have smoked with them and fed them for you have had them in your lodges. Already they are your friends. If you had wanted to kill them off, it should have been done before they got into the village. Now they are in so I think you should be friends to them and make peace."

The bundle also played an important part when Fishhook Village was built 6 years before I was born. The old men put Missouri River in charge of laying out the village. He replied, "I am glad you have selected me because I have taken good care of these skulls so we will surely have good luck."

He walked around on the site where the village was to be built singing the holy songs and then he said, addressing the Eagle Men, "I want to have the village here so that my people will increase and be safe. I want four good men who are holy and have had good dreams to decide on four places to build their lodges. I want them to help me so that we will have good luck and always conquer our enemies."

The older men met and selected Big Cloud first to put his lodge up to represent the east. Then when the weather was dry he could bring rain, for he had had dreams from Thunder. He was a good man and kind hearted. When he saw children with dirty faces, he washed them. When they cried, he would pick them up.

Big Cloud said, "I will do the best I can but I am not very powerful myself. But I had a dream so I will talk to the Thunder whenever we need rain. I will face to the east when we need rain and Thunder will do the things he promised me."

Again they talked it over and decided to pick a man for the south station. Bear-Looks-Out was named to put his lodge to the south side to help look after the village, bringing the buffaloes, calling the rain, and repelling the enemies. He said, "By myself I have no power or strength to carry out these things. In my dreams our Old-Woman-Who-Never-Dies promised to help me. I will ask her to help me. My grandmother, they appointed me to help direct this village and I want your help."

Then they appointed Bad Horn to select a spot for his lodge and he said, "By myself I cannot do very much, but my protector is a bear who will help us out. I will have my entrance to the north for the bears always den up on the north slopes with the door to the north. I hope that he will protect us and help us along."

Again they discussed the selection of the fourth man and named Missouri River; he agreed to take the direction from whence the Eagle Men had come. He stood up and prayed to the bundle.

After the four men who were the new leaders finished laying out the village, the people got along very well and there were no hungry people. This happened in the spring and there were good crops. A year later the Sioux came and tried to get into the village from the back side. They failed and four of them were killed. The people came out of their lodges and built fires where the Sioux could watch. They scalped and cut up the Sioux; they burned their enemies' bones until only the ashes remained. The women sang and all were happy. Nearly every year the enemies attacked the village but they could not get the people out. Only when the people went out hunting or on war expeditions were our enemies able to get at us. The people could not be run out of the village because they had these four men whom they had selected for their protectors and the two Eagle Men skulls which were part of this protection. [See pl. 12 for picture of this bundle.]

KNIFE CLAN BUNDLE

According to Knife clan informants, the bundle rites for this clan bundle followed the same pattern as that of the Waterbuster clan bundle. These rites, having lapsed somewhat earlier than the Waterbuster rites, were not actively performed after the death of Medicine Bird, the last bundle holder. Thus, it was not possible to obtain a detailed account of the rites and practices associated with the bundle. Medicine Bird obtained the bundle from an older member of the Knife clan from Awatixa. Since his clansmen were not interested in the bundle because of the costs of making the transfer after buffaloes became scarce, he left the bundle in his son's (Hunts Along) care. The latter was ill at the time this study was made and was unwilling to discuss the bundle as he was performing personal rites to the bundle in hopes of affecting a cure.

Bears Arm, who also belonged to the Knife clan, stated that the bundle consisted of two human skulls said to belong to two brothers who came from above to live with the Awatixa to help them. Formerly the two brothers, named Brush-Between-Horns and Goes-Along-Between-Hills, were eagles living in one of the Eagle villages in the sky. They entered the body of an Awatixa woman and were born in the village where they helped the people repel their enemies. When they were old, they told the people that they belonged to the Knife clan and that their skulls should be retained in the village; then the village would never be destroyed by the enemy. The bundle was kept by one of the most eminent members of the Knife clan who paid his clansmen for that privilege. Stirrup, the last bundle owner at Awatixa, was one of the Council of Twelve selected by the three villages at Knife River prior to 1837. According to Awatixa informants, the top leadership at this village was vested in two bundle owners, Blackens-his-Moccasin [66] who kept the Waterbuster clan bundle and Stirrup who kept the Knife clan bundle. The bundle never attained the same importance as the Waterbuster clan bundle after the death of Stirrup as several holders died or were killed in warfare until it reached Medicine Bird shortly before 1870.

SUMMARY

Five distinct clan bundle rites were reported for the Hidatsa: (1) A Waterbuster clan bundle which was owned by this group and kept by one of their most distinguished male members at Awatixa village; (2) a Knife clan bundle which was similarly owned and transmitted through the male clan membership of Awatixa village; (3) a Shell Robe bundle which was shared by the Awatixa and Mandans of the Prairie Chicken clan and kept by the Mandan (Bowers, 1950); (4) certain Thunder rites relating to Packs Antelope which were shared by the members of the Low Cap clan, one of their number retaining the bundle; (5) the Creek and Earth Lodge Making rites traditionally belonging to the Xura clan of Awatixa.

The clustering of clan bundles at Awatixa raises numerous problems concerning the bundle inheritance patterns for the three Hidatsa village groups. The clan was not an important property-owning group for the Hidatsa and Awaxawi, except for the eagle-trapping lodges which also were clan-inherited with the Mandan, which raises the question of the significance of clan bundles. In view of the greater emphasis on clan inheritance by the Mandan, it is suggested that the Awatixa borrowed this pattern from them. This belief is strengthened by the traditional relations which the Awatixa and Mandan have had over a very long time. In view of the fact that this Hidatsa village group has traditions of long residence on the Missouri near the Mandan, predating the arrival of the Hidatsa-River Crow and Awaxawi, it would appear that clan-inheritance of sacred bundles represents an older cultural stratum. This belief is further strengthened by the archeological record on the Upper Missouri where the late prehistoric-early historic site of this village group shows a very long period of occupation not equaled by any of the other Hidatsa groups for which we have traditional or archeological information.

Not only is there evidence of long and intimate contacts between the Awatixa and Mandan village groups but, as in the case of the Shell Robe bundle, ownership included all members of the Prairie Chicken clan of Awatixa and the Mandan villages but did not include

---

[66] For additional information on Blackens-his-Moccasin, see: Lewis, 1893, p. 184, and Catlin, 1841, vol. 1, p. 186.

the clansmen of Hidatsa and Awaxawi until after the building of Fishhook Village. In the case of this important sacred bundle, believed by both the Mandan and Awatixa to be very old, there were distinct village versions of the origin myth.

The two sacred bundles containing male human skulls were both clan bundles. As far as it was possible to determine, of all the earth lodge village groups on the Upper Missouri, only among the Mandan are other human skull bundles found. The Hidatsa and Awaxawi seem to have made more universal use of earth burials near the villages than the Heart River Mandan and Awatixa. The latter two employed scaffold disposal with secondary disposal through bundle burials of the bones, other than the skulls of males which were placed at Sun Bundle shrines situated at the edge of the village. Women, on the other hand, were more frequently buried in cache pits under or near their lodges.

When the bundle systems of the three Hidatsa villages are examined trait for trait, the Awatixa occupied a position intermediate to the Mandan with their highly developed clan-inheritance system on the one hand and the Hidatsa–Awaxawi on the other with a father-to-son system. It is interesting to note that it was only with the union of the three Hidatsa village groups at Fishhook Village that clans from the three village groups participated in these clan rites.

HIDATSA CULTURAL POSITION IN THE NORTHERN PLAINS

No reference to the Hidatsa communities was made in the historic accounts of traders and explorers prior to 1797 when Thompson distinguished them from their immediate neighbors, the Mandan, on the basis of linguistic and minor cultural differences. At this time they were living in earth lodge villages at the mouth of the Knife River. The village of the Hidatsa-proper was on the north bank, the village of the Awatixa was on the south bank at the river's edge, and the village of the Awaxawi was situated a short distance to the south on the spot where the courthouse in the town of Stanton, N. Dak., stands today. By the time of Lewis and Clark—1804–6—it was known that the Hidatsa and Crow were closely related linguistically, that they were previously one people, and that they had maintained close social ties even after the Crow had moved out onto the plains west of the Missouri River as nomadic hunters.

Although these early traders and travelers recorded several migration accounts for the Hidatsa and Crow, some of which are contradictory if one views the Hidatsa as a single unified group, these apparent contradictions tend to disappear if one examines each village group as an independent social unit. One version of Hidatsa-Crow history deals with the Mandan account of first encountering a strange people who appeared on the east bank of the Missouri River at the mouth of Heart River and called across. The Mandan, not understanding their language, said that "they want to cross" or *minitadi*, by which name the people of Hidatsa village were thereafter known. This version relates how the Minitadi tasted of the Mandan corn, which they liked, and how they agreed to return with their people in 4 days. This lengthened into 4 years at which time the Minitadi and the Crow appeared on the east bank of the Missouri and were ferried across in Mandan bullboats. They lived with the westside Mandan for a short time until a quarrel occurred between the Hidatsa and the Crow, the latter then moving out on the plains to the west as nomads, and the Hidatsa moving northward along the Missouri where they set up separate villages.

Historical anthropology of these village Indians must take into account general movements of related groups and specific movements of local groups. Mandan and Arikara migration myths tell of their southern origin downstream: the Mandan reached White River from the east, where they set up villages, and then migrated upstream until they reached the Heart River where some had lived so long that that area was thought of as "the heart of the universe." The Arikara had recently separated from the Skidi Pawnee to settle on the Missouri River in what is now the State of South Dakota where they planted their corn and built their earth lodge villages until losses from epidemics and pressures from the Sioux forced them, too, to migrate upstream, abandoning their ancient villages which were observed in ruins by Lewis and Clark in 1804.

Granting the validity of these migration myths as indicative of the general direction of population shifts in the Great Plains, the widespread movements of local groups to many localities during historic times is consistent with the long-time archeological picture of the region. Prior to 1930, those writing on the history of the three village tribes, the Hidatsa, Mandan, and Arikara, tended to treat each as a close-knit political group of related villages moving as a tribal unit when the wood and other resources were consumed. At that time it was believed that a single cultural tradition was shared by all of them. Other than the Mandan, whose late prehistoric archeology had been studied by Will and Spinden, little was known of the archeology of the Hidatsa and Arikara.

In 1930, a Logan Museum field party excavated the first rectangular lodge discovered on the Missouri. It was found to deviate sharply from the well-known circular lodge tradition. It was suggested that a second and earlier lodge tradition might exist locally on the Missouri River in areas formerly occupied by these three tribes. In this site, 39ST1, known today as the Cheyenne River site, surface features in part of the habitation area suggested other large rectangular lodges. Part of the area of the site had been occupied by the Arikara in historic times. Outlines of a rectangular lodge were discovered underlying the historic level in a stratigraphic position which preceded the earliest White contacts. A considerable interval between the two occupations was further evident by the fact that the outlines of historic Arikara graves cut the outlines of the ruins of these earlier lodges. So far as is known today, this was the first actual discovery of the reoccupation of an ancient village site by an agricultural group of a second tradition.

Those who had previously surveyed and excavated in earth lodge sites along the Missouri River in North Dakota and South Dakota took little note of this new evidence. Rectangular loghouses had commonly been built at the Mandan and Hidatsa villages near Knife River by White traders living with the Indians and married to Indian women. Although our researches at that time did not establish the presence of any European trade material in this association, pottery now known to closely resemble that of the Riggs site north of Pierre was found.   Not knowing at that stage of researches in the Plains what prehistoric Arikara pottery looked like, it was assumed by us that the difference in pottery at these two levels was due to the rapid deterioration of the potter's art under White trader influence and the introduction of metal vessels.   Numerous heavily grassed sites along the Missouri River showed similar lodge outlines, but the Logan Museum site maps of that time, and those prepared by Will and Spinden, were drawn to indicate circular lodges, it being assumed that surface disturbances by wind and water must have altered their original circular outlines.

A few years later, the North Dakota Historical Society with WPA funds excavated extensively in that State and confirmed the existence of rectangular lodges at Huff site in North Dakota.   This find was followed by numerous similar discoveries by W. H. Over and E. E. Meleen working in South Dakota.   In 1952, Woolworth excavated "Grandmother's Lodge," known by my informants as the "Sacred Lodge of the Old-Woman-Who-Never-Dies" who was held in reverence by the Hidatsa, Crow, and Mandan.   This lodge was found to conform to the same general rectangular dimensions of lodges in certain village sites downstream along the Missouri River to Chamberlain, S. Dak.   These discoveries provide us with a new image of the cultural history of the region.

When field researches there were first undertaken, it was generally assumed that agricultural villages were not at most more than a few hundred years old.   As early as 1924, George F. Will indicated that certain sites near the southern border of North Dakota, which his Mandan informants claimed were older than those at the mouth of Heart River, had types of pottery which he identified as characteristic of the older sites of Cannonball, Fort Rice, Shermer, Glencoe, Eagle's Nose, Bad Water, Holbrook, and Ward.   He distinguished them from the later sites such as Slant, Motsiff, Scattered, Boley, Sperry, and Burgois.   My Hidatsa informants identify only Scattered as their ancient residence.

A cultural history of the village Indians has been slow to evolve for a number of reasons: (1) The early researchers assumed that agriculture was late to reach the river valleys of the Great Plains and that the relatively homogeneous culture of the Hidatsa, Mandan, and Arikara which they saw in Historic times was characteristic of the entire period of their residence in the Plains; (2) knowing only one or two local areas, they had little knowledge of the large number of sites, running into the hundreds, which dot virtually every well-drained river terrace; and (3) methods and techniques for observation and analysis had to be developed in the field in conjunction with their researches.

By 1946, Mr. Will had been able to introduce time-depth into his field researches, employing tree-ring analysis techniques to old posts found in agricultural village sites near Bismarck. Based on observed cultural changes and differences existing within the same village and between villages, in 1939 I set a minimum date of A.D. 1300 for the small, unfortified, rectangular, lodge sites situated along the Missouri River from the Big Bend to the Clarks Creek regions, after which time this earlier native population began building the larger fortified sites with bastions.

However, recent carbon-14 tests on wood from these ancient rectangular lodge sites, now recognized as preceding the circular earth lodges, have established A.D. 700 as the earliest date for this agricultural tradition. And this date does not take into consideration still earlier Woodlands cultures in the Plains which bear evidence of limited agriculture.

Based on the survival of numerous items of the material culture of this rectangular-lodge tradition of the Missouri River Aspect after the transition to the historic circular lodges of the Mandan and Hidatsa, the architectural features of the ceremonial lodge of the Mandan, and their well-founded traditions of former employment of rectangular lodges, the history of the Mandan is now seen as a continuous cultural development on the Middle Missouri extending over a period of nearly 1,000 years. Beginning with the original Mandan researches by Will and Spinden, and employing all the techniques of the archeologist and ethnologist, we see emerging the image of the continuous valley residence of a single people—the Mandan of Lewis and Clark's era—which can be matched in few places in the United States.

Simultaneously with the abandonment of the small unfortified communities and the reorganization of this original population into larger fortified communities (the Oak Creek site in South Dakota; Huff, Ward, and Shermer sites in North Dakota), there was a general and large-scale invasion by a people with Central Plains Upper Republican cultural ties. These people quickly took over most of the valley upstream nearly to the North Dakota border. Locally, they united with the indigneous and other peoples from the east at the Arzberger site. There, one tradition in pottery (check-stamping and cord-roughened bodies), which is widely represented in the Lake Traverse, lower loop of the Sheyenne River, and the Red River Valley of eastern North Dakota, is well represented. These distinctive combinations of body types in association with crosshatched rims, dark color, and other diagnostic traits, characteristic of the somewhat later Schultz site on the Sheyenne River southwest of Fargo, N. Dak., have not been reported for locales upstream from the Arzberger site until one reaches the traditional homeland of the Hidatsa north of the Square Buttes in sites which my older Hidatsa informants identify as those they occupied before moving to the mouth of the Knife River.

This mass migration into the Missouri Valley of South Dakota seems to have come about as a consequence of an extensive drought in the central plains which occurred about A.D. 1450. It resulted in the displacement of many of the original inhabitants, the realinement of populations, and the introduction of many new cultural traits which produced local cultures now identified as belonging to the Chouteau or Slope Aspect. In South Dakota, there was a northward movement from the western tributaries of the Missouri River in Nebraska of the ancestral Arikara. There occurred simultaneously an eastward movement, along the tributaries of the Missouri River in South Dakota, of the ancestors of the southern Mandan who had already changed considerably both linguistically and culturally from those who had long lived on the Missouri. As our knowledge of the archeology of the sites of the Chouteau Tradition or Aspect grows, it is becoming increasingly evident, however, that a majority of these sites represents the various branches of the ancestral Arikara.

These newcomers to the Northern Missouri Valley introduced: A new house type, square to roughly circular in outline with the four-post support for the roof and weak peripheral wall posts; distinctive incised-decorated pottery designs; a high regard for catlinite; simple fortifications with or without bastions, which evolved to simple encircling ditches; distinctive flaking tools cut from the edges of buffalo vertebrae; and other tools from bone. A few cultural differences between these earliest sites suggest that regional differences probably already existed.

When these two populations of agriculturalists came together, there followed widespread cultural borrowing between those belonging to the Missouri Valley Aspect and those of the Chouteau or Slope Aspect. The most significant change for the people of the Missouri Valley Aspect was the adoption of the four-post roof support to a small square lodge with rounded corners by those who had formerly built large rectangular lodges. Those peoples of this tradition, living chiefly upstream from the Grand River, soon modified these small four-post lodges by the addition of rather heavy forked peripheral posts usually 12 to 13 in number, and 6–7 feet high, against which they leaned wooden slabs set back 5–6 feet to form a distinctive feature which in later years the Historic Hidatsa referred to as the *atutish* area. The southern groups downstream from the Cannonball

River continued to set the peripheral posts near the edge of the lodge as uprights, without the *atutish* section, until protohistoric times at the Rygh site. This Mandan–Hidatsa earth lodge type did not appear in the south until somewhat later at the Swan Creek site, upper horizon, and the Cheyenne River and Leavensworth sites.

In 1929, while excavating at the Larson site north of Bismarck, N. Dak., the field party from the Logan Museum excavated an earth lodge in the oldest and unfortified section of the site which showed that the *atutish* area was characteristic of their lodges at this time. Further excavations in the Hensler or Van Oosting site again revealed that the leaners had been set out 5–6 feet from the peripheral posts. Tree-ring dating for the Mandan village at the Larson site by Mr. Will showed occupation between A.D. 1615 and 1641. The Hensler site, although somewhat more recent in age, was still clearly precontact and in the Mandan tradition. A ceremonial lodge north of the "open circle" of the Hensler site had the traditional double row of eight central posts, a flat front facing the center of the open circle, a short entryway, roughly parallel long sides, and a rounded back that consisted of uprights set in slightly from the vertical. This lodge's upright back had been rebuilt by extending it back and forth several times.

Unlike the Mandan, who have traditions of once living in large rectangular lodges and who think of their ceremonial lodge as roughly rectangular rather than circular, the Hidatsa have no traditions of earth-covered lodges other than with the four-post frame, heavy peripheral posts, and the *atutish* area, or the small eagle trapping lodge set up on a four-post foundation like a tipi. This would indicate to me that the Hidatsa did not come onto the Missouri River to live until after 1615, as a minimum date. By this time, the rectangular lodge was no longer used as a residence by the Heart River or Northern Mandan. The Awatixa who have traditions of longest residence on the Missouri refer to the first lodges built there as having the *atutish* as described in the myth of the "Sacred Arrows" (see p. 305) when twins were ripped from their mother by a monster, one becoming known as *Atutish* or "Edge-of-the-Lodge," which is that section of the earth lodge extending from the peripheral posts to the wall where things were stored.

Some have thought that the Hidatsa came from the prairies as nomads, settled with the Mandan, and took over their culture in a matter of a few years. Reexamination of Hidatsa traditions, which I analyzed for this study in 1932 and 1933, and new information at hand on the archeology of the Northern Plains confirm native traditions of separate and independent migrations of the various Hidatsa and Crow groups coming to the Missouri at different times. When this study was undertaken in 1932, I was able to distinguish three distinct Hidatsa migration accounts. Those informants whose parents came from Awatixa village on the south bank of the Knife River claimed that they had always lived upstream from the mouth of the Heart River and they had no traditions of living elsewhere than on the Missouri River. The Awaxawi descendants gave an account of their ancestors' migrations which was essentially the same as recorded by Thompson in 1797; to the effect that they had previously lived along the streams to the east until a few generations prior to 1797 when they moved to the banks of the Missouri River. These informants claimed that their ancestors came to the Missouri River as agriculturalists and continued a way of life which was characteristic of their eastern residence. The Hidatsa-proper claimed to be the last to reach the Missouri River, coming there from the northeast as nomads, having "lost their corn" while residing north of Devils Lake. The various Hidatsa and Mandan traditions concerning the Crow Indians seem to have validity in that they believed that the Crow Indians residing west of the Missouri River came by two or more major migrations from their eastern homeland near the headwaters of the Red River of the North as agriculturalists, linguistically related to the Awatixa, while others came from the northeast as nomadic hunters as part of the Hidatsa-proper–River Crow linguistic group, known prior to their separation as the Mirokac.

This would then have been the picture of distribution of the Hidatsa and Crow groups five or six generations prior to 1797: The western branch of the Hidatsa–Crow would have been composed of an agricultural group—the ancestors of the Awatixa—living upstream from Square Buttes and a closely related nomadic group comprised of small bands living on the Plains to the west; a cluster of agricultural villages on the lower Sheyenne River and headwaters of the Red River, the survivors of this area becoming the Awaxawi when they moved to the banks of the Missouri River north of the Square Buttes; the Mirokac living as nomads in the Devils Lake area and to the north until they migrated southwestward to the Missouri. There some continued to live as nomads, to become the River Crow, and the others adopted the earth lodge and agriculture, settling upstream from the mouth of the Knife River as the Hidatsa-proper.

These native traditions of the various Hidatsa–Crow groups are borne out, in part, by recent archeological studies conducted in many areas of the Northern Plains traditionally occupied by these peoples. A significant group of sites on the Missouri River, between Square Buttes and the Knife River, traditionally occupied by the various Hidatsa groups, are found, from an analysis of lodge forms, village organization of lodges, and pottery types and frequencies, to be essentially alike and to differ in several respects from the contemporaneous Mandan living near the mouth of the Heart River. The diagnostic traits of this Painted Woods Focus are: Circular earth lodges with a well-defined *atutish* area or section; absence of specialized ceremonial lodges, open circles, or ceremonial areas; indiscriminate arrangement of lodges; absence of fortifications; distinctive pottery types and ranges not characteristic of the contemporary Mandan sites nearby. Type "S" rims fall well below the range for the Mandan while thickened rims, formed by the addition of a narrow band, are common. The incidence of check-stamped rims runs as high as 18 percent of the collection at the Fort Clark Station site a few miles downstream from the mouth of the Knife River. Check-stamped pottery bodies comprise 40 percent of the collection at the Upper Sanger site, and cord-roughened bodies comprise 6.6 percent at the Fort Clark Station site.

The contemporaneous Mandan sites show numerous differences from these identifiable earliest Hidatsa sites on the Missouri River. Lodges were identical for both groups and had the well-defined *atutish* section. The Mandan preserved an open area within the village, a specialized ceremonial lodge distinctive in structure from the habitation lodge, and a plaza complex consisting of an upright cedar post, an adjacent ceremonial lodge, and habitation lodges which faced the open circle.

There were numerous similarities in the pottery of the two traditions, the Mandan villages of the Heart River Focus and the Hidatsa villages of the Painted Woods Focus, which indicate that there had been a long period of intervalley contacts prior to the arrival of the Hidatsa on the Missouri. Evidence of this association is borne out by the fact that, trait for trait, these early Hidatsa sites on the Missouri closely resemble several sites in southeastern North Dakota along the lower section of the Sheyenne River. At the Shultz site near Lisbon, the pottery types and frequencies of types more closely resemble that found on the Missouri River in sites of the Painted Woods Focus than that found in traditional Mandan sites only 2 or 3 miles away. Check-stamp ware was never characteristic of the Missouri Valley or Chouteau traditions on the Missouri, but is very common in southeastern North Dakota and thence northward into Canada. It is found in the Devils Lake area and westward into the Mouse River drainage and thence westward to the Yellowstone River as far west as Forsyth, Mont., in a region that in late prehistoric times was traditionally occupied by the various Hidatsa and Crow groups. It appears occasionally in the Mandan sites near the Heart River by the time of the establishment of the Huff and Shermer sites, at least a century prior to the building of the first Hidatsa villages on the Missouri.

Its presence in these Mandan sites at this early date suggests that overland contacts between the Missouri and the Red River of the North existed long before the first Hidatsa–Crow groups settled on the Missouri. Extensive cultural exchange of other traits between the two areas continued until this westward movement of Hidatsa–Crow was terminated with the final arrival of the Mirokac.

Continued cultural borrowing between earth lodge peoples living along the Missouri River and these western tributaries of the Red River of the North even after the abandonment of the eastern area by the Hidatsa–Crow, is indicated by the many common traits of the historic Cheyenne of the same general region as noted by Strong in his excavations at the Biesterfeldt site. This site, however, shows closer cultural ties to the historic Arikara than to the Mandan or Hidatsa.

Thus, the record from native traditions, accounts of early discoverers, and archeology are in general agreement that the various Hidatsa and Crow bands reached the Plains from the western edge of the Woodlands as independent and separate groups. They came prior to the first White penetration of the Missouri Valley and after the Mandan had already become firmly established there. This penetration of the Plains seems to have been a friendly one as far as the Mandan are concerned; we find no mention in their traditions of any conflicts, and the earliest Hidatsa villages were not fortified. The earlier Mandans, with their rectangular lodge tradition, had built villages as far upstream as Clarks Creek near the mouth of Knife River. There may have been some settlements farther upstream, for the "Sacred Lodge of the Old-Woman-Who-Never-Dies," was of this tradition (of which the Hidatsa had no memories when this study was made).

We must assume that the various Hidatsa groups came to the Missouri Valley a few at a time. They settled above the mouth of the Heart River in areas abandoned by the Mandan as they moved from an independent village system to a more centralized tribal organization and built the large, long-occupied, and strongly fortified Slant, Motsiff, Scattered, Boley, Larson, and Double-ditch villages. Dialectic differences between these west-side communities of Nuitadi Mandans at the Heart River had disappeared until the later arrival of a small southern branch of Awigaxa Mandans, who had remained near the Grand River until after A.D. 1700, and a somewhat larger group known as the Nuptadi Mandan who had built at Double-ditch site prior to that date, they, too, coming north relatively late in prehistoric times. By A.D. 1700 the Mandan in the villages listed above were developing a strong tribal organization which was composed of the Nuptadi and Nuitadi linguistic groups. The Awigaxa Mandan, a peripheral linguistic group, also maintained friendly ties with the northern Arikara until the smallpox epidemics and the encroachment of the Sioux forced them to enter into new alliances for mutual defense.

The other two earth lodge groups, the Arikara to the south and the Hidatsa to the north, seem not to have achieved the characteristics of a tribal organization until after the smallpox epidemics of the 18th century.   There is archeological evidence that some of the original Arikara communities attempted consolidation at the Fort Sully site during protohistoric times, building one huge village of several hundred lodges and multiple ceremonial lodges.   The next major Arikara consolidation did not occur until about A.D. 1800.   Lewis and Clark, 1804, found them in the two Cottonwood (Leavenworth) sites and a third community on Ashley Island at the mouth of Oak Creek.   It appears that even at that time there was no particular tendency on the part of the Arikara to set up a unified tribal organization from among the survivors of the many abandoned villages mentioned by Lewis and Clark.   One group of Arikara, representing the survivors of the northern branch living near the Grand River in close association with the Awigaxa Mandan, made numerous resettlements of the old Greenshield site opposite Washburn, N. Dak., as close neighbors of the Awigaxa Mandans who had settled near there.   Peace could not be maintained between these northern Arikara and the Nuitadi and Nuptadi Mandan; old animosities were revived and conflicts soon arose.   As a result, these Arikara came to the Greenshield site to rebuild their homes several times between 1785 and 1820.   They then moved in with the other two Arikara groups at the Cottonwood sites where they were found during the Leavenworth campaign.   The Awigaxa Mandan eventually joined with the Nuitadi Mandan at Fort Clark and, after one final quarrel when they moved back downstream only to be reunited at Fort Clark a few years later, were absorbed by the latter.

The Hidatsa settlements on the Missouri upstream from their culturally related neighbors were, by and large, accepted by the Mandan without friction.   There is no memory of any intertribal conflict.   The Awatixa, who have longest traditions of residence on the Missouri, acted as a buffer against aggression by nomadic groups from the north, and their close linguistic and friendly ties with the Mountain or Western Crow gave the Mandan protection from that direction.   The long association of this group with their southern Mandan neighbors is reflected in their culture as described above; in trait after trait they more closely resembled the Mandan than the other Hidatsa groups.   With the single exception of temporary residence at Scattered Village with the Mandan where the present city of Mandan stands, they have generally lived upstream from Square

Buttes. Old Awatixa site on the south bank of the Knife River was their principal residence.

Traditional, historical, and archeological evidence indicate that the Awaxawi were the next group to settle on the Missouri River, coming there from the western tributaries of the Red River of the North by way of Devils Lake. They were agricultural Indians with a knowledge of the earth lodge and a culture that had already been strongly influenced by their distant overland contacts with the Mandan and the Awatixa Hidatsa. They settled in the Square Butte to Washburn area in closer association with the Mandan than with the Awatixa. The Hidatsa and River Crow came to the Missouri River as nomadic hunters and took over the unoccupied area upstream from the mouth of the Knife River. Some of these people adopted agriculture from the Mandan and their closely related linguistic neighbors, the Awatixa and Awaxawi, to become the Hidatsa-proper. Those who remained nomadic moved upstream and onto the lower Yellowstone River to become the River Crow.

Once established on the Missouri River, the more numerous Hidatsa and River Crow would not permit the other Hidatsa groups to settle above them on the river. War once broke out between the Hidatsa-proper and the Awaxawi when the latter attempted to move upstream beyond the Knife River and the Awaxawi, for a while thereafter, lived near Fort Yates with the agricultural Cheyenne.

When the smallpox epidemic of the last part of the 18th century broke out in the earth lodge villages on the Missouri River, the Hidatsa-proper and Awatixa were at the mouth of Knife River, the Awaxawi and Awigaxa Mandan were in the Painted Woods region, and the Nuptadi and Nuitadi Mandan were in the vicinity of the Heart River in six or more large villages. The combined Mandan-Hidatsa population must have been well in excess of 12,000 people, the Hidatsa groups constituting about one-third of the combined population. The combined Arikara population, apparently twice as numerous as the combined Hidatsa–Mandan population and living in twice as many villages between the Grand River on the north and the Big Bend to the south, suffered even greater losses than their neighbors to the north where the epidemic wiped out approximately 75 percent of the population.

Prior to this time, with the exception of the Mandan near the mouth of Heart River, this agricultural population on the Missouri River had been widely dispersed. Reorganization of the native population was hastened by the invasion of the Sioux in large numbers to the area. The Arikara concentrated near Grand River, the three Hidatsa groups concentrated at the mouth of the Knife River, and the Mandan moved upstream and settled a few miles below the Hidatsa for mutual defense against their common enemies. These mutual defense measures were taken just prior to A.D. 1800 as a means of protection against their more numerous nomadic neighbors.

By 1837–38, following another severe smallpox epidemic that nearly exterminated the Mandan and Hidatsa, the Arikara appeared on the Knife River, having been nomadic hunters in the Western Plains after their gardens had failed from drought a few years earlier. There they appropriated the Nuitadi Mandan village, and joined with the Mandan-Hidatsa survivors in a mutal defense pact against the Sioux and other nomadic neighbors. In 1845, Fishhook Village was built by the Hidatsa and Nuitadi Mandans. The other Mandans remained near the Arikara until after 1860 when they, too, came to Fishhook Village. Ten years later, most of the survivors of Hidatsa Village on the Knife River, under the leadership of Bobtail Bull and Crow-Flies-High, moved to the mouth of the Yellowstone where they lived until forced to return to the Fort Berthold Reservation. They established a settlement at Shell Village apart from the other Hidatsa.

To understand cultural differences and similarities among the various agricultural communities, one must take into account their separate histories. Hidatsa family, kinship, and clan loyalties have been strong while tribal loyalties have been weak. This has produced a system whereby some Hidatsa-proper bands have felt stronger loyalties to some River Crow bands than to their nearest neighbors, the Awatixa. Likewise, the Awaxawi have occasionally had closer ties with the Awigaxa Mandan or the earth lodge Cheyenne than with the Hidatsa-proper or the Awatixa. The Awatixa have had closer ties with the Mandan through cultural exchange than with the more nomadic Hidatsa-proper and, in the past, expressed little concern when many of the latter talked of rejoining the River Crow.

From what we have been able to determine, the Mandan had been more successful than the other groups in developing a tribal system. The Awigaxa Mandan, nevertheless, retained closer cultural ties with certain northern Arikara groups until after 1800. The Arikara, too, had their fraction group which was not completely integrated until after 1820.

At the time the first Whites reached the Missouri River during the 18th century, the Village Indians had a common basic culture which was of long standing in the river valleys of the Plains and had spread eastward to the tributaries of the Red River of the North. It was founded on common agricultural plants, tools, and technology. The summer villages were composed of semipermanent earth-covered lodges sufficiently large to shelter an extended family. Minor differences in design of lodges had disappeared. The winter season was normally spent in the lower wooded valleys where the population depended primarily on the animals they hunted. The eagle-trapping techniques had become standardized. Their material culture was exceedingly similar throughout several hundred miles of Village Indian occupation along the Missouri River and in such areas as the lower Sheyenne River to the east.

However, as one delves deeper into the archeology of the area, and comes to acquire greater understanding of these cultures through careful examination and with the aid of native informants familiar with their ancient culture, numerous differences come to light. Catlinite was uncommon in the village sites of the rectangular lodge tradition and in later Mandan sites, but it was common in sites of the Chouteau and Painted Woods tradition. On analysis of Mandan traditions and values, one learns that there was a strong prejudice against the use of redstone pipes for ceremonial functions which was not shared by the Arikara and Hidatsa. The Mandan preferred the large, carved, wooden pipe as did the Awatixa who had lived longest on the Missouri River near them. Shell beads were popular in the Missouri Valley tradition and unimportant in the Chouteau tradition.

The open circle or plaza of the Mandan was of long standing with them and their image of the community was built around this complex. Recent fieldwork in South Dakota and carbon-14 dates for that area indicate that this ceremonial complex was developed before the invasion of the region by Chouteau tradition peoples and that it was not adopted by the Arikara until nearly protohistoric times. Clearly indetifiable ceremonial lodge complexes, as yet unreported for the Arikara, antedate their first appearance in South Dakota by several centuries.

Even as late as 1933, Mandan informants were reluctant to discuss knowledge of this sacred complex. Hidatsa informants had no knowledge of sacred areas in their villages or separate ceremonial lodges, and archeology confirms this. Like the Mandan, the Awatixa believed that each village ought to have an outstanding sacred bundle owner stationed at each of the four directions within the village to sound alarms sent by their bundles whenever danger was at hand and to assist the head chiefs. This belief and practice was not shared by the other Hidatsa groups. It was the type of village organization that was employed when Fishhook village was built in 1845. There is neither traditional nor archeological evidence that the Hidatsa groups ever adopted the earth-covered ceremonial lodge.

We also find that the Awatixa, like the Mandan, commonly transmitted property of a sacred nature through the matrilineal line rather than from father to son as was the practice among other Hidatsa groups.

It is evident that the Mandan have influenced the Hidatsa more than the Hidatsa have influenced the Mandan. The oldest Hidatsa sites have distinctive types and frequencies of pottery that are not characteristic of the Mandan, and these had all dropped out by historic times with the adoption of the more popular Mandan types. Their age-grade military society system and women's age-grade societies were, in many instances, borrowed from the Mandan, even within the memory of the grandparents of native informants living in 1933. A common clan system was developing from two traditions, a 13-clan system of the Hidatsa-proper and Awaxawi, which was shared by the Crow, and a 7- or 8-clan system characteristic of the Awatixa. Their clan systems, through close contacts with the Mandan, were equated to extend cooperative ties across tribal lines.

It can be said that the Hidatsa enjoyed little of the cultural stability of the Mandan after their final arrival from the east. They had shifted from a marginal agricultural region to one possessing a highly developed agricultural system of long standing. Some had even come as marginal hunters and gatherers from the northeastern edge of the Great Plains and had undergone significant internal cultural changes brought about by their close association with Village Indians living near Heart River on the Missouri. They adopted social dances from the Sioux and passed them on to the Crow. They borrowed many curing rites from the Assiniboin which enriched their ceremonial life. Their ancient way of life was being rapidly enriched by their many new contacts on the Missouri when these processes were abruptly terminated with the extermination of the buffaloes, the conquest of their enemies by the U.S. Army, and their forced removal to the Fort Berthold Reservation.

BIBLIOGRAPHY

BECKWITH, MARTHA W.
  1938. Mandan-Hidatsa myths and ceremonies. Amer. Folk-Lore Soc. Mem., vol. 32.

BENEDICT, RUTH.
  1922. The vision in Plains culture. Amer. Anthrop., n.s., vol. 24, No. 1, pp. 1–23.

BODMER, KARL.
  1906. Travels in the interior of North America, 1832–1834. *In* "Early western travels, 1748–1846," ed. by Reuben Gold Thwaites, vol. 25. Cleveland.

BOLLER, HENRY A.
  1868. Among the Indians. Eight years in the far West: 1858–1866. Philadelphia.

BOWERS, ALFRED W.
  —— A history of the Mandan and Hidatsa. MS., Ph.D. dissertation, Univ. Chicago, 1948.
  1950. Mandan social and ceremonial organization. Univ. Chicago Press.

BRACKENRIDGE, HENRY M.
  1904. Journal of a voyage up the river Missouri; performed in eighteen hundred and eleven. *In* "Early western travels, 1748–1846," ed. by Reuben Gold Thwaites, vol. 6. Cleveland.

BRADBURY, JOHN.
  1904. Travels in the interior of America in the years 1809, 1810, and 1811. *In* "Early western travels, 1748–1846," ed. by Reuben Gold Thwaites, vol. 5. Cleveland.

BUSHNELL, DAVID I., JR.
  1922. Villages of the Algonquian, Siouan, and Caddoan tribes west of the Mississippi. Bur. Amer. Ethnol. Bull. 77.
  1927. Burials of the Algonquian, Siouan and Caddoan tribes. Bur. Amer. Ethnol. Bull. 83.

CATLIN, GEORGE.
  1841. The manners, customs and condition of the North American Indians. London.
  1867. O-kee-pa: a religious ceremony; and other customs of the Mandans. London.

CHARDON, FRANCIS A.
  1932. Chardon's journal at Fort Clark, 1834–1839. Ed. by Annie Heloise Abel. Pierre, S. Dak.

CURTIS, EDWARD S.
  1907 a. The Absaroke, or Crow, the Hidatsa. *In* "The North American Indian," ed. by Frederick W. Hodge, vol. 4. Univ. Press, Cambridge.
  1907 b. The Mandan. *In* "The North American Indian," ed. by Frederick W. Hodge, vol. 5. Univ. Press, Cambridge.

DENSMORE, FRANCES.
1923. Mandan and Hidatsa music. Bur. Amer. Ethnol. Bull. 80.
EGGAN, FRED, EDITOR.
1937. The social anthropology of North American tribes. Univ. Chicago Press.
GRINNELL, GEORGE B.
1923. The Cheyenne Indians, their history and ways of life. 2 vols. Yale Univ. Press.
HAYDEN, F. V.
1863. Contributions to the ethnography and philology of the Indian tribes of the Missouri Valley. Amer. Philos. Soc. Trans., n.s., vol. 12, art. 3, pp. 231–462.
HENRY, ALEXANDER.
1897. The manuscript journals of Alexander Henry and of David Thompson, 1799–1814. Ed. by Elliot Coues. 3 vols. New York.
KURZ, RUDOLPH FRIEDERICH.
1937. Journal of Rudolph Friederich Kurz. Ed. by J. N. B. Hewitt, trans. by Myrtis Jarrell. Bur. Amer. Ethnol. Bull. 115.
LA HARPE, BERNARD DE.
1886. Relation du voyage de Bernard de la Harpe, Decouvertes et etablissements des Francaise dans l'ouest et dans le sud de l'Amerique Septentrionale 1614–1754. Ed. by Pierre Margry. 6 vols. Paris.
LA VÉRENDRYE, PIERRE GAULTIER DE VARENNES.
1927. Journals and letters of Pierre Gaultier de Varennes de La Vérendrye and his sons. Ed. by Lawrence J. Burpee. Toronto.
LE RAYE, CHARLES.
1908. The journals of Charles Le Raye. South Dakota Hist. Coll., vol. 4.
LEWIS, MERIWETHER.
1893. History of the expedition under the command of Lewis and Clark. Ed. by Elliot Coues. 4 vols. New York.
LIBBY, O. G.
1908 a. Typical villages of the Mandans, Arikara and Hidatsa in the Missouri Valley, North Dakota. Coll. State Hist. Soc. North Dakota, vol. 2, pp. 498–502.
1908 b. La Vérendrye's visit to the Mandans in 1738–39. Coll. State Hist. Soc. North Dakota, vol. 2, pp. 502–508.
LOISEL, —
1939. Tabeau's narrative of Loisel's expedition to the upper Missouri. Ed. and trans. by Annie Heloise Abel. Univ. Oklahoma Press.
LOWIE, ROBERT H.
1910. The Assiniboine. Amer. Mus. Nat. Hist. Anthrop. Pap., vol. 4, pt. 1, pp. 1–270.
1912. Some problems in the ethnology of the Crow and Village Indians. Amer. Anthrop., n.s., vol. 14, No. 1, pp. 60–71.
1913. Societies of the Hidatsa and Mandan Indians. Amer. Mus. Nat. Hist. Anthrop. Pap., vol. 11, pt. 3, pp. 219–358.
1917. Notes on the social organization and customs of the Mandan, Hidatsa, and Crow Indians. Amer. Mus. Nat. Hist. Anthrop. Pap., vol. 21, pt. 1, pp. 1–99.
1918. Myths and traditions of the Crow Indians. Amer. Mus. Nat. Hist. Anthrop. Pap., vol. 25, pt. 1, pp. 1–308.
1919. The Hidatsa Sun Dance. Amer. Mus. Nat. Hist. Anthrop. Pap., vol. 16, pt. 5, pp. 411–431.

LOWIE, ROBERT H.—Continued
   1935. The Crow Indians. New York.
   1954. Indians of the Plains. New York.
MACKENZIE, CHARLES.
   1889. The Missouri Indians, a narrative of four trading expeditions to the
         Missouri, 1804–1805–1806. *In* "Les bourgeois de la compagnie du
         Nord-Ouest," ed. by L. R. Masson, vol. 1. Quebec.
MATTHEWS, WASHINGTON.
   1877. Ethnography and philology of the Hidatsa Indians. U.S.Geol. and
         Geogr. Surv. Misc. Publ., vol. 7. Washington.
MAXIMILIAN. *See* WIED-NEUWIED.
MORGAN, LEWIS H.
   1871. Systems of consanguinity and affinity. Smithsonian Contr. to
         Knowl., vol. 17.
MULLOY, WILLIAM T.
   1942. The Hagen Site. Univ. Montana Publ. in Soc. Sci., No. 1.
PALLISER, JOHN.
   1853. Solitary rambles and adventures of a hunter in the prairies. London.
PEPPER, G. H., and WILSON, G. L.
   1908. An Hidatsa shrine and the beliefs respecting it. Amer. Anthrop.
         Assoc. Mem., vol. 2, pp. 275–328. Lancaster, Pa.
PROVINCE, J. H.
   1937. The underlying sanctions of Plains Indian culture. *In* "Social
         anthropology of North American tribes," ed. by Fred Eggan.
         Univ. Chicago Press.
REID, RUSSELL.
   1930. The earth lodge. North Dakota Hist. Quart., vol. 4, No. 3, pp.
         174–185.
SCHOOLCRAFT, HENRY R.
   1851. Information respecting the history, condition and prospects of the
         Indian tribes of the United States. Collected and prepared under
         the direction of the Bureau of Indian Affairs. 6 vols. Phila-
         delphia.
SPAULDING, ALBERT S.
   1956. The Arzberger Site, Hughes County, South Dakota. Univ. Michi-
         gan, Occ. Contr. Mus. Anthrop., No. 16.
STRONG, WILLIAM DUNCAN.
   1933. The Plains culture area in the light of archaeology. Amer. Anthrop.,
         n.s., vol. 35, No. 2, pp. 271–287.
   1940. From history to prehistory in the northern Great Plains. *In* "Essays
         in historical anthropology of North America." Smithsonian Misc.
         Coll., vol. 100, pp. 353–394.
THOMPSON, DAVID D.
   1916. David Thompson's narrative of his explorations in western America:
         1784–1812. Ed. by J. B. Tyrrell, vol. 12. Toronto.
WIED-NEUWIED, MAXIMILIAN ALEXANDER PHILIPP, Prinz VON.
   1906. Travels into the interior of North America, 1832–1834. *In* "Early
         western travels, 1748–1846," ed. by Reuben Gold Thwaites, vols.
         22-24. Cleveland.
WILL, GEORGE F.
   1909. Some observations made in northwestern South Dakota. Anthrop.
         Pap., n.s., vol. 11.

WILL, GEORGE F.
   1924.   Archaeology of the Missouri Valley.   Amer. Mus. Nat. Hist. Anthrop.
           Pap., vol. 22, pt. 6, pp. 285–344.
   1946.   Tree ring studies in North Dakota.   Agric. Exper. Sta. Bull. 338.
           Fargo.
WILL, GEORGE F., and HECKER, THAD. C.
   1944.   The upper Missouri River valley aboriginal culture in North Dakota.
           North Dakota Hist. Quart., vol. 11, Nos. 1–2, pp. 5–126.
WILL, GEORGE F., and HYDE, GEORGE E.
   1917.   Corn among the Indians of the Upper Missouri.   St. Louis.
WILL, GEORGE F., and SPINDEN, H. J.
   1906.   The Mandans, a study of their culture, archaeology and ethnology.
           Peabody Mus. Amer. Archaeol. and Ethnol. Pap., vol. 3, No. 4.
WILSON, GILBERT L.
   1917.   Agriculture of the Hidatsa Indians.   Univ. Minnesota Stud. Soc.
           Sci., vol. 9.
   1924.   The horse and dog in Hidatsa culture.   Amer. Mus. Nat. Hist.
           Anthrop. Pap., vol. 15, pt. 11, pp. 125–311.
   1928.   Hidatsa eagle trapping.   Amer. Mus. Nat. Hist. Anthrop. Pap.,
           vol. 30, pt. 4, pp. 99–245.
   1934.   The Hidatsa earthlodge.   Amer. Mus. Nat. Hist. Anthrop. Pap.,
           vol. 33, pt. 5, pp. 341–420, ed. by Bella Weitzner.
WINCHELL, N. H.
   1911.   The aborigines of Minnesota.   Minnesota Hist. Soc., St. Paul.
WOOD, W. RAYMOND.
   ——.   An interpretation of Mandan culture history.   MS., Ph.D. disserta-
           tion, 1961, Univ. Oregon.
WOOLWORTH, ALAN R.
   1956.   Archaeological investigations at Site 32ME59 (Grandmother's Lodge).
           North Dakota Hist., vol. 23, No. 2, pp. 79–102.

Reconstruction of Rock Village.

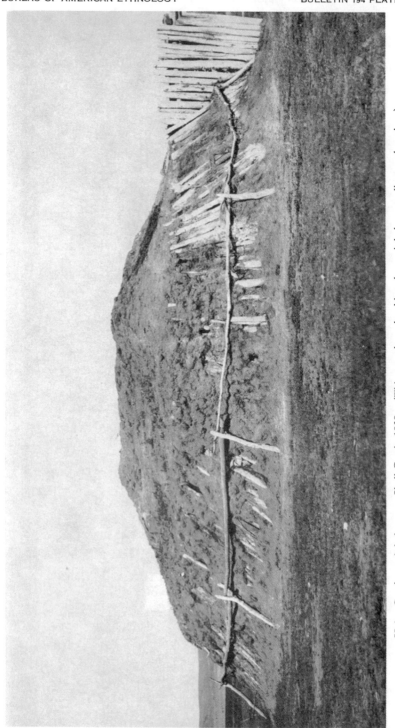

Hairy Coat's earth lodge near Shell Creek, 1929. (This was the only old-style earth lodge standing at that time.)

Pehriska-Ruhpa (Two Crows) in the costume of the Dog Band.　(Lithograph from original drawing by Carl Bodmer.)

Buffalo (Bull) Dance of the Mandan.   (Lithograph from original drawing by Carl Bodmer.)

Wolf Chief and wife, 1933.

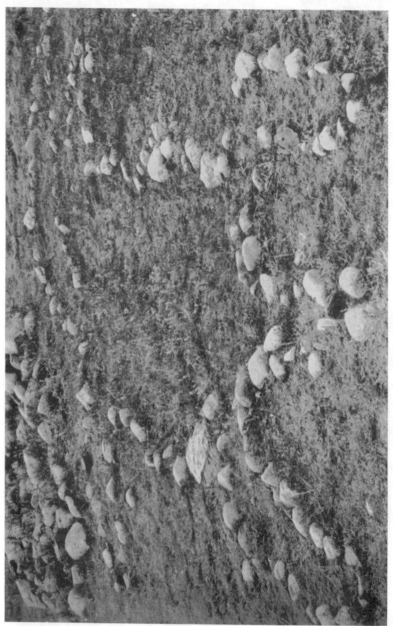

Turtle effigy near Price, N. Dak., 1929.

Roadmaker, of Awaxawi village.   (Lithograph from original drawing by Carl Bodmer.)

Scalp Dance of the Manitaries (Hidatsa). (Lithograph from original drawing by Carl Bodmer.)

The seven enemy warriors, 1930.

Buffalo skulls of a bundle owner, 1930.   (Extreme left of photograph retouched.)

Winter village of the Manitaries (Hidatsa). (Lithograph from original drawing by Carl Bodmer.)

Drags Wolf and Foolish Bear with Waterbuster clan bundle, 1933.

INDEX

54 10